KING ALFRED'S COLLEGE
WINCHESTER

To be returned on or before the day marked
below :—

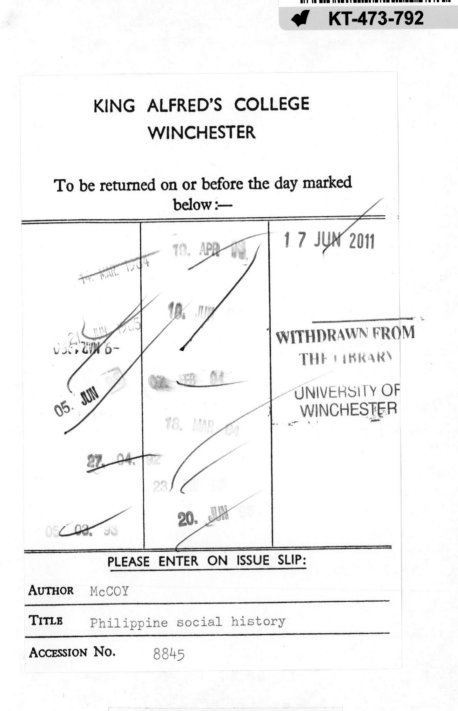

PLEASE ENTER ON ISSUE SLIP:

AUTHOR   McCOY

TITLE   Philippine social history

ACCESSION No.   8845

PHILIPPINE SOCIAL HISTORY

No.7 ASIAN STUDIES ASSOCIATION OF AUSTRALIA
Southeast Asia Publications Series

For our teachers

Horacio de la Costa, S.J.
and
Harry J. Benda

Philippine Social History:
Global Trade and Local Transformations

Edited by

Alfred W. McCoy & Ed. C. de Jesus

Published in Cooperation with
ATENEO DE MANILA UNIVERSITY PRESS
Quezon City, Metro Manila

UNIVERSITY PRESS OF HAWAII
Honolulu

UNIVERSITY PRESS OF HAWAII
2840 Kolowalu Street, Honolulu, Hawaii, 96822, USA

ATENEO DE MANILA UNIVERSITY PRESS
Loyola Heights, Q.C., Metro Manila
P.O. Box 154, Manila, Philippines

First published 1982
ISBN 0-8248-0803-7
© Asian Studies Association of Australia
Copyright in the Philippines by Ateneo de Manila

Simultaneously published in Australia by George Allen &
Unwin Australia Pty Ltd, 8 Napier Street, North Sydney,
NSW 2060, Australia

Distributed in Asia (excluding the Philippines) by Heinemann
Educational Books (Asia) Ltd, 41 Jalan Pemimpin, Singapore 2057

Printed in the Philippines by Vera-Reyes, Inc.
Typeset by Anna Tsakaros in Sydney, Australia

PREFACE

This volume grew out of a number of long dinnertime conversations between the editors at the de Jesus household in Manila during the early 1970s. One day at Manila's Magsaysay Center in April 1976, McCoy proposed, de Jesus approved, and a third party demurred, predicting accurately enough an enormous amount of work. Although the volume has developed far beyond the modest list of possible contributors and probable topics sketched out over lunch, its central purpose remains unchanged — to present the fruits of an important decade's research into Philippine social history.

We felt that a major period in the development of Philippine historiography was drawing to a close. In the late 1960s, following the release of a vast collection of 19th century provincial documents at the Philippine National Archives, several dozen Filipino and foreign scholars began research into regional social history. Within a few years almost every region was the subject of one if not two or more major research efforts. By the mid-1970s, however, work had slowed markedly and the once crowded reading room at the Philippine National Archives was empty. The time had come to assess the contribution of these regional studies to our understanding of Philippine history and the global process of social change.

This sudden surge of interest in Philippine regional history coincided with a wider scholarly debate, prompted by the writings of Andre Gunder Frank and Immanuel Wallerstein, over the nature of socio-economic development, or "underdevelopment", in the primary-producing regions of the globe. Although novel to many scholars of imperialism, these questions had been an integral part of Southeast Asian studies for several decades and, as such, had provided the conceptual basis for several of these Philippine regional studies. Despite the obvious relevance of the Philippine work to this wider scholarly debate, however, Filipinists played a minor role in it. The marked decline of support for all aspects of Southeast Asia studies in the United States during the 1970s coincided, unfortunately, with the publication phase of this regional research.

With the publication of this volume, the Filipinists have at last entered the debate. The Philippines experienced one of the most intensely documented transitions to modernity of any Third World nation. A unique combination of Spanish and American bureaucracies — legal, ecclesiastical, military and administrative — generated an enormous volume of records on almost every aspect of late colonial Philippine society. This documentation has allowed Filipinists to make one of the first comprehensive assessments of the socio-economic impact of European world trade upon the primary-producing regions of the Third World. It is our conviction that these essays, despite certain limitations, represent an important step forward in our understanding of these modern social transformations and merit the attention of scholars beyond the field of Philippine studies.

In the course of our work on this volume we received a great deal of support. Esther M. Pacheco at the Ateneo de Manila University Press and the editors of the ASAA Southeast Asia Publications Series took an early interest in this project.

Glenita Formoso McCoy and Melinda Quintos de Jesus read and commented on all drafts, and Brian Fegan assisted with the editorial work on a number of essays. Pam Millwood of the Australian National University's Human Geography Department drew all of the excellent maps, and Jennifer Brewster of the Pacific and Southeast Asian History Department did the final editing with great care. Professor Frank Crowley of the University of New South Wales encouraged this project during its infancy by providing both moral and financial support. Finally, the administrative staff of the School of History, University of New South Wales — Maria Giuffre, Sue Jones and Shirley Marshall — typed each of the essays several times with considerable patience.

A.W. McCoy & E. de Jesus
Sydney and Manila
May 1981

CONTENTS

MAPS

FIGURES

SOURCE ABBREVIATIONS

AFIO	*Archivo Franciscano Ibero-Oriental*	Madrid
AGI	*Archivo General de Indias*	Seville
AHN	*Archivo Histórico Nacional*	Madrid
AMAE	*Archivo de Ministerio de Asuntos Exteriores*	Madrid
ANRI	*Arsip Nasional Republik Indonesia*	Jakarta
APSR	*Archivo de la Provincia de Santíssimo Rosario*	Quezon City
AUST	*Archives of the University of Santo Tomas*	Manila
BH-PCL	*Beyer-Holleman Sources in Philippine Customary Law*	Canberra
BIA	*Bureau of Insular Affairs, Record Group 350, NARS*	Washington, D.C.
CO	*Colonial Office*	London
FO	*Foreign Office*	London
GPO	*U.S. Government Printing Office*	Washington, D.C.
HDP	*Historical Data Papers, PNL*	Manila
MAA	*Manila Archdiocesan Archives*	Manila
MN	*Museo Naval*	Madrid
NARS	*U.S. National Archives and Records Service*	Washington, D.C.
PIR	*Philippine Insurgent Records, PNL*	Manila
PNA	*Philippine National Archives*	Manila
PNL	*Philippine National Library*	Manila
PRO	*Public Records Office*	London
R.G.395	*Record Groups 395, NARS*	Washington, D.C.
UILL	*University of Indiana, Lilly Library*	Bloomington
USL	*University of Saint Louis Microfilms*	Saint Louis
YCO	*Ynchausti & Company (Elizalde & Co.)*	Iloilo City

INTRODUCTION

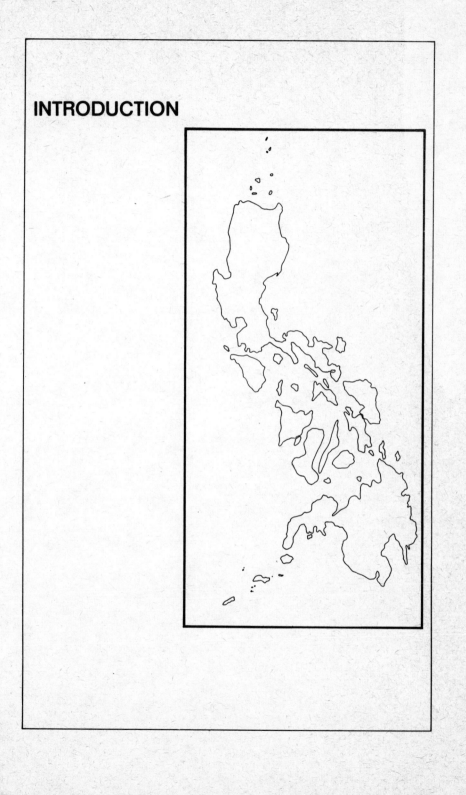

Introduction:
The Social History of an Archipelago

ALFRED W. McCOY

Two centuries ago most of the Philippine archipelago was still covered with virgin forests and sparsely inhabited. Spanish colonials occupied a few urban outposts such as Manila, and their control over Christian, tribute-paying "Filipinos" extended little further than the coastal littorals of Luzon and the main Visayan islands. As the Philippines entered the world economy in the late 18th century, the archipelago began an accelerated socio-economic transformation. Within the space of little more than a century, colonial armies subjugated the independent populations, peasant pioneers pushed back the forests, and agricultural exports soared.

Our understanding of these processes through which the Philippine archipelago entered the world economy has been deficient. Studies of Philippine society and history over the past century have not enjoyed strong institutional support, either colonial or national. The corpus of Philippine historical studies, as they had developed through the late 1960s, provided a detailed portrait of Manila politics during the late colonial period. For those interested in social history, the literature was inadequate.

Over the past decade, however, there has been a marked shift from political to social history. During the 1970s there was a sudden proliferation of social historical research, focused largely on studies of change at the regional or provincial level. Since little of this work has yet been published, this volume accordingly represents some of the first fruits of these labours. Although the focus of these essays is regional, provincial or local, the historical questions addressed are far from parochial. First, these essays raise some important questions for the study of Philippine national history, dealt with only briefly here and much more extensively in Ed. C. de Jesus' conclusion. More generally, these regional studies represent, collectively, one of the first comprehensive attempts to analyze the impact of world trade on the social history of agricultural export economies. As such, they seem to have some wider implications for the study of primary exporting societies around the globe.

Philippine Historical Studies

Our understanding of Philippine social history has developed far more slowly than that of Europe, the Americas or other Southest Asian nations such as Indonesia. In the most general terms, there have been two basic constraints on the

growth of Philippine social history: the unevenness of colonial scholarship denied
the field an adequate fund of historical and ethnographic data; and the postwar
emphasis on Manila-centric political history precluded discussion of broader questions. Until the early 1970s most American historians concentrated on colonial
politics, Filipino historians focused on the six years of revolution (1896-1902), and
social scientists were largely ahistorical in their research methods.[1] For a student
concerned about questions of social change, the studies of Indonesia were often
more stimulating. Dutch colonial scholars such as J.C. van Leur and postwar social
scientists, most notably Clifford Geertz, had put forward a number of useful theses
about the nature of Indonesia's social transformation during the colonial period.[2]

Throughout Southeast Asia, contemporary research has depended far more on
the scholarly legacy of the colonial period than is generally recognized. The ethnographic, sociological and historical researches by colonial scholars established a
rich fund of essential data that postwar students of Indonesia, Malaya and Vietnam were able to draw upon. Unlike several of Southeast Asia's major states, the
Philippines lacked a strong tradition of colonial scholarship. There were occasional
studies of significance, and individual Spanish or American scholars of distinction.
But neither the Spanish nor the American governments provided sufficient institutional support, in the colony or in the metropolis, for the continuous development
of Philippine studies. By the time of independence in 1946 there was, then,
nothing akin to the corpus of Dutch sociological and anthropological writing on Indonesia.

Viewed from the perspective of social history, Philippine studies developed
rather sporadically during the three postwar decades. The first decade of Philippine national independence was a time of sustained crisis that fostered a climate
unsuited to the conduct of objective scholarly inquiry. With the end of postwar
reconstruction and the weakening of the Huk revolt by the mid-1950s, scholarship
resumed after a 15 year hiatus. Over the succeeding quarter-century there appear
to be three general phases in the development of Philippine historiography, each
lasting the better part of a decade. During the late 1950s and early 1960s three major scholarly studies succeeded in outlining the development of foreign trade
linkages from the 17th to late 19th centuries.[3] During the 1960s Philippine studies
was dominated by a rather unproductive interaction between history and social
science that did relatively little to advance our knowledge of social history. Only
one historian, John Larkin, followed up the foreign trade studies of the 1950s and
examined the social consequences of changing patterns in external trade. Larkin's
pioneering study of Pampanga Province prompted a wave of regional and local
research during the 1970s.[4] Viewed in retrospect, the foreign trade studies of the
1950s and the regional social histories of the 1970s are complementary explorations of a single process — the incorporation of the Philippine archipelago into the
European world economy.

The wellsprings of the post-1970 burst of regional historical studies were several
and, for the most part, separate. The prewar Filipino literati had left a legacy of
local historical writings.[5] The foreign trade research of the 1950s had indicated the

importance of the 18th and 19th century economic changes and, through Wickberg's work on the mestizos, shown the enormous documentation available in the Manila archives.[6] Fr. Horacio de la Costa, in his lectures and essays, had urged an examination of questions beyond Rizaliana and modern colonial history.[7] Perhaps most importantly, American historian John Larkin began using archival sources to study Kapampangan provincial history and, through several influential journal articles, urged scholars to undertake parallel local studies as a means of moving beyond the Manila-centric vision of Philippine national history. Since the Philippines was overwhelmingly rural, the history of the provinces, Larkin argued, would have to be written before the national history could be complete.[8] Of equal importance, research into other areas of Southeast Asia, particularly Indonesia, had a strong influence on the development of Philippine social history. Scholars such as Harry Benda, Benedict Anderson and Clifford Geertz defined questions in their studies of modern Indonesia that Philippine social historians applied to their regional research.[9]

In response to these and more diffuse influences, regional historians initiated separate studies that constitute, in sum, a comprehensive survey of social change across the archipelago from the late 18th to mid-20th century. Almost all of the major Christian lowland ethnolinguistic groups, representative areas of the Luzon cordillera and some of the larger Muslim groups have been the object of at least one study during the decade, while some regions attracted two or more researchers.[10]

A new image of Philippine society appears to be emerging from these studies of regional social history. Almost by accident, regional history has developed an analytic approach appropriate to an archipelagic nation. Instead of accepting the scholarly legacy of Philippine studies, the regional historians used the rich resources of the Manila archives and local repositories to weave a new fabric for Philippine social history.

The corpus of pre-1970 scholarship, when surveyed in its entirety, portrayed the Philippines as a society that was essentially "political" in nature. Like peasants in other "rural" or "folk" societies, the Filipino was the sum of the social and bureaucratic units in which he lived — extended kinship networks, the traditional village, the municipality and the nation. Restrained by traditional values of reciprocity, the Filipino lived in a state of cultural, political and economic "undevelopment" that served as a positive barrier to "modernization". While the economy faltered, politics boomed. Channelling all their conflicts and aspirations through the political system, the Filipinos were unified through an electoral-cum-bureaucratic structure running from the municipality to Manila. The historical origins of this system lay with the Spaniards who imposed unified parochial and municipal administrations over a disparate archipelago and the Americans who added an overlay of provincial and national government. Imposed upon an archipelagic *tabula rasa,* these bureaucratic legacies played a key role in the making of the Philippine nation.[11]

A markedly different view of Philippine society emerges from a reading of these essays. The Philippines is not simply the sum of its political systems nor is it the prisoner of its anti-modern "Philippine values". Instead of a village society bound by cultural patterns and political rules, there emerges the image of an intensely dynamic society, or series of societies, that has changed constantly throughout its four centuries of recorded history in response to economic, demographic and technological stimuli. Instead of the "political" image of Philippine society and the cultural image of a Filipino "folk" resistant to change, we can substitute data indicating a society whose merchants and peasants were skilled innovators. The only tradition is that of change, and the only enduring "values" are those of an essential rationality. Nor is the country's historical "underdevelopment" a simple function of imperial exploitation, but very much a collaborative enterprise between the indigenous elite and foreign interests.

In terms of method, these essays represent a new kind of marriage between history and social science. During the 1960s social science dominated the interdisciplinary dialogue: historians accepted the models of cultural anthropology and sociology without criticism and social scientists expropriated chronology as evidence for their monogenic paradigms or presentist concerns.[12] Instead of working from the present backward, the authors of these essays, three of whom are anthropologists and one a geographer, begin in the past and move toward the present — an essential component of the historical method. Instead of substituting hypotheses or "models" for data, these essays employ a variety of archival, oral and published documentation for their largely social and cultural analyses. The result is a fusion of methods and problematic concerns which constitutes, in the Philippine context, both a new kind of history and a new kind of social science.

The Study of Social Change

As long as Philippine historical study concentrated on national political history it dealt with particularistic problems that were of little import to those outside the field. These regional social histories, however, address themselves to questions of social change that have for some years concerned students of Europe, the Americas and other parts of Asia. As one of the latest to shift from political to social history, Philippine historiography was, during the 1970s, a beneficiary of methods and questions refined elsewhere. Now that many of these regional studies are reaching publication, it appears that Philippine social history is about to repay some of its intellectual debts.

These Philippine regional histories represent, in sum, one of the first comprehensive attempts at analysis of the complexity of the local social transformations that accompanied integration into the world economy. In one of his recent essays a leading student of the world trade system, Immanuel Wallerstein, expressed his concern over lack of any significant research on "the processes that made it possible for the capitalist world system to incorporate ... non-capitalist social systems outside it".[13] Similarly, sympathic critics of another analyst of global trade systems, Andre Gunder Frank, have commented on his failure to probe the relationship between "'external dependence' on the one hand and the 'internal' structures of underdevelopment on the other".[14] Scholars of European social history —

particularly those associated with the French *Annales* school — are providing us
with an increasingly complete portrait of the complex, internal changes which
underlay Western Europe's emergence as the "core" or "centre" of the world trade
system.[15] But we still know very little about the parallel processes of change which
accompanied the integration of Asia, Africa and Latin America into this world
capitalist system as "periphery" or "satellite" states. The sum of the Philippine
regional studies represent a significant step forward, perhaps among the first, in
filling this gap in our knowledge.

The inadequacy of the existing literature is most evident in Frank's widely read
essay, *Capitalism and Underdevelopment in Latin America.* Influenced by the
U.N. economist Raúl Prebisch and the Marxist literature on imperialism, Frank
found the roots of Latin America's economic underdevelopment in the 16th century. From the time of the Spanish Conquest, Europe's development and Latin
America's underdevelopment were reciprocal elements in the same historical process. Frank saw all economic exchange within this world capitalist system as a
series of exploitative "centre-satellite" relationships running from Madrid-Santiago
(Chile), to Santiago-hacienda, to hacienda-Indian village.[16] In particular, his rather
reductionist treatment of colonial societies and their transformation drew widespread criticism, including some from those sympathetic to the larger thesis.[17]

Subsequent research has done little to clarify these questions. Wallerstein has offered a more refined model of the 16th century world system. Instead of a series of
centre-satellite relations, he sees northern Europe, England and Holland as the
"core" of a world trade system supported by "semi-peripheral" areas like Italy and
"peripheral" regions like Latin America. Between the early 16th and late 19th century the "core", England, gradually extended its trading sphere to the "external"
areas — most importantly, Russia and Asia — thereby covering almost the entire
globe.[18] But Wallerstein does not discuss the processes of change that accompanied an external area's integration into the world system.

The scholarly debate over the impact of world trade on Third World societies
coincided, fortuitously, with the Philippine regional research of the 1970s.
Although not influenced by either Frank or Wallerstein, several of the Philippine
regional studies were already directed at complementary questions. Problems of
trade and empire had been central to Southeast Asian historiography for several
decades, and studies of their impact on Indonesian society by scholars such as J.C.
van Leur and Clifford Geertz had influenced many historians of the Philippines.
Moreover, the Philippine historical studies of the 1950s, particularly those by
Legarda and Wickberg, had outlined the broad dimensions of the colony's socio-
economic transformation during the 19th century and laid the foundation for more
detailed work. Drawing upon these currents within Southeast Asian historiography, Philippine regional researchers posed questions about the impact of
foreign trade upon local societies that suddenly became germane to a wider debate
over "underdevelopment" and "world trade systems".

Like much of Asia, the Philippines did not enter the world trade system until the
late 18th century. The consequent process of social change, as demonstrated in

these essays, was quite varied and complex. The archipelago's integration within the world economy was slow, uneven, protracted and largely non-cumulative. After the Spanish landing in the 1560s, Manila became the remotest outpost of Spain's Latin American empire, marginally linked to Europe through the trans-Pacific galleon trade. The Philippines offered few incentives for an intensive exploitation of local resources. The archipelago was too remote for bulk trade, produced neither pepper nor spices, and was too lightly populated for mines or plantations (580,000 people in 1606 versus Mexico's 11 million in 1519).[19] Manila was, however, well situated to serve Spain in its brief bid for an Asian trading empire in the first half of the 17th century. Responding to dislocations in the global silk market, Manila became an entrepôt re-exporting Chinese silks and luxury goods to Europe via Mexico. Manila's trade statistics peaked in 1605, went into a protracted decline after 1650, and did not make a sustained recovery until 1787.[20] During the early 17th century, Spain also used Manila as its naval base in an abortive challenge to Dutch dominion over the Moluccas, the spice islands of eastern Indonesia. With the decline of the China trade and end of the Dutch wars by 1650, the Philippines became a missionary province and Manila an outpost of empire sustained by its surrounding haciendas.[21]

With the quickening of Europe's world trade in the 18th century, colonial pressures on the Philippine archipelago, at a low ebb for over a century, began to accelerate. Manila had been separated from 16th century Europe by time and distance. Improved maritime technology and industrial growth breached those barriers and brought Manila within Europe's reach from the late 18th century onwards. With the exception of corvée labour for naval construction during the Dutch wars of the 17th century, Spanish colonial administration had rested rather lightly on the archipelago. Outside of Manila and a few regional centres, Spanish monastic missionaries were generally responsible for colonial administration. Scattered and poorly financed, the missionaries lacked the means or the economic incentive to control most localities effectively. When the Spanish did apply pressure, as during the Dutch wars, intense but localized resistance was the result. Only on the large haciendas ringing Manila, the friar estates, did a transformed pattern of socio-economic relations develop during the first centuries of colonial rule. In his essay on this region Roth describes social relations on the haciendas and their operation as commercial rice and cattle estates producing the food surplus to sustain the Manila colony.[22]

The archipelago developed its first new links to intra-Asian, European and North American markets in the early decades of what we might call, in Braudel's terms, the Philippines' "long 19th century". Between 1780 and 1920, roughly speaking, most of the archipelago experienced a socio-economic transformation — a process which constitutes the central theme of the essays in this volume.[23] The clearing of Philippine frontiers was high social drama complete with the sudden migrations, land grabbing and aboriginal slaughters that accompanied the process in America, Australia or the Argentine. Migrating outward from the crowded Ilocos coast of northwestern Luzon, peasant pioneers cleared the Central Luzon Plain and the

The Philippines, Islands and Regions

ILOCOS COAST

LUZON

PACIFIC OCEAN

SOUTH
CHINA
SEA

Manila

Bikol
Peninsula

Mindoro

VISAYAN

Samar

Panay

Leyte ISLANDS

Negros Cebu

Bohol

Palawan

SULU

SEA

MINDANAO

Sulu

Land over 500 metres

0   75   150   km   300

Archipelago   CELEBES SEA

Cagayan Valley. Quitting a similarly parched and overcrowded ecosystem in western Panay, Ilongo pioneers cleared the rain forests of Negros Island for vast new sugar plantations. By the 1870s the archipelago's several regions produced a range of commercial crops for intra-Asian and international markets — tobacco in the Cagayan Valley of northeastern Luzon, rice and sugar in Central Luzon, *abaca* (hemp) for sailing cordage in the Bikol Peninsula, sugar in the Western Visayas, and Chinese foodstuffs in Sulu.

It is one of the truisms of Philippine historiography that these economic transformations were the fundamental cause of the failed national revolution (1896-1902) and the ultimate emergence of the modern nation state.[24] Judging from new evidence provided by these regional studies, however, the processes of socio-economic transformation also generated strong centrifugal forces that weakened the emerging nation. Rather than a unified nationalist elite, the Philippines had developed a series of distinct regional elites with divergent, if not conflicting, economic interests. Tagalog entrepreneurs who leased their rice lands from the Spanish church estates ringing Manila had every reason to support the nationalist revolt. Pampangan and Visayan sugar planters, who owned their own plantations, had equal cause to rally to the side of Spain and the colonial order.

The origins of national disunity spring then from the very processes of socio-economic transformation during this "long" 19th century. The Philippines did not develop as a unitary colonial economy oriented towards a single satellite entrepôt at Manila. Instead, the archipelago emerged as a series of separate societies that entered the world economic system at different times, under different terms of trade, and with different systems of production. This diversity of response was, in large part, the result of the influence of the Anglo-American merchant houses that dominated the export economy. Areas such as Bikol, Cebu and the Western Visayas developed separate ties to global markets through local branches of Anglo-American merchant houses. Operating with minimal support from Spanish colonial authorities, Anglo-American firms tolerated diversity in local production systems and made no attempt, through the imposition of political controls, to regularize patterns of production. Only in the Cagayan Valley of northeastern Luzon and several lesser areas did the colonial government, through its Tobacco Monopoly, control the new commercial agriculture.[25] By their uniqueness, however, these areas simply added to this patchwork pattern of diversity. In other areas, Anglo-American merchants dealt with an independent Muslim sultanate in Sulu, large-scale Chinese mestizo sugar planters in the Western Visayas, and small scale Filipino hemp farmers in Bikol. Whereas in Java traditional production systems were exploited or preserved, in the Philippines production was more commercialized, or capitalist, from the outset. Emerging regional elites consequently played a critical entrepreneurial role in the growth of Philippine exports and some local peasantries began to operate as rural wage labourers. The archipelago thus became the first area in Southeast Asia to develop indigenous commercial elites employing modern production methods and a rural wage labour market.

The variety and complexity of these social transformations were, in fact, greater than indicated previously in the literature on either world trade or Philippine history. Many of the critical regional transitions began in the late 18th century, *not* in the mid 19th, and were *not* the product of direct contact with the European-American markets.[26] In the 18th century Britain became an active agent in the intra-Asian trade and began handling an enormous variety of local commodities. In Sulu, for example, British merchants bartered arms and specie for products aimed at balancing the drain of her China trade such as sharks' fins, sea cucumbers or birds' nests. Dealing with Chinese mestizo merchants who called at Manila, British country traders imported Indian cloth and exported local textile products from Panay and the Ilocos coast.[27] In both regions, the transition to commercial agriculture in the mid-19th century was preceded by the growth of handicraft weaving industries in the late 18th century.

Several of these essays indicate that the early 19th century textile industry may have played a key role in the transition to export agriculture during the mid 19th century. Although there have been a number of references to the textile industry in the Philippine literature, its extent and significance have not been appreciated.[28] The emergence of native entrepreneurs, capital and wage labour in two important core regions of the archipelago was largely the product of the early 19th century weaving industry. Developing traditional handicraft weaving into a large-scale inter-island and international commerce, Chinese mestizo entrepreneurs drew women weavers into Iloilo City and created an urban centre of 71,000 people by 1857 — a population then as large as that of Chicago, Sydney, Valparaiso or Caracas. Profiting from a trade in cloth and indigo, the Ilocano mestizos raised the city of Vigan whose streets of fortress-like houses stand as mute testimony to their economic skills. The subsequent collapse of the weaving industry at Vigan and Iloilo in the 19th century generated the "push" for Ilocano and Ilongo peasant pioneers to migrate onto the Central Luzon and Negros frontiers — which then became the most commercialized and important agricultural areas in the archipelago. If the 18th century textile industry did reach such a high level of development, then the indigenous input of initiative and capital played a far greater role in the archipelago's transformation than previously imagined. The extent to which the proto-industrial textile growth of the late 18th - early 19th centuries created the preconditions — capital, labour and entrepreneurship — for the subsequent surge in export agriculture has not yet been determined. Judging from the history of the Negros sugar industry presented here, it was of major, perhaps paramount, importance.

In his work on the 16th century world system, Wallerstein argues that there was a marked tendency for slave systems to develop in the Latin American "periphery", tenanted agriculture in the Italian "semi-periphery", and wage labour in the English "core".[29] During the Philippines' long 19th century things were a good deal less tidy. A similar range of labour control systems was evident within the archipelago. The Sulu sultanate operated a slave system; the Chinese mestizo planters of Negros passed quickly through tenancy to wage labour and debt bondage; and Central Luzon planters used tenancy. Local elites used the most ap-

propriate and economical labour control strategy, which was largely determined by
the special needs and history of the region. In the main export areas local elites
were faced with a similar problem — how to secure, control and motivate adequate
labour in labour-deficit areas during periods of rapid economic expansion. In Sulu
the Muslim sultanate was faced with a critical labour deficit and responded by
raiding Christian Filipino regions to secure an adequate slave labour supply. In the
Western Visayas, Chinese mestizo sugar planters had antecedent careers as textile
entrepreneurs and used traditional tactics of wage payments and debt bonding
developed in their primitive weaving factories to create a wage labour market in
the cane fields. In Central Luzon the use of tenant farmers on both sugar and rice
fields was the product of pre-Hispanic production methods further developed in
the friar estates and a rational response to the problem of forest clearance in a
labour-deficit and capital-deficit production system.

None of these categories adequately describes the remote highland or insular
people who were marginally involved in cash crop activities. Although the commercial sector of their economies was initially limited, they still maintained linkages to
cash economies in the more developed regions. During most of the archipelago's
long 19th century the highland economies remained tangential to accelerated commercial activities in the lowlands. Through colonial military operations, both the
Igorots of the Luzon Cordillera and the Bukidnon of Mindanao's northern plateau
were forced into more extensive lowland contacts. Gradually their local economies
were commercialized.

The internal economic structures of individual export regions at the periphery of
the world system are quite complex and appear almost as microcosms of the global
system. Indeed, the entire range of "core" through "external" economic relations
found in the world system are also apparent in each export region of the Philippine
archipelago. The Western Visayas region, for example, comprises two large
islands, Panay and Negros, facing each other across a narrow and easily navigable
ocean strait. By 1900, after a half-century of rising sugar exports, the entrepôt Iloilo City and the belt of sugar plantations along the western coast of Negros Island
opposite made up the "core" of the region's export economy. Although its
geographical extent was quite limited, the core plantation sector made strong
demands upon many non-sugar-producing localities for capital, labour, materials
and subsistence food crops. The rice-growing districts along the wide plains of Iloilo Province on Panay's southeastern coast became the region's "semi-periphery".
Formerly the region's core, this area maintained its population and continued to expand, albeit not at the same rate as the plantation sector, as an important source of
rice for the Negros sugar districts. The overpopulated, narrow coastal plains of Antique Province in western Panay became the region's "periphery". The province suffered a permanent population loss through migration to Negros and became the
source of seasonal contract labour for cane-cutting on the sugar plantations. Areas
of Capiz Province on Panay's northern coast also played a peripheral role as suppliers of woven palm-leaf sacks for the shipment of export sugar. The region's "external" areas consisted largely of the southern quarter of Negros Island which har-

boured unsubjugated pagan villages in its forest fastness. Although the degree of integration with the export core varied with each locality, both the level of economic activity and population were largely determined by demands emanating from the core. This pattern was most typical of the more active export regions — Sulu, Cebu, the Western Visayas and Central Luzon. For other less "developed" regions, such as Samar and the Luzon Cordillera, foreign trade was not so dominant and the level of internal integration among localities was consequently much lower. By virtue of the Philippines' role as a "satellite" or "peripheral" zone in the world system, however, a parallel set of relations did *not* operate among the individual regions of the archipelago.

Beyond Regional History

Although the volume of regional studies and the energy of individual researchers are admirable enough, publications, until now, have been few and inter-regional or international comparisons fewer. Without some reflection, Philippine social history runs the danger of sinking into a "neo-antiquarian swamp".[30] Surveying the vast numbers of European local studies, the *Journal of Social History* commented in 1976: "The obvious question is when to stop, or better yet, when to combine. How many English villages need family reconstitution before sound generalization is possible?"[31]

Or, to put the question somewhat differently, how many Philippine provinces need to be studied before we can begin to make some meaningful inter-regional or perhaps national generalizations about the process of social change in the colonial Philippines? It would, of course, be equally damaging to attempt a premature national synthesis before sufficient evidence is in hand — in effect, allowing hypotheses to disregard evidence. Having broken the Philippines apart into regional blocs, is it, in fact, our aim to reassemble a national historical edifice, or are we social scientists using these regions as evidence for the resolution of more universal questions about the nature of social change?

Several of these studies seem to indicate that the local/national axis may not be the only fruitful focus for future research. The essays on Sulu, Iloilo City and Central Luzon demonstrate that external linkages to world markets, not to Manila, were the dominant stimuli for local transformations. This does not deny, of course, the gradual development of centralized political and religious systems during the colonial period. After the initial Spanish contact in the 16th century, however, these Manila-centred systems were not the main sources of stimuli. Manila became a simple conduit for more powerful economic links to intra-regional, intra-Asian and international trade networks. With the opening of provincial ports to direct foreign trade after 1855, centrifugal forces, already building, gained momentum. During the Philippines' long 19th century, Central Luzon's rice trade developed for the Asian market, Bikol's hemp cultivation for the American market, and the Western Visayan sugar industry for the world market. Hence the emergence of Iloilo City, Cebu and Sulu as commercially sovereign entrepôts maintaining independent ties to external trade networks. The 19th century boom in export agriculture did not initiate a simple upward curve of national integration; it also provided the economic base for the growth of regional autonomy. The new logistic networks led from the countryside, to the regional entrepôt, to the global markets — not to Manila, except in those areas of Central Luzon where she performed the role of a regional entrepôt. In this type of economic system, elite loyalties were complex and contradictory. The sugar planters of the Western Visayas, for example, became citizens of the world market in the 1860s but did not become citizens of the Philippine Republic until 1946 — a difference of nearly a century that left them with strong anti-national economic interests and close political ties to their premier sugar customer, the United States.

Future research into regional social history, in the Philippines and other primary exporting nations, might consider external linkages as an integral component of the local social structure. In so doing, a new model for analysis of these relations might serve as a useful starting point. There is a natural, and perhaps misleading, tendency to conceptualize these relations in hierarchical terms as a ladder leading from the locality, to the national/colonial capital, to the world market:

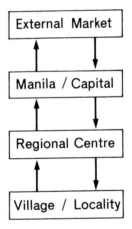

In the case of the Philippines and other areas of Southeast Asia, the region might be better understood as an independent point operating in a shifting network of linkages:

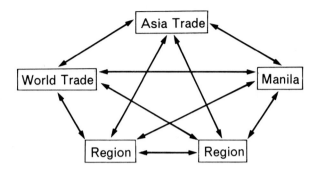

In analyzing the processes of social change, the linkage approach might lead to an examination of those external factors which play a role in local transformations. A complete portrait of local social dynamics is not possible without consideration of such factors. In primary exporting societies, closed national-regional networks are probably the exception.

Although such a model deals primarily with trade linkages, its application might improve our understanding of political relations in primary exporting nations. Carl Landé, for example, has analyzed Philippine politics in terms of dyadic ties reaching upward on the ladder from the locality through the province to Manila.[32] Writing on Southeast Asia as a whole, James Scott has described politics in terms of patron-client dyads originating in the locality and extending to the national/colonial capital.[33] Applying the linkages model would, for example, lead to an extension of these networks to include patron-client ties between regional economic elite and foreign factors or corporations, or between national/colonial political leaders and foreign governments.

Our greatest insights might spring from comparative studies with areas outside the Philippines. For example, there might be some meaningful comparisons possible between patterns of seaborne trade in the closed maritime basins of Europe and Asia where navigation developed relatively early — such disparate areas as the Mediterranean, the northwestern quadrant of the Indian Ocean, the Java Sea, the Sulu zone, the central Philippines, or Japan's Inland Sea. During much of this millenium, all have had a high level of internal trade and been linked periodically through a global commerce. Alternatively, we might consider comparisons between the social histories of individual regions; for example, Central Luzon and eastern Java, or Central Luzon and western Sicily.[34] Adopting a different focus, we might attempt an analysis of the historic interaction between external trade and internal social change for insular Southeast Asia, much as Braudel has done for the Mediterranean. Such studies could establish important commonalities or highlight contrasts that would illuminate our understanding of both the global trade system and its separate components. The results might prove a useful counterweight to the local-national political axis about which studies of Southeast Asia have for so long revolved.

NOTES

Brian Fegan, Jeremy Beckett, Robin Lim, Norman Owen, and Glenn May commented extensively on earlier drafts. In particular, Brian Fegan made a number of major contributions to the argument during both the preliminary and final draftings.

1 Almost all recent surveys of the academic literature on the Philippines have been in agreement about the considerable advances made during the 1970s. Their assessment of the previous two decades of scholarship has been uniformly negative, ranging from the polite critique to the devastating assault. See, Mark McDonald Turner, "Interpretations of Class and Status in the Philippines: A Critical Evaluation," *Cultures et développement* 10 (1978), 265-96; Robert Lawless, "The Foundation for Culture-and-Personality Research in the Philippines," *Asian Studies* 5 (April 1967), 101-36; Norman G. Owen, "Trends and Directions of Research on Philippine History: An Informal Essay," *Asian Studies* 12 (August-December 1974), 1-17; John A. Larkin, "Introduction," in, John A. Larkin, ed., *Perspectives on Philippine Historiography: A Symposium* (New Haven: Monograph Series No. 21, Southeast Asia Studies, Yale University, 1979), 1-11; Norman G. Owen, "Interdisciplinary Contribution: A Historian's View," in, Larkin, ed., *Perspectives on Philippine Historiography,* 65-74; Bruce Cruikshank, "Philippine Historiography: Accomplishment and Promise: 1955-1976," in, Donn V. Hart, ed., *Philippine Studies: History, Sociology, Mass Media and Bibliography* (De Kalb: Occasional Paper No. 6, Center for Southeast Asia Studies, Northern Illinois University, 1978), 1-97.

2 For some examples of the generally high standard of colonial and foreign scholarship on Indonesia see, J.C. van Leur, *Indonesian Trade and Society: Essays in Asian Social and Economic History* (The Hague: W. van Hoeve, 1955); B. Schrieke, *Indonesian Sociological Studies: Selected Writings, Part One* (The Hague: W. van Hoeve, 1955); Clifford Geertz, *The Religion of Java* (New York: Free Press, 1960); Clifford Geertz, *Agricultural Involution: The Processes of Ecological Change in Indonesia* (Berkeley: University of California Press, 1963); Harry Benda, *Continuity and Change in Southeast Asia: Collected Journal Articles of Harry J. Benda* (New Haven: Monograph Series No. 18, Southeast Asia Studies, Yale University, 1972); O.W. Wolters, *Early Indonesian Commerce: A Study of the Origins of Srivijaya* (Ithaca: Cornell University Press, 1967); Benedict R. O'G. Anderson, *Java in a Time of Revolution: Occupation and Resistance, 1944-1946* (Ithaca: Cornell University Press, 1972); Claire Holt, ed., *Culture and Politics in Indonesia* (Ithaca:

Cornell University Press, 1972).

3 Edgar Wickberg, *The Chinese in Philippine Life, 1850-1898* (New Haven: Yale University Press, 1965); Benito F. Legarda, Jr., "Foreign Trade, Economic Change and Entrepreneurship in the 19th Century Philippines" (doctoral dissertation, Harvard University, 1955); Serafin Quiason, *English "Country Trade" with the Philippines* (Quezon City: University of the Philippines Press, 1966).

4 John A. Larkin, *The Pampangans: Colonial Society in a Philippine Province* (Berkeley: University of California Press, 1972); John A. Larkin, "The Place of Local History in Philippine Historiography," *Journal of Southeast Asian History* 8 (September 1967), 306-17.

5 Perhaps the best example of the influence of the Philippine tradition of local historiography on the new social history is the use that American social historian John Larkin made of the writings of Pampangan historian Mariano Henson. See, Mariano Henson, *A Brief History of the Town of Angeles in the Province of Pampanga* (San Fernando: Ing Katiwala Press, 1948); Mariano Henson, *The Province of Pampanga and Its Towns* (Angeles: By the Author, 1965); Larkin, *The Pampangans.*

6 Wickberg, *The Chinese in the Philippines,* 253-54.

7 Horacio de la Costa, *The Background of Nationalism and Other Essays* (Manila: Solidaridad, 1965), 23-30.

8 Larkin, "The Place of Local History".

9 Benda, *Continuity and Change in Southeast Asia,* 121-53; Wolters, *Early Indonesian Commerce;* Benedict R. O'G. Anderson, "The Idea of Power in Javanese Culture," in, Holt, *Culture and Politics in Indonesia,* 1-69; Geertz, *Agricultural Involution.*

10 The essays contained in this volume are a representative but incomplete compendium of the work being done in the field. For examples of other work see, Cesar Abib Majul, *Muslims in the Philippines* (Quezon City: University of the Philippines Press, 1973); Reynaldo Clemeña Ileto, *Magindanao, 1860-1888: The Career of Dato Uto of Buayan* (Ithaca: Data Paper No. 82, Southeast Asia Program, Cornell University, 1971).

11 This image of the Philippines was not the product of a single scholar or school of analysis. It emerges from a survey of the postwar social science and historical literature on the Philippines. For perhaps the most succinct summary of this viewpoint see, Onofre D. Corpuz, *The Philippines* (Englewood Cliffs, N.J.: Prentice-Hall, 1965). For some samples of the sociological literature on Philippine folk values, see, Frank Lynch, *Social Class in a Bikol Town* (Chicago: Research Series 1, Philippine Studies Program, University of Chicago, 1959); Frank Lynch, "Social Acceptance Reconsidered," in, Frank Lynch and Alfonso de Guzman II, eds., *Four Readings on Philippine*

Values (Quezon City: IPC Papers No. 2, Institute of Philippine Culture, Ateneo de Manila University, 1973), 1-68; Mary Hollnsteiner, "Reciprocity in the Lowland Philippines," in, Lynch & de Guzman, *Four Readings in Philippine Values,* 69-91.

12 For some instances of interaction between history and social science during the 1960s and early 1970s see, Theodore Friend, *Between Two Empires: The Ordeal of the Philippines, 1929-1946* (New Haven: Yale University Press, 1965), 15-30; Carl H. Landé, *Leaders, Factions, and Parties: The Structure of Philippine Politics* (New Haven: Monograph Series No. 6, Southeast Asia Studies, Yale University, 1965), 24-57; Hollnsteiner, *The Dynamics of Power in a Philippine Municipality,* 28-62; and Benedict J. Kerkvliet, "Peasant Society and Unrest Prior to the Huk Rebellion in the Philippines", *Asian Studies* 9 (August 1971), 164-213.

Among historians, David Steinberg was perhaps the least critical in his use of social science concepts. For an extended critique of Steinberg's writing on the World War II period see, Alfred W. McCoy, "'Politics by Other Means': World War II in the Western Visayas, Philippines," in, Alfred W. McCoy, ed., *Southeast Asia Under Japanese Occupation* (New Haven: Monograph Series No. 22, Southeast Asia Studies, Yale University, 1980), 191-245; David J. Steinberg, *Philippine Collaboration in World War II* (Ann Arbor: University of Michigan Press, 1967).

13 Immanuel Wallerstein, *The Capitalist World-Economy* (Cambridge: Cambridge University Press, 1979), 135-36.

14 David Booth, "Andre Gunder Frank: An Introduction and Appreciation," in, Ivar Oxaal, Tony Barnett, and David Booth, eds., *Beyond the Sociology of Development: Economy and Society in Latin America and Asia* (London: Routledge & Kegan Paul, 1975), 70-72.

15 Peter Burke, ed., *A New Kind of History from the Writings of Febvre* (London: Routledge & Kegan Paul, 1973); Fernand Braudel, *The Mediterranean and the Mediterranean World in the Age of Philip II* (New York: Harper & Row, 1972); J.H. Hexter, "Fernand Braudel and the *Monde Braudellian*," *Journal of Modern History* 44 (December 1972), 480-539; Fernand Braudel, "Personal Testimony," *Journal of Modern History* 44 (December 1972), 448-67.

16 Andre Gunder Frank, *Capitalism and Underdevelopment in Latin America: Historical Studies of Chile and Brazil* (New York: Monthly Review Press, 1967), 3-33, 98-120.

17 Philip J. O'Brien, "A Critique of Latin American Theories of Dependency," in, Oxall, *Beyond the Sociology of Development,* 7-27.

18 Wallerstein, *The Capitalist World Economy,* 1-36; Immanuel Wallerstein, *The Modern World-System: Capitalist Agriculture and the Origins of the*

European World-Economy in the Sixteenth Century (New York: Academic Press, 1974), 301-57.

19 For a good summary of Spanish colonial policy see, John Leddy Phelan, *The Hispanization of the Philippines: Spanish Aims and Filipino Responses, 1565-1700* (Madison: University of Wisconsin Press, 1967), 93-120.

20 Pierre Chaunu, *Les Philippines et le Pacifique des Ibériques (XVIe, XVIIe, XVIIIe siécles.) Introduction méthodologique et indices d'activité* (Paris: S.E.V.P.E.N., 1960); Pierre Chaunu, "Le Galion de Manille," *Annales E.S.C.,* 6 (October-December 1951), 447-62; Jacques Bertin, Serge Bonin, Pierre Chaunu, *Les Philippines et le Pacifique des Ibériques (XVIe, XVIIe, XVIIIe siécles) Construction Graphique* (Paris: S.E.V.P.E.N., 1966).

21 William Lytle Schurz, *The Manila Galleon* (New York: E.P. Dutton, 1939), 342-57; Wallerstein, *The Modern World System,* 335-44; Nicholas P. Cushner, S.J., *Spain in the Philippines: From Conquest to Revolution* (Quezon City: IPC Monographs No. 1, Ateneo de Manila University, 1971), 101-52.

22 See also, Dennis Morrow Roth, *The Friar Estates of the Philippines* (Albuquerque: University of New Mexico Press, 1977); Nicholas P. Cushner, *Landed Estates in the Colonial Philippines* (New Haven: Monograph Series No. 20, Southeast Asia Studies, Yale University, 1976).

23 The best general description of these economic changes is found in Legarda, "Foreign Trade".

24 Cushner, *Spain in the Philippines,* 186-229; Teodoro A. Agoncillo, *The Revolt of the Masses: The Story of Bonifacio and the Katipunan* (Quezon City: University of the Philippines Press, 1956), 1-17; Teodoro A. Agoncillo, *A Short History of the Philippines* (New York: New American Library, 1969), 63-99.

25 Cushner, *Spain in the Philippines,* 186-209; Benito Legarda, Jr., "American Entrepreneurs in the 19th Century Philippines," *Explorations in Entrepreneurial History* 9 (1957), 142-59.

26 Most of the literature on the Philippines emphasizes the economic changes initiated by foreign merchants through the growth of links to European-American markets in the mid and late 19th century. See, David Joel Steinberg, ed., *In Search of Southeast Asia: A Modern History* (New York: Praeger, 1971), 155-164, 229-35; Wickberg, *The Chinese,* 65-93; Legarda, "Foreign Trade"; Cushner, *Spain in the Philippines,* 197-209.

The literature on dependency tends to place a considerable emphasis on direct links to European-American markets as the critical factor in these social transformations. See, Frank, *Capitalism and Underdevelopment,* 67-73; Jonathan Fast and Jim Richardson, *Roots of Dependency: Political and Economic Revolution in the 19th Century Philippines* (Quezon City:

Foundation for Nationalist Studies, 1979), 13-53; Wallerstein, *The Modern World-System,* 301-24.

27 Quiason, *English "Country Trade,"* 62-111.

28 Wickberg, *The Chinese,* 81-83; Cushner, *Spain in the Philippines,* 190-93.

29 Wallerstein, *The Modern World-System,* 301-02, 347-57, 85-93; Wallerstein, *The Capitalist World-Economy,* 17-20.

30 Elizabeth Fox Genovese and Eugene Genovese, "The Political Crisis of Social History: A Marxian Perspective," *Journal of Social History* 10 (Winter 1976), 214-15.

31 Peter N. Stearns, "Coming of Age," *Journal of Social History* 10 (Winter 1976), 245-55.

32 Landé, *Leaders, Factions and Parties;* Carl Landé, "Networks and Groups in Southeast Asia: Some Observations on the Group Theory of Politics," *American Political Science Review* 67 (March 1973), 103-27.

33 James C. Scott, "The Erosion of Patron-Client Bonds and Social Change in Rural Southeast Asia," *Journal of Asian Studies* 32 (November 1972), 5-37; James C. Scott, "Patron-Client Politics and Political Change in Southeast Asia," *American Political Science Review* 66 (March 1972), 91-113.

34 The literature on Mediterranean societies raises some intriguing comparative questions for the Philippines. See, Anton Blok, *The Mafia of a Sicilian Village, 1860-1960: A Study of Violent Peasant Entrepreneurs* (New York: Harper & Row, 1974); Sydel F. Silverman, "The Community-Nation Mediator in Traditional Central Italy," in, Jack M. Potter, et. al., eds., *Peasant Society: A Reader* (Boston: Little, Brown, 1967), 279-93.

LUZON

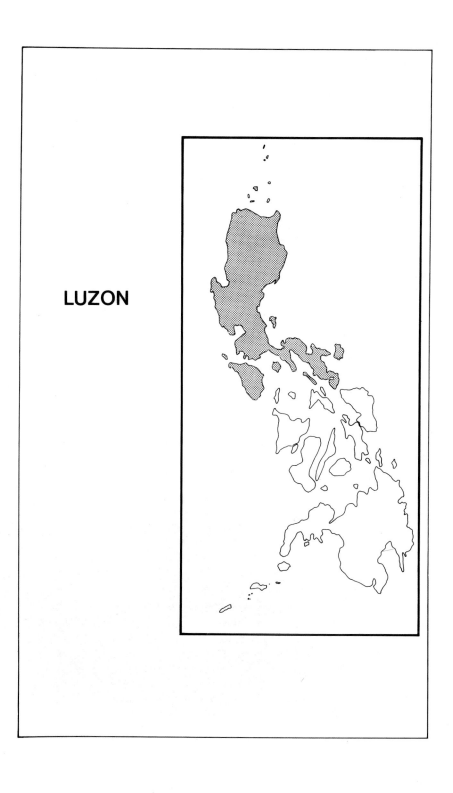

Control and Compromise in the Cagayan Valley

ED. C. DE JESUS

It would be unpardonable, after John Phelan's analysis of Philippine Hispaniza-tion, to assume anything more than an approximate correspondence between the intent and the effect of Spanish colonial policies. As Phelan demonstrated, a combination of several forces imposed severe limitations on Spain's capacity to transform Philippine society according to its preconceived plans.[1]

The archipelago's many languages and scattered settlements, as well as Spain's own limited manpower resources, posed problems for even the basic task of com-municating the decrees that originated in Manila, Mexico or Madrid. Ensuring that colonial subjects received and understood their orders was only the first require-ment. Comprehension did not necessarily engender compliance. The *indios,* par-ticularly the *indio* elite, often managed to deflect the force of government measures which threatened their interests. *Indio* officials imitated the posture adopted by Spanish colonial administrators when confronted with unpopular orders from the home government — they complied in principle, but not in prac-tice.

Despite their government's tendency to proclaim universal codes grounded in im-mutable moral and legal principles, Spanish provincial officials recognized the need to redefine objectives to fit local circumstances. Research into local history has documented the way the idealism of higher officials in Madrid was balanced with the realism of local officials in the Philippine provinces. Different regions presented distinct configurations of opportunities and constraints to Spanish col-onizers. The Spaniards had to take account of each area's specific geography and resource base as well as its existing social and political leadership, and forged com-promises often concealed in the common rituals and regulations of colonial rule. The history of the Cagayan Valley during the 18th and 19th centuries provides an example of this process of accommodation between central dictates and local con-straints.

The Regional Setting

Occupying the northeastern corner of the island of Luzon, the Cagayan Valley encompasses a well-defined region of some 26,000 square kilometres bounded on the north by the China Sea and on the other three sides by mountain ranges. In the west, the Cordillera Central system, with maximum elevations reaching close to 3,000 metres, cuts off the valley from the Ilocos coastal region. The highlands of the Caraballo, rising to between 1,750 to 1,850 metres, block the passage in the south to the Central Plain of Luzon. Along its eastern edge, the Sierra Madre mountain range begins its ascent, exceeding elevations of 1,850 metres before plunging sharply on the other side into the waters of the Pacific Ocean.[2]

A corruption of the Ilocano word for river, *carayan,* may have given the region its name. For the Ilocano guides of the Spanish explorers, the land across the mountain was the region of the river which the Spaniards called the Rio Grande de Cagayan.[3] Rising on the Sierra Madre mountains near the southern end of the valley, the Rio Grande pushes north, picking up the waters of other rivers along its 600 kilometre course, and pouring them out past the town of Aparri into the Babuyan Channel.

The precision with which one can delineate the physical contours of the Cagayan region contrasts with the vagueness of the term "Cagayan" when used for an administrative area or to identify the valley's indigenous population. Until well into the 19th century, the province of Cagayan extended over the entire valley. In 1839 security considerations and administrative convenience prompted the government to reduce the burden on Cagayan's governor by designating Ilagan and the towns further south as the new province of Nueva Vizcaya. Another reorganization took place in 1856 when the province of Isabela was created from portions of Cagayan and Nueva Vizcaya.[4]

The 19th century redistribution of administrative responsibilities only partially accounts for the ambiguity of the term "Cagayan". The area's linguistic and cultural diversity makes the term somewhat imprecise even during the earlier period when administrative boundaries coincided with the valley's geographical limits. The Spaniards recognized that there was not a single "Cagayan" people or "Cagayan" language; there were instead the Ibanags, Itaves, Gaddanes and others, each speaking a distinct dialect.[5] For the Spaniards, however, the only distinction that mattered was that between Christians and *infieles* or pagans. Thus, the Diocese of Nueva Segovia, to which Cagayan belonged, distinguished between established parishes and frontier missions. While the basis of the division was essentially religious, it also had its political aspects. For practical purposes, mission territory remained outside the effective control of the colonial government. Strictly speaking, "Cagayanes" referred to any of the indigenous inhabitants of the valley; in the literature on the valley, however, the term frequently applied more narrowly to the people who had accepted the Christian Church and the Spanish King. The extension of the term "Cagayanes" was in this sense rather flexible, expanding in scope with the consolidation of the Spanish spiritual and political conquest.

Some of the earliest reconnaisance missions conducted by the Spanish *conquistadores* on Luzon reached as far as Cagayan. The Spaniards needed a port on the northern or eastern coast of the island to serve as a way station for the Acapulco galleons.[6] In 1572, only a year after the conquest of Manila, Juan de Salcedo, grandson of the *conquistador* Legaspi, sailed from Vigan on the western coast of Luzon, rounded Cape Bojeador, touched various points on the northern coast of Cagayan, including Aparri, and continued on around Cape Engaño to the port of Lampon in Tayabas on the eastern coast of the island. But Salcedo made no attempt to push inland against the obviously hostile inhabitants or to plant perma-

The Cagayan Region in the 19th Century

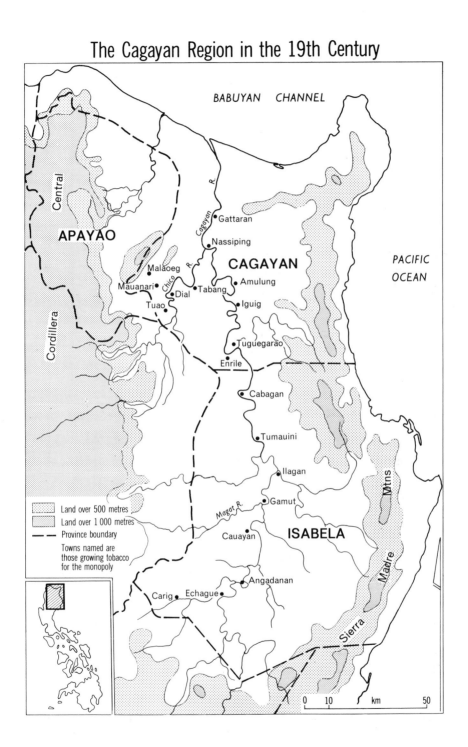

BABUYAN CHANNEL

Central

APAYAO

Cordillera

Cagayan R.

Gattaran

Nassiping

CAGAYAN

PACIFIC OCEAN

Malaoeg

Mauanari

Chico R.

Dial

Tabang

Amulung

Tuao

Iguig

Tuguegarao

Enrile

Cabagan

Tumauini

Ilagan

Magat R.

Gamut

Cauayan

ISABELA

Sierra

Madre Mtns

Angadanan

Carig

Echague

Land over 500 metres
Land over 1 000 metres
Province boundary
Towns named are
those growing tobacco
for the monopoly

0   10   km   50

nent bases in the area.[7]

With their attention focused on the galleon trade, the early Spaniards were little inclined to bother with a remote, untamed territory which lacked any readily exploitable sources of wealth. But China, the source of the silks shipped by the galleons to Mexico, did hold an interest for the Spaniards, and they saw Cagayan as virtually at its doorsteps. One official explained: "Although the land [Cagayan] is of much cost and no profit, it is a foothold and stepping stone by which to enter the realm of Great China."[8]

But if the Spaniards could use Cagayan as a staging point for an expedition into another country, might it not also serve as a springboard for an assault on Spanish Manila? Indeed, the troops despatched by Governor Ronquillo Peñalosa in 1581 to establish a base on the "frontier of China" discovered that *wako,* northern "pirates", had already built a fort at the mouth of the Cagayan River.[9] After destroying a pirate ship off Cape Bojeador, Captain Pablo Carreon sailed his force of Spanish soldiers and supporting Tagalog, Kapampangan and Visayan recruits up the river and built his own fort behind the Japanese base. The Japanese tried to remove the threat at their back but Carreon's force withstood the Japanese attack and chased the remaining *wako* out to sea. But the fear that the Japanese would return to invade the colony gave the Spaniards another reason for keeping watch on Cagayan.[10]

Having disposed of the "pirates", Carreon continued up the Rio Grande to a place called Lal-lo or Lalloc where he established the city of Nueva Segovia. By 1588, Nueva Segovia had a Spanish population of about 85 people. In the early 17th century the city sheltered 200 Spanish residents, not including the Spanish soldiers and officers manning the fort. Mindful of the "proximity to China", the government maintained a regular garrison in Nueva Segovia consisting of 50 to 100 and more men.[11] But as hopes of conquering China and fears of an attack by Japan gradually faded, so did Spanish interest in Cagayan. By 1622, only 20 Spanish civilians and 50 soldiers remained in the city.[12]

Colonial Administration

The colonial government, in fact, never kept sufficient troops in the field long enough to impose complete control over Cagayan. The Spaniards emerged as the single most powerful force in the valley, partly because of superior weapons and the assistance of *indios* from other provinces, but principally because the indigenous population lacked a rallying point which could unify the valley's independent kinship communities. Thus the Spanish military managed, without great difficulty, to overcome the limited resistance that these fragmented groups could mobilize. To be able to govern the area effectively, however, the colonial government needed the missionaries to persuade the people to accept Spanish sovereignty.

Mission work in the valley began in earnest only in 1595, when the arrival of 15 missionaries from Spain permitted the Dominican Order to accept the spiritual administration of the province which had previously been entrusted to the Augustinians.[13] In the same year, Pope Clement VIII made northern Luzon into a separate bishopric. Its first bishop, Fray Miguel de Benavidez, O.P., chose Nueva Segovia, the capital of Cagayan province, as the diocesan see.[14]

The shortage of qualified personnel seriously hampered early missionary activity. Primitive and perilous travel conditions placed sharp limits on what a handful of priests, however dedicated, could accomplish. Language problems further increased the demands on the limited manpower resources. The Dominican chronicler Diego de Aduarte reports the difficulty with which the older priests learned foreign languages, a problem compounded by the multiplicity of linguistic groups in the valley.[15]

The shortage of linguistically competent missionaries was a perennial problem in Cagayan. Some 200 years after Aduarte's time, the Dominican provincial was constrained to refuse Fray Juan Guidoti permission to return to Spain, alleging the urgent need in Cagayan for priests conversant with the language. Fray Carlos pointed out that the man assigned to Tuguegarao, then with a population of 12,600, was a 73-year-old priest, deaf, nearly blind and so sickly that he had to be carried up to the altar in a chair to celebrate Mass. The priest at Lalloc was also old and sick, and there was no one at all to minister to the people of Iguig, Amulung, Gattaran and Nassiping. These six towns, with a combined population of 17,800, had no one to attend to them except the two old priests at Lalloc and Tuguegarao.[16]

As in the other areas of the archipelago, Spanish priests and officials in Cagayan found it necessary to solicit the co-operation of indigenous leaders to promote the process of conversion and pacification. This strategy had received the sanction of both Church and State. The 1582 Synod of Manila declared: "The Viceroy or Governor is in conscience bound to appoint native judges and governors in places that are already peaceably settled. It is equally binding upon the King to see that this is accomplished."[17] Unfortunately, there is little information about these pre-conquest "native governors". Outside the Muslim areas where a clearer hierarchy was evident, the Spanish *conquistadores* used the term "king" for the more powerful leaders who ruled whole coasts or small islands and borrowed the indigenous term *datu* for the more common local chiefs who usually controlled less than 100 families or no more than a few villages. Although we know little about the complex process by which the independent *datu* were transformed into a colonized local elite, known collectively as the *principalia,* the actual regulations make it clear that such a transformation did occur. Spanish canonical and civil law recognized that the people had native officials, whose title to rule Spanish colonials could not arbitrarily repudiate. The principle laid down by Philip II in 1594 recognized this point:

> It is not right that the Indian chiefs of Filipinas be in a worse condition after conversion; rather should they have such treatment that would gain their affection and keep them loyal . . . Therefore, we order the governors of those islands to show them good treatment and entrust them, in our name, with the government of the Indians of whom they were formerly the Lords.[18]

The decision to recognize and to use the established social and political hierarchy, however expedient in practice, nonetheless represented a fundamental departure from the preferred state of affairs. The missionaries in Cagayan justified the imposition of Spanish colonial rule as a step that would liberate the people from the tyranny of their own chiefs.[19] In the end, however, colonial rule served to legitimize and reinforce the superior status of local tyrants. The pre-conquest rulers, by and large, maintained their positions and privileges as village and town officials in the colonial administrative order.

These *principales,* as the *cabezas de barangay* and *gobernadorcillos* were collectively designated, became responsible for preserving public order in their communities and collecting tribute and labour dues from their subjects. Technically, they were subject to the supervision and control of their provincial governor, or *alcalde,* and to their parish priest. But their role as intermediaries between the indigenous community and the colonial rulers allowed them opportunities for converting political influence into social and economic power at the expense of their subjects.

The *Discurso Paranético* which *Audiencia* Judge Gómez de Espinosa published in 1657 documented some of the ways in which the *principales* contrived to oppress the commoners or *cailanes.*[20] The authority vested in the *principales* by the Spaniards to requisition goods and services for local or central government projects gave them the leverage over the rest of the community. Goods so requisitioned were often paid for at prices fixed by the government, invariably lower than market rates, and ordinary citizens really had no way of knowing whether the *cabeza* actually used the articles they delivered to support official projects or whether he appropriated them to feed his family or to resell for a profit.

No subterfuge was necessary for some *cabezas.* According to Gómez de Espinosa, they simply took from the people whatever struck their fancy — a hunting dog, cow or bull, perhaps, or a piece of jewelry — and offered as payment a beating with whip or stick. Similarly, *cabezas* impressed the people to work on their fields, repair their houses, or row their boats. Nor were they above hiring out corvée labour to private parties who needed extra hands to cut wood or build houses. The willingness of people to pay cash for exemption from corvée labour was yet another source of *cabeza* income.

Gómez de Espinosa's memorial did not specifically cite abuses by Cagayan *principales.* But the Ordinances of Good Government promulgated for Cagayan by Joseph Ignacio de Arzadún y Revolledo in 1739, following a tour of inspection of the province, confirmed that its *principales* were not unfamiliar with the extortionate practices described in the earlier document.[21]

In addition to the advantages inherent in their official position, conditions peculiar to Cagayan provided other means for *principales* to augment their influence. Parish priests in other provinces collected cash fees for baptisms, marriages and burials, as well as the three *reales* which tribute-payers contributed for the expenses incurred during the three feast days which each town celebrated. But the *indios* of Cagayan did not have the money to cover these charges. Instead, the people supplied the parishes with goods and services through the *principales.* They brought rice, fish, chicken and eggs for the priest's table and served as oarsmen or porters in his travels. While the arrangement had official approval, the potential for abuse was great.[22] In 1841-1842 complaints against the system reached all the way to the *Audiencia,* the colony's high court, which still ruled favourably on this practice.[23]

The Spaniards never succeeded in controlling the highlands surrounding the Cagayan Valley. Until the end of the Spanish regime, therefore, Cagayan remained a frontier area where Christian communities and pagan tribes co-existed uneasily. In an effort to pressure these communities of *infieles* to accept Christianity and Spanish rule, the government passed an edict in 1642 proscribing "all intercourse, communication or trade with the heathen, apostate, and fugitive Indians, negroes and Zambals, who inhabit the mountains and hills, and are not reduced to the royal obedience, under penalty of 100 lashes and two years' service in the harbour of Cavite".[24] The revised Ordinances of Good Government issued in 1696 reaffirmed the general prohibition against commerce with the *infieles.* But enterprising *cabezas* and *gobernadorcillos* continued to trade salt, cotton, cloth and metal tools and tobacco for mountain bees-wax and gold. The *principales* of the frontier towns, according to the missionaries, encouraged the pagans to defy the Spaniards in order to preserve the clandestine trade from which they profited.[25]

The uprising which shook the central and southern towns of Cagayan in 1762 provides a glimpse of the relationship which had developed under colonial rule between *principales* and commoners. Starting from Ilagan, the rebellion rippled down the Cagayan River as far as Tuguegarao and spread along the Chico River to Piat, Tabang and westwards to Malaoeg. For the Spaniards, the trouble in Cagayan was a minor incident; their main concerns were the defence of the colony against the British and suppression of far larger revolts led by Juan de la Cruz Palaris in Pangasinan and Diego Silang in Ilocos. The Cagayan uprising was significant, however, as the first rebellion in the valley not led by the *principales.* In fact, they were among its targets.

In Ilagan, the main centre of the uprising, the rebels dragged the *gobernadorcillos* and the *cabezas* to the town tribunal and there whipped them "in the manner they used to whip the commoners". A dramatized reconstruction of the Ilagan "mutiny" pieced together over a century later from the town's collective memory portrayed the rebels as loyal subjects and faithful Christians. They insisted that they had respected their holy religion and obeyed the King and his representatives. But they did have one grievance: "They could no longer suffer that the governors and the *principales* treat them as slaves, beating them without mercy for the slightest fault; and . . . they have resolved to put an end to this tyranny by teaching them a lesson." The stage rebels then took the *gobernadorcillo* and sentenced him to 25 strokes, inflicting the same punishment on some of the *cabezas.*[26]

The actual rebellion was short lived. The rebels advanced against Nueva Segovia but failed to win over the *indios* who instead co-operated with the city's garrison in repulsing the attack. In the reprisal that followed, 33 rebels were hung at the gallows. Among those executed were Silang's emissary from Ilocos and a rebel ally from Pangasinan. As a security measure while they were campaigning against the British and Silang's followers, the Spaniards exiled 217 men from the rebel towns to the northern section of the province. When the order for their release came in 1765, only 124 of the exiles were still alive.[27]

The suppression of the 1762 rebellion was as much a victory for the *principales* as for the Spaniards. However much they might have sympathized with the commoners, the Spaniards could not condone violence against *cabezas* and *gobernadorcillos* who were still the legally constituted authorities. By recognizing Spanish sovereignty and accepting baptism, native chiefs were thus able to impose over the commoners a dominance suspiciously similarly to the pre-conquest despotism denounced by the missionaries — with the additional support of Spanish soldiers to protect them.

Tobacco Monopoly

The Spanish dependence upon the *principales* was most evident in their administration of the Tobacco Monopoly. Although the introduction of commercial crops changed the composition of local elites in most of the archipelago, the traditional Cagayan *principalia* seem to have made the transition without any substantial loss of influence. Established to produce for local consumption and not for export, the Tobacco Monopoly operated by designating certain limited areas near Manila as official production zones, or *coleccion*. The Monopoly made its profits by purchasing all tobacco in the *coleccion* at artificially low prices and then selling direct to consumers in designated Monopoly marketing areas, like Cagayan, at inflated prices. Any illicit cultivation within the marketing areas would obviously reduce Monopoly sales, and the system's success required the rigorous prohibition of all local tobacco cultivation.

When the government designated Cagayan a Monopoly marketing area in 1785, many Spanish officials predicted that it would virtually paralyze provincial trade.[28] Tobacco was then Cagayan's principal commercial crop, much sought after by the *infieles* in the mountains, snuff and cigar manufacturers in Manila, and traders from Pangasinan, Zambales and Ilocos. It was also an article of general consumption, serving as the people's "bread and wine" and the "most effective medicine for the cure of all their deficiencies."[29] Those opposed to the Monopoly's introduction feared that the attempt to ban tobacco cultivation in the valley would result in open rebellion. While conceding the importance of the crop to the economy of the province, other officials believed that the people would accept the Monopoly provided only that one condition was observed: the officials in charge of the government tobacco shops and the Monopoly guards had to be appointed from among the *principales*, "for they have much authority over the common people and do not like *indios* from other provinces coming to command them."[30]

Although the Tobacco Monopoly apparently provoked an uprising among the newly Christianized communities, the older towns submitted to the government order without resistance.[31] But the provincial economy could not cope with the disruption of trade patterns caused by the prohibition of its principal commercial crop. The decline of commerce, coupled with a series of typhoons, floods and a plague of rats and locusts in 1788 and 1789 left the Cagayan destitute and led to the flight of people to other provinces.[32]

Cagayan managed to collect a portion of the 1789 tribute tax only by such extreme measures as flogging debtors and throwing them into prison. The following year, the governor found it necessary to suspend collections altogether. Manila approved the decision and extended the period of relief from 1789 to 1792. To avert famine in the province, it also ordered Pangasinan to send to Cagayan up to 420 *cavans* and Ilocos up to 540 *cavans* of rice from the stocks they held for the royal treasury's account.[33]

In addition to the relief measures, the central government also initiated an investigation into the causes of the crisis that had overtaken Cagayan. Without ignoring the disastrous effects of bad weather and plagues, the governor and the missionaries pointed to the Tobacco Monopoly as the underlying source of Cagayan's economic problems. Unless the government permitted the province to resume planting tobacco, they anticipated a continuing drain of manpower. The governor estimated that Cagayan had already lost between 4,000 to 5,000 people from deaths and desertion.[34]

Other officials, however, remained resolutely opposed to exempting Cagayan from the Monopoly and rejected the idea that it was responsible for the province's problems. They admitted that the Cagayanes had been deserting their province, moving out as far as Manila to enlist as soldiers in the garrisons, ship out as seamen on trading vessels, or serve in private homes as cleaners, cooks and coachmen. But they insisted that emigration had been going on well before the establishment of the Monopoly.

It was not necessary, according to these officials, to postulate resistance to the Monopoly as the explanation for the flight from the province. The Cagayanes, apart from being shiftless vagabonds by nature, only sought to escape from their tribute obligations and, above all, from the oppression of the *principales*. Rather than blame the Monopoly, the missionaries should look to the "intolerable burden of personal service" imposed on the people and the harsh treatment suffered at the hands of their *gobernadorcillos,* under whom they were only "a little less than slaves". With all the compulsory labour required in public works and extorted by private persons, the people "hardly had any time to look to their own interests and attend to the fields from which they provided for their families' maintenance."[35]

The disagreement between Spanish officials and missionaries over what really ailed Cagayan dragged on for a few more years. The stand-off favoured the *status quo*; it was easier for Manila to allow the Monopoly to continue than to initiate a change in policy by granting an exemption to Cagayan. Eventually, however, ecology and geography prevailed over policy, and the government gradually relaxed its ban on tobacco-growing in the province.

The quality of Cagayan's tobacco crop had never been called into question. The region's soil and climate were particularly suited to tobacco. The colonial government also began to realize that Cagayan's isolation offered some advantages. Bounded on three sides by mountain ranges, the valley would be far more defensible against smugglers than the province of Bulacan where the government then cultivated tobacco for the Monopoly. A special investigator appointed to study the *coleccion* estimated that smugglers took between one-third to two-thirds of its crop.[36]

In 1797, 12 years after the original decree placing Cagayan under the Monopoly and prohibiting cultivation, the government began authorizing specific towns to grow tobacco for the Monopoly. In 1805, the government closed down the Bulacan *coleccion*. By 1830, the *coleccion* in Cagayan had grown to 21 towns with over 9,500 tributes. In that year, Cagayan surpassed Gapan, the government's first *coleccion,* in the quantity and quality of the crop it delivered to the Monopoly.[37]

With Cagayan's development as the Monopoly's principal *coleccion* came the instrumentalities by which the colonial government administered a tobacco-growing region. Foremost among these was the office of *caudillo* or overseer. For closer supervision of the tobacco farmers, in 1784 Governor-General Basco had authorized the appointment of a *caudillo* for every group of 50 farmers. His role was to supervise tobacco cultivation and then to ensure that the farmers delivered all the tobacco leaves that they produced to the Monopoly.[38] In return, the *caudillo* enjoyed exemption from corvée labour and tribute dues. Other benefits later granted by the government included a commission based on the size and quality of the *caudillo*'s tobacco deliveries.[39]

In the Cagayan *coleccion,* the post of *caudillo* routinely went to the *principales*. Don José Ferrer, appointed by Manila in 1831 to conduct an investigation of the *coleccion,* saw no practical alternative. He recognized that the *principales* acted like petty tyrants in exploiting the commoners, the *gente pleveya*. Without their intervention, however, he doubted the government's ability to derive the slightest profit from the community. In his view, the Cagayan *indio* would not work without artful persuasion or open pressure. Ferrer argued against choosing the *caudillo* from outside the *principalia* since to do so would add unnecessarily to the class of tyrants oppressing the people. Denying the *caudillo* appointment to the *principales* would in no way weaken their control over the people; they already had it within their means to force compliance to their commands. Commoners elevated above their station might be tempted to abuse their newly acquired powers.[40]

The establishment of a *coleccion* in Cagayan did not materially enhance the power of the *principales* over the commoners, although the many rules promulgated to govern the *coleccion* probably opened up more opportunities for the arbitrary exercise of that power. But the importance of Cagayan as a source of tobacco leaves attracted a burdensome load of bureaucratic attention. The meticulous record-keeping required by the Monopoly deprived the *indio* of the protection that obscurity had provided. Moreover, the *coleccion,* because it did offer the people a means of livelihood, gave them a stake in the established order and made it more difficult to decide on desertion as a way of evading pressure from the *principalia*. Thus, the *coleccion* indirectly reinforced *principales*' dominance by helping to encourage a more stable and a more docile population.

The *principales* gained another benefit. Government and missionary policy, from the early days of the conquest, had always aimed at gathering the people who were used to living in small, scattered clusters into larger settlements which were more easily controlled and Christianized. The Spaniards had found it difficult to implement this policy in Cagayan. The people preferred to maintain their houses close to the fields they were cultivating and the government did not have enough resources to enforce resettlement.[41] Throughout the 19th century, the missionaries continued to press for the policy of consolidation. The colonial government, however, had changed its priorities to accommodate the requirements of the Monopoly. Faced with the need to expand tobacco cultivation, it condoned the dispersal of the population in small settlements along the course of the Cagayan River where the best tobacco lands were located.[42] The persistence of the pattern of scattered settlements made it more difficult for governors or missionaries to control the abuses of the *principales*.

There were cases, needless to say, when governors or missionaries took the initiative in exploiting the community.[43] Even in these cases, however, they needed the assistance of some *principales* to serve as collectors or enforcers. Other *principales* might then become the victims of exploitation, but they would always have ways to shift some of the burden to the commoners.

The Monopoly favoured the *principales* in a third way. In the Central Luzon provinces, the *principales* had to face competition from the economically powerful Chinese and their mestizo offsprings. By the mid-18th century, wealthy landowners and merchants of largely mestizo stock had begun to capture *gobernadorcillo* offices in the province of Pampanga.[44] In his essay below, Marshall McLennan suggests that in Nueva Ecija, as in Pampanga, the pre-Spanish *datus* who had become *principales* under the Spaniards also failed to maintain their ground against mestizo encroachment.[45] Nicholas Cushner posits an even earlier date for the decline of the Tagalog *datus*. By the late 16th century, according to Cushner, their power had begun to diminish as control over land and labour resources passed to other Tagalogs of non-*datu* descent and to mestizos and Spaniards.[46] Elsewhere in this volume, Cullinane and McCoy show how the Chinese mestizo merchants of Cebu and Iloilo extended their control beyond the cities to emerge as dominant regional elites by the late 19th century. Cagayan, however, had nothing to offer the Chinese. Government control of the principal industry in the valley left little scope for individual entrepreneurship. Until well into the 19th century, the Chinese were conspicuous in Cagayan by their absence and, needless to say, no Chinese mestizo group emerged.[47] The *principales* were thus spared the challenge of a formidable competitor for economic and political power.

The Chinese began moving into the valley only in the 1870s when the government, under severe budgetary pressures, began to pay the farmers of the *coleccion* in *papeletas,* or certificates of credit, rather than cash. Government delays in redeeming these certificates — sometimes for as long as three years — enabled the Chinese to develop a business in discounting the *papeletas*. To meet immediate subsistence needs, farmers were willing to sell their *papeletas* for as low as 20 to 50 percent of face value.[48]

The abolition of the Monopoly in 1880 opened up more economic opportunities for the Chinese, and they began to gain greater prominence in the Cagayan provinces. Apart from their participation in the tobacco trade, they also moved into the retailing of consumer articles. Indeed, they combined the two activities, paying for the tobacco they purchased from the farmers with pieces of textile and other merchandise. They established their *tiendas de sari-sari,* or general merchandise stores, in the towns and built up another traditional line of business, money-lending. Within ten years of the Monopoly's abolition, the Chinese had established a substantial economic base in the valley.[49]

Relatively free from central government controls as long as they delivered acceptable tobacco to the Monopoly, and shielded for a long time from external competition by the remoteness of the region and the curbs on private enterprise, the *principales* could concentrate on consolidating their power over the commoners and, when possible, enlarging it at each other's expense. Elite status in the Cagayan Valley was unquestionably a prize of great worth. In other places, the burdens of office-holding may have indeed discouraged people from aspiring to the positions of *cabeza* and *gobernadorcillo.*[50] In Cagayan, this was not the case. The post of *gobernadorcillo,* the highest administrative office to which an *indio* could be appointed, was an object of keen competition. The office became even more attractive during the period of the Monopoly because the *gobernadorcillo* was also concurrently the *caudillo* of the *coleccion.* The political power, social prestige and economic benefits that went with the appointment invited attempts at manipulating elections to keep the post under the control of one individual or family. Ambitious *principales* resorted to bribes and threats to win votes from their colleagues, arranged marriages to cement political alliances and courted the support of the provincial governor and the parish priest.[51]

Competition for political office was, for all practical purposes, an exclusive game only the *principales* could play. Commoners might enter the ring, ironically enough, only when a corrupt governor or parish priest intervened in the electoral process to promote purely personal interests. Thus, Thomas Danao, Vincente Lazam and Domingo Cannu, three *principales* of Tuguegarao, complained in 1827 that the parish priest, Fray José Tomas Figuerola, selected the *gobernadorcillo* and other town officials from among his servants and familiars, even though these were only commoners (*en origen de la calidad de Pleveyos*). The complainants attributed the influence of these commoners to their spouses, apparently a formidable family of five sisters — Liberata, Josefa, Tecla, Ambrocia and Rosa Maguddatu — whom they also accused of enjoying a scandalously close relationship with the parish priest.[52]

The complaint detailed the various ways in which these officials exploited the people. Using the needs of the priest and the parish as the excuse, they provided themselves and their households with goods and services. People were sent to the mountains for as long as three months at a time to cut wood, allegedly required for the repair of the church but actually going into the construction of private houses. Girls assigned to take care of the church ended up in the homes of the Maguddatu sisters to sew, weave, wash clothes and perform other household chores.[53] The bill of particulars again emphasized the great leeway available to the *principales* for abusing legitimate claims to goods and services.

Loose control from Manila doubtless made it possible for some priests and governors to elevate commoners to the rank of *gobernadorcillo* on their own arbitrary authority. It seems more plausible to assume, however, that they would usually choose their retainers from among the *principales*. One of those against whom the complaint was directed bore the same surname, Lazam, as one of the complainants, suggesting some intra-*principalia* rivalry in the community (or, alternatively, that one of the complainants had the same lowly origins as those he was denouncing). It is also interesting to note that three of the surnames which appear in the 1827 document surface in later *gobernadorcillo* records: Battung (Aparri, 1856); Argonza (Lalloc, 1861 and Enrile, 1871); and Lasam/Lazam (Tuguegarao, Solana, Enrile and Iguig, 1876-1877).[54]

Conclusion

The abolition of the Monopoly exposed Cagayan's *principales* to challenges from the Chinese and other outsiders and released social and economic forces disruptive of elite continuity. Protected from external competition for so long, some of these *principales* lost their grip on political power, but only at about the same time that Spain itself was losing its grip on the colony.[55]

Constrained by unique regional circumstances, the colonial government had to accept the necessity of compromising some of their conflicting religious, political and economic objectives. The net effect of these Spanish accommodations appears to have been the consolidation of the power of the traditional *indio* elite which had ruled as *datus* before the conquest and as *cabezas* and *gobernadorcillos* under the colonial regime. The conditions created by Spanish policies in Cagayan buttressed the privileged position of the *principales,* allowing them to maintain their dominance over the community much longer than their counterparts in other provinces.

NOTES

1 John L. Phelan, *The Hispanization of the Philippines: Spanish Aims and Filipino Responses, 1565-1700* (Madison: University of Wisconsin Press, 1959).

2 For the geography of the Cagayan Valley, see, Frederick Wernstedt and Joseph Spencer, *The Philippine Island World: A Physical, Cultural, and Regional Geography* (Berkeley: University of California Press, 1967), 17-19, 314-29; T.M. Burley, *The Philippines: An Economic and Social Geography* (London: G. Bell and Sons, Ltd., 1973), 77-78; Julian Malumbres, *Historia de Cagayan* (Manila: Santo Tomas, 1918), 9-12.

3 José Burgues, O.P., "Descripcion general del Valle de Cagayan (Hacia 1897)," Archivo de la Provincia de Santíssimo Rosario (hereafter, APSR), Mss. Cagayan.

4 Gregorio Arnaíz, O.P., "Missiones Dominicanos en el Valle de Cagayan". APSR, Mss. Cagayan, vol. 1, doc. 17, 16-17, *Colección de Autos Acordados de la Real Audiencia de Filipinas* (Manila: Imprenta de Ramirez y Giraudier, 1861-1866), 5:207.

5 On the ethnic and linguistic diversity of the valley, see, *El Archipielago Filipino: Coleccion de Datos* (Washington, D.C.: GPO, 1900), 1:26-27, 40-41. See also, Felix Keesing, *The Ethnohistory of Northern Luzon* (Stanford: Stanford University Press, 1962), 168ff.

6 Arnaíz, "Missiones Dominicanos," 2-4.

7 Malumbres, *Cagayan,* 19-20; Pablo Fernandez, O.P., *Dominicos donde nace el sol* (Barcelona: Tall. Graf. Yuste, 1958), 34. According to Carlos Quirino, Salcedo also "sailed up and down the Cagayan River". "Juan de Salcedo: The Last Conquistador," in, *The Beginnings of Christianity in the Philippines* (Manila: Philippine Historical Committee, 1965), 135.

8 "Gaspar de Ayala to Felipe II," Manila, 15 July 1589, in, Emma H. Blair and John A. Robertson, *The Philippine Islands, 1493-1898* (Cleveland: Arthur H. Clarke, 1903-1909), 7:124.

9 "Gonzalo Ronquillo de Peñalosa to Felipe II," Manila, 16 June 1582; "Juan Baptista Roman to Viceroy," Cabite, 25 June 1582, in, Blair and Robertson, *The Philippine Islands,* 5:26, 5:192-93.

10 "Gonzalo Ronquillo de Peñalosa to Felipe II," Manila, 1 July 1582; "The Second Embassy to Japan," April-May 1593, in, Blair and Robertson, *The Philippine Islands,* 5:197, 9:39.

11 Domingo de Salazar and others, "Relation of the Philippine Islands," in, Blair and Robertson, *The Philippine Islands,* 7:37-38; Antonio de Morga, *Sucesos de las Islas Filipinas* (Cambridge: Cambridge University Press, 1971), 288; "Description of the Philippine Islands," in, Blair and Robertson, *The Philippine Islands,* 18:101.

12 "Miguel Garcia Serrano to King," Manila, 31 July 1622, in, Blair and Robertson, *The Philippine Islands,* 20:234-35.

13 Diego de Aduarte, "History of the Dominican Missions," in, Blair and Robertson, *The Philippine Islands,* 30:284-85. Fernandez, *Dominicos,* 34-35.

14 Malumbres, *Cagayan,* 357.

15 "History," in, Blair and Robertson, *The Philippine Islands,* 30:304; 31:38-39, 263-64, 294-95; 32:102.

16 Fray Carlos Arbea to Governor-General, Manila [Ca. 1830]. APSR, Mss. Cagayan, vol. 14, doc. 29, fols, 330-33.

17 Quoted in J. Gayo Aragon, O.P., "The Controversy Over the Justification of Spanish Rule in the Philippines," in, Gerald H. Anderson, ed., *Studies in Philippine Church History* (Ithaca, N.Y.: Cornell University Press, 1969), 12-13.

18 Quoted in Morga, "History," in, Blair and Robertson, *The Philippine Islands,* 16:155-56.

19 Aduarte, "History," in, Blair and Robertson, *The Philippine Islands,* 30:193, 295-98.

20 James S. Cummins and Nicholas P. Cushner, S.J., eds., "Labor in the Colonial Philippines: The *Discurso Paranetico* of Gómez de Espinosa," *Philippine Studies* 22 (1974), 190-91.

21 John L. Phelan, ed. "The Ordinances Issued by the Audiencia of Manila for the Alcaldes Mayores (1642, 1696, and 1739)," *Philippine Social Sciences and Humanities Review* 24 (1959), 377-80, 383-84, 384-85, 386-87, 389-90, 398.

22 Vincente Gómez, O.P., "Sobre estipendios de los misioneros dentro de Cagayan," 30 October 1777, APSR, Mss. Cagayan, vol. 11, doc. 10, fols. 32-35.

23 APSR, Mss. Cagayan, vol. 11, doc. 16.

24 "Ordinances of Good Government," 1642, 1696, 1768, in, Blair and Robertson, *The Philippine Islands,* 50:214.

25 Julian Malumbres, *Historia de Isabela* (Manila: Santo Tomas, 1918), 70; William Henry Scott, *The Discovery of the Igorots: Spanish Contacts with the Pagans of Northern Luzon* (Quezon City: New Day Publishers, 1974), 65; Blair and Robertson, *The Philippine Islands,* 50:248-49.

26 In Malumbres, *Isabela,* 72. Commoner leadership and an anti-*principales* strain also distinguished the uprising in Pangasinan and made it different from any of the earlier rebellions in that province. See, Rosario Mendoza Cortes, *Pangasinan, 1572-1800* (Quezon City: University of the Philippines Press, 1974), 182-85.

27 Manuel Ignacio de Arsa y Urutia, Nueva Segovia, 19 August 1763; Franco de la Torre to Cagayan Alcalde, Manila, 18 May 1765, APSR, Mss. Cagayan, vol. 12, doc. 2.

28 Governor General José Basco de Vargas issued the order establishing the Tobacco Monopoly in the Philippines on 13 December 1781. When first promulgated, however, the order only covered Manila and the provinces of Tondo, Cavite, Batangas, Tayabas, Laguna de Bay, Pampanga, Bataan and Bulacan. By 1786, the Monopoly extended over the entire island of Luzon. See, Edilberto C. de Jesus, *The Tobacco Monopoly in the Philippines: Bureaucratic Enterprise and Social Change, 1766-1890* (Manila: Ateneo de Manila University Press, 1980), 29-56.

29 José Mariano Cubella, Nueva Segovia, 17 February 1785. Archivo General de Indias (hereafter, AGI), Ultramar 638.

30 Joaquín de la Cuesta, Ilocos, 16 July 1785, AGI, Ultramar 633.

31 Malumbres, *Isabela,* 79; Scott, *Igorots,* 158-60.

32 Philippine National Archives (hereafter, PNA), EPC 1751-1847, 64, 686-723; 64, 725-64.

33 PNA, EPC 1751-1847, 64, 502-603; 64, 534; 64, 541-43.

34 Manuel de Garay to Felix Berenguer de Marquina, Nueva Segovia, 16 May 1791. PNA, EPC 1737-1847, 64, 524-29.

35 Melchor de la Lama, 7 December 1732. "Testimonia de expediente sobre poner siembras de tavaco en la Provincia de Cagayan," AGI, Ultramar 638.

36 "Copia del oficio que pasó el Señor Superintendente General de estas Yslas al Factor General Don Pedro de la Peña, en 22 de agosto de 1796, y planos propuestos para extender las siembras de tobacco a la provincia de Cagayan e isla de Marinduque," AGI, Ultramar 634.

37 Pedro de la Peña to King, Manila 20 June 1821, AGI, Ultramar 634; José Ferrer, "Expediente en que se trata de promover las siembras de Cagayan hasta el grado de perfección posible; formar un reglamento que fije las respectives funciones de los empleados de acquella colección y medios que puedan ponerse en planta para evitar en lo sucesive las vejaciones a que han expuestos los naturales de dicha provincia por varios de sus colectores. . .," Piezá, 1831, PNA, Tobacco Monopoly, fols. 60-66; de Jesus, *Tobacco Monopoly,* 207-09.

38 Don Joseph Basco y Vargas Balderrama, y Rivera, Cavallero del Orden de Santiago, etc. "Los repetidos excesos . . .," Manila, 28 January 1784, PNA, Tobacco Monopoly.

39 *Instrucción general para la dirección, administración e intervencción de las rentas del estanco y sus colecciones, aprobados por 5. M. en Real Order del 10 de agosto de 1850* (Madrid, 1849), art. 371-72, 82.

40 Ferrer, fol. 67.

41 Ferrer, fol. 74.

42 Malumbres, *Isabela,* 214; "Comunicacion del Superior Gobierno al Provincial sobre el expediente promovido por varios parrocos de la Isabela para que los habitantes se concentren y no vivan esparcidos, 27 de abril de 1865". APSR, Communicaciones con las autoridades eclesiastricas y civiles, 1866 a 1888, Legajo No. 7, vol. 1, doc. 33, fols., 17-18; Remigio Tamayo, O.P., on Tuguegarao, 17 February 1877, APSR, Mss. Cagayan, vol. 14, fols. 241-42; Bonifacio Corrugjedo, O.P., on Echague, 10 February 1877, APSR, Mss. Cagayan, vol. 14, fols. 237-38; "Relación del P. Buenaventura Campa sobre Echague, año 1899," APSR, Mss. Cagayan, vol. 15, doc. 30.

43 See de Jesus, *Tobacco Monopoly,* 140-42, 149-53.

44 John Larkin, "The Evolution of Pampangan Society" (doctoral dissertation, New York University, 1966), 52-80; Edgar B. Wickberg, *The Chinese in Philippine Life, 1850-1898* (New Haven: Yale University Press, 1965), 127 ff.

45 "Land and Tenancy in the Central Luzon Plain," *Philippine Studies* 17 (1969), 61-62. See also his "Peasant and Hacendero in Nueva Ecija: The Socio-Economic Origins of a Philippine Commercial Rice-Growing Region" (doctoral

dissertation, University of California, Berkeley, 1973), 95, 349-50.

46 *Landed Estates in the Colonial Philippines* (New Haven: Monograph Series No. 20, Southeast Asia Studies, Yale University, 1976), 17-18.

47 Numero de almas de la provincia de Cagayan administrada por los religiosos del sagrado orden de Predicadores, 29 de diciembre de 1803, APSR, Mss. Cagayan, vol. 1, doc. 11.

48 José Jimeno Agius, *Memoria sobre el desestanco del tabaco en las Islas Filipinas* (Binondo: Bruno Gonzalez Moras, n.d.), 7-10; Malumbres, *Cagayan,* 112-16; P. Guel, O.P., "Descripción de Malaueg, 1872," APSR, Mss. Cagayan, vol. 15, doc. 1; Bonifacio Corrujedo, O.P., on Ilagan, 27 December 1878; Pedro Garcia, O.P., on Enrile, 8 February 1877; Juan Antonio Alonso, O.P., on Tuao, 14 February 1877, APSR, Cagayan, Documentos Sueltos, 1740-1905, vol. 1, doc. 13.

49 Rafael Tejada, "Memoria de la provincia de Cagayan en la Ysla de Luzon," Tuguegarao, 1 May 1888, PNA, Cagayan, p. 21; Pedro Nolasco de Medio, O.P., "Noticias de Cagayan con motivo de la Exposición Hispano-Filipina de 1887," Malaueg, 16 December 1886, APSR, Mss. Cagayan, vol. 17a, fols. 249-50; Wickberg, *The Chinese,* 101.

50 Horacio de la Costa, *Asia and the Philippines* (Manila: Solidaridad Publishing House, 1967), 77-78.

51 The post of *cabeza de barangay* or village chief, awarded to the pre-Hispanic *datus,* was passed on from father to son. The *gobernadorcillo* served as the chief administrator of a town or *pueblo,* consisting of several villages, each under a *cabeza.* An electoral group of incumbent and ex-*cabezas* nominated three candidates for *gobernadorcillo* to the Governor-General through the *alcalde.* Unless the parish priest or the *alcalde* could raise valid objections, the Governor-General usually confirmed the candidate who received the highest number of votes. See, Edilberto de Jesus, "Gobernadorcillo Elections in Cagayan", *Philippine Studies* 26 (1978), 142-56.

52 "Conflictos sobre elecciones en Tuguegarao (1827) y en otras ocasiones," APSR Mss. Cagayan, vol. 14, doc. 28; fol. 505; 513 v.

53 "Conflictos sobre elecciones (1827)," fol. 509 v; 513 v.

54 See references in, de Jesus, "Gobernadorcillo Elections," 149-56.

55 Agustín Calvo, O.P., "Memoria de esta provincia de Cagayan en 1886," APSR, Mss. Cagayan, vol. 13, doc. 9.

The Spanish Occupation of the Cordillera in the 19th Century

WILLIAM HENRY SCOTT

The great chain of mountains which rises abruptly from the sea below Pasaleng on the provincial boundary between Cagayan and Ilocos Norte in the Philippines is called the Gran Cordillera Central. It quickly climbs to altitudes of 2,000 metres to divide Kalinga-Apayao from Ilocos Norte, and in Kalinga itself has crests reaching 2,400 metres. These heights continue southward through the old sub-province of Bontoc until they reach their peak of 2,926 metres on Mount Pulog in Benguet. Then they descend to the plains of Pangasinan, though a spur about 1,500 metres high called the Caraballo Sur runs off to the southeast of Baguio and divides the province of Nueva Vizcaya from Nueva Ecija. Most of the major river systems of northern Luzon have their headwaters on the Cordillera, and four of them rise within a few kilometres of one another on Mount Data. On the west, the Suyoc River flows into the Abra. On the northeast, the Chico River flows into the Magat and then into the Cagayan. On the south, the Agno — the most famous of them all because of its gold deposits — drains into the Pangasinan plain and Lingayen Gulf.

The Abra takes its name from the Spanish word for opening or gap, and originally referred to the *Abra de Vigan,* that dramatic natural gateway the stream has cut through the Malaya range of the Ilocos coast to reach the South China Sea. The name of the Chico River (i.e., "little") is another Spanish heritage — it comes from *Río Chico de Cagayán* by which the Spaniards distinguished it from the larger *Río Grande de Cagayán* into which it flows, now simply called the Cagayan. Under the Republic of the Philippines, this whole area constituted the Mountain Province with five sub-provincial divisions — Apayao, Kalinga, Bontoc, Ifugao and Benguet. In 1966 the Mountain Province was itself divided into four new provinces — Kalinga–Apayao, Ifugao and Benguet out of the old sub-provinces of those names, and Mountain Province, now merely the former sub-province of Bontoc, seat of the old provincial capital. Common geography and history, however, have caused the new divisions to be popularly referred to as the four mountain provinces.

Filipinos born on the Gran Cordillera Central are generally known as Igorots, though they might more accurately be referred to by the names of six different ethno-linguistic groups into which they can be divided — Isneg (Apayao), Kalinga, Bontoc, Ifugao, Kankanay and Ibaloy. When the Spaniards first met them trading gold in Pangasinan, Ilocos and Ituy (Nueva Vizcaya), they were called Ygolotes — later to be respelled Igorrotes — but mountaineers farther north on the Ilocos coast were called by the ordinary term applied to mountain dwellers all over the archipelago — *tingues* or *tinguianes,* from the Malay word for "high, elevated" (*tinggi*), a term nowadays restricted to the natives of Abra. In the Cagayan valley, the Spaniards simply called the Kalingas and Apayaos *infieles* (pagans) as they called the Ibanags and Gaddangs of the Cagayan valley itself. But when they went up the Apayao River in the early 17th century, they called the mountaineers there by the indigenous term *mandaya,* which literally means "those up above". Then when they made expeditions in to the Baguio gold mines in 1620 and Kayan in 1668, they called the people there Igorots too, and when they built a fort at Bagabag in 1752 against Ifugao attack from the west, they also called them Igorots. But whatever they were called, they all had one thing in common — they resisted assimilation into the Spanish empire.

The Spaniards ordinarily called the indigenous populations of their empire both in the Americas and in the Philippines *indios,* and as the subject people modified their native customs under foreign domination, quickly formed their own image of the *indio.* He was a brown-skinned person who wore pants instead of a G-string, attended mass, paid tribute, obeyed Spanish laws, and only went to war when the government told him to. The mountain peoples of northern Luzon — whether called Igorots, Tinguians or Mandayas — obviously did not conform to this pattern, so they were collectively referred to as *tribus independientes* rather than *indios.* But they were independent tribes only in the sense that they were composed of independent people, not that they were organized into independent *naciones.* They had no tribal governments or tribal boundaries, did not fight tribal wars or claim descent from common tribal ancestors, and are today called tribes simply for want of a better word to indicate their separate cultural and linguistic identities. Rather, they were villages of more or less related persons who, like the inhabitants of pre-Hispanic *barangays,* recognized no central authority, and took heads or slaves when they went to war, but made no political conquests. And because they had neither king nor castle — *ni rey ni roque,* as the Spaniards said — and so could not make formal declarations of war, all their killings are recorded in Spanish accounts as crimes whether they were committed for purposes of rustling cattle or defending their "brutish independence".

Spanish clergy, of course, were just as eager to convert these Filipinos as any others, and the Augustinians approached them from the west, the Dominicans from the east. Both orders alternated over the years between posting missionaries in pagan villages on the Cordillera, and trying to attract pagans down as catechumens to Christian settlements in the lowlands. Thousands of Igorots did go down to be baptized, but only one or two missionaries ever stayed on the Cordillera more than ten years. Some died, a few were killed and a few driven out, but most got sick or discouraged. Sometimes they accompanied troops or even led them and sometimes they went in with escorts, but often they hiked in alone. In Manila, archbishops and governors-general were agreed that Christianization was the primary duty of empire, but missionaries and commanders in the field were less united in their ideas of how to accomplish it. Friars were often so critical of the military campaigns which seemed to accompany the process, that they were accused of en-

Cordillera Region of Northwestern Luzon

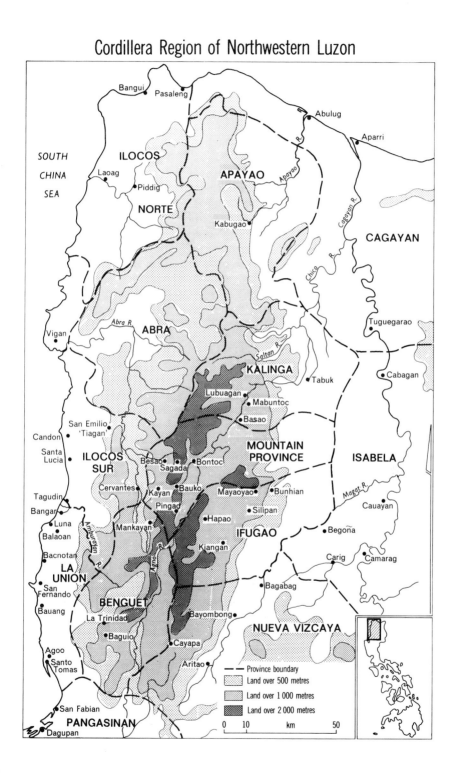

couraging Igorot resistance. But everybody was agreed that the Igorots would be better off both materially and spiritually in a great and progressive Christian kingdom than wandering naked through the mountains in undisciplined liberty with neither king nor master to look after their common weal. Consequently, it was felt that the collection of tribute and exploitation of gold mines would be just compensation and necessary support for a church and state that could and would provide better government than they could provide for themselves.

What first attracted Spanish conquistadors to the Cordillera was Igorot gold, but after 50 years of costly and unsuccessful attempts to occupy the mines, they made only one more try — in 1668 — and then gave the project up. So, too, an attempt to exploit the copper mines of Lepanto in the 1860s was a failure, and no governor ever seriously tried to tap the wealth of forest products and manpower they kept mentioning when recommending punitive expeditions against an Igorot independence that grew more galling over the centuries. But as early as the second or third generation of the Conquest, two aspects of colonial occupation had arisen which created an enmity with the Igorots that would last until the end of the Spanish regime — first, the need to protect Spanish subjects against non-Spanish subjects, and second, the desire to control all trade between them. A tendency for lowlanders to escape to the mountains aggravated the situation, but basically it was these two aspects which determined the course of highland–lowland relations for 300 years — and caused the Spanish observers such confusion by their ambivalence. For in the former case the lowlanders were allied with the Spaniards against the Igorots, and in the latter case allied with the Igorots against the Spaniards.

It was neither gold nor Gospel, however, which finally took the Spaniards onto the Cordillera in force, but tobacco. In 1782 the colonial government declared a Monopoly on the production and sale of this crop which put the colony on a paying basis for the first time in 225 years of occupation. The Monopoly promptly became an object of Igorot sabotage as they grew and sold it contraband themselves or carried it all the way across the Cordillera from Cagayan for clandestine sale in Ilocos. The colonial government eventually responded with a series of 45 punitive excursions in the 1830s which were unsuccessful in planting permanent military bases on the Cordillera itself. Alarmed by these results, they then undertook the first — and most destructive — military invasion of independent territory in Luzon since the 16th century. Armed with all-weather firearms with metal cartridges, they set up a series of politico-military *comandancias* on the more accessible western face of the Cordillera by the 1860s and, after the introduction of the Remington repeating rifle, established similar zones on the more isolated and independent eastern watershed. It is this cumulative action which is the subject of this essay, where it is conceived of as a military occupation rather than a conquest because it neither produced civil governments nor absorbed Igorot tribes into the colonial culture. It did, however, have obvious political — and less obvious economic — effects on the traditional life styles of the Igorot people, and paved the way for their incorporation into an American colony in the next century. And even more important, it set the pattern for highland-lowland relations which persist until the present time.

Headtaking in the East

In 1800 all Luzon north of Pangasinan was theoretically divided into the two provinces of Ilocos and Cagayan, plus the frontier mission of Ituy (Aritao) and Paniqui (Bayombong) which technically belonged to no province. On the eastern, or Cagayan, side of the Cordillera, Ifugao-Gaddang hostility provides a classic example of the relations between independent and subjugated Filipinos during the Spanish period. The Magat River valley had been one of the most prosperous areas in the archipelago when the conquistadors first saw it in the 1590s, and it took them 150 years to persuade the warlike Gaddangs to submit it to colonial jurisdiction. This political realignment had taken place with comparatively little armed conflict and so exemplified a fond Spanish distinction between *pacificación* and *conquista*. Ifugao robberies, extortion and killings were accordingly regarded as unprovoked attacks upon innocent Spanish subjects in legitimate Spanish territory, and theologians were not asked, as they had been in the 17th century, to justify making war against them. Rather, friar opinion was sought all during the 19th century on how best to contain or conquer such recalcitrant pagans.

The Ifugaos, of course, saw the situation in a different light, as the Spaniards themselves were well aware. One commander reported in 1836:

> Their enmity with the Christian towns seems to come from the fact that in older times they used to occupy the terrain which today belongs to the Missions of Paniqui, and from their having been dispossessed by the Gaddangs who are the ones reduced to Christianity there.[1]

Even when they did make up their minds that it would be more advantageous to live at peace with their Gaddang neighbours, it was hard to do so. When some of them started making fields near Cauayan in 1818, they encountered antagonism from the fort commander there. The local priest analyzed this behaviour as actual reluctance to reduce them to peaceful control:

> . . . for in that case he would lose all the money he is given for every convoy, which is six pesos . . . and, in addition, the constant business they make in salt and wine, from which he takes no little cash . . . and all this gain would go unrealized if the Igorots were reduced and left us in peace.[2]

This analysis expresses a friar sympathy based not only on evangelical zeal but on a rather surprised respect for Ifugao dignity upon seeing it during visits to their own villages. Fray Juan Molano wrote approvingly of the Ifugaos of Kiangan in 1801: "They are much given to labour as can be seen from the huge *payaos* (irrigated fields) they have, for there is no doubt that tremendous sweat went into their construction."[3] He was also struck by the excellence of their houses — all constructed without saws or other carpenter's tools from solid planks carried in from great distances and decorated with figures carved into the beams and mouldings. Nor did he miss the fact that they considered themselves masters of their own destiny and responded to his advances with self confidence:

> I talked to them about whether they would like a *gobernadorcillo* and the rest, to which they immediately agreed, but in reference to a Father (about which I hadn't spoken a word), they all said they didn't want one now or under any circumstances, that we should just be friends, and that I might come there when I liked for two or three nights but no more for their Anito or Buni, as they call him, would not permit them to have a priest, and they said further that having to take care of a priest would interfere much with their field work.[4]

Nevertheless, Father Molano concluded that when sufficient personnel were available, it would not be difficult to begin work there. Such optimism was typical of missionary reactions to Ifugao behaviour for the next 100 years. Following some of the punitive devastations of their villages which occurred on an average of once a decade from 1750 until the end of the Spanish regime, an intrepid friar would venture into a more or less hospitable reception and conclude that the harvest was ripe for the gathering. But once these hardy mountaineers had rebuilt their houses and recovered their economy, they would quickly reassert their independence, a turn of events the colonial government considered literal treason and frequently reacted to with punitive action.

Friars often took charge of these expeditions themselves to prevent the bloodshed and pillage which was perhaps understandably committed by lowland forces whose livestock, neighbours and families may have suffered personal Igorot attacks. The commander of an expedition in 1813, for instance, had treated his victims so treacherously that his own subordinates reported it in a formal complaint against him — while the Ifugaos rendered their own complaint in more traditional fashion by taking three Cabagan heads five years later. Fray Juan Prieto accordingly led a force of Cabagan civil militia in 1818 in hopes of apprehending the individual head-takers without attacking anybody else. Considering the difficulty of the situation, he was remarkably successful. Nobody was killed, only one innocent person was even wounded, and no household goods or valuables were looted, though the head-takers themselves made good their escape with their wives and children. And most remarkably of all, he recovered the three heads. As he proudly reported to his provincial later, not even the most professional troops had ever inflicted so fair a punishment with no loss of life, and never had such battle trophies been recovered at all — "since, according to what I have heard, and what those say who are accustomed to taking heads, both Christians and pagans, they would rather die than give up what they took in their forays, or *ngayao,* as they call them".[5]

Gold Mining in the West

On the western face of the Cordillera, no such hostile polarization developed between the Igorots and their Ilocano neighbours, mainly because they were spared the intensive military pressure that characterized the Cagayan–Magat frontier. The gold-seeking invasions of the first 50 years had all been focused on the Baguio mine fields and had created no general havoc, and from the *conquistador* standpoint had accomplished nothing. They left the Igorots in full possession of their gold, and even Igorot revenge on lowland populations participating in the expeditions quickly subsided in consideration of the profits of their mutual commerce. Nor had a harsh barrio-burning incursion in 1759 gained the Spaniards anything more than the retreat of the inhabitants of the mountaintop villages they destroyed. So, too, a far-ranging expedition onto the heights of the Cordillera in 1667-1668 had accomplished nothing though it had practically been invited into the area in the first place. An Igorot chieftain had had a falling out with local rivals and had gone down to ingratiate himself with Spanish authorities by persuading them of the wealth of the Suyoc–Mankayan gold mines and offering his services as guide. The resulting expedition made its headquarters in Kayan, and 32 years later one Miguel Mestizo — probably the son of one of the Spanish soldiers, to judge by his name — was appointed Maestre-de-Campo of Kayan. His great grandson-in-law Dekdek was holding the same title when the government made a tobacco-cutting raid on his town in 1811.

Kayan had a reputation in the early 19th century as the main source of the clandestine contraband tobacco flooding Ilocos. It was located at the crossroads of an old east–west trade route from Ifugao to the coast and a north–south route by which coin-of-the-realm was obtained from Abra smugglers in exchange for Kayan tobacco, Mankayan gold, and local manufactures such as *bolos,* spears and copper pots. In December 1817 this commerce was interrupted by the death of an Igorot in Tagudin and a retaliatory killing of an Ilocano from neighbouring Bangar, so Dekdek went down to re-establish friendly relations with Mayors Simón de los Reyes and Agustín de Valencia of the two lowland towns. On 14 January 1820, the three of them signed a peace-pact which defined their mutual boundaries, and each party guaranteed the lives of members of the opposite party in their own territory (or payment of ₱50 per murder), to apprehend refugees and criminals crossing the border, and to indemnify thefts at twice the value of the stolen goods.

To the north of this Kayan–Tagudin trade route was the higher Tirad Pass, gateway to another Igorot trade route from Bontoc to Candon, a lowland community with a long tradition of intimate Igorot contacts. Unlike other Spanish towns in Ilocos, it retained its native name: *kandong* is a species of tree, and under one such tree Igorot traders used to gather until it was chopped down by a friar and a church built in its place. At the time of the Conquest, Igorots had occupied territory in this region much closer to the sea than they did later. Salcedo found no towns along the coast between Bauang and Balaoan in 1572, though the area was even then being filled in by lowland migrations. Agoo was an Ilocano settlement in Pangasinan, and the fact that Namacpacan (later Luna) became a mission outstation of Pangasinan-speaking Bauang in 1599 instead of Ilocano-speaking Balaoan suggests a northward expansion from Pangasinan. Thus when Colonel Yldefonso de Aragón, Commandant of the Royal Engineering Corps, reported in 1819 that there were settlements of "tamed" Igorots within two or three hours of every town from Agoo to Bacnotan, he may well have been speaking of communities that had been there before any *conquistador* arrived to introduce the concept of "taming" in the first place.

Highland-lowland partnership in the early 19th-century gold trade still fit the description of Dr. Antonio de Morga of two centuries earlier:

> With the gold still unrefined or purified, they go down to trade with the Il-ocanos at certain places where they give them the gold in exchange for rice, pigs, carabaos, and other things they lack, and the Ilocanos finish its refinement and purify it perfectly and it passes through the whole land through their hands.[6]

Prominent citizens of the towns between Bangar and Santo Tomas lived solely off the profits of carrying Igorot gold to Manila on commission, and even in Pangasinan Don Yldefonso wrote: "It is a rare town from which travellers do not set out annually for the capital, carrying gold from the Agno or the Igorots."[7] A certain Capitán Agpalo of Namacpacan had a reputation for such lavish spending on business trips to Vigan that it was suspected he and his Igorot partners enjoyed a monopoly on some secret mine all their own. Lowlanders were now panning gold not only in the Agno flood plain around Asingan but on the beaches of San Fabian and Dagupan as well, and three or four small boats a year from the Batanes Islands with a cargo of semi-precious stones to exchange for Igorot or Tinguian gold constituted those forsaken islanders' only commerce with Luzon.

The Tobacco Monopoly—Revenuers and Bootleggers

The colonial government had by this time long given up the romantic Hapsburg dream of exploiting some Igorot *El Dorado* hidden away in the interior heights of the Cordillera. But it was now attracted back to the Cordillera by something even more important to its economy than gold — tobacco. When the Tobacco Monopoly was established in 1782, the Igorots suddenly found themselves with a lucrative cash crop on their hands as lowland smokers looked for an untaxed supply. Igorot response was prompt, and by 1796 their contraband crops were offering enough competition to move Tobacco Commissioner Melchor Lalama to plan a huge invasion of their territory. But just then Spain declared war on England and the memory of the British occupation of Manila 35 years before was still fresh enough to discourage deflecting the colony's defence forces to the hinterlands of northern Luzon. Nor was the anxiety quickly relieved. In 1805 almost the entire Spanish fleet was destroyed in the Battle of Trafalgar, and when French armies invaded Spain in 1808, the government ordered missionaries not to make excursions onto the Cordillera for the duration of the war so as not to give the Igorots any excuse for uprisings. Not until December 1826 when a contingent of veteran infantry and cavalry reached the colony was it feasible to take action. Then Lieutenant Colonel

Guillermo Galvey was appointed *Comandante del País de los Igorrotes y Partidas del Norte de Pangasinán* — Commandant of the Land of the Igorots and Outposts of Northern Pangasinan. In January 1829 he started out on ten years of raids intended to cut the trade off literally at its roots — that is, in the mountain fastnesses on both sides of the Gran Cordillera itself.

Galvey was a proud Spanish officer of stout body and stouter heart, with a natural curiosity and knack for picking up local languages, who was probably more highly motivated by love of adventure and romance of empire than the interests of the Tobacco Monopoly. A commander of quick decisions and unflinching courage, he was more than once wounded taking personal risks in the name of military honour — and twice almost paid for it with his life. He had the ingenuity of a *conquistador* of old for surviving in hostile territory and more than once erected forts without tools or carpenters, far from his source of supplies. The force of both his personality and his arms won him the respect of many of his Igorot foes: he always treated them with dignity in face-to-face parley, called those who submitted to him after defeat his friends, and left not a disparaging word about them in his diaries. He also burned their fields by the hectares and houses by the hundreds, destroyed their economy in whole valleys, and decimated their populations with smallpox. He was the greatest despoiler of the Igorots that Spain ever sent onto the Cordillera.

In February 1837 Galvey set out on what was intended to be the crowning achievement of these incursions — the carving up of the whole western and south-eastern flanks of the Cordillera into four military commands with forts in Abra, Benguet (that is, La Trinidad just north of Baguio), Ifugao and Mankayan. As it turned out, the plan was a costly and colossal failure which left no troops at all on the Cordillera by the end of the year. As far as military conquest was concerned, like Galvey's 44 other expeditions it only proved what had been known for two centuries — that a determined *conquistador* with firearms and enough cargo-bearers could cut his way to the very heights of the Cordillera, but could not maintain himself there permanently. From the standpoint of the Cordillera populations despoiled, however, the effects were obvious, far-reaching and long-lasting. Twenty-five years later they were described by German scientist Carl Semper in the following terms:

Everywhere you can find traces of a greater population than that of the Igorots of the upper Agno [today], and the valley of Benguet and its side valleys. In the valleys you find traces of destroyed *rancherías* and the stone walls they used to build around their houses; on the hillsides you can see fields arranged in terraces supported by stone walls but now covered with high grass; you can still see the remains of former irrigation systems and earthern walls and ditches indicating the separation of the mountains and valleys into divisions: all these are traces of a once more extensive cultivation. Today most villages bear the stamp of misery and deprivation: the fields are badly maintained, the stone walls around the houses dilapidated, and the great *rancherías* which existed in Galvey's time have been deserted; instead you only find individual houses in the depths of the canyons or on top of a hill.[8]

The Occupation Begins

Galvey's command was the first of a series of politico-military zones — *comandancias político-militares* — which were to cover the whole Cordillera by the end of the century — at least on paper. It included nine towns detached from civil jurisdiction in Pangasinan and Ilocos Sur between the Amburayan River and San Fabian. This is the area where the Spaniards found Chinese and Japanese ships trading for gold in the 16th century, and it contained coastal stretches they still had to cross at forced march in the 17th because of imminent Igorot attack. Galvey set up headquarters in a hamlet he called San Fernando, from which he made his incursions into Benguet by following the same route used by Conquistadors Aldana, Carreño and Quirante in the 1620s. Today it is the seaport from which the total output of the former Igorot gold and copper mines is shipped abroad in foreign vessels.

The military province of Abra and the military district of Benguet were created in 1846, and the next year a third command, in Tiagan on the crest of the Malaya range astride an Igorot trade route from Abra to the Ilocos coast. By 1850 the shape of things to come was clear: in that year Galvey's old Land-of-the-Igorots command was absorbed into the new military province of La Union, a punitive expedition escorted mining engineer Antonio Hernández into Mankayan to examine the copper deposits there, and the military governor of Nueva Vizcaya marched across Kalinga from Ifugao to Abra hoping to blaze a trans-Cordilleran trail and listing 2,100 households as submissive en route. In 1853 the district of Kayan was created just north of Mankayan — and later renamed Lepanto because government dispatch offices kept misdirecting its mail to Cagayan. In 1856 Tomás Balbas y Castro staked the first Spanish mining claim on the Cordillera and moved in with 120 Chinese immigrants. In 1857 the command of Bontoc was established in the very heart of Igorot territory on the eastern heights of the watershed. And from here, military occupation was rather adventurously extended downstream in 1859 with the establishment of the Saltan *comandancia* where the river of that name flows into the Chico in the malarial plains of Tabuk. A logistic — and sanitary — disaster, it was abandoned in the 1870s.

Conditions on the eastern side of the Cordillera, meanwhile, remained as hostile as they had been since the Dominicans first opened Pangasinan–Cagayan communications in 1739. The creation of the military province of Nueva Vizcaya in 1839 had not ameliorated the situation, and in 1846 energetic Governor-General Narciso Clavería went to have a look for himself. What he saw moved him to prompt action — to build a new fort at Begoña on the Magat River itself, and to appoint a new military governor, his own aide-de-camp, the brilliant young Mariano Oscáriz. Oscáriz took up his post early in 1847 and headed right up into Ifugao. He burned every village on the way up, destroyed all the tobacco, taro and *camotes* he found, cut the ripening grain and pulled down all the dikes so the water ran out of the terraces, and lost only one man. Planting the Spanish flag in the centre of a deserted Mayaoyao, he delivered an ultimatum which he described in the following terms:

I told them that the Governor General in Manila was tired of suffering the deaths which they continually made, and had decided not to let them live in that land any longer; that I had come to their country to do some damage and see how many men were needed to destroy all their fields till not one stone was left on stone, and that I would return when I was ready; and that the only way they could prevent this from happening was to agree to the following conditions: they would leave 40 hostages in Begoña; pay an annual recognition of one *ganta* of rice per person; not cross the Ibulao or Magat Rivers except at the fort in Begoña, where they would report to the commander, who would give them safe conduct to the town they were going to; that the hostages would be held responsible for carrying out these conditions and any murder committed; and that some chiefs should accompany us through the towns of Buglu, Bunhian, and Higu on our return to the Magat River, making their people carry our loads.[9]

The Mayaoyao Ifugaos had met their match. Their chiefs dutifully presented themselves in the capital at Camarag with the requisite hostages, built a little warehouse across the river, started buying clothes and salt for the first time in years — and asked for military aid against some Ifugao enemies. Missionaries took up residence in Mayaoyao and nearby Bunhian, and later in Lagawe and Kiangan, while Oscáriz kept his image polished with quick decisions and stern retaliations. Two generations later, Ifugaos were still telling how he threatened to take two or three of their heads for every one they took, how he skilfully palmed the ball when loading a rifle to fire blank charges at his own men to make them seem bulletproof, and how he once paced up and down a file of close-mouthed suspects in the public plaza in Camarag, revolver in hand, and shot down five at random to loosen the survivors' tongues enough to name the culprits.

Oscáriz attributed the new Ifugao docility to intelligent self-interest — the desire for free trade and an unwillingness to lose every town and terrace for the sake of a few leaders' head-taking prestige. To this analysis must be added the charismatic contribution of those Spanish friars who spent their short lives hiking in and out of head-taking villages between battles. By their courage and endurance, their affection and gifts, they often attracted followings with deep personal loyalty; and by their prevention of military excesses and defence of the local people against soldiers' abuses, they projected an image of a just and benevolent conquest. Nor was their proselytizing without its effect: by avoiding aggressive attacks on the local religion they found ready audiences when embarrassed shamans could not answer their questions. Thoughtful pagans could see the material and military power of these representatives of a deity who claimed authority over the whole world, and if the concept of a god who loved their enemies as much as he loved them was confusing, a monarch who cherished and protected his people was not. So, as pagans had done in other parts of the Cordillera in other centuries, Ifugao parents with no intention of giving up the faith of their fathers themselves were willing to have their children instructed and baptized. Thus everybody in Lagawe under 21 was baptized 15 years after a priest took up residence there in 1851.

In 1852 Oscáriz was transferred to Zamboanga (where he lived up to his reputation by killing two chieftains in hand-to-hand combat when scarcely recovered from battle wounds), and as soon as his magical presence was removed, an Ifugao of Silipan killed a Christian of Bagabag. The new governor, José Ochoteco, mounted an expedition, failed to catch him, burned another village instead, and indignantly refused a Silipan offer of another man to be beheaded in his place or to marry his victim's widow. The following July, two men of Lagawe engaged the garrison soldiers there in a conversation while their companions carried in the tribute rice and suddenly grabbed one soldier's *bolo,* wounded two of the troops, made off with 13 rifles, and burned the fort to the ground. In 1854 the people of Bunhian sacked the church, and Oscáriz's old Lieutenant Mariano Lumidao went up with 30 troops from Carig to take punitive action. He held a secret parley in the forest with the local *gobernadorcillo,* who returned the chalice and agreed to restore everything else if the cargo-bearers drafted for the march back would be released on reaching Carig, but Lumidao betrayed the agreement by throwing them all in prison. Such desultory tactics restored Ifugao political power to Ifugao hands, and exposed the friars to revenge once the troops withdrew after having billeted themselves in mission buildings.

Efforts at Evangelization

By 1864 there were only two missionaries left in Ifugao — José Lorenzo in Kiangan and Victorino García in Lagawe — and they were not to last much longer. On 14 August 1868, Father Lorenzo was killed trying to collect a ten-peso debt. He had loaned this sum to a man of Kiangan named Bumidang who promised to repay it at harvest time, and although he did not refuse when the time came, he kept putting it off until the missionary decided to go and collect it from his granary in person. This was not an unusual Ifugao practice, but it was done by them under arms so that the debtor would appear to be giving it out of good judgment rather than lack of valour. Father Lorenzo, however, ordered his few companions not to carry spears when they set out. Bumidang said nothing when the priest confronted him frankly with his intentions, but when he actually saw the bundles coming out of his granary — and ones he had set aside for seeds at that — he turned on the friar and felled him with one blow of a club. Father Lorenzo staggered away with the support of two little boys and was finished off with a spear on the way back to his church.

Fray Juan Villaverde rushed up to Kiangan, but was too late to do anything more than give Father Lorenzo a decent Christian burial and take over what turned out to be a discouraging and lonely assignment. There was no sign of those many baptisms left in the surrounding villages, and the really faithful converts had migrated down to the Christian towns. He passed two years with no company but two watchdogs who kept prowlers away at night, and was several times actually surrounded and his life threatened. Then, on 6 April 1870, he was called to Lagawe to administer the last sacraments to his only colleague, Father García, whose battered body was found at the bottom of a ravine that morning. (Men had entered his residence in the middle of the night, stripped the friar, thrown him naked off a precipice, and then placed his underclothes in the girls' sleeping quarters to initiate vicious gossip.) Open warfare had broken out meanwhile between Lagawe and Silipan, four men from Kiangan had been killed on the road to Bagabag the month before, and a week later a garrison soldier was speared to death. In 1871, three more soldiers were killed on the Kiangan–Bagabag trail, and when Father Villaverde finished mass during a fiesta that year, a spear aimed at him passed through his vestments and stuck in the door behind him. The last Spanish missionary in Ifugao decided his time had come, packed up, and left.

Father Villaverde concluded, not surprisingly, that no missionary could safely reside in pagan villages, but unwisely, that the solution to the problem was to relocate, by force if necessary, all pagan tribes in the lowlands where they could learn to farm — and obey — like lowland Filipinos. Governor-General Fernando Primo de Rivera accordingly delivered an ultimatum on 14 January 1881, for all unsubjugated Filipinos to submit to vassalage by 1 April in exchange for land grants and one year's maintenance, or suffer military invasion twice a year with the destruction of all their fields and goods and the confiscation of their livestock. To make the point clear, a contingent of Manila infantry and artillery arrived early in March, bringing with them the highest calibre canons Filipino manpower ever dragged across the Caraballo Sur.

The Igorot response was prompt and probably predictable. Father Buenaventura Campa summarized the Ifugao attitude as follows: "The Mayaoyaos all around declined to abandon the soil which saw their birth [and] the vast majority in Kiangan and Silipan were disposed to defend their brutish independence at the cost of any manner of sacrifice."[10] The Kalingas of Balatoc were so obstreperous that a Spanish officer led their Lubuagan and Bangad enemies in to discipline them with 49 deaths, and Lepanto Commandant Luis Sarela had a hairbreadth escape when he was surrounded near Hapao and had to be rescued by Pingad allies. Even the Spanish personnel in Benguet's sleepy little capital in La Trinidad just barely escaped with their lives when the garrison, government house and church were burned to the ground by a "crazy Igorot". Even after the deadline, the military governor of Abra had to send an expedition in to Mabuntoc, Kalinga, and spent the whole month "pacifying" villages that were obstructing road-building efforts across Kalinga from Abra to Cagayan. Bontoc was only foiled in an attempt to raise a real insurrection by lack of co-operation from Lepanto neighbours, but did make an attack with local allies. The Bontoc fort was too well protected by dry moats and stockades to be reached with fire. The rebels lured the troops on duty out by burning a lowlander's house, then killed four of them outright and wounded many — five of whom died aftewards — seized two Remington rifles, fired all the public buildings, and took to the hills to celebrate the four heads taken despite a loss of some 70 on their own side.

In between such military crises, however, the thankless, frustrating office of frontier politico-military command was more dull than dangerous, though never routine. Enforcing the public labour and collecting the tribute payments that would legitimize the occupation took up much of the commanders' time and energies. In October 1889, for example, Sacasacan successfully escaped road-building labour by threatening the Igorots of Daneo where a detachment of soldiers from Basao had planned to pick up guides for a punitive expedition against them. As the Spanish presence made itself more forceful on the western side of the Cordillera, the migration trend of Filipino *remontados* (runaways) fleeing foreign domination in the lowlands was reversed. In 1877 the government had complained about the loss of revenue in the populous provinces of Central Luzon due to this flight, but 12 years later Tiagan commandant Luis de Salazar said that Igorot migration trends "produce such a pile of petitions for transfer, resettlement and licence that it alone constitutes the most assiduous work of this command".[11]

The governors themselves were torn between sympathy for Igorot economic plight and disgust with the way they spent their wealth when they had any. When a decree attempted to extend vassalage to 15-year-olds, the Bontoc commandant promptly replied that the Igorots could not possibly meet the new payments because they would total more than the value of the preceding four years' rice production. More than one commander reported plagues of locusts as an excuse for not meeting tribute quotas. But the Lepanto commandant recommended in 1877 that full tribute be imposed in his district on the grounds that there was a large amount of money in circulation and that Suyoc miners bought all their food with cash. Father Angel Pérez grumpily added that they were evidently rich enough to have gone without work for three months when Chief Oitavi sacrificed 200 cows for his father's funeral. Nobody seems to have recalled Father Prieto's 1850 observation that "the majority of these pagans don't pay tribute because they don't have fields but live off *camotes* and the rice they earn by working the fields of others".[12]

The Occupation and Economics

Both administrators and friars believed that Igorots introduced into the colonial economy would eventually profit from such labours as the road-building they tried so hard to avoid, and hopefully introduced new crops and tools to stimulate commerce. Father Julián Malumbres took wheel-barrows and a coffee-husking machine in to Kiangan and provided his little school with a Singer sewing machine and western-type loom, and the local commandant set up a forge and personally gave instruction. In Lepanto, however, Father Pérez was not able to persuade Bauko potters to use a potter's wheel he provided, or the lumbermen of Malaya (Cervantes) to switch to saws from *bolos* and headaxes when hewing out hardwood boards for sale — though, he admitted, there was the problem of buying the saw in the first place. Everybody introduced seedlings of various kinds by the thousands — oranges, lemons, cacao, etc. — sometimes out of their own pockets, but the coffee trees that promised so lucrative a future were found mainly in the plantations of farmers such as a lowland schoolteacher, an ex-corporal or a discharged Spanish soldier. Native capitalists in the Agno valley, however, did successfully market this crop once they overcame the opposition of neighbours who not unreasonably feared an increase in public taxes and so poured boiling water on the plants at night. None of these innovators, however, was an economic planner, and such economic changes as actually took place under the Spanish occupation were basically Igorot responses to such opportunities as occurred to them rather than results of government or mission programs.

The Igorots of Tiagan, a day's hike above the Candon-Santa Lucia plain, where in 1877 it was possible to sell ₱8,000 of cattle for hard cash (not counting the unrecorded traffic), presumably felt no need for whatever economic advantages may have attached to the *comandancia político-militar* which was placed astride their Abra trade route in 1847. At least, Father Pérez said of them 50 years later: "They have not been able to make up their minds they have lost their independence, so they consider having to work on public projects for the State an abuse."[13] Those of the Amburayan valley defended a reputation for hard-headed valour for a half-century after Galvey first cut all their tobacco plants. They were finally subjected to military control only after the abolition of the Tobacco Monopoly had deprived them of their smuggling profits so suddenly that the next generation thought the ₱70,000 a year fondly recalled by their parents was just a fairy tale. Nor did the enterprising *caciques* of Benguet need military conquest to impose new business opportunities on their gold-producing, cattle-raising, vegetable-peddling economy. Such commercial liabilities as head-hunting they had discarded before Spain even moved into La Trinidad, but slavery was so commonplace that when the government began sending expeditions across the mountains into Ifugao, Benguet leaders could far-sightedly forestall revenge by electing Ifugao slaves as *gobernadorcillos*.

But the imposition of colonial authority on the Cordillera did have its effect upon the economic life of the people. When Bontoc commandant Pérez Royo remitted tribute collections of ₱1,445.50 in 1889, he estimated that the value of his *comandancia's* whole rice production was ₱3,985.00. This would have been significant enough had it meant that everybody was taxed a quarter of his income, but what it really meant was that those who lived at subsistence level off root crops would soon be reduced to debt peonage to the well-to-do owners of terraces to whom they would have to turn for loans or hire. Such Igorots were themselves aware of this market value of their labour. When some of them were tried in Vigan in 1890 for the murder of a lowland cloth merchant and his Bontoc companion but acquitted, they demanded ₱100 from the witnesses against them as indemnification for the time lost in jail. Service as a *polista* at public labour was just as real a payment as tribute rice, and men were known to claim exemption on the grounds of a working-age son's attendance at school. Those with any connection with the colonial government were exempted by law, of course — all manner of *gobernadorcillos,* barrio captains and ex-officials, even church boys and priests' servants — and they entrenched themselves so well that by the end of the Spanish regime, when the ordinary Igorot was asked his occupation, he replied "*polista*".

The failure of the 1881 ultimatum — and the Villaverde plan for reducing pagans along with it — called for some new assessment of the missionary scene. One was provided in 1889 by Villaverde's comrade of the cloth, Father Malumbres, and its reasoning was simple. Since Igorot robbery and murder arose from their sanguinary instincts and superstitions which required sacrifices and were aggravated by lowland abuses, nothing less than resident missionaries preaching the Christian Gospel in their midst would change their violent life styles. To enable these missionaries to do their work, military protection would have to be provided by more commands like those already in existence. Governor-General Valeriano Weyler took the suggestion and created the command of Quiangan (Kiangan, Ifugao) that same year, and reactivated the old Saltan command in Tabuk under the title of Itaves in 1890. In 1891 he created three more — Amburayan at the mouth of the river of that name between Ilocos Sur and La Union, Cayapa east of Baguio overlooking Nueva Vizcaya, and Apayao in the delta of the river which was then called Abulug. (Another command, that of Cabugaoan, in the headwaters of the Apayao River, only existed on paper: its commandant never moved higher onto the Cordillera than Piddig, Ilocos Norte.) Official appeals to both the Augustinians and Dominicans produced two dozen missionaries in residence in these districts by 1896, most of them within prudent distance of garrison troops whose precarious control of the area was dependent upon their ability to make use of local feuds.

Whether the use of modern firearms supplemented by Spanish-directed village vendetta might have eventually created enough order to permit Christian evangelists to reach the pagan heart and end all this bloodshed, it had nevertheless not done so by the end of the Spanish regime. The occupation of the Cordillera was still a military occupation, dependent on lowland sources for its foods, funds and guns, and its points of occupation were lonely outposts in the midst of unsubmissive tribes. The estimated 40 percent of the population paying ₱0.50 a year as a token of vassalage and the 25 schools and missionaries listed in 1898 were not evenly distributed — one quarter of them were in territory soon afterwards transferred to Ilocos Sur and La Union. In the District of Lepanto, it is true, no headtaking raids were reported in the 1890s west of the watershed running between Besao and Sagada. But the 8,118 Ifugaos listed as submissive in the Quiangan command were policed by 305 *guardias civiles* — an average of one soldier for every 26 taxpayers — and the mountain population of Kalinga-Apayao does not show up in Spanish tribute figures at all. The last official act of a Spanish commander on the Cordillera illustrates the final condition of the occupation. Bontoc commandant Eduardo Xandaró heard there were *Katipunan* sympathizers in Sagada and fell on that town at dawn on 11 July 1898 with a large force of auxiliaries from five villages who went home with 84 heads.

Results of the Occupation

The Spanish occupation of the Cordillera came to an end as abruptly as their occupation of the rest of the archipelago. Following the declaration of Philippine independence on 12 June 1898, Filipino forces invaded Benguet where the few Spaniards in La Trinidad held out until the end of the month before escaping up the Agno valley to find temporary refuge in Bontoc until its surrender on 3 September. At that time, census figures listed the total population of the various *comandancias* as 240,847, broken down into 129,444 vassals and 111,403 independent mountain dwellers. Judging from more accurate statistics in the early American period, however, another 50,000 unregistered mountaineers should be added to this number. A more realistic census, therefore, would show a total population of Cordillera peoples of some 290,000, with about 130,000 paying *reconocimiento* fees and one-third of these living in territory which never became part of the four mountain provinces. Whatever independence these figures may represent, it cost the Igorots dearly: they missed out on all those acculturated advantages that sent lowland Filipinos like Graciano López Jaena to ornament the Spanish press with graceful prose and José Rizal to hobnob with European scholars in half a dozen foreign languages while highland Filipinos were being exhibited in the 1887 "Igorot Village" in Madrid along with the other native plants and animals. And whatever subjugation the same figures represent, it cost the Igorots no less dearly, for the results of the Spanish occupation of the Cordillera were grim indeed.

Where they established military control, it is true, the Spaniards built horse trails and made it possible for Igorot travellers, lowland merchants and friar missionaries to move freely through former enemy territory. They introduced coffee, cacao and citrus fruits which made Igorot dining less monotonous and added Vitamin-C to their diet, though this mainly profited lowland and Spanish settlers. They increased the power of a handful of Igorot leaders, taught a few hundred how to read and write, intentionally or unintentionally caused thousands to migrate to the lowlands, and left 8,000 baptized Christians when they departed. But they also seized Igorot pigs, chickens and rice or purchased them at unfair prices. They helped reduce the poor to debt peonage by demanding the same tribute from everybody while exempting the rich and powerful from forced labour. They punished one village by leading against it its enemies from another, and they burned houses, cut crops, pulled down walls — and introduced smallpox and syphilis — in no less than 75 expeditions in the 19th century alone. But the grimmest result of the occupation was subtler, more tragic and longer lasting — the creation of a distinction between lowland and highland Filipinos which contrasted submission, conversion and civilization on the one hand with independence, paganism and savagery on the other.

NOTES

1 "Memoria sobra la ocupación militar de los montes habitados por Indios no reducidos," Biblioteca Central Militar y Archivo del Servicio Histórico Militar, Madrid, Item 7.230 (4-1-9-12), fol. 7v.

2 Letter from Cauayan, 22 September 1818, in Julián Malumbres, *Historia de Isabela* (Manila: Tip. Linotype de Santo Tomas, 1918), 163-64.

3 Letter to Fray Pedro Galan from Bayombong, 5 August 1801, Archivo de la Provincia del Santísima Rosario (hereafter, APSR), Quezon City, MS, Sección "Cagayán," Cartas.

4 *Ibid.*

5 Letter from Cauayan, 24 August 1818, APSR, MS, Sección "Filipinas," Vol. 118, fol. 252v.

6 Antonio de Morga, *Sucesos de las Islas Filipinas* (Madrid: V. Suárez, 1909), 182.

7 Yldefonso de Aragón, *Descripción geográfica y topográfica de la Ysla de Luzon o Nueva Castilla con las Particulares de las 16 Provincias o Partidas que comprehende* (Manila, 1819), 5:10.

8 Carl Semper, "Reise durch die nordlichen Provinzen der Insel Luzon," *Zeitschrift für Allgemeine Erdkunde* 13 (1862), 88-89.

9 "Diario de operaciones de la columna expedicionaria que en 29 de marzo de 1847 salió del Fuerte de Begoña," APSR, MS, Sección "Cagayán," Relaciones.

10 "Los Mayaoyaos y la raza ifugao," *El Correo Sino-Annamita* 26 (1893), 195-96.

11 Luis Salazar del Valle to the Central Government from San Emilio, Tiangan, 2 September 1889, Philippine National Archives, Comandancias.

12 Letter to Fray Francisco Gaínza from Mayaoyao, 1 October 1850, APSR, MS, Sección "Cagayán," Cartas.

13 Angel Perez, *Igorrotes: Estudio geográfico y etnográfico sobre algunos Distritos del Norte de Luzón* (Manila: El Mercantil, 1903), 236.

Changing Human Ecology on the Central Luzon Plain: Nueva Ecija, 1705-1939

MARSHALL S. McLENNAN

During the 19th century, particularly the second half, European colonial powers extended direct political control or economic spheres of influence over the entire Southeast Asian region. In each of these colonies, and even in Thailand, a restructuring of local economies occurred which effectively integrated Southeast Asia with the European system of world commerce. The manifold consequences of this integration cannot be understated. European capital investment fostered new agricultural systems devoted to the production of tropical export crops and the development of mining and mineral resources. Colonial primate cities emerged to mediate the export of primary products and the inflow of European manufactures.[1] Within the domestic economies, a restructuring of trade and labour relations took place. As a result, internal exchange relations serving essentially subsistence needs gave way to those characteristic of the marketplace.[2]

One of the most dramatic events in the economic transformation of Southeast Asia was the clearing of tropical forests from the major river valleys.[3] The late 19th and early 20th century witnessed large, spontaneous migrations of indigenous peoples into the sparsely occupied deltas — the Irrawaddy in Burma, the Menam in Thailand, and the Mekong in Vietnam.[4] These pioneers cleared the land, channelled the waters, and created the export rice granaries which made good the insufficiency of cereals production elsewhere in Asia and the world.[5]

Similar developments occurred in the Philippines, though with some variations. As the region's oldest colony, the Philippines was generally more responsive to European influence and its major lowland expanse, the Central Luzon Plain, was opened to pioneers in the early 19th century, some 50 years earlier than most areas of Southeast Asia.[6] The earlier commercializaton of rice production in the Central Luzon Plain established it as an exporter of rice for the China trade, a commerce which was particularly vigorous for the period 1820-1860.[7] By the 1870s, however, the progressive increase in the production of rice in Cochin China and the emergence of Saigon as a rice entrepôt of world importance depressed Philippine production and restricted it to domestic trade.[8]

Socio-economic change has not been the only consequence of clearing forests from the great tropical lowlands of Southeast Asia. Commercial agriculture places far different demands upon the environment than does subsistence agriculture. The subsistence farmer is conservative of his habitat, while the commercial farmer is a cog in a system geared to external forces beyond his control. Commercial agriculture has the capacity, over time, to both alter and damage the local ecology.

The transformation of the Central Luzon Plain from forest, swamp and lake to an endless web of rice paddies is a particularly revealing instance of man's abuse of the environment to the point where its productive capacity is threatened.

In all the lowland valleys of Southeast Asia, wet rice fields have replaced tropical forests and local economies have been restructured to facilitate a rapid rise in commercial rice production. Although the end-product, rice, is the same throughout the region, the impact of these transformations, particularly upon social patterns, varies greatly from one locality to another. Even within a single region, the Central Plain of Luzon, the processes of change have taken distinct forms in each of its five lowland provinces.

The almost overwhelming variety and complexity of these changes across the whole of the Central Luzon Plain makes generalization difficult and inexact. If, however, we shift our focus from the whole of the Central Plain to just one of its five constituent provinces, then these elusive complexities become far more manageable. Lying near the centre of the Plain, Nueva Ecija Province evolved from a formless marshland into one of the archipelago's key rice granaries between 1700 and 1940 — a transformation which makes it an apt area of historical study. During this period migration, forest felling and changing land use had an enormous impact upon its environment. The rate of change accelerated dramatically during the early decades of the 20th century when the province's economy was restructured for commercial rice production and its classical wet-rice hacienda system matured.

The Regional Setting

During the first 200 years of Spanish rule, the Central Plain's population was largely concentrated on the coastal margins at each end of the valley and its interior was almost unpopulated. Prior to the mid 19th century, the central lowland was still divided between just three provinces — Pampanga, Bulacan and Pangasinan. The region now comprising Nueva Ecija, eastern Pangasinan and southern Tarlac belonged to Pampanga and was loosely referred to as Upper Pampanga.

Nueva Ecija was created in 1705 when Governor Fausto Cruzat y Gongora organized the easternmost segment of Pampanga into a military *comandancia* to intimidate the warlike pagans of the Sierra Madre range and facilitate their conversion to Christianity. While the territorial dimensions of the district fluctuated between 1705 and 1848, and at one time even included the Polillo Islands, the district remained centred upon the mountains. In 1848 the *comandancia* was abolished and Nueva Ecija was reorganized as a province independent of Pampanga. Over the next decade there were a number of territorial adjustments which had the cumulative effect of changing Nueva Ecija from a mountain district to a lowland province at the heart of the Central Plain. Excepting the loss of four northern municipalities to Pangasinan Province in 1901, Nueva Ecija has maintained its 1858 boundaries until the present.

The Central Luzon Plain of which Nueva Ecija is a part occupies a flat sedimen-

The Central Plain of Luzon

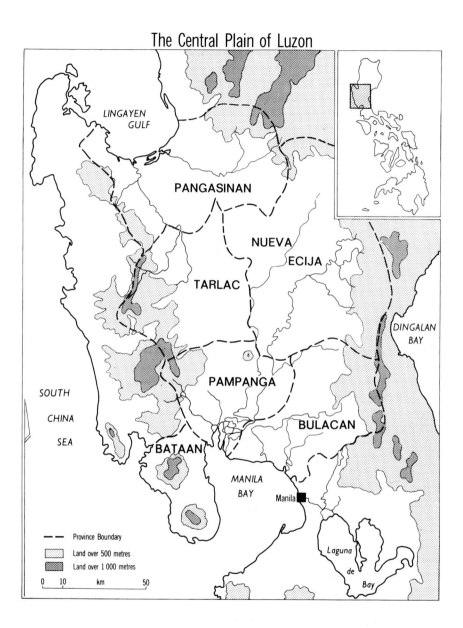

LINGAYEN GULF

PANGASINAN

NUEVA ECIJA

TARLAC

DINGALAN BAY

SOUTH CHINA SEA

PAMPANGA

BULACAN

BATAAN

MANILA BAY

Manila

Laguna de Bay

Province Boundary

Land over 500 metres

Land over 1 000 metres

0   10   km   50

tary basin some 200 kilometres long and 50 to 65 kilometres wide, opening to the
sea at both the north and south. The Plain's western and eastern margins are rim-
med by the Zambales mountains and the Sierra Madre respectively, while a trans-
verse range, the Caraballo Sur, separates it from the Cagayan Valley on the northeast. At its lowest point, in the proximity of Lake Canarin, a divide of less than 18
metres elevation separates the Plain into northern and southern catchment areas.
The northern catchment is drained by the Agno River and the southern watershed
by the Pampanga River and its chief tributaries, the Chico Pampanga and Peñaranda rivers. Since the landscape is so consistently flat and drainage consequently impeded, the Central Plain has a number of extensive fresh-water swamps. Most extensive is the Candaba Swamp, a product of rainy season overflow from the Pampanga River. In centuries past it embraced a considerably larger area, and was linked with the swampy trough of the Chico Pampanga River. In fact, as late as the
early 19th century a continuous belt of swamps and lakes, some of which have now
disappeared in the aftermath of deforestation, bisected the Central Plain from the
Lingayen Gulf to Manila Bay and allowed inland navigation between the Ilocos
Coast and Manila.[9] Within this depression, flood hazards are an annual problem
owing to poor drainage, and the establishment of permanent human settlements is
a recent development arising from mounting population pressure upon the land
elsewhere in Central Luzon.

It is, however, the great rice-producing plain lying between the Chico depression
and the eastern uplands which has emerged as the main focus of settlement and
economic development in Nueva Ecija. This crescent-shaped belt, the premier rice-
producing region of Luzon, extends northward from the southern boundary of
Nueva Ecija all the way to San Manuel in Pangasinan. It comprises clay and silt
loams which are fertile, well-drained and yet moisture retentive. Loose and easily
ploughed, it is these soils which are the basis of the Central Plain's productivity.

A tentative reconstruction of the biotic landscapes found in Nueva Ecija prior to
19th century forest clearance suggests the presence of five common types of
associations.[10] Two of these types, the *buri* and *molave* formations, were climax
associations. The *buri* palm (*Corypha elata*) is endemic to fresh-water swamps
throughout the Central Plain, but dense stands also once grew along the borders of
many streams and rivers in Nueva Ecija and elsewhere, and on higher ground
where the palm mixed with other forest types. Spanish accounts clearly establish
that the plump-stemmed *buri* palm was once found in almost pure stands along the
length of the Chico River drainage area, but by the 1950s most of it had disappeared. The second forest association is the *molave* formation, which is associated
with the long dry season characteristic of the Central Luzon Plain. This formation
takes its name from *molave* (*Vitex paryiflora*) and comprises an open forest type of
mixed composition. *Molave* forests are believed to have occupied the interstice between the Chico depression and the mountains to the east.

The three other biotic associations were almost certainly the product of human
activity — second-growth woodland associations called *calaanan* in Tagalog; park-
savannas with a brush or scrub appearance called *parang*; and grasslands con-

The Central Plain of Luzon; Physical Features

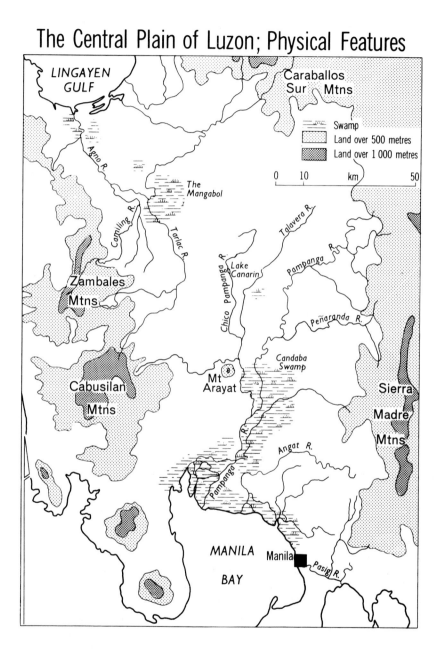

LINGAYEN GULF

Caraballos Sur Mtns

Swamp
Land over 500 metres
Land over 1 000 metres

0   10   km   50

Agno R.

Camiling R.

The Mangabol

Tarlac R.

Talavera R.

Chico Pampanga R.

Pampanga R.

Lake Canarin

Zambales Mtns

Peñaranda R.

Candaba Swamp

Mt Arayat

Cabusilan Mtns

Sierra Madre Mtns

Angat R.

Pampanga R.

MANILA BAY

Manila

Pasig R.

sisting predominantly of *Imperata cylindrica* and *Saccharum spontanieum* called *cogonales*. While their specific distribution at successive periods of human occupance has not been reconstructed, the overall historic progression has been one of replacement of woody growth by herbaceous associations. Since the turn of the century, if not before, the eastern municipalities of Nueva Ecija have been referred to as the *"parang* districts".

The Italon Mission Field

Spain expended the energy of two generations of missionaries to staff parishes for the wet-rice cultivators located on the two littorals of the Central Plain. This effort only marginally touched the region that was to become Nueva Ecija. Although the Augustinian friars established missions and towns (*cabecera*)[11] at Gapan and Cabiao in the 1590s, mission-founding in Nueva Ecija remained virtually at a standstill throughout the 17th century.[12] Only at the close of the century did a new period of missionary activity reassert itself along the margins of Christian settlement. This activity was directed less at extending the areas occupied by the Christian Tagalogs and Kapampangans than converting the mountain heathens. The Italon mission was established along the edge of the Plain, and a number of hill tribes were settled in a series of villages in the intermontane basins and on the edge of the Plain. After about 1720, however, the Augustinian missionaries appear to have been struggling to hold the mission front they had so vigorously established. Ecological circumstances characteristic of the region occupied by the missions on the edge of the Plain may have contributed to the ultimate defeat of the missionary endeavour. These missions, as it turns out, were located in the piedmont zone, the natural habitat of the malaria-bearing mosquito, *Anopheles minimus*. On either side of this zone, in the mountain and out on the plain, the habitat was malaria free. Unaware of the health hazards, the Spanish missionaries located their string of missions within the malaria zone for two reasons. First, the piedmont was in close proximity to the highlanders whom they wished to convert. Second, they believed permanent-field farming to be the only form of rural economy compatible with the village life they intended to impose upon the former shifting cultivators and forest wanderers.

With the gradual collapse of the Italon mission field, the focus of settlement in Nueva Ecija shifted permanently onto the Plain. The few surviving mountain settlements slipped into an obscurity from which they have not yet escaped. Most of the lowland settlements, though they often struggled at the brink of extinction, survived as secular settlements and eventually were revitalized by Ilocano pioneers and the commercial rice economy that followed in their wake.[13]

The frontier missions served as centres of Christianization for some 40 years and had some impact upon the local environment. As the priests were withdrawn one by one, some of the converts, instead of returning to the mountains, practised shifting cultivation in the lowlands and thereby contributed to the spread of second-growth woodland associations on a small scale. The missions, prior to their demise, also must have brought about environmental changes in the vicinity of their settlements. For example, in his summary of Augustinian efforts in north-eastern Nueva Ecija during the early 18th century, Mozo lauded the work carried on by Father Alexandro Cacho:

> He formed villages, opened roads, established schools, built churches, and felled groves; and what was but a little while before a gloomy and impenetrable forest afterward burst upon the sight of the astonished traveller as a broad plain, which the directing hand of the indefatigable Augustinian converted into a fertile field and beautiful province.[14]

Even allowing for hyperbole, the environmental impact of the missions must have been locally significant. The agricultural activities of a half dozen or more missions and their surrounding *visitas* for some 40 years probably left behind the second growth forests, *parangs* and *cogonales,* encountered by Ilocano pioneers 150 years later.

Ilocano Movement into Nueva Ecija

The migration of Ilocanos from their home on the narrow northwest coast of Luzon is a well known but little analyzed aspect of Philippine social history.[15] Prior to the 19th century, Ilocanos expanded primarily along their native north-west coast. Prompted by rapid population growth and consequent environmental deterioration in the home provinces, Ilocano migration began to accelerate some-time after 1810-1820. Large groups, sometimes consisting of whole communities and led by local gentry, began to migrate in wagon caravans or by sea to establish new villages in the virtually unoccupied interior of Pangasinan. By the 1840s Ilocano pioneers were beginning to penetrate beyond Pangasinan into Nueva Ecija, both directly from the north and circuitously by way of Tarlac.[16]

In their movement southward onto the Central Plain, Ilocano wagon caravans were able to follow existing roads and cart trails to the edges of settlement and then work their way a few kilometres across country, usually along natural river levees, to some likely site and establish their settlement. In large part the patterns of their movements were determined by the nature of the frontier. By the early 18th century, long before the onset of the Ilocano migrations, a thin veneer of set-tlement stretched across the length and breadth of the central lowland. Scattered and isolated, the individual interior settlements represented nuclear pockets of lowland Christian society surrounded on all sides by the frontier. As each *pobla-cion* and barrio was formed, it became an instrument for the taming of the sur-rounding countryside, a nodal point in the wilderness from which colonists issued forth to push back the frontier and expand the domesticated landscape. Throughout the 19th century, then, the process of migration was always served by existing settlements within the locality undergoing intensive colonization.

Most caravans knew in advance something of their destination. It was not un-common for itinerant merchants from the Ilocos Coast to locate a desirable place for settlement, return to Ilocos for their family, and lead a few adventurous

The Ilocano Migrations

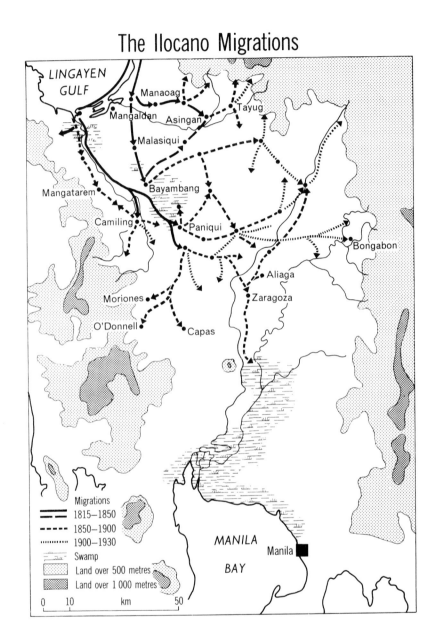

LINGAYEN
GULF

Manaoag

Mangaldan   Asingan   Tayug

Malasiqui

Mangatarem

Bayambang

Camiling

Paniqui

Moriones

O'Donnell   Capas

Aliaga

Zaragoza

Bongabon

Migrations
1815—1850
1850—1900
1900—1930
Swamp
Land over 500 metres
Land over 1 000 metres

0   10   km   50

MANILA   Manila

BAY

relatives or townsmen to the new land. In other cases, groups wishing to migrate dispatched land seekers to make a reconnaissance, and professional guides also led groups to unoccupied land. As the Ilocano movement gained momentum, it became possible for the later groups to rely upon relatives and fellow townsmen who had already migrated. Stories of lush lands lying untouched, available for the taking, filtered back to the Ilocos Coast and prompted mass migration.[17] Beginning late in the 19th century, the tide of migratory rice harvesters from Ilocos to Central Luzon added to the influx of pioneer families. After the November rice harvest in Ilocos, hundreds of families shifted south to Pangasinan, Tarlac, and Nueva Ecija between December and April to assist labour-short farmers in their harvest. Many Ilocanos used this seasonal migration as a means to seek a new home.[18]

Normally the immediate destination of the Ilocano caravans was some frontier barrio or town. Those who arrived with their families and sufficient capital frequently became sharecrop tenants (*kasama*) for relatives or other settlers with large land claims. This enabled the newcomers to settle in, then search out and clear a likely homestead in their spare time. Others became dependent labourers for relatives who had preceded them to the frontier. They were called *kasugpon*, meaning "helpers within the family circle". Many *kasugpon* were young, adventurous bachelors from among the relatives remaining in Ilocos who lacked the capital and provisions to start their own farmstead.

As soon as tenants and helpers had accumulated enough savings to buy a *carabao* (water buffalo) and other necessities, they sought out land to claim as their own.[19] If they planned to remain within the settlement where they had become established, it was usually necessary to accumulate sufficient capital to buy some land from one of the original settlers. Land was cheap and often could be purchased for a *carabao,* an axe, or a *bolo* (machete).[20] Otherwise, they sought out unoccupied land some distance away and moved to their new farmstead to begin a swidden farm (*kaingin*). In some cases unclaimed land still remained in the vicinity of the pioneer village, and so while working for others, the helper or tenant could clear land in his spare time. The *kasugpon-kasama* system was advantageous to both old and new pioneers. It afforded the newcomer security and made migration possible on a very limited grubstake. Conversely, it provided badly needed but scarce labour for colonists trying to provide an inheritance for their children by working a farmstead beyond the labour capacity of their family work force.

Not all groups went through a settling-in stage before making a bid to establish their farmstead. Many, especially in the case of a group migration, lingered in the frontier community only long enough to learn the location of unclaimed land suitable for agriculture. Once they had located a suitable place, they set to clearing, living in their carts until by co-operative effort they erected small houses from the felled trees, bamboo and *cogon* grass. Having brought seeds, cuttings, domesticated animals and crude tools with them, they planted their clearing and lived on dried food reserves while awaiting the first harvest. Usually they could supplement these provisions with locally caught fish, crustaceans and game, and with gathered fruits, roots and greens. Roots, both planted and growing wild in the forest, were especially important for the first several years until land could be prepared for paddy.[21]

Some of the Ilocano migratory groups demonstrated a unique synthesis of European individualism and a more traditional communalism. Having accepted the European concept of private ownership of land, many pioneers sought possession of their own private parcels. Nevertheless, vestiges of traditional communal tenure concepts remained very much alive, and some pioneering ventures were organized in a way reminiscent of pre-Hispanic *barangay* colonization.[22] An American colonial schoolteacher later observed that it was common for groups of four to 20 Ilocano families to migrate to the Central Plain under the leadership of a headman, who would acquire land in his name even though everyone in the group had contributed. The group built their houses together in a common enclosure and cooperated in clearing the land. Although each family was assigned a private parcel, peak labour periods such as planting and harvesting were a communal effort.[23] Historical accounts of the towns and barrios of the Central Plain provide many examples of this type of settlement. Mid-19th century settlers from Paoay, Ilocos Norte, established the barrio of Calem in Guimba by such means. The barrio history reports: "Captain Andres Salvador and his companions passed this place and decided to cut down the trees. They began to *kaingin* . . . Salvador owned the land and his companions became his tenants."[24]

One sociologist has called this practice the "colonial system of pioneering", but "*barangay* settlement" better captures the essence of the organizational relationship.[25] Not only did communal labour practices survive, but so too did traditional social stratification based on patron–client relationships. For many peasants, individual land ownership was not yet as valued as the security inherent in being the follower of a powerful leader (*amo*).[26] In traditional *barangay* society access to land was one of the benefits to be derived from dependency. Individual ownership of land was a mixed blessing, and its advantages only came to the fore with the gradual commercialization of the economy in the 20th century.[27]

The Nueva Ecija Hacienda

At the beginning of the 19th century the interior of the Central Plain was a thinly inhabited fringe between settled coastal strips to the north and south. Unlike the older Tagalog, Kapampangan and Pangasinan coastal villages, the interior settlements had no traditional gentry class (*principalia*). Later in the century, a provincial elite did emerge in Nueva Ecija, but its members came as land speculators from Bulacan, Pampanga or, to a lesser extent, Pangasinan and Ilocos rather than from the ranks of a local gentry. Those from Bulacan and Pampanga were predominantly of Chinese mestizo ancestry.[28]

Spanish colonials were among the first to exploit Nueva Ecija's resources. With the loss of Spain's New World empire and the demise of the galleon trade early in the 19th century, Spaniards began to recognize the archipelago's domestic resources. Since the lands of the well-populated littorals were securely in the hands of Filipino and Chinese mestizo gentry, these Spaniards acquired estates (haciendas) in the interior. Unable to secure sufficient labour to carry on agricultural pursuits, they stocked the land with grazing animals.

Spanish estates devoted to extensive land use began to appear late in the 18th century in the less settled part of Bulacan and Pampanga. As population increased near the estates, they shifted to a more intensive exploitation of the land. In Pampanga these estates concentrated increasingly on sugar and rice, while in Bulacan they turned to a number of commercial crops.[29] Consequently, livestock-raising shifted to the sparsely populated lands in the interior. Nueva Ecija, which in the past had provided a mere trickle of forest products, emerged in the second half of the 19th century as the main source of meat for the Manila market.[30] Although local *principalia* raised some stock on small ranches in the northern part of the province, large-scale ranching was most important on the Spanish-owned haciendas located in the central part of the province.[31] The largest hacienda in Nueva Ecija, with some 3,000 head of cattle, was the Sabani estate, occupying more than 6,000 hectares in what is today the municipality of Gabaldon.[32] By 1889 the provincial herds were reported to comprise 35,500 head of cattle, 38,500 *carabao,* 10,000 horses, and 70,000 pigs.[33] By then, however, rinderpest had begun to infest the livestock herds, and shortly thereafter large-scale ranching came to an end in Nueva Ecija.

While cattle-ranching played an important role in the early development of central and northern Nueva Ecija, it was the government Tobacco Monopoly that brought commercial agricuture to the province's southwestern corner. Late in the 18th century, the Gapan area was designated as a growing district for the Monopoly, effectively harnessing southern Nueva Ecija to the colony's nascent commercial economy. Since tobacco growers were required to devote themselves exclusively to the cultivation of the crop, they had to purchase rice and other necessities. Some of the early Ilocano pioneers were drawn into the area by the opportunity to produce rice for the tobacco towns.

Tobacco was grown primarily on the well-drained sandy terraces and levees of the Pampanga River and its major tributary, the Peñaranda.[34] With the end of the Tobacco Monopoly in 1881, these sandy soils, which are poorly suited to rice cultivation, began to be utilized for growing sugar cane and maize. Even before the end of the Monopoly, sugar had become a locally important crop on the heavier soils away from the rivers. It was primarily in association with sugar production that the smaller haciendas of southern Nueva Ecija and Cabanatuan were organized during the last quarter of the 19th century. While local *principalia* landowners grew some sugar, the bulk of production came from six Spanish-owned haciendas — four in Cabanatuan, and one each in Jaen and Cabiao. In 1870 only 499 hectares were planted to cane in Nueva Ecija, but by 1886, five years after the end of the Tobacco Monopoly, sugar cane was reported to be a crop "in ascendency".[35] In 1889 the combined output of the Nueva Ecija haciendas was 65,434 *pilones,* of which 61,300 *pilones* were shipped to Manila.[36] But Nueva Ecija's production, however, never approached that of Pampanga, Bulacan or Pangasinan.

With the appearance of large-scale centrifugal milling in the Philippines during the 1920s, commercial sugar production concentrated in the most efficient producing areas. On the Central Luzon Plain, only Tarlac and part of Pampanga, because of the sandy texture of their soils, successfully converted to modern sugar cultivation. Conversely, cane production disappeared from Nueva Ecija and Bulacan because their loamy soils retained too much moisture for the best production of sugar. In Nueva Ecija, only the Hacienda Buencamino, founded in 1912, continued to grow cane for centrifugal milling.

Municipalities of the Central Luzon Plain, 1960

In summary, the impact of Spanish-owned landholdings in Nueva Ecija was manifested first by the appearance of large estates with small areas devoted to rice farming and larger areas to livestock production. Late in the century smaller haciendas appeared in the southern municipalities, where more labour was available, and exploited the potential for sugar production. The period of cane farming lasted some 20 to 30 years, while livestock-raising collapsed after about 1890 because of rinderpest and foot-and-mouth epidemics. In both the northern and southern parts of the province, the *principalia* emulated Spanish livestock-grazing and sugar production, though at a lower level of capital investment. The newly emerging gentry was also largely responsible for organizing rice cultivation, which became increasingly important in the more populated parts of the province. During this century, pioneer rice farmers and sugar haciendas began felling the province's forests. The pioneer settlers, mostly from the Ilocos Coast, made rapid inroads in the still substantial stands of forests. Late 19th century sugar production had a major impact as well on the forests in the southern part of the province. The boiling of cane juice consumed vast amounts of wood, just as charcoal-making for iron-smelting was responsible for deforestation in Europe until coal was substituted in the early 18th century.[37]

Emergence of a Mestizo Elite

The provincial elite who ultimately emerged as the principal landowners in Nueva Ecija were predominantly of Spanish and Chinese mestizo stock. The elite acquired land in several ways. Most importantly, royal grants or purchase from the royal domain laid the basis for the pattern of estate holdings that developed in much of Nueva Ecija during the second half of the 19th century. The earliest estates were primarily Spanish-owned, but only a few of the present-day Spanish mestizo *principalia* are descended from the original estate owners. Migrating from the adjacent provinces of Pampanga and Bulacan,[38] these Spanish mestizos purchased their estates from the original Spanish grantee[39] or purchased land from the royal domain.

Chinese mestizos also became established among the province's landholding elite during the late 19th century, extending their holdings northward from Pampanga and Bulacan as each *pueblo* became integrated into the market economy.[40] The primary means of acquiring land was by extending mortages (*pacto de retroventa*).[41] Land was assimilated parcel by parcel, and the result was a pattern of "scattered holdings" which made the Chinese mestizos the dominant element among medium and small landlords. Only toward the end of the century did these mestizos begin to emerge as a prominent element among large *hacenderos*.[42] A number of Chinese mestizos from San Miguel de Mayumo, the northernmost town of Bulacan province, were active in organizing haciendas in Nueva Ecija while continuing to reside in their native town. Don José de Leon, for example, originally owned only some 250 hectares in Bulacan, but eventually controlled some 5,000 hectares scattered throughout southern Nueva Ecija.[43]

The change of colonial administrations from Spanish to American in 1899 enabled the province's *principalia* to consolidate their grip upon the land. Most Spanish-owned haciendas passed into *principalia* hands during the initial years of the American administration. Faced with reorganizing estates that had been temporarily seized by the revolutionary government and uncertain as to their prospects under the Americans, most Spanish *hacenderos* sold their holdings. Few Americans found the hacienda system an attractive investment, leaving the provincial elite without rivals for control of the land.

Maturation of the Hacienda System

The first two decades of the American period witnessed the most prolific expansion of *principalia*-owned rice haciendas ever to occur on the Central Luzon Plain. The various town histories in the *Historical Data Papers* provide the best glimpse of the process, although their chronology is frequently ambiguous or inaccurate. Nevertheless, it seems clear that from 1890 to 1925 the province's haciendas grew at the expense of the public domain and smallholders. The subsequent period from 1925 to 1941 was one of maturation devoted to developing haciendas laid out during the preceding period of expansion. While the earlier stage saw the *hacenderos* directing leasehold tenants (*inquilinos*) in forest-felling,[44] the next period was one of converting leasehold tenancy to sharecropping and developing complementary credit systems. The later period of consolidation was aided immensely by completion of a railroad line between Manila and Cabanatuan and the American road-building program, which fully integrated Nueva Ecija into the network of domestic commercial relationships.

In the initial period of claiming land, ambitious *principalia* recruited tenants with the promise of free or nominal rent during the early years of occupance in exchange for their clearing designated land. Opening land by this means was called the *canon* or fixed-rent system.[45] The main thrust of migration into Nueva Ecija coincided with the period of hacienda extension. As labour became more plentiful and forest clearance came to an end during the decade of the 1920s, the haciendas first began to raise the fixed-rent and then to switch to the *kasamahan,* or sharecropper system. The census statistics reveal the transition in Nueva Ecija. In 1903 there were 2,215 fixed-rent tenants and only 290 share tenants (*kasama*). In 1918 fixed-rent tenants increased slightly to 2,796 but share tenants jumped to 1,798. By 1939 the census enumerated 50,831 share tenants and only 867 cash tenants. The transformation was complete.

The conflict inherent in a northward expansion of commercial cropping, as exemplified by the hacienda, and a southward expansion of Ilocano subsistence smallholders provides the dramatic element in the domestication of the land in Nueva Ecija. The conflicts which arose were the outcome of fundamentally different perceptions as to the appropriate use of the land.

While some land disputes arose from legitimate misunderstandings, others were the result of fraud. The Spanish administration made several attempts to systematize property rights by issuing land titles, the most noteworthy being the royal decrees of 1880 and 1894. But ignorance, illiteracy, and adherence to traditional concepts of land rights prevented most peasants from acquiring legal titles. Those who responded were primarily the *principalia*, and they often made claim to adjacent lands when filing their claims. Manipulation of land laws by *principalia* became particularly blatant in the interior of the Central Luzon Plain during the early years of the American administration. The Americans, flush with the success of their homesteading program at home, initiated a similar plan for the Philippines in 1903. In an effort to speed up the registration of titles, cadastral surveys of whole municipalities were undertaken in 1913. Procedural delays and public corruption, however, worked to the detriment both of homesteaders and long-established smallholders. Homesteaders were given no assistance in site selection.[46] Many settled on uncleared hacienda land and learned of their mistake only after investing labour in clearing the land. By the same token the cadastral surveys provided *hacenderos* with the opportunity to make claim to adjacent lands.

Predominant Form of Landholding in Prewar Nueva Ecija
(1960 Municipal Boundaries)

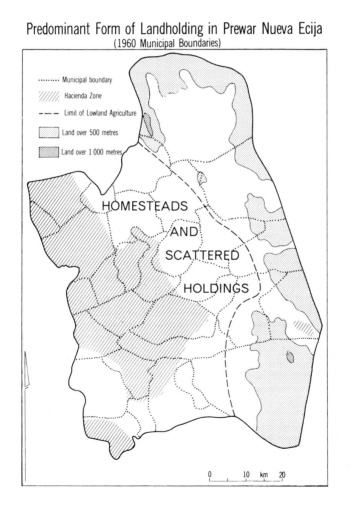

········· Municipal boundary

/////, Hacienda Zone

– – – Limit of Lowland Agriculture

Land over 500 metres

Land over 1 000 metres

HOMESTEADS AND SCATTERED HOLDINGS

0   10   km   20

Resurveys of haciendas became a further means to confiscate adjacent properties since most invariably found that the hacienda's lands were more extensive than previously supposed.

Conflicting land claims, when taken to court, were usually settled in favour of the hacienda, forcing many of the smallholders who had originally cleared the land to become tenants or depart the area. The most notorious land disputes occurred in the municipalities of Guimba, Nampicuan, Cuyapo and Talavera. So long as they were merely asked to pay fixed-rent (*canon*), many of the smallholders were willing to comply, probably looking upon this payment as a form of tribute to the powerful, rather than an acknowledgement that the land they occupied belonged to a hacienda. Matters came to a head during the 1920s when haciendas began to consolidate their grip upon the land by shifting from fixed-rent tenancy to sharecropping. The timing coincided with the completion of the road over Balete Pass from Nueva Ecija to the Cagayan Valley, and many of the displaced smallholders moved northward into Nueva Vizcaya and the Cagayan Valley to again seek land of their own.

The Human Ecology of Tenancy

The transition from smallholders to tenants in the early 20th century marked the consolidation of the hacienda system. Although many facets of prewar tenancy exploitation have already been detailed in an ample literature,[47] it is nevertheless important to link the hacienda system with a set of characteristics that Hans Bobek has called "rent capitalism."[48] According to Bobek, rent capitalism arises from the commercialization of a feudal economy in such a way that the original claims of the aristocracy upon peasant services are transformed into more explicitly profit-seeking obligations. Rent capitalism is a true form of capitalism to the extent that there is a striving for unlimited gain. In so far as it adopts accounting practices, it attains a high degree of economic rationality. It differs from modern capitalism in that it is not concerned with efficiency of production, but rather is satisfied with skimming off the proceeds by rent collection. It frees the owner from the duties and obligations of entrepreneurial management and capital-intensive investment.

A central feature of hacienda operations characteristic of rent capitalism is the elaboration of mechanisms which place the peasant cultivator in debt to the gentry class. In explaining this point, Bobek states: "It is an absolute ideal of the rent capitalist to get as many peasants as possible into debt so permanently that with all their yearly payments they can never liquidate the initial debt, which soon becomes legendary."[49] In a society characterized by rent capitalism, landlords are less concerned with stimulating higher crop yields than in elaborating means to increase rent collections. It is easier for landowners to increase income by expanding their control of labour than by encouraging their tenants to adopt progressive farm management techniques.

It was on the haciendas that the patterns of rent capitalism became most fully elaborated. The landlord with scattered holdings knew his tenants personally and was usually paternalistic towards them. While vestiges of paternalism remained on many haciendas, the greater distance between the *hacendero* and his numerous tenants promoted more impersonal relations that worked to the economic advantage of the landowner. On some haciendas paternalism became virtually a "dead horse".[50] This second stage of development, characterized by the techniques of rent capitalism, might be called the classical period of the rice hacienda on the Central Plain.

By the early 20th century hacienda-tenant credit relations were already quite complex. An American colonial, Victor Clark, observed that Filipino proprietors valued their land, as a rule, according to the number of families settled upon it.[51] Hence there was a propensity to divide cultivated lands into as many tenancies as possible. The optimal area that a nuclear family could till comfortably under the system of wet-rice cultivation was about three hectares. Many tenancies, however, were considerably smaller, some no larger than a half hectare. Even when income from other sources was significant, the average tenant had to borrow money or rice in order to survive on such a small farm. At the beginning of his contract with the landlord, the tenant usually had no reserve to feed his family. Hence the landlord gave him an advance, called *bugnos,* which was expected to be repaid by the tenant should he decide to terminate the tenancy arrangement. Moreover, until the rice seedlings were transplanted, the tenant and his family received a ration of rice to be paid back at harvest without interest. After transplanting, however, the tenant found it necessary to borrow at high interest rates, whether from his landlord or from some other source. Prior to World War II, interest rates ranged from 50 to 200 percent on loans usually extended for only six months or less. On the haciendas, debts were not settled with any regularity so that many tenants had no accurate knowledge of the amount of their debt.[52] The high rates of interest were based on traditional village subsistence practices predating market production. In a subsistence economy, borrowing a *cavan* of rice was thought to deprive the creditor of what the *cavan* would have produced had it been used as seed.[53] Hill and Moe have attempted to justify the high rates of interest as reimbursing landlords for rice stolen from the fields by their tenants prior to the harvest. They estimated this type of loss to range between 12 and 15 percent of the total crop. Hester and his colleagues have also pointed out that the risk of loss on loans is high.[54]

In extending credit to his tenants the *hacendero* was more interested in power than profits. Clark has shown that the main aim of these loans was to reduce the tenant to peonage: "The essence of peonage is the liability of a man to work for his employer so long as he remains a debtor to the latter, coupled with the practical impossibility of ever paying off this indebtedness. Peonage is a condition of tenancy." The idea that the tenant gains access to land by paying rent is almost fictional.[55] It was through debt — short term, long term, and the interest on both — that the landlord controlled the tenant and held him to the land.[56] In 1945 an American geographer observed :

It is to the advantage of the landlord to have the tenant indebted to him, not only because of the high interest rates but also because then the tenant may be forced to do all kinds of extra work and may not leave his holding. The debt binds the tenant to the land and makes him almost a slave of the landlord, who thereupon determines every step to be undertaken — the crop to be grown and the time of planting and harvesting. This control at times goes so far that literate tenants, who have the right to vote, are not at liberty to choose their own candidate but must cast their vote for the landlord's candidate.[57]

Similarly, Lasker noted:

The *kasama* who again has to borrow from his landlord soon after the crop has been divided and the debt has been paid will find it difficult to resist new charges arbitrarily imposed upon him — charges which, since the interest rate is settled by custom, often take the form of additional services or simply of cheating over the volume of his deliveries or over the value of supplies such as clothing. The net result is a tightening of the bondage from which the luckless debtor cannot hope to extricate himself.[58]

Another source adds:

For the payment of principal and interest, which is constantly growing until it acquires impossible proportions, the work of the tenant, his wife and children are demanded. When the children are old enough, they begin working as tenants working on the parental debts and the new debts acquired by themselves. The son who refuses to accept the debts of his father becomes an outcast in his own community.[59]

The hacienda also developed several new sources of income — charging tenants for compulsory use of its threshing machine, truck and house lots. These charges had no basis in tradition, and represented an intensified exploitation of the hacienda's potential for profit. In the mid-1950s, one observer of the province's tenancy conditions wrote:

Some years ago, the tenant still thrashed his palay by spreading it beneath the feet of two or three horses driven side by side in a circle around a bamboo pole. The farmer liked to do this, he was paid for thrashing the Hacendero's share, and his children got a great deal of fun out of it, to thrash in this manner. The Hacendero's huge trilladora (thresher) must do the job, and for every hundred cavans of palay thrashed, the tenant pays the landlord ten cavans.[60]

All the above observations were made about the 1920s and 1930s, the high-water mark of the Filipino rice hacienda. In postwar years, feeling the impact of the Huk rebellion and the consequent land reform program, the rice haciendas entered a period of retrenchment. The worst of abuses nearly disappeared, and interest rates declined somewhat. In addition, the size of haciendas and the scope of their operations decreased through division by inheritance, partition by the National Reform Administration, and conversion into mechanized agro-farms. Still, the never-ending round of poverty and debt continues for the tenant farmer and many a smallholder.

Although the reciprocal quality of patron–client ties was more often maintained in areas of scattered-holding tenancy, the fundamental principles of rent capitalism still applied, even if in a more beneficient manner.[61] In fact, among some of the lesser elite the manipulation of credit served not merely to increase their share of the harvest, but also to extend their networks of dependants by acquiring more land. However, for many of the lesser gentry, who had more traditional values and closer ties to their tenants, the full elaboration of the techniques of rent capitalism never became a primary goal. For many of the latter, credit remained essentially a tool for acquiring more property, especially after the disappearance of the free public land.[62]

The increase in farm rentals was not the only characteristic feature of the rice hacienda during its classical period. Most importantly, established haciendas often operated under the direction of an overseer. Some haciendas had been founded by *principalia* who never made their home in Nueva Ecija. The Bulakeño elite, in particular, seem to have taken advantage of the availability of land in sparsely settled Nueva Ecija, while maintaining their roots in Bulacan. Some local Nueva Ecija *principalia,* once their fortune and place in society were assured, retired to Manila. Others made their homes in Nueva Ecija, sometimes on their haciendas, more often in Cabanatuan or the nearest *poblacion.* Much has been said in contemporary literature regarding the relationship between absentee landlordism and peasant unrest.[63] Such may well be the case in Pampanga[64] and Bulacan, but in Nueva Ecija, and probably in Tarlac as well, *principalia*-owned haciendas which replaced the earlier Spanish livestock ranches and sugar estates were, in essence, ventures in land speculation in which *hacenderos,* tenants and pioneer smallholders alike were interlopers on the scene. While the question of absentee landlordism and its effect on Philippine rural society needs thorough scholarly exploration, in the case of Nueva Ecija the issue seems almost extraneous. The Nueva Ecija hacienda was itself symptomatic of the growing commercialization of the Philippine economy and was intrinsically a more rational system of labour and resource exploitation than the older scattered-holding system.

A final characteristic of prewar Nueva Ecija was an agriculture characterized by monoculture. Even when Pangasinan was the primary producer of rice surpluses throughout most of the 19th century, monocrop agriculture was never characteristic of that province except on the eastern haciendas, which were then a part of Nueva Ecija. Although the 19th century saw the beginnings of regional crop specialization, monoculture developed only during the American colonial period. Simultaneously, Nueva Ecija replaced Pangasinan as the premier rice-producing province of the Philippines.

Monocropping was the logical outcome of the patterns of hacienda development in Nueva Ecija. During the pioneering stages, while tenants were still clearing the land and being charged a nominal rent, diversified swidden-cropping habits prevailed. But once each tenant's holding had been laid out in paddy fields, the landlord or his overseer took a more direct interest in promoting the production of rice as the premier cash crop. Moreover, as the forest disappeared, many of the small streams, lakes and ponds also vanished. And with the water went the opportunity to cultivate other crops in the dry season. In those few areas where irrigation water was available in the dry season, farmers either cultivated one late-maturing rice variety annually or raised two rice crops per year. Hence conditions of increasing aridity accompanied the period of hacienda consolidation in Nueva Ecija, thereby limiting opportunities for crop diversification. The Cabanatuan-Manila rail link led to an early development of marketing facilities for the rice surpluses, further integrating smallholders, scattered-holdings landlords and the haciendas into a system of rice monocropping.[65] Only in the southern tier of municipalities of Nueva Ecija, in particular Gapan and San Isidro, was some semblance of crop diversity maintained.

Homesteading and Land Speculation

Homesteading, too, has left its mark upon the tenure patterns of Nueva Ecija. When the Public Land Act was passed in 1903, introducing the homestead system into the Philippines, sizable sections of public land were still available in the Central Luzon Plain in parts of northern and eastern Nueva Ecija. Except among the Ilocanos, who tended to migrate in groups, initial Filipino response to homesteading was apathetic. The American homestead system had been developed among a people accustomed to a pattern of dispersed settlement, but lowland Christian Filipinos were more gregarious.[66]

Despite the drawbacks of the homestead program the number of applicants began to grow steadily after 1912.[67] Nueva Ecija, close and accessible to the littorals of both Manila Bay and the Lingayen Gulf-Ilocos region, quickly felt the impact. Between 1904 and 1932, homesteaders filed approved claims for 46,887 hectares in Nueva Ecija, approximately 16 percent of the arable land.[68] While homesteads were established throughout Nueva Ecija, the main area of settlement was a broad stretch of public land in the northeast lying between Bongabong, San José, Muñoz and Talavera.[69] Despite opposition from *hacenderos* who tried to block confirmation of their land titles, homesteaders succeeded in establishing a pattern of small holdings. Although none of the Philippine censuses was carried out at the opportune moment to mark the peak of smallholder ownership in northeastern Nueva Ecija, the era of homesteading is reflected in the high percentage of owner-operated farms reported in these municipalities by the 1939 census. After 1939, however, landlords made considerable inroads into the homestead areas as revealed by the dwindling percentages of owner-operators enumerated in the 1960 census.

Whether claimed by *hacenderos* or homesteaders, public land suitable for agriculture was on the point of disappearing in Nueva Ecija by the end of the 1920s. With the disappearance of the frontier, opportunities to acquire large tracts of land also vanished. The great Ilocano migrations into the Central Luzon Plain ran their course in just over 100 years, beginning about 1815 and ending around 1925 with a final, convulsive surge in response to the homestead program. Even as the last great torrent of Ilocano immigrants poured into Nueva Ecija another significant but more subtle movement — which would ultimately displace or make tenants of the vast majority of the Ilocano pioneers — was starting to materialize. Beginning around 1915, there was a migration of Tagalog capitalists, not peasants, that was to prove significant in the further integration of Nueva Ecija with the national economy. Except for the few wealthy individuals like José de Leon, who were able to purchase haciendas, speculation took the form of acquiring small pieces of land through purchase or mortgage foreclosure. Financing and credit mechanisms had replaced the axe and the plough as the means to acquiring land.

Initially speculation in land was limited primarily to the southernmost municipalities of Nueva Ecija, but gradually, as many homesteaders found they could not survive, land acquisition by moneyed people spread northward, carrying a pattern of scattered-holding tenancy with it.[70] Homesteaders who lacked capital reserves were prone to borrow, become overextended and ultimately end as tenants on their former homesteads. Natural disasters also took a toll of homesteaders. The case of Barrio Popolon in Bongabon is typical. During one season in the early 1920s rinderpest killed all the *carabao* of the barrio. The land lay uncultivated, and to survive, the people had to sell their farms. Today they are tenants, and the barrio farmlands are owned by a few well-to-do families.[71] The process of attrition among independent farmers has continued to the present, and as the number of Ilocano owner–operators declines, Tagalog landlords with scattered holdings continue to increase.

The Commercial Economy

The commercialization of Nueva Ecija's economy and its integration into external markets was a slow, cumulative process that took two centuries to complete. The first stirrings of Manila's nascent commercial economy began to be felt in Nueva Ecija late in the 18th century. The creation of the Tobacco Monopoly in 1781 rapidly tied the southern river towns to the colonial economic system.[72] Nevertheless, Nueva Ecija's participation in interprovincial trade was marginal in the first half of the 19th century. After mid-century, livestock raising, pushed out of areas closer to Manila by the growing intensity of land use there, expanded into Nueva Ecija, and from about 1870 onward the production of sugar also assumed some importance. In turn, traders from Nueva Ecija sought salt, dried and smoked fish, coconut oil, and various *nipa* products from the coastal provinces.[73] By the last third of the 19th century a commercial economy of some significance dealing in the export of rice, sugar, tobacco and livestock had developed in Nueva Ecija. Despite the distances to markets and the extreme transport difficulties in the central and northern districts of the province, pioneer farmers sought commercial outlets for their surpluses. A constant flow of exports materialized moving toward Manila via Dagupan and Guagua, the main ports in the Agno and Pampanga deltas. The quest for estates within Nueva Ecija, as in Tarlac, was also an expression of the penetration of the region by commercial influences.

By the 1880s, Nueva Ecija had become a major rice exporter shipping some 500,000 *cavans* of *palay* to Manila each year — far more than Pampanga, once Manila's leading supplier. Between 1870 and 1887 the province's annual rice production increased from 700,000 to 1.5 million *cavans*.[74] The leading rice-producing municipalities were Gapan (270,000 *cavans* in 1885) in the south and Aliaga (182,000 *cavans*) in the centre of the province,[75] while Cabanatuan, Gapan and San Isidro became the main points for shipment to Manila. For the better part of the 19th century and the first two decades of the 20th, Pangasinan remained the leading rice-producing province of the archipelago. Stimulated by American road-building and public lands programs, haciendas and homesteads proliferated in Nueva Ecija during the second and third decades of the 20th century and empty lands were quickly turned to paddy. In the early 1920s Nueva Ecija edged past Pangasinan as the new rice granary of the Central Plain, and by the mid-1930s Nueva Ecija was producing eight to nine million *cavans* per year, about one-fifth of total national production.

Despite the commercialization of the economy, the only significant change in the province's productive process betweeen the 1880s and 1960s was an increasing substitution of hired labour for reciprocal labour. The practice of hiring labour gained strength particularly among the hacienda tenancies. Given a socio-economic system characterized by rent capitalism, this is not surprising. Capital investment focused upon one element only — land. As the frontier faded into history and Nueva Ecija became a labour surplus rather than a land surplus area, the easiest path by which landowners could increase their income was by the acquisition of more tenancies, not by investment in the improvement of land with the goal of increasing yields. Hence there were few socio-economic pressures upon the peasantry to adopt improved cultivation techniques. Even *principalia* investment in the construction of private irrigation systems is less an exception to this generalization than it might appear. Irrigation canals were a means to guarantee annual production and expand the tillage within a *hacendero's* holding, not essentially a means to increase yields.

Despite a shift in transport service from river craft to rail and trucks, Cabanatuan and Gapan continued to function as collection points for the rice harvests. In 1909 there were six rice mills in the province, two each in Cabanatuan and Gapan, and single mills in Sta. Rosa and San Isidro. By 1935 there were 42 mills, 13 located in Cabanatuan and ten in Gapan.[76] No other municipality possessed more than three mills, and one of these, Sta. Rosa, could be considered part of the greater Cabanatuan milling complex.

From the beginning the milling process was heavily dominated by Chinese, especially in Cabanatuan, and was attractive to them since it strengthened their control over market distribution. Walter Robb tells of an American who "tried the milling game" in Cabanatuan early in the century and lasted only a few years in competition with the Chinese. He tried to buy for cash, mill the rice, and ship it to Manila for a straight miller's profit. Since the Chinese millers operated on the basis that rice was a medium of exchange and the basis of credit, they were able to gain control of the crop while it was still growing in the field and cut off the hapless American's access to sufficient grain for profitable operation.[77]

To the Chinese operator, the mill served merely as one point of leverage over the many facets of the rice-marketing process. The distribution system began with the mill's numerous agents — networks of rice dealers who linked the cultivators with the mills. Competition between mills was minimal since each had developed its own clientele among growers and landowners over the years.[78] While some of the dealers moved about the countryside loaning money against future harvests, others operated sundry stores to attract farmers in need of credit. The shopkeeper extended the farmer loans with little or no interest, and later purchased the latter's surplus rice at a rate somewhat lower than the prevailing market price. The rice dealer purchased rice from the farmer when prices were low, often before the harvest, and sold later in the year when prices were higher. The mill operator stored the unhusked rice he had acquired and milled it when he speculated that the commodity had reached its peak price.

From Cabanatuan and Gapan rice moved southward by rail and truck to Manila. In Manila the grain came under the control of the Tutuban Rice Exchange (established in 1922), many of whose members were part or full owners of Nueva Ecija rice mills.[79] The complete Chinese control of the prewar Manila rice market is reflected in the names of the founders of the exchange — Tan Sio, Chan Kiau, Chung Quiat Tao, Chua To Key, Cheng Liaoco, Co Hue Ty, Poa Nguanco, Lim Koon Hong and Ty Eng An. At the Tutuban Rice Exchange there were several types of buyers — Manila wholesale merchants, Manila retailers, brokers and commission merchants, provincial wholesalers and provincial retailers. While much of the rice was consumed in Manila and the adjacent suburbs, considerable grain moved on to supply rice-deficit areas elsewhere in the islands, such as Cebu, Leyte, the Bikol provinces, Samar, Negros and Masbate.[80]

The 1930s was the period of florescence of wet-rice monoculture in Nueva Ecija. Most of the lowland forests and grasslands had been cleared; hacienda development had reached a stage of maturity; fixed-rent tenants had been transformed into sharecroppers dependent upon their landlords for their security; elaboration of road and irrigation systems provided an ever more stable foundation for the functioning of the emergent agricultural system; and a Chinese-dominated rice distribution network had grown which functioned as an instrument of product concentration.

Impact upon the Environment

The expansion of wet-rice and sugar-cane cultivation into the interior of the Central Luzon Plain has effected revolutionary changes in the environment. Pioneering set in motion a widespread process of deforestation, followed axiomatically by a gradual aridification of the lowland environment.

The first concerted period of forest-felling accompanied the founding of missions on the Central Plain during the late 17th and early 18th centuries. When many of these missions began to be abandoned on the eastern side of the plain in Nueva Ecija during the mid-18th century, the missions' fields were quickly transformed into grass and scrub which became the breeding grounds for locust swarms. Once established, the grasslands and locusts undoubtedly served to perpetuate each other. In some cases stands of secondary forests eventually reappeared on formerly cultivated land, but frequent firing of grass and scrub tended to maintain open associations.

Nevertheless, at the beginning of the 19th century *molave* and *buri* palm forests still covered vast areas of the interior. The great era of forest felling occurred between about 1820 and 1925. The primary impetus to deforestation was the process of pioneer colonization — the clearing of land for agriculture by Ilocano and other smallholders in the 19th century, and by homesteaders and tenants of *hacenderos* in the early 20th. Nevertheless, lumbering, the fabrication of sugar and charcoal, and the periodic firing of grazing land all contributed to the eradication of woodlands. First to disappear from the Central Plain were the *molave* forests, while certain of the *buri* palm forests along the swampy fringes of the Chico Pampanga River were not felled until the 1950s.

Despite the monsoonal precipitation regime, the Central Luzon Plain at Spanish contact was characterized by moist conditions. The heavy alluvial clay soils that stretch the length of the Central Plain formed a swampy environment. Published materials from the 19th century and maps from earlier periods reveal the presence of large and small lakes that have subsequently disappeared. Only Lake Canarin and a few smaller lakes survive in the interior of the Plain today, and these have become virtually seasonal lakes like the Mangabol. The expansion of irrigation facilities has redirected drainage patterns. The lowland forests once retarded the flow of water to the sea, modifying the seasonal highs and lows. With the disappearance of these forests, the rivers become engorged and flood-prone throughout the rainy season while the land bakes in the sun during the dry months.

But the growing aridity of the Central Plain finds its causes beyond the Plain proper as well. Lumbering and swidden farming in the surrounding uplands have stripped much of the watershed of its forests. At the end of World War II, a building boom in the Philippines, Japan and the United States created a tremendous market for Philippine lumber. Commonwealth forest laws were relaxed under the Republic. The pine and mossy oak forests of the Central Cordillera fell prey to the lumbering boom, and the cleared land, much of it in the Mount Data National Park and Central Cordillera Forest Reserve, was opened for homesteading early in the 1950s by Executive Order 180. Market gardening, which was localized in the Trinidad, Lucban and Guisad valleys prior to the war, began to expand along the Mountain Trail toward Bontoc early in the 1950s. Today there are over 1,000 hectares of vegetable terraces where moss forest once stood.[81] The mossy humus-rich soils that formed under these forests were excellent conservers of water, and the streams and rivers arising in these areas provided a steady supply of water to the lowlands the year round. Today the moss forests have all but disappeared, and the resulting decline in hydro-electric generation at the Central Cordillera's power plants is reflected in Manila's recurring power "brownouts". Springs have vanished with the forests; gullying and slope slippage in the uplands is matched by increased rates of sedimentation behind reservoir dams; and rainy season runoff is rapid with consequent flooding of farmland in the Central Luzon Plain.

It can be surmised that because of the deforestation of the Plain and the adjacent mountains, flooding in the lowlands is more extensive than in past centuries. Certainly the effects of flooding and typhoon damage is more serious today in the Central Plain than in the 18th and 19th centuries. While storm damage has always caused hardship, subsistence farmers, especially those on the pioneering frontier, had alternative resources such as hunting and gathering to fall back upon until new crops could be harvested. Peasants caught up in a system of commercial rice cultivation in a fully occupied area have no such alternatives. Their only recourse is to borrow to survive. Not only does storm damage force them to borrow, it precludes paying off former obligations, thereby compounding indebtedness. Today the problems posed by natural disasters are as much economic as dietary.

While the rainy season brings the threat of floods, the shrinking dry season supply of stream water exaggerates the effects of drought. In recent years the farmers of Nueva Ecija have been attempting to raise a second crop — rice, maize, tobacco or vegetables — during the dry season, but are finding the watercourses running dry during the hot months with increasing frequency. After the drought of 1968, the government made shallow-well pumps available to farmers on easy terms for tapping the water table. There has been a considerable response to this program in Nueva Ecija. *Hacenderos* and other landlords have also installed deep-well pumps, not only to ensure a water supply for their own tenants and for farms they manage themselves, but also to exploit the opportunity to sell an increasingly scarce resource to neighbouring cultivators. It can be predicted that the long run effect of these pumps will be to reduce the depth of the water table. Given the rapid rate of siltation of dams in the Cordillera Central in the aftermath of deforestation, it is even debatable whether the recently completed Pantabangan Reservoir dam, behind which has formed a 17,000 hectare lake providing irrigation water for 81,000 hectares the year round, will prove a long-term solution to the water needs of the Central Plain.

Opportunities to supplement harvests with riparian resources are also diminishing in the Central Plain. The widespread disappearance of lakes and ponds and contraction of the swamps has reduced the habitat suitable for many fish, frogs, freshwater crustaceans and other aquatic life. In recent years the increasing use of insecticides has introduced another ecological deterrent to the preservation of aquatic food resources in the interior of the Central Luzon Plain. One example of the effects of aridity upon the availability of food is provided by the farmers of San José, Nueva Ecija, who now take their fish nets all the way to the Mangabol swamp in Tarlac to fish in the dry season.[82] To a great extent, however, the people of the

interior have come to rely upon the coastal districts of the Lingayen Gulf and
Manila Bay for fish and other water life. For the poorer segments of society, the
depletion of local riparian resources means that much of the time they must forego
traditional foods in their daily diet. Their ancestors on the littorals of Luzon may
have supplemented a basically aquatic diet with rice. Today, however, rice monoculture is mirrored in the daily fare.

The accelerating cycle of flood and drought — exemplified in the destructiveness
of the 1972 floods — is the most obvious manifestation of a pervasive deterioration
of the environment of the Central Plain. Yet the same process of economic transformation which now threatens the region's environment has made the Central
Plain the Philippines' most important granary. Continuing environmental destruction will mean the decline, if not the ruin, of the region's productivity. The loss of
such an important food-producing region would be a social and economic disaster
of the first magnitude.

NOTES

1 The concept of the primate city, of which Manila is an example, originated
with Mark Jefferson, a geographer. He observed that the primate city is
supereminent within a country in terms of population and is characterized
by unequalled functional diversity and national influence. See, "The Law of
the Primate City," *Geographical Review* 29 (April 1939), 226-32. The
economic objectives of Western colonialism were particularly conducive to
fostering the growth of primate cities in political dependencies. In this
regard see, T.G. McGee, *The Southeast Asian City: A Social Geography of
the Primate Cities of Southeast Asia* (New York: Praeger Publishers, 1967);
Robert R. Reed, "The Colonial Origins of Manila and Batavia: Desultory
Notes on Nascent Metropolitan Primacy and Urban Systems in Southeast
Asia," *Asian Studies* 5 (December 1967), 543-62; and Robert R. Reed, "The
Primate City in Southeast Asia: Conceptual Definitions and Colonial
Origins," *Asian Studies* 10 (December 1972), 283-320. For analysis of the
evolution of colonial urbanism in the Philippines, see, Robert R. Reed,
"Hispanic Urbanism in the Philippines: A Study of the Impact of Church and
State," *University of Manila Journal of East Asiatic Studies* 11 (March
1967), 1-222. Entry of the Philippines into the European-dominated system
of international commerce is seminally treated by Benito Legarda, Jr.,
"Foreign Trade, Economic Change and Entrepreneurship in the Nineteenth
Century Philippines" (doctoral dissertation, Harvard University, 1955); see
also, W.E. Cheong, "The Decline of Manila as the Spanish Entrepot in the
Far East, 1785-1826: Its Impact on the Pattern of Southeast Asian Trade,"
Journal of Southeast Asian Studies 2 (1971), 142-58, especially page 151;
and Thomas and Mary C. McHale, *Early American-Philippine Trade: The
Journal of Nathaniel Bowditch in Manila, 1796* (New Haven: Yale University
Press, 1962).

2 For an analysis of the distinction between redistributive and market exchange economies, see, Karl Polanyi, Conrad M. Arensberg, and Harry Pearson, *Trade and Market in the Early Empires* (New York: The Free Press, 1955), especially chapter 13. It should be noted, nevertheless, that market exchange norms remained highly coloured by redistributive vestiges in the Philippines, particularly as regards landlord-tenant relationships. For the reciprocal relationship between economic exchange and the organization of labour for production in the context of colonialism, see Immanuel Wallerstein, *The Modern World-System: Capitalist Agriculture and the Origins of the European World Economy in the Sixteenth Century* (New York: Academic Press, 1974), chapter 2, especially pages 100-03.

3 Forest clearance as a major theme of human modification of the earth and domestication of the landscape has been intensively explored by European geographers and economic historians. For a general review and extensive bibliography, see, H.D. Darby, "The Clearing of the Woodland in Europe," in William L. Thomas, Jr., ed., *Man's Role in Changing the Face of the Earth* (Chicago: University of Chicago Press, 1956), 183-216. In the same volume forest clearance in tropical areas is tangentially analyzed, with accompanying bibliography, by H.H. Bartlett, "Fire, Primitive Agriculture, and Grazing in the Tropics," 692-720.

4 Michael Adas, *The Burma Delta: Economic Development and Social Change on an Asian Rice Frontier, 1852-1921* (Madison: University of Wisconsin Press, 1974); Lucien M. Hanks, *Rice and Man; Agricultural Ecology in Southeast Asia* (Chicago: Aldine, 1972); and Pierre Gourou, *L'Utilisation du Sol en Indochine Francais* (Paris: Centre d'Etudes de Politique Etrangère, 1940).

5 E.H.G. Dobby, "Rice in South-East Asia," *Malayan Journal of Tropical Geography* 1 (October 1953), 57-58.

6 Aside from Adas' monograph concerning the Irrawaddy delta in Burma, the only major English language study of pioneer occupance and commercialization of wet rice agriculture in a Southeast Asian riverine valley is that of Marshall McLennan, "Peasant and Hacendero in Nueva Ecija: The Socio-Economic Origins of a Philippine Commercial Rice-Growing Region" (doctoral dissertation, University of California, Berkeley, 1973). For occupance in the Central Luzon Plain in the period preceding the initiation of commercial influences in the 19th century, see, Daniel Doeppers, "Hispanic Influences on Demographic Patterns in the Central Plain of Luzon, 1565-1780," *University of Manila Journal of East Asiatic Studies* 12 (September 1968), 11-96; and Rosario Mendoza-Cortes, *Pangasinan, 1572-1800* (Quezon City: University of the Philippines Press, 1974); and, Marshall S. McLennan, "Population Growth, Migratory Movements, and Agricultural Commercialization in the Central Luzon Plain, the Philippines, 1732-1939" (unpublished paper, 29th Annual Meeting of the Association for Asian Studies, New York, 27 March 1977).

7   Legarda, "Foreign Trade," 249-78; and Nicolas Tarling, "Some Aspects of the British Trade in the Philippines in the Nineteenth Century," *Journal of History* 11 (1963), 287-327.

8   Ramon Gonzales Fernandez, *Annuario Filipino Para 1877* (Manila: Plana y Ca., 1877), 48.

9   Information on the size of the Mangabol swamp is reproduced from Daniel F. Doeppers, "Spanish Alteration of Indigenous Spatial Patterns on the Central Plain of Luzon, 1565-1780 " (M.A. thesis, Syracuse University, 1967). The most useful source regarding the former existence of an inland waterway is Yldefonso de Aragon, *Descripcion geográfica y topográphica de las islas de Luzón o Nueva Castilla* (Manila: A. Gonzaga, 1819-1821), 5:3-4. For comment on the waterway and additional sources, see, McLennan, "Peasant and Hacendero," 114-16, and for evidence concerning the former extent of swamps and the presence of now extinct lakes, see pages 15-20, 24-29.

10 For a tentative reconstruction of natural vegetation associations in the Central Luzon Plain, see, McLennan, "Peasant and Hacendero," 26-35.

11 The term *cabecera* referred, from the 16th through 18th centuries, to a parish seat; after about 1850 until the end of Spanish rule, to a provincial capital. *Visita* was a 17th century ecclesiastical term for a village with a chapel where services were periodically observed.

12 McLennan, "Peasant and Hacendero," 284-85.

13 The surviving settlements are San Nicolas, Tayug, Umingan, Lupao, San Joseph (today San José), Bongabon and Santor. A detailed account of the mission endeavour may be found in McLennan, "Peasant and Hacendero," 284-91.

14 Quoted in, Emma Blair and James A. Robertson, *The Philippine Islands, 1493-1898* (Cleveland: A.H. Clark, 1903-1909), 48:70.

15 Although primary consideration is given to the Ilocano migration into Nueva Ecija, a preliminary attempt to review the origins, causes and dimensions of the entire Ilocano movement may be found in McLennan, "Peasant and Hacendero," chapter 6. See also, Tomas Fonacier, "The Ilocano Movement," *Dilliman Review* 1 (1953), 89-94; José P. Apostol, "The Ilocanos in Zambales," *Journal of History* 4 (1956), 3-15; and Henry T. Lewis, *Ilocano Rice Farmers; A Comparative Study of Two Philippine Barrios* (Honolulu: University of Hawaii Press, 1971), 19-38.

16 Northern Tarlac was still part of Pangasinan province at the time it was being settled by Ilocano pioneers.

17 The richest source of accounts concerning the Ilocano migration and pioneer living in Nueva Ecija, Pangasinan and Tarlac is the collection of *Historical*

Data Papers (hereafter, *HDP*) located in the Philippine National Library. By executive order of the president, the Bureau of Public Schools in 1952-1953 undertook the preparation of histories for all the towns and villages in the Philippines. Since the individual papers were prepared by schoolteachers with no training in historiography, they must be evaluated and used with considerable caution. Regarding the study area, they chronicle the folk memory of, and also beyond, the second and third generation descendants of the original settlers. Despite these limitations, the *HDP* provide a diversity of information concerning the Ilocano movement on a scale unmatched by any other source.

18 Frederick V. Field and Elizabeth B. Field, "Philippine Interisland Migration," in Bruno Lasker, ed., *Filipino Immigration to Continental United States and to Hawaii* (Chicago: University of Chicago Press, 1931), 406; Hugo H. Miller, *Economic Conditions in the Philippines* (Boston: Ginn and Co., 1920), 312-13; and Miller and Mary E. Polley, *Intermediate Geography* (Boston: Ginn and Co., 1932), 39-40.

19 "History and Cultural Life of the Municipality of Nampicuan," *HDP,* 46-47. Lewis also found a two-stage settlement process in the Cagayan Valley (*Ilocano Rice Farmers,* 29).

20 "Historical Data of Pangasinan," *HDP,* 449, San Manuel section.

21 Pioneering activities such as site selection, home construction, clearing and field preparation, and use of natural resources in the local environment are described in, McLennan, "Peasant and Hacendero," 256-61, 265-69.

22 A *barangay* was a village settlement of the preconquest Philippines, which consisted of one or more kinship groups and their dependants representing a socio-political territorial community.

23 Cited by Miller, *Economic Conditions,* 224-25, 277.

24 "History and Cultural Life of Guimba," *HDP,* 234.

25 Serafin E. Macaraig, *Social Problems* (Manila: Educational Supply Co., 1929), 315.

26 *Amo,* the Ilocano equivalent of the Tagalog term, *apo,* a grandfather, master, patron or charismatic leader, or elder person of authority or higher dignity.

27 This point is made by John A. Larkin, *The Pampangans: Colonial Society in a Philippine Province* (Berkeley: University of California Press, 1972), 304-07, about the Kapampangan peasantry, and by Ben J. Kerkvliet, "Peasant Society and Unrest Prior to the Huk Revolution in the Philippines," *Asian Studies* 9 (1971), 164-213 for Nueva Ecija. See also, James C. Scott and Benedict J. Kerkvliet, "How Traditional Rural Patrons Lose Legitimacy: A Theory with Special Reference to Southeast Asia," *Cultures et Développement* 5 (Summer 1973), 501-40, especially pages, 527-30.

28 The *Estadisticas* section of the Philippine National Archives contains municipal enumeration sheets for the never-completed civil census of 1896. In many cases the birth, marriage and death records specifically distinguish Filipino–Malay, Spanish mestizo, and Chinese mestizo individuals. Comparisons of surnames to landholder lists provided evidence that Chinese mestizos were predominant among the larger landholders in a number of Nueva Ecija municipalities.

29 By the late 19th century, Bulacan was importing its livestock needs from Nueva Ecija, Pangasinan and Zambales. *Guia Oficial de Filipinas, 1889* (Manila, 1889), 80.

30 U.S. Bureau of Insular Affairs, *A Pronouncing Gazetteer and Geographical Dictionary of the Philippine Islands* (Washington: GPO, 1902), 704. See also, Joaquin Rajal y Larre, "Memoria de la Provincia de Nueva Ecija en Filipinas," *Boletin de la Sociedad Geografica de Madrid* 27 (1889), table 2, 344.

31 *Ibid.,* 291, 299-301.

32 For a description of the Sabani estate, see, Estaeban de Peñarrubia y Clemente, *Memoria Descriptiva del Valle del Sabani, Propiedad de D. Manuel Ramirez y Carbajal* (Manila: Ramirez y Giraudier, 1866).

33 Rajal y Larre, "Memoria de Nueva Ecija," 314.

34 In the 19th century the Peñaranda River was known as the Rio Gapan.

35 The 1870 figure is reported in Augustín de la Cavada, Mendez de Vigo, *Historia geográfica, geológica y estadística de Filipinas* (Manila: Ramirez y Giraudier, 1876), 74. The 1886 comment may be found in the *Guia Oficial de Filipinas, 1886* (Manila, 1886), 806.

36 Rajal y Larre, "Memoria de Nueva Ecija," table 1, 342-43. Whether these figures include smallholder production is not stated. A *pilon* was an earthenware pot used to transport sugar. Each *pilon* held about 150 pounds of sugar, but removal of impurities in Manila by their adherence to clay placed over the open tops of the pots — called the claying operation — reduced the sugar to about 100 pounds. Charles Wilkes, *Narrative of the United States Exploring Expedition During the Years 1838, 1839, 1840, 1841, 1842* (Philadelphia: C. Sherman, 1850), 5:289. For an eyewitness account of the claying process, see, Robert MacMicking, *Recollections of Manilla and the Philippines During 1848, 1849 and 1850* (Manila: Filipiniana Book Guild, 1967), 177.

37 J.E. Spencer, "On Charcoal Burning, and the Role of the Charcoal Burner," in, Christopher Salter, ed., *The Cultural Landscape* (Belmont, California: Duxbury Press, 1971), 116-22.

38 The origins of these families and their economic background prior to migration to Nueva Ecija are elements in the emergence of the hacienda system in the Central Luzon Plain which await investigation. The same is true of the Chinese mestizo families who entered the province to acquire landholdings. In the case of the Chinese mestizos, they may represent merchants who began to invest their commercial wealth in land at this time in response to the newly emergent competition of Chinese immigrants.

39 As related to the author by Roberto V. Gonzalez, grandson of the *hacendero* Francisco Gonzalez.

40 For the rise of the Chinese mestizo to a place of prominence in Philippine economic history, see, Edgar Wickberg, "The Chinese Mestizo in Philippine History," *Journal of Southeast Asian History* 5 (1964), 62-100. See also, Larkin, *The Pampangans,* 48-56.

41 McLennan, "Peasant and Hacendero," 142-47.

42 The patterns of Chinese mestizo landholdings in 1896 for several municipalities are reviewed, with tables, *Ibid.,* 344-49; John A. Larkin, "The Evolution of Pampangan Society: A Case Study of Social and Economic Change in the Rural Philippines" (doctoral dissertation, New York University, 1966), 86. Specific marriage alliances in Nueva Ecija are identified in McLennan, "Peasant and Hacendero," 349-50.

43 Nueva Ecija, Office of the Assessor, "List of Declarents or Owners of Fifty or More Hectares of Land in Nueva Ecija," *HDP,* 434, Cabanatuan, Barrio San José section; "History and Cultural Life of Talavera," *HDP,* Barrios Tabacao and Valle sections; "History and Cultural Life of Guimba," *HDP,* 386, 636; "Historical and Cultural Data of Sta. Rosa, Nueva Ecija, and Its Barrios," *HDP,* Barrio LaFuente section; and an interview with a former overseer of the de Leon family.

44 Ricardo Monet, "Memoria de la Provincia de Nueva Ecija, San Isidro, 27 Octobre de 1892," *Memorias,* Philippine National Archives. The provincial governor explicitly states that agriculture in Nueva Ecija was exercised by means of the *inquilinato* system, whereby the tenant paid a fixed annual rental to the landowner.

45 *Canon* means "rent" and so the *canon* system is the same as the *inquilinato* leasehold, but since sources usually use the term *canon* in conjunction with pioneering and and clearing, therefore it may also generally connote that the lessee is being granted an unusually low, or perhaps even free, rent for the first several years in exchange for his heavy labour input.

46 Karl J. Pelzer, *Pioneer Settlement in the Asiatic Tropics* (New York: American Geographical Society, 1945), 111.

47 Many of the most useful sources on tenancy relationships and the role of credit in the 19th and 20th century Philippines are identified in McLennan, "Peasant and Hacendero," note 95, 533.

48 "The Main Stages in Socio-Economic Evolution from a Geographical Point of View," in Philip L. Wagner and Marvin W. Mikesell, eds., *Readings in Cultural Geography* (Chicago: University of Chicago Press, 1962), 218-47, especially pages 233-40.

49 *Ibid.,* 235-36.

50 For the decay of paternal practices on a hacienda in Talavera, see, Kerkvliet, "Peasant Society and Unrest," 166-69.

51 "Labor Conditions in the Philippines," *U.S. Bureau of Labor Bulletin* 10 (1950), 776. Similar views to those advanced in this paragraph are expressed in several unpublished manuscripts written by James N. Anderson, Department of Anthropology, University of California, Berkeley, which he kindly allowed the author to read.

52 Evett D. Hester, et. al., "Some Economic and Social Aspects of Philippine Rice Tenancies," *Philippine Agriculturalist* 12 (1924), 396.

53 A *cavan* is a measure of grain approximately equal to 75 dry litres. This explanation for the origin of Philippine interest rates on the borrowing of rice is attributed to Horacio de la Costa by Beatrice Hidalgo de Miranda, "The Administration of the Dominican Ricelands: A Study of Socio-Economic Conditions" (seminar paper, Ateneo de Manila, 1959), 23. Of course the village subsistence economy that gave rise to such traditional rates of interest was also characterized by debt peonage.

54 Percy A. Hill and Kilmer O. Moe, "The Cultivation of Rice," *Journal of East Asiatic Studies* 9 (1960), 117; Hester, "Some Economic Aspects," 395.

55 Clark, 775-76.

56 Armando M. Dalisay, "Types of Tenancy Contracts of Rice Farms in Nueva Ecija," *Philippine Agriculturalist* 26 (1937), 163.

57 Pelzer, *Pioneer Settlement,* 94.

58 Bruno Lasker, *Human Bondage in Southeast Asia* (Chapel Hill: University of North Carolina Press, 1949), 131.

59 Hester, "Some Economic Aspects," 396.

60 M.D. Manawis, "The Life of the Nueva Ecija Peasant," *Manila University Journal of East Asiatic Studies* 4 (1955), 280. See also, Miller, *Economic Conditions,* 32.

61 In an unpublished paper, "Peasants as Prey," James N. Anderson provides a penetrating analysis of the elaboration of mutualistic relationships and the distortion of peasant dependency in relation to the growing commercialization of the Philippine economy during the 20th century. See also, David Reeves Sturtevant, "Philippine Social Structure and Its Relation to Agrarian Unrest" (doctoral dissertation, Stanford University, 1958), 51-52 for the

mutualistic aspects of traditional tenancy; also Ansil Ramsey, "Ramon Magsaysay and the Philippine Peasantry," *Philippine Social Sciences and Humanities Review* 30 (1965), 65-68; and Larkin, "The Evolution of Pampangan Society," 57-58, 60, 110-15.

62 For an intriguing appraisal of *pacto de retroventa* as a credit mechanism in 19th century Pampanga, see, John Larkin, "The Causes of an Involuted Society: A Theoretical Approach to Rural Southeast Asian History," *Journal of Asian Studies* 30 (1971), 783-95.

63 See U.S. Mutual Security Agency, *Philippine Land Tenure Reform Analysis and Recommendations* (Manila: Special Technical and Economic Mission, 1952), A17-18, for statistical data concerning the place of residence of all owners of land exceeding 24 hectares in the Central Luzon Plain.

64 Larkin, "The Evolution of Pampangan Society," 128-219. A movement of scattered-holdings landlords to Manila and the provincial capitals would have had a traumatic impact upon traditional patron–client relationships. The hacienda system, however, is itself another manifestation of the retreat from traditional relationships.

65 In analyzing the switch in rice varieties cultivated in the Cagayan Valley from *pagay iloko* to *pagay tagalog* that was prompted by the greater suitability of the latter variety to mechanical threshing, Lewis (*Ilocano Rice Farmers,* 73) observes that smallholder practices had to conform to changes that became prevalent on the haciendas: "The dependence and interdependence of the patterns of work and co-operation, together with the particular technological demands of the rice system used, requires a high degree of conformity among small farm operators in a given area; it is highly unlikely that single cultivators would or could make innovations or adopt new techniques which conflict with existing practices . . . The larger farm operator, controlling as much as 300 hectares, is able to change and direct what amounts to an ecological community of his own — a complex social and technological system of interdependent parts."

66 Pelzer, *Pioneer Settlement,* 110-111.

67 *Ibid.,* 111.

68 Philippine Islands, Department of Agriculture and Commerce, *Statistical Handbook of the Philippine Islands, 1932* (Manila: Bureau of Printing, 1933), 33. However, the *Statistical Bulletin* ([Manila: Department of Commerce and Communications, Bureau of Commerce and Industry, 1918], 2:200), reports that between 1904 and 1918, 5,402 homesteaders were granted 69,717 hectares in Nueva Ecija.

69 Sam H. Sherard, "Agricultural Conditions in the Province of Nueva Ecija," *Philippine Agricultural Review* 4 (1911), 131, 137. See also, the 17 July 1908 provincial governor's report by Manuel Tinio. U.S. National Archives,

Social and Economic Records Section, record group 350, file 91, vol. 950, 2-3.

70 For a revealing account of land speculation in Nueva Ecija by a Manila barber see, Walter Robb, "Little Biographies of Men of the Crowd," *American Chamber of Commerce Journal* 9 (December 1929), 15, 17.

71 "Historical Data of Nueva Ecija", *HDP*, 433, Bongabon-Popolon section.

72 In 1781 the Gapan tobacco district was a part of Pampanga province. When Nueva Ecija was organized as a province in 1848, and the tobacco district placed within its jurisdiction, the entire province was designated a producer for the state Tobacco Monopoly.

73 Aragon, *Descripcion geográfica,* 5:12.

74 The sources for 1870 and 1887 are appendices and tables in Cavada and Rajal respectively. Both authors generally fail to specify the year for which statistical data apply. Certain tables, however, are explicit; therefore the assumption has been made that all data apply to the same years.

75 Philippine National Archives, Estadisticas, Nueva Ecija. See, McLennan, "Peasant and Hacendero," 398, for municipal production of *palay,* sugar and tobacco within Nueva Ecija in 1885.

76 José E. Velmonte, "Palay and Rice Prices," *Philippine Agriculturalist* 25 (1936), 406.

77 Walter Robb, "Cabanatuan: Rocky Ford," *Filipinos, Pre-War Essays* (Manila: Araneta University Press, 1963), 95-96.

78 Velmonte, "Palay and Rice," 390.

79 *Ibid.,* 394.

80 "Rice Distribution in the Philippines and the Tutuban Rice Exchange," *Philippine Journal of Commerce* 12 (April 1936), 13, 36.

81 P.A. Rodrigo, "The Tragedy of Vegetable Growing in the Mountain Province," *Philippine Farms and Gardens* 5 (October 1968), 16-17, 23, 25, 27.

82 Conversation with Mr. Belgrano Cahigal, Central Luzon Agricultural College, Muñoz.

The Social History of a Central Luzon Barrio

BRIAN FEGAN

T he Central Luzon village is not a closed community, nor is it a microcosm of the larger society. It is not the archetypal "Asian" village — a timeless, tightly-knit economic, ritual and political unit. The history of a Central Luzon village must be written as a part of a wider regional history. Since the beginning of the colonial period, villagers' relations with external intermediaries have set the tenor of village life. In the first centuries of Spanish rule those intermediaries were the missionary Spanish friars. In the 19th century, however, rent capitalists drawn from the Chinese mestizo communities of Manila and Central Luzon opened the region to world markets by fostering the settlement of new agricultural villages outside the friar-dominated towns. Providing a further elaboration of these external influences, 20th century political entrepreneurs linked the villagers to the national polity. In each period these intermediaries have profited from a partial monopoly of villagers' contacts with the wider systems, but have had to compete for that monopoly, and occasionally faced opposition when villagers have tried to withdraw from the wider system in protest at their superiors' rapacity.

A "barrio" is no more than a neighbourhood or hamlet with a name which is recognized by the state as its smallest unit of local government. Each barrio has come into existence through a gradual accumulation of population. That process has produced a parallel fragmentation of older villages, as once subordinate hamlets hive off to form separate barrios. This uneven, spontaneous pattern of development has denied the Central Luzon barrio a strong economic or political identity. Such limited coherence as it does have derives largely from a thickening of the web of relations that tie families to neighbours and those kin that do live in the village. Outside intermediaries use relations with rival village leaders to ration the distribution of the few scarce benefits or resources they control, thereby manipulating a factional competition that drives the villagers apart. Moreover, villagers themselves have essentially shallow roots in the barrio, and orient themselves outward and upward in their loyalties and life prospects. Just as their ancestors came from several places, so they have lived and worked elsewhere, and their kin and children are similarly scattered by the search for a living.

An anthropologist trying to write a history of such a village has to draw on the work of specialists who have studied the region's history. Despite this liability, the anthropologist has the advantages of a unique local familiarity and special perspective which enables him to reinterpret the historians' work and reflect upon its limitations. His own sources, the living people of a given locale, can do what documents cannot — add important material that escaped the urban record keepers, point out the continuities of persons and problems through the decades, and offer insightful interpretations of events. Since the poor, unlike the rich and powerful, commit little to writing and preserve less, their oral version of the past deserves recording lest history be written only from above. This village history, then, attempts to trace the broader currents of regional developments and examine these from the point of view of the people in one of its villages.

Barrio Buga is a village of San Miguel de Mayumo, the northernmost municipality in the Tagalog-speaking province of Bulacan. Its houses and farms lie along the Bulo River, just at the fringe of the low hills rising east to the Sierra Madre Mountains and the plain sloping imperceptibly westward to the fringe of Candaba Swamp. It is about 75 kilometres north of Manila, just upstream from Highway 5. Like the town of which it is a part, Bo. Buga's creation, extent and periodic redivision have been the *post facto* work of outside authorities who have simply extended official recognition to new social units spawned by population growth. All of what is now the town of San Miguel remained an unpopulated frontier until the late 17th century and Buga itself was a wilderness until the 1880s. The town was first settled in the 17th century when Tagalog and Kapampangan pioneers pushed in from the south and west respectively to create an identifiable settlement — a fact recognized by the Church in 1689 when it made San Miguel a *visita,* or satellite chapel, of the Gapan parish church just to the north. Further population brought state recognition in 1725 when the colonial government created the municipality of San Miguel. But the area around Buga was lightly settled until two centuries later. The Church established a *visita* there in 1922 and the state made it an official barrio in 1962. (See map on page 68 for San Miguel's location.)

Cross Section of San Miguel, Bulacan

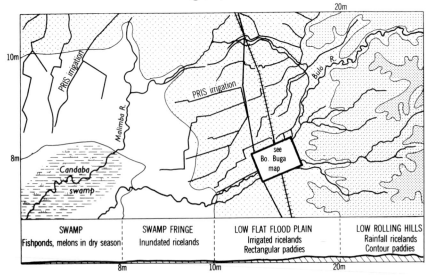

More population, in turn, led to the emergence of separate and rival centres, recognized first by the Church and then by the state — separation of San Ildefonso from San Miguel town in 1877, and separation of Bo. Sapang from Bo. Buga in 1972. As even this brief chronology indicates, population growth has played a critical role in the region's history — first by allowing an extension of the existing social patterns under frontier conditions, and then by changing the society internally when the frontier came to an end.

Early Settlement and Colonial Stasis

The area that is now the municipality of San Miguel was wilderness at Spanish contact in the 1570s, and was not settled for the first 150 years of Spanish colonial rule. Its first settlers came from *pueblos* to the south and west where the social patterns imposed by the resident Augustinian friar-curates[1] had already had more than a century of "time to simmer".[2] It is not clear whether they were fleeing the burdens of life in the established *pueblos,* were pioneers trying to establish subsistence-oriented communities at the frontier, or sought to exploit local resources for trade. They came from two sources: Kapampangan speakers from across Candaba Swamp settled its eastern margin, while Tagalog speakers from around Angat moved along the foothills of the Sierra Madre, settling further up the river valleys. In 1689 Augustinian missionaries set up a *visita* in the San Miguel area, and by 1725 the population was sufficient for Church and state to found a municipality named San Miguel de Mayumo.[3]

We know little about the town during the first century of its history. Population

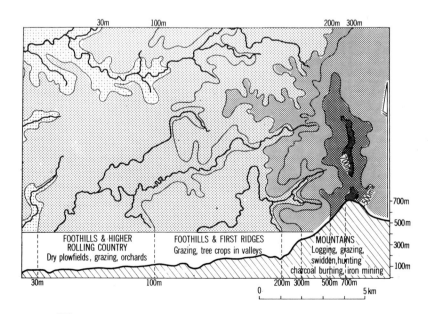

had reached only 1,821 people by 1760, when there were 440 married couples, or households, paying tribute.[4] The parish headquarters shifted around 1763 from the foothills to its present site on the river,[5] indicating the increased importance of trade, for the river was the town's highway to market. About a third of the town's *gobernadorcillos,* or municipal mayors, in the 40 years from 1763 to 1802 had Chinese-origin surnames,[6] indicating members of this commercially oriented stratum were already important by the end of the 18th century.[7] In addition to products hunted and gathered in the forest, grassland and swamps, the area supplied cattle from the 12,000 head that grazed on the Hacienda Buenavista.[8] There was also a stock market at Bo. Partida in the foothills where cattle from deeper in the interior were auctioned and made up into herds for the drive down the *Daang Tulisan,* the Robbers' Trail, to Manila.[9] After 1781 San Miguel was included in the Tobacco Monopoly area based at Gapan about 15 kilometres north.[10] These intimations of early commerce indicate that by the end of the 18th century the Augustinian friars were beginning to lose that monopoly of contact with the outside world that they had held in earlier times, when their efforts to stop new ideas reaching their flock — from other Spaniards or the pagan Chinese — had been assisted by the mercantilist economic policy of the colony.

19th Century Economic and Demographic Growth

From about 1830 onward San Miguel became part of the capitalist world system. After the port of Manila was opened to foreign trade in the early 19th century, Spanish and Chinese mestizo merchants, who had acquired some capital in earlier forms of trade, devised new ways of combining capital and labour in order to procure crops for the world market. During the 18th century native entrepreneurs had been largely limited to roles as buy-and-sell merchants or land lessees on the Hacienda Buenavista, a church estate that extended into the town's southern fringe, but still managed to acquire ownership of large tracts of forest land in San Miguel and the uncleared plains to the north. As entrepreneurs and peasants began pushing north beyond the church-owned haciendas of southern and central Bulacan in the 18th century,[11] San Miguel became the jumping-off point for movement into the interior, and one of the first places where capital and commercial expertise were invested in land speculation.

When export agriculture began to develop in the early 19th century, San Miguel's resident Chinese mestizo merchants let blocks of unsettled land to *kasama* sub-tenants whom they directed to grow the new commercial crops of indigo, sugar or rice. The mestizos lived in town, spoke Spanish and were oriented to the outside world through their trading and family contacts in other towns. As Spanish speakers, they understood the intricacies of the Spanish colonial legal system and its land-titling procedures. When the market for sugar and rice boomed from the 1820s, the mestizos, through their control over land and capital, were primed to become influential intermediaries between the new world markets and Central Luzon's peasant pioneers.

By the mid-19th century more than one-tenth of the town's population was categorized as Chinese mestizos on the tribute lists. These cannot have been cultivators, for if a mestizo was a farmer he could be reclassed as an *indio,* exempted from paying the heavier mestizo tribute.[12] In 1851 there were 398 Chinese mestizos and 3,409 "natives" listed as taxpayers; in 1858, 540 and 4,458; and in 1860, 627 and 5,212 respectively.[13] The large proportion of mestizos indicates the importance of commerce in the town's economy, probably because of its location as the nearest free town outside the friar estates to the south and the Tobacco Monopoly area to the north.

Two great changes stand out in the town's social history during the 19th century: the increase in population after about 1830, and the substitution of commercial crops for the earlier trade in cattle and forest products. At the frontier there was a temporary correspondence of interest between a capitalist class seeking crops suitable for the external market and new peasant households searching for land and equipment to set themselves up as cultivators. This mutual accommodation of interests was dependent on the existence of the frontier and doomed to pass with its closing. Once the frontier was closed and there were no profits to be made from clearing new lands, landlords began a more intensive extraction of produce from their tenants, and the peasants, pressed by a rising population of competitors for access to land, were increasingly disadvantaged.

Conditions for cultivators were better at the frontier than in the older settled areas. In the late 18th century, some tenants on the friar estates did not own even such equipment as buffalo, plough, harrow and *bolos,* and had to rent them from the estate or an *inquilino.*[14] The estates had stripped the cultivators of all means of production and reduced them to mere labour. Buzeta, writing in the late 1830s, indicates that in lower Bulacan irrigation permitted two commercial crops per year around Baliuag; but the cultivators appear to have been day labourers.[15] Although there was ample unoccupied land open to those with their own equipment, these impoverished peasants were forced to accept positions as tenants to gain access to an essential "establishment fund" of land and basic farm equipment. Accommodation between landlord and tenant within the new export economy was based, then, on two complementary strategies — peasant cultivators aimed at acquiring an "establishment fund", while export merchants employed a more complex "rent capitalist" approach.

Establishment Fund and Rent Capitalism

The anthropologist Eric Wolf has proposed a scheme for understanding the level of production that cultivator households must reach if they and the society of which they are part are to survive.[16] In any agricultural society cultivator households must produce enough to supply three "funds" — a "caloric minimum fund", i.e. enough to feed themselves; a "replacement fund" to feed livestock, put aside seed and renew the working equipment of the farm household; and, a "ceremonial fund" to underwrite the costs of gifts and feasts that maintain relations between separate households in the community. Where power holders outside the cultivator class exert claims on its product or labour, it has to meet a fourth "fund of rent". It is on the latter fund that the society's status as "peasant" rests.

Although useful, this scheme has one major drawback — it is static. It works well where the area of land in cultivation, the number of households, the number of farms, the wider economy or the political system are not changing. But where, as in the modern Philippines and much of Southeast Asia, these are changing, it needs a dynamic factor. To Wolf's four static funds we need to add a dynamic fifth, "the establishment fund".[17]

In addition to its repeated annual expenditures, a peasant household must set aside part of its production in order to help each of its children set up a like household with means of production or living that will enable it to maintain a lifestyle comparable to that of the parent generation. This is a conscious concern of families in all societies. Even if it were not a conscious goal, it is a structural requirement of a stable agrarian system. If an increasing proportion of peasants' children cannot be established with the means to be proper peasants, then they come to constitute a separate and growing under-class — so that in that sense, the agrarian system changes. Attention to the questions of *how* peasants transmit life chances to their children, *how* households are established, and from *where* the resources are found directs inquiry away from static typologies of inheritance and residence rules to a range of important questions — changing pressures on the environment; new arrangements between classes; migration; the reduction of leisure to produce more crops per area from farms divided by inheritance; changes in crops and techniques; changes in the availability of land, labour and capital; and the opening of new income niches in the economy and political system.

While peasant attitudes can be explained through the idea of an establishment fund, merchant behaviour can be best described through the concept of "rent capitalism". The geographer Hans Bobek[18] has defined a type of economic behaviour that he calls "rent capitalism". It is a true form of capitalism in that the capitalist gains control of part of the product of others' labour by having control of their means of production, sells that product for money, and then reinvests part of his surplus to expand his operations. The rent capitalist profits by securing claims to the product of small-scale farmers and artisans — by laying out capital to buy land or gain it through mortgage, extending credit to peasants at high interest for movable means of production, and extending subsistence credit in emergencies. But rent capitalism is distinguished from "productive capitalism" because the capitalist does not apply capital to the productive process itself. He does not draw together the means of production and labour that he controls into one large production unit, does not drive the pace of the production process, and does not invest capital in the technological improvement of the instruments of production. Therefore rent capitalism, Bobek argues, is static. Although rent capitalism does appear a static system once in operation, I would argue that there are at least two ways that it can transform an economy. First, as Barbara Ward has shown, when merchants enter a previously isolated area they give new manufactured goods to the inhabitants on credit, and then require them to pay in a product suitable for the world market — effectively transforming a pre-capitalist economy.[19] In this way local handicrafts, usually textiles, are destroyed,[20] while the land and labour of the inhabitants are drawn into supplying commodities for the world market. Second, where a booming market for export crops coincides with an expanding population whose peasant households are seeking an establishment fund to work idle land at the frontier, then rent capitalism can transform a wilderness into a settled agricultural landscape tied to the market system within a couple of generations.[21] The secret of rent capitalist accumulation under such conditions is the way in which entrepreneurs, by extending a remarkably small amount of low-risk capital, can secure both enormous capital gains and a continuing income from a marketable crop. During the 19th century, particularly between the 1830s and 1890s, rent capitalism had just this impact on Central Luzon.

The peasant pioneers of Central Luzon found that the rent capitalists already had title to the best land and were forced to make arrangements with a landowner. Those unable to bring movable components of an establishment fund — work-beasts, axes, *bolos,* ploughs, harrows, seed, household equipment and a stock of rice to support them to first harvest — were also obliged to seek these on credit. Most landlords granted peasants a pioneering contract which allowed them three or four years to transform the forest through swidden farming to paddy before a share of the stipulated market crop was due.

Thus the peasant's labour converted a landowner's low-cost, idle land to productive land, without the landowner risking the great sum of capital he would have tied up had he hired wage labour. For a small outlay the entrepreneur could then realize capital gains by sale, or use the land as as security for loans. Moreover, he had assured himself annual supplies of a profitable commodity without further outlay in wages, and shifted the risks of production to the tenant-debtor. After a bad harvest the rent capitalist squeezed the peasant hard enough to leave insufficient grain for his family's caloric minimum and replacement fund, and then loaned him rice at high interest. The capitalist kept the peasant alive in bad years but never allowed him a good year, for then past debts and interest were recovered. The productive process on the several small peasant farms into which his estate was divided required no supervision by the rent capitalist or a paid staff. The rent and interest payments that the peasant met were something that he had to take into account in driving his family's labour. What Chayanov and Sahlins[22] have described as the peasant's capacity for self-exploitation in a production unit where labour has no wage cost was, in this case, a rate of exploitation set by the landowner-creditor.

The tenant-debtor was also persuaded to drive his own and his family's labour because he had the illusion that he was a self-employed entrepreneur whose income and future depended on his own skills in developing the farm, subject, of course, to the legitimate demands of an inactive "partner" for return to scarce capital. In so far as the tenant-debtor was successful, the rent capitalist usually managed to skim off part of what might have been the peasant's profit.

Rent capitalism heightened political and cultural distinctions between the town capitalists and village tenants. For the previous 250 years, the population of the *pueblos* had been under close control of the Spanish missionary priests. Commercial agriculture then dispersed the poor outside of the *pueblos* to scattered frontier villages. Church control over peasant religion declined since there were not sufficient priests to maintain frequent circuit visits. The alienation of the village from the priest allowed a peasant reinterpretation of Catholic ritual and led to the emergence of the anti-colonial millenial variants so evident in the peasant movements of the 19th century.[23]

Rent capitalism required that the merchant reside in the town rather than on the land. At his residence-cum-warehouse, the rent capitalist could receive deliveries of crops from dispersed tenants and debtors; negotiate tenancy contracts and loans with old and new tenants; lend money or rice to distressed independent cultivators; watch the market and engage in timely buying and selling of commodity crops; and have access to the legal processes in cases involving purchase and mortgage of land or recovery of debts.

Residence in town helped distinguish the rent capitalists as a separate cultural stratum. They lived under the shadow of the church belfry and remained far closer to Catholic orthodoxy than did the peasants who saw priests only for life crisis rituals or high holy days. High cash incomes allowed conspicuous consumption and adoption of a foreign lifestyle. Their children went to the parochial school, and were fluent in Spanish. As the century drew on, wealthy families sent their sons to universities in Manila and abroad where — freed of the stultifying orthodoxy of religious schools and censors — they became intellectual citizens of Europe, earning for themselves the unofficial title *ilustrado,* or enlightened.

The colonial government continued to draw on these men of wealth and culture to fill local offices. The measure of legitimacy afforded by office and accompanying titles, *Don* and *Kapitan,* added to that great informal power — based on wealth and an entourage of tenants, overseers, guards and domestic servants — which earned them the Spanish term of opprobium *caciques,* chiefs. In the countryside their power exceeded that of the weak colonial state. This class, drawn from remnants of the old colonial *principalia,* and augmented by the commercially oriented Chinese mestizos, had emerged as both an endogamous, cosmopolitan status group culturally distinct from the peasants and as power elite impatient with colonial restrictions that excluded them from formal office commensurate with their informal power.[24]

Prosperity at the Frontier 1830-1890

While the frontier lasted, peasant cultivators had a considerable measure of prosperity. Aside from access to the free resources of nature to help meet their several funds, the land rent was set low enough that most did not bother to change landowners in search of better conditions. While rents remained low, and free resources of the forest lasted, an increasing proportion of peasants came to own their own instruments of production. The ordinary developmental cycle of the domestic group also helped to create a certain prosperity. Consider as a model a young couple who marry at age 20, have a child the first year, and an additional one every three years thereafter. For the first years after marriage, the growing number of children depends on only two adult workers, whose product must be enough to meet all four essential funds. Once the children reach the age of 13 or 14, however, they begin to make an increasingly important contribution to household income. Twenty years after the couple's marriage there will be four or more workers contributing to the family's income — the wife, a child of 20 about to marry, and two others aged 17 and 14.[25] If there are unused resources about, or room for intensification of the farm work, the family can pay off its debts and begin to set aside an establishment fund for the next child to marry. This model does, in fact, describe what happened to many on or near the frontier at the century's turn. There was enough land on the fringe of settlements for a family to help a member clear a block, or to make swiddens in the forest There was plenty of grassland, so that the boys could help create savings by tending a string of buffalo. The calves could provide workbeasts for children marrying, be retained as a form of saving for sale in emergency to keep the family out of debt, or worked to provide additional income. Moreover, there was a labour shortage at peak transplanting and reaping seasons near the frontier, so that children from about 13 up could earn cash and rice to contribute to family income.

Frontier families pooled their resources to establish a young couple as a self-sustaining household. In the marriage negotiations between parents, each family stated what components of their establishment fund it would be responsible for in a process of matching contributions of goods and labour.[26] Aside from workbeasts, other farm equipment such as yokes, harness ropes or wooden harrows could be made by skilled older kinsmen from forest materials. Kinsmen could also co-operate in the initial clearing of a farm, building a house and making essential household equipment. Moreover, a young couple breaking in a farm on the frontier fringe could continue to live with parents and be helped by family labour for a year or so while they established themselves as a production unit.[27]

Turn of Century Bust

The coincidence of interest between rent capitalists and peasantry came to an end in the 1890s. The period from 1890 to 1914 was disastrous for the peasantry because of epidemics of man and beast, locusts, wars, changes of regime, banditry, collapse of foreign sugar markets, and general economic depression. The landowners reacted to all these threats to their economic interests by squeezing tenants harder.

Some indications of the scale of this disaster can be gleaned from crude population figures. The graph of population growth up to the 1880s, if continued at that slope, would have increased the population of the San Miguel-San Ildefonso area from 26,659 at 1887 to about 35,000 in 1903. But instead, population actually fell in those 16 years by 6,414 to 20,245 in 1903, some 15,000 below the projected figure. This disastrous decline was not the result of emigration, for other towns and the two provinces of Nueva Ecija and Bulacan show similar downward trends.

The troubles began in the late 1880s with a series of rinderpest epidemics, a disease that killed thousands of buffalo in 1887-1892 and recurred sporadically until about 1914. Simultaneous epidemics of foot-and-mouth also weakened buffalo. The many peasants who lost their draught beasts were unable to continue as small-holders or tenants since they had lost both their savings and the major means of production that gave them some independence from a landowner. Rent capitalists took advantage of this situation to impose new charges on the peasantry.

Compounding the disastrous impact of buffalo disease, war and human epidemics further reduced prosperity and population. In 1882 a cholera epidemic was so severe the dead were buried by cartfuls in common graves. In 1894 small-pox cost "thousands of lives". In 1902 cholera struck again while the town was oc-cupied by U.S. forces.[28] During the first phase of the Philippine Revolution in 1896-1897, Spanish and Filipino forces fought protracted battles near San Miguel — confiscating scarce buffalos and foraging for food.[29] In the second phase of the war against Spain, local revolutionary forces, which included members of promi-nent San Miguel *ilustrado* families, defeated the Spanish in San Miguel in October 1898, and held the town for a short time.[30] In April 1899 U.S. forces occupied and burned the town, razing parts of barrios San Agustin, San Juan, Sta. Rita and San Vicente.[31]

The peasants of San Miguel thus began this century weakened by disease, war, severe draught animal losses, and continuing locust plagues.[32] Sugar cultivation had collapsed, leaving many millstones lying about in villages as the only testimony to a once important industry. Much rice land was abandoned for want of

Population Increase, San Miguel 1760—1970

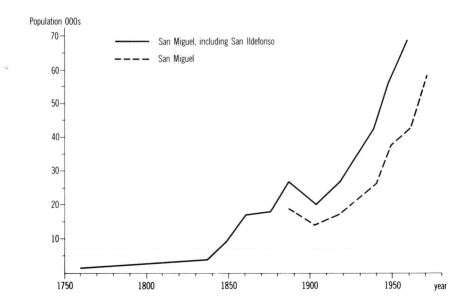

labour or draught animals, and many families, having lost their workbeasts and unable to keep their farms, were forced to eke out a living by subsistence farming on marginal land or wage labour.

The disasters of this period were interpreted by folk-catholic peasants as signs, like the plagues that struck down pharaoh's Egypt, that the rich in town and the colonial regime (whom they equated respectively with the Sanhedrin of Jerusalem and Pilate) had lost the support of God. Mystical leaders led bands of peasants into the hills in imitation of Moses leading the children to the Promised Land. Elderly peasants say that the foothills of the Sierra Madre abounded with "Colorum" religious sects in 1900 to 1906, distinct from both the anti-American revolutionaries and the bandits who attacked outlying settlements. Downstream, along the fringe of Candaba Swamp, the *Santa Iglesia* movement had many adherents.[33]

The landowners in the town also suffered from the epidemics, fires and falling rice receipts. But they gained politically by the change of regime. Although municipal and provincial government offices were made elective, in the first decades of the American regime voting was restricted to the wealthy by property and literacy qualifications. Among the members of San Miguel landowning families who attained office beyond the municipal level were Don Felipe Buencamino, one of the founders of the pro-American *Partido Federal* in 1900; Col. Pablo Tecson-Ocampo, who resisted until 1901 and then became the first civil governor of Bulacan; and Don Ceferino de Leon, representative and senator.[34] Indicative of their rapid recovery, San Miguel's capitalist families continued to extend their holdings into Nueva Ecija in the first years of the century. Felipe Buencamino acquired lands in Nueva Ecija and Pampanga; the Tecson-Ocampo family in Sta. Rosa, Nueva Ecija; and the de Leons several large haciendas in Nueva Ecija.[35]

Recovery and Renewal of the Frontier

By 1918 human and buffalo populations had recovered from the turn of the century disasters. As buffalo gradually increased, families that had been reduced to landless labourers were able to bring land back into cultivation and become peasants again. The recurrent locust plagues abated. Brigands were eliminated by the colonial constabulary, or took up peaceful occupations as times improved. By the 1918 census San Miguel's population had recovered to 17,988, just below its 1887 level of 19,397. Elderly peasants say that most families by then had farms as tenants, and many once more owned their own movable means of production in the form of buffalo and farm equipment.

But tenancy conditions were worsening. The leading families who remained had become a kind of aristocracy culturally distinct from the peasants. Their power, limited to one town under the Spanish regime, was now augmented by having members in provincial and national politics. The overworked native priests could not moderate abuse of power by the local elite, as some Spanish friars had.

From 1890 onwards, large landowners began to change the conditions of tenancy on their estates by raising annual rents, and forcing tenants to change to the sharecrop system. Each change had the effect of obliging the tenants to hand over more rice. Share tenancy invited conflict, for if a landowner's receipts were 50 percent of the crop he had an incentive to push up the yield of each tenant and to inspect the harvest so that all was presented for division. The net result was the imposition of a new rationality. Whereas under the old fixed rent system the landowner had no reason to concern himself with the efficiency of a tenant as long as he paid, the new share-crop system gave the landlord an incentive to evict any tenant who was aged, sick, widowed or inefficient.

The interposition of overseers (katiwala) into the landlord-tenant relation breached the former relationship of mutual trust. Hacienda landowners busy with politics or the management of other estates in Nueva Ecija, and those resident in another town or Manila, were not available to exercise patron–client relations. Landowners began to interpose a professional estate manager, paid on an incentive system, to gather rents. The system of extending credit and recovering debts informally between owner and tenant was replaced by book entries administered by the manager through a staff of overseers, most of whom took a little extra for themselves. On the large estates share tenants devised stratagems to conceal the total harvest and bribed the overseers to look the other way. The introduction of overseers into such a tense harvest division set the stage for intimidation of the peasants and abuse of their women.

The transition from fixed rent to share cropping was a profound change in the social history of Central Luzon, and bears closer examination. The idea of kasamahan or "partnership", often translated as "share tenancy", involved an ideology of the mutual requirements of capital and labour. A capitalist provided the land and advanced cash for expenses, while the tenant contributed his family's labour and certain equipment — in this century buffalo and tools. After deducting the costs of seed and some hired labour, they shared the net crop equally. The capitalist was a kind of "sleeping partner", the tenant the "active" partner. Ideally each addressed the other as "kasamá", partner, and shared a relation of mutual respect and trust, in which each was ready to provide resources the other lacked.

But many peasants did not accept this ideology, and regarded the landowner as an exploiter. They held that the land had been expropriated by fraudulent title over the heads of customary owners, or by forging loan documents signed by non-literate smallholders.[36] The capital, they held, had been obtained by cheating — charging illegal interest on loans and demanding pay in undervalued products. Tenants believed they had paid the value of the land and the principal on loans many times over, yet the balance grew continually because of unjust interest. They should, therefore, take the land, refuse to pay more rent, and renounce their debts. The peasants were the "real" farmers; landlords played no part in production, and had no right to its fruits. Such views seem to have been held quite early in the 19th century, judging by Spanish and American reports of peasant denunciations of the mestizo landowners. This radical ideology had been the basis of 19th century peasant uprisings against land grabbing and the anti-landlord outbreaks of 1896 to 1904.[37] It was later articulated in 20th century peasant–nationalist conspiracies,[38] and reinforced by socialist ideas that spread from radical Manila printers to tenant unions from 1917 onwards. Those most likely to embrace this radical ideology were smallholders threatened by debt with loss of their land, and the fixed-rent tenants whose reduction to share cropping was proceeding rapidly.

By the end of World War I, several years of booming wartime rice prices and the regeneration of buffalo stocks should have placed the peasantry in a position to recover their lost prosperity of decades past. But there were two great changes which prevented such developments — landlords were tightening the conditions of tenancy, and peasants, inspired by the rise of an anti-capitalist ideology, were inclined to resist. The full impact of these changes on Central Luzon are most aptly illustrated by the study of conditions at the village level.

Bo. Buga at the Century's Turn

In the 1890s Buga held few families, and people were still moving in — Kapampangans from Candaba and Tagalogs from further south in Bulacan. There was no irrigation. The area to the east, upstream from the village, was still uncleared with patches of *buri* palms along watercourses, and many trees and bamboos. On the floodplain of the Bulo River, Hacienda De Leon was mostly cleared, but only part of the land was bunded; much of the land at the Bakod River end of farms was still grassland, used for grazing because the soil was poor and flood-prone. Only the land with better soil and drainage was used for rice, and this was planted to early maturing varieties that ripened seasonally in November. The sandier soil towards the Bulo River levees was used for maize in the wet season, and after the rice harvest some paddy fields were planted with a quick maturing maize crop. North of the river there was still forest and brushland in the area of present farms 19 to 28, on the Hacienda Sevilla. Further to the east, land had been cleared for sugar cultivation in the 1870s, to supply a stone sugar mill that stood near the northern end of farm 29. During the 1890s, the mill was abandoned and the land had reverted to brush.

By the time the wars of 1896-1901 had ended there was much idle land — both uncleared forest and cultivated fields that had reverted to brush for want of men and buffalo. Buffalo losses to rinderpest epidemics continued until about 1912. Many smallholders were forced to abandon, sell or mortgage their land for want of buffalo, or to get money to buy beasts. Others were obliged to reduce the area within their boundaries that was actually farmed, and/or to stagger plantings — by using varieties with different seasonal ripening — so as to be able to complete ploughing and harrowing.

Many peasants eked out a living as transplanters and harvesters in season, and reverted to making swiddens in the receding forest, or planted hoe crops of maize and sweet potato on the sandy stream levees. The women, as well as working on the farm, wove sleeping mats from *buri* palm leaves, *buntal* hats, and nets; men made charcoal for sale, collected *buri* leaves, fished in the wet season or went away in the dry season to work as carpenters, construction hands or harvesters.

Landowners took advantage of the scarcity of buffalo to charge an annual rental of ten *cavans* of rice per beast. A farmer needed two buffalo to do the heavy work of converting idle land to paddy or to prepare for planting, and thus had an extra charge of 20 *cavans* on his share of the net crop. According to the late Miguel Macapagal, a tenant paying buffalo rental was more like a hired hand than a farmer, because he had to guard and tend the buffalo throughout the year but had no rights to the calves. Since land, buffalo and seed all belonged to the landlord, such peasants had lost control of the means of production, and accordingly lost income and independence.

Tenancy Conditions and Protest

The accounts of village informants show how these changed tenancy conditions impinged on the lives of individual peasants during the first two decades of this century. On the established Hacienda De Leon, south of the river, tenants worked on 50:50 crop shares, with the transplanting expenses shared; but could borrow rice rations only at 100 percent interest. Don Felis de Leon required tenants to

Farms in Barrio Buga, San Miguel

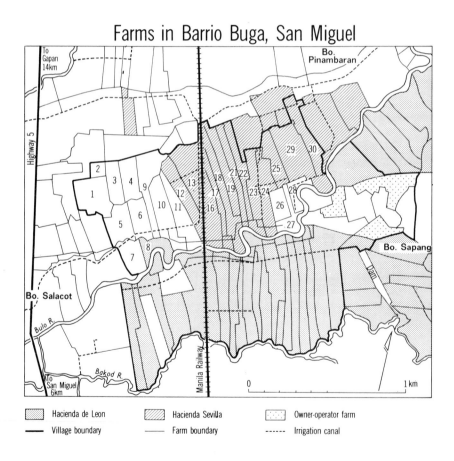

haul the harvested rice to his house in town, deliver him firewood without pay, give him half of any mangoes or bamboos, and help without pay in his household at fiesta. Peasants say, moreover, he had an eye for pretty village girls, and sired several children by different young women of peasant families. But he set up the mothers of his children with farms and "recognized" some of the children. Old tenants say that Don Felis was *mabait,* kind as landlords go. He used to ride about the estate, praise diligent tenants, and, in the early years of the century, trusted their report of the harvest rather than interpose overseers to police the threshing.

On the Sevilla–De Leon estate north of the river some forest remained, and much of the land became overgrown with tall grass after the canefields had been abandoned during the 1890s. Dionisio Macapagal recalls that his father was a tenant for Don Felis at first, but lost his buffalo, fell ill and lost his farm. After their father died, Dionisio's mother and her four sons lived as landless labourers until about 1914 on De Leon land. Then the eldest son· Emiliano, who was then a strong bachelor in his 20s, spoke to Don Catalino Sevilla, who assigned him two buffalo and a piece of overgrown land to convert to paddy. The conditions were that the tenant pay ten *cavans* of rice for each buffalo, but no land rent for three years — by which time it should have been converted to rice paddy. Next year the second brother Guillermo took on the adjacent land, now farm number 29, on the same conditions. Both brothers expected that after three years, when they had converted the brush to paddy land, they would be asked to pay a fixed annual rent of perhaps five *cavans* of rice per *cavan* of seedlings. By 1917 or 1918 both brothers had worked hard for several years, converted the greater part of their farms, built houses in the dry season from local forests, and looked forward to marrying.

But as soon as both farms were established, Don Catalino presented new conditions — 50:50 harvest shares, 100 percent interest on rice rations, and, most importantly, outrageous interest on cash loans. Any money borrowed was to be recovered from the tenant's share of the crop at the rate of one *cavan* of rice per peso loaned, although the price of rice, even at harvest time, ranged from two pesos to ₱2.50, and in 1918-1919 rose to around six pesos per *cavan* because of a shortage. Don Catalino still charged ten *cavans* per year compulsory buffalo rent, though there was no longer a shortage of draught animals. He now demanded delivery of firewood to his house in town, half of the bamboos, and was planning to employ overseers to police the harvest.

Emiliano and Guillermo Macapagal considered these changes unjust. They spoke to neighbours, and in 1918 or 1919 led a delegation of about ten of Don Catalino's tenants to protest. A key complaint was buffalo rental. By this time many tenants were able to purchase their own, or to hire them cheaply, and were thus in a position to abandon a tough landlord and take on a new farm. Some believed that the estate's obligatory buffalo rental was so high that they had paid the full price of the beasts several times over. They wanted to pay no more than 50 percent interest on rice rations and repay cash debts during harvest at the rate of ₱1.50 per *cavan* instead of one peso. Finally, they wanted the crop share ratio to be 60:40 in favour of the tenant, rather than the 50:50 Don Catalino demanded, even though this was still higher than the fixed rent they had been promised.

When the delegation reached Don Catalino's house in town, only the Macapagal brothers and the wives of two other tenants went in to present the petition. The other men were too embarrassed. Don Catalino refused to accept their proposals and restated his conditions. The two women raised no objection, but the elder Macapagal brother Emiliano said that if Don Catalino would not return to the old conditions or accept their proposed terms, then he would leave him. Guillermo said that he would do likewise.

Don Catalino came out of the house and told the other tenants that he would not agree to their petition. Would they agree to his conditions? He asked the two women first, then each of the men in turn. All consented. He then asked the Macapagal brothers, but they refused to yield and soon left the hacienda in protest. Dionisio Macapagal says that his brothers quickly found new tenancies on land of the Morales family, who were small proprietors living in the next barrio. The conditions were 60:40, no buffalo hire, equal sharing of expenses, and full deduction of 20 percent of the gross crop for the costs of the harvest from reaping through to threshing. The Morales family did not use overseers to police the harvest, and lived as rich peasants rather than absentee landlords.

Other peasants say the Macapagal brothers did not leave but were evicted because they were the ones who had organized the petition. Whatever the case, many farmers were sympathetic to the tenancy conditions that Emiliano had proposed, and used to visit the Macapagal houseyard to discuss them.

The Context of Local Protest

The times were very restless. In the years during and following World War I, landowners were trying to tighten conditions, and tenants, with access to ample buffalo and unoccupied land, could afford to abandon a tough landlord and seek better conditions. News of spreading tenant protests in other barrios of San Miguel came from kinsmen, the marketplace and young men working away at the harvest. Reports of events in Manila, lower Bulacan and Nueva Ecija spread quickly up and down the railway. In the dry season men from Tagalog and Kapampangan sides of the seasonally drained Candaba Swamp met and discussed conditions in that no-man's land where they went to gather *buri* palm leaves for mats, to catch fish and to plant melons. All around the fringes of the swamp the exploits of the *Santa Iglesia* cult and recent execution of its leader, the radical mystic Felipe Salvador, were still fresh.

In 1918 or 1919 two men, Jacinto Manahan and Lopé de La Rosa, visited Emiliano Macapagal in the barrio and invited him to help organize a branch of their tenant union, *Timbulan Anak Pawis* or Association of Sons of Sweat,[39] which quickly gave way to the *Kapatiran Magsasaka,* the Brotherhood of Farmers.[40] The Macapagal brothers' houseyard became a gathering place for discontented peasants interested in a tenancy union or patriotic issues.[41] Men in their 70s interviewed in 1971-1973 recalled that the *Kapatiran* was the most influential of the early peasant unions. Its ultimate objectives were to make people equal and to secure independence for the nation. Its immediate objectives were more prosaic — more favourable crop shares of 60:40; equal sharing of crop expenses between landlord and tenant; no forced buffalo rents; a maximum of 50 percent interest on loans; no compound interest on outstanding balances following a crop failure; liquidation of cash debts at two pesos per *cavan*; no free delivery of firewood; no free household services to landowners by an indebted tenant or his family; and an end to landowners using force, authority and the opportunity given by domestic service to rape or seduce peasant girls. The union's members also wanted the right to join the union without the threat of eviction, and later, following the extension of the suffrage after 1916, the right to vote without direction.

The *Kapatiran Magsasaka* belongs to one of the two main ideological and organizational strands in the early history of Central Luzon peasant unions. The first, which includes the *Kapatiran,* was derived from the radical social ideas of Andres Bonifacio's revolutionary *Katipunan* of the 1890s, had the organizational form of a brotherhood, and mixed radical class aspirations with both nationalism and millenial ideas. This strand, like the *Katipunan,* adapted ideas from folk-catholic images in the *Pasion* epic and Easter Vigil ceremony.[42] It promised renewal of society by a liberator who would come out of the East with guns to free suffering sons of the nation with the help of the redemptive acts of an armed brotherhood of initiates. This strain is well represented in the *Katipunan* of the 1890s; the *Santa Iglesia* of Felipe Salvador to 1912; the *Ricartista* organizations in 1914-1920; the *Kapatiran Magsasaka* peasant union in 1918-1934; and various smaller movements such as the so-called "Colorums" of Tayug and San José, Nueva Ecija (1924 and 1931), *Tanggulan* (1927-1931), *Sakdal* (1928-1935) and *Ganap* (1935-1942).

The second ideological strand took up new ideas from European anarchist and socialist writings smuggled in at the century's turn by returning *ilustrados* such as Isabelo de los Reyes and Dr. Dominador Gomez. These were disseminated in Tagalog pamphlets and newspapers by the radical printers' union, *Union de Impresores,*[43] whose leaders were founders of a series of trade union federations, including the *Union Obrera Democratica* of 1902 and the *Congreso Obrero* (1911-1928). By the late 1920s leaders of this strand, including the peasant activists Jacinto Manahan and Juan Feleo, had been abroad to communist conferences in Asia and Europe; and in 1929-1930 they founded the Communist Party of the Philippines (PKP).

Despite the divergence of ideas and organizational patterns between the two strands, their leaders were in contact with each other. Peasant members held syncretic folk-Marxist ideas, adapted through the earlier idiom of folk-catholic ideas. Except on the issue of sources of external support — critically a source of arms — both strands shared a view that the landlords and America were the enemy, and had such a hold on the political system that peaceful reform was impossible. The first stream looked to Japan as a source of guns. The urban intellectual leaders of the second more Marxist stream felt a rising was out of the question, but ordinary members and middle-level leaders had vague hopes of guns from Russia.

The *Kapatiran Magsasaka* belongs to the first stream. It was organized in 1920 in Baliuag, Bulacan by Attorney Vicente Almazar[44] as a successor to the *Union ng Magsasaka* — another Bulacan union which had launched the Philippines' first tenant strike in 1918 and actually won a collective bargaining contract.[45] Influenced by urban trade union activity in Manila just to the south and other tenant movements on the Central Luzon Plain to the north, Bulacan's peasants combined elements of both in their unions of this period. Jacinto Manahan, for example, who had visited the Macapagal brothers in 1918-1919, was a member of the Manila printers' union, *Union de Impresores,* and a native of Bulacan, Bulacan where the first peasant strike and union began. He soon emerged as the most popular and successful organizer of peasant unions in the region and was active in San Miguel. The town's official history agrees with Buga peasants in placing Manahan there in 1919 as co-founder of a *Union ng Magsasaka* branch, which soon faded, and again in 1920 as founder of a *Confederacion del Trabajo* branch.[46] In 1922 Manahan called a national conference of the peasant unions that had proliferated after the successful 1918 strike,[47] and pulled together the large and potent confederation popularly known as the *Kalipunan* or KPMP. *Kapatiran* members in Bo. Buga also considered themselves part of KPMP.

The *Kapatiran Magsasaka* took the organizational form of a brotherhood of initiates, with its ritual closely derived from Bonifacio's revolutionary *Katipunan*.[48] Its patron and spokesman was General Teodoro Sandico, an ex-revolutionary commander and a perennial candidate for office on populist–nationalist platforms. Speaking to large crowds wherever they went, he and Attorney Almazar promoted the ideals of unity and mutual aid, and attracted recruits to the union. Once initiated into its secrets, members were empowered to recruit like-minded fellows from their home villages, and instruct them in the ideals of the brotherhood, preparatory to examination and initiation. The initiation ceremonies were conducted at night in a large houseyard shielded by trees. The new member was led there by his sponsor blindfolded, examined on the ideals of the union, and then instructed on unity and mutual aid among members. He was warned that if he revealed the *Kapatiran*'s secrets or membership to outsiders, joined the landlord-organized *Katipunan Mipanampon,* broke a strike or accepted the farm of a member evicted from his tenancy, he would be punished by death. Then Sandico, Almazar, or in their absence the municipal leader, branded the initiate on the right shoulder with the red-hot triangular-shaped iron of the plough harness. His blindfold was then removed to reveal to his "formerly blind eyes" the rest of the brothers illuminated by bamboo torches, lit from the fire used to heat the iron.

Formation of the *Kapatiran Magsasaka* brought a euphoric sense of unity and common purpose to the villagers. None can talk about the period of its heyday from 1922 to about 1933 without emphasizing the intensity of mutual-aid arrangements for farm work, and the enthusiasm with which people participated in the life crisis rituals of fellow members.

One reason for this unity may be that the union came at a crucial time in the internal class composition of the village and the surrounding area. Those who had lost their farms during the hard years from 1890 to 1915 had once more become farmers. Reclaiming abandoned land and breaking in new farms still provided a safety valve to absorb the new families either just marrying or coming in from further south. The village, like others, was internally class homogeneous: all economically active households farmed, virtually all farmers were tenants, and most expected their children to become tenants. Thus, the village had a potential for unity against the economically and culturally distinct landowners in town. The exciting new idea of the union — reinforced by elements of folk-socialism, and by its ritual form recalling the *Katipunan* of 1896 — provided an ideology and organizational structure to tap that potential.

Class homogeneity also meant that there were few landless labourers and thus a labour shortage in the village. The mutual-aid ideology of the union encouraged a proliferation of exchange labour arrangements that met this need. Those arrangements, according to old people who can remember conditions before 1920, were not traditional, but had arisen during the period of the *Kapatiran* and broke down by the 1950s. There had "always" been dyadic exchange-labour arrangements between pairs of households, but the *Kapatiran* fostered village-wide co-operation. Old people say the union's group work was merry; young men and women enjoyed the opportunity to show their strength and skills, and to court, while for tasks like transplanting there were songs to provide rhythm and unison. Moreover, people felt more equal because of their common participation. When a *Kapatiran* member died, the union brothers were called to join kin and neighbours in the three-day wake for the dead. Informants say that the funeral processions of members were impressively long — partly because the organization took the opportunity to show its strength in such quasi-disguised political processions immune to police harassment.

But the *Kapatiran*'s mutual aid ideology had a reverse principle that a peasant who did not join, particularly one who joined the strike-breaking *Katipunan Mipanampon,* was excluded from exchange labour, publicly shunned, and was buried alone. When in 1972 I asked a number of men aged 60 or more what they recalled of the unions, each proudly rolled up his sleeve to show me the scar of the *Kapatiran*'s triangular brand, and after naming national and village leaders, turned bitterly to denounce two villagers who joined the *Katipunan Mipanampon.* One of these, still a pariah 40 years later, acquired the insult-name of *lampong,* "wildcat", which rhymes with *Mipanampon* and is a reminder that he "walks alone". This man was rewarded with the tenancy of one evicted when the landlord found he was a member of *Kapatiran.* "Wildcat" later lost the farm, so the story goes, because aside from being unable to find work-partners, or to hire labour, his farm was sabotaged. His seedbeds were oversown with weeds, his dykes opened and closed to damage the crop. In other villages, the buffalo of strike-breakers were maimed or stolen, and their sheaf stacks set afire.

Strict landlords in San Miguel reacted to the *Kapatiran* by forming a branch of *Katipunan Mipanampon.* This anti-union organization originated in Pampanga, where it was founded by Zoilo Hilario, and was paralleled in lower Bulacan by the

Samahan ng Magsasaka at Nagpapasaka formed by Don Emilio Rustia of Baliuag.[49] Both were founded in reaction to the success of the anti-landlord tenants' unions. The strict landlords who set up *Katipunan Mipanampon* gave it strength by recruiting their overseers, indebted or loyal tenants, and landless men promised a tenancy. In San Miguel, as elsewhere, the landlords who organized these unions were connected with the ruling *Nacionalista* Party, whereas the unionists supported rival *Democrata, Sakdal* and *Frente Popular* candidates.

Tanggulan and Sakdal in the Village

In the 1920s and 1930s San Miguel's radical peasants considered the *Nacionalistas* the party of rich men who had sold out national independence for personal gain under the American regime. They supported opposition parties but were unable to make much difference in the outcome of elections. Few peasants had the vote, and some landowners could force their tenants to vote as directed. Democracy seemed a sham, and the rich, the *Nacionalistas* and the Americans unmovable. The Great Depression at the end of the 1920s exacerbated tensions in Central Luzon as landowners continued to change to share-tenancy; interposed more overseers to force up the revealed harvest; and evicted tenants who were old, sick, inefficient, joined tenant unions, or did not vote as directed.

Like their fellows elsewhere, radical peasants in Buga were not content to seek amelioration of their conditions as a class of tenants. As citizens they wanted some say in governing their town and nation, and as patriots wanted total and immediate independence from the United States. From 1929 to 1931 the barrio radicals joined the *Kapatiran* and *Tanggulan* movements to work for these aspirations. Dionisio Macapagal, younger brother of union activists Emiliano and Guillermo, was one of many tenant farmers who joined both these organizations, the KPMP, and *Sakdal*. From his perspective, and that of others like him, involvement in all these movements was part of a continuous commitment that renders the differences in organizational names and leaders unimportant. In 1928 Dionisio was a young unmarried man, working a tenant farm owned by a small proprietor, and, was an initiate of *Kapatiran Magsasaka*. As a *Kapatiran* member, he also joined an affiliated secret patriotic society, the *Tanggulan,* founded jointly by Patricio Dionisio, a lawyer and journalist from lower Bulacan, and Attorney Vicente Almazar, founder of the *Kapatiran.*[50] To new initiates like Dionisio, it was revealed that *Tanggulan* proposed to rise against America and its *Nacionalista* collaborators because it was impossible to gain national independence, brotherhood for all citizens, improved conditions for tenants or justice for the common people so long as the rich and foreigners worked together to oppress them and the political system was closed to peaceful reform. Like the earlier *Ricartista* organizations, *Tanggulan* promised that Japan would land guns on the east coast — the essential condition for a national rising. The *Kapatiran–Tanggulan* network extended over the whole of Tagalog-speaking Central Luzon and had parallels in the Ilocano-speaking areas.

In 1931 the leaders of *Tanggulan* were arrested in Manila,[51] decapitating the organization. Two years later *Kapatiran*'s local leader, Attorney Almazar, died, leaving the union to devolve into a set of unco-ordinated mutual-aid groups. Buga's radical peasants continued as members of the KPMP peasant confederation, and had contacts with Kapampangan unionists across the swamp. But KPMP had no armed wing, and was not radical enough for them on the nationalist issue. They opened contacts with Lopé de la Rosa, a former KPMP organizer, who led an armed band of folk-socialist rebels based on Bo. Mandile several kilometres downstream on the swamp fringe. It was, however, the *Sakdal* message — heard from orators at demonstrations, strikes, election rallies and funerals — that captured peasant aspirations. Like *Kapatiran–Tanggulan, Sakdal* had had an outer and an inner organization — the outer concerned with electoral politics, the inner with an armed conspiracy. In practice the inner *Sakdal* conspiracy was composed, at least in northern Bulacan, of ex-*Tanggulan* members and local leaders. Dionisio Macapagal, together with many residents of Buga and an adjacent barrio, joined *Sakdal,* but also continued as members of the KPMP peasant union.

In May 1935 the local *Sakdal* unit was scheduled to join a nationally co-ordinated rising, aimed initially at the capture of San Miguel's town centre. Members assembled on the assigned evening, with their uniforms and an assortment of arms. Scouts had been sent north to Gapan and Sta. Rosa in Nueva Ecija to find out why the promised arms had not yet come, and south to San Ildefonso, where the *Sakdal* conspiracy was very strong among the discontented tenants of Hacienda Buenavista. The scouts reported that there were no arms on the way, though some organizers still hoped that Japanese aircraft would drop them. South in San Ildefonso the rising would go ahead, but it seemed nothing would happen to the north unless the situation developed favourably. The *Sakdal* unit was confused. Dionisio Macapagal says that the married men like him were the first to decide. Without arms the nationalist rising looked like suicide, and they had responsibilities to wives and children.[52] They proposed that the unit disperse and await developments. He went home, hid his uniform, and went to bed ashamed to talk to his wife or comrades.

In the aftermath of the *Sakdal* debacle, many members switched to unequivocal support of the KPMP, while others, still trusting in the myth of the guns from the Land of the Rising Sun, affiliated with a series of small organizations in Bo. San Ildefonso that continued the *Tanggulan–Sakdal* tradition. These had names like *Oras Na, Araw Na, Dumating Na, Nagkaisa Na, Handa Na,* which evoked the immediacy of violence, and were all, according to Dionisio, fanatic and pro-Japanese. They faded later into the *Ganap* Party, which welcomed the Japanese at the start of World War II as Asian brothers who would liberate Filipinos from the United States.

Left-Wing Unions and Wartime Guerillas

From 1935 to 1942 the peasants shifted their union memberships from *Kapatiran Magsasaka* to the KPMP, a mass peasant union affiliated with the Communist Party. After the *Kapatiran*'s leader died in 1933, it devolved into a set of village-based mutual aid groups. The *Sakdal* and *Tanggulan* debacles left the pan-Asian pro-Japanese strand of peasant nationalism discredited and the KPMP had begun to denounce Japanese imperialism. Sometime in the mid-1930s a *Kapatiran* orator from Buga allegedly revealed its secrets to the landowner–politician Regino Sevilla, who was also a founder of the strike-breaking *Katipunan Mipanampon.* Sevilla used the revelation of the names of *Kapatiran* leaders to approach certain of them, and persuade them to become campaign organizers for him. In return he left them in control of their tenancies, but armed them and encouraged them to rustle the buffalo of KPMP supporters, and to beat up KPMP leaders. Some *Kapatiran* remnants were thus effectively turned into an adjunct to the strike-breaker union, and its leaders into a kind of *mafia.* When Sevilla was elected mayor in 1937 he used both these extra-legal forces and the municipal police to break strikes and harass members of the leftist unions, as did his successor Eugenio Tecson.

When the Japanese invaded in late 1941, the residents of Buga fled to the hills because the road and railway bridges over the Bulo River were military targets. Harassed by bands of roving men in the refugee camps, they eventually returned to the village. In Buga and Pinambaran several former *Tanggulan* and *Sakdal* members at first welcomed the Japanese as Asian brothers come to liberate them from the Americans. Dionisio Macapagal remained true to the *Tanggulan–Sakdal* tradition but says that few *Ganap* became genuine collaborators or acted as hooded informers used by the *Kenpeitai* to point out anti-Japanese guerillas.

The war years were a time of extreme political danger since there were three armed governments in the area enforcing conflicting demands — the Huks, USAFFE guerillas and the Japanese with their armed collaborators. Early in the occupation, about April-May 1942, the KPMP unionists were contacted from a headquarters in Bo. Batasan and asked to form a *Hukbalahap* unit.[53] Arms from the abandoned U.S. Army camp at Bo. Sibul Springs were brought in by Kardeng de Guzman, and others arrived from the Bataan-Corregidor battlefields via union contacts. As armed violence became a part of village life in the war and postwar years, two brothers with a talent for organization, Andron and Kardeng de Guzman, emerged as the dominant local leaders.

Kardeng de Guzman had become village leader of *Kapatiran Magsasaka* after the death of his cousin Emiliano Macapagal in 1928 and soon thereafter acquired his martial skills. Once universal manhood suffrage was extended in the mid-1930s, landlord politicians — Don Catalino and Don Regino Sevilla on one side, and Don Mariano and Don Serafin Tecson on the other — sought to control the new peasant vote by arming their barrio followers. Some armed peasant leaders turned to political entrepreneurship. By the outbreak of World War II, Kardeng had built up a considerable local power base through possession of arms and was acting as a broker for his followers with national politicians. Several months after the Japanese invasion in 1941, Kardeng affiliated his armed band with guerilla units formed from remnants of the United States Armed Forces in the Far East (USAFFE). When a USAFFE unit named Anderson's Guerillas set up a base in the mountains east of Bo. Buga, Kardeng made contact through his eldest son Rubing, a High School student who was a member of San Miguel's reserve officer training unit. USAFFE units remained in the area throughout the war, dominating the hilly country to the east of the village.

During the 1930s, another de Guzman brother, Andron, had shifted from the *Kapatiran* to the left peasant union KPMP and developed contacts with Kapampangan socialists. In the mid-1930s San Miguel was a centre of Socialist Party activity in Central Luzon. Socialist leader Luis Taruc had attended San Miguel High School and operated a tailor shop at the edge of town. During this period Andron was attracted to the socialist message and became involved in left-wing union activities. In 1942 he became the local organizer for the Communist-affiliated *Hukbalahap* guerillas, and his unit dominated the flat, irrigated areas of dense population to the west of Highway 5. Since it straddled the informal boundary between two rival guerilla organizations, Bo. Buga had to maintain relations with both. Kardeng's band affiliated with the USAFFE guerillas in the mountains to the east, while his brother Andron's Huk unit controlled the flat lands to the west.

Kardeng and Andron developed a way of keeping their units out of each other's way to avoid incidents in the village. Until his arrest in 1943, Kardeng stayed in the village, while Andron based his unit downstream in Bo. Salacot. When he wanted to enter the village Andron's unit sent a scout to check that the Japanese were not there and consulted Kardeng to make sure there were no strangers who might inform. Each unit conducted its ambushes and raids away from the barrio, preferably near a collaborating village, and tried to head off any other unit contemplating an action too near to home that might bring a Japanese retaliatory raid. Both units augmented their supplies by ambushing the trucks of merchant "collaborators" on the highway, and distributed some of the proceeds among villagers that harboured them.[54] Thus to a certain extent these two armed forces acted similarly, in terms of the Robin Hood logic of a bandit force whose survival depends on the preservation of its popular support by distribution of loot, and occasional daring actions against hated authorities.

There were, however, important differences between the two guerilla organizations. The USAFFE spent most of their time hiding in mountain camps where they collected intelligence, awaited the return of U.S. forces and practised the military rituals of drill, saluting and report writing. In contrast, the Huks gave form to the ideals of the prewar nationalist organizations by establishing an efficient alternative government which tried to change the social order. Living scattered among the barrios, San Miguel's local Huk units involved villagers in policy decisions, settlement of disputes and punishment of offenders. In their recollections of the war, Buga's villagers insist that the Huk units behaved well. Although they had guns, they did not demand or seize what they wanted. They approached people humbly and respectfully. To obtain rice they participated in the harvest for the usual pay. Some say that Huk guerillas stacked their arms and went about begging for rice house-to-house at mealtimes in pairs, like beggars. Huk unit commanders consulted with village leaders before entering any barrio. The peasants' anti-

landlord sentiment was captured neatly by the Huk policy of denying the rice
harvest to the landowners, on the military ground that once the owner brought his
share to town the Japanese might seize it. The Huk policy had the effect of polariz-
ing the situation further by forcing landowners to collaborate with the Japanese in
order to collect their share of the harvest.

The war and occupation caused national shortages in manufactured goods, and
Japanese occupation money inflated so rapidly that people turned to barter to get
their needs. Many peasants acquired urban goods by bartering rice, which was
desperately short in Manila, for lamps, sewing machines, watches, etc. The
favourable terms of the barter trade were enhanced by a series of good harvests
and a Japanese-sponsored wastelands project to bring idle land into cultivation.
Shortages of gasoline and diesel led peasants to revert to handmilling their rice,
further reducing cash expenditure. The villagers found an odd prosperity in rever-
sion to a subsistence-cum-barter economy.

Although the local Huk and USAFFE units established a *modus vivendi* that
kept the village free of violence, they had to cope with a Japanese system of local
government directed by a headman responsible to the occupation authorities. The
traditional method of agreeing with superiors verbally, but appearing to be inefficient in carrying out unpopular orders — playing the stupid peasant — was complicated by the presence of pro-Japanese *Ganap* supporters in the village.[55]
Moreover, although Kardeng and Andron were able to keep amicable relations between their units within the village, the USAFFE and *Hukbalahap* organizations at
the higher levels were at odds. Those landowners who joined the resistance had affiliated with USAFFE, reinforcing the anti-Huk bias of American guerilla officers.
There were frequent disputes over territory and some occasional armed clashes between the two forces.

After Liberation in early 1945, Kardeng returned to the village and acted as a
tough leader rather than a rebel, dealing with a variety of forces — the Huk, his
nominal superiors in the Civilian Guards, the Army and politicians — as an independent local leader. He was everyone's friend, and played his strengths in such
a way that whichever major group should come out on top he would be able to look
after the interests of his family and supporters. Every account of this powerful
man's behaviour agrees on his being an exemplar of the exchange system. If anyone
treated Kardeng with proper respect, or did him a favour, then Kardeng would
overwhelm him with hospitality, gifts, and support in his disputes and troubles.
But if anyone insulted Kardeng or injured any of those under his protection, then
Kardeng would retaliate in the way that person most feared. Kardeng was able to
keep up his over-generosity by augmenting his own resources with things received
in exchange — the free gifts and help of supporters, plus the gifts of independent
powerful men to indicate friendship and recognition of spheres of influence. But he
also preyed upon the resources of strangers and enemies. During the war
patriotism had legitimated profitable hijacking and ambushing of trucks and carts
of "collaborator" merchants on the highway, and rustling buffalo from collaborators and enemies.

In the immediate postwar years, Kardeng became an active political entrepreneur and was elected municipal councillor with the highest vote. Later he became an elder and caucus member of the Liberal Party machine. Part of the basis of his power remained, however, his ambiguous local position. His brother was a Huk commander in San Miguel, but Kardeng became an overseer and a Civilian Guard. During the 1950s and 1960s, he maintained a small private army equipped with wartime weapons, manned by his ex-USAFFE troops and his brother's Huk veterans, and commanded by his sons. Kardeng's men practised a measure of guarded predation on strangers and enemies outside his exchange system. During the Huk rebellion (1946-1952), Kardeng did not interfere with his brother Andron's Huk unit, but kept the old tactical arrangement that all raids must be away and the home village kept a peaceful haven. Thus Kardeng operated in a consistently pragmatic manner, concerned to do the best he could for himself and his supporters in a world taken for granted.

Andron, in contrast, was repeatedly described as *napakabait,* extraordinarily good or simple, and built his forces by acting as an exemplar of anti-exchange behaviour more appropriate to a saintly religious leader, or a curer. Whichever way one approached Andron initially, with courtesy or insult, he took this to be something only *sa balat,* part of external behaviour, and sought its true roots in one's *loob* or inner person. Several ex-Huk speak of their relations with Andron as a kind of moral conversion process, in which they first came into contact with him out of curiosity or chance, but were so impressed by his example of non-exploitative inter-personal relations that they wanted to bring about a world in which all men behaved that way. If the inner person (*loob*) of all men was good, there could no longer be rich and powerful oppressive landlords, moneylenders, and officials. When Huk soldiers offended against the rules of the organization, Andron had the offender brought before him, probed the facts and motivations of the case, and brought the man to see in what way he had behaved without regard to his fellowman. Having achieved such recognition, the offender was asked to propose his own punishment. The whole process might take several days, and have an extraordinary effect on the offender. The essence of the accounts people gave was that Andron acted in terms of an ethical system in which the stranger was not treated as victim, a friend was supported only if he was right, an enemy forgiven, and the individual made to consider abstract ethical behaviour. This contrasts sharply with Kardeng, who acted by a dyadic balancing of gifts and injuries in an exchange system, beyond whose limit the stranger must be assumed a predator or legitimate prey.

Stories about Andron and Kardeng claim that both were *matapang,* brave, and had *anting-anting,* magical amulets. In Kardeng's case, this was an invisible coat of mail that repelled any weapon aimed at him between the neck and upper thigh. In an early postwar incident, about 1947, when Kardeng was one of the kingmakers in municipal politics, Civilian Guard enemies ambushed him beside the town church and sprayed him with Thompson sub-machine gun fire. According to local legend, Kardeng's amulet deflected all the bullets from his torso, but he was struck several times in the thighs and legs. He recovered with a limp, and the ambush party was eliminated soon after.

The Postwar Village

At war's end the village had altered its appearance. The number of houses had increased and new clusters appeared. Villagers who had migrated to Manila or the town in search of work before the war, returned in wartime to Buga where rice, fish and firewood were available.

During the war and the disturbed 1945-1954 period, a number of families moved their houses close to those of strong local leaders with arms. In Buga proper a number of new households, and several established ones, moved under the wing of Kardeng de Guzman who found them work in his complex of blackmarket operations. Kardeng and his followers repaired U.S. army trucks abandoned in the fighting, and "bought" others from black American servicemen for a case of local rum or a prostitute. Some say that trucks hijacked several kilometres away were brought there, their contents distributed and the vehicles cannibalized for parts. There was a lucrative market for hauling logs from the mountains and milled lumber to Manila where war damage generated a great demand for construction materials.[56]

A second housing cluster had gathered beside a right-of-way on the boundary of the Hacienda De Leon and adjacent lands belonging to other owners. These houses clustered about that of Adong Feliciano, a prewar *Kapatirang Magsasaka* member who had emerged in wartime as a strong local leader capable of holding at bay the conflicting demands of USAFFE, Huk, Japanese and bandit groups. Like Kardeng, Adong became a political broker in the immediate postwar years, but slipped because he failed to find other enterprises to support his followers, and later mixed his roles as protector of his house cluster with that of overseer for the De Leon estate.

In the aftermath of Liberation, the pro-Japanese *Ganap* members had a mixed fate. A few joined the Japanese retreat north to Mountain Province.[57] Several from Pinambaran and Buga were rounded up by USAFFE, but the intervention of Andron and Kardeng de Guzman reprieved several, including their kinsman Dionisio Macapagal. Any captives not spoken for by a USAFFE influential or a landowner were eliminated. Surviving members of the *Tanggulan, Sakdal* and *Ganap* organizations later found acceptance with the PKM peasant union (the successor to the prewar KPMP), organized by men who were *Hukbalahap* and Communist Party leaders.

The postwar decade was worse than the war, as the landowners tried to recover control of their lands, collect back rents and break the new union. The peasants had lived for three years free of close landlord control, gained some experience in self-government, and had arms and experience in using them. Moreover, the postwar Huk and its allied union, the PKM, now provided an overarching organization, led by famous wartime guerilla leaders like Luis Taruc, encompassing all Central Luzon. In response, landowners organized "Civilian Guard" units to back up their overseers in policing the harvest, and to eliminate suspected PKM/Huk members.[58] The Civilian Guards and Constabulary intimidated villagers — beating men who failed to defer, demanding pigs and chickens for their meals, and abusing village girls. Several families had male members taken to the swamp and drowned, on suspicion of support for PKM/Huk, or because they had tried to protect a woman. Villagers stopped using the river for bathing or drinking because of the number of corpses floating there. The Civilian Guards were often ex-USAFFE, and received half salary from the government and half from the landowners' association. Their abuses stiffened peasant resistance. Villagers had hoped that Japan's defeat would mean an end to conflict, and that independence would bring peaceful social reforms through the ballot box. The unseating of Democratic Alliance congressmen elected from Central Luzon in 1946, the disappearance of PKM leader Juan Feleo, and the unhappy discovery that they were "wanted" forced many peasants and former Huk to dig up their guns and become outlaws. Men on the run reformed their wartime units, rather than wait passively to be eliminated. In Bo. Buga most *Hukbalahap* veterans supported the PKM and its armed wing, renamed the HMB, and reformed their unit under the leadership of Andron de Guzman.

As conflict between the Huk units and the landlords' Civilian Guards escalated, the Philippine Army and Constabulary began a series of forced evacuations to separate the guerillas from their supporters. Downstream towards the swamp a number of isolated house clusters and smaller *sitios* were forced to relocate their homes in concentrated lines along Highway 5 and other major roads. Other *sitios* and whole barrios were abandoned by households trying to avoid the constant attentions of the government forces. They moved to ribbon settlements along Highway 5, and to a squatter area, derisively called "Grace Park",[59] on the fringe of the town.

Between September and November 1948, the army forced all peasants in San Miguel to evacuate with their livestock and valuables to a concentration camp in the township, in order to starve the Huk and cut them off from information.[60] Simultaneously, the army tried to destroy the Huk units in the field and catch leaders like Andron de Guzman. Anyone outside the town was shot on sight and villagers could leave the camp to attend to their farms only under army escort. In the concentration camp the soldiers and Civilian Guards used torture to obtain information. The peasants lost much livestock, and several children died in the unsanitary conditions.

Villagers speak of this period only with difficulty, preferring to forget the terror and abuses they suffered. A number of longlasting family feuds date back to these killings and betrayals. Some local elite participated in pacification campaigns and posed for commemorative photographs beside Huk corpses. The dreaded Skull Batallion of Col. Napoleon Valeriano murdered eight peasants attending a wake and displayed their corpses along the highway with placards reading "Huk". One *Nacionalista* Party leader summed up elite attitudes when he told the writer that the Army had wanted to burn Bo. Buga to the ground and eliminate its population, but was persuaded to desist by certain "weakling sentimentalists" and "politicians".

Sometime after the Army's 1948 campaign, Andron de Guzman called his men to a meeting and told them that he had decided to surrender. Although undertaken to help the people, the struggle, he said, was bringing them excessive suffering and had no hope of winning. He released each of his Huk soldiers from his "active" role, and said that it was up to each to make whatever arrangements he could to return to peaceful life. Several of his men went to Manila or Nueva Ecija where they were not known and later filtered back into the village when times were quieter. Others switched allegiance to Andron's brother Kardeng who guaranteed to protect them from the authorities. Andron himself surrendered in Manila to avoid being eliminated by local officials. Through a third brother, Graciano de Guzman, then a major overseer on De Leon estates in Nueva Ecija, he arranged to have Doña Narcisa Buencamino de Leon, owner of LVN Movie Company, and her relative Doña Trinidad de Leon (widow of President Manuel Roxas), both owners of San Miguel haciendas, secure guarantees that he would not be shot on surrender. He was later released to become a guard in Doña Narcisa's LVN Movie Company safely distant from San Miguel.

After the Rebellion

By 1954 the rebellion had petered out. Downstream on the Candaba Swamp fringe several barrios retain a strong rebel tradition that now appears cut off from any general movement. They are spoken of as "old Huk", but in practice "Huk" had come to mean social banditry rather than rebellion. Landlords do not visit these areas, and the overseers behave circumspectly, not pressing the tenants too hard to force up the revealed harvest.

The unprecedented floods of July–August 1972 saw a remarkable instance of this social banditry. A convoy of government relief trucks bound north from Manila to Nueva Ecija was stranded by a collapsed bridge at the southern approach to the small Bakod River bridge on Highway 5. As the drivers chatted with locals selling snacks, they remarked that the rice would not be distributed free to flood victims because a powerful politician had "sold" it to business associates in Cabanatuan City who would hold it for the expected famine price. The following evening at dusk a flotilla of large motorized canoes, each holding four to six armed men and towing a string of three or four empty boats, came upstream from the swamp fringe. The drivers had no choice but to help unload their trucks into the canoes. The armed men said they would distribute the rice downstream in the worst-flooded villages, made jokes offering to issue receipts signed by "Commander Noah" payable by the "Central Luzon Relief Fund", and left after filling their petrol tanks from the trucks. Villagers from the swamp fringe area later said that the "Huks" had distributed sacks of rice throughout that night. Each recipient was told to switch the grain to his own sacks and dump the tell-tale government sacks in the flood. This action prompted diversion of a Philippine Marine unit with amphibious vehicles to the area to carry out a Civil Action program and issue relief medicines. The residents were certain that if they had had no rebels then they would have had no relief. This incident and others like it were, to a large extent, most of what remained of a once powerful movement that 20 years earlier had seemed poised to seize national power. Fundamental changes in village population, class structure and political organization that developed from the 1940s largely destroyed the conditions which produced the tenant movements, and make their revival an unlikely prospect. The most important underlying factor in the decline of armed peasant movements is the emergence of a fast-growing new class within the village — the landless labourers.

The end of the land frontier meant that additional households could not be established with livings as peasants. From the 1920s onwards, the number of farms in Bo. Buga increased only slightly while the number of households doubled.[61] Since only one child in each household could hope to succeed to the tenancy, the rest had to be capitalized for some new, non-agricultural pursuit or fall into the landless rural labourer class.

Some new livings became available through the political system. When the peasants got access to education and the vote in the 1930s, they used patron–client electoral politics to expand education and the civil service. The process by which upper peasant families acted as political ward-heelers for the two landlord-dominated parties, in return for getting their own children into civil service jobs, may have prevented conversion of the militant class consciousness shown in the peasant movements of the 1917 to 1954 period into a peasant class party.[62]

After the disturbances of the 1940s, there was a marked increase in the number of peasants' children who became teachers and civil servants. While prewar students had had to board in town to attend San Miguel High School, great improvements in postwar roads and transport allowed barrio students to commute daily from home. Peasant families still made considerable sacrifices to send their children to high school. They had to forego a teenage child's labour on the farm and his earnings as a contribution to household income, and spend scarce cash on school fees, uniforms, transport and books. A reduction in available household labour meant tenant farmers had to spend more to hire labour, reduce leisure to do more of the work on the farm, and to take on "sideline" wage work. But by working harder and depressing personal consumption, peasant parents managed to put aside the resources for their children's education. The cost of an education for a civil service position became the postwar substitute for a farm as an establishment fund. In the calculation of property division for inheritance and in arranged marriage negotiations, the extent to which a child's or suitor's life chances have been provided for by expenditure on education became a valid consideration.

But no government in a poor country could expand the civil service fast enough to make places for all school graduates. There were two kinds of informal rationing. First, governments progressively inflated the educational qualification for civil service entry, for instance, from six to 13 years' schooling for teachers. Second, the scarce positions were, until Martial Law in 1972, rationed through politicians who dispensed them judiciously to graduates recommended by influential local vote-brokers. Thus, as well as working harder and consuming less to meet rising costs of their children's education, peasant parents had to campaign vigorously to deliver the votes of kinsmen, friends and landless clients to politicians of the landed class. Absorbed in this process of bartering votes for civil service placement, peasants lost as a class because they were unable to form a class-interest party or to rationally support third party candidates whose chances of delivering patronage jobs were slim. Village communities became factionalized along party lines by more affluent peasants campaigning for competing landlord politicians. An inflated civil service recruited in this way inevitably had to accept low salaries, while officials realistically, if cynically, came to devote themselves to ignoring the processing of any paperwork until suitably rewarded.

By the early 1970s it had become apparent to peasants that the civil service frontier had closed to their children. Only the richest peasants could afford to send a child to college in Manila, for fees, board and pocket money were costly. The national political system began to lose legitimacy when it could no longer hold out promise of positions, just as the agrarian system had done two generations earlier.

The Losers — Landless Labourers

Throughout the 1920s and 1930s, the ratio of households to farms stayed at little over one to one in the villages, and internal class differences were consequently minor. But from the 1940s onward, those young couples who had not been established with either a farm or a civil service placement began to accumulate in the villages as landless labourers, fostering a sharpening class division within the villages.

At first, the landless labourers presented a problem for the exchange labour system. They could not be repaid in exchange labour for they had no farms. They needed wages. Simultaneously, tenants needed to hire labour to replace their older unmarried children who were in high school, or who, having graduated, would not stoop to field work while on "stand-by" waiting for a civil service post. The mutual-aid ideology of the unions of the 1920s and 1930s could be translated into exchange labour only between households with farms. When extended to the landless, mutual-aid meant giving them work opportunities at fair pay rates. After the 1950s, the exchange labour systems collapsed for all tasks except those using buffalo, since the lack of available fodder made it difficult for the landless to keep draught animals. During the 1970s feast labour was restricted to ploughing and harrowing with buffalo.

By the early 1970s, a second and more numerous generation of landless labourers was competing for work. Responding to the glutted labour market, tenant farmers lowered all their payments to landless labourers — harvesting shares declined from one-fifth to one-seventh of the crop, and real transplanting wages dropped by 50 percent. In Bo. Buga, a system developed whereby a gang of landless labourers would contract to transplant or to weed without payment, in return for the exclusive right to harvest that farm. The tenant farmer today is, in most households, the only member to do farm work, and that is reduced to ploughing, harrowing and supervising, for cheap or free labour can be easily got from the landless. Those peasants' children fortunate enough to have received an establishment fund as civil servants have left the village. Those not so fortunate have stayed to be exploited by the tenant farmers.

Landless labourers are in a weak bargaining situation because of the general labour surplus which is constantly exacerbated by the introduction of new labour-saving technology. In the 1970s, the Green Revolution and limited land reform have encouraged mechanical ploughing, direct seeding to eliminate labour-intensive transplanting, chemical weeding, and an entrepreneurial strategy of cost cutting to facilitate repayment of bank loans. Under pressure from these rationalizing forces, tenant farmers have been forced to abandon customs which gave the landless access to work — decisions made less painful as kinship between them and the second generation landless grows more distant.

Within the village the landless labourers' bargaining position is further weakened by their poor claim, in either custom or law, to houselots. A tenant farmer has a right to a houselot on his farm, or if there is no suitable site within his farm boundaries, to a site elsewhere on the landowner's estate. The houselot is a valuable element in a rural family's livelihood, for there it can store hay for fodder, stable buffalo, raise pigs and chickens, grow vegetables, and carry on a variety of backyard industries such as custom carpentry or vehicle repair. But a family that lacks a farm lacks also a houselot right. It must approach a farmer to recommend that the landowner grant (as a temporary privilege) a small portion of the farmer's existing houselot area.

Many landless labourers are unable to take a strong bargaining stand against the farmers over wage rates because they depend on good relations with farmers to gain access to scarce houselots and scarcer jobs. Each year, usually in the dry season, Buga's tenant farmers evict a few landless households to punish them for joining another political faction or for speaking out against wage cuts. Thus, tenant farmers have become a new class in the villages. They have received a certain affluence and security of tenure through the combined effects of the failed Huk rebellion, government programs and changing technology. And their position has been strengthened by the formation of a class beneath them, the landless. Political entrepreneurs among the tenant farmers have managed to monopolize political power in the villages, and to prevent the landless class playing the leading role in village elections that their numbers might indicate. The villages no longer stand united against the landlord class in town. They are divided by internal class conflict.

The following illustration shows the kind of changes that have taken place on two typical tenant farms as the number of households outstripped the number of farms in the village. If each farm had one tenant household containing a married couple and the six children typical of that day in 1930, then by 1970 there would be three houses per farm. After the lapse of 40 years, a third generation would be marrying and setting up new households (Farm I). Even if family size were to fall, the number of families must soon increase, and the kinship between the farmer and the new households become more distant. Under these conditions, one can predict that these new households will continue to flock to urban slums since they will re-

Population increase & pressure on house-lots, 1930 to 1970

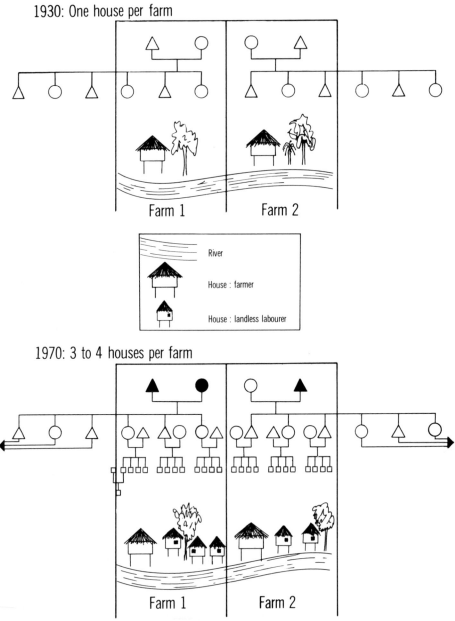

1930: One house per farm

Farm 1   Farm 2

River

House : farmer

House : landless labourer

1970: 3 to 4 houses per farm

Farm 1   Farm 2

main unemployed squatters in the villages. Despite a constant emigration to Manila, Nueva Ecija and neighbouring villages, the number of households in Bo. Buga doubled from some 60 in 1942 to 125 only 30 years later.

The landless labourers have nothing to gain from Marcos' Martial Law land reform, which, if implemented, would only benefit some tenants. It offers absolutely no land rights or wage guarantees to the largest and fastest-growing class in the villages. Without secure access to land, the landless cannot build pig pens or chicken pens, plant vegetables or try other backyard enterprises to supplement their falling seasonal wages. Aside from seasonal farm work, they live precariously (*"isang kahig, isang tuka,"* one scratch, one peck) by every family member taking on any income-producing activity available — by selling green fodder to buffalo owners, by combing the watercourses for fish or frogs, by hemming handkerchiefs, by gleaning the harvested fields, or by begging from their more affluent neighbours. A few landless are lucky enough to have relatively steady jobs as drivers or road workers, but they have to compete for these with tenant farmers who have better education and more extensive extra-village contacts.

The landless labourers consume few manufactures; almost all their income goes on food. Despite their enormous numbers, they are too poor to constitute an internal mass market for cheap consumer goods produced in urban factories that otherwise might employ them.

Conclusion

Population increase in San Miguel did not proceed in the direction of agricultural "involution" as in Java. Absentee landlordism and a high-risk agriculture produced a pattern of relatively large, indivisible tenant blocks. When the agricultural frontier closed, extra households could only be established outside the agricultural sector. Some found livings in the civil service after parental investment in their education. On the national scale, this process produced a degree of "bureaucratic involution". Those who were not established as peasants, in white-collar positions or in other secure-income niches, accumulated as landless labourers in the villages. Their presence broke down exchange labour, created class division within the village, and generated a steady flow of squatters for Manila's slums. The proportion of urban slum dwellers and rural landless who work for legal wages is relatively low. A high proportion gain a precarious living by hustling as dependent petty entrepreneurs, who work longer and harder for less pay than the legal rates set in the organized sectors of the economy.[63] The operators have the illusion that they are petty entrepreneurs favoured by a rent capitalist with the privilege of access to a means of living. The number of petty entrepreneurs competing for custom in the tertiary sector is a kind of "services involution" brought on by population increase and scarce capital.

Central Luzon's peasants were united for one generation after the close of the agricultural frontier when their villages held a homogeneous class of tenant farmers. During that time the villagers stood as tenants against landlords in the

By the 1970s, the villages had become internally class-stratified, and the ﾡ numerous landless class now has nothing to gain from tenant unions or land ﾵsfer to tenants. The tenant issue has shifted to provinces such as Nueva Viz-ﾩya and Isabela in Cagayan Valley or to parts of Mindanao where the frontier is just now passing. For a short time villagers there may unite around the tenancy issue, but the problem of the landless will become acute within a generation. Revolutionary, reformist or counter-insurgency programs that concentrate on the issue of tenancy are irrelevant to the newest and fastest growing class — the landless labourers found in both city and village. For this class the political and economic system has failed utterly. The landless are fragmented, weak and friendless. Although silent, the landless, by virtue of their numbers alone, may yet play a major role in the shaping of their nation's problematic future.

NOTES

1 John L. Phelan, *The Hispanization of the Philippines* (Madison: University of Wisconsin Press, 1959).

2 George M. Foster, "What is a Peasant," in, Jack M. Potter, et. al., eds., *Peasant Society: A Reader* (Boston: Little, Brown and Co, 1967).

3 Marshall McLennan, "Peasant and Hacendero in Nueva Ecija: The Socio-Economic Origins of a Philippine Commercial Rice-Growing Region" (doctoral dissertation, University of California, Berkeley, 1973), 469.

4 Emma Blair and James Robertson, eds., *The Philippine Islands, 1493-1898* (Cleveland: A.H. Clark, 1903-1909), 42:105.

5 The Historical Data Papers, "History and Cultural Life of San Miguel, Bulacan". (Typescript, Ca. 1950-1951.) Copies were held in 1972 in the National Library, Manila. (Hereafter, *HDP*.)

6 *HDP*, 6-7.

7 The analysis of surnames follows John A. Larkin, *The Pampangans: Colonial Society in a Philippine Province* (Berkeley: University of California Press, 1972), 48-62.

8 McLennan, "Peasant and Hacendero," 117.

9 *HDP*, 181.

10 McLennan, "Peasant and Hacendero," 125; *HDP*, 165.

11 Dennis M. Roth, *The Friar Estates of the Philippines* (Albuquerque: University of New Mexico Press, 1977).

12 Eliodoro Robles, *The Philippines in the Nineteenth Century* (Quezon City: Malaya Books, 1969), 77.

13 *Guia de Forasteros de las Islas Filipinas,* 1851, 1858, 1860 (Manila: Various publishers). The figures may relate to the preceding year in each case. Of six Guias located, only these show *Mestizos de Sangley* as a separate category.

14 Roth, *Friar Estates,* 88-90.

15 Manuel Buzeta and Felipe Bravo, *Diccionario geográfico, estadístico, histórico de las Islas Filipinas* (Madrid, José de la Peña, 1850-1851).

16 Eric R. Wolf, *Peasants* (Englewood Cliffs: Prentice-Hall, 1966), 4-10.

17 Brian Fegan, "Establishment Fund, Population Increase and Changing Class Structures in Central Luzon," *Canberra Anthropology* 1 (October 1978), 24-43.

18 Hans Bobek, "The Main Stages of Socio-economic Growth from a Geographical Point of View," in, Philip L. Wagner and Marvin W. Mikesell, eds., *Readings in Cultural Geography* (Chicago: University of Chicago Press, 1962), 218-47. I would add to Bobek's account that unlike the productive capitalist, the rent capitalist does not have to meet wage costs to obtain a product for sale and therefore has no incentive to multiply the productivity of labour by investing in improved means of production. The absence of a wages nexus between capitalist and labour may account therefore for the technological stagnation of rent capitalism.

19 Barbara Ward, "Cash or Credit Crops?", *Economic Development and Cultural Change* 8 (January 1960), 148-63.

20 See, Norman Owen, "Textile Displacement and the Status of Women in Southeast Asia," in, Gordon P. Means, ed., *The Past in Southeast Asia's Present* (Ontario: Secretariat, Canadian Society for Asian Studies, 1978).

21 I would argue that similar conditions applied in Lower Burma and Negros Occidental in the Philippines in the mid-19th century, and in Central Thailand, much of Malaya, and southern Vietnam a little later.

22 Marshall Sahlins, *Stone Age Economics* (London: Tavistock, 1974), chapters 1 and 2.

23 A priestless folk-catholicism had among the elements available to it for re-interpretation the *Pasion,* a verse epic of the story of Christ, a tradition of devotional fraternities, syncretist curers who claimed a supernatural gift of healing often combined with claims to be mediums in contact with super-naturals, attendance at church life-crisis rituals, and annual rituals. See, Reynaldo Clemeña Ileto, *Pasyon and Revolution: Popular Movements in the Philippines, 1840-1910* (Quezon City: Ateneo de Manila University Press, 1979).

24 Philippine historical and social science writing uses the blanket term "elite" rather loosely to refer to any persons of wealth, power or prestigious life style. The term "class" is used within the tradition of American studies of "social class", i.e. prestige rating within a local community. Both usages run the risk of attending only to cultural evaluation of status, while neglecting

power and "class" in the sense used by either Weber or Marx, and European sociologists. I restrict the term to its political sense.

25 The model of a changing ratio of hands to mouths, and a cycle of prosperity tied to the life-cycle of the domestic group follows A.V. Chayanov, *The Theory of Peasant Economy* (Homewood Illinois: Richard D. Irwin for the American Economic Association, 1966). See also, Sahlins, *Stone Age Economics*. The extension to the establishment fund is mine.

26 See, James N. Anderson, "Some Aspects of Land and Society in a Pangasinan Community," *Philippine Sociological Review* 10 (January-April 1962), 41-58; Francis J. Murray, "Increasing Population Pressure and Changing Marriage Modes in Central Luzon," *Anthropological Forum* 3 (November 1972), 180-88; Daniel Scheans, "The Ilocano: Marriage and the Land," *Philippine Sociological Review* 13 (1965), 57-62.

27 The process of pioneering new land is described by McLennan, "Peasant and Hacendero," 253-61. The Malay process seems similar, see, E.K. Fisk, *Studies in the Rural Economy of South East Asia* (Singapore; Eastern Universities Press, Ltd., 1964), chapter 3; and Ragnar Nurske, *Problems of Capital Formation in Underdeveloped Countries* (Oxford: Basil Blackwell, 1958). Nurske points out the potential for capital formation concealed in rural underemployment; the Chinese communists attempted to mobilize it.

28 *HDP*, 19; the information on epidemics in San Miguel is paralleled by McLennan, "Peasant and Hacendero," 207. He notes a "multitude of comments" from Nueva Ecija towns on the severity of cholera in 1882, and that it recurred in 1889 and 1902.

29 *HDP*, 166.

30 *HDP*, 9.

31 *HDP*, 160, 176, 189, 195.

32 Locusts increased to plague proportions on the ungrazed pastures and on farmland that reverted to grass, after the rinderpest epidemics.

33 See, Ileto, "Pasion"; Milagros Guerrero, "Luzon at War: Contradictions in Philippine Society, 1898-1902" (doctoral dissertation, University of Michigan, 1977), 175-85.

34 "All About Our Town and Schools: San Miguel Bulacan" (Typescript, 1966.) This source has no page numbers, and is based on *HDP* but updates it with some new data. A further revision was in process in late 1972.

35 See also, McLennan, "Peasant and Hacendero," 350.

36 Complaints that the friar estates, Spanish haciendas, *principalia* and the rich acquired land by fraud are common. Spanish colonial decrees of 1880 and 1894 facilitating legal title exacerbated the problem, for the rich and lawyers took the opportunity to title customary lands held by less legally agile smallholders.

37 Guerrero, "Luzon at War".

38 In Central Luzon these include larger movements like the *Ricartista, Tanggulan* and *Sakdal* lower-class nationalist conspiracies as well as smaller movements such as "Colorum" that shared their ideas and goals. See, David R. Sturtevant, *Popular Uprisings in the Philippines, 1840-1940* (Ithaca, N.Y.: Cornell University Press, 1976).

39 The first recorded labour fraternity in San Miguel may have been the *Timbulan Anak Pawis* founded by a triumvirate of peasants in Bo. Salangan in 1912. See, "All About". The *HDP* gives the date as 1921, but both accounts agree that it made a donation of 100 *cavans* of *palay* to build the Salangan school, which "All About" lists elsewhere was founded in 1912, though another list shows a school site was formally donated by a landlord in 1922. The date matters because the earliest tenant union otherwise recorded was founded in Bo. Matungaw of Bulacan, Bulacan in May 1917. Second, the name foreshadows *Kalipunan Anak Pawis* which was founded in 1928 in Manila as a labour confederation. Lopé de la Rosa of Bo. Mandile, near Salangan, became a foundation member of KAP and the Communist Party of the Philippines in the late 1920s.

40 The *HDP,* on page 16, claims Benigno Cristobal and Jacinto Manahan were organizers of *Union ng Magsasaka* in 1919, Manahan of a *Confederacion del Trabajo* chapter in 1920, but says *Kapatiran Magsasaka* began in 1922. Though names of these organizations were unstable, unionism as an idea and a form of protest organization was spreading.

41 The *Ricartista* organization consisted of armed groups of a lower-class nationalist brotherhood, organized with military ranks, and modelled on the *Katipunan* of 1896, with goals of (national) liberty, equality and fraternity. See, Maria P. Luna, "General Artemio Ricarte y Garcia: a Filipino Nationalist," *Asian Studies* 15 (1971), 229-41.

42 Brian Fegan, "Light in the East: Pasion, Vigil, and the Idiom of Central Luzon Peasant Movements 1896-1970," (unpublished Ms., 1978).

43 Guillermo Capadocia, "The Philippine Labor Movement," typescript ca. 1950, Military Intelligence Service, Armed Forces of the Philippines, Personal File: Guillermo Capadocia, 7-20.

44 Rolando E. Villacorte, *Baliwag: Then and Now* (Caloocan City: Philippine Graphic Arts, Inc., 1970), 233.

45 Capadocia, "Philippine Labor," 29. The UIF conference of 31 March 1918 adopted this collective-bargaining policy. It was quickly successful, and provided a model for other organizations.

46 *HDP,* 18.

47 Capadocia, "Philippine Labor," on page 54 says: "Jacinto Manahan, a printer working at the Bureau of Printing and a member of the Union de Impresores de Filipinas (UIF), being a resident of Bulacan, Bulacan, took notice of the spreading organization of the peasants. He brought the matter to the attention of the leaders of the Congreso Obrero de Filipinas (COF). He was assigned by the COF to contact and help the peasant organization". Manahan called the August 1922 conference that resulted in establishment of the KPMP peasant confederation. Though its initials in Spanish and English differ this was a continuous organization from that date. Note that this suggests that urban radicals connected to Manila trade unions and later to emerge as founders of the PKP set up the first tenant unions, guided their early tactics, then drew them together into a confederation under urban radical leadership. Kerkvliet has argued the contrary — that peasants reacted spontaneously and locally to landlords ceasing to act as patrons to their tenants, and that these grassroots organizations only later coalesced into wider organizations and acquired loose, over-arching urban leadership. His view gives little role to ideas or leadership. See, Benedict J. Kerkvliet, "Peasant Society and Unrest prior to the Huk Revolution in the Philippines," *Asian Studies* 9 (August 1971), 173; and his *The Huk Rebellion: A Study of Peasant Revolt in the Philippines* (Berkeley: University of California Press, 1977).

48 Fegan, "Light in the East".

49 Villacorte, *Baliwag*, 233.

50 Sturtevant, *Popular Uprisings*, 206.

51 *Ibid.*, 210.

52 The nationalist and radical ideas, and the political realism of Central Luzon peasants are dismissed by Sturtevant, *Popular Uprisings*.

53 *HDP*, 93-94; *HDP* for Bo. Batasan claims "... the Hukbalahap was organized in this barrio by Luis M. Taruc, one of the foremost leaders of the dissidents at present, on 29 March 1942".

54 The highway barrio, Salacot, claims a history of banditry back into the Spanish period, (*HDP*, 117-18). *Sitios* Ilog Bulo and Sacdalan of Bo. Salacot were Huk wartime strongholds: "The place became notorious by the mysterious disappearances of members of the Philippine Constabulary, *Ganaps*, and other Japanese spies that happened to visit the place unexpectedly in small numbers. Merchants passing by were stopped and their illicit goods were confiscated for the supply of the fighting men of the guerilla armies". (*HDP*, 128.) Compare Francis J. Murray, "Local Groups and Kin Groups in a Tagalog Tenant Rice-Farmers Barrio" (doctoral dissertation, University of Pittsburgh, 1970), 38-39.

55 The *HDP*, 113, for Bo. Pinambaran stresses the strength of *Ganap* there.

56 The David and Tayag mills opened in 1946 at Bo. Sibul Springs. The logging boom peaked again in 1963-1967 when Felix Tayag was mayor, until NAWASA agents tried to stop deforestation of the watersheds ("All About Our Town").

57 *HDP,* 113.

58 See also, Kerkvliet, *The Huk Rebellion.*

59 For example, *Sitios* Pamumbunan and Pulong Kawayan of Salacot, (*HDP,* 124-5); Bo. Mandile in 1950 had only ten houses left of 200 pre-1948 (*HDP,* 95); Bo. Magmarale was forcibly evacuated in 1950 on suspicion of "conniving with the Huks" (*HDP,* 89).

60 *HDP,* 32; only Bo. Sibul Springs, held by a strong Civil Guard detachment, was not evacuated. The commander was Major Felix M. Tayag, owner of a lumber mill extracting logs from the mountains, Vice-Mayor 1951-1955, Mayor 1963-1967 (*HDP,* 211).

61 San Miguel's population was 27,178 at the 1918 census, 58,712 in 1970.

62 Expulsion of the Democratic Alliance congressmen in 1946 made it clear that the political system had no place in it for the left. But the tension between millenarian hopes of radical social change and short-term pragmatic self-interest could be handled by peasant elders overtly playing the pork-barrel and patron–client game in electoral politics, while covertly supporting the rebels.

63 That is, they rent a one-man sized chunk of capital from the current generation of rent capitalists. This new rent capitalism in the secondary and tertiary sectors of the economy parallels landlord-tenant relations in the primary sector. Native capitalists have little option but to invest capital in rent capitalist fashion: the return is better (given the position of the Philippines in a world market economy dominated by the U.S. and Japan, and open to manufactured imports from advanced economies with larger markets) than in manufacturing. Local capital tends to be driven back into bidding up the price of land, and into rent capitalist services industries, because of the difficulty of entry to productive capitalist investment in manufacturing, and low taxes on landholding.

Church Lands in the Agrarian History
of the Tagalog Region

DENNIS MORROW ROTH

U ntil the turn of the 20th century, monastic haciendas were the dominant form of land tenure in the region surrounding Manila. Throughout most of the Spanish colonial period, ecclesiastical estates occupied nearly 40 percent of the surface area in the four Tagalog-speaking provinces of Bulacan, Tondo (now known as Rizal), Cavite and Laguna de Bay, and within this generally fertile zone of the Philippines they controlled the largest share of the most productive soil. Thus, a knowledge of these estates is a key to an understanding of the agrarian history of the Tagalog region. But such knowledge has an even more immediate value for Philippine scholarship. Spanish and American writers of the late 19th and early 20th centuries pointed to agrarian unrest on the friar estates as one of the main causes of the 1896 revolt against Spain. Some American officials identified the estates as the overriding source of the revolt. These officials, anxious to prove that the Filipinos were unfit for self-government, had a motive in exaggerating Tagalog participation in the revolt, while on the other hand denying that it had a wider, national base. But even if allowances are made for politically inspired hyperbole, the general unanimity of Spanish and American sources must be taken as compelling evidence that the estates played an important role in the events of 1896.[1] Our purpose in this essay is to follow the historical development of the estates and in so doing to show those conditions which helped to bring an end to Spanish colonialism in the Philippines.

The Estates

On the eve of the Philippine Revolution of 1896, four religious orders owned 21 haciendas in the provinces surrounding Manila. Seven years later the American colonial government, fearful of further outbreaks of agrarian unrest if friar land-ownership continued, bought 17 of these estates for division and sale to Filipinos. Four ecclesiastical estates remained. Three decades later they were to become principals in the *Sakdal* uprising of 1936. Over the next few years, the Church sold the remaining estates, largely to the Philippine government, thus ending three and a half centuries of large-scale ecclesiastical landownership in the Tagalog provinces.

During the 19th century the Dominicans, owners of ten estates, were the largest landlords in the region, followed by the Augustinians with seven, the Order of St. John with the large Hacienda Buenavista in Bulacan, and the Recollects, owners of two valuable and intensively cultivated estates in Cavite. The Archdiocese of Manila owned the remaining estate — the Hacienda of Dinalupihan in Bataan Province.[2]

The haciendas ranged in size from the Augustinians' mini-estate of Binagliag (294 hectares) in Angat, Bulacan, to the sprawling, though still somewhat sparsely populated Hacienda Buenavista, measuring nearly 30,000 hectares. The larger haciendas included entire towns within their confines. This was particularly true in Cavite and Laguna. There hacienda boundaries conformed very closely to the municipal boundaries which had been established as administrative and pastoral units. The reason for this close correspondence of town and hacienda seems to lie in the fact that in Cavite and Laguna all of the haciendas formed a compact, contiguous group. From Muntinlupa in the north and Calamba in the south, Laguna de Bay in the east and Naic in the west, there stretched an unbroken expanse of friar land. The almost complete identity of names for haciendas and the towns they encompassed was one expression of these provinces' cultural geography. Only the town of Bacoor, Cavite, most of whose lands were part of the Hacienda San José, did not take its name from an estate.

Before the late 18th century, few of the haciendas in Cavite and Laguna were separate municipalities. Either they were included within larger administrative units, as were the Cavite estates, or they were not accorded the full trappings of municipal status. Such was the case in Laguna where the haciendas were surrounded by Laguna de Bay, other haciendas, and the provincial boundaries of Cavite and Batangas, thus making it impossible to parcel them among other towns.

The unwillingness to confer full municipal status on the haciendas was based on the Law of Indies' requirement that each *pueblo de indios* have land which was owned (either collectively or individually, depending on the indigenous forms of tenure) by its inhabitants. Thus a sort of legal fiction had been devised in order to prevent conflicts over landownership. When the need for this fiction lapsed in the late 18th century, it was natural for Spanish officials to establish new towns following the boundaries of the estates.

However, in Bulacan and Tondo the haciendas did not form a compact group (though there were contiguous haciendas in Tondo), and consequently the coincidence of town and haciendas was not as complete there. Some towns in these two provinces were entirely encompassed within the estates, but there were others where landownership was divided between the haciendas and the Filipino citizenries. Again, cultural geography was reflected in town names. In Bulacan, where the religious haciendas were more dispersed than elsewhere, only the town of Santa Maria de Pandi bore the name of an estate.

In most outward respects, there was little to distinguish the 19th century hacienda towns from other Philippine towns. Like most towns, they had a municipal centre (*municipio*) with a centrally located plaza where the parish church, a government building and perhaps a jail usually would be found. The residence of the friar administrators (the *casa hacienda*) and a granary (sometimes combined in one building) were the only visible evidence marking the presence of a friar estate. The *municipio* was the home for the wealthier citizens of the town — the traders, artisans and tenants who leased but did not actually till the land. Outside the *municipio* and scattered throughout the several thousand hectares of rural land-

Spanish Religious Estates, Central Luzon, 1896

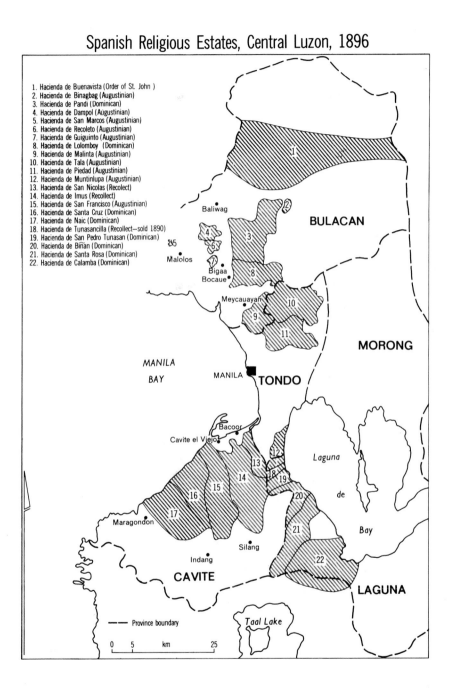

1. Hacienda de Buenavista (Order of St. John)
2. Hacienda de Binagbag (Augustinian)
3. Hacienda de Pandi (Dominican)
4. Hacienda de Dampol (Augustinian)
5. Hacienda de San Marcos (Augustinian)
6. Hacienda de Recoleto (Augustinian)
7. Hacienda de Guiguinto (Augustinian)
8. Hacienda de Lolomboy (Dominican)
9. Hacienda de Malinta (Augustinian)
10. Hacienda de Tala (Augustinian)
11. Hacienda de Piedad (Augustinian)
12. Hacienda de Muntinlupa (Augustinian)
13. Hacienda de San Nicolas (Recollect)
14. Hacienda de Imus (Recollect)
15. Hacienda de San Francisco (Augustinian)
16. Hacienda de Santa Cruz (Dominican)
17. Hacienda de Naic (Dominican)
18. Hacienda de Tunasancilla (Recollect—sold 1890)
19. Hacienda de San Pedro Tunasan (Dominican)
20. Hacienda de Biñan (Dominican)
21. Hacienda de Santa Rosa (Dominican)
22. Hacienda de Calamba (Dominican)

Baliwag

BULACAN

Malolos

Bigaa
Bocaue

Meycauayan

MORONG

MANILA
BAY

MANILA

TONDO

Bacoor

Cavite el Viejo

Laguna

de

Bay

Maragondon

Silang

Indang

CAVITE

LAGUNA

Province boundary

Taal Lake

0   5   km   25

scape were the barrios where the peasants lived near the fields they cultivated as sharecroppers (subtenants) and agricultural labourers.

Thus the class structure of an estate's Filipino population was much the same as that of non-hacienda towns — with one very important difference. The Filipinos of the non-cultivating agricultural class did not own the land which they rented out to sharecroppers. As we will see, this social structure was the product of a historical evolution, for at one time in the history of the estates there was no distinction between tenant and cultivator.

Origin of the Estates

The friar estates trace their beginnings to the land grants which were made to the early Spanish *conquistadores*. During the late 16th and early 17th centuries, approximately 120 Spaniards received grants within a 100 kilometre radius of Manila.[3] Generally a land grant consisted of a large unit of land known as a *sitio de ganado mayor* (equivalent to 1,742 hectares) and several smaller units called *caballerias* (42.5 hectares). Larger grants measured two or three *sitios* and may have included a *sitio de ganado menor* (774 hectares).[4]

Spanish law required that land grants not encroach on areas already occupied by Filipinos. This injunction may have been followed in some instances, particularly in those areas which were thinly populated at the time of conquest. But in other areas where population density was greater, this principle was disregarded. Violations had become numerous enough by 1596 to provoke a decree from Philip II, warning against any further usurpations of Filipino land. By that time much of the land surrounding Manila had already been distributed and a pattern of landownership begun which was to continue until the beginning of the 20th century.[5]

The Spanish *hacenderos* were quick to show their unwillingness and inability to exploit their lands. By 1612 the original land grants had been consolidated into 34 *estancias* (ranches).[6] Spanish landowners sold their lands to other Spaniards, who, in turn, mortgaged or donated their estates to the religious orders. Spanish success in owning lands in other parts of the Empire poses the question of their failure in the Philippines. Three explanations suggest themselves. The Spanish population in the Philippines was highly transient and its impermanence was not conducive to settled landowning. A small Spanish population, together with the absence of mining and other large-scale economic activities, restricted the market for livestock products which were the mainstay of the early estates. And, perhaps most importantly, the attractions of the high profits to be made on the speculative Manila galleon trade turned the Spaniards' attention almost exclusively to trans-oceanic commerce. With the Spanish abandonment of ranching and agriculture, the field was left to the religious orders.

The religious orders acquired their estates in a variety of ways. Several of the largest haciendas were donated to the orders by Spaniards seeking spiritual benefit. Some lands were purchased directly from their Spanish owners. More commonly, large outlays of cash were not necessary because the estates were heavily mortgaged to religiously endowed funds known as *capellanías*. The orders simply assumed the old mortgages when the properties were transferred to them at auction.[7]

Filipino donors and sellers also contributed directly to the formation of the religious estates, though to a lesser extent than the Spaniards. These transactions, however, appear to have varied regionally. In Cavite and Laguna there are no recorded instances of donations and only a few sales. In Tondo, donations and sales by Filipinos were numerous. There were fewer (and smaller) land grants in Tondo than in the other provinces, perhaps because of the high population densities there. Thus, land obtained from Filipinos figured larger in the development of its estates. The Augustinian Hacienda of Meysapan in Tondo began with a land grant made to the Augustinians but was considerably enlarged as a result of sales and donations. The Jesuit Hacienda of Marikina, also in Tondo, had a similar history.[8] In Bulacan, Filipinos sold land to Spaniards and religious orders but with less frequency than in Tondo. Donations of land were quite common in Bulacan but these lands were administered as separate *capellanías* and were not encompassed within the boundaries of the larger estates. Sales and donations of land by Filipinos were thus concentrated in those areas (Tondo and southern Bulacan) which were closest to Manila, were most developed commercially, and had the densest populations at the time of conquest.

Former Filipino chiefs and headmen were invariably the ones who sold or donated land. Collectively known as *principales* by the Spaniards, they were converted into village and town officials by the colonial government. *Principales* often dealt in large tracts of land. Did they have a right to do so under Filipino customary law or had the "shocks and near social chaos produced by the conquest" allowed them to appropriate communal lands and to collude with buyers and recipients of donations?[9] A confident answer to this question waits on more research into pre-Hispanic land tenure systems but indirect evidence suggests that such expropriations occurred. Those lands which were donated by *principales* in the name of an entire village are particularly open to question. According to Cushner, such donations are suspect because, although individuals might expect spiritual gain, "no possible advantage accruing to entire villages is mentioned in the documents concerning donations made in the name of villages".[10]

Most Filipinos living in the late 19th century knew nothing of the actual origins of the friar estates. The propaganda of that era told them that the religious orders did not have titles to their haciendas. This belief, though strengthened by the anti-friar agitation of the moment, had deeper roots in the Filipino consciousness. In 1697 the government commanded the friars to present their titles in a civil court. The orders refused, invoking ecclesiastical immunity. The judge charged with surveying lands threatened them with confiscation and asserted that they were usurpers of Filipino land. Eventually, the government conceded the issue and accepted an extra-judicial settlement.[11] This jurisdictional dispute re-surfaced several times in the early 18th century. The intermittent wrangling had its effect on the Filipinos, many of whom began to believe the Spanish judiciary's most extreme rhetoric. Historical research has shown that the friars had title to most of their lands. But did the Filipinos' belief that the orders were usurpers of their land have some real basis?

Several estates were surveyed in 1699 and 1754 and these surveys can be compared with those made by the Taft Commission in 1903. However, care must be taken because, although land grants supposedly consisted of standard land units, the actual dimensions of the grants may have deviated from these measures. It is not known how much later surveys may have altered the original grants. In only one case can we speak with reasonable assurance. In 1745 the haciendas of Biñan and Santa Rosa in Laguna measured 6,142 hectares after having been stripped of all land that exceeded the original land grants as a result of their involvement in the agrarian revolt of that year. In 1903 the surveyors found that they contained 8,489 hectares. Thus, Biñan and Santa Rosa expanded by more than 2,000 hectares between 1745 and 1903.[12]

The Early Period

The Spaniards brought with them to the Philippines their ideas of landownership and their experiences from the New World. They met a people of different culture and confronted new ecological and economic conditions. The process of mutual adjustment was gradual and so the late 16th century and much of the 17th was a time of experimentation on the estates. The ways in which they were administered and made use of Filipino labour varied more in these early decades than they would at a later period.

The initial preoccupation with cattle-ranching soon gave way to more diversified hacienda economies. Stock was still run, but on most estates its economic importance was overshadowed by rice, sugar and tropical fruits. The economically sophisticated Jesuits devoted more of their lands to sugar than the other orders, although their operations were small compared to the sugar culture which arose in the 19th century. The Jesuits and the Augustinians used methods which they brought from the New World. (There is no indication that sugar was grown on the Dominican and Recollect estates before the 19th century.) The sugar was grown on specifically reserved plots which were worked by labourers or by tenants contributing gratuitous labour. The sugar was refined in the haciendas' mills and then marketed by the orders. By the late 18th century methods of sugar production began to change. Tenants grew their own sugar which was then refined in the hacienda mill. By the 19th century all aspects of sugar production were in the hands of the tenants.

Rice was the main crop and it was grown in several ways. Sharecroppers were present on some estates, and on a few, such as the Jesuits' San Pedro Tunasan, they may have been in the majority. In the 18th century direct contracts between haciendas and sharecroppers became less common and in the 19th they vanished. A variation of the sharecropping agreement was occasionally used by the Jesuits. Rice land was worked by a group (compañía) of labourers and the crop was then divided between the hacienda and the workers.[13] However, wet rice is not amenable to group methods of cultivation because of the need to regulate water supply which is best superintended by a tenant or small owner. This method was the least common and perhaps was discontinued when the Jesuits discovered that it was not particularly suited for rice cultivation.

Most commonly rice land was rented to tenants (*inquilinos*) for a fixed annual rent. With the disappearance of sharecropping contracts and *compañías,* the *inquilinato* became universal on all of the estates. The Dominican friars charged rent in two ways. On irrigated haciendas, such as Biñan and Santa Rosa, a fixed number of *cavans* (44 kilograms) of *palay* (unhusked rice) was paid for each unit of land.[14] On the unirrigated haciendas, such as Pandi and Lolomboy, rent was expressed in terms of money but was paid in kind according to the price of *palay* at harvest time. Because they did not have irrigation, their paddy fields depended on the vagaries of the rainfall. In good years they could produce as much as the irrigated haciendas, but in general their yearly production was less predictable. By charging rent in money, the variability of yields was taken into account. Following good harvests, the price of *palay* would be lower and the hacienda could collect a larger number of *cavans.* In bad years when the price was higher, the gross number of *cavans* in rent was lower. In the late 18th century there was an increasing trend away from translating money into *palay* on the unirrigated haciendas, a phenomenon which reflected the monetizing effects of the growth of a Philippine export trade. Tenants were then able to acquire cash for the rents without going through the hacienda market.[15]

At harvest time the tenants also paid back the loans which the hacienda administrator had extended to them during the year. These loans were considerable in the 17th and 18th centuries but were no longer made to the more well-to-do tenants of the 19th century. In 1784 Ciriaco Gonzalez Carvajal, Judge of the Royal *Audiencia* (high court) and the first Director of the Society of the Friends of the Country, wrote the most detailed description of the haciendas' financial operations. Although he was a critic of the religious orders and may have selected examples of high interest rates to show them in a bad light, his basic facts can be confirmed by archival records:

> For each water buffalo he pays three pesos at harvest time, 12 *reales* [one and a half pesos] for a harrow, eight *reales* for the plough, and four *reales* for the machete. The rental of these tools is equivalent to about one-half of their price when sold by the Chinese at the fair, while a water buffalo costs at the most eight pesos.
>
> In the same manner the tenants are charged for the advances of rice according to its monetary value which fluctuates from day to day. A *cavan,* which costs two or three *reales* in February during harvest time, increases in August and the two succeeding months to as much as eight *reales.*
>
> When the harvest arrives, the *hacendero* (who is usually a layman contrary to the regulations established by Your Majesty, your governors, and officials) requests the assistance of the justice officials or assumes the responsibilities

himself and prevents the tenant from selling any rice until he satisfies the rent and whatever else he may owe. With this manoeuvre the *hacendero* pressures the tenant, who immediately pays him the seed and the rent.

At the same time the price of the harvest is set, determined by the *hacendero* and some leading natives of his faction, who have subleased their lands to other people who are their partners. The price is usually two *reales* a *cavan*. This accomplished, the *hacendero* liquidates his other accounts with the tenants. He charges 12 *cavans* for each water buffalo, six for the harrow, four for the plough, two for the machete, and for each *cavan* loaned in the months of August, September and October, he takes at least four. From the smallest harvest a tenant can harvest 250 *cavans* from a *quiñón* [5.76 hectares] of land, which is about the largest he can work. From this he pays ten for seed, 50 at the most in rent, 12 for the water buffalo, six for the harrow, four for the plough, two for the machete, and for the seven that were loaned to him so he could eat, he pays 28. Deducted from the 250 *cavans* he obtained from the harvest, he is left with 138 which, sold at harvest time at two *reales,* make 34 pesos and four *reales.* From this the tenant has to pay the salary and the meals of those who help in the planting and harvest, his own clothing, tribute, the expenses of his household, and the other obligations to which he is subject.[16]

Exempted Labour

The transfer of estates from unsuccessful Spanish landowners to the monastic orders was accomplished with relative ease. Their transformation into profitable enterprises was more difficult. In order to make them productive, the religious orders invested thousands of pesos in the improvement of their estates. Dams and irrigation works were built on a large scale and money advanced to prospective tenants and labourers to entice them onto the estates. But in addition to their own efforts, the religious (and the few remaining lay) owners called upon the colonial government for help in supplying their labour needs.

In Latin America the state aided the *hacendados* and miners by providing them with drafts of corvée labour, known as *repartimientos*. Indians were taken from their villages and forced to work in the mines and on the haciendas for specific periods each year. *Repartimientos* for Spanish colonists were abolished in the New World at about the time that land was being granted in the Philippines, so the practice was not introduced into the Philippines. However, the state continued to draft labour for its own needs. Timber for ships and galleons had to be cut in the mountains, and naval yards built and maintained. The Filipino peasant living in one of the provinces near Manila gave up a month each year to these tasks, and if the call came at the wrong time he might be unable to plant or harvest his crops. A payment known as *topa* could be made to officials for a replacement to be found, but few were able to raise the necessary cash. The desire to avoid these distasteful tasks gave the *hacenderos* another way of obtaining labour, and an institution arose which might be called an indirect *repartimiento*. Landowners would petition the government to exempt some of their charges from forced labour. The *casas de reservas* (exempted households) could then be full-time workers on the haciendas. Armed with the powers of exemption, the *hacenderos* could attract Filipinos to their estates or keep the services of those already there.

In the 17th century the colonial government granted a specific number of exemptions to a hacienda. The original grant was sometimes followed by others which increased that number. When the Dominicans acquired Biñan and Santa Rosa in the mid-17th century, they inherited the 74 *reservas* on the estates. By 1684 the number granted had increased to only 84, but in 1704 it had grown to 168. In 1716, at the request of the tenants of the hacienda, the Dominicans negotiated with the government for 213 exemptions.[17]

This piecemeal method was largely replaced in the remainder of the 18th century by a policy of complete exemption. The entire population of Biñan and Santa Rosa was exempted by sometime in the 1730s, and soon thereafter other large haciendas were given the same treatment.[18]

Although the *casas de reservas* belonged to a special administrative category, they did not constitute a separate class of labour. Exemptions could be given to either tenants or landless peasants, depending on the decision of the particular hacienda administration. The Dominican *reservas* were invariably tenants, with the exception of those non-tenants included in the blanket exemptions to Biñan and Santa Rosa. As far as we know, all of the Dominican crop lands were rented to tenants and thus it was in the best interest of their cultivation that tenants be exempted. The Jesuits rented to tenants but also kept some land, called a *demesne* in medieval Europe, which was cultivated under their supervision. In his study of the Jesuit estates, Cushner distinguishes between tenants and *reservas* but does not say how the *reservas* were used.[19] If some of them were landless labourers, it seems logical to assume that the Jesuits exempted them so they could work on the *demesnes*. On the other hand, exempted tenants could also be required to perform gratuitous labour on *demesnes* as was the case with the Augustinian Hacienda of Pasay during the 1740s.[20]

The institution of exempted labour largely accomplished its main purposes of populating the estates and making them dependable suppliers of agricultural products for the Spaniards in Manila. Biñan and Santa Rosa grew and prospered as a result of the liberal policy of exemption which the government had adopted towards them and they quickly became the Dominican's most profitable properties. Other estates experienced similar benefits, particularly those which had been granted blanket exemption.[21]

The institution also had its negative side, at least for the Filipinos. More exemptions meant that more Filipinos were siphoned off from the non-hacienda villages which then had to fill their labour quotas from diminishing population bases. Consequently, the burden of forced labour grew increasingly heavy on the Filipinos living outside the estates. Moreover, this burden could not be measured solely in terms of the official number of exemptions. Governmental supervision was inadequate and it became relatively easy for the *hacenderos* to exceed their quota of exemptions.[22] Sometimes they would merely issue their own receipts of exemption or they might refuse entry to local Filipino officials who were responsible for gathering labour gangs. For instance, the Hacienda of Imus in Cavite did not have a grant of exemption. Nevertheless, Filipino officials charged that they were not permitted on the estate.[23] Unable to keep the *hacenderos* within the limits of their grants, officials may have been persuaded that it was easier simply to exempt an entire hacienda. The 17th and early 18th centuries were filled with complaints and petitions from Filipinos outside the haciendas who felt they were being discriminated against and who wanted relief from excessive labour obligations. When the agrarian revolt of 1745 broke out, one of the grievances of the rebels was the institution of exempted labour and the abuses which had infected it.

By the turn of the 19th century, most of the grants of exemption had lapsed or had been revoked. Biñan and Santa Rosa were the last holdouts, keeping their exempt status until 1832.[24] During the last century of Spanish rule, population growth had replaced extra-economic pressures as the main determinant of hacienda growth and exemptions were no longer essential to their development. In addition, the most dreaded form of forced labour, timber cutting in the mountains, had been abolished, thus diminishing the value of exemption.[25]

The Revolt of 1745

The Philippine peasantry reacted to economic hardship and cultural disorientation under Spanish rule with periodic outbursts of militant nativism and religious messianism. The friar estates were fertile grounds for inchoate protest, but in the region where the friar estates were located unrest took the form of "social banditry". During the 18th and 19th centuries banditry was endemic in Cavite and southern Tondo, areas in which the estates were unusually dominant. Cavite's continuing reputation for outlawry owes something to its geography, the character of its people, but also to the three centuries during which large estates controlled so much of its land. Caviteños who were unwilling or unable to rent land from the haciendas swelled the ranks of the many bandit gangs which infested the roads and occasionally attacked the towns and haciendas of Cavite, Tondo and Laguna. In 1762-1764, during the period of the British invasion of the Philippines and the Spanish government's additional preoccupation with the revolts in the provinces of Pangasinan and Ilocos, bandits temporarily seized the haciendas and two Dominican lay administrators were killed.[26] Soon thereafter the Augustinians abandoned their once-productive Hacienda of Meysapan in southern Tondo because of continual bandit depredations.

However, in 1745 five provinces near Manila erupted in an agrarian revolt which directly expressed Filipino anger with the estates. The basic issues in the revolt were land usurpation by the haciendas and the closing of the haciendas' land to common use for pasturage and forage, a right which had been stipulated in the Laws of the Indies and had been the traditional practice on the haciendas.[27]

The flashpoint of the rebellion was a dispute between the Hacienda of Biñan and the neighbouring town of Silang, Cavite, over several thousand hectares of land which both claimed. The dispute had been simmering since the turn of the century, but not until 1740 did the Dominicans begin formal proceedings to gain control of the land. Three years later a fraudulent survey was conducted which included the disputed land within the boundaries of the hacienda. The results of the survey were then hastily ratified by the Royal *Audiencia,* which had failed to evaluate the facts of the case adequately and overlooked the grossly incorrect units of areal measure used by the surveyors.[28] The errors which permeated all aspects of the decision gave the citizens of Silang ample reason to believe that money rather than justice had been the arbiter. The Dominicans took possession of the land and in early 1745 began to expel the people of Silang and to replace them with tenants from Biñan. In the meantime another unfavourable *Audiencia* decision had been handed down against the town of San Mateo in Tondo and in favour of a contiguous Augustinian hacienda.[29] But the situation on the haciendas remained quiet until the end of April 1745.

Undoubtedly encouraged by these decisions, the Recollects requested that a new survey be made of their Hacienda of Imus. The *Audiencia* sent several officials, but armed residents of Old Cavite, Bacoor and Parañaque threatened them and they were forced to withdraw after having included some land in the hacienda which these towns maintained was theirs.[30]

On 30 April the revolt began in earnest. Rebels from Silang and other Cavite towns destroyed the boundary markers placed by the administrator of Biñan and then besieged him and 16 of his tenants in the *casa hacienda.*[31] They were not harmed, however, and all eventually escaped to Manila. The Augustinian Hacienda of Santa Cruz de Malabon in Cavite was the rebels' next target. Livestock was slaughtered, tenants were threatened, and the administrator was forced to flee to the safety of the Port of Cavite.[32] Such was the pattern repeated throughout the course of the revolt. Residents from surrounding towns would occupy the religious haciendas (the five or six lay-owned estates were not molested), while the tenants looked on or occasionally became the object of the rebels' ire. Only a few tenants appear to have been active participants.[33]

News of the events in Laguna and Cavite reached Manila, and a Spanish municipal official was commissioned to pacify the rebels with a minimum of force. His negotiations with the *principales* of Silang were disrupted by the common people of the town who demanded the immediate return of the disputed land.[34] The revolt broke out anew, spreading rapidly to many of the estates in Cavite, Laguna and Tondo.

A new commission was given to Pedro Calderon y Henriquez, a judge of the *Audiencia,* who set out for the provinces with 27 heavily armed cavalrymen. Calderon believed that most of the Filipinos' grievances were justified. However, he was fearful that too many specific concessions would undermine the authority of the government and lead to more outbreaks against the haciendas.

Rather than accede to particular demands, he thought it more prudent to encompass them in general proclamations. First, he issued a general amnesty for all except the "principal instigators of the revolt". He promised that all the religious haciendas would be surveyed and that free access would be granted for pasturage and forage in the hacienda uplands. He also issued another decree regarding abuses with *reservas* on the estates, and in most of the towns he left the inhabitants in control of the land which they claimed, on condition that they deposit the rents with the treasury until he could determine legitimate ownership. Calderon, however, was careful to say to the Filipinos that most of the haciendas' land had been acquired legitimately and could not be returned.[35]

Calderon's combination of firmness and concession was successful. Violence was avoided except in San Mateo where a Spanish soldier was killed and the town put to the torch.[36] Disturbances then broke out in Bulacan, sparked by a barrio in Meycauayan which was bordered by two haciendas. One thousand men described as bandits occupied the *casa hacienda* at Lolomboy but decamped when Calderon approached with his troops, reinforced by a Filipino contingent from Pampanga.[37]

In October 1745, four months after Bulacan had been pacified, the towns of Rosario, Taal and Balayan in Batangas (south of Cavite) rose against the Jesuit haciendas of Lian and Nasugbu because of alleged land usurpation and the closing of the commons. Here there was the necessity for a larger military operation because the rebels refused to submit to Calderon. Many were killed and 30 to 40 were sentenced to prison terms.[38] Had all the provinces erupted simultaneously, Spanish military strength would have been seriously tested. With the British poised to attack at a sign of weakness, Philippine history may have taken quite a different course.

Change

The revolt of 1745 preceded by a few years a turning point in the socio-economic history of the friar estates. It occurred midway in their history and coincided approximately with the end of the first phase of that history. It also presaged a new era on the estates. The Filipinos who reacted against the expansion of the estates and the system of exemption underscored excesses which had become part of the *hacenderos'* search for land and labour. On the other hand, the attempt to close the haciendas' commons showed that new ideas of landownership were in the air and foreshadowed the economic forces which would soon impinge on the estates.

Until the second half of the 18th century the estates' social structures were relatively simple. Cultivating tenants grew subsistence crops, paid their rents, and turned to the administrators for loans. The lines of hacienda authority were firmly drawn, so firmly that most of the tenants, regardless of any grievances they might have had, did not take part in the revolt of 1745.

In the last century and a half of the estates' existence, five interrelated developments took place which greatly altered their social structures. First, before the late 18th century, tenants leased on the average one-half a *quiñón* (2.9 hectares) or less of rice land which they worked themselves. By the 19th century, tenants frequently leased a *quiñón* or more which they subleased to sharecroppers. In other words, a two-tiered hierarchy consisting of *hacenderos* and cultivating tenants was supplanted by a three-tiered hierarchy consisting of *hacenderos,* non-cultivating tenants and sharecroppers. Second, the *hacenderos,* who were no longer so involved in the cycle of productive activities, stopped extending loans and withdrew to a position of passive rent-collecting. Next, export crops, particularly sugar, assumed a much larger role on several of the estates. Rapid population growth increased the competition for land. Finally, declining fertility of rice land coupled with rising rents resulted in decreasing crop shares for the tenants.

Following the British occupation of Manila (1762-1764), Spanish colonial policy began slowly and haltingly to open the Philippines to world trade. Lacking a manufacturing base of its own, the Philippines' "comparative advantage" lay in the export of tropical agricultural products. Most of the Chinese were expelled from the Philippines in 1765 and were not permitted to re-enter in large numbers until the 1840s. In the absence of competition from the Chinese, the commercially oriented Chinese mestizos, offspring of Chinese men and Filipino women, were in the van of economic change for more than 50 years. In the early 19th century, foreign commercial firms (mostly British and American) were permitted to establish themselves in the islands. Within a few years these firms, working with the once again numerous and well-organized Chinese, assumed the lead in promoting export production and in supplying the Philippines with manufactured goods from abroad.

One of the consequences of the type of export growth experienced by the Philippines was that its fruits fell almost exclusively to a highly select group of the population. The new exchange and monetary economy intensified the sway of the moneylender and usurer in Philippine rural society without establishing the foundations for industrial development or a viable internal market. Whether such a basis might have been laid in the absence of colonialism is, of course, impossible to determine; but the actual result of the course pursued in the Philippines was an economy characterized by an up-and-out flight of capital and a rigid class structure.

In the provinces surrounding Manila an increase in the concentration of landownership and in the number of sharecroppers followed the advent of a commercial economy. Various forms of dependent land tenure had always existed in the Philippines, but the late 18th and 19th centuries saw a vast extension of these relationships throughout the Tagalog countryside.

Sharecropping also became institutionalized on the friar estates — no longer in its previous form as a direct contract with an *hacendero* but as a sublease with a tenant. By the close of the Spanish era in the Philippines, most of the friar lands were cultivated by sharecroppers whose meagre income was diminished by the two nonproducing strata of rent collectors above them. After the tenant had paid the hacienda the fixed rental and taken half of the remaining gross production for himself, not much could have been left for the sharecroppers who did the work and assumed most of the expenses of cultivation.

This had not always been the situation on the friar estates, but appears to have developed parallel with the concentration of landownership and the spread of tenancy throughout the Philippines, though it was governed by some unique characteristics of its own.

In the early 18th century, a regime of small tenant cultivators was typical on most of the haciendas. Records for the years 1707 and 1712 show that the average leasehold on the Augustinian Hacienda of Mandaloya in Tondo was less than one-half a *quiñón* (2.9 hectares), an indication that subleasing was virtually nonexistent.[39]

Until the late 18th century, the haciendas of Biñan and Santa Rosa were also worked by tenants in large measure. The administrators loaned large amounts of money, rice and tools to the tenants of these estates.[40] Had the lands been sublet by the tenants, the hacienda would not have felt the obligation or the need to provide them with these loans, the curtailment of which coincided roughly with the absorption of most of the land by noncultivating leaseholders.

Prior to the changes in tenure, the typical tenant of the Hacienda of Biñan occupied on the average one-half a *quiñón* of rice land, according to a government document of 1756.[41] Carvajal, writing in 1784, used the example of a tenant working the land himself, although he stated that some of the *principales* sublet their lands to sharecroppers.

By the beginning of the 19th century the Augustinian friar, Martínez de Zúñiga, observed that most of the land of Biñan was in "the hands of the rich" who cultivated it by means of sharecroppers. He did not say whether this was a recent development, but the implication, both in his description of Biñan and of other haciendas in Tondo, is of newly evolved relationships which were congenial to the desires of the administrators to ensure the collection of the rents with a minimum of bother.[42]

The growth of subtenancy did not proceed uniformly throughout all the friar haciendas. Those closer to Manila in the provinces of Tondo and southern Bulacan had a greater proportion of sharecroppers at an earlier date than others farther removed from the capital and its commercial activity. In 1745 there were several tenants with large holdings on the Hacienda of Makati in Tondo.[43] By the 1760s the average leasehold on Makati was exactly one *quiñón*, a figure which points to a relatively high incidence of subtenancy.[44] The 1769 registry of the Hacienda of Pandi in Bulacan recorded five tenants renting 58 *quiñónes* of rice land out of a total cultivated area of 390 *quiñónes*.[45] The number of sharecroppers on Pandi must have already been considerable at this date. On the other hand, some of the haciendas of Cavite lagged behind for a time and did not begin to have high rates of subtenancy until the 19th century.[46]

In the late 18th and 19th centuries, Chinese mestizos moved onto the religious estates, making up a significant part of the new class of noncultivating tenants. On some haciendas such as Biñan and Santa Rosa where there had always been a large Chinese mestizo population, this was merely a second wave. On others, such as Pandi and Lolomboy, mestizos who had been present in the early 18th century must later have withdrawn or else lost their corporate distinctness by merging with the Filipino population, since there are no names of Chinese mestizos in the 1769 registries of the haciendas.[47] They were active, however, in the municipal centres of the haciendas from which, according to the administrators, they did all the buying and selling with the tenants of Pandi and Lolomboy. When they began acquiring land on Pandi and Lolomboy in the late 18th century, the tenants grumbled to the Dominicans that "we, the Filipinos of the town, should be preferred over all others, particularly the Chinese mestizos who have no right to land".[48]

Because of their previous accumulation of commercial capital, the Chinese mestizos were in a position to finance agricultural production. In order to accomplish that objective, the Filipino peasant first had to be persuaded to part with his land, but the endemic conditions of sharp seasonal fluctuations in his reserves, and the small and variable crop yields made him chronically vulnerable and only required that the land become valuable enough for someone to covet who had enough money. On the friar estates these conditions were exacerbated by the necessity of making rental payments. Once the tenant cultivator had parted with some of his surplus to the hacienda, it was much easier to pry loose the rest from him and for the noncultivating tenant to insinuate himself between the hacienda and the former tenant. In turn, the hacienda administrators reacted to these developments by preferring to rent to the new class of tenants who could be counted upon to pay, even if this sometimes clashed with their professed policy against subleasing.

Another factor which may have hastened the exit of the cultivating tenant was the increasingly high interest rates charged on the loans made to him by the hacienda. The documentation is by no means conclusive on this point, so it must be taken as entirely provisional until a more detailed study of this period can be made. Interest rates for loans on Biñan in the 1740s were usually about 33 percent from sowing to harvest, but by the mid-1750s they had begun to climb to between 50 and 60 percent.[49] Thirty years later Carvajal described rates of several hundred percent.

The sharecroppers (and landless labourers) occupied the bottom rung of the hacienda social order. Their position on the estates was economically and socially more insecure than that of the tenants. In the eyes of the judiciary the subleasing agreement had no binding effect on the hacienda administration. As a consequence, when a tenant was expelled for nonpayment of rent, the sharecropper was liable to find that his share of the crop or his tools and animals had been attached in order partially to cover the debt of his former lessor. He could also be forced off the land along with the tenant. A few expelled tenants might stand up for their sharecroppers and plead against these proceedings on the grounds that the organization of the estates made the sharecroppers indispensable. However, such reasoning carried little weight in the local courts of law.[50]

On other occasions the immediate pressures on the sharecroppers came from the tenants. Since the hacienda's rent was usually deducted from the total harvest rather than merely from the tenant's share, the cropper in effect paid one-half of the rent. Sometimes an indebted tenant could attempt to forestall eviction by stepping up the exactions from his sharecroppers. As early as 1778 such practices were causing acrimonious disputes on the Hacienda of Pandi, but the sharecroppers did not have much recourse because their existence was closely tied with the tenants.[51]

The reciprocal ties that bound tenants and sharecroppers were probably more fragile than the patron–client relationships that existed between the independent Filipino landowners and their share tenants. Since the tenant's holdings were to some extent dependent on the whim of the administrator, the awareness of his own precarious situation may have been added incentive for him to wrest the maximum amount of short-term utility from his sharecroppers. But it would be an error to suppose that the cleavage between sharecroppers and tenants was sharply drawn in the late 19th century before the appearance of agricultural labour unions and socialist ideologies with their specific appeals to the peasantry. Nevertheless, there is some evidence that spontaneous associations of sharecroppers were beginning to develop by the 1880s in the province of Cavite. The friars, rather than the tenants, seem to have been their main preoccupation.[52]

The spread of sharecropping on the estates was an immediate boon for their administrators. Rent collection was put on a more secure and regular basis. In addition, the *hacenderos* no longer had to involve themselves in productive activities. However, the subleasing practice had a long-term drawback, glimpsed by Martínez de Zúñiga during his travels at the turn of the 19th century.[53] The clear lines of authority which had once run from *hacenderos* to cultivators were disrupted by the interposition of noncultivating tenants. The cultivators now had their primary relationships with other Filipinos whose greater wealth made them less dependent on the haciendas. Social differentiation made the structural equation unstable. Economic difficulties catalyzed it into the revolt of 1896 on the estates.

The prosperity of tenants and subtenants hinged on how much the land produced and on how much they paid in rent. Descriptions of yields and rents varied with the perspective of the observer. Friars and their supporters asserted that rents absorbed only a nominal proportion of gross production. Tenants, on the other hand, maintained that they kept very little after rents and expenses had been deducted.

A lack of detailed records prevents us from being precise about rents and yields but there is enough evidence to outline the general trend. In the late 18th century the best irrigated rice land on the friar estates produced from 250 to 400 *cavans* of unhusked rice per *quiñón*. Maximum rent was 50 *cavans* or one-fifth to one-eighth of gross production.[54] This relatively favourable situation began to deteriorate in the 19th century as the tenants and their sharecroppers were caught in a squeeze between rising rents and falling crop yields.

The official hacienda records present an ambiguous account of rentals. On the estates where rent was traditionally paid with a fixed number of *cavans* of *palay,* such as Biñan, the registries show only a nominal increase. For example, sometime in the 1860s rent on Biñan and Santa Rosa was raised from 50 to 53 *cavans* per *quiñón,* and at about the same time a charge of 16 *cavans* was added for the second annual but smaller yield crop known as the *palagad.*[55] The *palagad* may have been grown on these estates before this period, but there are no records of rent being collected for it. The tenants of Lolomboy and Pandi paid more than double the amount of money for a *quiñón* of first-class rice land (₱35) than they had a century earlier, but the price of *palay* had since doubled, and thus the rent as measured in *palay* increased only about seven or eight *cavans*.[56] On other estates where rental payments had been changed from money to *palay,* the increase was somewhat larger. In the 18th century the tenants of the Hacienda of San Francisco de Malabon in Cavite had paid ₱14 for a *quiñón,* or the equivalent of about 28 *cavans* in current prices. At the end of the Spanish period it was 50 *cavans.*[57]

However, the more significant effect on the tenants is not readily apparent from the hacienda records. All of the 18th and early 19th century documents dealing with the matter are unanimous in equating a *quiñón* of land with either ten or eight *cavans* of seed, but in 1903 Marin y Morales said that in Cavite a *quiñón* held only five *cavans.*[58] The testimonies of Cavite tenants before the Taft Commission confirm this statement.[59] Either the land area measured by the *quiñón* had shrunk (there was a saying in Cavite that every year the land, as measured by the administrators, grew bigger than it actually was), or else farming practices had changed over the years and fewer seeds were used in planting a given area of land. Both may have acted in tandem.

In 1890 the administrator of Biñan reported that the best land produced 240 *cavans* a *quiñón,* 60 of which was paid in rent.[60] Dominican records for 1896 covering all of their haciendas show that rent took from one-third to one-sixth of the rice crop.[61] The first systematic records of rice production in the Philippines were not begun until 1910, seven years after the estates had been purchased by the American colonial government. The friar lands were then under the management of the Bureau of Lands which was investing money in the upkeep and expansion of irrigation works, while selling off plots to tenants. The country was recovering from the rinderpest epidemic and locust plagues which had struck the islands at intervals beginning in the mid-1880s. Thus, crop production in the second decade of the 20th century may have been better than it was during the last two decades of friar ownership.

From 1910 until 1925 the province of Cavite produced on the average 20 *cavans* of unhusked rice per hectare.[62] Approximately 60 percent of the province's rice land was found on the former friar estates. By making the conservative assumptions that only one rice crop was grown and that all of the province's remaining rice land was planted to the upland variety yielding only five *cavans* a hectare, we infer that the estates averaged 30 *cavans* during this 16-year period.[63] Under these circumstances, the best land probably yielded from 35 to 45 *cavans* a hectare (about 200 to 260 *cavans* a *quiñón*). Rents in Cavite ranged from 50 *cavans* a *quiñón* on San Francisco de Malabon to 60 *cavans* on Imus.[64] These figures agree quite closely with those given by the Cavite tenants before the Taft Commission in 1903.[65]

Rentals for sugar lands were generally less than those for paddy fields. Originally they were based on the rates charged for the infrequently exploited upland rice fields. From the middle of the 19th century to the 1896 revolution the rental for sugar land doubled. From ₱15 for a *quiñón* of first-class land in the 1840s, it was increased to ₱20, then ₱25, and finally ₱30 where it would remain until the revolution.[66] If bad crops or prices prevented a tenant from satisfying the annual rent, he had to pay double the following year.

Sugar land was leased to tenants under a three-year contract. In most cases the tenants did not have to pay rent for three or four years until the land had been cleared or had begun producing an income. Spokesmen for the friars, such as Father Marin y Morales, used this aspect of the contracts as evidence of the hacienda's fair treatment of the tenants.[67] It was, however, only prudent business sense which dictated this concession, for if rent had been required immediately, the lands would never have been cultivated.

The sizes of many of the leased lands on the Hacienda of Calamba were relatively large. Several were above 50 hectares. José Rizal's family had one of the largest (380 hectares), although their land was classified as third-class, the least productive type.[68] The rents themselves, in good years, were not particularly onerous. In fact, the Spanish traveller and writer, Sinibaldo de Mas, had actually recommended the renting of sugar lands as more remunerative than their purchase.[69] The main objection, however, was not the amount of the rental — although this, too, became an issue when sugar prices slumped in the 1880s — but the conditions of tenure. Renting sugar lands was seldom practised in other provinces such as Cebu and Pampanga. The land was either purchased outright, or obtained through a mortgage known as the *pacto de retro*. In many instances the mortgagee would obtain the use of the land, and should the mortgagor default on the loan, he could ultimately get full ownership of the land. Despite Sinibaldo de Mas' advice, renting sugar land must have had drawbacks which did not recommend it to sugar growers. Primarily because of the relatively large investment required in sugar cultivation for work animals and milling devices before the introduction of the modern sugar central, short-term leases must not have offered a sufficient guarantee to the stability of the investment. This was one of the objections cited by Rizal in his letters to the government concerning conditions on the Calamba estate.[70] John Foreman, an English visitor to the Philippines, accurately described the effects of these contracts. They did not specify the land that was to be rented or its size. All aspects of the contracts were vague, and the tenants were thus at the mercy of the administrator.[71]

All of this was exacerbated in the 1880s and again in 1894 when sugar prices dropped precipitously as the result of competition with European sugar beets and recessions in the industrialized world. The friar estates were not alone in feeling the effects of depression. Hard times were reported from officials in other areas. However, the tenants had a more tangible object on which they could affix blame for their troubles.

Conclusion

Those Tagalog provinces with the largest concentrations of friar landholdings led the way in the revolt of 1896. To be sure, the origins of the revolt should not be sought solely, or even primarily, in the conditions on the friar estates. Many factors lay behind the struggle against Spain. Nevertheless, agrarian unrest on the estates can be seen as a powerful force uniting all Tagalog social classes. Despite their differences, non-cultivating tenants, sharecroppers and agricultural labourers had one overriding interest in common — all desired the end of friar landownership.

Spanish and American officials referred in general terms to the existence of agrarian unrest on the estates. Unfortunately, neither their statements nor the archival records discovered so far shed much light on the actual dynamics of that unrest as it led up to the outbreak of 1896. That task remains for historical research. However, two things seem reasonably clear. The revolt was particularly intense within the boundaries of the estates and, consequently, their inhabitants were the leading participants in the early phases of the armed conflict.

Such was not the case in 1745 — then the hacienda populations had been the eye of the hurricane. Nor did the revolt of 1896 follow the typical pattern that historians and social scientists have seen in agrarian conflicts which have occurred throughout the so-called Third World. According to the analysis which is now generally accepted, populations living directly under the authority of landowners are usually too dependent (both psychologically and materially) on their overlords or too vulnerable to violent suppression to risk open revolt.[72] Rather, the revolutionary tinder has most often been supplied by independent peasantries living on the peripheries of the estates or in areas outside the main centres of state power.

What was different about the friar estates in 1896? The answer seems to lie in the complex social structure which had evolved on the estates during the last century and a half of their existence. As non-cultivating tenants interposed themselves between *hacenderos* and peasant cultivators, the *hacenderos* lost their claims to legitimate authority and their hold over the inhabitants of their estates. Increasingly they were perceived as simple rent-collecting excrescences. Lines of authority and dependency were loosened. They were irrevocably broken when the economic difficulties of the late 19th century severely affected all elements of hacienda society.

NOTES

1 Rizalino Aquino Oades, "The Social and Economic Background of Philippine Nationalism, 1830-1892" (doctoral dissertation, University of Hawaii, 1974), 229; William Howard Taft, "Addresses, Pamphlets, etc. Relating to the Philippines" (Washington D.C., Library of Congress).

2 The estates were as follows: Dominican — Naic (Cavite), Santa Cruz (Cavite), Lian (Batangas), Tunasan (Laguna), Biñan (Laguna), Santa Rosa (Laguna), Calamba (Laguna), Pandi (Bulacan), Lolomboy (Bulacan), Orion (Bulacan); Augustinian — Binagliag (Bulacan), Dampol (Bulacan),Malinta (Bulacan), San Francisco (Cavite), Muntinlupa (Laguna), Tala (Tondo), Piedad (Tondo); Recollect — Imus (Cavite), San José (Cavite); Order of St. John — Buenavista (Bulacan); Archdiocese of Manila — Dinalupihan (Bataan). The haciendas of Lian and Tunasan belonged to the Colegio de San José from the 17th century onward and were administered by the Jesuits. After the expulsion of the Jesuits in the 18th century, they were administered by the Colegio's secular

clergy. When the Colegio was incorporated into the University of Santo Tomas in 1875, the haciendas came under Dominican administration until 1915 when the Colegio and its estates were again transferred to Jesuit administration. The Hacienda of Buenavista came under the jurisdiction of the Archdiocese of Manila when the Brothers of San José were disbanded in the latter half of the 19th century.

At one time the Jesuits had been the dominant landowning religious order. Following their expulsion from the Philippines in 1768, the Jesuit estates were confiscated by the government and sold to lay Spaniards and Filipinos. The Jesuits did not acquire agricultural land when they returned to the islands in 1859, but two of their former estates reverted to ecclesiastical ownership in the 1830s when the Spanish owners of Calamba and Naic sold out to the Dominicans.

3 University of Indiana, Lilly Library (hereafter, UILL), Philippine MSS. 1632-1640, folios 152-69.

4 Nicolas Cushner gives areal equivalencies which are 20 percent larger than these. See, his *Landed Estates in the Colonial Philippines* (New Haven: No. 20, Southeast Asia Studies, Yale University, 1976), 73, 132. His measures are too high because he equates a *vara* with an English yard. Actually, it was equivalent to 32.91 inches or 0.836 metres. See, Zoilo Espejo, *Cartilla de agricultura filipina* (Manila: Imp. de Ramirez y Giraudier, 1870), 98-99. A *sitio de ganado mayor* measured 3000 *pasos* on a side (5000 *varas*) and a *menor* 2000 *pasos*. These measures were the same as those used in Mexico.

5 Archives of the University of Santo Tomas (hereafter, AUST), Cédulas Reales, microfilm roll 31. It is not possible to decide which lands were taken from Filipinos by examining the names of towns in existence during the early years after the conquest since most of the haciendas did not become municipalities until the late 18th and 19th centuries. Therefore, the absence of a town name for an area occupied by an hacienda does not mean that it was unoccupied at the time land grants were distributed.

6 Archives of the Province of Santíssimo Rosario (hereafter, APSR), Haciendas, tomo 12, folios 136.

7 APSR, Haciendas, tomo 15.

8 Cushner, *Landed Estates,* 26-28.

9 Cushner, "Meysapan: The Formation and Social Effects of a Landed Estate in the Philippines," *Journal of Asian History* 7 (1973), 38.

10 Cushner, *Landed Estates,* 20.

11 Charles H. Cunningham, "Origin of the Friar Lands Question in the Philippines," *American Political Science Review* 10 (August 1916), 465-80.

12 Dennis M. Roth, *The Friar Estates of the Philippines* (Albuquerque: University of New Mexico Press, 1977), 98.

13 Cushner, *Landed Estates,* 50.

14 AUST, Libros, tomo 24, folios 278-80.

15 APSR, Haciendas, tomo 4, folios 212-14.

16 AUST, Libros, tomo 13, folios 122-26.

17 AUST, Libros, tomo 10, folios 218-23.

18 AUST, Libros, tomo 13.

19 Cushner, *Landed Estates,* 52.

20 University of Saint Louis Microfilm Collection (hereafter, USL), Sección Jesuítica, microfilm roll 816, "Testimonio de gavelas que se cobravan a los Indios".

21 Philippine National Archives (hereafter, PNA), Cedulario 1755-1758, folios 54-55.

22 APSR, Haciendas, tomo 4.

23 AUST, Libros, tomo 55, folio 270.

24 APSR, Haciendas, tomo 15.

25 This kind of labour was abolished sometime in the late 18th or early 19th century.

26 APSR, Historia Civil, tomo 1, folio 129.

27 APSR, Libros, tomo 55, folios 200-250.

28 *Ibid.,*folio 483.

29 *Ibid.,* folio 240.

30 USL, Sección Jesuítica, microfilm roll 816.

31 AUST, Libros, tomo 55, folio 545.

32 *Ibid.,* folio 269.

33 *Ibid.,* folios 200-80.

34 *Ibid.,* folios 410.

35 *Ibid.,* folio 472.

36 *Ibid.,* folio 400.

37 *Ibid.,* folio 434.

38 USL, Sección Jesuítica, microfilm roll 816, "Carta del Obispo de Nueva Segovia".

39 UILL, Philippine MSS. 1583-1631, folios 231-32; Cushner, *Landed Estates,* 107.

40 AUST, Libros, tomo 24, folios 278-80.

41 APSR, Haciendas, tomo 4, "Colección de Cartas".

42 Joaquín Martinez de Zúñiga, *Estadismo de las Islas Filipinas* (Madrid: Minuesa de los Rios, 1893), 1:47.

43 AUST, Libros, tomo 55, folios 387-88.

44 Cushner, *Landed Estates,* 49.

45 APSR, Haciendas, tomo 10, folios 90-96.

46 PNA, Erecciones de Pueblo de Cavite; AUST, Becerros, tomo 21, folio 50; PNA, Protocolos de Cavite, legajo 1291, folio 262.

47 APSR, Haciendas, tomo 10, folios 90-120.

48 AUST, Folletos, tomo 74, folios 198-99.

49 AUST, Libros, tomo 24, folios 278-80; APSR, Haciendas, tomo 4, "Biñan — 1766".

50 PNA, Terrenos de Bulacan, tomo 1, 1769-1888.

51 *Ibid.,* expediente 1.

52 PNA, Terrenos de Cavite, tomo 4.

53 Martínez de Zúñiga, *Estadismo,* 1:47.

54 PNA, Erecciones de pueblo de Cavite, tomo 1, legajo 75; APSR, Haciendas, tomo 14, folio 230.

55 AUST, Libros, tomo 5, folios 150-60.

56 APSR, Haciendas, tomo 14, folios 96-120.

57 AUST, Libros, tomo 24, folios 416-18. In my book (*Friar Estates,* 140) I mistakenly gave the rent as 53 *cavans.*

58 Valentín Marin y Morales, *Ensayo de una síntesis de los trabajos realizados por las corporaciones españolas de Filipinas* (Manila: Universidad de Santo Tomas, 1901), 1:218.

59 U.S. Bureau of Insular Affairs, *Fourth Annual Report of the Philippine Commission* (Washington: GPO, 1904), 1:142-203; AUST, Libros, tomo 90.

60 AUST, Folletos, tomo 79, folio 192.

61 APSR, Haciendas, "Prospectus of the Philippine Sugar Estates Development Company, 1896".

62 Philippine Islands, Dept. of Commerce and Industry, *Statistical Bulletin* (Manila: Bureau of Printing, 1918-1927).

63 This figure is quite close to those reported for the Cavite estates during the years 1924-1928. See, Philippine Islands, Bureau of Lands, *Annual Report of the Director of Lands* (Manila: Bureau of Printing, 1925-1929). However, the 1928 figures for the Laguna estates are clearly errors or misprints

because they show them producing 200 *cavans* of unhusked rice and 700 *pilones* (61 kilos) of sugar per hectare — both impossibilities.

64 Marin y Morales, *Ensayo,* 1:218.

65 U.S. Bureau of Insular Affairs, *Fourth Annual Report,* 1:142-203.

66 APSR, Haciendas, tomo 17.

67 Marin y Morales, *Ensayo,* 2:699.

68 AUST, Libros, tomo 91.

69 Sinibaldo de Mas y Sans, *Informe sobre el estado de las Islas Filipinas* (Madrid: I. Sancha, 1843), 2:21.

70 José Rizal, *Escritos políticos e históricos* (Manila: Comisión Nacional del Centenario de José Rizal, 1961), 39.

71 John Foreman, *The Philippine Islands* (London: S. Low, 1892), 154.

72 For an excellent theoretical discussion of this issue see, Urzua Frademan, *La Demanda Campesina* (Santiago: Universidad Católica de Chile, 1969).

The Provincial and Municipal Elites of Luzon During the Revolution, 1898-1902

MILAGROS C. GUERRERO

E arlier studies of the Philippine Revolution and the Filipino–American War have concentrated on their cosmopolitan *ilustrado*[1] leadership and various aspects of the conflict between the Malolos Republic and the United States. They are, however, remiss in neglecting the role played by the provincial and municipal elites in the Revolution and their consequent entrenchment in positions of power throughout the country. Yet one of the most obvious and significant features of the political situation during the years 1898-1902 is the emergence of these local elites as the real victors of the Philippine Revolution. The ground rules established by President Emilio Aguinaldo for the country's political reorganization as it was slowly freed from Spanish control enabled the elites to be the final arbiters of the direction that the Revolution would take in many towns. Often, the wealthy and educated Filipinos who occupied provincial and municipal offices used the ideals of the Revolution as a means to promote their interests. Rampant graft and corruption characterized the administration of many a municipality, exacerbating the grievances of the peasant masses and contributing to their radicalization. The perpetuation of the colonial regime at the provincial and municipal levels also helped give rise to peasant messianic movements. The elites and even the Aguinaldo government regarded these movements as "fanatical" and "subversive". Unfortunately, some contemporary students of the Philippine Revolution tended to agree with this partisan view and looked at the peasant reaction to elite entrenchment during the Revolution as "discordant, non-integral elements", with "little or no relevance to the nerve-fraying drama in Manila, Kawit or Malolos".[2]

The events of 1898 had a tremendous impact on the Philippine elite, particularly among the *ilustrados* concentrated in Manila. In less than a year, the most prominent men of the country had to shift their allegiance from the Spanish colonial government to the revolutionary regime established by Aguinaldo. But no sooner had they done this when, recognizing the pragmatic political and economic reasons for withdrawing their support from Aguinaldo and the Revolution, they transferred this allegiance to the United States. Although the effects of the Revolution were felt throughout the archipelago, its impact on the elites was most pronounced in Manila and Central Luzon. The Revolution began at Manila, spread first to the surrounding provinces and fought its major battles in Central Luzon. Elite participation in the Revolution was most important during its second phase (1898-1902), and it was these years which had the greatest impact on the postwar settlement between the elite and their new colonizers.

The Revolution

Despite the absence of what may presumably be regarded as organized *ilustrado* leadership after General Aguinaldo and the Biak-na-Bato Republic went into exile in December 1897, the Revolution in Luzon did not abate in the Tagalog Provinces but, in fact, spread rapidly to Central Luzon and the Ilocos Provinces.[3] "Illicit societies" and "bandit bands", which operated along the lines of the *Katipunan*[4], waged guerilla war against Spanish forces throughout Luzon, killing Spanish priests, civil officials and their numerous Filipino sympathizers. Recruitment into various *Katipunan* and *Katipunan*-like associations during 1897 and early 1898 proceeded at a rapid pace. Indeed, according to the journalist, Wenceslao E. Retana, "for every *Katipunan* of 1896, there [were] now ten such organizations".[5]

In Pangasinan, the *Guardia de Honor*,[6] a peasant society whose membership numbered 40,000 in August 1897, seems to have worked hand in hand with the *Katipuneros* in the continuing insurrection. Spanish repression served only to increase its following not only in Pangasinan but also in La Union and Zambales.[7] In Zambales itself, the *Katipunan* continued to operate under the leadership of two brothers, Teodoro and Doroteo Pansacula, who advocated the common ownership of property (*comunidad de bienes*) and the distribution of the property of the rich among the poor. They maintained that "it was already time for the rich to be poor and for the poor to become rich" and that the uneducated should govern the towns while the intelligent should be subordinated to them.[8] The rich and educated citizens of Zambales naturally labelled the Pansaculas and their followers "robbers" and "bandits" and co-operated with the Spanish troops in persecuting the movement. This only led to the exodus of more Zambaleños into the rebels' mountain redoubts.

In Pampanga and Tarlac, guerilla resistance was led by messianic peasant organizations such as the *Cruz na Bituin* (Crossed Stars) and the *Santa Iglesia* (Holy Church), which espoused the brotherhood of men as well as the redistribution of land and property.[9] In particular, the *Santa Iglesia* prophesied that Philippine independence would be accompanied by a social-levelling process. These beliefs, though heavily laden with religious ideas, must have filled the hearts of the rich Kapampangans with apprehension. The Kapampangan elite, as J. Larkin cogently points out, joined the Revolution only in late May and June of 1898 when the Filipino rebels in most of Central Luzon had defeated the Spanish forces.[10] After they had joined the expeditionary forces sent by Aguinaldo to the province, the Kapampangan elite refused to recognize the social revolution taking place in their midst and sought to eliminate the *Santa Iglesia* leadership and control the base of the movement. When the brotherhood resisted, they branded it a group of bandits deserving a total persecution.

Indeed, in many towns throughout Luzon, well-to-do Filipinos as well as many municipal officials refused to join the Revolution during 1897 and early 1898. Some were not content with playing the role of fence-sitters but actually turned against the insurgents by actively supporting the friars and the Spanish forces.[11] Thus, while it is true that Spanish control over Luzon weakened increasingly, the

Central Luzon, 1900

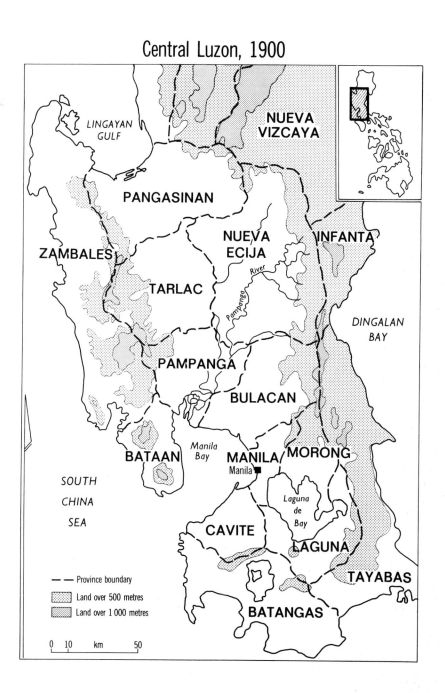

LINGAYAN GULF

NUEVA VIZCAYA

PANGASINAN

ZAMBALES

NUEVA ECIJA

INFANTA

TARLAC

Pampanga River

DINGALAN BAY

PAMPANGA

BULACAN

BATAAN

Manila Bay

MANILA

Manila

MORONG

SOUTH CHINA SEA

Laguna de Bay

CAVITE

LAGUNA

TAYABAS

BATANGAS

— — Province boundary

Land over 500 metres

Land over 1 000 metres

0   10   km   50

Spaniards in Manila felt confident that as long as Aguinaldo remained in his Hong Kong exile, the colony would remain secure in Spanish hands and the prominent Filipinos would be loyal to Spain. Under the latter's influence, recalcitrant Filipinos might be persuaded to accept the *pax hispanica*.

When rumours of the Spanish-American War reached Manila and the provinces on 22 April 1898, this feeling of confidence was buoyed by protestations of loyalty from Aguinaldo's lieutenants who were quick to offer their services to Basilio Augustin, the Spanish governor. Thus encouraged, the governor created a Filipino militia which incorporated some of Aguinaldo's military leaders. He also created a consultative assembly, which included the cream of the Philippine elite: Pedro Paterno, Ambrosio Rianzares Bautista, T.H. Pardo de Tavera, Joaquin Gonzalez, Maximino Paterno, Ariston Bautista and Cayetano Arellano.[12]

Pedro Paterno, the leader of the assembly, lost no time in demanding reforms for the colony, particularly an autonomous government and representation in the Spanish *Cortes*. Then, with "the evils of Spanish colonization over", the Filipinos would struggle "side by side" with the Spaniards against the United States.[13] These demands were made on 31 May 1898, a dozen days after Aguinaldo returned from Hong Kong with the help of the Americans. By then, rebels in Cavite and adjoining Tagalog provinces, heartened by Aguinaldo's call to arms, were fighting with even greater intensity. Desperate for Filipino support, the governor acceded to Paterno's wishes. Copies of manifestos containing these reforms were published in both Tagalog and Spanish and distributed throughout Manila. Then Paterno demanded on 13 June that Philippine autonomy, as promised, be put into effect. The colonial government, despite its weak position, was ill disposed to buckle down before the consultative assembly. Aguinaldo, who had returned from exile several weeks earlier, had already declared independence the day before. When he received a Tagalog translation of the manifesto, he noted tersely on its margin: *"Tanghali ca na!"* ("You are pretty late!").[14]

Indeed, in light of Aguinaldo's return, the elite's plan to obtain autonomous status under Spain was probably too late. Insurgent leaders who continued the struggle in his absence acknowledged him as their supreme leader. Demoralized by insurgent victories, many Spanish civil officials and residents, such as those in Batangas and Ambos Ilocos, were less concerned with determined resistance than with debating and fighting among themselves as to the most effective means of evacuating to Manila.[15] The Spanish *Guardia Civil* suffered from massive desertions. Commanders of the newly established Filipino militia also eventually deserted to the Aguinaldo camp. The impression that the Americans were allies in the struggle for independence helped Aguinaldo considerably.

The most prominent of the deserters from the Filipino militia was Felipe Buencamino, commander of the important Anda Salazar regiment in Manila. His defection signified the Filipino elite's abandonment of the Spanish government. Still believing in the legitimacy of Spanish hegemony in the Philippines, he went to Cavite to dissuade Aguinaldo from embarking on an insurrection that he feared would only degenerate into a civil war. But from Cavite he sent word to Manila that he had been "converted" to the revolutionary cause. He declared that it was the spontaneous resurgence of the Revolution that led him to follow Aguinaldo, "a humble being, almost unknown". Only a movement guided by "a special divine dispensation", he wrote Governor Augustin, could enable Aguinaldo to obtain the adherence of rebel militias in ten provinces in less than 20 days after his return and to surround the city of Manila. In a letter dated 9 June 1898, he particularly urged the governor to surrender to Aguinaldo immediately, because "the North American squadron is at our disposal whenever we desire to use it".[16]

Two months later, it became clear to Buencamino and the other *ilustrados* in Luzon that the Philippine Revolution did not have the support of the United States. Although the Filipino rebels had virtually surrounded Manila, the Americans outmanoeuvred Aguinaldo by negotiating a secret agreement with the Spaniards whereby the latter agreed to surrender to the Americans if the Filipinos were excluded from the forces of occupation. On 13 August 1898, after a mock battle, the Americans entered Manila. Aguinaldo's exclusion showed the cosmopolitan elite that the United States was a more important factor to reckon with. Within a short period of time, they had to rethink their position. They had shown themselves quite prepared to accept an autonomous status for the Philippines under continued Spanish control; they would also welcome the same arrangement under the United States.

But the *ilustrados* also recognized the uncertainty of the political situation. Despite the patently disadvantageous position of Aguinaldo in Manila, he had the support of the entire Tagalog region. And during the last half of 1898, there was still the possibility that Aguinaldo might succeed in dislodging the Americans from the city. Provincial and municipal officials from Central Luzon and the Ilocos provinces continued to send protestations of support for Aguinaldo. As yet, there was no intimation whatsoever that the Americans planned to push northward beyond Manila. Thus, while the cosmopolitan elite[17] were doubtful that the Revolution would succeed, they extended their support to Aguinaldo. The latter, acutely aware of the lack of talents among the active insurgent leaders, invited the wealthy and educated Filipinos to serve in his government.[18]

Establishment of Local Government

As the Spaniards were routed, taken prisoner, or forced to flee to the uncertain peace of Manila, Aguinaldo called for the reorganization of Philippine provincial and municipal governments as fast as town and countryside were seized from the enemy. His decree of 18 June 1898 provided the basis for such a plan. In so far as Aguinaldo and Apolinario Mabini, his political adviser, were concerned, political reorganization was the ultimate outcome of the victory of the Filipinos over their colonial masters and the logical step after the declaration of independence. The passage of the decree, however, was also prompted by important tactical considerations. With the administrative structure of the country completely in the hands of the Filipinos, successful reorganization would prove to the outside world the Filipinos' capacity to govern themselves. "The foreign powers shall change their opinion of us," Mabini asserted. "They cannot but give way to what they see."[19] The program of political reorganization would also give Aguinaldo a means by which revolutionary plans and goals could be pursued. The holding of elections and the consequent broadening of the government would be a validation of the Revolution and a certain move toward legitimizing the Aguinaldo leadership. Indeed, with the American presence in Manila, it was necessary to consolidate Filipino control outside the city and widen the foundations of the revolutionary government.

In accordance with the provisions of the decree, most of the towns of Cavite, Bataan, Batangas and Pampanga held their elections in June and July; Manila, Tayabas, Pangasinan and Ambos Ilocos in August; Abra, Ambos Camarines and Nueva Ecija in September; Nueva Vizcaya and La Union in October; Isabela, Catanduanes, Albay and Sorsogon in December.[20] The elections, in effect, followed the liberation of the provinces.

Political reorganization was, however, strongly affected by the actions of local and provincial elites that were perhaps of greater significance than General Aguinaldo's various directives ordering immediate elections. To illustrate this point, we might compare the nature of political reorganization in Manila, the Bikol region and the Western Visayas.

In Manila the government experienced serious difficulties in holding municipal elections owing to its occupation by the Americans. There was a feeling of hesitation and uncertainty among the revolutionary leaders as to whether it would be wise to bring about political reorganization in the city and its suburbs. At the same time, however, there existed a sense of urgency that elections be held there — to shift the balance of power against the Americans. Despite this quandary, Aguinaldo nevertheless appointed Ambrosio Flores governor of the province of Manila, with instructions to hold elections as expeditiously as possible. Mabini, however, questioned the validity and effectiveness of elections in the area, particularly in the suburbs closest to the Walled City,[21] fearing that conflict (*disgusto*) with the Americans would ensue if the insurgents made their direct influence and authority visible. Following Mabini's counsel, Aguinaldo ordered Flores to suspend the elections and to order those who had been elected to refrain from exercising their office until the "problem" with the Americans had been resolved. Instead, propaganda and recruiting committees which had been operating in the city and environs were ordered to maintain some kind of control over the American-occupied towns, as well as to function as underground municipal assemblies.[22]

Nevertheless, the elections in Manila seem to have taken place. However, there is no indication from the Philippine Insurgent Records that elections were held in the towns where the Americans were in sole command.[23] By the end of September 1898, Flores had carried out Aguinaldo's directives; provincial officials had been chosen and the towns had elected their presidents.[24] Many of the chosen town presidents had been municipal captains under Spain and continued to be accepted and respected by their constituencies.[25]

In an undated "Notes on the Provincial Government of Manila", Flores observed that the Americans failed to perceive the political advantage that they might obtain by recognizing the newly established presidents, who were "disposed to serve under their direction" and would have been "the most efficient and valuable assistance to the American administration; for as they know the language, the locality and the inhabitants, none could be better than they in maintaining order". Instead, the Americans "have pursued them unceasingly", preventing them from freely exercising their office and investing the problems of government in individuals who "do not even know the laws they propose to apply". Flores added that peace could have been restored in Manila if the insurgent officials and the Americans co-operated with one another. "Diplomatic and governmental relations and all public services would have been benefited, and friction of any kind become impossible had the American government recognized the municipal governments instituted by the Revolutionary government."26

It is doubtful whether these notes were made available to either Aguinaldo or Mabini. If they had been, neither would have approved Flores' motives for political reorganization once amicable relations between American authorities and the Aguinaldo camp deteriorated after the U.S. Army captured Manila. At any rate, by mid-August 1898, Aguinaldo indicated his preference for underground governments in Manila by approving an admittedly irregular election in the suburb of Tondo by eight *principales* who chose among themselves the officials of the populous town. The group — which included the parish priest, the incumbent president and three ex-presidents — presented their "letter of adherence" to Aguinaldo in Bacoor, Cavite, deploring the "anomalous situation" in which they "could not live under the constituted authority of the legitimate government of the country". They asked what they might do "to avoid disorder, the anarchy arising from the lack of legitimate authority and to maintain the necessary faith in and harmony with the foreign domination".27 Aguinaldo conceded that, contrary to the electoral law, the government for Tondo would have to be organized clandestinely, and "in the most opportune manner" possible.28 Accordingly, under the supervision of Leandro Ibarra, the Secretary of the Interior, four Tondo *principales* chose among themselves the town president and councillors (or delegates) by conveniently putting four office titles into a hat. Upon drawing them out, they constituted themselves as the municipal government of Tondo.29 Some *principales,* however, objected to the irregularity of Tondo's political reorganization and at least three strong protests were sent to Aguinaldo between 20 August and 14 November 1898 before the President finally called for a second election, this time in faithful accordance with the provisions of the June 18 decree.30

In contrast, political reorganization in the Bikol provinces was unusually placid.31 The Revolution did not spread to the region during 1896-1897 nor was there any organized and widespread guerilla resistance during Aguinaldo's exile. Conditions there remained uneventful even after Aguinaldo's return and the resurgence of the struggle against Spain in Luzon. While leading citizens of Albay, Ambos Camarines and Sorsogon were aware that independence had been declared on 12 June and that the call to arms had been sent from Cavite to all parts of the country, they did not take any action either favouring or opposing the endeavours of their counterparts in the Tagalog region. Only when news reached Legaspi, Albay in late August that the Spaniards in Manila had been routed by the Americans and that General Vicente Lukban and his troops were advancing toward the Bikol peninsula,[32] did the Spanish community in Albay — civil officials, priests, businessmen, long time residents — feel impelled to abandon their posts and residences and head for Manila.

The Spanish officials handed over the administration of Albay to a Committee of Provisional Government, a select body constituted by prominent Albayanos. Elias Ataviado, who wrote our main source material for the events in the Bikol region in 1898-1899, pointed out that the transfer of Albay from its colonial position to that of a province of a sovereign nation was accomplished "without the shedding of blood".[33] On 22 September, the day after the Spaniards left Legaspi, the committee convoked an assembly of the most prominent *principales* of the capital as well as the towns of Legaspi and Daraga, and elected provincial and municipal officials of the province. In Catanduanes and Sorsogon, the Spanish authorities transferred the command of their jurisdiction to Bikolano leaders. The latter was entrusted to the parish priest of the capital. In Ambos Camarines, on the other hand, the Bikolanos seized control of the towns and imprisoned many Spaniards. Thus, by the time General Lukban reached Camarines early in September 1898 and General Vito Belarmino was placed in command of Albay in late October, the *principales* of these provinces had almost finished laying the basis for the reorganization of the provincial and municipal structures that would deal with the political situation in Manila and Malolos.[34]

News of the establishment of a revolutionary government in Luzon also galvanized the elites of Western Visayas into action. By July 1898, a plot against the Spaniards by the principal citizens of Iloilo was already underway. "Conspirators" headed by Roque Lopez and Pablo Araneta organized the Iloilo *principales* — some of whom, like Aguinaldo's lieutenants, had volunteered or had been recruited into the Spanish militia — against the forces of General Diego de los Rios, who were at this time bracing themselves against an imminent American attack. By mid-August, revolutionary committees were already established in the key towns of Iloilo. Hostilities erupted in November, with the insurgents succeeding in isolating the Spanish forces in the towns of Molo, Jaro and Iloilo. The victorious "conspirators" established a provisional revolutionary government on 17 November with Roque Lopez and Vicente Franco as president and vice-president respectively. In contrast with the mood of the takeover of the towns of Luzon, anti-Spanish feeling was not evident. The Spanish troops were allowed to occupy the "neutral" town of La Paz as "guests" of the insurgents. The capitulation of the principal town of Iloilo was effected later in December when the Spanish troops under de los Rios surrendered to the insurgents.[35]

The Negros elite followed the same pattern of revolutionary organization. There, the wealthy *hacenderos* established their own armies, usually drawing up the militia from peasants labouring in their estates. Lopez encouraged the Negrenses to co-ordinate their efforts with their counterparts in Iloilo, particularly because

Iloilo was dependent upon Negros for rice and other staples. Thus, almost simultaneously with the upsurge of insurgent activity in Iloilo, the Negros leaders effected the capitulation of the Spaniards in the island. On 6 November, the Spanish governor in Bacolod, who hoped in vain for reinforcements from Iloilo, was forced to accede to the terms of capitulation that the *ilustrados* of Negros Occidental drew up.[36] This was followed by the establishment of a provisional government under Aniceto Lacson and organization of municipal assemblies, patterned after the model laid out in Aguinaldo's June 18 decree. In Negros Oriental, on the other hand, de la Viña and other *principales* of the province led the assault upon the Spanish authorities. The task was an easy one, for the governor and his men in Dumaguete had already evacuated to Cebu when the insurgents reached the provincial capital. The remaining Spaniards capitulated without resistance on 24 November.[37]

The elite of Western Visayas, however, did not intend to recognize the supremacy of the Malolos Republic. The officials of the Iloilo provisional revolutionary government changed its name into the Federal State of the Visayas and envisaged the region as an equal member of a federal system to be composed of the three major island groups of the archipelago. Thus, even as the prominent Iloilo leaders pledged their loyalty to the government in Luzon, one immediately senses from their protestations that they merely regarded Aguinaldo as the first among equals.[38] This feeling was further bolstered by the recognition accorded them by the leaders of Cebu who submitted the proceedings of the political reorganization of the province to the government in the Visayas instead of sending them to Aguinaldo.[39]

There was not even this token recognition of Aguinaldo's leadership among the Negros elite. Juan Araneta was appointed by Aguinaldo as the politico-military governor of Negros. While he accepted the office, he refused Aguinaldo's instructions that a provisional government be established in the island. The people of Negros, he declared, had already chosen a cantonal government. Araneta was merely expressing the view of the Negros elite that the province should have its own government and its own constitution under a Federal Republic where Malolos could at best exercise nominal control.[40] Araneta's refusal to form a government oriented to Malolos was not the only rebuff to Aguinaldo. The Negrenses also failed to send any delegates to the Malolos Congress when it convened in September 1898. Aguinaldo had to appoint some of his trusted aides to represent both Negros Occidental and Negros Oriental in the legislature to present a picture of solidarity to the outside world.[41]

That the *ilustrados* of Iloilo and Negros were only paying lip service to the revolutionary government in Luzon became manifest when the Americans arrived in Iloilo on 28 December.[42] It did not take long for the Iloilo *ilustrados* there to relay to General Marcus Miller (who commanded the expedition to Iloilo) their feeling that the Visayas could not survive under an independent Philippine Republic and that it would be, in fact, better off under the protection of the United States. Their economic interests dictated this position: they feared that failure to co-operate with the Americans might have disastrous effects on the economic well-being of Iloilo. They were also thinking of the material benefits that might be gained from collaborating with the new conquerors. The War Commissioner of the Federal Council expressed these thoughts in his letter to Aguinaldo:

> The economic and agricultural problem, which is very bad in this province is greatly worrying us; owing to the most scanty crops of palay and sugar cane which are expected . . .
> If the Americans would undertake railway, mining and industrial enterprises here, there would be plenty of cattle and the labourer would have a place to earn the bread for their children, with the advantage to the managers of having sufficient labour.
> The attitude of this Government [i.e., of the Visayas in Iloilo], and therefore of those it represents, which has had to be assumed towards the Americans, has been and is a great source of worry to both, for although the instructions which you sent us here are to repel them, the respect for the decision of the Congress of Paris and the critical economic and military situation of this region makes us waver in our decisions.[43]

The American attack on Iloilo on 11 February and the resistance of the insurgents under General Martin Delgado, who adopted a scorched-earth policy as they retreated from enemy advance, inflicted grave damage on the city. The Iloilo elite promptly opened negotiations with Miller. Through Pablo Araneta, they attempted to persuade the insurgents still entrenched in Iloilo to vacate their positions since they were no longer needed. In retaliation, General Delgado threatened with death those Ilongo collaborators who would take the oath of allegiance to the United States.[44] But this was a desperate gesture because from late February 1899 the insurgents of Iloilo waged a hit-and-run resistance against the Americans while the provincial elite supported the American campaign against it.

Afraid that Negros might suffer from the same destruction, the government in Bacolod raised the American flag on 12 February. A commission was hastily organized — composed of four prominent *hacenderos* led by Juan Araneta — for the purpose of negotiating with General Miller in Iloilo.[45] The latter warmly welcomed them, advised that they confer with General Otis in Manila and provided them with free transport. In Manila, the commission requested troops to protect them from irregular Tagalog forces who, they said, had begun to foment rebellion in the island because the leading citizens welcomed American control. It assured Otis that they would accept American sovereignty if the United States would allow the continuation of the Negros cantonal government. Otis granted this petition but insisted that American occupation was necessary because this would demonstrate the recognition of American sovereignty by the people of Negros — a condition that the commission accepted. While the Negrenses were allowed to frame a constitution for their government, this was not taken too seriously by either side. For Otis later appointed a military governor for the entire island, and the Negros elite accepted the arrangement, happy that they would be spared the injurious effects of the Revolution that even then had virtually ravaged the whole of Luzon.[46]

With the reorganization of the provincial governments, notwithstanding the early collaboration of the Iloilo and Negros elites with the Americans, Filipino officials gave every indication that they had reached full political stature, free from the restrictions imposed by the colonial regime and that practically omnipresent censor of local administration, the Spanish friar. Consequently, the provisions of the June 18 degree, which provided the impetus for change, and the consequent transition from colonial to revolutionary government are not without interest. The decree stipulated that only citizens of 20 years of age or above who were "friendly" to Philippine independence and were distinguished for their "high character, social position and honourable conduct, both in the centre of the community and the suburb", were qualified to vote. These criteria would have excluded all but the so-called *ilustrado* or *principalia* class, an exceedingly small minority in each town, which had dominated the economic and political structures during the Spanish regime.[47] These men were to choose among themselves the *jefe local* or president of the town and three councillors: the councillor of police and internal order, the councillor of justice and civil registry, and the councillor of taxes and property. The *principalia* was also required to choose the *cabeza* or headman for each barrio in the municipality. The president, three councillors and the headmen constituted the town's *junta magna* or popular council. The presidents of the towns, after consultations with their respective assemblies, were to elect by a majority of votes the governor of the province and three councillors, with duties and responsibilities similar to those of municipal officials. The town presidents and the elected provincial officials in turn were to elect from among the *principalia* of the province their representatives to the Congress in Malolos.[48]

The collection of taxes and rents and the maintenance of peace and order remained the most important responsibilities of the municipal president. The councillor of justice and civil registry was expected to help him in the formation of courts, keeping the various registers and holding the census, while the responsibility of the councillor of taxes and property was the collection of all taxes and the administration of public funds.[49] Reorganization followed the centralized pattern of administration of the Spanish regime. Consequently, the provincial governor and councillors and, on the national level, the delegates to the Malolos Congress were vested, in a much more complex manner, with the same duties and responsibilities as their municipal counterparts.

Challenges to Elite Dominance

The structure and function of the provincial and municipal governments of Aguinaldo's reorganization plan was patterned after the colonial reforms of 1893,[50] which contained virtually all the provisions discussed above. The June 18 decree, however, provided for the appointment of a military chief for each province. Aware of the possibility that the military in wartime conditions might gain ascendancy and perhaps be more inclined to oppose civilian supremacy in the government, Aguinaldo specified that the military chiefs were not empowered to intervene in the government and administration of the province and could, in fact, obtain assistance for the defence of their areas only through the chiefs of the province and the municipalities.[51] This was a justified fear, for as we shall point out later, the rivalry between the civilian and military elements in the government was a divisive factor in the war against the United States.

Indeed, some of the most contentious elections in 1898 arose from the conflict between the military commanders and the civilian election commissioners. The conflict arose from differences in interpreting what was in the first place a vague and confusing article in the June 18 decree. This was Article 9, which stipulated that the government would name for each province a commissioner specially vested with the power to establish revolutionary governments. It further added, however, that the military chiefs who wrested the towns from the Spaniards were election commissioners by virtue of their office.[52] The military commanders rightly interpreted this as implying that as soon as the Spaniards were routed, they could begin the political reorganization of the liberated areas. In many towns, this process took place without much difficulty, even with the appointment of a civilian election commissioner who, following Aguinaldo's specific instructions that he honour the elections supervised earlier by the military commander, simply took over the unfinished task of reorganization from military hands.

While election proceedings in most areas were characterized by the co-operative supervision of the civil commissioner and the military commander, Aguinaldo's instructions were sometimes disregarded and differences in interpreting the decree used merely as arguments by which a military leader waged a struggle for political ascendancy. The conflict between Manuel Arguelles, election commissioner in Tayabas, and General Eleuterio Marasigan, head of the expeditionary forces, illustrates the difficulties of overlapping functions. Marasigan was chiefly responsible for a campaign of harassment against Spanish outposts in the province. When Aguinaldo appointed Arguelles election commissioner to Tayabas on 29 June 1898,[53] Marasigan had already begun the political reorganization of the province. Arguelles therefore refrained from reversing Marasigan's authority lest the people be "scandalized".[54]

The debate might have accelerated into a real struggle for power in Tayabas if Marasigan had stood his ground.[55] In his last letter to Arguelles, he remarked rather petulantly that they were wasting their time debating an unimportant issue; his mission in Tayabas was not to seek high political office but to save his countrymen from the enemy and fight for independence.[56] On 26 July, Aguinaldo resolved their differences in favour of Arguelles who was provisionally vested with the powers of the civil governor until all the towns in Tayabas had held their elections.[57]

The preoccupation with specificity of duties and fear of overlapping responsibilities also characterized the relationship between the military commander and election commissioner in Laguna. General Paciano Rizal, military commander of the province and brother of the martyred hero, apparently gave little help to the civil commissioner sent by the President. Rebuked by Aguinaldo for his non-cooperation, Rizal replied that he deliberately avoided any participation in the process of political reorganization so that he might not be accused of meddling in civil affairs.[58]

Fortunately for Aguinaldo, these differences in the interpretation of the law did not escalate into full-blown conflict that would have prevented the establishment of provincial governments. Despite these antagonisms, the election commissioner remained one of the most important elements in the process of reorganization, for without him, no election could take place. Taylor claimed that the election commissioners dictated the direction and structure of the elections, so much so that reorganization was "a mere form", lacking the spontaneity of the democratic process.[59] Yet a careful reading of many election proceedings shows that, contrary to his prejudiced view, prominent citizens managed reorganization on their own terms while complying with the provisions of the presidential decree and with little opposition from the commissioners.

The commissioners, members of the political elite themselves, would have acknowledged the validity of the existing power structure in town and countryside at the demise of the colonial regime. In the first place, most of the election commissioners were highly respected, prominent citizens in the provinces to which they had been assigned.[60] Secondly, because hundreds of towns had to be "reorganized", the commissioners were constrained to appoint sub-delegates or deputy commissioners to expedite the elections. Such deputies were equally prominent and influential individuals and were thus likely to be respected and obeyed by the *principales*.

Indeed, one may very well agree with Larkin's view that because of the elite's exclusive control of the electoral process, Aguinaldo's conservative policy of political reorganization "merely perpetuated *cacique* society and government".[61] This was hardly surprising. Firstly, Aguinaldo was a member of the municipal aristocracy, and although less educated and less propertied than the other luminaries of the second phase of the Revolution, doubtless shared the same views and goals peculiar to the *principalia* of the time, particularly that of the Tagalog region — specifically, the transfer of political power into their hands and the elimination of priestly control on the government. Conservatism was also good political and military strategy. Recognizing the "dearth of talents" in the top echelon of the government, Aguinaldo appointed wealthy and highly educated Filipinos who were at one time indifferent and sometimes strongly opposed to the Revolution. Believing that the *ilustrados'* inclusion in the government would bring not only expertise but also prestige, Aguinaldo appointed to his Cabinet prominent Filipinos like Pedro Paterno, Felipe Buencamino and Gregorio Araneta, despite complaints from friends and rebel leaders who did not possess the wealth, education and experience that Aguinaldo considered necessary for running the affairs of the nation.[62]

On 7 June 1898, before the passage of the electoral decree, Aguinaldo advised General Tomas Mascardo to leave local chiefs in Tarlac in their former offices lest their removal cause widespread disturbances in the province.[63] Presumably, similar commands to insurgent leaders in other provinces were also issued. This order suggests that Aguinaldo considered the support of the municipal bureaucracy extremely necessary for the success of his government. To have immediately implemented a policy which required absolute adherence and loyalty from the incumbent officials — there is no evidence that he entertained such a notion — would have imperilled his plans for a successful political reorganization. Aguinaldo must have realized the potentially dangerous and vexing issue of removing men of power and influence, particularly because the Tagalog expeditionary troops sent to the non-Tagalog regions did not have any reservoir of educated men who could take over the civil administration of these areas. The leaders of the Cavite troops sent to Cagayan, for example, conceded that they found it difficult to take over the civil government, owing to a severe lack of *ilustrados* among their soldiers.[64]

Yet, despite the repeated assertions that only Filipinos of position, educational attainment and honour were elected to office,[65] this was not always the case. In some towns, "uneducated" and "poor" citizens were voted into office by an electorate lacking in the qualifications of the old *principalia.* The prominent citizens did not take part in the elections or were allegedly defrauded of their rights by the "vulgar mob". For instance, the *principalia* of Solano, Nueva Ecija and Urdaneta, Pangasinan opposed the confirmation of popularly elected "uneducated and ignorant persons" who, in their minds, were "totally incapable" of governing, and demanded from Malolos a nullification of the elections.[66]

Such elections raise important questions. What was the status of the power structure in the municipality before the elections took place; what were the attitudes of the general populace toward the Revolution and those of the *principalia;* and what was the masses' actual participation in the Revolution? What factors were responsible for these deviations from traditional electoral practices? To what extent might these unusual elections be interpreted as mass opposition to the traditional political elite, who were to be further entrenched in power by fiat of the revolutionary government? The massive files of the Philippine Insurgent Records (PIR) yield their treasures so very slowly and the answers to these questions may require an examination of their entirety. In the case of Solano, it should be pointed out that the protested election was the second one to be held under insurgent auspices. Early in April 1899, the town had been the centre of much unrest, owing to the refusal of the citizens to pay their taxes and their demonstrations against the continued perpetuation by their elected officials of the onerous ways of the colonial government. Along with the demand for the abolition of taxes, particularly of the certificate of citizenship which replaced the *cedula personal,* might have been a desire, unexpressed in the reports, for a change in the leadership of the town.[67] The very men who had been removed from office by the election of the non-*ilustrados* were the ones who protested the "illegal" election. Very likely, the second election reflected more clearly the will of the people. Aguinaldo and his commissioners, however, tended to take the side of the *principalia,* so much so that such elections were regularly voided and others called to install more "qualified" persons.

Survival of Local Elites

A notable result of the requirement allowing only individuals who possessed *principalia* status to acquire public office was that Aguinaldo and his commissioners many times approved the election of officials who were obviously Spanish sympathizers. To be sure, they could not have been wholly responsible in this regard. Since the *principales* of the towns chose their officials from their own ranks, it was inevitable that any Filipino who possessed the necessary qualifications and was highly regarded by the local elite but whose sentiments favoured the fallen government might be elected to office. Moreover, it was quite difficult for the election commissioners to determine who among the local elite had worked for or against the Revolution, particularly in towns where, after clashes with the Spaniards, the *principales* were the very first citizens to have been approached by the commissioners or the very first group to welcome the insurgent troops into their towns. No small measure of pragmatism — some contemporary works on the Revolution would brand it opportunism[68] — on the part of the *principalia* was involved in their decision to embrace the revolutionary cause. Needless to say, if such a switch did not entail honest service to the revolutionary government, the latter was shortchanged immeasurably, as Daniel Tirona, commanding officer of the Tagalog expeditionary troops in Cagayan, unhappily discovered.

The appointment of native Cagayanos instead of Tagalogs to positions in the provincial government of Cagayan, wrote Tirona to Aguinaldo, would be "good politics" and therefore advantageous to the Republic.[69] He had no difficulty in finding well-qualified Cagayanos, but he later admitted that he was "deceived" by the patriotic stance of the wealthy *principales* of Cagayan, particularly by Vicente Nepomuceno, who was elected provincial president with his support.[70] These *principales,* the very first Cagayanos to welcome the Tagalog troops, were patriots "only in words", who later refused to commit themselves to the struggle for freedom. Tirona claimed that requests for aid to the Tagalog troops as the latter prepared for the American blockade of the Cagayan coast in mid-1899, as well as for help in collecting war taxes, fell on deaf ears.[71] Only after Nepomuceno had been elected provincial president did Tirona discover that, as Judge of the Court of First Instance, he had taken bribes for releasing revolutionary partisans imprisoned by the Spanish. Though "a pro-friar and a Spanish sympathizer" and "exploiter of the poor", his fellow *principales* voted for him. His "closeness" to Tirona, implied the Cavite official, prevented the disaffected from reporting the above information and airing their grievances to the Malolos government.[72] Tirona was convinced that Nepomuceno would use his office for self-aggrandizement since the first administrative act of the Cagayan president was to assign an annual salary of ₱2,000 to himself, a sum considerably larger than the ₱420 provided by the central government for the province.[73]

Thus, the elitist provisions of the June 18 decree and the practical, strategic need of the Aguinaldo government to rely upon the municipal officials for the continuation of the Revolution led to the preservation of the elite. Though one might see many new faces in places of authority, socially they looked so much like their predecessors during the Spanish regime that no significant social change in the political leadership of the provinces is discernible. The provincial presidents were invariably men of stature and wealth who more often than not rose from the ranks of the municipal elite. Many were educated and continued to maintain sufficient contact with the cosmopolitan elite in Manila — enhanced by the establishment of the Malolos Republic — so as to claim importance and prominence beyond their respective spheres of influence. Most of the presidents elected during 1898 and 1899 in Luzon had at one time or another occupied important positions open to Filipinos in the colonial government.[74]

The municipal officials were similarly situated. A comparison of (1) the list of municipal officials in the *Guías Oficiales* over an eight-year period (1890-1898); (2) the list of municipal presidents prepared by the Malolos Republic; (3) data from numerous *actas de elecciones* (minutes of election proceedings) during 1898-1899; (4) data on municipal officials and "original" and "prominent" families in towns throughout Luzon from the *Historical Data Papers;* and (5) the scattered "loyalty" reports prepared by the United States Army shows that the municipal elite was essentially unaltered, and that local government offices simply rotated within its ranks. This observation is further bolstered by checking the information from these sources with those in the *Reports of the Philippine Commission* during the first five years of the American regime.[75]

The continued control by the elite of the municipal administrative machinery is further reflected in the number of actual voters in the elections of 1898-1899. For instance, Lipa, Batangas, a town with a population of 9,315, held elections in 1898 in which the president was chosen by a mere 25 votes. In the populous town of Bacolor, Pampanga, only 73 qualified voters were present to reorganize the municipal government.[76] In Vigan, Ilocos Sur, only 116 were qualified as electors out of a population of 19,000; 72 out of 6,101 souls in Gamu, Cagayan; 111 out of 6,240 in Cabagan, Isabela; and 73 out of a population of 13,811 in Ilagan, Isabela.[77] Failing to discover any kind of mass participation in the electoral process, Taylor deplored that the people "did not care, at any rate, they were not consulted".[78] Thus, one can agree with Le Roy's view that "the Filipino upper class organized and ran the Philippine Republic while it lasted".[79]

The elitist nature of the Republican government was also reinforced by the continued dominance of families which had controlled local politics during the colonial regime. In explaining this phenomenon, the authors of the local history of some towns in Luzon did not find it strange that, whatever the political situation, a family might "monopolize" positions in the government because these were given to "men of means and resources" and were traditionally transferred among members of the same family.[80] During the Revolution, this political advantage was enhanced by the fact that some individuals who belonged to prominent families joined the *Katipunan* and were involved, often as leaders, in revolutionary activity between 1896 and 1898.[81] In many an *acta de elección* may be encountered a majority of qualified electors with the same surname, a pattern that leads one to suspect that such electors might have been consanguinally related, especially if such names tally with the so-called "first", "original" and "prominent" families listed in the *Historical Data Papers*.[82]

The continued entrenchment of political powerful families in some municipalities, however, produced a negative reaction not only from rival *principales* who protested the system of politics but also from the common folk. A common cause of complaint was the lack of revolutionary fervour among these families and their perpetuation of corruption and abuse of power. Undoubtedly this aspect of municipal politics alienated many from the revolutionary government. For example, Gregorio Evangelista, *capitan municipal* of Kandaba, Pampanga during the early 1890s, was elected town president under insurgent auspices in July 1898 while two nephews were elected councillor of justice and councillor of taxes and rents respectively. A brother-in-law was elected head of the *población* or the central barrio. No elections were held for *cabezas* of the outlying barrios; instead a report on the *cabezas* of Evangelista's preference was merely drafted for submission to Aguinaldo. The election itself was surrounded by much fraud and deception, claimed irate residents in their petition to Aguinaldo. The election commissioner was absent from the meeting and only Evangelista and his brother-in-law, the military commander of the town, supervised the elections. Despite the expectations of the common folk (*los polistas*) that they would be allowed to participate in the elections — nearly 1,000 had assembled in the church for the purpose — their ballots, which the Evangelistas collected at the beginning of the meeting, were simply disregarded.[83]

The complainants were equally distressed by the fact that a man hated by the people (*hindi gusto ng bayan*) should retain power with the consent of the Malolos government. The Evangelistas and their relatives had been ardent sympathizers of the Spaniards; during the "first insurrection" (1896-1897), they fed and supported the *Guardia Civil* and the Spanish soldiers sent into the town to suppress the rebels. Now that the Revolution had succeeded, the Evangelistas would ally with the victors. Evangelista, through his subalterns and not through the *cabezas,* collected all the taxes from the townspeople. These collections, however, were never appropriated for the general welfare of the town but reportedly went to his private coffers. How could a man like him be allowed to continue serving as president of their town? Twice, the Kandaba citizens requested the government to nullify the elections and to hold another electoral meeting. There is no record of any response to their complaint. But a list of municipal presidents drawn up in 1899 still showed Evangelista to be the president of Kandaba.[84]

The Insurgent Records, as far as I have explored them, provide scanty information on the nature of the support for these powerful families and the character of the factions (*partidarios*) responsible for the opposition to familial politics. There is also little evidence that the Republic did anything to correct the evil aspects of regnant familism. Given the problem of dealing with American intervention and the Republic's constant search for support throughout Luzon, the government might not have had any alternatives to recognizing the domination of the politics and administration of many a locality by entrenched and powerful families.

While the municipal elite by and large continued to remain in positions of power and influence they had traditionally held, it should be pointed out that many *principales,* who were elected by their colleagues, did not seem to have been interested in joining the ranks of Republican officialdom. A considerable number of elected officials submitted resignations (*renuncias*) which pleaded "old age" or "ill health".[85] Taylor, struck by the uniformity of the reasons behind the resignations asked rather querulously: "Were there ever so many officials sick at one time?".[86] Indeed, it seemed as though an epidemic had struck many qualified municipal officials. Aguinaldo himself was sceptical about these excuses, and to obtain his approval, medical certificates of unfitness had to be submitted. But most of these resignations had to be accepted because the apathy and disobedience that might ensue would have subverted the government.[87]

These resignations, however, did not create a marked dearth of municipal officials, for as the re-election proceedings attached to the *renuncias* would show, there were other members of the *principalia* who were willing to fill the vacated positions. Of interest here is the observation that coercion was not used to complete political reorganization. But it is equally interesting to note that the number of resignations increased remarkably between the months of January and March 1899, when rumours of the impending war, the widening rift between Aguinaldo and the Americans, and the news of the final outbreak of hostilities on 4 February percolated throughout Luzon.[88] These factors undoubtedly exacerbated uncertainties and fears regarding continued service under the Malolos Republic.

Be that as it may, it can be seen from the foregoing discussion that the provincial and municipal elites enjoyed robust political health. The Revolution was not a challenge against which they had to prove themselves capable of survival; in fact, the Revolution did not question their ascendancy. Aguinaldo needed the elite despite lower class reaction in many towns against its continued predominance. The elite responded with its support — its patriotism and pragmatism perhaps working in remarkable combination. Some of the rebel leaders who continued the resistance against Spain in Aguinaldo's absence were wealthy and educated men. Aguinaldo acknowledged their leadership by continuing their military commissions, which in turn substantiated their authority beyond their respective municipalities and offered a much wider latitude for obtaining and exercising power and influence. The Generals of the Revolution — such as Francisco Macabulos, Casimiro Tinio, Mariano Llanera, José Alejandrino and Simon Tekson — are good examples.[89] On the other hand, personnel files (*hojas de servicio*) scattered throughout the PIR suggest that middle-ranking officials (colonels, lieutenants and captains) also had roots in the *principalia,* though generally of less prominent and affluent status.[90] Many municipal officials founded *Katipunan* chapters in their towns and led their members into skirmishes with the Spaniards. Some military officials were former students in Manila who abandoned their studies when the Revolution broke out. With political reorganization, they seem to have retained, or have preferred to keep, their military appointments even as other members of the local elite would have taken over positions open to them in the municipal government.[91] Thus, it may be said that the Revolution gave the provincial and municipal elites an altered configuration. Constituting a new layer within the elite, municipal bureaucrats-turned-military-officials could, if they so desired, contest the old class from which they were a spin-off.

Civil-Military Conflicts

As noted earlier, with political reorganization the functions of the civil and military officials became inextricably intertwined with each other. In the early months of the revolutionary government, officials of the insurgent army and the reorganized governments functioned more or less as a united force, with the civilian elements more powerful than the military. It was not long before some military officials laid claims to the same prerogatives as those traditionally possessed by the municipal bureaucrats and the relationship between them came to be characterized by friction and conflict. The functions of the military at times overlapped those of the civil officials, while confusion arose from the assertions of military officials that they had the right to undertake the responsibilities of the latter. Jealous of their positions in their respective jurisdictions, civil officials protested this arrogation in their letters to General Aguinaldo and other officials in the central government, and stressed the need for a sharp division between their powers and those of the military.

Aguinaldo's injunction that — with the exception of enemy attacks and other exigencies — military officials should act only with the consent of the civil officials was more honoured in the breach than in the observance. The outbreak of the war with the United States served to widen the cleavage between the military and the civil officials. Aguinaldo decreed on 4 February that in view of the hostilities with the Americans, he was granting the military greater powers than the civil officials throughout Luzon. This order apparently did not sit well with the latter and Malolos felt a rather rancorous reaction from them. Consequently, Aguinaldo declared that the pre-eminence of the civil officials had never been questioned and that their position vis-a-vis the military should be as prescribed by Article 9 of the June 18 decree.[92]

Protests against the military were widespread, affecting most of the provinces of Luzon. In Pangasinan, which was already divided into two zones to accommodate two rival groups of provincial officials, those of the eastern zone charged that the military commander's intervention in civil affairs confused the municipal bureaucracy who did not know whom to recognize and obey as the final authority in the province.[93] The same situation obtained in Ambos Camarines where both provincial and municipal officials accused the provincial military commander of usurping their functions and prerogatives. The latter's declaration of martial law upon the outbreak of the war was deeply resented by the civil authorities, who claimed that the attendant reconcentration of people in the provincial capital and the conscription of able-bodied men to reinforce the militia caused panic and anxiety among the people. Indeed, the declaration of martial law led rapidly to the suspension of commerce and the paralysis of agriculture. The military commander, they charged, actually revived the "bitter times of 1896" when the Spaniards suspended the constitutional rights of the Bikolanos. For a province that was hardly affected by the Revolution in 1896-1897, however, it was understandable that the civil officials should be concerned about the harmful consequences of the declaration of "a state of war" upon their economy.[94]

The reports of many provincial and municipal bureaucrats provide impressive evidence that they considered the military a threat to their paramountcy in politics and the latter's intervention in civil affairs a stumbling block to good government. In Bataan, Zambales, Tayabas and Isabela, the provincial military commanders were reported as having "invaded" the office of provincial officials, leaving the latter virtually powerless and with very few tasks to undertake while remaining fully responsible for whatever abuses the military might have committed.[95] Civil officials in other areas echoed the same complaint. The authority of the civil officials, as much as that of the military, noted one councillor of rents and taxes in Nueva Ecija, emanated from a legitimate government, not from one made farcical by military intervention.[96] Even the Spaniards, declared yet another official, first sought the town official's permission before they instituted domiciliary searches or arrested any constituent.[97]

In many towns the military authorities vied with the local officials in the collection of taxes, the conscription of personal labour (*polo*) and other traditional responsibilities of the civilian authorities. It should be pointed out, however, that the collection of the same tax by both civil and military collectors was not unusual. The military was said to have even assumed routine duties, such as the dissemination of orders and circulars from the central government in Malolos, much to the discomfiture of municipal officials, who perhaps saw themselves disadvantaged by the consequent reduction of their contact with the populace.

The military had grown "independent" of the civil government, said an anonymous writer sometime in February 1899, and had "arrogated to themselves the powers of the colonial civil guard and the municipal police".[98] Several officials addressed themselves to this troubling aspect of rising militarism. The president of Bataan feared that the military authorities in his province were intent on organizing a faction or an independent military organization which could grow beyond his control. Thus, even as the towns lay defenceless against roving *tulisan* bands, the military commander of the province refused to give the militia's surplus arms to the municipal police forces; instead these were awarded to favourites (who were neither soldiers nor policemen) who constantly menaced the peace and order of the towns by their rowdy behaviour. On the other hand, the president of the town of Antipolo claimed that the province of Morong (now Rizal), was plagued by the abuses of the insurgent militia under General Pio del Pilar. The soldiers were more interested in pillaging the countryside and in gambling (which despite Aguinaldo's prohibition of the vice was openly encouraged by del Pilar) than in preparing for the conflict with the Americans. So disorganized were del Pilar's troops that when the Americans attacked the town of Cainta in early April 1899, they retreated in complete disarray. The townspeople, indignant at this display of cowardice and lack of discipline, resolved to disarm the soldiers and fight the Americans themselves.[99]

Manuel Arguelles, one of Aguinaldo's advisers, warned the latter that the rise of militarism did not augur well for the health of the Republic, which needed "a robust civil administration" to survive.[100] A diametrically opposite view came from Daniel Tirona, military commander of the Cagayan Valley, who said that the military was needed to provide a check on a civil bureaucracy endowed with the "spirit of absolutism" inherited from Spain. He wrote the president that all of northern Luzon — Ilocos, Cagayan, the non-Christian mountain districts, La Union, Tarlac and Pangasinan — should be placed under the stewardship of one single general, who could restore order and put a stop to the factionalism between the military and the civil officials.[101]

The central government, to be sure, was deeply troubled by the civil–military conflict but appeared unable to solve the problem. The Secretary of War issued a circular warning to his subordinates that it would be "a fatal error to substitute Spanish militarism with Filipino militarism". He reiterated Aguinaldo's injunction of 1 March 1899 that the army's function was limited to the active support of the civil authorities. As such, military officials did not have any jurisdictional, disciplinary or even tax powers over the people. With the outbreak of the war with the United States, their only duty was to fight the "North American invaders". He warned that any military official who infringed on the prerogatives of the civilian bureaucracy would be punished severely.[102] On the other hand, Mabini, who favoured the institution of a military dictatorship when the war began, was defeated by the Congress — naturally partisan to the civil officials — which refused to pass his proposal that the military commander be made the sole authority in each province. Mabini did not insist on the passage of his decree for two reasons: Aguinaldo did not wish to favour any party in the conflict while he (Mabini) was aware of the unceasing complaints against the military throughout Luzon. Mabini also felt that it might be too difficult to remove an erring and abusive official from his command.[103] The President must have considered the problem an insurmountable dilemma for there is little in the Aguinaldo correspondence that can tell us how he might have solved the problem. Indeed, to have simply solved the problem in favour of either group would have escalated the conflict. That knowledge must have determined his indecision.

Alienation of the Masses

One fact, however, is indisputable: aside from the awesome spectre of divisiveness, which threatened to rend the fabric of legitimacy that the Malolos Republic had carefully woven around itself, the conflict had a profoundly disturbing impact on the populace. The consequent proliferation of officials doing the same work, whatever their garb, was to create, as Le Roy aptly puts it, "more bosses" for the masses.[104] Both the civil and military authorities made demands for personal services, in violation of Aguinaldo's decree that abolished the *polo y servicios*.[105] The extortionate levy of old and new taxes, and the embezzlement of public funds by government officials exacerbated popular discontent.[106] Mabini rightly recognized that this growing sentiment demanded as much attention as the struggle for power among the local leaders for:

> if the people are with us, though we can not conquer today, we may entertain the hope that we shall shout victory tomorrow; if not, we are to be defeated. Great is, indeed, our danger in fighting against the Americans, but still greater is the peril which we have at home, the . . . abuses which may give rise to a new revolution.[107]

From the voluminous correspondence between citizens and their leaders and among government officials themselves, two letters reflecting the conditions obtaining in Pangasinan seem representative of similar but less detailed reports from other parts of Luzon. The first, Cecilio Apostol's letter to Aguinaldo,[108] and the second, an anonymous complaint to Mabini, were written almost a year apart. They are quoted here at length to illustrate the magnitude of administrative problems that the Malolos Republic had to wrestle with. Less than a month after Aguinaldo declared independence in June 1898, Apostol saw only confusion and a mad scramble for power among the elite:

> There exist here [in Pangasinan] two Departmental Provinces, one calling itself that of Northern Luzon and of which Don Vicente del Prado is the President, and the other which calls itself that of Northern and Central Luzon, presided over by Don Juliano Paraiso. Besides these two gentlemen, there are two governors in the province, one Civil Political Military, living in Lingayen, named Don Felipe Bartolome, and another living in Real Guerrero, a town of Tayug, named Don Vicente Estrella. And in addition, there are a large number of Administrators, Inspectors, Military Judges, Generals . . . and they cannot be counted. It is a pandemonium which even Christ, who permitted it, cannot make anything out of. Indeed the situation is indefensible. It reminds me of the schism in the middle ages when there were two Popes, both legitimate, neither true. Things as are clear as thick chocolate, as the Spaniards say.
>
> Article 9 [of the June 18 decree] says that the Superior Government will name a commissioner for each province with the special duty of establishing there the [political] organization set forth in the decree. Very well so far: which of the so-called Presidents of Northern or of Northern and Central Luzon is the commissioner appointed by that Government to establish the new organization in that Province? Are military commanders named by you for Pangasinan? I would be very much surprised if either of them could show their credentials.
>
> But poor, ignorant creatures, in so far as the republican form of government is concerned, in order to avoid worse evils, took them at their word, obeyed them like automatons, hypnotized by the title of "Insurgents" which they applied to themselves. But when I had the opportunity to read the said decree, doubts were forced upon me, I began to suspect — may God and they pardon me — that they were trying to impose upon us, so slyly, an affair shielded by the

motto "loyal service to the mother country" when in fact they came to these towns "for business".[109]

Ten months later, an irate unidentified resident of Pangasinan described virtually the same political scenario to Mabini:

> Since the decree of the national loan was issued, many of the residents have asked themselves in wonder, where have the sums collected gone to?... What are those sums? Where are those Mondragon guns that fire 60 shots a minute? Was there ever so great a fraud! If they do not properly account for how these sums have been employed the province will consider them [the provincial and municipal officials] thieves.
>
> [The military commanders], taking advantage of the present situation, force all males, without distinction of [social class], to drill with arms, and order them to do guard duty each day...
>
> The local chiefs of the province... are despotic kings in their respective pueblos, with the exception of one who is the local chief of Urbiztondo... What is the result of the abuses committed by the local chiefs? Disapprobation, ill humour and a great deal of regret for having worked for independence because there were certain orders and customs which it was intended to abolish, and instead, they continue practising them, and that which previously was to be despised in the Spaniards, is respected now among the local chiefs. Furthermore, as the people know that the provincial chief takes no notice of the complaints against the local chiefs, the residents thereof endure, suffer and say, "A thousand times better the Spanish government than this".
>
> There are persons who have even said: "I was very glad and content when the separation from the Spanish Dominion was obtained, but now we have to swallow very bitter pills which the Spaniards never forced us to take."[110]

The central government could not be expected to remain indifferent to these conflicts, but in Malolos the deliberations of the Congress over the constitutional program for the country and the even more vital business of contending with the Americans seemed to outweigh all other problems. The government, to be sure, followed a paternalistic orientation, a fact attested to by the steady stream of correspondence to Malolos on practically all aspects of life that demanded Aguinaldo's attention. Aguinaldo, for his part, responded with numerous exhortations on good government. But while he stood at the helm of the Republic, he lacked the means to impose centralized control and seemed powerless to curb the excesses of government officials in towns distant from the political centre. Indeed, it is difficult to see what the central government could have done to check official abuse in the provinces when it depended upon the very men responsible for it. This fact was not easily lost on some discerning Filipinos. "If your magic power reaches them, your will and orders do not,"[111] an anonymous citizen from Ilocos wrote Aguinaldo — a remark that calls to mind the frustration expressed by an unidentified citizen with regard to official apathy toward graft and corruption in the 1850s: "The governor-general is in Manila (far away); the king is in Spain (farther still); and God is in heaven (farthest of all)."[112]

Aguinaldo himself felt frustrated at his inability to curb widespread misgovernment. In December 1898, less than eight months after he assumed the leadership of the Revolution, he offered to resign the presidency and called for his replacement by a more qualified man. In a poignant letter to the Filipino people, he acknowledged his "incompetence" to tackle the problems that plagued the fledgling Republic and the personal and deep pain caused by civil and military officials who "put their own welfare before the common good" and "show themselves brave to excess with the townspeople".[113] However, his letter of resignation, which was to have been distributed in pamphlet form, was suppressed by his Cabinet, particularly by his advisers, Mabini and Buencamino. In Buencamino's view, Aguinaldo's resignation would only worsen the political situation, "ruin the whole nation before the eyes of the foreigners" and "cause the death of our Revolution".[114]

Still, it appears that the government attempted to provide a solution to these problems. The Secretary of the Interior instructed provincial officials and designated special investigators to make inspection trips to towns under their jurisdiction with the express purpose of reporting to the government cases of misgovernment and recommending the proper course of reform.[115] It would not appear, however, that many such inspection trips were made, especially to the towns that needed them most. Moreover, the punishment for abuse of power, even for the most serious case of maladministration, was simple removal from office. As the provincial president of Nueva Vizcaya wryly observed, removal from office was not a punishment at all, but a virtual exoneration of one's guilt.[116]

In the absence of any effective checks by the central government, rampant abuse of power characterized local administration in many parts of Luzon. Yet a government newspaper in Barasoain, Bulacan, *Ang Kaibigan ng Bayan* (The Friend of the People) sought to attribute the state of political affairs to the people's inexperience in governing themselves:

> We are constructing our freedom on the ruins of the Spanish government. . . But since we began only yesterday, we have not yet prepared all that is necessary to build the temple of freedom. Why should we wonder and detest the events that daily take place in our country? Why should we look for perfection when this state is difficult to attain within a short period of time?[117]

The author of this remark, however, seems to have missed the fact that most of the civil officials responsible for the disaffection in the provinces had served in the colonial government. The ground rules established by Aguinaldo for political reorganization, it may be reiterated here, carefully preserved the colonial elite, to the exclusion of even a few non-elite elements who might have been elected to office by the citizenry — not by the *principalia* — on the basis of their active support of the Revolution. Only the Spanish colonial master had been done away with; on the provincial and municipal levels, the same actors performed the same unchanging roles. The consequent incongruities of political reorganization during the Revolution, e.g., the firm entrenchment of municipal officials who had openly supported or sympathized with the Spaniards and the use of unbridled authority by many a local official, led to widespread discontent and frustration. The perpetuation of the same aspects of colonial rule served to weaken the reformist and integrative goals of the Revolution, alienated many citizens from the Republican government and contributed markedly to the process by which the peasants of Luzon found their voice and resisted, in their limited way, the seemingly concerted attempts of the political elite to thwart their expectations of the rewards of the Revolution. As the political elite were quick to claim the leadership of the Revolution, so too did members of the peasant masses demand that they also should partake in the rewards of the Revolution through the implementation of good government and the abolition of taxes and forced labour. When these were not forthcoming or were consistently blocked by provincial and municipal elites, many peasants joined tax riots, demonstrations and messianic movements. If the Filipino elite were the ultimate victors of the Revolution, then the masses in town and countryside were the unwitting victims. One senses in the hundreds of complaints about official abuse in the Insurgent Records that insult had been added to injury. During the second phase of the Revolution, the peasant masses knew only too well that the Spanish civil official or friar was no longer on the scene to be blamed as the final architect of the continuing corruption in government and society.

NOTES

For the sake of brevity, these abbreviations have been used for documents from the Philippine Insurgent Records (PIR), U.S. National Archives and Records Service (NARS): Selected Documents (SD); Old Series of Documents (OS Pa.); New Series of Documents (NS Pa.); and Unnumbered Unidentified Packages (Unno. Pa.).

1 Meaning the "enlightened ones" or those members of the intelligentsia who were not only educated but also possessed some degree of economic preeminence in the colony. The Tagalog term *maginoo* (respectable person, implying noble or aristocratic lineage) was also used in describing the elite. *Principalia* was also a popular term during the 19th century; it broadly refers to the Filipino elite and includes incumbent and former *gobernadorcillos* (municipal governors), *cabezas de barangay* (heads of *barangays* or barrios), *cabezas* who had served for ten years, and the *maestros de niños* (schoolteachers). In a bifurcated society where the *principalia* constituted the elite, the rest of the population was usually referred to as *timawas* or *cailianes* (plain, ordinary citizens). See, Eliodoro Robles, *The Philippines in the Nineteenth Century* (Quezon City: Malaya Books, 1969), 60-63. Unfortunately, very few studies have been made on the various aspects of the social structure, particularly that which concerns the distinction between

Spanish and indigenous perceptions of the elite and the masses. But see, Norman G. Owen's analytical study of the Kabikolan elite, "The *Principalia* in Philippine History: Kabikolan, 1790-1898," *Philippine Studies* 22 (1974), 297-324.

2 David R. Sturtevant, *"Guardia de Honor* — Revitalization Within the Revolution," in, David R. Sturtevant, *Agrarian Unrest in the Philippines* (Athens, Ohio: Southeast Asia Series No. 8, Center for International Studies, Ohio University, 1969), 1.

3 Reports of the civil governors of the Tagalog, Central Luzon and Ilocos Provinces in, "Memorias sobre la situacion politica de las provincias del Archipielago, 1897-1898," Archivo Historico Nacional (Madrid), Seccion de Ultramar, Legajo 5157.

4 The *Kataastaasang Kagalang-galang na Katipunan ng Mga Anak ng Bayan* (Highest and Most Respectable Association of the Sons of the People) or *Katipunan,* for short, was a separatist society founded by Andres Bonifacio in July 1892. It was responsible for the outbreak of the Revolution in the Manila area. For a detailed study of this society and the first phase of the Revolution, see, Teodoro A. Agoncillo, *The Revolt of the Masses: The Story of Andres Bonifacio and the Katipunan* (Quezon City: University of the Philippines Press, 1956).

5 W.E. Retana, "La Insurreccion," *La Politica de España en Filipinas,* 15 May 1898, 188.

6 David R. Sturtevant in his *Popular Uprisings in the Philippines, 1840-1940* (Ithaca, N.Y.: Cornell University Press, 1976) contends that the movement was not an integral part of the Revolution. On the basis of numerous documents on the brotherhood that he did not use, however, I take the opposite view that the *Guardia de Honor* movement was just such a unique type of political organization as the Pangasinan peasants might have been expected to form during the Revolution. The conditions obtaining in the province during the Revolution contributed to a rapid radicalization of the peasantry, leading them to oppose the Aguinaldo government and later the American military authorities who were partisans of the elite. See, Milagros C. Guerrero, "Luzon at War: Contradictions in Philippine Society, 1898-1902" (doctoral dissertation, University of Michigan, 1977), 186-214.

7 Wenceslao E. Retana, "La situacion," *La Politica de España en Filipinas,* 15 April 1898, 146-47.

8 Ruperto Blanco to EA, 4 October 1898, Philippine Insurgent Records (hereafter, PIR), NS Pa. 183½, R.409; Pagpapatotoo ng Bayang Botolan, 4 October 1898, 183.47½, R.409; Teodoro Pansacula, *et.al.,* Report of 15 July 1898, PIR, SD 964.2, R.57; Wenceslao Viniegra to EA, 13 November 1898, PIR, SD 964.3, R.57.

9 Modesto Joaquin to EA, 12 August 1898, PIR, NS Pa., 61.126, R.251. For an understanding of the goals of the *Santa Iglesia* movement and their complaints against the Pampangan elite, see, Kasaysayan ng mga ipinagdadamdam at karaingan ng comandante Felipe Salvador sa mahinahong pasia ng Kgg. na Presidente ng G.R. [Account of the resentments and complaints of Major Felipe Salvador, submitted to the just and gentle decision of the Honorable President of the Republic], 14 January 1899, PIR, SD 1284.1, R.79.

10 John A. Larkin, *The Pampangans: Colonial Society in a Philippine Province* (Berkeley: University of California Press), 111-19; Guerrero, "Luzon at War," 181.

11 Manuel Sastron discusses in detail the cooperation of the Filipino provincial and municipal elites with the Spaniards during the first phase of the Revolution. See, *La insurrección en Filipinas y la Guerra Hispano-Americana* (Madrid: Imprenta de la Sucesora de M. Minuesa de los Rios, 1901).

12 Among those who expressed their willingness to fight the Americans in defence of Spain were Emiliano Riego de Dios, Secretary of War of the Biak-na-Bato Republic; Baldomero Aguinaldo, Don Emilio's cousin and his Secretary of the Treasury; and Generals Pio del Pilar and Artemio Ricarte. See, *ibid.*, 368; *Gaceta de Manila*, 9 May 1898.

13 See the English translation in John Foreman, *The Philippine Islands* (New York: Scribner's, 1899), 590-92.

14 Quoted in Teodoro A. Agoncillo, *Malolos: The Crisis of the Republic* (Quezon City: University of the Philippines Press, 1960), 144.

15 Extracto ng labanan sa Provincia ng Batangas [Description of the capture of Batangas], n.d., PIR, SD 1100.5, R.65; JP (Cagayan) to EA, 7 November 1899, PIR, SD 1101.6, R.67. See also, *Principales* of San Isidro, Nueva Ecija, *Certifico,* 14 October 1898, in *ibid.*

16 Felipe Buencamino to Governor Basilio Augustin, 9 June 1898, PIR, SD 918.2, R.54.

17 I use the phrase "cosmopolitan elite" to refer to those *ilustrados* whose influence and authority extend beyond their home provinces, e.g., Pedro Paterno, Cayetano Arellano and Joaquin Gonzalez.

18 Agoncillo, *Malolos,* 240.

19 Apolinario Mabini to Galicano Apacible, n.d., The National Heroes Commission, *The Letters of Apolinario Mabini* (Manila, 1965), 48.

20 J.R.M. Taylor, Notes on records of elections, PIR, SD 1165.8, R.72; SD 1200.8, R.74; and SD 1201.1, R.74; See also, election reports (June 1898 — January 1899), PIR, NS Pa. 272, Encls. 29, 31-47, 42-45, 57-58, 61, 66, 70, 71, R.511; PIR, SD 1200.6, R.74; Election reports (December 1898), PIR, NS

Pa. 286, Encls. 179-204. Elections were also held in the settlements (*ran-cherias*) of the Amburayan district in November, where native Igorot officials were chosen. *Actas de elecciones* in various *rancherias* of Amburayan, November 1898, PIR, OS Pa. 5, Encls. 45-46, R.111.

21   A. Mabini to EA, 7 September 1898, PIR, SD 384.4, R.5. See also, Mabini, *Letters,* 58. At the end of the 19th century, the towns of San Miguel, Quiapo, Malate, Santa Ana, Paco and Pandacan constituted Manila's suburbs or *arrabales.*

22   EA to Ambrosio Flores, 7 September 1898, PIR, SD 114.3, R.11.

23˙ List of approved town elections, PIR, SD 897.2, R.52; list of local presidents [1899?], PIR, SD 268.4, R.22; *Actas de elecciones,* Pandacan, Paco and Malate, 3, 4 & 6 August 1898, PIR, SD 1138, Encls. 3, 6, 8, R.70.

24   Ambrosio Flores to EA. Letters of 27 and 29 August 1898, PIR, SD 1016, Encls. 1 & 3, R.69.

25   Ambrosio Flores, *Notas del Gobierno Provincial de Manila,* n.d. PIR, SD 301.12, R.23.

26   *Ibid.*

27   Residents of Tondo to EA, 20 August 1898, PIR, SD 1138.1, R.70.

28   EA. Decree of 20 August 1898, *ibid.*

29   Sec/Interior to EA. Memo of 20 August 1898, *ibid.*

30   John R.M. Taylor, *The Philippine Insurrection Against the United States, A Compilation of Documents with Notes and Introduction* (Pasay City: Eugenio Lopez Foundation, 1971), 2:144-45.

31   Elias Ataviado, *The Philippine Revolution in the Bicol Region (August 1898 — January 1899)* (Manila: Encal Press, 1953), 101-63.

32   The insurgent troops assigned to the Bikol region would have arrived before September if it had not been for the conflict between Generals Lukban and Malvar. Considerable friction developed between the two leaders over men and arms, with Malvar possessing more troops and munitions. Upon the surrender of Tayabas to the insurgents, Malvar would have taken all the captured arms if it had not been for Aguinaldo's firm intervention that Lukban be given at least one-half of the captured rifles. *Ibid.,* 145-46. The conflict between Malvar and Lukban is hinted at in Estanislao Legazpi's letter to Apolinario Mabini, 31 August 1898, PIR, SD 1089.3, R.66.

33   Ataviado, *Revolution in Bicol,* 111.

34   *Ibid.*

35   See, the *hojas de servicio* of Quintin Salas which is actually an account of the involvement of various members of the Iloilo elite in wresting power from the Spaniards in, Robert H. Noble, A Compilation of Insurgent Documents During the Insurrection in the Philippine Islands from 1898-1902, Pertaining Chiefly to the Visayan Group, PIR, 3:204-11, R.637; *Acta* of 18 November 1898, SD 920.5, R.54.

36 Juan Araneta to the President, Comite Central de Visayas, 6 November 1898, PIR, SD 311.2, R.23; Articles of surrender of the Spanish garrison, 7 November 1898, PIR, SD 315.1, R.23; Juan Araneta, "La Rendición de Bakolod," *La Independencia,* 28 December 1898.

37 Aniceto Lacson to EA, 7 November 1898, PIR, SD 315.1, R.23; Proclamation of the members of the provincial government of Negros, 7 November 1898, PIR, SD 77.4, R.9; Maria Fe H. Romero, *Negros Occidental Between Two Foreign Powers (1888-1909)* (Bacolod: Negros Occidental Historical Commission, 1974), 108-11.

38 Roque Lopez to EA, 5 December 1898, PIR, SD 705.3, R.39; Roque Lopez to the People of the Visayas, 27 December 1898, PIR, SD 912.2, R.53.

39 *Acta* of 26 January 1899 in Actas del gobierno provisional de la revolución, 17 November 1898 — 17 May 1899, PIR, BK. C-6, R.90. See also, James Le Roy, *The Americans in the Philippines* (Boston: Houghton Mifflin, 1914), 2:113.

40 Melecio Severino, Certificate of 28 November 1898, PIR, SD 77.3, R.9. See also, Romero, *Negros Occidental,* 104-05.

41 *Ibid.*

42 United States, War Department, *Annual Report of the Major General Commanding the Army, 1899* (Washington, D.C.: GPO, 1899), 2:62-64.

43 J. Hernandez to EA, 4 December 1898, PIR, SD 705.2, R.39.

44 Unfinished letter to Sec/War (Baldomero Aguinaldo), 14 March 1899, PIR, SD 52.1, R.8.

45 Romero, *Negros Occidental,* 134.

46 *Ibid.,* 136-62.

47 Aguinaldo did in fact decree on 20 June that only those individuals who owned property sufficient to serve as security for the amounts entrusted to their care and custody could be elected councillors and commissioners of revenue. EA, Decree of 20 June 1898, printed pamphlet, PIR, SD 206.3, R.18.

48 EA, Decree of 18 June 1898, in, Taylor, *Philippine Insurrection,* 3:114-15.

49 EA, Decree of 20 June 1898, Rule 34-42, *ibid.*

50 U.S. Philippine Commission, *Report of the Philippine Commission to the Secretary of War for the Year 1900* (Washington: GPO, 1901), 1:444-59.

51 Decree of 18 June 1898, articles 8-9, in, Taylor, *Philippine Insurrection,* 3:115.

52 *Ibid.*

53 EA to Manuel Arguelles, 29 June 1898, PIR, NS Pa. 212.54, R.438.

54 Manuel Arguelles to EA, 15 July 1898, PIR, NS Pa. 212.54, R.438. A similar
    situation obtained in Leyte in mid-1899 when Ambrosio Moxica was ap-
    pointed by Aguinaldo as civilian election commissioner. General Vicente
    Lukban arrived in late 1898 to accomplish the insurgent occupation of Leyte
    as well as undertake essentially the same tasks vested with Moxica. But
    when already in Leyte, Moxica received instructions from Aguinaldo pro-
    hibiting him from holding re-elections in towns where Lukban had already
    held one. Moxica, in his discussion with Lukban, claimed that his official in-
    structions were to the contrary. Although he was later to engage Lukban in
    the struggle for leadership in the island, Moxica resolved the confusion by
    confirming the results of the Lukban-supervised elections, claiming that
    such a decision was necessary so that the government might not suffer from
    "a loss of prestige" among the people. Ambrosio Moxica to EA, 17 July 1899,
    PIR, SD 1077.1, R.65. For a brief treatment of the Lukban-Moxica struggle
    for power, see, Donald Chaput, "Leyte Leadership in the Revolution: The
    Moxica-Lukban Issue," *Leyte-Samar Studies* 9 (1975), 3-12.

55 Uneasy in sharing powers with the military commander in the exercise of
    civil functions, Arguelles informed Marasigan that, in accordance with the
    June 18 decree, civil jurisdiction over the towns now rested with his office
    while the latter possessed purely military responsibilities. Marasigan
    asserted that the same law provided that "if the province is threatened or oc-
    cupied by the enemy, the military chief of the highest rank may assume that
    power of the provincial chief until the danger has disappeared". Manuel
    Arguelles to E. Marasigan, 16 July 1898, Lucena, Tayabas, PIR, NS Pa.
    212.54, R.438.

56 Marasigan to Arguelles, 18 July 1898, PIR, NS Pa.212.45, R.551.

57 EA, Decree of 26 July 1898, Bacoor, Cavite, PIR, NS Pa. 403.45, R.551.

58 Paciano M. Rizal to EA, Sta. Cruz, Laguna [July 1898], PIR, OS Pa. 51.41,
    R.134.

59 Taylor, Note on elections, n.d., PIR, SD 1201.5, R.74; Taylor, Note on elec-
    tions, n.d., PIR, SD 1165.4, R.72; Taylor, Note to the election proceedings of
    San Fabian, Pangasinan, January 1898, PIR, SD 907.2, R.53.

60 General Francisco Macabulos, a prominent Chinese mestizo merchant and
    political figure in La Paz and the provincial capital of Tarlac, successively
    filled the office of *Teniente mayor, cabeza de barangay* and justice of the
    peace of Tarlac before he joined the Revolution. E. Arsenio Manuel, *Dic-
    tionary of Philippine Biography* (Quezon City: Filipiniana Publications,
    1970), 2:299. The election commissioners for the other provinces in Luzon
    were similarly situated. Manuel Tinio, Vicente Camara, Mariano Llanera,
    José Alejandrino, Miguel Malvar, Manuel Arguelles and Domingo Samson,
    who were election commissioners for Ambos Ilocos, Zambales, Nueva Ecija,
    Bontoc, Batangas, Tayabas and Albay respectively came from wealthy

families and occupied positions of authority and influence in the colonial government. For references to Domingo Samson, see, Ataviado, *Revolution in Bikol.*

61 Larkin, *The Pampangans,* 118.

62 Agoncillo, Malolos, 240.

63 EA, Memorandum of 7 June 1898, PIR, SD 1080.3. R.66.

64 Major José Leyba wrote Aguinaldo that though there were a few capable men among them, proven in battle against the Spaniards, they were nevertheless uneducated (*walang abot*), and their appointment to positions in the provincial or municipal administration might become a source of conflict with the Cagayanos because most of the *principales* in practically all the towns were *ilustrados*. Maj. José Leyba to EA, 1 November 1898, PIR, SD 10.7, R.5.

65 See for example, Daniel Tirona, Notes on Town Government [1900?], prepared for Taylor, PIR, SD 279.10, R.22. Tirona prepared these notes after his surrender. He also assisted Taylor in interpreting captured Republican documents.

66 Citizens of Urdaneta, Pangasinan to EA, 10 October 1898, PIR, NS Pa. 293.110, R.540; Residents of Solano, Nueva Vizcaya to EA, 25 April 1899, PIR, SD 231.1, R.19; See also, *Actas de elecciones populares,* Bauan, Batangas, July 1898, PIR,NS Pa. 98.80, R.286; *Principales* of Guiguinto to JP (Bulacan), 12 July 1898, PIR, SD 1101.6, R.67. Such situations made for rancorous and protracted political reorganization but they demonstrate that the process was controlled very strongly by the local or municipal *principalia*. In San Carlos, for example, a distinguished *Katipunan* leader was elected with 40 votes against his opponent who drew 25 votes. During the elections — where 181 *principales* were in attendance — he reportedly threatened to shoot anyone who opposed him. Though all 181 approved his election, 30 of these protested to Aguinaldo that "brilliant" and "irrefutable service in the revolution" was not enough qualification for office. The social position of Faustino Gonzales, the president-elect, was "unknown" (*desconocida*), his conduct "dishonourable". Both Aguinaldo and the provincial council had already approved the election but decided to call for another one. The first election was held on 19 August 1898, shortly after the liberation of the province from Spanish control; the re-election was held on 12 March 1899. See, *Acta de eleccion* (San Carlos, Pangasinan), 19 August 1898; *Principales* of San Carlos to EA, 23 August 1898; JP (Pangasinan) to Sec/Interior, 3 November 1898; *Acta de eleccion,* 12 March 1899; all in PIR, SD 1137, R.70.

67 JP (Nueva Vizcaya) to Sec/Interior, 10 April 1899, PIR, SD 187.5, R.16; Wenceslao Valera (Military Commander of Bayombong) to Sec/War, 3 April 1899, PIR, OS Pa. 53.60, R.135.

68 The "opportunism" of the *principalia* is one of the main themes of such works as: Amado Guerrero, pseud. (José Ma. Sison), *Philippine Society and Revolution* (Manila: 1971) and Renato Constantino, *Dissent and Counterconsciousness* (Quezon City: Malaya Books, 1970).

69 Daniel Tirona to EA, 23 January 1899, PIR, SD 349.4, R.24.

70 *Ibid.*

71 Daniel Tirona to Sec/War, 25 February 1899, PIR, SD 219.1, R.18.

72 Tirona to EA, 23 January 1899.

73 The budget for 1899 assigned ₱540.00 for the civil governor of Manila, a first-class province; ₱480.00 for a second-class province such as Albay; ₱420.00 to Cagayan, a third-class province; and to Morong, a fourth-class area, ₱360.00. See, General Estimates of State Expenditures and Receipts, 1899, in, Taylor, *Philippine Insurrection,* 4:329-32. Tirona's experience was apparently not an isolated one. In Bauang, Batangas, the popular council raised an uproar when the provincial president, Don Manuel Genato, removed the councillors of justice and taxes and appointed his favourites to the vacated positions, the latter being men who were supposedly fence-sitters during the "first Revolution" and utterly lacking in patriotism, having been spies for the Spanish curate. Genato could not have retained his favourites without further incurring the wrath of the townspeople, so he saved his face by calling for a new election. Espediente contra Eugenio Aranas y Andres Buendia, por abusos cometida de sus funciones [December 1898], Eugenio Aranas y Andres Buendia, Sobre arbitriades de D. Manuel Genato, 20 December 1898, Junta popular (Bauan) to Miguel Malvar, 19 December 1898; Acta de eleccion (Bauan, Batangas), December 1898; all in PIR, NS Pa. 239.33, R.474.

74 United States Army, Department of Southern Luzon (hereafter, DSL), Memorandum on Vicente Camara for the Division Commander, October 1901, PIR, SD 773.1, R.44; Anthony Tuody, compiler, *Album Historico de la primera asamblea filipina* (Manila: Bureau of Printing, 1908), 50-56; see also, Andres Moralle (Civil Governor, Isabela) to Governor-General Primo de Rivera, 23 February 1898, in, Legajo 5157, Ministerio de Ultramar, Archivo Historico de la Nacion, Madrid; Filipinas, Gobierno Superior, *Guia oficial, 1896* (Manila: 1896), 565.

75 List of local presidents in the provinces of Cavite, Batangas, Laguna, Nueva Ecija, Tarlac, Pampanga, Manila, Bulacan and La Union, [1899], PIR, SD 268.4, R.22; Zambales, *Relacion de los funcionarios civiles,* 8 July 1898, PIR, SD 166.8, R.15; GO, 1890-1898 (Manila: 1890-1896); Philippine National Library, *Historical Data Papers,* 1953 (hereafter, *HDP*); descriptive cards of insurgents (Arrests in Tarlac), n.d., U.S. Army, Department of Northern Luzon (hereafter, DNL), 3rd District, RG 395, Entry 2244; U.S. National Archives and Records Service (hereafter, NARS).

76 Resumen general de los padrones [de la provincia de Batangas], 15 December 1898, PIR, SD 936.2, R.56; Taylor, note on elections, n.d., PIR, SD 1200.3, R.74; Taylor, Note on elections, n.d., PIR, SD 1201.1, R.74.

77 Taylor, Note on certain records of elections in the PIR, SD 1165.8, R.72.

78 Taylor, Notes on elections, n.d., PIR, SD 1201.5, R.74.

79 James le Roy, *Philippine Life in Town and Country* (New York: G.P. Putnam's Sons, 1905), 183. I have in fact come across only one election in which "all classes participated" (*todo el vecindario de todos clases*): "*principales,* property owners and labourers from the age of twenty years." The election took place in the town of Bucay, Abra, where Don Andres Bravo received 460 votes while all his four opponents received a total of 11 votes among themselves. *Acta de elección,* Bucay, Abra, 3 September 1898, PIR, SD 1200.8, R.74. Bravo was also elected first municipal president under the Americans. See, Capt. Thomas Ashburn to the Adj. Gen., Bangued, 21 February 1900 (Bangued, Abra), U.S. Army, DNL, p.4, RG 395, Entry 3061.

80 History and Cultural Life of Bocaue, Bulacan, *HDP*; see also, the "History and Cultural Life of Calumpit, Bulacan," *HDP*; "History and Cultural Life of Sta. Rita, Pampanga," *HDP*.

81 See, for example, Mariano Ponce's glowing references to the revolutionary activities of prominent Filipinos in Manila and the provinces in *Cartas sobre la revolución* (Manila: 1932), 47, 53, 86, 100.

82 In the *HDP,* the term "first" or "original" families usually meant those families which were responsible for the settlement and development of their towns and upon which the Spaniards depended for good municipal administration. The *HDP* also list the prominent families of each town. To give just one example from so many: in the town of Santiago, Ilocos Sur, the municipal officials, from the president to the councillor of justice, were all surnamed Siping, while in Bantay, in the same province, the *principales* elected Pio Pilar y Paz municipal president. Of the 12 barrios listed in the *acta,* six had *cabezas* surnamed Paz while three had barrio heads surnamed Pilar. *Acta de elección,* Bantay, Ilocos Sur, 18 August 1898; *Acta de elección,* Santiago, Ilocos Sur, 20 August 1898; PIR, NS Pa. 98, Encls. 24-25, R.285.

83 Residents of Kandaba to EA, 29 July 1898, PIR, NS Pa. 183.13, R.409; List of local presidents . . . [1899], PIR, SD 268.4, R.22.

84 *Ibid.*

85 Taylor, Note on elections, PIR, SD 1200.3, R.74. See also, letters of resignation from various officials in PIR, OS Pa. 5, 30-36, R.111; PIR, NS Pa. 183.45, R.409.

86 Taylor, Note on election proceedings in Pangasinan, 27 September 1898, PIR, SD 1200.6, R.74.

87 Taylor, Note on Elections, n.d. PIR, SD 1201, Encls. 1 & 8.

88 I am inclined to agree with Taylor's observation that the proportion of resignations was very large during late January 1899. See, Taylor, Note on elections, n.d., PIR, SD 1200.3, R.74.

89 [Military commanders of Cavite, Manila, Bulacan and Nueva Ecija], 20 June 1898, in Taylor, *Philippine Insurrection,* 3:218-20: List of Military Chiefs and their stations, December 1898, *ibid.,* 3:636-37.

90 See, for example, the personnel file of various rebel leaders, 1898-99, PIR, NS Pa. 173, 90 encls., R.400; PIR, OS Pa. 19, R.116.

91 EA, Decree of 1 March 1899, PIR, SD 866.8, R.49.

92 *Ibid.*

93 JL (Tayug) to General Gregorio Mayor, 24 July 1898, PIR, NS Pa. 99.453, R.287.

94 Jefes Locales (Nueva Caceres, Ambos Camarines) to EA, 22 February 1899, PIR, SD 192.2, R.17.

95 P. Leon to Sec/Interior, Balanga, Bataan, 21 April 1899, PIR, SD 2003.1, R.81; JP (Zambales) to EA, 9 January 1899, PIR, SD 988.2, R.60; JP interino (Tayabas) to EA, 22 September 1898, PIR, SD 1246.3, R.76; JP (Isabela) to EA, 16 July 1899, PIR, SD 1157.1, R.71.

96 Rafael Viarid to General Alipio Tecson, San Antonio, Nueva Ecija, 2 January 1900, PIR, NS Pa. 232.95, R.465.

97 JL (Caloocan, Manila) to General Licerio Geronimo, 6 October 1900, PIR, NS Pa. 293.177, R.538.

98 Unsigned memorandum on the militia, [February 1899], PIR, SD 478.1, R.29.

99 Letter to Sec/Interior, [Author's name illegible], 21 April 1899, PIR, SD 2003.1, R.81; R.M. Lacandola to EA, 18 April 1899, PIR, SD 17.3, R.12. See also, Taylor, *Philippine Insurrection,* 2:197.

100 Arguelles was president of Tayabas until his appointment to the Philippine Commission in Manila in January 1899. Manuel Arguelles to EA, 22 September 1898, PIR, SD 1246.3, R.76.

101 Daniel Tirona to Sec/War, 25 February 1899, PIR, SD 219.1, R.18. In another confidential letter, he asked that he be appointed to this task and be permitted to organize the militias of these provinces into one army, a request which did not get any response from Aguinaldo. Tirona to EA, n.d. [early 1899], PIR, SD 349.12, R.24.

102 Sec/War, Circular letter, n.d. [mid-1899], PIR, SD 192.1, R.17.

103 Apolinario Mabini to EA, 26 February 1899, PIR, SD 656.6, R.37.

104 Le Roy, *Philippine Life in Town and Country,* 183.

105 EA, Decree of 5 January 1899, PIR, SD 609.4, R.34.

106 The following constitute a mere fraction of documents on maladministration in the PIR. They are, as nearly as I can make out, representative of hundreds of similar materials not cited here. See, Residents of Candaba, Pampanga to EA, 29 July 1898, PIR, NS Pa. 183.13, R.409; JL and *cabezas* (Tambobong, Bataan) to EA, 13 August 1898, PIR, OS Pa. 53.53, R.135; Espediente de los residentes de Manaoag, Pangasinan al Presidente, 20 August 1898, PIR, SD 1165.9, R.72; Agustin Dizon to the Editor, *La Republica Filipina,* 23 November 1898, PIR, SD 2017.1, R.81; JL (Paombong, Bulacan) to EA, 15 December 1898, PIR, OS Pa. 53.73, R.135; Espediente sobre Pablo Rivera, JL (Bambang, Tarlac), 6 January 1899, PIR, OS Pa. 5.39, R.111; Felipe Salvador to EA, 14 January 1899, PIR, SD 1284.1, R.79; JP (La Union) to Sec/Interior, 22 January 1899, PIR, SD 1262.1, R.77; Anonymous letter to Mariano Alimurung, Macabebe, Pampanga, February 1899, PIR, NS Pa. 53.36, R.134; JP (Tarlac) to Jefe Militar (Tarlac), 4 March 1899, PIR, SD 1262.2, R.77; JL (Alcala) to JP (Pangasinan), 25 March 1899, PIR, SD 1088.1, R.66; JP (Morong) to EA, 18 April 1899, PIR, SD 17.3, R.17; Unsigned letter to EA, 18 April 1899, PIR, SD 305.1, R.23; JP (Tarlac) to Sec/Interior, 4 June 1899, PIR, OS 53.68, R.135; Pablo Ocampo to Sec/Interior, 21 September 1899, PIR, OS Pa. 53.61, R.135; R. Roman to Sec/Interior, 24 November 1899, PIR, SD 47.8, R.7; Anonymous letter to EA, n.d., PIR, OS Pa. 53.35, R.134; Espediente de la denuncia contra el JL (San Juan, Abra), n.d., PIR, OS Pa. 5.71, R.111.

107 Mabini to EA, 28 February 1899, in, Taylor, *Philippine Insurrection,* 4:27-28.

108 Cecilio Apostol was a popular nationalist poet whose patriotic pieces were published in *La Independencia,* a newspaper so radical that the American authorities repeatedly tried to suppress it but to no avail. He later joined the *Nacionalista* Party founded by Pascual Poblete in 1901, which was also suppressed by the Americans for its platform of absolute political independence for the Philippines.

109 Cecilio Apostol to EA, 10 July 1898, in, Taylor, *Philippine Insurrection,* 3:176-81. See also, PIR, SD 7.7, R.5. I have altered Taylor's sometimes too literal translation.

110 Unsigned letter to A. Mabini, [April 1899], in, Taylor, *Philippine Insurrection,* 4:63-64.

111 Unsigned letter to EA, n.d. [late 1898?], PIR, SD 1180.2, R.74.

112 John Bowring, *A Visit to the Philippine Islands* (London: Smith, Elder, & Co., 1859), 315.

113 "Aguinaldo's Appeal to his Filipino Brothers," December 1898, in, Taylor, *Philippine Insurrection,* 3:418-24.

114 Felipe Buencamino to EA, 22 December 1898, in, Taylor, *Philippine Insurrection,* 3:438-39.

115 Sec/Interior to JP (Pangasinan), 23 November 1898, PIR, SD 1101.1, R.60; see also, Notes for Inspection reports, 23 November 1898, PIR, SD 278.1, R.22.

116 EA, Decree of 29 April 1899, PIR, SD 1194.1, R.74; JP (Nueva Vizcaya) to Sec/Interior, 24 November 1899, *ibid.*

117 Editorial, *Ang Kaibigan ng Bayan, Diariong Tagalog,* 14 October 1898.

Abaca in Kabikolan: Prosperity without Progress

NORMAN G. OWEN

At the beginning of the 19th century the Bikol region, or *Kabikolan* — occupying Luzon's narrow, southeastern extremity — was, as it had been for centuries, a backwater in the Philippine economy.[1] It was largely self-sufficient in rice and most other food crops, though it imported some coconut oil from neighbouring Samar. The gold mines of Camarines Norte, which had excited the Spanish *conquistadores* two centuries before, had never turned out to be the bonanza hoped for by generations of optimists. The specialty of the region, abaca or "Manila hemp", was an excellent hard fibre without a visible external market. Some was used to produce cordage for local consumption and the royal shipyards of Cavite; some was used in the hand-weaving of textiles which were worn locally and traded to other regions of the Philippines on a small scale.

By the end of the century, abaca accounted for nearly 40 percent of the Philippines' rising exports and Bikol produced nearly half the total crop. In 1900, the town of Legazpi, which had not existed 50 years earlier, was the most important of the "hemp ports" which the American invaders captured from the Filipino revolutionaries to ensure the flow of abaca to the ropemills of New England and New York — suppliers of naval cordage to Atlantic shipyards and of binder twine to the wheat farmers of the Midwest.[2] In the early decades of the 20th century Albay was, according to some estimates, the richest province in the Philippines.[3]

By the outbreak of World War II Kabikolan was once again a backwater, though not so isolated or impoverished as it had been 140 years earlier. Its pre-eminence in abaca production had long since been lost to Davao, whose Japanese-operated plantations were more efficient. In coconut production, it lagged behind Laguna and Tayabas [Quezon] provinces. Rising tenancy and the disappearance of handicrafts were symptoms of a relative decline which even the completion of the railway linkage to Manila could not reverse.[4] Politically, the Bikol provinces were all but impotent, leaving national leadership to Tagalogs, Visayans, and even Ilocanos and Kapampangans. Whether or not the Kabikolan situation had actually worsened in absolute terms during the American period is not clear. What is clear is that the region had not lived up to the 19th century promise of further development.

Besides its intrinsic local interest, then, a study of Kabikolan in the 19th and early 20th century sheds light on an insufficiently studied problem in Third World history — the paradox of truncated development. Like many other countries, the Philippines underwent a transformation in this period, from an essentially subsistence economy to one dominated by the export of primary products: first sugar, indigo, tobacco, abaca and coffee; later sugar, timber, minerals, coconut products and fruit. Where this transformation occurred without direct Western involvement in production (through forced cultivation or foreign-owned estates) it has been under-represented in the historical record. We are just beginning to understand the process of "commercialization" and how it created in some areas short-term prosperity without long-term progress. Analysis of the rise and fall of the abaca industry in Kabikolan may serve as a case study, with the acknowledged limitation that, like all case studies, it will prove to be in some senses irreducibly unique.

Setting the Stage

For better or worse, the economic history of Kabikolan owed a great deal to its physical geography.[5] Its combination of a rainfall regime without a marked dry season, and volcanic slopes, fertile and well drained, provided the ideal environment for abaca. Furthermore, there were fertile, if narrow, rice-growing plains nearby — along the coast and in the central valley from Albay to San Miguel Bay — which at the beginning of the 19th century supported a sedentary population capable of supplying labour to the growing abaca industry. This was in contrast to the situation in much of the Eastern Visayas and Mindanao, where terrain equally suitable for abaca was not in such proximity to settled rice-growing plains. The chief geographical disadvantage of Kabikolan was its remoteness from the main currents of commerce and development in the Spanish Philippines. The land route to Manila was tortuous, and the sea route from the most convenient ports (on the Pacific side of the peninsula) passed through the dangerous San Bernardino Strait, whose rocks and currents could sink even the mighty galleons. It was possible to avoid these straits by sailing from ports on the western coast, but these ports, except for Sorsogon, had poor communication with the agricultural interior and were exceptionally exposed to the elements and the depredations of "Moro" raiders.

It was the threat of the Muslim marauders, as much as any other factor, which accounted for the backward state of Bikol development prior to 1825. The complete story of this centuries-long conflict between Muslims and Roman Catholics in Philippine waters remains to be told, but from the perspective of Kabikolan between 1750 and 1825, it made no difference what the roots, rights and wrongs of the struggle were. The simple fact was that "Moros" showed up year after year to attack shipping and pillage the coasts, particularly the smaller and more isolated settlements along the Sibuyan Sea, Catanduanes and Camarines Norte. At the peak of these raids, even the major ports of the region and the boats of the Spanish government were not immune from attacks, and towns well in the interior lived in a state of terror later revealed in their folk histories. As in the Visayas, these raids discouraged the establishment of regular trading routes and the accumulation of immovable capital in coastal towns, and were thus a substantial impediment to commercial growth. Sometime early in the 19th century, the tide turned in Kabikolan. The ultimate causes for the decline of the Moro threat must be sought elsewhere. In Kabikolan, at least symbolically, the shift may be dated to 1818, when provincial maritime militias finally defeated the raiders in a sea battle. It was actually decades before the threat entirely vanished, but after that date raids appear to be smaller, less frequent and directed against more remote sites within the region.[6]

The other major obstacle to economic development before the 19th century was Spanish colonial policy, which was both restrictive and exploitative. The restrictions were most evident in the nominal prohibition of all external trade from the Philippines save the two galleons a year to Mexico and the Asian vessels carrying Asian goods (mostly for the galleon trade) allowed to enter Manila. The exploitation consisted primarily in the extraction by forced sale or taxes of surplus agricultural production and corvée labour. The combination of these two factors reinforced subsistence tendencies in the local economy, since the opportunities for profitable trade were not commensurate with the likelihood that any voluntarily increased production would be rapidly expropriated. The "Bourbon Reforms" of the late 18th century were intended to remedy many of these wrongs and to stimulate commercial production. Embodied in such innovations as the Tobacco Monopoly, the Royal Philippine Company, and the Economic Society of Friends of the Coun-

The Bikol Region

try, these reforms represented a significant shift in Spanish intentions for the Philippines, and may actually have had some stimulating effect on the economy of Central Luzon. In Kabikolan, however, the major Bourbon innovation, a silk-weaving project, proved to be a complete fiasco, producing little silk and much hardship.[7] Most descriptive accounts suggest that the region was scarcely more commercialized in 1825 than it had been in 1750.

Eventually, however — half a century after the first of the Bourbon Reforms — Spain carried through a certain liberalization of trade and permitted greater private enterprise in commerce. The loss of Mexico forced a reorientation of Manila's trade, and the technically illegal visits of English and American merchants, tolerated from the late 18th century, became vital to the Spanish mercantile economy in the 1820s. By 1817 there was a United States consul in Manila; during the 1820s several foreign merchant houses were established there; and successive Spanish administrations actively encouraged commerce, culminating in the official opening of Manila to foreign merchants in 1834, under Governor-General Pascual Enrile.[8]

The opening of the Philippines to the world market system was the last critical precondition for 19th century development in Kabikolan. The chief contribution of the Spanish government was to get out of the way, which it did reluctantly, slowly and inconsistently.

Abaca in the World Market

The first vessel carrying abaca to the West left Manila in 1818 for a world fibre market entering an era of unprecedented expansion. In England and the United States, it was to be the age of the whaler and the clipper ship; later in the century, as sail began to fade, other uses for hard fibres developed, of which the most important was binder twine for the mechanical grain harvester developed by Cyrus McCormick of Chicago. True hemp, of which Russia was the chief source, proved inadequate both in quantity and quality to these new demands, and the cordage industry scoured the world for substitutes. Abaca proved to be the finest of these, better even than true hemp. Later in the century henequen (sisal), sunn hemp, istle and New Zealand flax also became international trade commodities, though only the first of these could compete with abaca. These fibres had little in common save that they could be made into some kind of cordage to meet the growing demand; most are not even of the hemp family, abaca being a kind of banana and henequen a kind of cactus. But despite numerous imperfections in the market, throughout the 19th century there was a growing interchangeability of these fibres. A world market developed, integrating technological innovations and the economic cycles of the industrial nations with the costs of production and transportation of these fibres from the less developed countries in which they were grown. It was this linkage to a global fibre market which created the abaca industry of Kabikolan.[9]

The intermediaries in this linkage were importers and fibre brokers in England and the United States, merchant houses in Manila, and middlemen in the abaca-growing provinces of the Philippines. Of these, the most critical were the British and American merchant houses of Manila — such as Ker & Co.; Smith, Bell & Co.; Peele, Hubbell & Co.; and Russell & Sturgis — whose role has been studied elsewhere.[10] By accepting orders from Atlantic importers, mobilizing local capital and setting up a procurement system in the provinces, they provided both the structure and the funding necessary for the infant abaca industry. They were scarcely altruistic in this; they made every effort to exploit the Filipinos by creating a purchasing monopoly or pool which could depress local prices while keeping the export price up. But in the long run they failed; the monopoly was never achieved, and the two largest American houses eventually went bankrupt.[11] By then, however, the export industry was well developed and firmly locked into the world fibre market.

One obvious consequence of this connection was that the price of abaca always depended heavily on events external to the Philippines, beyond the control not only of the Filipinos but of their colonial rulers as well. Familiar events in the history of the West — the "hungry" 1840s, the Crimean War and the American Civil War, the industrial depressions of 1857, 1873, 1893 and 1907, etc. — are clearly visible in Manila price quotations. Furthermore, the export linkage carried these same fluctuations to Kabikolan, where they are reflected in such diverse indicators of economic activity as local land and crop prices, wage rates, government revenues (including cockfight admissions) and even the rate of marriage.[12]

Abaca in the Provinces: 1825-1875

It is much more difficult to find information on the provincial abaca industry than on the Manila export trade, for most merchants and travellers rarely left the capital, while the Spanish priests and bureaucrats in the provinces rarely concerned themselves with any activity that was not demonstrably immoral, subversive or taxable. Nevertheless, we can reconstruct certain aspects of the 19th century abaca trade. Prior to the 1820s, there was no "trade" as such. The governor compelled the production and forced sale of whatever amount of abaca the royal cordage-works needed or he wanted for his own business. But as the export trade developed, a hierarchy of provincial brokers and middlemen grew up to handle the abaca between the fields and the exporters.

Abaca was typically grown neither on huge western-style estates nor by individual peasant proprietors, but on lands owned by municipal elites and worked by the peasant majority. The normal labour relationship was a version of sharecropping adapted to the peculiarities of abaca cultivation. Simple wage labour was generally used for clearing the land, planting the trees and weeding the fields during the two to three years before the plant was ready to harvest. Once harvesting began, no further planting was necessary; the same field would continue to yield fibre indefinitely. The real effort in the industry was in harvesting and preparing the fibre — cutting down the ripe stalks, stripping the fibre from the surrounding pulp, drying it and bundling it for sale. This was arduous labour, and the standard basis of payment was that the labourers received one half of all the fibre they stripped, normally sold directly back to the landowner at the prevailing provincial market price. There were a myriad of minor variables which may have made these labour arrangements more or less favourable from time to time — the provision of rations, the obligation to weed, the right to cultivate food crops between the rows of abaca, the obligation to carry the fibre to market, or the advance payment of head taxes by the landowner. But essentially the arrangement was constant. The labourer shared in the profits of abaca as they rose and fell in rhythm with the world fibre market.[13]

The landowner in turn sold the abaca either in the town market or directly from his fields, to an abaca buyer, usually an agent (*personero*) of some provincial merchant. Many of these *personeros* were Ilongos or Ilongo–Chinese mestizos who had originally come to Kabikolan as part of Iloilo's expanding trade. The merchants were predominantly Spaniards, although by the 1860s the Manila houses were sending out young Americans to supervise provincial purchasing.[14] During this period, the Bikolanos by and large stuck to agriculture itself, rather than the commerce in agricultural products. Although Chinese grew in importance in the retail trade of Kabikolan after the 1850s, they were of relatively little importance in the exportation of abaca until later in the century.

From the fragmentary data on the economics of the abaca trade which have survived from this era we can get a rough sense of how the profits were distributed. George Peirce came to the Philippines from New England in 1856 as a 19-year-old clerk for Peele, Hubbell & Co. By 1862 he was responsible for buying one-third of all the abaca exported from the Philippines and his salary had grown from less than ₱1,000 to ₱5,000 a year. Accepted into the partnership in 1868, by 1873 his share was worth roughly ₱150,000 on paper, and he was by no means the wealthiest of the partners. At the next level of the trade, some of the Spanish provincial merchants regularly engaged in property transactions involving thousands of pesos and were able to borrow more than ₱10,000 from the American houses. Felix Dayot, Peele, Hubbell & Co.'s agent in Tabaco, put up a house and warehouse worth ₱6,500 as security for his debts to them in 1862; in the same year, within a space of two months, another Spaniard bought more than 70 parcels of abaca land for a total price of over ₱4,500; and neither of these two was worth a fraction of the fortune of the Muñoz clan. On the *personeros* we have far less information. Some of them ranked with the lesser Spanish merchants, buying and selling property and putting up bonds of thousands of pesos, but others, particularly the subagents (*personeritos*), had to borrow sums as small as ₱20 or less to obtain capital with which to buy abaca.[15]

Finally, we can estimate the cash income of an abaca-stripper or a wage-labourer during times of peak prosperity at ₱75 a year or less, an amount which might be supplemented by subsistence activities such as growing food crops, fishing or hunting. If the 19th century land registers are at all reliable, only about one out of five Bikolano families in Albay owned their own land; the rest must have worked on the fields of others for a share of the crop. In periods of depression, the cash income of such workers might fall by a third, perhaps compensated for in part by a proportionate increase in subsistence activities.[16] American merchants, on the other hand, would suffer in the slump not just reduced profits, but the net loss of tens of thousands of dollars. Two years after George Peirce reached the peak of his fortune, his estate was bankrupt. Nevertheless, despite the proportionally greater risk they incurred, it would be difficult to argue that American merchants profited less from the abaca trade than Bikolano labourers did.

Abaca in the Provinces: 1875-1925

A number of occurrences in the early 1870s suggested the possibility of a radical transformation of the abaca industry. A prolonged boom in world fibre prices (1865-1873) encouraged expanded production and increased competition in Kabikolan. The completion of the cable from London to Hong Kong and the opening of British banks in Manila altered the international economics of the trade, leading some of the merchant houses to fail in the depression that followed the boom. The introduction of the steamship in the inter-island trade gave increased leverage to those with the extra capital to invest in such innovations, as did the use of screw-presses and stone warehouses for abaca. Chinese economic activities in the Philippines continued to expand rapidly in new directions.

In the last quarter of the 19th century there were in fact certain signs of change within the abaca industry. Internationally, the attempt of the National Cordage Company to corner the American fibre market led to hitherto unreached price peaks in Manila and the provinces (1889), although the failure of the N.C.C. led to another depression (1893). Earlier, as the American agency houses in Manila had gone bankrupt, their share of the export trade was taken up by British houses; these, along with a few of the larger Spanish firms, came to control the dominant share of the inter-island trade as well. Meanwhile, within Kabikolan, the pioneering role of Ilongos as middlemen in abaca buying had been contested by other immigrants, Tagalogs and Chinese in particular. The latter group, able to combine abaca procurement with small-scale retailing of foodstuffs and imported goods, eventually supplanted most Filipino middlemen. Throughout the industry, a new spirit of legalism and competitiveness can be seen — in the tendency to treat land as a commodity, in attempts to enforce legal contracts between merchants and *personeros,* in mutual mistrust between landlords and labourers over the terms of their standard agreement, and perhaps in certain rare hints of enclosure or usurpation of communal lands.[17]

Underneath all this, however, the basic technology and organization of abaca production remained unchanged. Despite innumerable "improved" hemp-stripping machines invented in the late 19th century, nothing actually proved more efficient than the 17th century light *cuchilla,* which could be carried out to the fields where the abaca grew. As all other machines required the entire stalk to be brought to them — only to throw 98 percent of the weight away after stripping — their labour cost was prohibitive.[18] Landholding patterns were only slightly altered by expansion of landed wealth, since most entrepreneurs acquired multiple scattered plots worked independently rather than consolidated estates.[19] Although a few Spaniards invested in large contiguous "plantations", such a form of ownership offered no economies of scale, and thus no advantage over the traditional pattern of smaller plots. On both kinds of holdings, arrangements between labourer and landlord — 50:50 share harvesting — remained constant.

The American occupation of Kabikolan, commencing in 1900, also seemed to promise change. Surely a new political system, with new laws on landholding and homesteading, a new export tax on abaca (1899-1913), a new national system of fibre classification (1915), and access to a major market, new sources of capital and "yankee enterprise" should have had some impact on the industry.[20] There were indeed some changes — growth of export production, an increase in the number of large estates (though they never became the dominant form of production), and an apparent rise in tenancy.[21] But over the first 25 years of American rule, the comparisons with the Spanish era are more striking than the contrasts. Prices fell during world depressions (1907-1912), rose during wars (1914-1918), and crashed again afterwards, despite all efforts of the colonial government to maintain them. Internal transportation was slightly improved by the construction of a better road system, but most of the factors of production and marketing were unchanged. Agricultural technology in Kabikolan in the 1920s was identical to that utilized in the 1820s — even as the Japanese in Davao were developing new ways of rationalizing abaca planting and harvesting. Despite putatively superior scientific knowledge, the Americans could not shelter the abaca industry from the periodic destruction of drought, typhoons, plant disease and rinderpest, which by killing the *carabaos* disrupted transportation from the fields to the markets. Access to the American market was not the bonanza for abaca that it had been for sugar, since abaca was already on the free list. (Quite possibly free access of Philippine cordage to the American market might have made some difference had it been introduced earlier or extended beyond 1935.) Meanwhile, the Chinese continued to dominate abaca purchasing in Kabikolan, and foreigners (Americans and British) the export trade. Bikolanos, as always, cultivated the fields and took their cut of the profits from the bottom.

The Decline of Bikol Abaca

In 1924 Kabikolan produced nearly 70,000 metric tons of abaca, 38 percent of the total production of the Philippines in that year. By 1932 its production had fallen to less than 30,000 metric tons, scarcely more than a quarter of a national industry which was itself in decline. American consumption of Philippine abaca fell more than 50 percent between 1925 and 1933, though Japanese demand took up some of the slack. In Kabikolan, the yield per hectare was slipping even as the price of abaca was plummeting, so that by one calculation the gross returns per hectare of abaca land in Albay fell more than 60 percent in a single year (1930-1931).[22] Although there was some slight recovery of both the local and the national industry later in the 1930s, neither regained the kind of prominence or prosperity it had once enjoyed. The abaca boom, for a century the mainspring of the Bikol economy, was over.

A number of factors contributed to its decline. In the global market the production of henequen, which had always trailed abaca before 1913, nearly tripled between 1910 and 1935, while abaca production, after many fluctuations, ended up where it began. Henequen harvesting in Yucatan (Mexico) had been mechanized early in the 20th century, and the cultivation of the plant was easily expanded to new areas, particularly Indonesia and Africa, after World War I. The only advantage abaca held was its superiority for certain specific kinds of cordage, but this diminished in importance with the relative decline of shipping as a consumer of fibres. (After World War II nylon was to take even this last area of unquestioned superiority from "Manila rope".)

Meanwhile, within the Philippines, Davao, with its industrially organized and partially mechanized Japanese plantations, had increased its share of total abaca production from 3.5 percent in 1915 to 45 percent in 1934. The Bikol fields, some of them worked continuously for a century, were beginning to show signs of exhaustion. The Bikol landowners and labourers were locked by a century of tradition into a pattern of operations antithetical to that of the Japanese estates, which were large contiguous holdings worked by wage labour gangs, rather than scattered plots worked on a basis of individual share stripping. Even nature seemed to conspire against Kabikolan. Unlike Davao, which was south of the typhoon belt, Bikol remained exposed to typhoons and was afflicted by a number of plant diseases after a century of virtual immunity. Finally, the system of scattered holdings had prevented the emergence of abaca millionaires in Kabikolan, which in the context of 20th century Philippine politics meant a lack of national influence capable of obtaining special favours for the industry.[23]

The course of economic history is strewn with the bones of industries which time and technology passed by: whaling in New England, tin mining in Cornwall, indigo in South Carolina and the Philippines, and opium in British India. Abaca in Kabikolan, like each of these, flourished in its own time. There was nothing illusory about the wealth it created. For a century, abaca brought relative prosperity to Kabikolan — not just to merchants and landowners, but also to ordinary labourers and peasants. Assessed by estimated incomes, government revenues, attractiveness to immigrants and descriptive evidence, it appears that conditions were noticeably better for most Bikolanos in 1925 than they had been in 1825. Nor is this finding unique. Global terms of trade were generally favourable for tropical products in the late 19th and early 20th centuries. In spite of "colonial exploitation", there are several known cases of increased prosperity during these years in Third World countries which were to fall into the profoundest poverty by the 1930s.[24]

The critical question, finally, concerns neither the rise nor the fall of a particular industry, but the capacity of the country or region to turn temporary growth into sustained development, capable of increasing even when the original industry fails. Clearly New England had that capacity; clearly Kabikolan did not. To explore this question we need to move beyond the abaca industry to the total Bikol economy and how it affected and was affected by Bikol society and values.

The Subsistence Economy of Kabikolan

In the Bikol provinces, as elsewhere in the Philippines, the staple crop was rice, grown principally on the plains in drainage-retention paddy fields. Nineteenth century descriptions of Kabikolan all mention rice along with abaca as the two principal products of the region.[25] But since Bikol rice was locally consumed and its cultivation was no different from what travellers had already seen elsewhere in Luzon, once mentioned it tended to be overlooked in these accounts. Crude estimates of consumption and production suggest that rice cultivation in Kabikolan actually expanded considerably during the 19th century — perhaps even doubled — but it failed to keep up with population growth.[26] An existing intra-regional trade in rice, chiefly from the fertile Bikol plain around Nueva Caceres to the deficit areas of Camarines Norte and Albay, grew rapidly as the region's population growth showed a distinct shift toward upland areas suitable for abaca cultivation and coastal towns accessible to trade — both lacking self-sufficiency in rice. But by the 1870s the region as a whole was importing rice from Saigon and Pangasinan indirectly by way of Manila. Kabikolan, though it continued to feed a majority of its own inhabitants, remained a chronic grain-deficit region thereafter.

Although the relative decline in rice production clearly had some connection with the rise of abaca, it should not be assumed that the competition for resources was always direct. Rice is grown best on the plains, abaca on the slopes, so the two crops were complementary in their use of terrain. There may have been some competition for capital — in directly productive goods, in infrastructural investment and in the maintenance of labour necessary to clear new fields. But there was a potential complementarity of capital as well. The same carabaos that ploughed rice paddies could haul abaca to the ports, and the same roads, warehouses and piers which expedited the export of abaca could also be used for the importation of rice, textiles and other consumer goods. Had abaca growing not attracted local capital, it is theoretically possible that more might have been invested in irrigation. Yet there is no evidence that an expanded irrigation system was ever seriously contemplated in Kabikolan before World War II. As for labour, rice growing has a distinctly seasonal demand pattern — two peaks at the time of transplanting and harvest, with a slack period in between and a lengthy "off-season" during the drier months; while abaca can be harvested year round, perhaps best during the dry season. Thus there was also a potential complementarity of labour demand, and it is probable that many rice cultivators also stripped some abaca in the off-season, while many abaca strippers took time off to work in the rice harvest. Analysis of baptismal records in one Albay town indicates a distinct increase in the number of conceptions occurring in the dry season after harvest — also the time of most town fiestas — suggesting that the rhythm of the rice-growing cycle continued to hold sway even in the heart of the abaca district.[27]

The Bikolanos also continued throughout this period to engage in many other subsistence activities — cultivating supplementary staples (corn and root crops) along with a multitude of fruits and vegetables; fishing in seas, lakes, rivers, even the flooded fields; hunting and gathering forest products; keeping livestock for agricultural labour (*carabaos*) and domestic consumption (pigs and chickens); and making their own pots, hats, mats, tools, textiles, boats and houses from local materials. As always, such subsistence activities are overshadowed in the historical records. But careful examination of the sources will show that they persisted well into the 20th century despite the tide of commercialization. Even the products most heavily imported into Kabikolan — rice and textiles — displaced local production only in limited areas. During times when trade was disrupted by war (especially 1898-1901) or by declining export prices (especially the 1930s), many Bikolanos increased their subsistence activities, neglecting the abaca fields and cultivating root crops which helped them survive the bad years. A century and a half after the first commercial exports of abaca, the Bikol economy could still be described as "consisting basically of a subsistence-oriented agriculture, with overtones of commercial agriculture".28

The chief advantage to the Bikolanos of the continuing subsistence economy was that it reduced the risks of commercialization. Without rejecting the opportunities for larger profits offered by abaca and other industries, they kept open the option of reverting to more traditional means of livelihood rather than trusting themselves entirely to the mercies of the market. In the absence of any direct evidence as to Bikolano motives, it is this prudent minimizing of risks, rather than "oriental economics" or peasant ignorance, to which we must attribute the persistence of subsistence.

Other Commercial Industries

Related to the myth of peasant ignorance is the assumption that the previously unrecognized superior virtues of market-oriented production, once experienced, will inevitably lead to a displacement of subsistence. In this simple model of development, the rise of an export trade in abaca should have brought in its train the commercialization of all other elements of the Bikol economy, slowly but surely, in a linear process of modernization. The reality, however, is far more complex.

Before abaca fibre was ever exported, there were several commercial industries in Kabikolan producing commodities for sale in the Manila market: gold, textiles, sea-slugs (*balate, trepang*), cordage, civet and forest products. During the 19th century new commodities were also shipped from the region — coal, cattle and horses, timber and rattan, ships, and essence of ilang-ilang — as some of the earlier industries flourished and others faltered. In the 20th century it was the coconut industry which emerged as the most important, eventually replacing the faltering abaca trade as the region's chief export. Meanwhile, other industries had developed aimed primarily at the regional market, such as distilling coconut "brandy", rice milling, and growing sugar and contraband tobacco.

To write the individual histories of these industries is not only beyond the scope of this essay, but quite possibly beyond what the available sources will permit. In many cases we cannot even be sure which of these industries were government sponsored, which were promoted by European capital, and which were the product of local enterprise, much less how production was organized. But what is evident is that these industries do have individual histories; thus no linear model of increasing commercial awareness does justice to their rise and fall.

The cordage trade, for example, disappeared by the middle of the 19th century, presumably victim of the superior technology of Manila rope mills. Civet also disappeared; why, we do not know. The local ship building industry rose to sudden prominence in the 1840s but declined precipitously before the end of the century, thanks primarily to the widespread use of the steamship in inter-island travel. The same innovation, however, sparked new ventures in coal mining. Bikol textiles apparently ceased to be common currency outside the region by the mid-19th century, displaced by imported machine-woven cottons; yet early in the 20th century a new export market developed for some of the finer Albay *sinamay* fabrics. Tobacco was grown illegally as long as the government Monopoly kept the cost of better cigars high; with the end of the Monopoly in the 1880s the inferior local product could no longer compete. Coconuts had grown in Kabikolan and been used for a wide variety of domestic purposes from time immemorial. Not until the 20th century, however, when advances in chemistry multiplied the uses to which vegetable oils could be put (soap, margarine, nitroglycerine, etc.), did an export market for copra develop. The gold industry of Camarines Norte, meanwhile, followed a cyclical pattern all its own, with periods of dormancy and localized depression broken by bursts of mining activity in the 1790s, the 1820s and 1830s, the 1870s, the 1890s, and the 1910s, culminating in a tremendous boom following the devaluation of the American dollar (and consequent jump in the price of gold) in 1933.

From a survey of all these enterprises, a few salient generalizations emerge. First, of course, is the fact that each industry was unique, and therefore that no single model of development suffices to explain them all. Second is the high degree of instability of many of them, and therefore the high risk involved in investment of money or energy. Third, possibly related to the second, is the evidence that many of these industries were initiated or later controlled by non-Bikolanos — Spaniards, particularly in mining, ship building, cattle ranching, and the cultivation of sugar and ilang-ilang; Chinese, in distilling and rice milling; Americans, in 20th century mining; and sometimes even Ilongos or Tagalogs. By the same token, outsiders were responsible for many other innovations that completely failed: the 18th century silkworm project; dreams of exporting cotton, indigo, pepper, cacao and rubber from the region; a multitude of bankrupt mining ventures; efforts to mechanize the abaca industry; a costly and disastrous project to dig, at public expense, a sea-level canal linking Nueva Caceres to the Sibuyan Sea. With rare exceptions, however, outsiders did not participate in the subsistence sector. In those few cases where they did, the Tagalogs and Ilongos who invested in rice lands tended to be those who married Bikolanos, became involved in local politics, and wound up assimilated into the indigenous society of Kabikolan.[29]

Transportation, Commerce and the Bureaucracy

Improvements in infrastructure and the expansion of commerce and the bureaucracy, unlike the productive enterprises discussed above, followed an almost linear path during the 19th and early 20th centuries. Progress was often slow, and it is clear that, by most indices of modernization, early 20th century Kabikolan still lagged behind not only Manila, but such regional centres as Iloilo. There is no question, however, that significant changes had occurred, and the progress seems to have been cumulative rather than cyclical.

At the end of the 18th century there were "neither wheels, nor roads for them", according to one observer, and transportation consisted of "horses, cows, and carabaos, and shoulders . . . canoes, *cascos,* and sampans, or mini-boats".[30] A hundred years later — even before the American flurry of investment in public works — there were good carriage roads with stone bridges in the most important districts of Albay and Camarines Sur, and serviceable roads for horses and carabaos in all of them, while steamers connected the coastal ports with each other and with Manila, docking at new wharves and unloading abaca from new warehouses. One major shift in trading patterns had occurred. The western ports, which flourished between the 1820s and 1860s, had declined in importance relative to the Pacific ports of Legazpi, Tabaco, Nueva Caceres and Daet, all of which had better access to the major centres of population and agricultural production.[31] Meanwhile, the telegraph connected Kabikolan to Manila in the late 19th century, and within the first decade of American rule a railroad link was begun, though it would not be completed until the 1930s.

Reinforced by, and reinforcing these improvements in transportation was an enormous expansion of commerce. We know of little activity in the early 19th century beyond irregular voyages to Manila carrying local produce and the visits of itinerant peddlers to Bikol towns. By the end of the century, there was regular steamship traffic with Manila (as well as an ongoing sailing trade) which carried tens of thousands of tons of abaca out of Kabikolan and returned laden with rice and textiles. There were weekly or semi-weekly public markets in most sizeable towns, paying a substantial market tax. There were Spanish department stores in the provincial capitals; and there were ubiquitous Chinese merchants, whose spheres of operations ranged from substantial general stores to tiny shops. By the early 20th century these Chinese were said to dominate the import, export and retail trade of Kabikolan, although they had not created any of them; they had simply penetrated a commercial system which had evolved over the previous century. Despite the claims of their enemies, however, there remained room for competition by Bikolanos and by other outsiders at many points within the system.[32]

The proliferation of the Spanish bureaucracy coincided with the growth of transportation and commerce in time, though it was virtually independent of them. Its primary impetus came not from local conditions but from peninsular Spain, which, having lost most of its American colonies by 1825, had far more attention and manpower to invest in the Philippines than it had spent there in the previous 250 years. The Mexican revolution deprived the Manila government of an important fiscal subsidy and shocked its officials into an awareness of the possibilities of an anti-colonial revolt — prompting the regime to increase its administrative control over the countryside as a means of raising revenue and insuring order. The extraordinary political instability of 19th century Spain compounded these developments by increasing the number of loyal followers of innumerable new governments who had to be rewarded with "places" in the bureaucracy, as well as the number of defeated opponents who had earned exile as far from Spain as possible. The completion of the Suez Canal, cutting the voyage in half, also greatly increased the attractiveness of the Philippines for Spanish appointees. The result was a multiplication of officials in the provinces as well as in Manila. The Roman Catholic church, though technically distinct from the colonial bureaucracy, was subject to many of the same influences, and in the latter half of the 19th century also sent far more friars to the Philippines than ever before.[33]

For Kabikolan, one obvious result was an unprecedented growth of the official presence in the provinces. Early in the 19th century, a typical province might have just two regular Spanish officials: a Governor, who served as tribute collector, military commander and judge; and a treasury administrator, who supervised the Tobacco Monopoly with the aid of a few Filipino soldiers. There were also various commissioners, collectors, distributors and retailers of tobacco, warehousemen, militia officers and clerks, but these seem to have been positions without formal salaries, filled on an *ad hoc* basis from among local Spanish and Filipino residents. In all Kabikolan, moreover, there were just 18 Franciscan friars and a handful of secular priests, so that several of them were forced to administer two or more parishes.

A half-century or more later, the same Bikol province might have, among others, a civil governor; a judge; a public prosecutor and public defender; attorneys and jailers; a treasury administrator (before the end of the Tobacco Monopoly) with his retinue of inspector, warehouseman, *carabineros,* distributors and vaccinators; officials reporting directly to specialized branches of the central government (engineers and assistants, chief telegraphers and operators, agronomists, etc.); a Spanish-officered contingent of the *Guardia Civil*; and two schoolteachers in every town. By the 1880s there were also more than 40 Franciscans in Kabikolan as well as an increased number of secular priests.[34]

Although the top positions in these bureaucracies were reserved for Spaniards, there were plenty of second- and third-echelon posts (such as vaccinators, public scribes, secular priests and school teachers) as well as minor auxiliary positions open to Bikolanos and other Filipinos. This not only meant a source of income for them, but direct exposure to Western concepts of law and government and to the functioning of a highly articulated, if remarkably inefficient, bureaucracy. The cost, of course, was high. In purely economic terms, Spanish taxation removed from Kabikolan a large percentage of the increased revenues brought into the region by the abaca trade. Moreover, the new positions superseded certain traditional occupations. Among the provincial elite, local healers, herbalists and vaccinators gave way to Western-trained doctors, though they may have retained their influence with the masses. In the construction business, indigenous *maestros de obras* were displaced by Spanish engineers. And as the civil bureaucracy expanded, the Bikolanos were removed further and further from proximity to power. Early in the 19th century the mayor of the provincial capital would substitute for the governor in the latter's absence, while in later decades there was a host of Spaniards occupying intermediate positions. Nor were these displacements justified by superior honesty or efficiency — the doctors failed to prevent several late 19th century epidemics, the engineers built bridges that scarcely lasted longer than traditional constructions though costing many times as much, and the Spanish bureaucrats often abused their powers and stole all they could both from the Bikolanos and the colonial exchequer.

Urbanization and the Tertiary Sector

Accompanying the growth of commerce and the bureaucracy, which occasioned an influx of outsiders, was a nascent urbanization which included the rudiments of certain service industries by the turn of the century. Only the provincial capital of Ambos Camarines, Nueva Caceres (later Naga City), belongs clearly to the study of urbanization. It had a *población* with over 10,000 inhabitants, the diocesan secondary schools and seminary as well as most of the provincial bureaucracy, and a visibly dominant position in provincial society, culture and internal trade. In Albay, with the export trade divided between two ports (Legazpi and Tabaco), the capital in a third town (Albay), and much of the real wealth of the province in the abaca-market towns of the interior, it is harder to define what was "urban" at the turn of the century. Yet there was a 25 kilometre stretch of road from the interior valley to the coast which ran through six municipalities (Ligao, Guinobatan, Camalig, Cagsaua/Daraga, Albay and Legazpi) with a total population in 1903 of 194,000, of which nearly 25,000 were living in the *poblaciones*. As this linear strip also contained the provincial government, Albay's only secondary school (1895-1900), its principal ports and a clear majority of its bureaucrats and merchants, we are justified in considering it an "urban" cluster of sorts.[35] The port towns of Tabaco, Daet and Sorsogon each also had some claim to urban status at the turn of the century, but were clearly of less size and significance than Nueva Caceres and the Ligao–Legazpi complex.

Within these urban areas we find whatever glimpses of a "modern" sector the historical records afford. Here were the secondary schools, the provincial offices, the courts, the ecclesiastical centres, the "reformed" municipal governments open to Spaniards as well as Filipinos, the newspapers, the lawyers, tax-farmers and professional witnesses. Here too were most of the merchants, the banking facilities they provided (acceptance of deposits at interest, letters of credit on Manila), the major warehouses and abaca presses, the Spanish department stores and the earliest and most important Chinese shops. Here too were most of the small number of Bikolanos and outsiders employed as bakers, barbers, carpenters, clerks, coachmen, launderers, seamstresses, shop-attendants and tailors. These urban centres also seemed to host a disproportionate share of gambling, certain kinds of

manufacturing (such as distilling), and perhaps the adumbration of a proletariat —
a floating labour force looking for work on the docks, in the warehouses or at construction labour.

Even by the standards of the time, however, the urbanization of Kabikolan was
underdeveloped. Before 1900 there were no banks, one short-lived Spanish newspaper, and just three secondary schools in the entire region. Even most of the service industries mentioned were very scanty indeed. One reason for this was that
Kabikolan stood to Manila as Manila stood to the industrial West, in a kind of colonial dependency. Manila supplied banking and marketing facilities (along with
commercial initiative), higher education, machinery (screwpresses, steamboats and
sewing machines), luxury imports and Western-style foodstuffs for the urban elite,
sometimes even building supplies such as timber and rattan which might well
have been procured locally. Above all it supplied skilled labour, in the broadest
sense — cooks, carpenters, abaca press operators, buyers and brokers, Tagalog
clerks and technocrats, as well as Spanish bureaucrats, Anglo–American merchants and Chinese shopkeepers. Not surprisingly, the immigrants in 19th century
Kabikolan were heavily concentrated in the urban areas, where the greatest opportunities for quick profits might be found. One result of this was that local resources
and manpower were never developed as fully as they might have been. The new industries had little "multiplier effect" on the Bikol economy. The complementary
result was that a significant proportion of the abaca-based prosperity of Kabikolan
was drained off to Manila by merchant houses, taxation, the importation of goods
and the remission of salaries. In the 20th century the pull of Manila would sometimes work in a different way, to remove from Kabikolan some of its nascent entrepreneurial talent (such as the Spanish mestizo Juan Madrigal) and to foster
absentee landlordism.

Bikolanos and "Outsiders"

It is very easy to overdraw both the distinction between urban and rural
Kabikolan and the boundaries between outsiders and Bikolanos. This was not a
classic "dualistic" society like British Malaya, where two distinct cultures involved
in two distinct economies lived side by side. Every municipality, even the most "urban", included rural barrios, and the population of the *población* usually retained
close ties to the surrounding countryside. Economically, Kabikolan showed a con-
tinuum from strictly commercial operations to pure subsistence; the abaca industry itself ensured that most Bikolanos were part of the market economy, sharing in its rises and falls. Socially and politically, the lines between ethnic or
linguistic groups were often blurred by intermarriage and acculturation. Some of
the most important Bikol families of the 20th century descended from 19th century immigrants of Spanish (Garchitorena), Tagalog (Abella), Tagalog-Chinese
mestizo (Samson) and Ilongo-Chinese mestizo (Locsin) ancestry, all of whom came
to identify with the region and its culture.

Nevertheless, the generalization may be ventured that the Bikolanos less completely internalized such Western values as risk taking, profit making and progress

than did the outsiders in Kabikolan during this period. The rise of the abaca industry clearly demonstrated that the Bikolanos were as capable as anyone of responding "rationally" to economic incentives. Not only did they work regularly in the fields, but surges of new planting accompanied every significant rise in prices. Other kinds of behavioural evidence, however, suggest that traditional values remained strong, particularly in the spheres of rice growing and local politics.

Rice growing, as noted above, was the core of the traditional subsistence economy of Kabikolan. It was largely ignored by outsiders, who calculated that it was economically much less profitable than abaca, or indeed almost any cash crop. The price of rice paddies remained high, however, and there is some evidence suggesting that rice was held in particular esteem by the indigenous elite, the *principalia*. In debates over the legal separation of new towns from old, for example, both proponents and opponents of the separation shared a rhetorical assumption that rice growing was the only sound and suitable basis for a municipal economy, unlike ephemeral cash-cropping or commerce. Scattered evidence on landholding suggests that rice paddies were proportionately more concentrated in the hands of the *principalia* than abaca fields. Nor were such priorities confined to the more backward elements of the provincial elite. During a period from 1847 to 1860, encompassing the first great abaca boom in Albay, the dean of the most influential Bikolano family, Sinforoso Imperial de Vera, had the purchase of 21 rice paddies notarized, but not a single field of abaca.[36]

The other obsession of the *principalia* was political influence, which could be acquired and demonstrated through either of two routes. One was municipal elections, which were bitterly contested in late 19th century Kabikolan — unlike Central Luzon, where truly influential Filipinos were said to shun local office. Elections occasionally had to be repeated because of charges and counter-charges of corruption, some of which even reached the ears of Madrid. Powerful families, such as the Durans of Polangui, used a variety of municipal offices to exercise social and economic dominance over an entire town. The other route was through the colonial bureaucracy, using a knowledge of the Spanish language and a willingness to be useful to the colonialists. The classic example is again Sinforoso Imperial de Vera, who, besides being a municipal official in two different towns (at different times), served the Spaniards as translator, schoolteacher, court assistant, special commissioner for the prosecution of gambling, public defender and official witness. He also helped secure for one of his sons the posts of court assistant, member of the provincial board on labour service, and commissioner for criminal prosecution; for another son, official witness and eventually public scribe.[37] Both families, the Durans and Imperials, went on to be major forces in 20th century Bikol politics.

What do rice growing and local politics have in common? Essentially, both offer the possibility of controlling other people as well as acquiring monetary wealth. Outsiders, having no particular desire to acquire Bikolano clients, looked only at the monetary returns of rice growing, which were comparatively meagre. To a Bikolano, or an outsider wishing to integrate himself into Bikol society, to control rice lands meant also to have the power to be a patron. A rice tenant is much more dependent on his landlord than an abaca stripper is.[38] Furthermore, rice is necessary and permanent. The owner of rice paddies does not depend on the fluctuations of an external market he cannot control; whatever the crop is, he owns it, and the shorter the supply the greater influence this ownership gives him over those who must eat. And as population pressure began to be felt in 20th century Kabikolan, the position of the landlord was further enhanced.

Similarly, in a Philippine context, political office has always implied the power not only to benefit the common weal and to enrich the office holder, but also to do favours for friends. One can detect in the fragmentary evidence on 19th century politics signs of those patterns of patron–client relationships reinforced by control of public office that have so often been described in the 20th century. Indirect testimony pointing in the same direction is derived from the history of the office of public scribe. Under the Spanish system, this office was for sale, with the assumption that the revenues it produced (fees for notarization, etc.) would recompense the holder for the cost of acquisition. Early in the 19th century Spaniards held the post in Camarines, but later in the century they were outbid by Filipinos. We cannot prove that the Filipinos who purchased the office there and in Albay did so because in addition to its nominal revenues it offered powers which could be converted into political favours and obligations. But it is striking that both offices eventually wound up in the hands of two of the most politically powerful families in turn-of-the-century Kabikolan — the Abellas of Camarines Sur and the Imperials of Albay.[39]

Another hint of the continuing importance of manpower control in Kabikolan lies in the growing number of people whose occupation is defined not by what they did but by the fact that they served — "dependants", "servants", "agents", "domestics", etc. Unlike peasants, whose basic livelihood was derived from their own productive labour, such "servants" were full-time retainers, who lived directly on wages or favours from their master, and whose only profession was to do whatever he told them. The evidence for this development is tenuous, at best, but it is consonant with what we know of the 20th century Philippines and the evolution of peasant societies in general.

In the absence of direct corroboration, this interpretation of 19th century Bikol society and values must remain speculative. But it does offer something other than the putative "passivity and peacefulness" of the Bikolanos to account for their comparatively minor role in commercial activities within the region. It also helps to explain both how certain families rose to prominence in 20th century Bikol politics, and why Bikolano politicians never achieved real national influence. On the national scene, it was not enough to control a loyal local constituency. A would-be leader needed also access to substantial wealth (far more than rice growing ever offered) and some appreciation of or experience in the more modern sectors of the economy. The same choices which had served the Bikol *principalía* well within their own region inhibited them in the larger national context.

Two Conclusions

There are two ways of approaching a general assessment of the history of Kabikolan from 1825 to 1925. The most obvious is to ask why a century of cash-crop prosperity failed to result in more permanent development. This question cannot, of course, be answered in isolation. To be meaningful, an answer would have to include other cases in which export growth *had* been utilized successfully as the basis for development. Such a comparison is beyond the scope of this essay; here we can only offer some crude hypotheses.

For the specific failure of the abaca industry it is not hard to find specific causes: falling world prices, rising world competition and changing world technology; plant disease and soil fatigue; and an established productive system incapable of radical change. Many of these are common, in one form or another, throughout the Third World. The great depression of primary products lasted roughly from 1913 to 1950, undercutting dozens of economies whose prosperity was based on the export of tropical produce.[40] Technology, almost by definition, is capable of rendering certain commodities, occupations and whole industries obsolete as it streamlines production. Environmental and cultural problems remain extraordinarily difficult to handle, much less predict, as the vicissitudes of the contemporary "green revolution" testify.

Population growth, in Kabikolan as elsewhere, also increased the pressure on agricultural land, tipped the balance of local power even farther toward the landowners, and generally inhibited progressive change, since the element of risk seems higher as the slack in the agrarian sector disappears. With unprecedented rates of natural increase, shrinking internal frontiers and no colonies of their own in which to expand, the Third World has faced demographic obstacles to development far more serious than those which the industrial West had to surpass.

Nevertheless, the suspicion remains that some adjustment should have been possible. Even if there was no way to forestall the collapse of the abaca boom, during the prosperous decades "developmental foundations" might have been laid — agricultural modernization, infrastructure growth, the rise of domestic entrepreneurial and administrative elites, and the generation of domestic finance (taxes and savings) capable of maintaining public services and high levels of capital formation.[41] The Bikolanos should somehow, we feel, have made themselves capable of creating new kinds of prosperity when abaca finally faltered, even as New Englanders had transcended the end of whaling.

Lack of initiative is one of the implicit charges levelled against the Bikolanos (and all Filipinos, and the entire Third World) as an explanation for their continued poverty. Had they had the entrepreneurial skills, the self-discipline, the inventive and innovative genius that characterized the West, it has been argued, they would have been as rich as the West. This study provides some evidence in support of the unsurprising view that cultural differences toward economic activity do exist, and that maximization of profits is not a universally accepted priority. But such a view, which tends toward "blaming the victim", hardly seems adequate as a total explanation of persistent poverty.

An alternative perspective would be to focus on lack of autonomy — the inability of the Bikolanos to control their own polity or economy. They gained their primary cash income by the sale of a single product to a world market almost wholly dependent on the economic cycles of England and the United States. They paid taxes and followed regulations promulgated first in Madrid, later in Washington. They sold their produce to Spaniards and Americans and bought rice and cloth from the Chinese. Had they wanted to compete, they would have had great difficulty obtaining access to capital or market contacts. Even the Philippine Assembly, like the later Senate, Commonwealth and Republic, was located in Manila and reflected that city's continued domination over the interests of the provinces. The Bikolanos never had the option of establishing their own tariffs, depending on their own markets, inviting or excluding their own choice of immigrants, creating their own infrastructure, supporting their own agricultural research, shaping their own destiny. Colonized doubly, by the West and by Manila, they experienced that absence of autonomy which characterizes the Third World.[42]

It is hardly necessary to add that there is no guarantee — or even particular probability — that the Bikolanos would have in fact used such autonomy to create self-sustaining economic growth. In the panorama of history, for every Japan which has succeeded in converting political independence into economic strength, a dozen Thailands or Mexicos have failed. Such examples, however, suggest the pervasive influence of imperialism — its endless efforts to manipulate even where direct colonial control is not held, its perpetual threat of intervention. A single study can hardly settle the universal question of Third World poverty, but clearly the "failure" of Kabikolan must be judged within the context of global imperialism, and putative lack of initiative must be balanced by demonstrable lack of autonomy.

There is another way to look at Bikol history, however, if we can suppress some of our historical hindsight long enough to do it. That is to look at the Bikolanos in their own history, not simply as progenitors of later generations to whom they are somehow responsible. Nothing in the available sources suggests that most Bikolanos, however much they cared for their families, intended to subordinate their individual dreams to their collective destiny, sacrificing the present for the future of their race or region. In the absence of evidence that such was their ambition, it is unfair to judge the Bikolanos of the 19th century for their failure to lay "developmental foundations" on which their posterity might build.

We have no clearly articulated statement of 19th century Bikolano values, but we can learn something about them from the sources we do have. The Bikolanos were and are devout Roman Catholics. They were good farmers, skilled artisans, adept sailors and brave fighters when they had to be. They enjoyed gambling, drinking and singing, and had one of the highest birth rates in the Philippines. Although they frequently complained about excessive taxes and abuses by the Spanish government, they were hardly in a state of revolutionary readiness by 1896, or even 1898. Not until after independence would rural radicalism take root in Kabikolan. Economically, the Bikolanos took no unnecessary chances, but they were quick to seize the opportunities for a higher income offered by abaca cultivation. Over the course of a century, the decisions made by the Bikolanos about their own lives seem to have resulted in marginally increased prosperity and a largely intact traditional culture. Their strategy, if we may call it that, blended the retention of many local institutions and values with the selective seizing of certain new opportunities. It is presumptuous of us to study their "failure" without also recognizing their success.

NOTES

Research on this topic in Spain and the Philippines (1972-1973) was funded by the Foreign Area Fellowship Program and the University of Michigan. While in the Philippines, the author was a Visiting Research Associate of the Institute of Philippine Culture, Ateneo de Manila University.

1 Unless otherwise indicated, all the data on which this paper is based are found in my doctoral dissertation, "Kabikolan in the Nineteenth Century: Socio-economic Change in the Provincial Philippines" (University of Michigan, 1976), although the analysis differs in certain respects.

2 Norman G. Owen, "Winding Down the War in Albay, 1900-1903," *Pacific Historical Review* 48 (November 1979), 557-89.

3 [Leonard S. Goddard], *The Province of Albay* (Manila: Albay Fair Association, 1912).

4 For a brief description of Kabikolan in the 1930s see, Robert L. Pendleton, "The Bicol Region: From the Notebook of a Soil Technologist," *Philippine Agriculturist* 23 (September 1934), 247-52.

5 On the geography of Kabikolan see, U.S. War Department, Division of Insular Affairs, *A Pronouncing Gazetteer and Geographical Dictionary of the Philippine Islands* (Washington: GPO, 1902); U.S. Bureau of the Census, *Census of the Philippine Islands . . . in the Year 1903,* (Washington: GPO, 1905); Robert Huke [et al.], *Shadows on the Land* (Manila: Bookmark, 1963); Frederick L. Wernstedt and Joseph E. Spencer, *The Philippine Island World* (Berkeley: University of California Press, 1967); Luis General, Jr., Lydia SD. San José, and Rosalio Al. Parrone, eds., *Readings on Bikol Culture* (City of Naga: University of Nueva Caceres, [1972]), 1-9.

6 On Moro raids in Kabikolan, see, Owen, "Kabikolan," 34-47, based on documents from the Philippine National Archives (Ereccion de Pueblos, Albay) and from the Museo Naval, Madrid, as well as the standard 19th century published accounts by Vicente Barrantes and José Montero y Vidal. For the larger context of raiding see, James F. Warren, "Trade-Raid-Slave: The Socio-economic Patterns of the Sulu Zone, 1770-1898" (doctoral dissertation, Australian National University, 1976), which for this period generally supersedes Cesar Adib Majul, *Muslims in the Philippines* (Quezon City: University of the Philippines Press, 1973).

7 The major manuscript sources on the Bikol silk-weaving project are found in
   the Museo Naval. On the Bourbon reforms the most comprehensive account
   in English is five articles by Maria Lourdes Díaz-Trechuelo in *Philippine
   Studies,* 1963-1966, based on her research in the Archivo General de Indias,
   Seville. See also, Díaz-Trechuelo, *La Real Companía Filipina* (Seville: Escuela
   de Estudios Hispano-Americanos, 1965); María Luisa Rodriguez Baena, *La
   Sociedad Económica de Amigos del País de Manila en el siglo XVIII* (Seville:
   Escuela de Estudios Hispano-Americanos, 1966); Benito Fernandez Legarda,
   Jr., "Foreign Trade, Economic Change and Entrepreneurship in the Nine-
   teenth Century Philippines" (doctoral dissertation, Harvard University,
   1955), 106-68; Nicholas P. Cushner, S.J., *Spain in the Philippines* (Quezon
   City: Ateneo de Manila University, 1971), 186-96; Edilberto C. De Jesús,
   "The Tobacco Monopoly in the Philippines, 1782-1882" (doctoral disserta-
   tion, Yale University, 1973), 17-62.

8 U.S. Department of State, *Despatches from United States Consul in Manila,
   1817-1899,* microfilm (Washington: National Archives, 1955); Legarda,
   "Foreign Trade," 171-90, 360-62, 397-429; Benito Legarda, Jr., "American
   Entrepreneurs in the 19th Century Philippines," *Bulletin of the American
   Historical Collection* (Manila) 1 (June 1972), 25-52; Museo Naval (Pascual
   Enrile papers).

9 Samuel Eliot Morison, *The Ropemakers of Plymouth* (Boston: Houghton
   Mifflin, 1950); *Cordage Trade Journal* (New York), 1890-1900.

10 Legarda, "American Entrepreneurs"; Norman Owen, "Americans in the
   Abaca Trade: Peele, Hubbell & Co., 1856-1875" (forthcoming); Nicholas Tarling, "Some Aspects of British Trade in the Philippines in the Nineteenth
   Century," *Journal of History* (Manila) 9 (September-December 1963),
   287-327.

11 See the correspondence of Peele, Hubbell & Co. partners George Henry
   Peirce (Stanford University Libraries), Richard Dalton Tucker (Peabody
   Museum, Salem), and Frederick Emory Foster (Lopez Memorial Museum,
   Pasay City), as well as papers dealing with the estate of Jonathan Russell
   (Baker Library, Harvard University).

12 Owen, "Kabikolan," 127-36, 393-402, using data principally derived from
   merchant circulars and Manila newspapers (such as *El Comercio*), *Cordage
   Trade Journal,* public works budgets (for wage rates) and cockfight revenues
   from documents in the Archivo Histórico Nacional, Madrid (Sección de
   Ultramar), land sales and public market taxes from documents in the
   Philippine National Archives (Protocolos, Albay, and Mercados Publicos,
   Ambos Camarines), and parish records from the towns of Polangui,
   Guinobatan, Camalig and Libog [Sto. Domingo] in Albay.

13 For period descriptions of abaca cultivation, see, Manuel Blanco, O.S.A.,
   Flora de Filipinas (Manila: Sto. Tomás, 1837), 246-50; U.S. Congress,

Senate, *Report from the Secretary of the Navy . . . Relative to the Cultivation and Manufacture of Hemp,* 29 June 1842, Senate Document, Vol. 2, No. 6, 27th Congress, 3rd Session, 1842-43; J[ean Baptiste] Mallat [de Bassilan], *Les Philippines* (Paris: Arthur Bertrand, 1846), 1:134-35, 2:279-80; José Felipe del Pan, "El Abacá," *Boletín Oficial del ministerio del Fomento* 32 (December 1859), 385-401; Feodor Jagor, *Travels in the Philippines* (1873; Manila: Filipiniana Book Guild, 1965), 222-34; Frederick Emory Foster [Forastero], "Letter descriptive of a visit to the Hemp producing districts of the Philippine Islands," 24 March 1876, Lopez Memorial Museum (No. 3310); Abelardo Cuesta y Cardenal, *Memoria sobre el beneficio de abacá á máquina* (Manila: R. Mercantil, 1887); "Cultivo del Abacá en la Provincia de Albay," 7 February 1892, Archivo Histórico Nacional (Ultramar, Legajo 473, Expediente 29); John Foreman, *The Philippine Islands* (London: Samson Low, Marston & Co., 1899), 324-33; Clarence W. Dorsey, "Report on Abacá or Manila Hemp Soils of the Philippines," 10 September 1902, in U.S. War Department, Bureau of Insular Affairs, Philippine Commission, *Report of the Philippine Commission For the Year 1902* (Washington: GPO, 1902), 1:642-52; Mariano Abella, "The Cultivation of Abaca," *Census of 1903,* 4:22-28; Philippine Islands, Department of the Interior, Bureau of Agriculture, *Abacá (Manila Hemp),* by H.T. Edwards and Murad M. Saleeby (Manila: Bureau of Printing, 1910).

14   References to Ilongos in the Bikol provincial trade come primarily from the Philippine National Archives (Ereccion de Pueblos, Camarines Sur, and Protocolos, Albay); for Spaniards and Americans see also the correspondence of the partners of Peele, Hubbell & Co. (note 11, above).

15   *Ibid.*

16   Income calculations are based on the daily wage rates (₱0.19-0.25) for unskilled labour (derived from public works budgets in the Archivo Histórico Nacional) and on the estimated share (₱0.23-0.35) of an abaca stripper cleaning one-half *arroba* (5.75 kg) of fibre per day and receiving one-half of the provincial price for abaca. It is assumed that actual employment was on the order of 200 days a year, allowing both for numerous fiestas and for periods of unemployment due to adverse weather conditions. For land registers, see Philippine National Archives (Estadisticas, Albay).

17   Morison, *Ropemakers of Plymouth,* 78-85; *Cordage Trade Journal;* Arthur S. Dewing, *History of the National Cordage Company* (Cambridge: Harvard University Press, 1913); *Under Four Flags: The Story of Smith, Bell & Company in the Philippines* (n.p., n.d.); Edgar Wickberg, *The Chinese in Philippine Life: 1850-1898* (New Haven: Yale University Press, 1965), 96-108; Philippine National Archives (Protocolos, Padrones de Chinos, and Estadisticas, Albay); "Los Chinos en Esta Provincia," *El Eco del Sur* (Nueva Caceres), 27 May 1894. See, Owen, "Kabikolan," 129-30, 157-71, for an overview of late 19th century change in the abaca industry.

18 Pan, "El Abacá," 390; Ramón González Fernández and Federico Moreno y
    Jéres, *Manual del Viajero en Filipinas* (Manila: Santo Tomás, 1875), 172-78:
    Cuesta y Cardenal; "Cultivo"; Foreman, *The Philippine Islands,* 324-26; Ed-
    wards and Saleeby, *Abacá,* 31-32.

19 Philippine National Archives (Estadisticas, Albay).

20 The major primary source on the abaca industry in the American period is
    the United States National Archives (Record Group 350, File 845).

21 Philippines, Commonwealth, Department of Labor, "Fact-Finding Survey
    Report," 21 January 1937, by Ramón Torres (typescript copy in the
    American Historical Collection, Manila); Pendleton, "The Bicol Region";
    Hugo H. Miller, *Principles of Economics Applied to the Philippines* (Boston:
    Ginn. & Co., 1932); *American Chamber of Commerce Journal* (Manila) 7
    (June 1927) and 10 (July 1930). Data on tenantry and other aspects of
    agriculture are often derived from the censuses of 1903, 1918 and 1939; see,
    Norman G.Owen, "Philippine Economic Development and American Policy:
    A Reappraisal," in, Owen, ed., *Compadre Colonialism* (Ann Arbor: Universi-
    ty of Michigan, Center for South and Southeast Asian Studies, 1971),
    116-18, on some difficulties in using these data.

22 [H.T. Edwards], "Report on Investigation of the Abaca Industry . . . 1925";
    Edwards, "Conditions in the Bicol Abacá Industry" [1932]; Mariano Gar-
    chitorena, *The Philippine Abaca Industry: Its Problems* (Manila: Bureau of
    Printing, 1938); all in United States National Archives and Records Service,
    (Record Group 350, File 845, items 808-A, 904-A, and 915).

23 *Ibid;* see also, Charles O. Houston, Jr., "The Philippine Abaca Industry:
    1934-1950," *University of Manila Journal of East Asiatic Studies* 3 (1954),
    267-86, 408-15.

24 W. Arthur Lewis, ed., *Tropical Development, 1880-1913* (London: George
    Allen & Unwin, 1970), 32-33 and *passim*; Michael Adas, *The Burma Delta*
    (Madison: University of Wisconsin Press, 1974); Norman G. Owen, "The Rice
    Industry of Mainland Southeast Asia: 1850-1914," *Journal of the Siam
    Society* 54 (July 1971), 139-41.

25 Descriptions of all or part of Kabikolan used in this and succeeding sections
    include among published works, Jagor, *Travels in the Philippines;* Felix de
    Huerta, O.F.M., *Estado geográfico . . . de la . . . Provincia de S. Gregorio
    Magno* (Binondo: M. Sanchez, 1865); Agustín de la Cavada y Mendez de
    Vigo, *Historia geográfica, geológica y estadística de Filipinas* (Manila:
    Ramírez y Giraudier, 1866); J[oseph] Montano, *Voyages aux Philippines et
    en Malaisie* (Paris: Librairie Hachette, 1886); Juan Alvarez Guerra, *Viajes
    por Filipinas: de Manila á Albay* (Madrid: Fortanet, 1887); Adolfo Puya Ruiz,
    Camarines Sur (Manila: "La Oceanía Española," 1887); Joaquín Pellicena
    Camacho, *Por el país del Bicol* (Legazpi: V.R. Vega, 1917); Mariano Goyena

del Prado, *Ibalón* (Manila: General Printing Press, 1940); and the reports of provincial officials in the annual *Report of the Philippine Commission, 1901-1908*. Manuscript descriptions may be found in the Archivo General de Indias (including reports on a diocesan visit of 1791-1792), the Museo Naval (including notes by members of the Malaspina expedition, 1792, and reports by provincial officials in 1807 and 1830-1835), the Biblioteca Nacional de Madrid (including reports on Camarines Norte in 1886), the Philippine National Archives (including reports on Albay in 1844, 1861 and 1885, and on Sorsogon in 1894), and the United States National Archives (including unpublished reports of provincial governors, 1909-1916).

26 See, Owen, "Kabikolan," 196-202, for these calculations.

27 *Ibid.*, 189-95; baptismal data from Guinobatan (Albay) parish records.

28 *Cordage Trade Journal* 20 (19 April 1900); Edwards, "Conditions," 7; Wernstedt and Spencer, *Philippine Island World,* 416.

29 Owen, "Kabikolan," 207-09, 456-58, analyzing data primarily derived from documents in the Philippine National Archives. Information on commercial industries in general is summarized in *ibid.,* 216-97.

30 Pedro Licup (Diocesan Chief Notary), in "Testimonio de la Visita Diocesana de Nueva Caceres año de 1791," Archivo General de Indias, Ramo de Filipinas, Legajo 1033.

31 See, Owen, "Kabikolan," 306-21, for an analysis of this shift, based on data from the Philippine National Archives (Ereccion de Pueblos, Albay), the Museo Naval, and the Archivo Histórico Nacional (Ultramar).

32 Philippine National Archives (Mercados Publicos, Camarines Sur; Padrones de Chinos, Albay; Protocolos, Albay); Archivo Histórico Nacional (Ultramar); Alvarez Guerra, *Viajes por Filipinas, passim*; Montano, *Voyages,* 90-100; Puya Ruiz, *Camarines Sur,* 94-96 and *passim*; *El Eco del Sur,* 1894; Wickberg, *The Chinese,* 96-98.

33 The expansion of the Spanish presence in the Philippines was noted by such 19th century authors as Jagor, Alvarez Guerra, Montero y Vidal, and José Rizal, *The Lost Eden (Noli Me Tangere)* (New York: W.W. Norton, 1968), 22. The best 20th century description of this expansion is Eliodoro Robles, *The Philippines in the Nineteenth Century* (Quezon City: Malaya Books, 1969).

34 For Spanish officialdom in Kabikolan see, the annual *Guía de Filipinas* and individual personnel files in the Archivo Histórico Nacional (Ultramar); on the Franciscans, see, Eusebio Gómez Plátero, O.F.M., *Catálogo biográfico de los Religiosos Franciscanos de la Provincia de San Gregorio Magno de Filipinas* (Manila: Santo Tomás, 1880).

35 Population data from the *Census of 1903*; descriptive data from Alvarez Guerra, Puya Ruiz, etc.

36 Philippine National Archives (Estadisticas, Ereccion de Pueblos, and Protocolos, Albay); Archivo Histórico Nacional (Ultramar).

37 Philippine National Archives (Ereccion de Pueblos and Eleccion de Gobernadorcillos, Albay); Archivo Histórico Nacional (Ultramar); Norman Owen, "The Principalia in Philippine History," *Philippine Studies* 22 (1974), 297-324.

38 Factors promoting closer relations between rice tenants and their landlords include the need for farming capital (seed, farm implements and draught animals), mutually agreed-upon arrangements for water control, sharp seasonal demands for extra labour (often necessitating borrowing), and simple physical proximity of lowland paddy-fields to lowland towns.

39 Archivo Histórico Nacional (Ultramar).

40 Lewis, *Tropical Development,* 29-43.

41 *Ibid.*

42 On the concept of subordination (absence of autonomy) in Southeast Asian local history, see, Ruth T. McVey, "Introduction: Local Voices, Central Power," in, McVey, ed., *Southeast Asian Transitions* (New Haven: Yale University Press, 1978), 1-31.

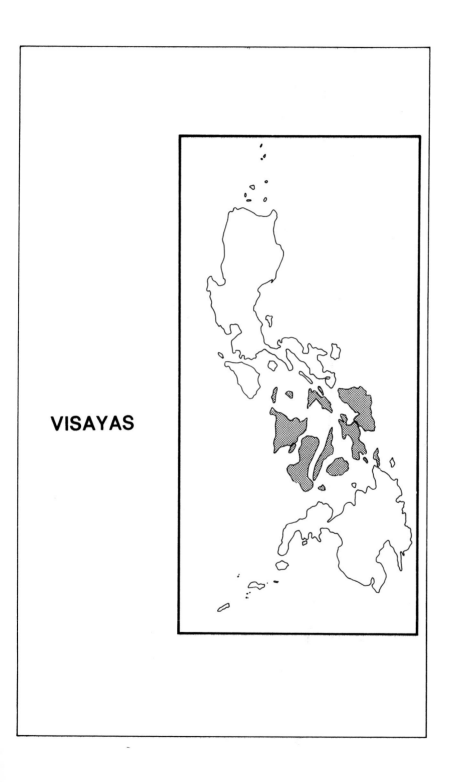

VISAYAS

Continuity and Change in the Economic and Administrative History of 19th Century Samar

BRUCE CRUIKSHANK

For most of its history the island of Samar has been a backwater. Although it is the archipelago's third largest island and over 5,000 square miles in area, little attention has been paid to this easternmost island in the central Philippines. An area may be considered a backwater on at least three grounds: little happened there; what happened there was overshadowed by events elsewhere; or, as a partial corollary to both of the preceding, it has commanded little attention from either administrators or historians. During the period of Spanish colonial rule, Samar qualifies on all three grounds.

To categorize an area as a backwater does not necessarily mean it lacks a certain charm, interest or history. It only means that its appeal and history are less perceptible than those of other areas. Samar, of course, does have a history, parts of which are interesting and even unique when compared to other regons of the archipelago. For most of the Spanish period, for example, Samar's parishes were headed by Jesuit and Augustinian friars, the Spanish "regulars". Native "secular" priests consequently acquired comparatively few parishes. Despite the strong missionary influence on the island, there were none of the friar-owned estates that aroused such strong anti-colonial conflicts in Cebu and in Central Luzon. Rebellions on Samar were relatively few. The most notable were the Sumoroy Rebellion of 1649-1650 and a cluster of revolts over 200 years later in 1884-1886.[1] Although there were marked advances in municipal, or *pueblo,* administration in the late 18th and 19th centuries,[2] Samar's population remained largely dispersed and there were no settlements approaching the size of the sugar haciendas of Negros, the friar estates of the Manila region, or the commercialized farming villages of Central Luzon. Like the whole of the archipelago, there was a marked rise in the island's population in the 19th century — from 42,000 in 1800 to 245,000 in 1896.[3] But even by the standards of a sparsely populated archipelago, Samar still retained the character of an undeveloped frontier at the end of the 19th century.

As is customary in much of the literature on the Philippines, all of these comparisons have been made from the perspective of the "developed" regions — Manila, Central Luzon, Cebu or Iloilo — with the implicit assumption that their socio-economic patterns were somehow more characteristic or significant. One may, of course, test this set of assumptions by simply reversing the perspective. Putting the question in its most extreme form, one might ask how the rest of the archipelago conformed to the patterns of life on Samar. Might not the slower tempo of change on Samar been more typical of much of the archipelago than the accelerated development of Negros or Central Luzon? The rapid economic changes in these areas are exciting, if not dramatic, and quite naturally have tended to dominate the literature. But when viewed from an archipelago-wide perspective, the events there may have been atypical. Certainly for Samar they were. From Samar's perspective the changes in those areas were too early and too grand in both scope and consequence. Before we can place the whole of the 19th century Philippines in perspective, we need to know as much about Samar as we do about the oft-discussed changes in Negros and Central Luzon.

Agriculture and Commerce

As late as 1860 Samar was an island of dispersed settlements only loosely bound together by a common religion, a lightly felt administrative structure, and a few ties between *pueblos* through the interchange of goods. Commerce was only of minor importance, represented in most *pueblos* by the periodic appearance of travelling merchants or the governor. Few other persons or events from the outside impinged on the Samareños,[4] most of whom were bound by age-old rituals of religion and the basic patterns of their crops and environment.

In 1859 the German naturalist and world traveller, Feodor Jagor, made a short and strenuous tour of Samar. The record of his journey to all parts of the island provides us with a description of life on the island before the significant changes of later decades. His travels began in July when he arrived in Laoang after taking three days to cross the becalmed San Bernardino Strait from the Bikol Peninsula. He then walked to Catarman and was rowed up the river to the Salta Sangley watershed between Catarman and Calbayog. After crossing the divide on foot, he spent the night at a chapel on the Calbayog side. The next morning, a minor *pueblo* official from Catarman, who had accompanied him this far, helped him locate a boat and rowers for the trip down the Calbayog River. They left about 7 a.m. and arrived at Calbayog about 11 p.m. The next day they left for Catbalogan in the afternoon, since a thunderstorm had kept them ashore during the morning, and arrived in Catbalogan that night. Jagor stayed in Catbalogan for a few days and made side trips to Calbiga. He then began his journey to the east coast through the rough interior via boat, litter (he had hurt his foot in Calbiga), and boat again. He rested for a few days on the way before finishing the trip to Paric by boat and portage. From Paric he by-passed Tubig and sailed directly to Borongan for several days. Then he proceeded to Guivan, rested there for some more days, then tried to sail to Tacloban, Leyte. Once more, though, he was becalmed and spent 31 hours on the water while being rowed to Tacloban. He returned once more to Samar, to Basey, but only for a brief visit from Tacloban.

Jagor's route and travels are an apt illustration of certain essential aspects of life on Samar. One detail constantly met in his book is the time and difficulties that travel involved. He was becalmed in the San Bernardino Strait and the Leyte Gulf, and had to rely on his feet, boats and Samareños to carry him on his way. At no time did he ride a horse or take a carriage, because the roads were so poor: "Samar has scarcely any other means of communications besides the navigation of the coast and rivers, the interior being roadless, and burdens have to be conveyed on the shoulders." Throughout his journey he relied on the priests and officials to help him hire porters, find accommodation and guide him. There were no inns. He stayed with priests, in government houses in the *pueblos,* and in a rented house in Catbalogan. Travellers were evidently rare, especially European ones.

Jagor observed almost no industry of any kind on Samar. Only at Borongan and Guivan did he note anything like a large-scale exploitation of Samar's natural products. Commerce was rudimentary and almost restricted to certain *pueblos* and areas. At Laoang there was "little tillage" and even fishing was neglected, whereas Catbalogan was the centre of maritime trade. He met merchants from Catbalogan who had come to Catarman to collect rice for transport to Albay, just as they car-

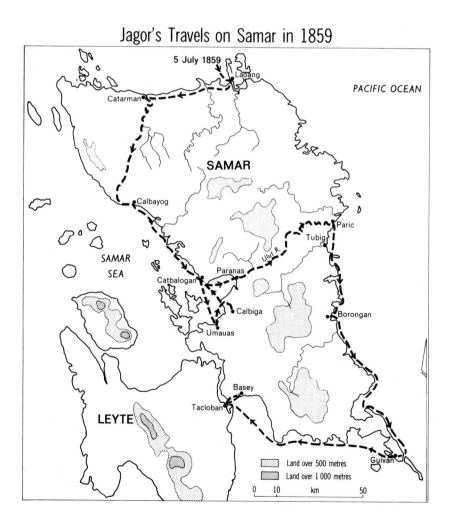

Jagor's Travels on Samar in 1859

ried goods to and from Manila and Guivan. Guivan was the centre of "the most important district in Samar".

By and large there were "no markets in Samar and Leyte". Trade and credit arrangements were simple and "less developed in eastern and northern Samar than in the western part of the island which keeps up a more active communications with the other inhabitants of the archipelago". Barter with rice and fabrics was usual, especially "in the interior where there is hardly any money". All sorts of forest products were grown and exchanged, but only coconut oil and rice were significant. Abaca was mentioned but only in passing. Not surprisingly, since commerce was minimal and money rare, honesty and family discipline were still strong on Samar; robbery and theft were rare. Families took care of their own poor — only in Catbalogan were there charity cases (and only eight of these), whereas in Albay (whose commercial development preceded Samar's) beggars "are not wanting".

Apparently there was little of note occurring on Samar. As a naturalist, Jagor of course described the vegetation and animals. Otherwise, topography and the travails of travel preoccupied him, with short asides on a *pueblo* election, "pirates", Samareño customs, agriculture and commerce. In 1859 Samar was still far removed from major political or commercial currents. The Spanish governor was appointed by Manila, supervised *pueblo* elections, and relied on the friars for effective local knowledge and control. Moro raids had ended but sea travel was still not completely safe. The major towns were Catbalogan and Guivan; Calbayog was only mentioned for the good view from the parish house. The few traders, working out of Catbalogan and Guivan, moved from place to place collecting small amounts of many crops, especially coconut oil, rice and forest products, and took them to Manila, Albay or Cebu.[5]

As Jagor indicated, Samar was a rural island. The number of major crops — coconuts, rice, and later abaca — was few, but the number of forest and sea products used by the Samareños was legion. Typical crops included rice, coconuts, abaca, bananas, sugarcane, tubers, tobacco, cacao, coffee and various fruits. From the sea came many kinds of fish, sea cucumbers (*balate*) and shark fins (*aletas de tiburon*). At the margins where the sea met the rivers grew mangroves and nipa palms, sources of a multitude of materials for the house as well as the cuisine. From the forests came honey, wax, wild pigs and other game, timber and rattan. Medicines and clothing also were taken from the immediate environment of the Samareños — from the famed seed of St. Ignatius (*igasud* in Samar-Leyte Visayan), used for a wide range of fevers and other ailments,[6] to cloth made from the abaca plant's fibre. With the ingenuity man has displayed throughout his history, Samareños produced a deceptively potent drink called *tuba* from coconut and nipa palms.[7] Coconut palms also yielded copra and oil, while abaca was the source of ropes and cloth, and pigs and carabaos yielded lard and hides. The variety of foods, plants and building materials was immense. The population did not, then, lack a basis for self-sufficiency. Samar had "nothing to envy in productions to other (regions) of the archipelago".[8]

Most of these products were used locally, but some were important in commerce.

In 1851, 35 boats carried away cargoes of abaca fibres and cloth, coconuts and oil, shark fins and sea cucumbers, turtle shells, pigs and lard, carabao hides, rattan and timber, rice, wax and other products with a total value of ₱121,000.[9] Samar, however, was a minor producer for the archipelago's commerce: ₱121,000 was only about ten percent of the total going to Manila from either the Visayas or the Zamboanga–Sulu area. Even Leyte sent products totalling about ₱56,000 more than Samar's.[10]

Within Samar itself, the variety of products should not conceal the importance of three plants. Rice, coconuts and abaca were the primary concerns of the Samareños and their most essential sources for food, trade and clothing. Samar, unlike Central Luzon, is not blessed with large plains which allow large-scale, rice monoculture. The north coast plain from Palapag to west of Catarman is the island's largest level lowland area available for rice cultivation, and its major source of rice exports, usually to the Bikol Peninsula. Jagor noted the presence of Catbalogan merchants in Catarman buying some of this rice for transport across the San Bernardino Strait. While the north coast was the major producer, all regions seem to have produced some rice.

It appears that most rice, even that grown on the north plain, was not "wet" or artificially irrigated rice but "dry" rice which depended upon the rains for moisture. In 1876, a governor of Samar said that the rice produced on Samar was "almost all of the mountain" variety, i.e. dry rice.[11] The method used to grow this dry rice was *kaingin,* or slash-and-burn, and was usually employed in hill or mountain country, generally in areas of second-growth forest. The cultivators cut down the trees and brush, allowed them to dry, and then set fire to them just before the rains were expected. Once the rains came, the seeds were simply dropped into holes that had been punched into the ground with sharpened sticks. After two years, when most swiddens had lost their fertility, the cultivators moved to a new area and had to allow eight to 15 years for the land to recover.

One of the main barriers to introduction of wet rice cultivation was lack of draught animals, carabaos, on the island. Wet rice cultivation depends heavily upon the use of carabaos for ploughing, "puddling" and harrowing, but they were scarce or non-existent on 18th century Samar. In 1784-1785 two Franciscan documents stated that there were no carabaos on the island,[12] but a number of 19th century sources show evidence of them[13] — a discrepancy perhaps explained by the Franciscan claim that the order reintroduced the draught beasts to Samar after 1835.[14]

Like many areas of the archipelago, Samar moved, at some point in the 19th century, from a net-exporter of rice to a net-importer. In 1870 Samar imported 50,600 *cavans* of husked rice and exported 114,445 *cavans* of unhusked rice.[15] It is one of the characteristics of Samar's commercial geography that it was, and is, easier to import rice from other areas of the Philippines to rice-deficient areas of Samar than from rice-abundant areas on the island's own north coast; hence the two figures. If we assume that it takes about two units of unhusked *palay* to make one unit of milled *arroz,*[16] the net surplus for all of Samar in 1870 was about 6,500 cavans of *arroz*. By 1876, no rice at all, even from the north coast, was exported, and about 25,000 *cavans of arroz* was imported.[17] By the 1890s, 60-65,000 *cavans of arroz* were imported, and none exported.[18]

Samar and Major Settlements in 1800

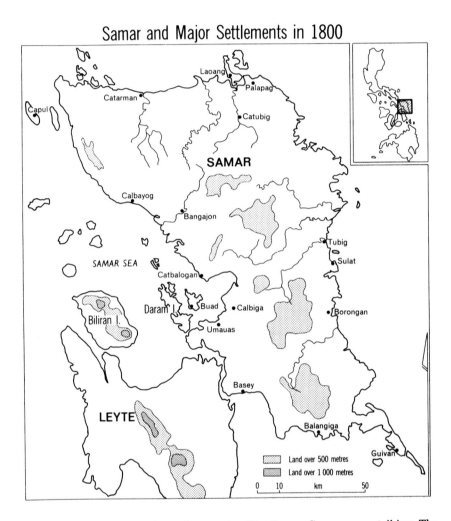

The contrasts between rice and coconut cultivation on Samar were striking. The main area of rice production was the north coast, while the south and southeast coasts were the centres of coconut palm holdings. Rice was produced largely for local food consumption, while coconuts enjoyed steady export demand and had a variety of uses (drinking wine, cooking oil, etc.). Coconut trees required little attention, but rice demanded a more constant cultivation. Rice fields were rotated, but coconut stands remained for many years.

Once the coconuts were harvested and the husks dried, the oil was extracted through an exceptionally crude process:

> The kernel is rasped out of the woody shell of the nut on rough boards, and left to rot; and a few boats in a state of decay, elevated on posts in the open air, serve as reservoirs, the oil dropping through their crevices into pitchers placed underneath; and finally the boards are subjected to pressure. This operation, which requires several months for its completion, yields such a bad, dark-brown, and viscid product that the pitcher fetches only two pesos and a quarter in Manila, while a superior oil costs six pesos.[19]

Nonetheless, Samar consistently produced and sold large amounts of coconut oil to merchants for sale to Manila.

The third of the three major crops grown on Samar was abaca, *Musa textilis,* a plant of the same genus as the banana and which looks quite similar to the uninitiated eye. It is native to the Philippines and northern Borneo. Grown throughout Samar, it has long been used as a source of rope and clothing, and is ideally suited to the island's mountainous terrain and frequent rainfall.[20] Three years after planting from seed or sprouts, the abaca plant is ready for stripping. It requires weeding only once or twice a year, can be harvested at any time, and will produce for some 15 years if carefully harvested. Its major enemies are strong winds, but by being planted in clearings with trees and bushes nearby it may be protected from these devastating effects.

Samar was a fortunate island for its people. Subsistence and commerce were both provided for. There were some regional variations and specialties (fish from the Catbalogan area; abundant rice on the north coast; abaca in the hills behind Calbayog, Tubig, Sulat and Borongan; and coconuts in the south), but all regions had enough for life and for trade. The three major crops offered a complementary relationship. Rice cultivation and fishing could be pursued seasonally, while the two main cash crops could be grown on the side, with minimal attention, to be harvested when the demands of fishing or rice growing slackened. Samar also had a complementary relationship between its coastal areas (with fish, nipa, mangroves and salt) and the interior (with abaca and forest products such as honey, wax, rattan and game).

Samar's history shows two major patterns of trade. The first, and oldest, was small-scale. It was dependent upon ambulatory Chinese mestizo merchants or government requisitions, and relied upon a variety of products. It was especially strong in the south, the Catbalogan area and the north coast. Responding to an increased world demand for abaca after 1860, a second pattern of large-scale trade emerged which was dominated by Chinese merchants and most important in the Calbayog area.

The character of the small-scale trade is revealed in the records of the island's 18th and 19th century trading expeditions. In 1779, after a ten-year absence because of the danger of Moro attacks, a fleet of 43 boats from Guivan and Leyte arrived in Manila carrying 30,280 litres of coconut oil, about 4,540 litres of lard,

and a large cargo of sea cucumbers, chocolate and cinnamon.[21] In the 1790s
Palapag sent four or five "large canoes with 14 oars" with wax, coconut oil, lard,
woven cloth and other goods to Manila, a round trip which took a month because of
the necessity to scout ahead for Moros.[22]

For the rest of the 18th century and well into the 19th, the pattern was the same:
small, sporadic groups of boats, sailing for Manila and the Bikol Peninsula, braving
the Moros in order to sell coconut oil, lard, wax, some "bad" tobacco, and abaca
fabrics.[23] Only five ships left from Samar for Manila in 1818,[24] but in 1829 there
were 31,[25] with the number rising to 41 in both 1833 and 1834.[26] In 1824, over
half of all the coconut oil sent to Manila came from Samar, about 435,000 litres, as
well as a substantial quantity of wax, turtle shells, sea cucumbers and shark fins.
The total value was over ₱35,000,[27] from a province whose annual revenues only
averaged about ₱18,000 in 1815.[28] In 1851, trips by 35 boats between Samar and
Manila carried cargoes totalling about ₱121,000 in value.[29]

Within Samar itself, certain regions were dominant both as sources and as trans-
shippers of goods. The south, especially Guivan, was active in the production of
coconut oil and sea products; it also collected and forwarded products from as far
north as San Julian on the east coast. Because of trade, Guivan and Basey may well
have been the wealthiest *pueblos* on Samar in the late 18th and early 19th centuries.[30] The north coast was also a frequent exporter, but mainly of its own goods
— rice, fabrics, wax, honey, and some fish, cattle and coconut products. The Catbalogan area was the major collector of goods from other regions for trans-
shipment to Manila. Its merchants drew goods from the whole west coast as well as
from the north coast; Santa Rita, Basey and Balangiga in the south; and overland
from the *pueblos* of Sulat, Tubig, Paric and Oras. Calbayog shipped some products
directly to Manila, but probably the bulk of its goods went via Catbalogan and its
merchants.

As in other areas of the Philippines, these merchants were primarily Chinese
mestizos.[31] In 1785, a Franciscan noted that the Samareños tended to sell their
rice, coconut oil, wax and woven cloth to Chinese mestizos, who then took them to
Cebu or Manila for resale.[32] Guivan was described as "very rich because of the
many Chinese mestizos there",[33] presumably because of the trade they conducted.
There apparently were some Samareño merchants as well, as a governor of Samar
observed in 1832:

> The little fishing and agriculture is in the hands of the most wretched [of the
> Samareños] who with much toil . . . pay their tribute tax [in kind], after which
> they live on the easily grown root crops . . . The rich class [of Samareños] or
> [Chinese] mestizos is entirely devoted to commerce . . . [34]

While not all of the merchants were Chinese mestizos, most of them were. Since
Manila and Cebu were the main entrepôts, those merchants who had connections
there would more easily receive advances, have storage facilities, and be more
adapted to the intricacies of trade. In all of these areas the Chinese mestizos had an

edge over the Samareños.[35]

While not all Chinese mestizos on Samar were engaged in trade, most had some connection with it. It follows, then, that the residence pattern of Chinese mestizos should indicate the major areas of trade. Catbalogan, the main collection port for trade goods, was probably the town with the most resident Chinese mestizos. Certainly, of all the Franciscan mission areas from 1778-1801, it was dominant, with about 300 Chinese mestizos living there, followed at a distance by Catarman (20 to 30) and Gandara (15 to 20). Catarman probably had Catbalogan representatives living there to ensure the collection of north coast rice and other goods for shipment to Manila. Gandara is an inland *pueblo* and its merchants probably were in charge of ensuring the accumulation of forest products from the interior. There were no resident Chinese mestizos on the east coast or other *pueblos,* but merchants probably visited regularly to advance money and collect crops. The volume of products in other *pueblos* probably did not warrant a resident Chinese mestizo population.[36]

Within Samar, the Chinese mestizos had just two major rivals for commercial dominance, the Spanish governor and the *gobernadorcillos.* Competition between the two trade networks was fierce. The governor and *gobernadorcillos* exploited their official positions to try to exclude the Chinese mestizos, while the mestizos used crop loans and higher purchase prices to woo customers. In 1792, for example, the Gandara *gobernadorcillo* tried to prevent all merchants, both Samareño and mestizo, from entering the *pueblo* to trade or to collect crops loans. The matter was resolved five months later when the Manila government supported the traders' rights to enter Gandara.[37] In 1806, Guivan *pueblo* officials asked that mestizo merchants be barred from the town during harvest, also the time for tribute collections, saying that they disturbed the market by offering higher prices for the crops. Not surprisingly, given his own trade interests, the governor backed this request, but was overruled by Manila since the law had imposed no restraint on trade by either local or "ambulatory merchants".[38]

By the 1850s the patterns of trade on Samar were changing. During the 1840s, governors were barred from commerce,[39] a decision which facilitated the sudden proliferation of Chinese merchants in provinces. During the 1830s, the Spanish government had progressively removed the barriers which had kept the Chinese out of provincial commerce — immigration restrictions, limitations on internal travel, and controls over occupation. Through superior organization and business techniques, the Chinese competed successfully with the mestizos and most simply found it easier to rely on the Chinese merchants rather than to trade at a loss.[40] The Chinese had begun to trade on Samar by 1847,[41] and in only five years were winning government monopoly contracts.[42] In 1862, there were 58 Chinese on Samar. Five of them had fixed-location stores, a beginning of the trend away from travelling, but most still operated "at different places in temporary or shifting stores for one or more months in a year".[54] By 1870, there were 356 Chinese,[44] and two decades later the number peaked at 1,892.[45] In 1864, the Chinese mestizos were residing in only 21 of the island's 31 towns, but by the 1890s they were dominant in every *pueblo.*[46]

The nature of the commerce on Samar changed in this period as well. The island's varied export trade shifted to an emphasis on abaca cultivation as the main commercial activity.[47] Between 1851 and 1870 abaca exports increased over tenfold, from 10,000 piculs or 680 tons,[48] to 114,000 piculs or 7,800 tons.[49] In 1875, 36,000 piculs of abaca were exported to all ports, amounting to a value of ₱162,000, or about 53 percent of all exports. Coconut oil exports were second with about 42 percent of the total.[50] In 1893, the annual imports and exports for Manila–Samar trade were summarized as follows:

> The imports from Manila through the ports of Catbalogan, Calbayog, Catarman, Guivan, Laoang, and Borongan are by means of steamships and sailing vessels. The first two ports are on a regular schedule while the others have ships arriving irregularly...The total value of imports can be calculated at ₱300,000, most of it through Calbayog.
>
> Exports are from the same ports and ships as imports...The total value of exports may be calculated at an average of ₱880,000 to ₱990,000 from abaca, ₱39,750 to ₱40,500 from copra, and ₱40,000 from dried fish. This totals from ₱953,750 to ₱1,070,500, most of which also leave from Calbayog.[51]

This quotation not only indicates that abaca had become king with about 92 percent of the value of all Manila-bound exports, but also demonstrates Calbayog's pre-eminence as a commercial port. Steamships had added a new element to Samar export trade patterns, and the number of arrivals and departures, steam and sail, increased markedly. In 1851, 35 boats made 55 trips to and from Samar. In 1869, incomplete records indicate that at least 39 boats went from Samar to Manila. Of the 21 whose origin was given, five were from Catbalogan, four were from Calbayog, and one was from either Catbalogan or Calbayog; six were from Guivan; four were from Borongan; and one was from Catarman.[52] In 1886, 80 boats went to Manila from Samar, 39 of which carried some abaca.[53]

Viewed across the span of a century, Samar's economy appears to have experienced some major changes. The patterns of trade had altered, the Chinese had emerged as prime merchants and were present in every *pueblo,* abaca was supreme, cash was more common, and shipping had increased. There were now in every *pueblo* Samareños who sold *tuba* and other locally produced foods and goods.[54] Nonetheless, the changes were not fundamental. The economy was still based on growing, harvesting and selling agricultural or fish products. There were no landed estates. Sales were still made by advancing money against future crops,[55] probably by Chinese and local patrons. The Chinese now loaned money at 36 percent annual interest, but they would still not loan money to Samareños, at least not to poor ones. There were no banks on Samar.[56] Most Samareños continued to live bound up in their traditional patterns. They were tied to the *poblaciones* by fiestas and relationships with their patrons, but they tended to live at least some distance away, involved primarily in farming and small-scale fishing. They engaged, as their forefathers had, in a variety of occupations: fishing, weaving,[57] wage work, making *tuba,* making copra and coconut oil, growing rice and root crops, building their homes from bamboo and nipa palms, and receiving advances in kind for their abaca and other cash crops. Change had come to Samar, but it was not revolutionary change.

The Administration of Samar

During the 19th century both the scale and scope of the provincial bureaucracy increased enormously. Until the mid-19th century provincial revenues were small, irregular and insufficient. From 1778 to 1800 the revenues for Samar averaged about ₱9,700 a year, while expenses averaged about ₱9,800. During the next 23 years revenues averaged ₱14,500 and expenses ₱14,200. Between 1846 and 1889, however, revenues rose from ₱29,300 to ₱76,400, while expenses increased from only ₱13,600 to ₱26,000 — leaving the province with a substantial surplus.[58]

By one of those seemingly inevitable laws of bureaucracies, the increase in the budget was paralleled by an expansion of the provincial administration. In the late 18th century, the Spanish secular administration on Samar was quite small, perhaps numbering no more than three or four Spaniards, and was largely in the hands of the governor. The government's 1857 official directory still showed only five Spaniards on Samar — the governor, a lieutenant-governor, two alcohol (*tuba*) licensing administrators and a tribute collector.[59]

During the latter half of the 19th century Manila increased both the size and complexity of provincial administrations. Responding to directives from Manila and Madrid, Philippine provincial governments added positions designed to increase revenues, administer formal justice and ensure security. This archipelago-wide process of administrative rationalization reached Samar in about 1860. Symbolic of the change was a request by the provincial governor in 1859 for permission to spend ₱65 to buy an iron strongbox in which to store the provincial revenues.[60] Like all buildings on Samar, the "royal house" (*casa real*), or the governor's office-cum-house, had a roof made of nipa palm fronds. Fires were not uncommon and the governor feared that one might incinerate the provincial receipts, then kept in a wooden strongbox. For the first time in its history Samar had revenues large enough to merit such an expense, and it was approved, like most matters, after being sent to Madrid for final confirmation. Over the next two decades the size and complexity of the island's administration grew steadily. By 1880, there were, in addition to the governor, four treasury officials, a judge, a prosecutor and three public work inspectors; eight years later there was also a notary public and an official from the Visayan Forest District; and in 1889, there was a public defender, an interpreter and a merchant registrar as well.

By the 1880s, it was obvious that a staff in Catbalogan alone was incapable of handling the administration and paper work of a province the size of Samar. In the mid-1890s, there were two judicial staffs (judge, prosecutor and public defender) and two treasury staffs, one in Catbalogan and the other in Borongan. As early as

1862,[61] the governor had suggested that Samar be divided into three administrative districts for smoother and more efficient administration. All officials and the Bishop of Cebu were in favour of the plan. The three regions were roughly the west, north and east coasts. In 1867, the plan was approved in Manila and by the Council of Administration in Madrid, but evidently it died somewhere in the hierarchy since no further action was taken.[62] A similar proposal was made in 1877 by a Franciscan of long experience on Samar.[63] In 1890 the idea was again put forward, this time by Governor-General Weyler, who favoured the establishment of two sub-commands of the north and east coasts for better administrative control. He argued that because of the poor communications, the governor in Catbalogan had little effective control in the north and the east coasts.[64] No final action was taken on this proposal due to red tape and requests by Madrid for more information. By contrast, the Franciscans by no later than 1890 had divided Samar into three vicariates for the west, east and north coasts.[65]

The Spanish realized that better communications with the towns were essential if better administrative control over Samar was to be achieved.[66] Contact between Catbalogan and Manila was improved first. In 1834, Governor-General Enrile told how he had made mail delivery in the archipelago regular and more frequent. One example he gave was the reduction of time for mail delivery between Manila and Catbalogan from 15 to ten days.[67] Steamship service also improved contacts with the rest of the archipelago. In 1872 a wharf for steamships and mail service was proposed for Catbalogan.[68] By 1893 two steamships from Luzon called at Catbalogan every ten or 15 days; the official mail ship docked at Calbayog every 28 days; and other steamships called irregularly for cargos at Guivan, Borongan, Laoang, Catubig and Catarman.[69] It is symptomatic of the new expectations that in 1894 a Franciscan priest complained that in Bobon "the mail service is very bad; it not only arrives late but frequently is lost as well".[70] One hundred years earlier such a complaint would have been unnecessary, since a rapid and reliable mail service had not been expected.

With the growth in administrative structure, that key aspect of a bureaucracy, paper work, increased in the last part of the 19th century. Every town had to submit records of every financial transaction, from the monthly payments of school teachers who were replacing the priests in the schools to reports on tribute collection, all with the signatures of the local officials and the approval (*visto bueno*) of the parish priest. Any repairs paid for from provincial or municipal funds had to be carefully detailed, approved and administered. In 1876 a provincial governor provided the most apt description of the rising tide of paper:

> The tempest of paper grows stronger each moment, the wind doubles from every direction at once, each surge succeeded by yet a greater one.
> We live under the complete dominion of paper . . .[71]

The Municipal Administration

The late 19th century was a period of significant development in the administration of Samar's municipalities. During the early centuries of colonial rule, the island's sparse population had remained scattered and generally resisted the attempts of Spanish missionaries to concentrate them in settlements. In the late 18th century, however, the pressure of Moro slave raiding seems to have facilitated friar attempts to relocate Samareños closer to the *poblaciones,* at least on the raid-prone north and west coasts. But *pueblo* formation was even more marked in the late 19th century. The number of towns rose from 15 in 1800, to 19 in 1854, to 40 in 1898. Fuelled by large immigrations from areas such as Cebu and Bohol, population growth was even more striking — rising from about 42,000 in 1800, to 110,000 in 1849, to 245,000 in 1896.[72]

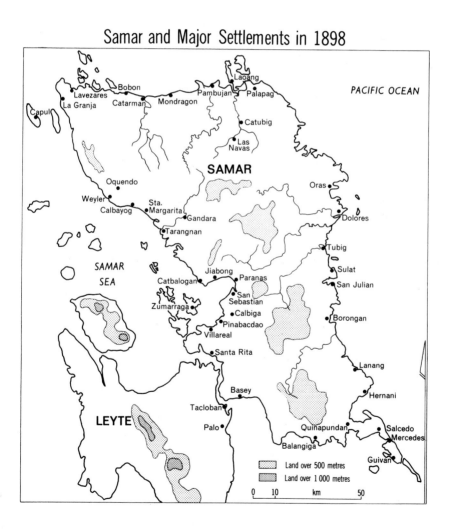

Samar and Major Settlements in 1898

Municipal budgets also increased dramatically in the late 19th century. During the previous century there were no municipal funds,[73] and they first appeared in the 1802 budget with a total of ₱1,407 for both income and expenditure.[74] Throughout the century the island's total municipal incomes increased steadily — from ₱5,282 in 1859,[75] to ₱11,040 in 1886, to ₱62,407 in 1896.[76]

The rise in the number of municipal officials and their duties paralleled budgetary increases. The rapid growth of population and towns alone ensured an increase in the number of *gobernadorcillos* and *cabezas de barangay,* with corresponding elections for certain town officials. The number of *cabezas de barangay* increased from 440 to 1846 to over 1,388 in 1893.[77] Other positions must have expanded in numbers as the size of the average town increased and as more *visitas* and barrios were established. In the late 19th century new municipal functionaries, notably schoolteachers and local police (the *cuadrilleros*), were appointed, whose selection, supervision and payment were partially the duties of the *gobernadorcillo*. In 1884 the tribute system was abolished and a new system of head taxes, the *cedula personal,* was imposed — a transition from a traditional complexity to a modern, paper-intensive one. The new tax system depended upon an annual, universal registration — that is, all persons who had any contact with the government had to have a *cedula,* and each year a new *cedula* had to be purchased.[78] The increase in provincial paperwork was enormous. Simultaneously, the Spanish government required all businesses and merchants to buy licences (the *Contribucion Industrial*), from the small stand selling *tuba* and odds and ends to large-scale merchants. In the 1890s comprehensive censuses of all buildings (*Fincas Urbanas*) were conducted, and all were ranked by use and size for tax classification. In 1895-1896, officials had to compile the first local census combining population, vital statistics, land holdings (by size and owner), and the number, type and owner of livestock (the *Estadistica*). These changes did not alter the dependence of the Spanish government upon the *gobernadorcillos* and other town officials. There were more demands and more supervision, but the actual operation of the new laws, the collection of taxes and the filling in of forms still depended on this class of Samareños.

Administrative Demands and Their Impact

While the Spanish presence loomed ever larger in the municipalities, many of the demands of the new colonial bureaucracy were less exacting than before. Indeed, an examination of three central aspects of Spanish administration — military draft, public labour demands (*polo*) and the *cedula* tax — confirms this thesis. Instead of weighing the relative burdens, however, Samareños may have disliked the direct, external interference in their affairs and resented the new system more than the old.

The conscription of young men to work or fight away from their homes is certainly an important measure of the impact of government upon its citizens. The threat of a draft in 1649 to serve in the Cavite shipyards seems to have been the basic cause of the 1649-1650 Sumoroy Rebellion on Samar. This was the only rebellion on Samar until the 1880s and the only one connected with conscription. In 1733, 734 men had been drafted to help fight the Moros, but there was no rebellion.[79] By the late 19th century, the process of drafting was systematic but apparently not excessive or resented. After the municipal elections, the governor would supervise the drawing of lots whereby every fifth unmarried young man was subject to conscription. In 1870 only 72 men from a population of about 150,000 were drafted,[80] from 1877 to 1881 only 82 a year,[81] and in 1896 only 129 men from a population of about 245,000.[82] Throughout this period there were only a few reports of men fleeing the draft and there were no rebellions.[83] Objectively, the draft seems to have declined in its percentage of exactions and, subjectively, few Samareños seem to have resented it enough to try to flee from it.

The evidence on the public labour requirement is less complete but what there is suggests that it too became less rigorous in the late 19th century. From the beginning of Spanish rule, either corvée duty or payment of an annual fee was required of most male Samareños. This labour was usually employed in building and maintaining local bridges, buildings and roads. Before 1884, a full 40 days' labour could be, but seldom was, required from those who could not pay for their annual exemption. After 1884 the length of service dropped to 15 days. Moreover, as abaca fibre became a widespread source of cash or credit, paid exemptions were probably more widespread.[84]

By 1860, families had to annually pay about two pesos in kind or specie for the miscellaneous taxes which made up the tribute, while unmarried men and women paid about one peso.[85] In the late 19th century, most Samareño adults had to pay two pesos a year for their *cedulas*.[86] This is quite an increase, but the price of abaca fibre rose from five pesos per picul in 1855[87] to ₱14 in 1889.[88] The price of *cedulas* was higher than the old tribute, but it was a price more easily paid in the late 19th century than the tribute had been in the early decades, at least in the abaca areas. Nonetheless, the *cedula* illustrates the growing presence of Spanish administration. Under the tribute system, the individual taxpayer had no direct contact with the Spanish provincial government. The *gobernadorcillo* was responsible for compiling lists of taxpayers, covering any non-payments from personal or local resources, and forwarding the correct total to the provincial government at Catbalogan. Although the *gobernadorcillos* continued to compile and collect under the *cedula* system, every adult taxpayer was now individually responsible for his own payment and subject to summary arrest for failure to show a *cedula* receipt.

With the new rules concerning *cedulas,* the impact of Spanish administration became greater on the individual Samareño because of the increase in the colonial presence. The *cedulas* provided a ready-made check on a person's legal and taxable incorporation in the administration. In 1855, the *cuadrilleros,* town-based rural militia, were established, increasing the range and efficiency of police authority.[89] Provincial police authority also increased. In 1880 the *Guardia Civil,* the provincial militia, was established, and within a decade had 90 men stationed in 13 *pueblos.*[90]

After the late 1870s, references to vagabonds became common, probably because there were now both more agents available to check on the Samareños and more concern about unadministered persons. From 1785 to 1879, references to vagabonds are absent or scarce. In 1879 three members of the *cuadrilleros* arrested and charged a man in a *sitio* of Borongan for vagrancy, because he did not pay his tribute nor have a profession. Even though he grew some root crops and was staying with his brother-in-law, he was remiss in his tribute, used to play truant from school when a child, and drank — in short, he was seen as an undesirable. Without the *cuadrilleros,* it is doubtful if that man would have been arrested; after his arrest he was brought to the *gobernadorcillo,* but there is no suggestion that he had wanted to arrest the "vagrant".[91] In 1880, an abaca-stripper from Balangiga was arrested for not paying tribute and for playing around with women. Even though one abaca grower testified to his good character, the government banished the accused to a penal colony in Mindanao.[92] During the 1880s such cases were frequent. For instance, in 1881 two persons from Guivan were arrested for being unregistered and without known support and were deported to a colonial penitentiary in Palawan.[93] In 1881 four persons from Villareal were arrested by the *Guardia Civil* on suspicion of belonging to a bandit group. For not being registered, not complying with their "personal and Christian obligations", and not having means of support, they were deported to the colonial penitentiary in Palawan.[94] In 1884, 12 persons from Paranas were apprehended. Since they too were remiss in their civic obligations, did not attend church, drank and gambled, and had no permanent residence, they were deported to Palawan.[95]

There was a parallel rise in Samar's prison population during the last three decades of the 19th century. Between 1775 and 1870 the number of prisoners usually totalled about 100 over the space of a year. By 1877 the number of persons jailed in the year had risen to 549 and, despite a decline in the 1880s, remained at least sporadically high during the last decades of Spanish rule.[96]

Although the actual number of Spanish administrators on Samar in the late 19th century remained small, the proliferation of regulations and regulatory agencies, increase in demands upon town officials, the growth in provincial and local police, and the imposition of the *cedula* made the colonial bureaucracy an unavoidable aspect of life for most Samareños. In 1894, a Franciscan noted these changes and complained about their impact on what had been the exclusive bailiwick of the parish priests.[97] Some of the complaints were ageless. For instance, he charged that the secretary to the governor was an extortionist who used his official position to make advances to whichever woman caught his eye. Other comments, though, reflect the changes that had taken place. He called the *Guardia Civil* "the foremost bandits of the province" because they robbed and mistreated the Samareños at will. He also noted that regulations and taxes on timber house construction, for example, had become a barrier to such initiatives.

Conclusions

Had the German traveller Feodor Jagor returned to Samar in 1894, some 35 years after his actual voyage, he could not have missed observing the signs of change. He surely would have noted the prevalence of abaca growing wherever he went, the presence in every *pueblo* of Chinese and Samareño stores, and the increased number of boats (especially steamships). He would have noticed the great growth in population in the Calbayog area and its importance as the centre of external commerce. If he had stayed in Calbayog for several days, he would have found more to comment on than the "commanding view of the islands" from the parish house. He would no longer have called the Guivan area "the most important district in Samar", and probably would have awarded that accolade to the Calbayog area. In Catbalogan he surely would have commented upon the increase in Spanish administrative offices as well as the new wharf. All the *poblaciones* he visited would have seemed larger and more populous than before.

But the continuities would have been just as remarkable as the changes. He might have taken steamships to and from Samar, avoiding the variable winds which had becalmed him before, but once on Samar he would have travelled by foot, boat and litter as before, though he might have used a horse or carriage on the Calbayog plain. The seasonal and natural descriptions would have been the same, as would have been his descriptions of crops, except for the prevalence of abaca cultivation. Clothing and houses would have been the same, though imported cloth and other goods would have been noticeable in a few houses. He would no longer have been able to say that robbery and theft were rare, though it is unclear whether he would have noted any decline in personal honesty and family discipline. Markets would have been more common, as would have been cash, but he would still have noted the absence of banks and that "trade and credit are less developed in eastern and northern Samar" than on the west coast. Change had come to Samar, but for most Samareños the continuities — in custom, clothing, rituals, housing, crops, food and political relationships — were of greater importance.

During his 1859 voyage Jagor had been the typical traveller — observant but with little perspective on changes and processes; relying on established institutions and authorities for help, company and explanations; concerned with travel conditions, reliability of servants, and quality of food and sleeping accommodations. The Samareños in his narrative have no depth or life of their own. They exist primarily as pastels to help fill out his book. In other ways, of course, Jagor was a more observant visitor to the archipelago than many other 19th century tourists. In any event, he was one of the very few who ventured a visit to Samar.

Even the social historian writing long after the fact shares the traveller's predilection for the exceptional — *gobernadorcillos,* prisoners, robbers and vagabonds. But it was the unexceptional Samareños who built the roads and bridges, manned the boats, carried the traveller's litter and settled the island. They supported the administrative hierarchy with taxes and labour; they built the churches and most of the offices. But who were these unexceptional Samareños? If their avoidance of office, arrest or imprisonment made them invisible to their own present and to ours, then perhaps we might glimpse them through their labours. The emergence of abaca in the late 19th century is perhaps the most convenient point of entry into this missing dimension and the questions that it raises. It has already been suggested that abaca and rice could have been complementary crops,

the former grown on hills and secondary land, demanding little attention and offering good returns; while the latter was grown as the mainstay of consumption, on
level and cleared lands, demanding seasonal expenditures of great energy and
watchfulness. As the exports of abaca increased, so must the supply of money and
credit, increasing the buying power of the Samareños. The nature of abaca allowed
it to be grown in many places, even in *poblaciones,* thus providing a cash crop for
all. In December 1894, an observer noted upon disembarking in Catbalogan:

> On the slopes of the higher mountains, behind the [*población*], the hemp-
> plants . . . grew luxuriously, and in front of many of the houses in Catbalogan
> the white fibre was out drying on clothes-lines.[98]

How much of the new wealth reached the Samareños and how involved in the
new commercial economy were they? Was the Samareño population homogeneous
and did the new wealth reach them equally? In 1832 the governor had described
Samareño society this way:

> The little fishing and agriculture is in the hands of the most wretched [of the
> Samareños] who with much toil . . . pay their tribute tax [in kind], after which
> they live on the easily grown root crops . . . The rich class [of Samareños] or
> [Chinese] mestizos is entirely devoted to commerce . . . [99]

This question involves two economic levels in society, what a contemporary
sociologist has called the "big people" and the "little people".[100] The relationship
between the two levels involves almost all aspects of life, social, political and
economic, from godfathers to factions and tenants. But it is the economic aspect of
the big–little relation that is at issue here. "Economic security, manifested if not in
great surplus, at least in solvency, is the hallmark" of the big people.[101] In 19th
century Samar, the big people were probably town officials, landowners and sellers
of abaca — that is, the *principalía* and their close relations. The little people were
tenants and labourers. Agriculture in Samar was probably based largely on a
shareholder system. There were not large estates on Samar as in Central Luzon —
most fields on Samar in 1896 averaged only about two hectares in size.[102]
Nonetheless, tenancy was common: in 1870, Cavada stated there were only 11,203
owners or landlords out of a total of 40,379 farmers.[103] This guess is probably
much too high, unless Cavada distinguished between farmers and farm workers,
omitting the latter from his total. The 1896 census, though incomplete (the population covered was 164,619 out of an 1896 total of 244,781), offers a fuller set of
statistics. Out of this partial population total there were only 3,735 owners of
5,717 fields. While the average size of a field was about two hectares, each owner
controlled about three hectares. If we assume that each owner represented a family,[104] the question becomes how many families controlled the land. If we divide the
total population in the census by five, the assumed average family size,[105] the
result is a total of 32,924 families. There were only 3,735 owners, big people,

listed. Consequently, it appears that about 11 percent of all families controlled the ownership of land in Samar in 1896.

A contemporary study of a village in Leyte concludes that "no tract of more than a hectare is worked by the owners alone".[106] Usually day labourers and tenants were used. There is no specific information on share tenancy for Samar, but there is some on wages for day workers. The governor of Samar reported in the early 1890s that an abaca worker could earn ₱17.50 a year, beginning with the harvest in the third year after land had been cleared, planted and weeded. This represented half the profits for five piculs of cleaned and dried abaca at seven pesos per picul.[107] As the price went up, so would the worker's earnings. Some earnings from the growth in commerce must therefore have trickled down to the agricultural labourers and tenants. It is interesting, however, how little such a labourer could earn, and then only in the third year from newly planted abaca plants.

In this same report, the governor comments that at least four-fifths of the arable land was unused. This seems strange at first — why did not the tenants and labourers merely take some of this land, most if not all untitled,[108] and set out their own fields? Some did, but it appears from the scanty evidence that most did not. The reasons for this seem to be the result of an interplay of crop requirements, patron–client relationships, and limits to the commercialization of Samar. The three major crops all required an investment in time and labour before returns could be realized. Newly planted coconuts require a wait of at least seven years; rice needs four or five months for clearing, planting and harvesting; and abaca plants can be harvested only in the third year. During this time the worker and his family must be fed and housed and his taxes paid. Rice involved the shortest wait, but only abaca and coconuts returned good market prices.

The patron would support his followers and encourage them to grow cash crops, but the usual arrangement seems to have been the share system. Credit and money advances would probably be subtracted from the client's share, with the possibility of debt and further, never-ending obligations. The patron, probably residing in the *poblacion,* presumably would also have first claim on the purchase of his client's crops as well as greater opportunity to claim the land as his. Alternative work such as dock labour in the ports was possible, for one-half of a peso a day,[109] but the amount of this work was limited.

Indications are, moreover, that commercialization had made only small inroads on Samar. Consequently, the patron–client relationship, involving a web of tradition, social ties and economics, probably was still quite strong. The governor's report mentioned that in addition to the great amount of available land not being used, rice production was still done without irrigation; abaca production was not as large as it could be because of shortage of labour; fields were still relatively small; there was no commercial harvesting of timber, nor was there a significant livestock industry; and mineral resources, few as they were, were not being tapped. Fishing remained an important industry in some *pueblos,* especially around the Maqueda and Villareal Bays, and salted fish were a major export from these areas. The governor went on to say, however, that there was no factory for salting the fish:

either the fishermen themselves or the buyers salted the fish "in their homes" and then resold it — obviously not a large-scale commercial process.

It is apparent how little information there is on the nature of Samareño society, relations between strata, and the impact of social, economic and political changes in the 19th century. We still lack information on transactions of land and other property, avenues of vertical social mobility, exposure to nationalist ideas, contested municipal elections and so forth. It is not possible to prove or disprove assertions that a "new social and economic class . . . stayed away from village politics, disdaining to take part in the elections, except to use their influence and resources to avoid being elected".[110]

This lack of materials for an intensive study of the social dynamics of the Samareño population, especially its elite, is unfortunate and makes it impossible to either confirm or challenge conclusions about social change made through studies of other regions. One would expect, though, that Samareño society was composed of a strong local elite made up of old families and upwardly mobile entrepreneurial families. We might expect that there were attempts to keep the little people in their expected place through the use of police as well as manipulation of land-ownership, tenancy contracts and patron-client ties. We might also assume that there were factional conflicts among the local elites, accompanied by attempts at forming supportive alliances with influential officials beyond Samar.

Similarly, this essay has had to neglect an analysis of the relation between economic changes on Samar and the demands of the world economy. Clearly Samar did not exist within a vacuum — the real centres of economic life were found in Cebu, Iloilo, Manila, Great Britain and the United States, to which the island's economy responded as a producer of raw materials.[111]

Despite its limitations, Samar's regional history does provide a new perspective on the wider history of the Philippine archipelago. Very briefly, it seems that economic changes, reinforced by tighter communications and administrative systems, are the key features in the archipelago in this period.

In the late 18th century, the Spanish began to move from exclusive fiscal dependence upon the Acapulco galleon's annual trading profits to a more locally based income — the government Tobacco Monopoly, new commercial crops and a more diverse maritime trade. During the 1820s the galleon made its last voyages and foreign-owned commercial houses were allowed to trade in the archipelago. Exports began to rise sharply in both quantity and value in the second quarter of the 19th century, led by sugar from Central Luzon and, later, Negros Occidental, and abaca from Bikol, Samar and Leyte. The Chinese, acting both independently and as agents of the foreign firms, advanced goods, loaned money and collected crops for exports, thus, as in Samar, bringing the new economy to most areas of the archipelago.

Samar was obviously a part of this whole process. Spanish emphasis on communications, road systems, mail service, administrative rationalization, taxes and growth in bureaucracies was archipelago-wide. The experience on Samar detailed earlier is a microcosm of the whole. Viewed, however, from the perspective of

Manila, Central Luzon or Negros Occidental — with which most of the literature is concerned — the changes on Samar came late and were incomplete. Apparently the impact of the new economy on Samar occurred after 1860 or 1870. The improvement of communications on Samar was only partial and administrative changes were not as marked as in other areas.

Studied from the perspective of Manila or Central Luzon, Samar's historical record might seem incomplete or even inconsequential. Much of the historical research on Luzon has been focused towards an explanation of the origins of the national Revolution (1896-1902). According to the existing literature, certain families in the more developed areas of the archipelago acquired unprecedented wealth from their involvement in the new agricultural economy. With wealth came significant changes in the social structure of the elite, often Chinese mestizo, whose prestige and position were no longer local and dependent upon municipal office. The greater wealth and interests broadened the families' horizons geographically, intellectually and, eventually, politically. Geographically the new elite had ties and interests from the *pueblo* to the province and to Manila. The new wealth enabled them to send their sons to institutions of higher learning in Manila and, eventually, Spain and Europe. As the intellectual boundaries of these students expanded, they began to attempt to change the ideas and institutions of the past, coming into conflict with conservative Spaniards and conservative institutions. In ways that are still not clear, these upper class reformists and ideological radicals were joined by lower level groups and attempted a political revolution. This simplified outline of the archipelago's 19th century history suggests some questions which remain to be answered about the quality of social change on Samar. Most probably, the answer to these questions about a backwater such as Samar would do very little to illuminate our understanding of the national Revolution itself.

One might, however, reverse this question and examine the relationship between Samar and the archipelago from Samar's perspective. One might well ask what Samar's history suggests about the established image of Philippine history. Strongly put, this viewpoint raises the question of how the history of the rest of the archipelago conforms to the patterns of Samar's history. It might suggest limitations to the general view and offer new questions for future research.

The history of 19th century Samar indicates that by no means every area of the archipelago experienced the early and disruptive economic change of Central Luzon, Iloilo or Negros Occidental. These more developed areas have dominated the literature, giving perhaps a false impression that the whole of the archipelago experienced change at this accelerated tempo. Even a cursory glance at the map will show that Central Luzon, lowland Negros and the densely populated areas of Cebu are but fragments of the archipelago. Major islands like Mindoro, Masbate, Leyte, Bohol and much of Mindanao probably moved at a pace closer to Samar's. And many areas of Luzon such as the Cordillera, the Ilocos coast or parts of Bikol may have shared more in common with Samar than Negros. Further research may indicate that, for most 19th century Filipinos, the norm was not the hacienda but the scattered subsistence settlement only partly committed to commercialized agriculture.

Not only does this regional backwater have a discernible history, but one that suggests new interpretations and directions of research into the larger history of the Philippine archipelago. The re-writing of that larger history may well end up stressing, as does Samar's, continuity rather than change.

NOTES

This essay is based on research conducted in 1972-1973 in the Philippines, Spain and the United States. This work was funded primarily by a Fulbright Hays Doctoral Dissertation Research Award and supplemented by grants from the East Asia Studies Department and Graduate School of the University of Wisconsin. I especially want to thank my research assistants who provided invaluable aid during my work in the Philippines in 1972-1973; Fr. José Dacudao, Concertina S. Masindo, Augustus T. Bacabac, and Godofredo Arellano; as well as the staff of the archives mentioned below.

1 For more information concerning rebellions and revolution on Samar, see, Bruce Cruikshank, "A History of Samar Island, the Philippines, 1768-1898" (doctoral dissertation, University of Wisconsin-Madison, 1975), 211-16; Bruce Cruikshank, *Pilgrimage and Rebellion on Samar, 1884-1886* (Madison: Center for Southeast Asia Studies, University of Wisconsin, 1979).

2 *Pueblos* are best translated as municipalities or municipal districts rather than towns or cities. The core of the *pueblo* was the *población*, the site of the municipal offices, church, rectory, jail, plaza, and homes of the most prominent citizens (the *principales*; as a group known as the *principalia*). Around the *población* but still within the *pueblo* were subsidiary settlements known as *visitas*, barrios, *rancherias*, and *sitios*, roughly arranged from the more settled and larger *visitas* (usually with a chapel for the use of a visiting priest) to two or three houses loosely clustered together in a *sitio*.

3 For a fuller discussion of the demographic and settlement patterns on Samar in this period, see, Bruce Cruikshank, "The Settlement of Samar in the Nineteenth Century," *Leyte-Samar Studies* 12 (1978), 30-63.

4 By *Samareño* I mean the non-Spanish and non-Chinese residents of Samar. The term is used for convenience and is not meant to imply that there was a feeling of Samar-wide sentiment or citizenship on Samar.

5 These summary comments on Jagor's travels are from his *Travels in the Philippines* (Manila: Filipiniana Book Guild, 1965), especially chapters 19, 20 and 22. Quotations were taken from pages 181, 211, and 212.

6 *Strychnos ignatii, Bergius.* There are a large variety of sources mentioning this remarkable drug. See, for instance, Manuel Blanco, O.S.A., *Flora de Filipinas, según el sistema sexual de Linneo* (Manila: D. Miguel Sanchez, 1845 [2nd ed., revised]), 61-62; Juan J. Delgado, S.J., *Historia general sacro-profana, política y natural de las islas de Poniente llamadas Filipinas* (Manila: Eco de Filipinas de D. Juan Atayde, 1892), 784-86; *El Archipiélago Filipino* (Washington, D.C.: GPO, 1900), 1:624; T.H. Pardo de Tavera, *Plantas medicinales de Filipinas* (Madrid: Bernardo Rico, 1892), 209-11; U.S. Bureau of Insular Affairs, War Department, *A Pronouncing Gazetteer and Geographical Dictionary of the Philippine Islands* (Washington, D.C.: GPO, 1902), 78; and Giovanni Francesco Gemelli Careri, *A Voyage to the Philippines* (Manila: Filipiniana Book Guild, 1963), 505-51, and 97, note 18.

7 See, John Foreman, *The Philippine Islands* (New York: Charles Scribner's Sons, 1899), 356-57, for a description of production techniques. Also see, H.D. Gibbs, "The Alcohol Industry of the Philippines Islands," *Philippine Journal of Science* 6 (April 1911), 99-146, and 6 (June 1911), 147-206; and Canute VanderMeer, "Corn on the Island of Cebu, the Philippines" (doctoral dissertation, University of Michigan, 1962), 76-78.

8 *El Archipélago Filipino,* 116.

9 Real Academia de la Historia, Madrid, Sección Filipinas: 9:4480.

10 *Ibid.*

11 Archivo Franciscano Ibero-Oriental (hereafter, AFIO), 96/46. Dry rice is still usual on Samar according to Michael P. McIntyre. See, his "Leyte and Samar: A Geographical Analysis of the Rural Economies of the Eastern Visayas" (doctoral dissertation, Ohio State University, 1951), 218-19.

12 AFIO, 95/9 (undated) and AFIO, 95/11.

13 See the record of a two-headed carabao born in Basey in 1824 (Philippine National Archives [hereafter, PNA], Ereccion de Pueblos, Samar, Legajo 122: no. 27 [1825]) and the reports of commerce in carabao hides in 1824 and 1851 (Archivo General de Indias [hereafter, AGI], Ultramar, Legajo 599; and Real Academica de la Historia, Madrid, Sección Filipinas: 9:4480).

14 Valentín Marin y Morales, O.P., ed., *Ensayo de una síntesis de las trabajos realizados par las corporaciones religiosas Españoles de Filipinas* (Manila: Santo Tomás, 1901), 2:596.

15 Agustín de la Cavada y Mendez de Vigo, *Historia, geográfica, geologica y estadística* (Manila: Ramírez Giraudier, 1876), 2:80.

16 Foreman, *The Philippine Islands,* 319; University of Chicago, Philippine Studies Program, *Area Handbook on the Philippines* (New Haven: Human Relations Area Files, 1956), 1:xxxi. The ratio given is by volume.

17 AFIO, 96/46.

18 PNA, Memoria de Samar, 1893. This change also occurred in the archipelago as a whole. See, Hugo H. Miller, *Economic Conditions in the Philippines* (New York: Ginn and Company, 1920). 33-38.

19 Jagor, *Travels,* 194; Foreman, *The Philippine Islands,* 358; Joaquin Martínez de Zúñiga, O.S.A., *Estadismo de las Islas Filipinas ó mis viajes par este país* (Madrid: Viuda de M. Minuesa de los Rios, 1893), 2:64; Fernando Fulgosio, *Crónica de las Islas Filipinas* [Madrid: Rubio, Grilo y Vitturi, 1871]) makes the same points, but he is generally unreliable. J. Mallat (*Les Philippines: Histoire, Géographie, Moeurs, Agriculture, Industrie et Commerce des Colonies Espagnoles dans l'Océanie* [Paris: Arthus Bertrand, 1846], 1:291-92) comments on the fetid odour of this concoction when, as so often, it was combined with fish scraps not sufficiently cleaned from the planks or troughs. The "pitcher" Jagor refers to is probably the *tinaja* (the translator uses this word on the next page), or large earthern jar holding about 12¾ gallons, which sold for ₱1.50 on the south coast in November 1855 (PNA, provincia de Samar, unnumbered legajo, 1804-1890: 1855-57).

20 See, J.E. Spencer, "The Abaca Plant and Its Fiber Manila Hemp," *Economic Botany* 7 (1953), 204-06; and S.W. Wardlaw, *Diseases of the Banana and of the Manila Hemp Plant* (London: Macmillan, 1935), *passim,* who points out that many diseases postdate 1900 or are easily controlled. Also see, Norman G. Owen, "Kabikolan in the Nineteenth Century: Socio-Economic Change in the Provincial Philippines" (doctoral dissertation, University of Michigan, 1976), chapters 2 and 3.

21 AGI, Filipinas, Legajo 645, exp, 5; José Montero y Vidal, *Historia General de Filipinas* (Madrid: Manuel Tello, 1887), 2:308.

22 Museo Naval (hereafter, MN), Ms. 136, Doc. 11, f. 363.

23 See, AFIO, 95/9 and AFIO, 95/11 for general statements about this trade.

24 AFIO, 111/4.

25 AGI, Ultramar, Legajo 664 ("Registro Mercantil de Manila").

26 MN, Ms. 1773, Doc. 19, ff. 164-65; and AGI, Filipinas, Legajo 824, exp. 454, ff, 27-28v. In 1835, the number fell to 33 (MN, Ms. 2187, Doc. 14, ff. 53-54). The totals of all shipping were certainly larger since ships to Cebu, Iloilo and Bikol are not included in these totals.

27 AGI, Ultramar, Legajo 599.

28 AGI, Filipinas, Legajo 878.

29 Real Academia de la Historia, Madrid, Sección Filipinas: 9:4480.

30 Martínez de Zúñiga (*Estadismo,* 2:65) describes Guivan as "very rich". When the Augustinians ceded their Samar parishes to the Franciscans in 1804, an inventory of the churches was conducted. The churches at Guivan and Basey, in comparison to the Franciscan ones inventoried in 1768, were much

larger, with more decorations, weapons and statues, than other Samar churches.

31 For the overall Philippine context, see, Edgar Wickberg, *The Chinese in Philippine Life, 1850-1898* (New Haven: Yale University Press, 1965), and his "The Chinese Mestizo in Philippine History," *Journal of Southeast Asian History* 5 (March 1964), 62-100.

32 AFIO, 95/11.

33 Martínez de Zúñiga, *Estadismo,* 2:65. Although this book was first published in 1893, in the same sentence he referred to the Augustinian priests at Guivan and Basey. This dates the information as referring to pre-1804 patterns.

34 MN, Ms. 1774, Doc. 41, ff. 70-78.

35 I am reading between the lines of Wickberg's works (see footnote 31, above). The other competitors, the Chinese and metropolitan Spanish, were restricted in their activities by the government or preoccupied with the galleon trade.

36 For sources of statistics and regional patterns, see, Cruikshank, "History of Samar," appendix 12.

37 PNA, Ereccion de Pueblos, Samar, Legajo 122: No. 9 (1792).

38 PNA, Errecion de Pueblos, Samar, Legajo 122: No. 33 (1806-1809). The dispute followed an 1804 order by the governor telling the *gobernadorcillos* to refuse entry to merchants during the collection of the tribute payments. He was supported by the Franciscans. The Manila government in early 1806 voided this order, since commerce once permitted in an area was open to all subjects (PNA, Ereccion de Pueblos, Samar, Legajo 122: No. 31 (1804-1806)).

39 Civilian governors were forbidden to trade in 1844 and military governors (Samar had one after 1830) in 1847, effective in 1848. However, as late as 1859, a Samar governor was found guilty of, *inter alia,* using his official position and powers to engage in trade. His successor was accused of rice transport and commerce schemes and other charges; he was cleared of the trade abuses but found guilty of the others. Archivo Histórico Nacional (hereafter, AHN), Ultramar, Legajo 5169, exp. 18; and, AHN, Ultramar, Legajo 5173, exp. 2.

40 Once again I am relying on Wickberg (see footnote 31, above) for the overall patterns. By 1848 a steady rise in Chinese population in the archipelago was clear. In 1857, Chinese or any foreigner could bid on government contracts; in 1863, they and other foreigners could practise any occupation and inherit property. In the 1870s, a cheap, regular and frequent steamship service was running between Manila and Hong Kong. In 1847, there were about 5,700

Chinese in the Philippines; in 1864, about 18,000; 1867, about 30,000; 1886, about 66,000 (maybe even 90,000). In 1849, 92 percent of the Chinese were in Manila, while in 1873 only about 50 percent were; by 1891, there were Chinese in every province.

41 PNA, Ereccion de Pueblos, Samar, Legajo 117-1: no. 4 (1847-1881).

42 PNA, Provincia de Samar, unnumbered legajo, 1786-1897: 1824-52.

43 AGI, Ultramar, Legajo 629.

44 Cavada y Mendez de Vigo, *Historia*, 2:72.

45 *Guía oficial de las Islas Filipinas, 1893* (Manila: M. Perez, 1893).

46 For sources and distribution see, appendices 12 and 13 of Cruikshank, "History of Samar".

47 The fibre from the abaca plant was in demand on the world market for cordage for sailing ships. Regular exports of abaca from the Philippines began in 1822, mainly from the Bikol Peninsula. For an overview, see, Owen, "Kabikolan," chapters 2 and 3.

48 The abaca exports were measured in piculs. A source for 1903 (U.S. Bureau of the Census, *Census of the Philippine Islands* [Washington, D.C.: GPO, 1905], 4:449) indicates that the picul and other weights and measures varied greatly in size. The standard weight was 63.262 kilograms or 139.5 pounds, but Leyte's picul weighed 69.012 kilograms or 152.1 pounds. The picul used on Samar was not listed, but for this calculation I have assumed it was the same as Leyte's, 152.1 pounds. Variations in measure and weights such as these probably reflect the new and non-integrated nature of the archipelago-wide commerce.

49 Real Academia de la Historia, Madrid, Sección Filipinas: 9:4480; Cavada y Mendez de Vigo, *Historia,* 2:80.

50 AFIO, 96/46.

51 PNA, Memoria, Samar, 1893. This figure for value of exports actually understates the total since the governor who wrote this report said that 100,000 to 120,000 piculs of abaca were exported from Samar to Manila, whereas the totals in 1891-1894 were about 2,000,000 piculs annually, making abaca's dominance even greater than he indicated (Bureau of Insular Affairs, *A Pronouncing Gazetteer,* 803).

52 These 1869 figures are from an incomplete set of *Revista Mercantil* in AGI, Ultramar, Legajo 604.

53 From *El Comercio* newspaper reports of Manila shipping, generously relayed to me in a private letter of 23 April 1973, by Norman Owen.

54 This statement is based on a preliminary analysis of the licence of business for Samar in the 1890s (PNA, Contribucion Industrial, Samar).

55 PNA, Memoria, Samar, 1893. Wickberg, *The Chinese,* 96-97.

56 The information on interest rates and banks is from PNA, Memoria, Samar, 1893.

57 Abaca cloth was still worn in a village in northeastern Leyte, though no longer made there, as late as 1955-1956. See, Ethel Nurge, *Life in a Leyte Village* (Seattle: University of Washington Press, 1965), 18-19.

58 The figures for the 1778-1823 period are arranged by governor's term of office, from one to seven years. I have totalled and averaged them. All are from AGI, Filipinas, Legajo 878, except for the 1803-1808 figures, which are from PNA, Provincia de Samar, unnumbered legajo, 1804-1890: 1809-1813. The 1846 figures are from PNA, Provincia de Samar, unnumbered legajo, 1841-1893: 1846. The 1873-1874 figures are from PNA, Provincia de Samar, unnumbered legajo, 1786-1897: 1873-1874. The 1889 figures are from AHN, Ultramar, Legajo 5340, exp. 565. For the 1875-1880 period, the administration estimated annual revenues and expenditures of ₱31,553 and ₱24,499 respectively; in fact, though, only about ₱19,600 and ₱17,400 respectively were collected or expended (AHN, Ultramar, Legajo 5285, exp. 19).

59 *Guía de Forasteros en las Islas Filipinas, para el año de 1857* (Manila: Amigos del País, 1856).

60 AHN, Ultramar, Legajo 5175, exp. 43.

61 Plans for divisions of Samar for administrative efficiency were not new. In 1747, Samar and Leyte were made into two provinces since the combination was too much for one governor to administer effectively (AGI, Filipinas, Legajo 454). However, six years later there were complaints from the Jesuits that this plan was not working well after all, and the two provinces were reunited; this was approved by the king in 1762, whose order was apparently received back in the Philippines in 1765 (AGI, Filipinas, Legajo 611). The two provinces were divided again, and for the last time, in 1777 (AGI, Filipinas, Legajo 791, exp. 46). This redivision was summarized and considered in Madrid in 1786 (AGI, Filipinas, Legajo 372). Madrid finally approved the redivision 22 years after it had been effected, in 1799 (AGI, Filipinas, Legajo 366, exp. 7). There is one document from the Franciscans favouring this redivision, dated 1782 (AFIO, 95/15).

62 PNA, Ereccion de Pueblos, Samar, unnumbered legajo, 1786-1898: 1867.

63 AFIO, 95/15.

64 AHN, Ultramar, Legajo 5339, exp. 526; AHN, Ultramar, Legajo 5327, exp. 384; PNA, Ereccion de Pueblos, Samar, unnumbered legajo, 1809-1898: 1890-1892. In this last source, the governor of Samar at one point suggests that Samar be divided into four administrative zones. It is interesting that at no time were the 1862-1867 proposal and approvals noted.

65 *Guía Oficial de Filipinas, 1890,* (Manila: Chofre, 1890).

66 See, for instance, AFIO, 96/46, dated 1876, where the governor complained in his own peculiar syntax:

"If communications are the nerves of the pueblos as some statesmen believe. If they are the arteries as some believe, charged with circulating and transmitting among the diverse social bodies the moral and material riches that surround them. If, as all agree, the pueblos achieve greater civilization as more and better ways of communication are opened. Whichever of these principles you accept, Samar represents a considerable backwardness on the scale of progress . . ."

67 MN, Ms. 1671, Doc. 7, ff. 15-16.

68 PNA, Provincia de Samar, unnumbered legajo, 1841-1896: 1872.

69 PNA, Memoria, Samar, 1893. There were 2,331 non-steampowered boats officially registered and active in Samar's waters.

70 AFIO, 95/49.

71 AFIO, 96/46.

72 Cruikshank, "Settlement of Samar," 30-63.

73 AFIO, 95/6; AFIO, 95/11, and AFIO, 95/8.

74 AGI, Filipinas, Legajo 878.

75 The 1851 figures are from PNA, Ereccion de Pueblos, Samar, Legajo 119-2; no. 10 (1851-1854), and the 1859 ones are from AHN, Ultramar, Legajo 5185, exp. 157. It is one of the curiosities of these figures that both revenues and expenses often cancelled out exactly.

76 The figures for 1875-1876 are from AHN, Ultramar, Legajo 5285, exp. 19; those for 1886-1887 are from AHN, Ultramar, Legajo 5342; and those for 1896-1897 are from AHN, Ultramar 5340, exp. 563. The sources of these funds were varied, but mainly they were from fees loosely attached to the basic tribute payment. See, Eliodoro G. Robles, *The Philippines in the 19th Century* (Quezon City: Malaya Books, 1969), 72-80.

77 PNA, Provincia de Samar, unnumbered legajo, 1841-1893: 1846. PNA, Memoria, Samar, 1893. The total for 1893 omits Catarman, whose figure was not given; the full total was probably around 1,440.

78 Robles, *Philippines in the 19th Century,* 244-47; Nicholas P. Cushner, S.J., *Spain in the Philippines: From Conquest to Revolution* (Quezon City: Institute of Philippine Culture, Ateneo de Manila University Press, 1971), 112; and Carl C. Plehn, "Taxation in the Philippines," *Philippines Social Review* 13 (February 1941), 146-51.

79 AGI, Filipinas, Legajo 705.

80 Cavada y Mendez de Vigo, *Historia,* 2:480.

81 Ignacio Salinas y Angulo, *Legislación Militar Aplicada al Ejercito de Filipinas* (Manila: Plana y Compañía, 1879), 1:232.

82 PNA, Provincia de Samar, unnumbered legajo, 1862-1896: 1894-1896.

83 From a preliminary study of PNA, Quintas, Samar.

84 From 1850 to 1859, the population of Samar increased from about 111,500 to 126,400 people, but the amount collected for exemption rose from ₱1,690 to₱9,807 (AHN, Ultramar, Legajo 5194, exp. 70). Information on later payments was not available. For general comments on *polo,* see Robles, *Philippines in the 19th Century,* 83; and O.D. Corpus, *The Bureaucracy in the Philippines* (Manila: Institute of Public Administration, University of the Philippines, 1957), 114, 125, note 52.

85 Robles, *The Philippines in the 19th Century,* 76.

86 *Ibid.,* 244-45. There were 16 classes of *cedula,* but almost all Samareños were of the tenth class, which paid two pesos apiece per annum.

87 PNA, Provincia de Samar, unnumbered legajo, 1804-1890: 1855-1857.

88 PNA, Provincia de Samar, unnumbered legajo, 1861-1897: 1889.

89 Salinas y Angulo, *Legislación Militar,* 1:210.

90 PNA, Memoria, Samar, 1893. The posts were in Catubig, Catarman, LaGranja, Calbayog, Paranas, Catbalogan, Villareal, Basey, Balangiga, Guivan, Borongan, Sulat and Oras. On its establishment, see, *Pastorales y demas desposiciones circuladas a los Parrocos de esta Diocesis de Cebu por los Señores Obispos o sus Vicarios Generales* (Manila: Santo Tomás, 1883 and 1884), 2:182-83; and Robles, *Philippines in the 19th Century,* 193.

91 PNA, Provincia de Samar, unnumbered legajo, 1846-1898: 1879.

92 PNA, Provincia de Samar, unnumbered legajo, 1859-1898: 1881.

93 PNA, Expedientes Gubernativos, 1880-1882, exp. 6, ff. 1-236b.

94 PNA, Expedientes Gubernativos, 1880-1882, exp. 7, ff. 37-85b.

95 PNA, Expedientes Gubernativos, 1884-1886, exp. 4, ff. 1-16b.

96 AFIO, 95/5; PNA, Provincia de Samar, unnumbered legajo, 1786-1897; 1824-1852; Cavada y Mendez de Vigo, *Historia,* 2:82; AHN, Ultramar, Legajo 5237, exp. 18; AHN, Ultramar, Legajo 5223, exp. 161; AHN, Ultramar Legajo 5225, exp. 66. See also, *Guía oficial de Filipinas. Anuario histórico-estadístico-administrativo. 1879* (Manila: Amigos del País, 1878); *Guía oficial de Filipinas. 1884* (Manila: Ramírez y Giraudier, 1884); *Guía oficial de Filipinas. 1885* (Manila: Ramírez y Giraudier, 1884), respectively. Montero y Vidal, *El Archipiélago Filipino,* 195, lists 57 jailed on Samar for criminal acts. I cannot explain the drop in number in the 1880s, but I suspect that the statistics are incomplete: in the first of the 1884-1886 rebellions, 257 persons were jailed temporarily in March 1884, while in late 1884 over

400 Samareños were jailed for an attack on Borongan. Either of these figures would inflate the total prisoners held in the mid-1880s into the range of prisoners held in the 1870s and 1890s.

97 AFIO, 95/49. Also see, Bruce Cruikshank, "An Essay on the Franciscans on Samar Island, the Philippines, 1768-1898," *Archivo Ibero-Americano* 38 (1978), 247-72.

98 Joseph Earle Stephens, *Yesterdays in the Philippines* (reprinted in *The Philippines Circa 1900*) (Manila: Filipiniana Book Guild, 1968), 259-60.

99 MN, Ms. 1774, Doc. 41, ff. 70-78.

100 The expressions come from the contemporary study of social composition in a town on the Bikol peninsula by Frank Lynch, S.J. (*Social Class in a Bikol Town,* [Chicago: Research Series No. 1, Philippine Studies Program, University of Chicago, 1959], 118, and *passim*).

101 *Ibid.,* 122.

102 This figure is based on a preliminary analysis of an 1896-1897 census on Samar (PNA, Estadistica, Samar). The statistics are not complete, omitting six *pueblos* altogether and some categories of information for other *pueblos*. It seems to have been the first census made on Samar and may be presumed to contain understatements and inaccuracies. The averages used are means.

103 Cavada y Mendez de Vigo, *Historia,* 2:83.

104 This overstates the number of families since some women were listed as owners and some children may have been listed as well. Moreover, I could not determine if owners of the same surname were from different families. Finally, concealment of true ownership may have been common. On the other hand, not all families may have been farmers. Many could have been fishermen, though occupations were probably combined. For the rough use to which I put these statistics, such considerations are not critical. At the most they emphasize that the contrast between owners and labourers was probably greater than I indicate.

105 Akira Takahashi (*Land and Peasants in Central Luzon: Socio-Economic Structure of a Philippine Village* [Honolulu: East-West Center Press, 1969], 83) says that "the average size of the households" was 5.2 in the Bulacan municipality he studied in 1963-1964.

106 Nurge, *Life in a Leyte Village,* 32.

107 PNA, Memoria, Samar, 1893.

108 PNA, Provincia de Samar, unnumbered legajo, 1804-1890: 1880; PNA, Memoria, Samar, 1893.

109 PNA, Memoria, Samar, 1893.

110 Corpuz, *The Bureaucracy in the Philippines,* 117.

111 Anton Blok, *The Mafia of a Sicilian Village, 1860-1960: A Study Of Violent Peasant Entrepreneurs* (New York: Harper & Row, 1974); Jane Schneider and Peter Schneider, *Culture and Political Economy in Western Sicily* (New York: Academic Press, 1976); Immanuel Wallerstein, *The Modern World-System: Capitalist Agriculture and the Origins of The European World-Economy in the Sixteenth Century* (New York: Academic Press, 1974). Closer to home, see also, Norman Owen's review of Michael Adas' book (*The Burma Delta: Economic Development and Social Change on an Asian Rice Frontier* [Madison: University of Wisconsin Press, 1974]) in the *Journal of Asian Studies* 35 (November 1975), 115-19.

The Changing Nature of the Cebu Urban Elite in the 19th Century

MICHAEL CULLINANE

T oday, standing beside a branch station of the Cebu City fire department, is a simple cross which is all that remains of one of the richest churches in the 19th century Philippines. Destroyed not by war or natural disaster, the exquisite Parian parish church was demolished in an act of vengeance aimed directly at Cebu's powerful Chinese mestizo community. * In 1849, after two decades of conflict, the Spanish governor-general ordered the suppression of the Parian parish and the destruction of its church; 30 years later the Spanish bishop of Cebu carried out that order and the church was disassembled stone by stone — a unique event in Philippine ecclesiastical history and even perhaps in the history of Christendom.[1] More importantly, this bitter, protracted conflict was but one indication of the rising influence of the mestizo minority in 19th century Cebu and its seminal role in the formation of the city's modern elite.

Since Edgar Wickberg's study of Chinese mestizos some 20 years ago, little has been done on this important ethnic minority. A number of historians have more recently re-emphasized the critical role of the mestizo elite in the formation of the economy and nationalism, but none has studied a specific mestizo community over a long time-frame.[2] Through the history of Cebu's community we can trace the evolution of the mestizo elite from a ghetto of wealthy merchants in the late 18th century to the nucleus of a powerful provincial aristocracy a century later. From the perspective of local history it is possible to view this elite within the urban environment in which it emerged and to isolate the economic, social and cultural factors that influenced its development over the decades.

The Urban Setting: Port and Hinterland to 1800

In many respects Cebu presents an unlikely environment for extensive human settlement. The long narrow island possesses a rugged interior with very few lowland plains, even along its coast. A porous limestone base and a limited rainfall have made Cebu unusually dry for a tropical setting. On only a few coastal lowland areas have Cebuanos been able to produce wet rice; their staple food has always

---

* The term Chinese mestizo (or *mestizo sangley,* as it was most frequently used in the 19th century) refers to a person of mixed Chinese and Filipino parentage. In the Spanish colonial context it also refers specifically to any person whose father was classified as a Chinese mestizo. Hereafter, and unless otherwise specified, the term "mestizo" will be utilized for "Chinese mestizo".

been a dry crop (mainly millet and corn). Deforestation and subsequent erosion over the centuries have left much of the island unsuitable for agriculture.[3] The difficulty of obtaining an adequate food supply on Cebu in the mid-16th century was one of the main reasons that the Spanish conqueror Legaspi abandoned the island in search of a more hospitable agricultural environment elsewhere in the archipelago.

Nevertheless, Cebu has always been a major population centre, primarily due to its key location astride the archipelago's main trade routes. Cebu lies in the very heart of the Visayas, surrounded on all sides by islands of varying sizes and importance, at the centre of a truly insular region of the Philippine archipelago. Situated along the middle of the east coast, Cebu City* has profited greatly from this favourable location. It enjoys a well-protected port area with a substantial, contiguous agricultural hinterland. It was predominantly commerce that drew people to Cebu; as one mid-18th century resident noted, it was a place "where no one can live without barter and trade".[4]

Long before the Spanish arrived, Cebu was an entrepôt that linked local traders with those of the Malay archipelago and the South China Sea. As Cebu was drawn into the Spanish political orbit, the port's commercial relations with the Malay world declined and eventually ceased. The 16th century traders from the south were replaced early in the 17th century by Muslim raiders in search of plunder and slaves from the emerging Christian settlements of the Visayas. Furthermore, Spanish colonial policy precluded the exploitation of Cebu's commercial potential; efforts to restrict the trans-Pacific trade to Manila deterred the development of competing port cities. By the middle of the 17th century Cebu had become a commercial backwater apparently unattractive to both Cebuanos and Spaniards.[5] When Cebu re-emerged as a major Visayan entrepôt in the first half of the 19th century, it did so not as a Malay trading port looking south, but as a link in an extensive commercial network centred in the markets of Europe and North America.

In spite of its economic decline, Cebu persisted as an administrative, military and religious centre in the Spanish colonial system. By the end of the 16th century it functioned as the capital of the sprawling province of Cebu. Fort San Pedro, probably the first major stone structure erected in the city, was one of the most important military installations outside of Luzon. The presence of Spanish and Filipino troops made Cebu and the nearby municipalities the safest coastal settlements in the Visayas. In 1595 Cebu became the seat of the largest Philippine diocese, which until 1865 included the whole of the Visayas and "Christian" Mindanao. The diocesan seat also attracted three major religious orders: Augustinians,

---

* Although Cebu City was not a city in the modern sense until the 20th century, it was recognized as such in the Spanish system and was consistently referred to as *la ciudad de Cebu* from the late 16th century on; it will, therefore, be referred to in this essay as the city of Cebu. Furthermore, "Cebu" will hereafter be used to refer to the city of Cebu; when the island or province of Cebu is meant, this will be specified.

Cebu Province Circa 1900

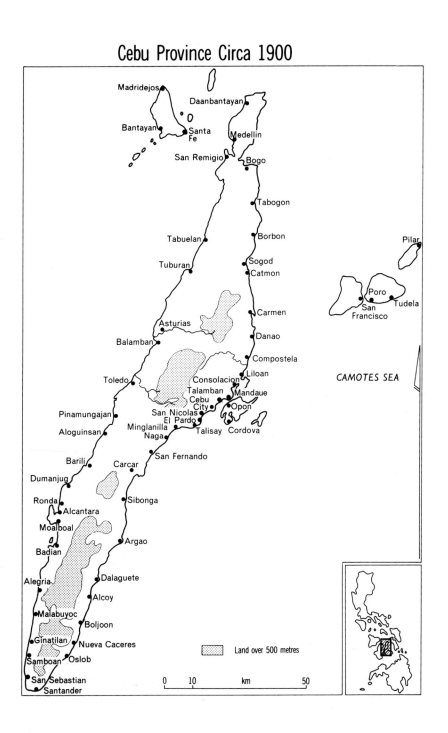

Madridejos
Daanbantayan
Bantayan
Santa Fe
Medellin
San Remigio
Bogo
Tabogon
Tabuelan
Borbon
Tuburan
Sogod
Catmon
Carmen
Asturias
Danao
Balamban
Compostela
Toledo
Liloan
Consolacion
Talamban
Mandaue
Cebu City
Opon
San Nicolas
Pinamungajan
El Pardo
Aloguinsan
Minglanilla
Talisay
Cordova
Naga
Barili
San Fernando
Dumanjug
Carcar
Ronda
Sibonga
Alcantara
Moalboal
Badian
Argao
Alegria
Dalaguete
Alcoy
Malabuyoc
Boljoon
Ginatilan
Nueva Caceres
Samboan
Oslob
San Sebastian
Santander

Pilar
Poro
San Francisco
Tudela

CAMOTES SEA

Land over 500 metres

0   10   km   50

Jesuits and Recollects. Each established a regional base in Cebu and constructed a church and convent (or monastery). The Jesuits also founded a school (Colegio de San Ildefonso), which became a diocesan seminary sometime after the expulsion of the Society in 1768.[6]

Throughout Spanish rule Cebu was relatively small in area. The settlement clustered around the port and along narrow estuaries, all within a kilometre of the shoreline, and was confined by swamp and marshland. Most observers agreed that Cebu was more a city in name than in reality. One traveller in the 18th century described it as "an assemblage of a few miserable huts" interspersed with "magnificently built" monasteries for only "two or three persons".[7] Except for Fort San Pedro, the only permanent stone structures until the 19th century were the church complexes of the Augustinians, the Recollects and the Parian, and the *colegio* (secondary school), church and residence of the Jesuits. Even the Cebu Cathedral remained an unimposing wooden building until well into the 19th century.

The port of Cebu was equally unimposing. Most of the smaller inter-island trading vessels probably manoeuvred their way through the mangrove swamp on Cebu's north side, past the islet of Tinago and up the estuary to the Parian district, then the Chinese residential area, where the market and trading centre were located. As this waterway began to silt up in the late 18th century, the main port area became the shoreline on the south side of the fort.[8] When Cebu was opened to foreign trade in 1860, ships calling at the port still had to anchor off the beach, much as the early Spanish vessels had done 300 years before.

Some of the best agricultural land of the island of Cebu lies along the coastal plain for 20 or so kilometres north and south of the Cebu port area. This fertile hinterland that spreads out between the small urban area and the coastal mountain range gradually came under the ownership of Spanish religious orders. Part of this land (mainly Banilad) had been granted to the Augustinians by Legaspi. Early in the 17th century the Jesuits also acquired substantial landholdings north of the city in Mandaue. Subsequently, both orders expanded their estates considerably through donations and purchases. By the beginning of the 19th century they had laid claim to nearly the whole lowland plain surrounding Cebu, as well as that extending along the nearby south coast. The Augustinians possessed two large estates which consisted of more than 9,000 hectares. The Jesuit estate in Mandaue, somewhat smaller in size, was given over to the diocese of Cebu in 1769 to support the seminary.[9]

In the early centuries of Spanish rule, the Jesuits and Augustinians attempted to convert their estates into grazing lands, but their cattle-raising schemes seem to have been unsuccessful. By the 18th century, the Augustinian lands south of the city were growing sugar and rice and most of the other estate lands seem also to have reverted to agricultural use. At the start of the 19th century the hinterland around Cebu was still basically underdeveloped and for the most part sparsely populated. Three decades later the commercial use of this land was increasing rapidly and by mid-century the whole area was heavily cultivated in sugar, mainly for export, and some rice for local consumption.[10]

The city of Cebu was originally intended to be a Spanish settlement. The conqueror Legaspi had designated the south side of the Pagina River as the "native" (Cebuano) settlement, and there in 1580 the Augustinians founded San Nicolas, the first *pueblo de indios* on the island. This jurisdictional division, however, was soon ignored by the local inhabitants. By the end of the 16th century many Cebuanos had established residence in Cebu and on its fringes, mainly by reclaiming the adjacent marshland. Moreover, a Chinese quarter, the Parian, had emerged across the narrow estuary on the city's north side. To minister to these wandering souls and to convert the Chinese and their offspring, the bishop of Cebu founded a secular parish in 1614. The parish of San Juan Bautista had a broad jurisdiction over the Chinese of the Parian, their descendants and all the natives residing within the ill-defined limits of the city. The Cathedral remained the exclusive church of the Spanish community. Administratively the whole urban area functioned under a Spanish municipal council (*ayuntamiento*), presided over by the governor.[11]

As the number of resident Spaniards diminished during the 17th and early 18th centuries, Cebu ceased to be a Spanish city. In 1751 all pretence to a Spanish community disappeared when the government disbanded the city council due to a lack of qualified members. Several administrative changes were made at this time. The council was replaced by three municipal jurisdictions (*pueblos*): the city proper, the Parian and Lutaos. The city proper, which consisted of the old Spanish city, became a "native quarter" (*pueblo de indios*), for it was now inhabited predominantly by Cebuanos and a small group of Spaniards and Spanish mestizos. The Parian remained the Chinese, or Chinese mestizo, quarter. Lutaos became a sprawling area intended to incorporate the Cebuanos and the descendants of the Lutaos[12] who had settled along the shoreline and in the swampy areas contiguous to the old city. The municipality of Lutaos had jurisdiction over all the indigenous inhabitants (mainly Cebuanos) living outside the city proper and the Parian.[13] Each of these municipalities functioned separately, had its own set of officers and was subdivided into its own tax-collecting units, or *barangays*.

An even more important change occurring at this time was the division of the city's three municipal units into two secular parishes. The parish of the city proper, centred at the Cathedral, continued to serve the resident Spaniards and Spanish mestizos, but now also served the Cebuanos living within the old city. The Parian–Lutaos parish, erected in 1614, served all those who resided outside the city proper, and soon came to be centred in the Parian, where the Church of San Juan Bautista was constructed by the end of the 18th century.[14]

For the next century the "city of Cebu" consisted of three civil and two ecclesiastical jurisdictions with no overarching administrative structure other than the authority of the governor and the bishop. By 1800 the small urban area of Cebu had expanded very little. However, a number of families from each of the city's municipal districts had taken up residence on the nearby hinterland. Considerable confusion and later controversy arose over this movement, for the extent of the

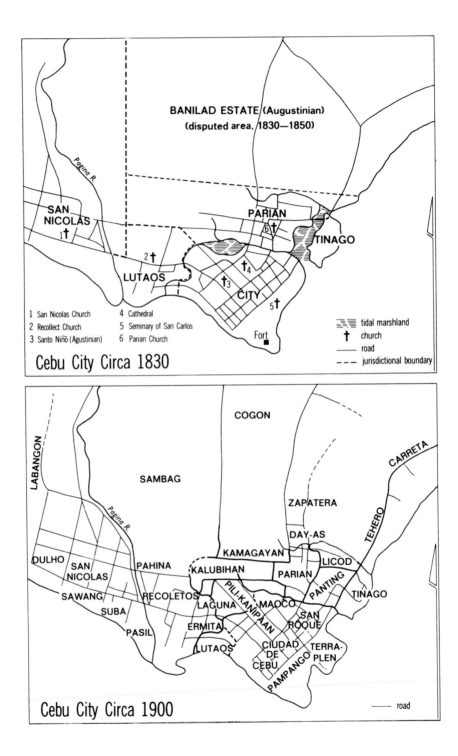

BANILAD ESTATE (Augustinian)
(disputed area, 1830—1850)

Pogina R.

SAN
NICOLAS
1 †

PARIAN
6 †

TINAGO

2 †

LUTAOS

† 4

† 3

CITY

5 †

Fort

1 San Nicolas Church   4 Cathedral
2 Recollect Church   5 Seminary of San Carlos
3 Santo Niño (Agustinian)   6 Parian Church

tidal marshland
† church
road
jurisdictional boundary

Cebu City Circa 1830

COGON

LABANGON

SAMBAG

Pogina R.

ZAPATERA

CARRETA

DAY-AS

TEHERO

DULHO

SAN
NICOLAS

PAHINA

KAMAGAYAN

KALUBIHAN

PARIAN

LICOD

PANTING

TINAGO

SAWANG

RECOLETOS

PILI-KANIPAAN

MAOCO

SUBA

LAGUNA

SAN
ROQUE

PASIL

ERMITA

CIUDAD
DE
CEBU

TERRA-
PLEN

LUTAOS

PAMPANGO

road

Cebu City Circa 1900

city's jurisdiction beyond the restricted confines of the old urban area was never clearly delineated. This situation was complicated by the Augustinian claim of ownership over all the land surrounding the city. Furthermore, the Augustinians also administered the two parishes bordering the city: San Nicolas to the south and Opon (with its *visita* of Talamban) to the north. Nevertheless, most of the inhabitants of the barrios nearest to Cebu continued their association with the city's three municipal districts and all but a few remained parishioners of the Parian-Lutaos church. As the expansion onto the nearby hinterland continued, an inevitable conflict emerged among the various claimants to jurisdiction over the outlying barrios.

The Emerging Elite: Chinese Mestizo Community, 1750-1840

During the second half of the 18th century Cebu was a city of Cebuanos and Spanish mestizos, dominated, commercially and socially, by a relatively small community of Chinese mestizos. From their base in the Parian, the wealthiest of these Chinese mestizos probably exerted more influence over the urban area than did any of the colonial authorities. Their only rivals for power were the provincial governors, the bishops and the influential members of the locally based religious orders, particularly the Augustinians. In the first half of the 19th century it would take the combined efforts of these three colonial forces and more than 20 years of litigation to curtail only a small portion of the mestizos' power.

The Parian was a rather small district linked to the city proper by three stone bridges over a narrow estuary. It had once possessed a substantial number of Chinese residents, but the declining commercial significance of Cebu led to gradual reduction of their numbers. By the end of the 18th century only a few Chinese remained. Early 19th century accounts clearly suggest that Chinese numbered very few indeed; the earliest population figures for the Parian indicate that in 1830 there were only six full-blooded Chinese living in Cebu. It is likely that the Parian was already a predominantly mestizo community by the early 18th century; by the end of that century there is little doubt that it was peopled almost entirely by mestizos, who inherited commercial opportunity from Chinese fathers and a Philippine-Hispanic-Christian culture from Filipina mothers.[15]

In the 1830s Cebu had some 325 Chinese mestizo tributes (*tributos* or tax-paying units, usually families), about one-quarter of the city's tribute-paying population. About three-fourths of these mestizos (roughly 250 tributes) resided in the Parian, while the remaining (about 80) were registered in the city proper. In addition, there were nearly 100 mestizo families residing on the lands surrounding Cebu, most of whom were enrolled on the Parian civil registers. Based on these tribute figures, we can calculate that the Parian had a total population of some 1,200 mestizos, 30 Spaniards or Spanish mestizos, and six Chinese.[16]

Lutaos at this time was purely a Cebuano municipal district with slightly more than 500 tributes within its recognized limits and another 70 or so transients settled on the lands behind Cebu. The city proper was inhabited by approximately 550 tributes; it also maintained jurisdiction over another 80 tributes (mainly Cebuanos) who were settled on the nearby hinterland. Some ten to 20 Spaniards and about 100 Spanish mestizos, aside from Spanish religious and military personnel, also resided in the city proper.[17]

In an urban population that numbered 10,078 in 1834, the Parian–Lutaos parish incorporated slightly more than two-thirds of the inhabitants of Cebu.[18] For these *ciudadanos* the Parian was the central focus of their religious and social life. In many respects the parish also united the two municipal districts politically, and in the litigations of the early 19th century they acted as one entity.

A select group of approximately 30 wealthy mestizo families appear to have comprised the elite of the Parian and its parish. It is clear that only a small part (perhaps ten percent) of the mestizos of the Parian made up the community's elite, as reflected in the early 19th century *principalia* and in most of the major economic transactions notarized in the city.[19] These families represented a close-knit, socially inter-related group that tended to confine its marriages, if not strictly within the principal families, then almost always within the larger mestizo community. Thus, when one of the most prominent mestizos of the Parian died in the 1820s, at least ten other prominent mestizo families were able to link themselves to him. To the extent that the mestizo elite married out, their partners were primarily Spaniards and Spanish mestizos, though at least one *gobernadorcillo* of the Parian married a *mestiza* from Manila. Some mestizos must have married Cebuanos from Lutaos and the city proper, but the existing records made little mention of it, indicating that such marriages were not occurring among the mestizo elite, for whom the most information exists.[20]

The dominance of the mestizo elite was based on wealth. Although relatively few sources exist to describe in detail their economic activities, a number of Cebu mestizos emerged from the 18th century as the leading commercial figures of the city, a distinction they shared with the Spanish governors.[21] By the 1820s Cebu was beginning to regain its position as the major entrepôt for the central and eastern Visayas and northern Mindanao. Muslim raids were by this time being more effectively curtailed, especially along Cebu's eastern coast. As the conditions for trade improved, mestizos of Cebu's Parian took full advantage of their opportunities; and, as the demand for Visayan products increased in Manila, they soon came to dominate this trade.[22] Early in the 19th century the most prominent mestizos appear in notarial documents as owners of inter-island trading vessels or stores and warehouses in the Parian, as retail and wholesale merchants with commercial agents throughout the Cebu trade area and in Manila, and as sponsors of domestic trading voyages for the distribution and collection of a wide variety of commodities.[23] These wealthy mestizo merchants operated out of the Parian, and, until the 1840s, showed little interest in acquiring land or property beyond this district. Their economic orientation was clearly commercial and for them there was little need to acquire interests outside their community.

On the other hand, the more numerous and less prosperous mestizos engaged in a variety of occupations. In the urban area they were, among other things, ship captains and supercargoes, artisans, warehousemen (*bodegeros*), retailers, and owners of small stores. Some functioned in these and other capacities as dependants of wealthier mestizo merchants. Increasingly, mestizos were among those moving to the nearby hinterland and engaging in agriculture. The earliest mestizos to settle in this area seem to have been herdsmen, who participated in the cattle-raising schemes of the Augustinians and Jesuits. Others appear to have been attracted by the late 18th century agricultural development activities of the Recollects north of Cebu.[24] This movement resulted early in the 19th century in small pockets of mestizo farmers, tenants or lessees (*inquilinos*), and landowners as far north as Danao. These mestizos were not, however, from among the Parian's leading families. The prominent and wealthy mestizo *principales* lived almost exclusively in the Parian, engaged in commerce, owned property primarily in the Parian as well, and participated actively in the life of their municipality and parish.

One exception to this general characterization of the mestizo elite was Don Blas, depicted as one of the Parian's wealthiest residents. Don Blas is said to have initiated an extensive cattle-raising venture of his own along Cebu's southeast coast (Sibonga to Naga) during the second decade of the 19th century. It does not appear that he sought ownership of the land in question, but instead tried to usurp the grazing rights on an immense part of the coastal plain, much of which was under cultivation by Cebuanos. This evoked strong reaction from the local population. In 1814 a large group of Cebuanos, led by Juan Diong, a locally prominent fighter against Muslim raiders, marched 40 kilometres to Cebu with *bolos* in hand to bring an end to the destruction of their farms by the cattle of Don Blas. A major rebellion was averted by the intervention of the most influential Augustinian of the time, Fr. Julian Bermejo, who personally convinced the rebels to return to their barrios and assured them that Don Blas' cattle scheme would be curtailed; and, so it seems, it was.[25] This enterprise, though indicative of the boldness of the mestizo elite, was unique; most of the wealthy mestizos devoted themselves to commercial activities and inter-island trading.

By the end of the 18th century the mestizo community had been substantially Hispanized in the Philippine sense of this term. The Parian itself resembled the typical Philippine *población* (town proper). In its heart was the Church of San Juan Bautista, which faced a relatively small triangular plaza, surrounded by municipal buildings and the wooden and stone houses of the *principales*. The whole district was little more than four city blocks by three, laid out in a somewhat irregular pattern. The traditional two-level *principalia* house consisted of the residence above and the family store and warehouse below on the street level. These family stores persisted well into the 20th century as neighbourhood shops providing essentials from brooms and matches to a variety of local delicacies.

Cebu's mestizos began to enter the colonial intelligentsia relatively early. Some families sent their sons to the local seminary, while others were beginning to send some to study in Manila. By the 1830s, one prominent Parian mestizo was acting as the provincial notary public, one of the highest appointive positions available to Filipinos. Mestizos also had long been competing successfully for government monopoly contracts.[26] Most importantly, many mestizos were attracted to the secular clergy.

The local component of the secular clergy began its growth in the late 18th century. An important factor in this growth was the reorganization of the old Jesuit *colegio* into the Royal Seminary of San Carlos, which was officially recognized in 1783.[27] Though most accounts stress that the seminary did not at first prosper, it did produce a growing number of "native" priests, an increasing proportion of whom were mestizos. In 1779 the diocese of Cebu had 25 secular priests, only three (or 12 percent) of whom were mestizos. By the 1830s, 61 seculars can be identified in the Cebu diocese, and by this time at least 24 (about 40 percent) were mestizos. More importantly, several of these mestizo priests had played (and were playing) critical roles in the administration of the diocese. At least three mestizos had held the office of Provisor and Vicar-General, the second highest office in the diocese. Archdiocesan organizational charts for 1834 reveal that four of the top six posts in the diocese of Cebu were held by mestizos.[28]

By the start of the 19th century the mestizos of Cebu were culturally and linguistically similar to the Cebuanos of the urban area. Although many of the mestizos, especially the *principales,* spoke some Spanish, Cebuano-Visayan was the language of the urban area. Chinese had long since disappeared from the Parian. Culturally the mestizos were far more Filipino than Chinese; and, as Wickberg has suggested for Manila, it was they who established the model for elite acculturation within the Filipino-Hispanic cultural setting. In Cebu this was particularly true, since only the mestizo elite possessed the wealth and contacts necessary for a higher life style.[29]

Regardless of their cultural and linguistic similarity with Cebuanos, the mestizos were seen to be racially different from the indigenous population. Their fair skin and "mestizo" features came to be associated with elite status. Furthermore, Spanish colonial policy made this racial distinction a legal one; Chinese mestizos were assumed to be economically more productive and were taxed at a higher rate than others. Moreover, in Cebu the great majority of these mestizos, and virtually all their *principales,* lived in the Parian, separate from the rest of the population. Thus, by the early 19th century the mestizos represented an ethnically homogeneous community whose social and economic position was strongly influenced, if not determined, by their racial origins. Unlike the Cebuanos of the city, mestizos of the Parian developed an identity beyond their families with a distinct community that had come to dominate the city's society.

Above all else, the Parian church symbolized the mestizos' position in Cebu. Not only did it reflect their devotion to Christianity and all the related social implications, but more importantly, it was theirs. The church had been constructed, decorated and maintained by the donations of the parishioners, mainly the mestizo *principales.* It owed almost nothing to the Spanish government or to any religious order. From its inception the Parian parish had been secular, initially administered by Spanish secular priests directly under the bishop of Cebu. By the end of the 18th century the Parian was administered by one of its own sons, the most prominent mestizo priest of the day, Fr. Pedro de San Rafael y Vasquez. He not only served as the Parian's parish priest for 38 years (1791-1829), but also helped to administer the diocese of Cebu as Provisor and Vicar-General under two bishops. Moreover, Fr. San Rafael was the highest-ranking member of the secular clergy during two periods when the diocese was vacant (1818-1825; 1827-1829). He is also credited with using the great wealth of his parish to sponsor major improvements of the Parian church. At the time the solid stone Parian church rivalled (if not in size, surely in decorativeness) the Augustinian church (Iglesia de Santo Niño) and dwarfed the decaying structure that served as the Cebu Cathedral. Descriptions of the "mestizos'" church stressed its elaborate interior with exquisitely carved wooden images (*santos*) and gold and silver inlaid walls.[30]

Among the Spanish authorities, the Augustinians had the most substantial investments and the only lasting commitment to Cebu. The highest-ranking civil official, the Spanish governor, was generally depicted as a self-serving individual who stayed in Cebu only long enough to accumulate sufficient wealth to assure a life of leisure on his return to Manila or Spain. When he left Cebu he liquidated his holdings and called in his debts. Often he left behind his name, inscribed on a bit of colonial masonry or loosely attached to an infant member of the city's Spanish mestizo population. Few indeed were the Spanish civil or military officers who remained in Cebu beyond their tour of duty. Until the 1830s there were very few permanent Spanish residents other than these officials and religious personnel.[31]

As the earliest missionaries, the Augustinians acquired considerable holdings in Cebu. Aside from their large landed estates in the surrounding hinterland, they held much property in the old Spanish city. By the end of the 17th century the Augustinians owned more than one-fifth of the lots in the city proper, making the order the largest urban landowner. By the 1820s the Augustinians held more than one-fourth, having acquired many of the urban lots of departed Spanish residents.[32] Outside the urban area, the Augustinians administered all but one of the parishes along Cebu's east coast.

In spite of these interests, the 18th century appears to have been a difficult time for the Augustinians. Muslim raids against their major parishes had greatly hindered the development of stable communities. By mid-century they began to turn over many of their parishes and missions to other orders. The number of Augustinians assigned in the Cebu port area declined significantly during the second half of that century, and the earlier developments on their landed estates seem to have fallen into decline, especially on the Banilad estate.[33] This general period of neglect appears to have ended early in the 19th century, when the Augustinians began to reassert their authority in the urban area and throughout the province. Through the efforts of Augustinians, particularly Fr. Julian Bermejo (resident in the Philippines, 1797-1851), the parishes of Cebu's southeast coast devised an effective defence system against Muslim raids. As a result, the municipalities began to emerge as more stable and more populous communities.[34] By the 1820s the Augustinians administered the parishes surrounding Cebu, possessed the largest estates in the province (including those encircling the city), owned much of the best urban property, enjoyed Cebu's largest church complex, and administered the cult of the Holy Child (Santo Niño), the most popular image in the central Visayas. Their only rivals for control over the urban area and a significant portion of its hinterland were the mestizos of the Parian.

When viewed in the light of mestizo–Augustinian rivalry and impending conflict, the 1814 rebellion along Cebu's southeast coast, discussed earlier, takes on broader implications. Juan Diong's uprising was not directed against the Spaniards, but against the efforts of an enterprising mestizo of Cebu's Parian to usurp the use of farm lands. Does the uprising reflect an early 19th century resistance to mestizo movement into the province? Or, was it a reflection of something entirely different? The curious link between Juan Diong and Fr. Bermejo and the later myth of the Santo Niño's miraculous intercession in the eventual settlement, suggest that the uprising may have been staged to keep urban-based mestizos from penetrating into the rapidly developing "Augustinian" parishes of the southeast. The whole affair may well have been an early manifestation of the growing controversy that erupted between the mestizos and the Augustinians in the third decade of the century.

Jurisdictional Conflict in the Urban Area, 1820–1850

The power, influence and sense of community of the Parian elite are well demonstrated in their long struggle with the colonial authorities, particularly the Augustinians, for control over the Parian parish. The conflict was unavoidable and the stakes were high. For the mestizos it meant the survival of their parish, which was the central focus of their community life and the institution through which they controlled much of the indigenous population and maintained a claim of jurisdictional control over the agricultural land behind the city. For the Augustinians it was a struggle to confirm their ownership and spiritual administration of all the city's hinterland and to consolidate their control over the municipalities surrounding the port area. In the larger context it was a struggle between the ruler and the ruled. It pitted mestizo wealth and contacts against a powerful and influential Spanish religious order and several of its backers. Both forces had the support of prominent Spanish clergymen, businessmen and officials, and, until the final stages of the struggle, both seemed to have equal access to legal and extra-legal mechanisms. The litigation was replete with religious, moral and racial allegations and appeals, and there can be little doubt that it also reflected very personal animosity, particularly between the *principales* of the Parian and the Augustinian bishop of Cebu. In the end, Spanish bureaucratic policy supported the Augustinian cause and brought a crushing legal defeat upon the mestizo community. The conflict ended in the administrative reorganization of the urban area and the dismantling of the mestizos' municipality and parish.

By the start of the 19th century Cebu's three municipalities and two parishes were crowded into a very restricted area. Confined by the Pagina River and the Augustinian estate, the three municipal jurisdictions had almost nowhere to expand. As their populations gradually increased, an unavoidable competition ensued for the limited available space. Within the urban area the alternatives for expansion were few. Two rather small barrios that emerged in the late 18th century from coastal marshland became the initial focus of controversy: Zamboanguillo and Tinago, on Cebu's south and north sides respectively. By the 1820s Zamboanguillo, which had become the site of the port, was sought both by the city proper and Lutaos, while Tinago was sought by the city proper and the Parian. The Augustinians claimed land in both districts.

The major issue in the later conflict, however, was control over a sizeable portion of the land contiguous to the city which the Augustinians claimed as part of their Banilad estate.[35] The commercial potential of the land does not appear to have been an issue in the early stages of the conflict; it was most certainly an issue in the later stages. The initial concern seems to have been over who had jurisdiction over the inhabitants themselves. The tendency was for settlers from the city to retain membership in their parish and municipality of origin rather than to enrol as parishioners of the distant Augustinian *visita* of Talamban, which the Augustinians insisted had spiritual jurisdiction over the whole Banilad estate, including the barrios nearest to the city. Eighteenth century Augustinian neglect of this area contributed to the jurisdictional confusion. By the second half of the 18th century the priests of the Parian had undertaken (or, as the Augustinians would have it, usurped) the religious administration in this area. The Parian priests ministered to the inhabitants of this area and enrolled them on their parish lists. These barrios became part of the Parian's spiritual domain, and, legally or not, were recognized by all (but the Augustinians) to be within the civil jurisdiction of the city as the heir of the long defunct city council (disbanded in 1751). On at least one occasion the mestizos demonstrated their willingness to fight to guarantee their priests' jurisdiction over these barrios.[36] Understandably, the Parian parish, dominated as it was by wealthy, assertive mestizos, posed a threat to Augustinian control over the area the order considered its own. Recognition of the Parian's spiritual jurisdiction would lead to the area becoming incorporated into the mestizos' municipality and could ultimately lead to permanent mestizo control over the land and its inhabitants.

In 1828 the conflict came into the open. Early in that year the Spanish governor ordered that the barrio of Zamboanguillo be incorporated into the city proper. Quickly the *principales* of the Parian–Lutaos parish, backed by their influential priest, Fr. San Rafael, protested and appealed the decision to the higher authorities. By the end of the year the conflict involved every prominent civil and religious official in the city. The parish priest of the Cathedral, himself a mestizo, declared that the mestizos of the Parian and their allies in Lutaos were attempting to encroach on the city proper both from the north (through Tinago) and from the south (through Zamboanguillo). Fearing the reduction of his already confined parish, the priest warned that if they were not stopped they would soon claim everything up to the walls of the Santo Niño church, the Cathedral and the Seminary. The Augustinians shared (if not created) these fears and their leading missionary, Fr. Bermejo, acted as one of the most ardent defenders of the inner city's position.[37]

As this initial controversy lingered in the court, two important changes that occurred within the Cebu diocese led to a widening of the conflict. Since 1827 Cebu
had been without a bishop, and the administration of the diocese had been in the
hands of prominent seculars, especially the ranking mestizo priest Fr. San Rafael.
In March 1829 the venerable Fr. San Rafael died. By the end of the year a new
bishop had been appointed for Cebu, Fr. Santos Gómez Marañon, the first Augustinian named to the post since the early 17th century. The new Augustinian bishop
wasted no time. He refused to name a new parish priest for the Parian, and simply
appointed an acting priest. In July 1830, three months before his own consecra-
tion, Bishop-elect Marañon wrote to the governor-general urging that the only
practical solution to the deplorable conditions existing in Cebu was the suppression
of the Parian–Lutaos parish and its incorporation into the Cathedral. The Spanish
governor, Manuel Romero, concurred with the bishop's recommendations and further proposed that the three municipal jurisdictions of Cebu be reorganized into a
single unit with two wards (*gremios*), one for the mestizos and the other for the
natives (*naturales*).[38] What began in 1828 as a controversy over two small urban
barrios had become a direct challenge to the existence of the municipality and
parish of the Parian.

In December 1830 the governor-general, acting almost entirely on the advice of
Bishop Marañon and the endorsement of Governor Romero, decreed the suppression of the Parian parish and its union with the Cebu Cathedral. Caught off guard
by this sudden turn of events, the mestizo community rapidly organized for the
struggle. Acting as a parish, they hired a legal representative in Manila and
prepared a lengthy appeal, answering each of the bishop's allegations and present-
ing a strong, well-documented defence. To expedite matters in Manila, the *principales* of the Parian also enclosed ₱1,000 with their appeal, to be given to the
governor-general to demonstrate their "recognition and gratitude for the benefits
that they hoped to receive".[39]

After receiving the Parian's appeal, the prosecuting attorney of the *Real Audiencia,* the colony's highest court, who had originally recommended that the parish be
suppressed, reversed his opinion. This resulted in the issuance of an order on 28 July
1831, to suspend the actual suppression until all the facts were known and a proper
decision could be reached. The suspension order, however, arrived too late in Cebu,
for on 14 July Bishop Marañon, with all the pomp and ceremony befitting a feast
day, formally incorporated the Parian parish into the Cathedral. With what appears to have been a degree of satisfaction, the bishop reported to the authorities
that the municipal officials of the Parian and Lutaos had even been made to kiss
the hand of the priest of the Cathedral in order to express loyalty to their "true
parish priest".[40]

Unable to force the suspension order, the Parian–Lutaos residents vigorously
pushed forward their litigation to convince the higher authorities that the suppression of their parish was unjustified and was simply an act of vindictive jealousy by
their enemies. By the end of 1831 nearly 30 members of the parish had applied for
permission to go to Manila to present their case in person.[41]

The central issue of the conflict soon became apparent. After obtaining the suppression of the Parian parish, the new bishop began to push for the recognition of Talamban as a separate parish. The Augustinians argued that all the inhabitants of their Banilad estate were under the civil and ecclesiastical jurisdiction of Talamban. By raising the *visita* of Talamban to a separate parish under an Augustinian priest, the bishop could then more easily demand that all the residents of the estate be enrolled under Talamban, thus facilitating his order's claim to and control over the disputed area.

As the years passed by, it became more and more evident that very little legal justification existed for the suppression of the Parian parish. That the Parian church was only a short distance from the Cathedral, as stressed by the bishop, was clearly not a valid reason to abolish the parish. The bishop's accusations regarding the exotic (Chinese-like) religious images and rites of the mestizos were countered by religious character references submitted by Spanish Recollect missionaries.[42] The only legitimate point of contention was what exactly was the jurisdiction of the old Parian parish; its right to exist could not be easily challenged. Bishop Marañon and his colleagues had difficulty obtaining support for their cause within Cebu. Their only persistent supporter was Governor Romero; when he left his post in Cebu he continued to work for the bishop by acting as legal advocate for the Augustinians and the *principales* of Talamban in their effort to gain parish status for their municipality and the right of jurisdiction over the whole Banilad estate.[43]

After eight years of litigation, the authorities in Manila were won over by the mestizos' representative. Rejecting a plea by Bishop Marañon (allegedly from his death-bed) in late 1838, the governor-general ordered that the Parian parish again be separated from the Cathedral and assigned its own priest. The *principales* of Parian and Lutaos praised the governor-general and, as "your humble servants", expressed their gratitude.[44]

Realizing that he had lost the bitter struggle with the despised mestizos, Bishop Marañon made one last effort to keep them from controlling any part of the Augustinian estate. For more than a year he managed to delay the implementation of the separation order, alleging that before the Parian parish could be restored, its jurisdiction must be explicitly delineated. Shortly before his death in 1840 the bishop ordered that all the inhabitants of the Augustinian estate of Banilad be permanently administered by the parish of Opon through its *visita* of Talamban. With this dying gesture, Bishop Marañon reduced the jurisdiction of the renewed Parian parish to the thin strip of land around the city proper.[45] Another decade of conflict and litigation ensued.

Fresh from their triumph over the bishop and his allies, the mestizos immediately began their struggle to retain jurisdiction over the disputed area, which by the early 1840s was being converted into commercial sugar lands. With renewed confidence, they now argued more openly that this territory was not only in their jurisdiction, but that Augustinian ownership of the land itself was open to question. In direct defiance of an order issued by the new governor in 1840, the municipalities of Parian and Lutaos enrolled all the disputed inhabitants on their civil registers, even though the Parian parish priest had complied with the dying bishop's order and allowed these "souls" to be enrolled on the ecclesiastical register of Talamban. The *principales* of the city proper complicated matters further by continuing to push a separate claim to the disputed area as the heirs of the Spanish municipal council. At the heart of the conflict, however, remained the intransigence of the mestizo elite, who refused to relinquish their control over the inhabitants of the disputed area. The situation was a legal nightmare with no foreseeable solution. In frustration, the new governor is said to have stated with regard to this litigation: "There is not force enough to extinguish its passions."[46]

By the 1840s the colonial atmosphere in the Philippines was beginning to show signs of change. Early 19th century Spanish efforts to improve the administrative apparatus, especially after the Latin American revolutions, led to a series of reforms aimed at increasing the efficiency of the government and improving control over the archipelago's inhabitants. To prevent local officials from interfering in trade as they had during much of the 18th century, the privilege of provincial governors to engage in commerce was revoked in 1844.[47] As the tasks of Cebu's governors became more wholly administrative, the mestizos, their former commercial rivals, continued to be their major adversaries in the struggle for local control.

Since the early 19th century, the Spanish had taken particular notice of the mestizos and their wealth, and were beginning to be concerned about mestizo control over the native population, especially in areas such as Central Luzon and Cebu. As Wickberg has noted, from the 1840s onward "Spanish conservatives were haunted by fears of an *indio* revolution led by *mestizos*".[48] To counteract such a turn of events, Spanish policy began to seek ways to reduce mestizo influence and prestige. Keeping these two groups of Filipinos apart became a major concern of the government. This concern was well expresed in Sinibaldo de Mas' famous report of 1842. He had warned that *indios* and mestizos must be kept "separate and at odds, so they can never form one mass nor have a common public spirit".[49]

These were surely the sentiments of the attorney-general of the colony's high court, the *Real Audiencia,* in the late 1840s. After reviewing the documents involved in the Cebu controversies, he concluded that the whole problem originated from the "ambition, insolence and wealth" of the mestizos, which had led them "little by little, though constantly, to usurp a territory that did not pertain to them".[50]

Soon after the newly appointed regional governor of the Visayas arrived in Cebu, it became obvious that his position toward the mestizos was hostile. In September 1847 he sent a concise, but rather detailed memorandum to Manila recounting the "evils" existing in Cebu and proposing a far-reaching reorganization of the entire urban area and its immediate hinterland. His proposal called for the incorporation of the cluster of municipalities into one City of Cebu, the establishment of two wards or *gremios* (one for mestizos and one for natives, *naturales*), ensuring recognition of the Cathedral as the integrated city's single parish by demolition of the Parian church, and formation of a new Talamban parish with partial jurisdiction over the Banilad estate. Although presented as a rationalization of Cebu's administrative districts, the action was clearly aimed at reducing the power and influence of the mestizos. In tracing the history of the situation, he stressed that through "cunning and disorderliness' the mestizos had come to better their own condition relative to the "indolent *indios*" by extending their property beyond the city.[51]

The new bishop, Romualdo Jimeno (a Dominican), endorsed the regional governor's proposals and at the end of 1848 the attorney-general in Manila vigorously sought the governor-general's approval, emphasizing that the unity of Parian-Lutaos must be terminated since it gave the people (mestizos and natives) "common cause". On 31 January 1849, the governor-general signed a decree which adopted almost to the letter the proposals of the Visayan regional governor, including the plan to demolish the Parian church.[52]

Two important appeals were immediately submitted. When faced with the responsibility of ordering the demolition of the Parian church, the bishop balked. He appealed at length that such an act was "too extreme" for the natives to witness, served no constructive purpose, and might turn many against the government. The church, he pleaded, should be utilized for religious services, the feast day of the patron saint and as an urban refuge or sanctuary, as it had been under Bishop Marañon; to tear it down would be truly "painful".[53] The attorney-general was outraged. Just short of accusing the bishop of being an enemy of the state, he declared: "All the influence, all the gold of the mestizos, all the anxiety to emerge triumphant in the scandalous dispute which was initiated by Bishop Marañon failed to demonstrate the legal origin of their Parish."[54] He argued that the destruction of the Parian church would not be repugnant or "painful" to anyone but the "richest of the mestizos, the most influential among them", who had little interest in religion; as for the *indio,* he proclaimed, he would have nothing to lose by the disappearance of the mestizo church. Nevertheless, the bishop's opinion was respected and the demolition order was suspended, but not revoked; the church could not have its own priest and was to receive no financial support.

A second important appeal was submitted by the *principales* of Talamban in union with their new Augustinian parish priest. They protested that the 1849 decree denied them access to a great many of their parishioners who resided in the disputed area. Although the Augustinians had succeeded in obtaining Talamban's recognition as a separate parish, the part of the Banilad estate long disputed with the Parian was placed within the jurisdiction of the City of Cebu in order to extend the urban area. After considering the appeals, especially a separate one by the Augustinian priest, the decree, once more against the advice of the attorney-general, was modified and the disputed area reassigned to Talamban and its Augustinian administrators.[55]

By 1850, after more than 20 years of "ruinous litigation", the controversy ended by decree in precisely the way Bishop Marañon had proposed in 1830. The mestizo elite had suffered a decisive defeat; they had lost their municipality, their parish and their claim to any jurisdictional control over the city's hinterland. In despair they mounted their resources and organized for a simultaneous appeal in Manila and in Madrid. Two local mestizo attorneys, Guillermo Osmeña and Catalino

Veloso, were empowered to pursue the case in the Philippine capital. The wealthiest and most prominent Spanish businessman in Cebu at the time, Nicolas de Olaquivel, carried an appeal of the mestizo ward (gremio de mestizos) to the court in Madrid. The appeal was elaborate and equally impressive, but the effort proved futile.[56] The Parian never re-emerged as a municipality and ceased forever to be the seat of an independent parish. The church remained standing, but did not function as a parish church; the sacraments were no longer administered there and masses were apparently conducted only on the feast days of the patron saint. Twenty five years later the church was finally torn down on the bishop's order, allegedly after a controversy over the mestizo elite's opposition to an Augustinian saying mass in the church during the saint's day.[57] By the time the last stone was removed, the centre of Cebu's society had already shifted away from the Parian.

Cebu in Transition, 1840–1860

The two decades between 1840 and 1860 have been described as a "watershed" period for Cebu province.[58] While these legal controversies were raging, the city and province of Cebu were beginning to be transformed economically. When the struggle began in the 1820s Cebu had already begun to re-emerge as a Visayan entrepôt; in 1850, when the litigation ended, Cebu was not only an active port in the inter-island trade, but had also become the distribution centre for rapidly rising commercial sugar production. The official opening of Manila to foreign trade in 1834 led to the widespread cultivation of commercial crops that were in increasing demand in world markets. During the 1840s, Cebu's hinterland and most of the lowland plains along the east coast of the island were turned over to sugar cultivation, crude milling devices were erected, and sugar was shipped to Manila for export. By mid-century Cebu province had become one of the Philippines' leading sugar producers and Cebu City was well on its way to becoming a major centre of commerce.[59]

Although the legal defeat of 1849 reduced the mestizo community's sphere of political influence, it did not result in the decline of individually powerful and wealthy mestizo families. Mestizo merchants and ship owners continued to play the leading roles in all aspects of the external trade with Manila and the Visayas; and, as sugar production increased, they reaped considerable profits. There can be little doubt that the mestizos were among the prime movers in the development of Cebu's sugar production.[60] But they were not alone in these pursuits. Another important element had appeared, a small but very influential group of Spanish merchants.

The earliest recorded Spanish merchants seem to have arrived in Cebu in the 1830s and, as the last of the trading governors disappeared in the 1840s, these men were already in position to take their place. Although there were no more than six (almost all from the mother country), these Spaniards played a critical role in the trade with Manila and the development of commercial sugar production, mainly by extending large amounts of credit to primary producers and mestizo middlemen. They acquired land in the city and in the nearby municipalities, and owned sailcraft, houses and warehouses. Through their commercial activities most of them accumulated considerable wealth and settled permanently in Cebu.[61] These Spaniards interacted quite closely with the leading mestizo merchants, not only by loaning them money and engaging in business, but also by sharing the highest positions in the urban society. At least two of these Spaniards married into prominent Parian mestizo families; several lived in the Parian itself; and when the leading mestizo of the day died in 1849, two Spanish merchants served with a mestizo as the executors of his estate. These Spaniards demonstrated little fear of a mestizo-led conspiracy or uprising; they were content to profit from their association. One of these wealthy Spaniards, as noted, even represented the mestizo elite in its appeal to the Spanish crown to restore the Parian parish.[62]

A few members of the Cebuano ward (*gremio de naturales*) also took an active part in the economic changes. Several of its *principales* and a few prominent residents of the Cebuano municipality of San Nicolas owned trading vessels, had contacts in Manila, engaged in sugar contracts with local farmers, and were beginning to acquire lands in the sugar-producing districts of the province's east coast. None of these *naturales* seem to have acquired as much wealth as the leading mestizo and Spanish merchants and a very few were able to convert their new wealth into a comparable social status within the local society.[63]

Before the rapid commercialization of sugar, the mestizo elite had shown very little interest in acquiring lands outside the Parian or beyond the immediate hinterland adjacent to the city. Nevertheless, as discussed earlier, a number of non-elite mestizos had found their way into many of Cebu's municipalities by mid-century, even to the distant island of Bantayan. The largest numbers of mestizos in the 1850s were concentrated in those municipalities nearest Cebu, especially to the north.[64] Wherever these mestizos settled, most of them seemed to have broken their ties with the Parian and to have identified with their new communities. They came to view themselves more as mestizos from Carcar, from Mandaue or wherever, rather than from Cebu or the Parian. Only a small number of the early mestizo migrants emerged as *principales* or significant landowners, while some disappeared into the ranks of Cebuano townspeople. Only in a few places (such as Talamban, Mandaue and Bantayan) did they become dominant figures in the economies and societies of their new municipalities.[65]

For the first time in the 1840s the commercialization of sugar led the mestizo elite of Cebu's Parian to acquire substantial agricultural lands. At the same time the rapid development of the port of Cebu also encouraged wealthy mestizos to acquire lands in the city proper.

The earliest landed interest of the mestizo and Spanish merchants was directed at the prime sugar lands closest to the city, mainly in the Banilad religious estates, Talamban and Mandaue. They soon acquired the usufruct rights to much of this area; as lessees (*inquilinos*) they paid the annual land rent for the right to cultivate the land or to have it cultivated. Although most of this land was already occupied and under cultivation, the wealthy Parian mestizos and Spaniards gradually acquired the leases through purchase or through the indebtedness of the cultivator.

In such cases the prior occupants invariably remained on the land as tenants and divided the crop with the new leaseholder, whose primary obligation was to pay the rent to the Augustinians or to the Seminary.[66] Their control over much of the land and tenants on these estates was strengthened by the fact that wealthy merchants also supervised the collection of the rent. From the 1840s until at least the 1870s (and probably longer), three mestizos and one Spaniard leased the right to collect the rent on Augustinian lands — a confluence of controls that probably permitted them to exert a more direct influence over tenants and cultivators.[67]

These same merchants also began to acquire landholdings in other sugar-growing municipalities. Initially they seem to have preferred simply to buy sugar from provincial producers rather than to acquire their own land and directly supervise its cultivation. However, in order to stimulate sugar cultivation, urban-based merchants began extending credit to provincial landowners, who in turn mortgaged their lands and properties or sold them under the notorious agreement to resell (pacto de retrovento). Failure to comply with the terms of the contract and, most commonly, failure to deliver an agreed-upon quantity of sugar or other products, resulted in the land falling into the hands of the moneylender and the former owner becoming a tenant.[68]

By mid-century mestizos and some Spanish merchants were already acquiring landholdings in municipalities beyond the urban area, primarily along Cebu's southeast coast. A few prominent mestizo families of the Parian had also begun to stake out particular areas within certain municipalities; here they systematically built up their holdings both through purchase and foreclosure on loans. Gradually some elite families of the Parian sent sons to reside in the province and to manage their families' provincial lands.

The development of the urban area itself soon led many of the wealthy merchants to show an interest in property in the inner city and the new port area. The first area of speculative development was a strip of swampy shoreline between the estuary of Lutaos and the south side of the fort, mainly Zamboanguillo, which had become Cebu's port area in the early 19th century. There were then no permanently constructed buildings in this area, but by the 1830s most of the marshland had been reclaimed and the estuary diked. Through merchant investment, Lutaos and Zamboanguillo soon emerged as one continuous commercial district and property there increased in value.

Most of the land in the city proper had come under the ownership of four entities: the Augustinian order, the Diocese of Cebu, the Seminary of San Carlos and the City of Cebu. These major landowning bodies controlled more than 80 percent of the city proper. Through four separate organizations they leased lots in the urban area in exchange for a fixed annual fee, also known as canon. Right to the use of these lots and to the ownership of the houses and other buildings on them could be bought and sold at will, but the occupants, or the actual leaseholder of the lots, were obliged to pay the rent.[69]

By the 1850s wealthy mestizos and Spanish merchants were gradually acquiring lots and houses in the city and the Lutaos area, not only in the vicinity of the port, but also in the more residential sections of the city (Pampango and San Roque). Some of this interest in urban property was in short-term speculation, but as the centre of Cebu's social and economic life shifted away from the Parian, mestizo merchants sought more and more property in the city proper, both for residential and business purposes. Nevertheless, on the eve of Cebu's major economic boom, the city's wealthy and influential mestizos still lived in the fairly cohesive community of the Parian from where they continued to maintain a strong influence on every aspect of urban life.

The Changing Urban Environment, 1860–1890

In 1860 the Spanish government issued a decree opening the port of Cebu to direct foreign trade.[70] In 1863 foreign vessels began to appear at Cebu to take on cargoes of sugar and hemp for direct shipment to ports outside the Philippines. By 1866, in response to the new economic opportunities, four major foreign business houses had established agencies in Cebu. Within a decade after the opening of the port the economic situation in Cebu had changed markedly. Although some trade with Manila continued, sugar and hemp, the primary export products, now moved directly to foreign markets, mainly through the agency of British and American commercial houses. Cebu became "an emporium for Visayan products" and the third most important port in the archipelago.[71]

The presence of highly capitalized foreign export firms altered many of the earlier economic relationships. The trade in major export commodities to Manila, previously dominated by mestizo and Spanish merchants, almost ceased to exist. While a number of mestizos and Spaniards continued to ship Visayan goods to Manila, most of these merchants now dedicated themselves to the collection of sugar and hemp from Cebu and other Visayan and northern Mindanao areas and to the transport of these products to Cebu to sell to the foreign business houses. Much of this inter-island trade was conducted by family partnerships, while a few companies emerged as consortiums of a number of Cebu-based merchants. Local entrepreneurs quickly established a "symbiotic relationship" with the foreign commercial houses by linking their own economic activities with those of the exporters.[72]

Foreign merchant houses rapidly became the port's leading creditors. By loaning large sums to local merchants, mainly mestizos, they established a commercial network that reached deep into the Cebu trade area; more than ever before the municipalities of Cebu and neighbouring provinces became economically linked to the city. This money, together with local capital, was distributed into the sugar, abaca and later tobacco growing areas of the region through agents (*personeros*) who supervised the collection and shipment of these products to the port of Cebu. Here they were processed, weighed, stored and sold to foreign merchant houses for export. These activities were not unlike those the mestizo and Spanish merchants had been engaged in since the 1840s. However, extensive credit from the foreign business houses allowed Cebu's merchants to expand their operations far beyond their pre-1860 dimensions. At the same time, however, it made local merchants and agriculturalists increasingly dependent on distant foreign markets and demands and prices set in Europe and North America.[73]

The expanding economy created great opportunities for profit in commercial agriculture. In 1879 the British vice consul, C.R.B. Pickford, one of the earliest commercial agents assigned to Cebu, reported:

> Keen competition and the large amount of capital required for plant and advances, have at times rendered the trade unremunerative to Europeans: but the natives have reaped the benefit of this state of things, and agriculture has received an impulse which it would not otherwise have done.[74]

Although there is much evidence to demonstrate that a number of provincial landowners were among the "natives" to reap this benefit, there can be little doubt that a relatively small group of city-based merchants, led by the wealthy mestizos, profited most.

One of the most significant results of the sequence of economic changes was the growing attachment of most of Cebu's dominant families to the land. Investment in land and property became an almost universal preoccupation of the leading city merchants, whether mestizos, Spaniards or later immigrant Filipinos. By the 1880s there were very few indeed who did not possess a number of urban lots, houses, warehouses and stores in the city and agricultural lands in the provinces. Moreover, a number of principal families of both the "native" and mestizo wards (*gremios*) who had not been active in commerce emerged at this time as prominent property owners; through commercial agriculture several acquired considerable fortunes.[75]

The rapid commercialization of agriculture had a significant impact on the provincial land tenure system and settlement patterns. By the 1870s most of the best lands of the east coast of Cebu had already been acquired and put under cultivation, primarily by urban-based merchant families. An investigation by the Spanish colonial treasury as early as 1862 revealed that the good lands were owned by the mestizos, while only very small portions belonged to the Cebuanos. More than a decade later a German traveller claimed that the land of Cebu "mostly belongs to the mestizos, and is let out by them, in very small allotments, upon lease".[76] Since most of the land of Cebu's north and west coasts was just beginning to be exploited by 1870, these accounts pertain mostly to the older, more settled east coast where the earliest developments in sugar cultivation had occurred.

During the late 19th century there were three new areas of intensive sugar cultivation on Cebu island — the municipality of Carcar 40 kilometres south of the city, the northwest coast and the *contracosta,* or west coast. The availability of a substantial coastal plain led to a significant increase in production, especially after 1860. In Carcar, wealthy mestizos of the Parian elite came to own a large portion of this area and the municipality became dominated by urban-based mestizos.[77] The best sugar lands proved to be those located mainly along the northwest coast,[78] an agricultural frontier that was not opened to widespread commercial exploitation until the 1870s and 1880s. Most of the province's largest private estates were eventually established in the newly developing municipalities of the north and west coasts (from Barili around the north to Borbon), where almost all the best lands were planted in sugar (and later tobacco) for export. A large proportion of the agricultural settlers and later tenant cultivators appear to have come mainly from the more populous east coast of Cebu and from other provinces, particularly Bohol. The major landholders and estate builders were a mixed group of local *principales,* mestizos (both Chinese and Spanish) from Cebu, Cebuanos from the east coast, and immigrant Spaniards and Filipinos. Even the long-resident British agent, C.R.B. Pickford, took his own advice and acquired a very large sugar estate in Toledo on Cebu's *contracosta.*[79]

The landed estates acquired by these enterprising individuals were not all in Cebu province. Bohol and Leyte were also important areas in the expanding economy. The coastal plains of western Bohol were cultivated mainly in sugar, while the more rugged coastal areas of western and southern Leyte and northern Mindanao developed into a major abaca-growing region. Nearly all the sugar and hemp from these areas was transported to Cebu for export. Although the mestizos of Cebu played an important part in these activities, they did not monopolize the economic opportunities. Large-scale sugar production and the exploitation of abaca had attracted many newcomers who emerged as wealthy and influential residents of the provinces. Most of these new merchant–landowners maintained close contacts with Cebu and came to participate in its elite society.

The acquisition of provincial lands also led to an elite emigration from Cebu. Most of these elite families, however, did not wholly uproot themselves; on the contrary, most left behind parents or siblings and retained their urban property. A number of brothers, cousins, or in-laws of the leading merchants established themselves in the municipalities and fed business into the family's ventures in Cebu, often obtaining loans from their wealthy merchant relatives. Of the original 30 or so principal families of the mestizo *gremio* in the early 1850s, most had clearly established branches of their family in the provinces by the 1890s. There were very few Parian mestizo families who did not have links with one or more prominent provincial families by this time; for some the links were substantial.[80] The expansion of the urban elite into the city's widening hinterland was the beginning of the formation of a province- and region-wide elite.

Among the important changes brought about by the opening of Cebu's port was the influx of Chinese, who came to play an increasingly dominant role in the urban economy. Although a few Chinese merchants were beginning in the 1850s to engage in retailing and to compete in the inter-island trade (especially with Manila), they did not play a significant part in these activities. Nevertheless, they were perceived as a threat by the mestizo and Spanish merchants of Cebu, who in 1859 protested against Chinese participation in the Manila trade, especially in export products, and argued that the Chinese should be restricted to "retail shopkeeping".[81] After the opening of the port in 1860, the number of Chinese in the city grew steadily — from 30 in 1857, to 611 in 1870,[82] and settling at about 1,400 (all males) in the 1890s.[83] The Chinese had come to stay and would have a lasting impact on the city.

The newly arrived Chinese resided almost entirely in a small district adjacent to the port (mainly in the old Zamboanguillo–Lutaos area) and were organized into a separate Chinese ward (*gremio de chinos*). Lutaos served as the new Chinese quarter; all of the Chinese stores and warehouses were located in this crowded district and along its adjoining streets. Unlike the 18th century Parian-based community, these Chinese remained predominantly non-Christian. In the mid-1880s only 13 percent were Christian; even fewer married local women or maintained close ties with the Christian community.[84]

Initially the Chinese had their greatest impact on the import trade and the distribution (wholesaling and retailing) of goods which were purchased or obtained on credit in Manila and shipped to Cebu. This was the well-known *cabecilla*-agent system and was described in 1878 by the British vice-consul of Cebu:

> The Chinese dealers have the trade entirely in their own hands . . . Our bazaar consists of 54 Chinese shops, most of which are connected with Chinese firms in Manila, whose business it is to make up the assortments required for this market. The trade is conducted on the most economical principles, and European competitors would have no chance with these Chinese distributors of goods, who have one or more shops in all the principal villages on the coast and in the outlying districts.[85]

Not only were Europeans unable to compete, but local merchants were soon having equal difficulty in doing so; the Chinese *cabecilla*-agent system "dealt a blow to the wholesaling trade" of Cebu's mestizos. This "blow", however, should not be overestimated, for it clearly did not at first eliminate mestizos or other merchants from inter-island trade, especially the shipping of export products to Cebu. In conjunction with their wholesaling activities, the leading Chinese merchants also became important moneylenders and shipowners of the city and provinces. Later in the century Cebu-based Chinese merchants established their own *cabecilla*-agent system throughout the Cebu trade area for the wider distribution of their imported goods and for the collection of export commodities (especially hemp and tobacco). It was not until the early 20th century, however, that the Chinese came to dominate this latter part of the trade as well.[86]

The expansion of the colonial bureaucracy in the late 19th century brought an influx of Spaniards into Cebu. In 1860, Manila established a regional Political-Military Government for the Visayan Islands at Cebu and within a decade there were seven new administrative departments in the city. The number of Spaniards rose from 17 in 1857[87] to 224 in 1870, creating a distinct Spanish colony for the first time in the city's history.[88] Although Spaniards were found in nearly all major economic pursuits, only a few became exceptionally wealthy. Many combined bureaucratic posts or the practice of their professions (medicine and law) with commercial activities. Even without much wealth, most of the resident Spaniards enjoyed considerable prestige within the larger society. The presence of this compact but very visible community of influential Spanish residents contributed to the rapid transmission of Spanish material culture and language throughout the small urban area. For the first time in three centuries a fairly numerous body of Spaniards themselves became models for Filipinos to observe and emulate.[89]

In spite of the presence of an increasingly influential Spanish community, the indigenous urban elite continued to dominate Cebu's society. Young men from elite backgrounds readily availed themselves of the growing educational opportunities in Cebu and Manila. Armed with education, degrees and a knowledge of Spanish, they found employment at all levels of the colonial government. They were acting as magistrates, solicitors, interpreters and clerks of the Court of First Instance and the *Real Audiencia,* justices of the peace in the city and provinces, and secretaries and clerks in almost all the offices of the local bureaucracy. Although few became municipal teachers, most of the city's renowned private tutors were from the local elite. Furthermore, the sons of prominent city families, particularly Chinese mestizos, continued to play a leading role in the secular clergy and in the running of the diocese under the Spanish hierarchy.[90]

Through their wealth and influence a number of prominent individuals wielded significant power in both city and province, making it difficult for even the colonial government to control them. They were capable of managing and sustaining long litigations against anyone who challenged this power and their "general use of bribes" frequently resulted in success in the courts.[91] One particularly good example of this power was the conflict that arose in the early 1870s between the Spanish governor and the wealthiest mestizo merchant, Gabino Veloso. The governor jailed Veloso for refusing to pay the lease on certain rural properties. Veloso in turn filed formal charges against the governor for arbitrary arrest and harsh treatment of several heads of local tax-paying units (*cabezas de barangay*) for allegedly defaulting in their tribute-collecting duties; he further charged the governor's secretary with tampering with the account books to create the appearance of indebtedness by the *cabezas* in question. After a long and exhaustive investigation, a Spanish committee concluded that although Veloso was a dangerously powerful local figure — a *cacique* — the case against the governor and his colleagues was sound. The authorities were forced to reprimand the governor, but immediately reinstated him and privately, it seems, encouraged him to try to curtail the excesses of *caciques* such as Veloso.[92]

The Veloso case stands out as an example of how the situation had changed since the earlier litigation between the mestizo community and the Augustinians. Although Veloso was able to call upon a wide variety of supporters throughout the city and province, his struggle was primarily a personal one and did not represent community-wide action. Veloso's case did not reflect a continuing effort of the mestizo community to assert its collective influence over Cebu; it reflected instead the effort of one powerful Cebuano aristocrat to manifest his dominance within the larger society. In another sense, the Veloso case exemplified the changing environment. It occurred at a time when the number of Spanish bureaucrats in Cebu was increasing and when these civil officials were beginning to wield a more pervasive authority over the lives of Filipinos. Don Gabino was unwilling to accept this change and resisted with some success. There is also some evidence to suggest that Veloso may have viewed his action against the governor as representative of the contemporary effort of the emerging Filipino "national" elite to obtain a higher place within the colonial society and polity.[93] Nevertheless, Veloso was not implicated in the disturbances of 1872 and played no role in the early stages of the "propaganda movement". Don Gabino's power was individually (or familially) focused; he died in 1881 as a man "whose influence in Cebu and Manila was all-encompassing".[94]

The late 19th century transformations of Cebu's trade, government and education system soon mirrored themselves in the city's changing life style. Religious festivities were becoming more elaborate and, more importantly, there were an increasing number of civic events. The installation or arrival of a new governor, a royal birthday and other non-religious occasions now inspired popular manifestations, such as parades with bands and banners. There were also other forms of entertainment and recreation, including dramatic presentations and horseraces. Foreign and Manila-based circuses and dramatic and operatic troupes frequently performed in Cebu. Public buildings were improved, standards for maintenance and appearance of houses were imposed, plazas were made more attractive and benches and kerosene lamps were installed within them and along the major thoroughfares to facilitate the citizens' *paseos,* and the first pumping machine was acquired to combat frequent and destructive fires. In 1867 the local seminary began to function also as a secondary school (*colegio*) for young men; in 1880 a similar school was opened for women. In 1886 the inauguration of the higher court, the *Real Audiencia,* led to the establishment of the first local newspaper, the *Boletín de Cebú.* By 1890 Cebu was still "a nice little place", but was rapidly becoming much more urban and cosmopolitan.[95]

Cebu's Aristocracy in the 1890s

In the last decade of Spanish rule Cebu possessed an urban aristocracy that was easy to identify at the top but harder to identify at lower levels. Though fairly open and based mainly on wealth, it continued to be dominated by the leading families of the pre-1860 period. As far as can be determined, it consisted of less than 75 families.[96] Writing in 1903, the Cebu journalist Antolin Frias recalled the tight circle which had comprised the upper stratum of the city's society during the last three decades of the 19th century:

> I, who have the whim to believe, as all those who live with memories and illusions, that "the time past was best", take delight in bringing to mind those days in which the Velezes, the Osmeñas, the Climacos and others like them brightened the Cebuano sky like stars of the first magnitude; they stood out more by the height through which their wealth had ranked them, and as such, they were honoured with respect and admiration by their own and by foreigners.[97]

The central core of this aristocracy remained the 30 to 40 inter-related Chinese mestizo families descended from the *principales* of the old Parian. These mestizos retained their corporate identity through their ward (*gremio*) which functioned until the end of Spanish rule. Representatives of the wealthy mestizo families never ceased to play a leading role in the *gremio*; direct descendants of almost all members of the *principalia* of the mestizo *gremio* of the 1850s served the same body in the 1890s. Thus, in what was probably the last election for local offices under Spanish rule, in 1896, the winning candidate for the *gremio* captain was Mariano Veloso, the son of Gabino Veloso and heir to one of the largest fortunes in the Visayas. Members of most of the other prominent mestizo families took part in this election as candidates, office-holders and electors from the *principalia*.[98]

Although these wealthy mestizos continued to dominate the larger elite, they did so more as the traditional urban aristocracy than as Chinese mestizos *per se*. In 1890 the Parian church had been gone for more than a decade. The plaza of Parian had become little more than a small neighbourhood park surrounded by the old residential area. Wealthy mestizo families now lived throughout the city and province and regularly participated in the activities and institutions of the larger urban area and beyond. Their association with the "mestizo community" had become less important than their membership in the "urban aristocracy". Active participation in their *gremio* and its offices was simply one way to achieve local recognition. The ease with which prominent mestizos declined elective posts in the *gremio* in favour of appointments to the more prestigious city council clearly indicated their new orientation. Cebu's ethnically cohesive elite of the mid-century had transformed by the 1890s into a multi-ethnic aristocracy. Specific ethnic origin seemed less important for membership than the collective experience of having emerged as dominant in the local society after a half century of social and economic change. In spite of a declining emphasis on ethnicity, it is nonetheless essential to stress that it was an elite with mestizo roots (both Chinese and Spanish); very few of its recognizable members can be classified as "Cebuano" or *indio*.

Spanish mestizos made up an important part of the expanded elite. Most were the descendants of those Spaniards who had settled in Cebu before 1860. Under the colonial administration, Spanish mestizos were classified separately and, though they might have been culturally similar to Chinese mestizos and Cebuanos, their ethnic origin restricted them from participation in the indigenous governments. Many chose to become "natives", a change that could be legally attained through petition, but was probably more often carried out informally. Although a few of Cebu's Spanish mestizos retained this status and remained administratively outside the *gremios,* most enrolled in the Cebuano ward, the *gremio de naturales*; only one Spanish mestizo is known to have been incorporated into the *gremio de mestizos*.[99]

Another small but subsequently important part of the urban and provincial elite of the 1890s was a number of immigrants, mainly Spanish and Chinese mestizos from Manila. Many came initially to fill posts in the bureaucracy, while some came to avail themselves of the economic opportunities. As they met with success in their various endeavours, their wealth and increasing prestige drew them into the elite; most eventually solidified their ties through intermarriage or *compadrazgo* relationships.[100]

Few Cebuano *naturales,* even among the *principales,* attained enough wealth, property or prestige to achieve urban elite status. Some obtained minor posts in the bureaucracy through local secondary education, but only a handful could be considered wealthy or prestigious, and by the 1880s even their *gremio* had come under the control of locally prominent Spanish mestizo "natives" and immigrant non-Cebuanos.

Although many of Cebu's older generation of Spaniards and Spanish mestizos became integrated into the urban elite, the new (post-1860) generation remained somewhat apart. Enlargement of their population, as discussed, made it possible for them to maintain an ethnically focused community within the urban area. Similarly, very few Chinese participated in Cebu's urban elite. Most wealthy Chinese, like the foreign business community (at the time mainly British), had little interest in converting their local commercial success into social or political prestige within Filipino society; they remained for the most part separate from it.[101]

The multi-ethnic nature of the urban aristocracy is best represented in Cebu's city council, re-established in 1890. Unlike the earlier *ayuntamiento,* the new city council was not limited to Spaniards. From the outset it was an institution with far more prestige than responsibility, which seemed to make membership on it highly coveted. The councillors (between 15 and 20) were appointed semi-annually, on the nomination of the Spanish governor, who presided over the body.[102]

Between 1890 and 1898 some 61 residents of Cebu served on the *ayuntamiento.* Twenty five of them were peninsular Spaniards (nine had lasting commitments to Cebu, of whom at least five were married to Filipinas), 17 were Chinese mestizos (from 13 families), eight were local Spanish mestizos (four from the *gremio de naturales*), four were immigrant Filipinos, four were residents of San Nicolas, and only one was Cebuano from the *gremio de naturales.* The councillors represented the wealthiest and most prominent families of Cebu. About half of them were merchants, but many of these had multiple occupations, usually combining commercial activities with some form of landholding. Twenty five percent of the councillors were landowners, seven (11 percent) were lawyers, and nine (15 percent) held (or had held) offices in the Spanish bureaucracy.[103]

Intermarriage played a major role in establishing and maintaining aristocratic identity. The earlier tendency of the leading mestizo families to select marriage partners from their own community or from prominent Spanish and Spanish mestizo families continued. The result was a rather inbred inner elite core. By the century's turn there was some leavening of the elite as the children of the wealthiest, post-1860 Spanish and mestizo immigrants became acceptable marriage partners.

A major portion of elite social life rotated around the family. Most elite families had at least one large house. Wealthier families often had two or more houses in one location; these formed a compound, sometimes enclosed by a wall. As the place of residence for the extended family, the house frequently contained an array of servants and usually three generations of family members. A major complaint by foreigners at the turn of the century was that Cebu had no hotel — it had remained a small city oriented toward families.[104]

Since the house or compound was the focal point of the family's social life, to possess a large, well-furnished house in which to maintain relatives and entertain was an essential attribute of elite status. Weddings, baptisms, departures and arrivals of relatives, associates or dignitaries were all occasions for sponsoring elaborate banquets and dances, complete with one or more orchestras and various kinds of musical and dramatic presentations, often performed by the family members themselves. Each of these festivities required significant preparations of food and entertainment for numerous guests, with emphasis on conspicuous consumption and lavish hospitality. To be able to host such affairs on a regular basis required considerable and sustained wealth. Thus the great aristocrat, Don Mariano Veloso, was praised as follows: "No one, like him, could give such brilliant 'soirées' in his magnificent mansion on the Plaza Libertad, no one could surpass him in extravagance and ostentation, being, as he is, the Croesus of Cebu."[105]

Access to wealth was, therefore, the critical factor in gaining acceptance in the urban elite, for without it a family could not participate in the aristocratic life style. Almost all the other traits popularly attributed to the elite (such as illustrious, honourable, of good standing, charitable, extravagant, prestigious and the like) derived from wealth or were contingent upon it. Wealth in Cebu of the 1890s was something to be proud of, something to flaunt. The Spanish system perpetuated the emphasis on wealth as an essential to high standing in the community since it was the primary prerequisite for office-holding.[106]

The major social events of the year were the primary meeting places of the elite society. At the various religious services, banquets and cultural events, the members of the aristocracy mingled with prominent Spaniards, exhibited their opulence and demonstrated their familiarity with up-to-date European material culture. As elsewhere in the Philippines, the elite developed a taste for the Spanish *zarzuela* (light opera) and *comedia.* By the 1880s local troupes had been formed and performed at the city's major festivities and in many of the larger, more prosperous towns throughout the province. In 1895 the first permanent theatre building was completed in Cebu, the *Teatro Junquera,* an elaborate edifice that became the focal point for the social and cultural life of Cebu for the next three decades.[107]

Elite women were rather restricted in their social life outside the family. Their education had been confined to the home and limited to the learning of domestic skills. After 1880 many young women were able to acquire the rudiments of a Spanish education at the *Colegio de la Inmaculada Concepcion* under the *Hermanas* (later *Hijas*) *de Caridad,* a local religious order. The *colegio,* which appears to have functioned mainly as a training ground for elite women, stressed such acceptable female skills as sewing, embroidery, singing and piano playing, all of which became important for women who professed elite status.[108]

The main role of many elite women, especially married ones, was that of household manager. The wife (or other female relatives) of the family head generally took responsibility for running each large household. These managerial tasks frequently prepared such women to participate in the running of some of the family's business activities. Many an elite household maintained a store that sold a wide variety of domestic items (sari-sari) and that often bought agricultural goods marketed in the city by small producers from the nearby municipalities. Some women expanded the scope of the family store by specializing in the making and sale of baked delicacies, dress-making and embroidery work, sometimes on a fairly large scale. Several elite women, especially those unmarried or widowed, went far beyond domestic and household-centred concerns and became major forces in the expansion and maintenance of family fortunes. Women such as Damiana Veloso, the unmarried daughter of Gabino Veloso, were very active in business, land acquisition, money lending and other commercial matters.[109]

The urban elite of Cebu became intricately linked to the Spanish colonial society of the late 19th century. Its wealth, life style and high status in that society had been attained under Spanish sovereignty; few of its members had much cause for discontent. As long as their economic advantages could be maintained, the aristocrats of Cebu seemed to have no serious objections to the colonial condition. Their search for reforms was solely within the realm of economic matters, jointly with local Spaniards. Political grievances may well have been a topic of conversation among the elite, but there is no evidence of any public discussion or demonstration of these sentiments. The city's elite avoided involvement in controversy and seemed unwilling to jeopardize its socio-economic position by advocating political reforms. Similar to the Veloso case of the 1870s, open grievances were primarily individual or personal; collectively the elite of Cebu demonstrated loyalty to the socio-political system that permitted it to remain wealthy and influential.

The five children of Gabino Veloso typify fairly well the general attitudes and activities of the Cebuano aristocracy in the 1890s. Melchor left for Spain to travel and study, but seems to have avoided the nationalist reformers of Barcelona and Madrid. Damiana, Buenaventura and Mariano immersed themselves in managing their father's business interests, and enjoyed the benefits of wealth and prestige. Buenaventura and Mariano held influential positions as city councillors, and Damiana was a devoted servant of the church. With their illegitimate half-brother, Rafael, they all participated wholeheartedly in the aristocratic life style of the urban society and demonstrated little awareness of (let alone involvment in) the political and revolutionary activity occurring in Manila and its environs in the 1890s. Although they experienced wide geographic contacts and enjoyed fairly advanced education, there is no evidence that they or their aristocratic peers had developed a "national" consciousness. It would take the trauma of rebellion and war with a foreign invader to elicit even a nominal demonstration of nationalistic sentiment from the Cebu aristocracy.[110]

Loyalty and Dislocation: Elite Response to Rebellion

The response of Cebu's elite to the news of the Tagalog rebellion of August 1896 was immediate and enthusiastic support for the Spanish colonial government, based initially on what appears to have been genuine loyalty and only later on a spreading fear of Spanish repression. The city's aristocracy generously donated money to the Spanish cause, and almost all its young men turned out for the newly organized Loyal Volunteers (*Voluntarios Leales*), a local militia created at first to protect the province from the internal threat of Tagalog-inspired subversives and rebels, and later to serve as a home guard against an impending external invasion by the "treacherous" Americans. During the early years of unrest in Luzon, life in Cebu seems to have gone on normally.

In the latter part of 1897 and in early 1898 the seeds of rebellion were sown in Cebu, primarily among low-level urban bureaucrats, some discontented *principalia* of the municipalities near the city (particularly San Nicolas), a large part of the urban labour force, and numerous tenants, small landholders and landless peasants. On 3 April 1898, the long loyalty of the Cebuanos to Spanish rule ended abruptly in a violent outbreak in San Nicolas that quickly spread into the city and down the south coast. For four days the rebels, who were led by a charismatic leader with alleged *Katipunan* contacts and supernatural attributes, held sway over the city, while the Spanish community and many of its aristocratic supporters were confined to the fort, Santo Niño convent, and Seminary. When Spanish reinforcements arrived, they drove the rebels into the hills after a bloody encounter. For several days after the Spanish retook the city, bodies of hundreds of dead rebels and citizens caught in the fighting were burned in large open fires around the city and in San Nicolas. Commerce came to a halt and Cebu became a dismal, chaotic city whose remaining inhabitants lived in fear of returning rebels and revenge-seeking Spanish. The tranquil life of colonial Cebu had come to an end.[111]

Although most of the city's aristocracy survived the rebellion and its bloody aftermath, the events of April surely left most of them stunned and confused. Many families fled from the city to live on their provincial lands, others took refuge in their homes, afraid to leave and forced to survive as best they could. Although the Spanish-American War spread to the Philippines in May 1898 and Manila fell to the Americans several months later, Cebu continued to be ruled by a paranoiac Spanish general until the end of December.

When the Spanish departed in December, leaving the city and province to a small clique of hand-picked urban aristocrats, an uneasy peace prevailed. In February 1899 the Cebu leadership affiliated with the Philippine Republic and awaited the next move of the Americans. Even the elite seemed inclined to resist the invader, for the Spanish had apparently conducted a vigorous anti-American propaganda campaign. In late February an American gunboat appeared and presented the ruling clique with a simple ultimatum: surrender the city or prepare for war. Within 24 hours the Cebu elite, acting in character, decided to surrender. A small detachment of United States Marines landed, raised their flag, and American rule began in Cebu.[112]

Conclusion

Late in the 18th century a small group of Chinese mestizos in Cebu's Parian formed the earliest identifiable "Filipino" urban elite. Based on wealth acquired through commerce, the mestizos emerged as a powerful and cohesive ghetto elite. Until 1849 the Parian functioned as a separate municipal district and parish within the larger framework of the City of Cebu. After a long legal struggle in the 1830s and 1840s, the mestizos lost their municipality, parish and later their church, but retained their ethnic identity through the *gremio de mestizos*.

The economic and administrative changes that occurred in Cebu after 1860 had a profound impact on the urban elite. A far more pervasive colonial bureaucracy, controlled by peninsular Spaniards, was implanted in the city; its most prestigious members took a place at the apex of Cebu's society and Spaniards began to set the cultural tone for elite life. By the 1890s several Chinese merchants controlled a large part of the trade of the port. Although most of the pre-1860 merchants remained wealthy and prominent, they now shared their socio-economic position with new elements who had taken advantage of the numerous opportunities prevailing throughout the region. Moreover land, not commerce, became the primary source of wealth for most of the indigenous elite, and control over the most commercially productive land in the Cebu trade area was dispersed among a somewhat heterogeneous group. Cebu City became to the province what Manila was to the larger Philippines — an administrative and economic centre with strong ties to its hinterland. Paralleling this fundamental change, the close ties of the mestizo elite to the old Parian collapsed as the multi-ethnic urban aristocracy acquired land and linkages that embraced the whole of the city, province and region.

At the century's turn the Cebu elite demonstrated its resilience by emerging from revolution, war and the advent of a new colonial regime stronger than ever before. By the 1890s the city's aristocracy enjoyed a rather satisfying life style under Spanish colonial rule and remained loyal to Spain during the early phases of the Philippine Revolution. Yet, by the end of 1898, members of the urban elite had emerged as the local leaders of the "nationalist" struggle against American colonial expansion. As long as significant elements of the elite continued to resist, the Americans found it very difficult to pacify the province. By the end of 1901, however, the full collaboration of the elite had been achieved. In less than a year, although more obviously divided politically than ever before, the major elements of the old aristocracy came into control of the city and province. By 1904 its most promising candidate for future political leadership was an ambitious young attorney named Sergio Osmeña. His meteoric rise to national prominence was indicative of the Cebu elite's capacity for survival.

Osmeña was a direct descendant of one of the wealthiest and most prominent leaders of the old Parian; he was a product of the Cebuano aristocracy of the 1890s. Having obtained a Spanish education in Cebu and Manila, he enthusiastically demonstrated his adherence to Spain's rule as an ardent anti-revolutionary propagandist in 1896 and 1897. For this he was honoured, on the eve of Cebu's uprising, with a special award of loyalty from the Spanish government. The American invasion, however, interrupted any plans he might have had to exploit his relationship with Spanish officials. Rejecting an initial instinct to resist the invaders, he chose early collaboration, while at the same time identifying himself with the growing intellectual nationalism espoused by the last generation of *ilustrados* trained under Spanish rule. While expounding nationalist sentiments in his popular local newspaper, he carefully familiarized himself with American ideals and institutions and developed a reputation among the new colonial rulers as a conservative and rational spokesman of Filipino upper class opposition to permanent American sovereignty. By the time the fighting was over, Osmeña was already well versed and well established in the American colonial structure. With the support of the dominant socio-economic elements of the city and province, the Catholic Church, and most of the influential agents of the colonial government, he emerged in 1905 as the most powerful Cebuano politician; by 1906 he was also one of the most important national leaders. For the next 35 years he and his law school classmate Manuel Quezon ruled Philippine national politics. When Quezon died in exile in 1944, Osmeña ascended to the presidency of the Commonwealth of the Philippines; the following year he returned to the Philippines with General Douglas MacArthur to take over the leadership of his war-torn country. After his first and only political defeat in 1946, Osmeña retired to private life, but not before he turned the mandate of local power over to his son Sergio Junior. Through Osmeña and the system of electoral politics imposed by the Americans, the aristocracy of Cebu, though somewhat altered by the new regime, came to enjoy a more pervasive control over the lives of Cebu's inhabitants than it did under Spain.[113]

This study of Cebu's urban elite is perhaps the first close examination of any Philippine elite group during the whole of the colonial period. As such, it raises a number of questions with wider implications for our understanding of Philippine social and political history. With little definition and less documentation, most histories of the modern period have postulated a number of major theses about the nature and influence of the "Filipino elite". The elite emerged after 1850 in response to the rise of export agriculture; were led to a strong anti-colonial nationalism through the acquisition of wealth and education; and eventually, with varying degrees of commitment, led the national revolution against Spain and America.

Cebu's history would seem to indicate that these theses are only partially correct. For the Cebu urban elite the critical economic changes began in the mid-18th century, not the mid-19th. And the subsequent rise of export agriculture broadened the elite's ethnic base to produce a provincial aristocracy, but did not change the overall dominance of the old Parian mestizo families. The correlation between this new wealth and growing nationalism seems, at best, an indirect one. Instead of moving rapidly from a familial–local to national consciousness in the late 19th century, Cebu's elite shifted from an ethnic "mestizo consciousness" to one combining provincial and class sensibilities. Indeed, it would appear that the early 19th century "mestizo consciousness", a variety of ghetto identity, may have been as strong an influence on the emerging anti-colonial nationalism as was European liberalism. A parallel study of Manila might show that, as in Cebu, the formative mid-century conflicts came from parochial, not proto-national, issues. In Cebu's case, the late-century elite were comfortably Hispanicized, remained loyal to Spain, and at no point supported the Revolution during its anti-Spanish phase.[114] The middle-stratum Cebuano "elite" of San Nicolas, an area roughly equivalent to Manila's revolutionary quarter, Tondo, did support the Revolution, but they were far remov-ed from the society's upper strata. Once the Americans arrived off shore, most of Cebu's aristocracy surrendered immediately, and its most promising young aspirants, notably Sergio Osmeña, soon began a close collaboration with the new colonials that was to last beyond formal independence in 1946. It is testimony to the sophistication of Cebu's aristocrats that they — together with those from other regions of the archipelago — had the wealth, education and political skills to make the transition from parochial, to regional, to national power. At each stage in this century-long evolution, the Cebu elite was guided by a sensitive understanding of its essential self-interests. Such rational calculations dictated opposition to the Augustinians in defence of the Parian parish, loyalty to Spain in the face of national revolution, early collaboration with America, and an advocacy of an eventual in-dependence. Had Cebu's friar estates become the oppressive, unavoidable presence that they were in the Tagalog provinces about Manila, then Cebu's elite might have had cause to feel the national passions of their Tagalog peers. But that remains hypothetical.

The analysis of Cebu's emerging regional economy provides some understanding of the commercial framework which underlay the aristocracy's intellectual posture. While formal Spanish colonial policies imposed a uniform administrative structure and tended towards national integration, the economic changes of the 19th century moved in an opposite direction. In the mid-18th century, the City of Cebu was bound to Manila by ecclesiastical, bureaucratic and mercantile ties. By the end of the 19th century, Cebu had become an autonomous entrepôt dealing directly with the centres of a global economy. The city had tightened its hold over a greatly expanded hinterland and effectively drawn western Leyte, Bohol, northern Mindanao and eastern Negros out of Manila's orbit. For this extensive region, the lines of capital, shipping, imports and exports led first to Cebu and from there to the centres of the world economy. Responding to these economic realities, several administrative, ecclesiastical, and educational changes in the late 19th century strengthened the region's ties to Cebu City. When Cebu emerged as the ar-chipelago's second city in the early decades of this century, it did so as an autonomous cultural centre with a vibrant Cebuano-language media (newspapers, theatre, radio, cinema, and education) which resisted for some time the en-croachments of a Tagalog-based national language. Clearly export agriculture had promoted regional autonomy, not national integration.

Finally, Cebu's history indicates the potential significance of Philippine urban history. The emergence of the Cebu elite and the economic development of the region were inextricably bound up with the city. There has been a general tendency to equate Philippine "local" history with the rural — country municipalities, provinces or regions. The national political history of the Philippines, for example, might profit from historical studies of Manila's communities — Tondo, Binondo or Quiapo. Indeed, until we know a good deal more about the development of Manila, Vigan, Iloilo or Bikol's urban complex, the history of the archipelago will remain incomplete.

NOTES

Research for this essay was made possible by a Fulbright-Hays Pre-Doctoral Research Grant (1972-1974) and the assistance of the University of San Carlos (Cebu City), Department of Research and Scholarships (1974-1976). I wish to thank Fe Susan Go, Norman G. Owen, Morton J. Netzorg, Alfred W. McCoy and the late Rev. Josef Goertz, S.V.D. for contributing to earlier versions of this essay.

1 This case will be discussed in some detail later in this essay.

2 Edgar Wickberg, "The Chinese Mestizo in Philippine History," *Journal of Southeast Asian History* 5 (March 1964), 62-100; John Larkin, *The Pampangans: Colonial Society in a Philippine Province* (Berkeley: University of California Press, 1972); Norman G. Owen, "Kabikolan in the Nineteenth Century: Socio-economic Change in the Provincial Philippines" (doctoral dissertation, University of Michigan, 1976); Bruce L. Fenner, "Colonial Cebu: An Economic-social History, 1521-1896" (doctoral dissertation, Cornell University, 1976).

3 Canute Vandermeer, "Population Patterns on the Island of Cebu, the Philippines: 1500 to 1900," *Annals of the Association of American Geographers* 57 (June 1967), 316-20.

4 Juan J. Delgado, *Historia general sacro-profana, política y natural de las islas del Poniente Llamadas Filipinas* (Manila: Imprenta de El Eco de Filipinas de D. Juan Atayde, 1892), 62.

5 Fenner, "Colonial Cebu," 43-57; Daniel F. Doeppers, "The Development of Philippine Cities before 1900," *Journal of Asian Studies* 31 (August 1972), 779-82; Juan de Medina, "History of the Augustinian Order in the Filipinas Islands," in, Emma Helen Blair and James Alexander Robertson, eds., *The Philippine Islands, 1493-1898* (Cleveland: Arthur H. Clark Company, 1903-1909), 23:161-63; Delgado, *Historia general,* 62; Manuel de Azcárraga y Palmero, *La Libertad de comercio en las islas Filipinas* (Madrid, 1871), 66-69.

6 Felipe Redondo y Sendino, *Breve reseña de lo que fué y lo que es la diócesis de Cébu en las islas Filipinas* (Manila: Estab. tip. del Colegio de Santo Tomas, 1886); *Reseña histórica del Seminario-colegio de San Carlos de Cébu, 1867-1917* (Manila: E.C. McCullough & Co., 1917); Manuel Buzeta and

Felipe Bravo, compilers, *Diccionario geográfico, estadístico, histórico de las islas Filipinas* (Madrid: José C. de la Peña, 1851), 1:542-55; Francisco Colín, *Labor evangélica de los obreros de la compañía de Jesús en las islas Filipinas* (Barcelona: Imprenta y Litografia de Henrich y Companía, 1900, edited by Pablo Pastells), 1:37.

7 Guillaume Joseph de Gentil de La Galaisiere, *A Voyage to the Indian Seas* (Manila: Filipiniana Book Guild, 1964), 138; a similar view was expressed at the start of the 19th century by Joaquín Martínez de Zúñiga, *Status of the Philippine Islands in 1800* (Manila: Filipiniana Book Guild, 1973), 433.

8 Alfredo Velasco, *La Isla de Cebú* (Cebú: Establecimiento Tipográfico "El Boletin de Cebú," 1892), 14; Medina, "History," 161; Rodolfo Fajardo d'Almeida, "Fundación y vicisitudes de la parroquia de San Juan Bautista," *Lungsoranon* (16 July 1941), 16, 19. I wish to thank Fe Susan Go for sharing her copy of the Fajardo d'Almeida work, which was published in the Catholic organ of the Cebu diocese beginning with the date indicated; since her copy appears in clipping form, the dates of subsequent issues where this series appeared are not given.

9 Fenner, "Colonial Cebu," 57-66; Philippine National Archives (hereafter, PNA), Protocolos, Cebu Province, 1414, 31 October 1897; *Report of the Philippine Commission to the President. . . 1904* (Washington: Government Printing Office, 1905), 1:761-66; *Reseña histórica del Seminario-colegio de San Carlos,* 253-54, 268.

10 Medina, "History," 159-60; Fenner, "Colonial Cebu," 62-65; Archivo Histórico Nacional, Seccion de Ultramar, Filipinas, Gracia y Justicia, 1853, legajo 2174, expediente 43, "Los feligres de la suprimida parroquia de Parian y Lutaos en la diócesis de Cebú solicitan reestablecimiento de dicha parroquia" (hereafter, AHN, 2174), pieza 5 (hereafter, P-5), "Contestación de Fr. [Mateo] Perez," 28 January 1833, 10-13. I wish to thank Norman G. Owen, R. Bruce Cruikshank and the late Rev. Josef Goertz for helping to locate and to acquire the above mentioned collection of documents from AHN; microfilm copies of these materials were used at the Cebuano Studies Center, University of San Carlos, Cebu City, Philippines.

11 Velasco, *Isla de Cebu,* 11, 14, 18; Fajardo d'Almeida, "Fundación," 19; "Description of the Philipinas Islands," in, Blair and Robertson, *Philippine Islands,* 36:100-01; Redondo y Sendino, *Breve Reneña,* 150; AHN, 2174, P-5, "Contestacion de Fr. Bermejo," 12 February 1833, 2-10; "Contestación de Fr. [Mateo] Perez," 28 January 1833, 10-13.

12 Lutaos were Samals from the coastal areas of Mindanao and Sulu; sometime in the first half of the 17th century a sizeable group of these people settled in the coastal marshland and mangrove swamp area just south of Cebu. This area came to be known as Lutaos, though by the 19th century much of the marshland had been reclaimed and the district inhabited almost entirely by

Cebuanos. Francisco Combés, *Historia de Mindanao y Jolo* (Madrid: Vda. de M.M. de los Ríos, 1897), 28-29; AHN, 2174, P-5, "Contestación de Fr. [Julian] Bermejo," 12 February 1833, 2-10

13 AHN, 2174, P-3, "Testimonio literal de la separacion, division, y ereccion del pueblo del Sr. San Juan Bautista . . .," 2 March 1830, 9-24; P-5, "Ynforñe del Yllmo. Sr. Obispo de Cebú al Superior Gobierno," 7 March 1833, 24-35.

14 Fajardo d'Almeida, "Fundación," 19; AHN, 2174, P-5; "Ynforme del Yllmo. Sr. Obispo de Cebú al Superior Gobierno," 7 March 1833, 24-35.

15 Fenner, "Colonial Cebu," 56; AHN, 2174, P-1, "Relacion de los tributantes del Parian y Lutaos," 22 July 1830, 20; P-5, "Ynforme de Yllmo. Sr. Obispo de Cebú al Superior Gobierno," 7 March 1833, 31 (the Bishop reported that "There are no Chinese; [they are] very scarce."); Joaquín Encabo de la Virgen de Sopetran, "Informe sobre los naturales de la diócesis de Cebú"(1815), *Missionalia Hispánica* 6 (1949), 390-91.

16 AHN, 2174, P-1, "Relación de los tributantes del Parian y Lutaos," 22 July 1830, 20; P-5, "Relación que manifiesta el número de tributos asi de naturales como de mestizos havidos en el ano prócsimo pasado de 1832 . . .," 18 February 1833, 24.

17 *Ibid.*

18 Manila Archdiocesan Archives (Manila) (hereafter, MAA), "Mapa de almas del Obispado de Zebú, año de 1834 . . . provincia de Zebú . . . parroquia de la Cuidad". I wish to thank Peter C. Smith for permission to use these data from his file.

19 These estimates are based on considerable work with the following materials; PNA, Protocolos, 1818-1860, Cabezas de Barangay, Provincias, Cebu province, and many of the documents in AHN, 2174, as cited in note number 10.

20 *Ibid.* Specific references to Protocolos documents have not been made here in order to conserve space. After identifying the principal families from these records, efforts were made to construct genealogies for as many of them as possible; the comments here are based on the results of these efforts.

21 Fenner, "Colonial Cebu," 53-55; Delgado, *Historia general*, 62-63; Encabo de la Virgen de Sopetran, 391, 396-97; Tomas de Comyn, *State of the Philippines in 1810* (Manila: Filipiniana Book Guild, 1969), 37-40.

22 Wickberg, *The Chinese*, 78, 82-85; Fenner, "Colonial Cebu," 87-97; Buzeta and Bravo, *Diccionario geográfico*, 393; Fabian Rodríguez, "Un buen religioso y patriota español," *Revista Agustiniana* 11 (1886), 20-24; *Mapa general de las almas que administran los padres agustinos calzados en estas islas Filipinas sacado en el año de 1820* (Madrd: Imprenta que fué de Garcia, 1820), 5; Jean B. Mallat de Bassilan, *Les Philippines: Histoire, Géographie,*

Moeurs, Agriculture, Industrie et Commerce des Colonies Espagnoles dans l'Océanie (Paris: Arthur Bertrand, Editeur, 1846), 1:311.

23 *Ibid.*; PNA, Protocolos, Cebu province, 1818-1860.

24 *Ibid.*; AHN, 2174, P-5, "Contestación del Fr. [Mateo] Perez," 28 January 1833, 10-13; "Contestación del Fr. [Julian] Bermejo," 12 February 1833, 2-10; *Provincia de San Nicolas de Tolentino de la congregacion de España e Indias* (Manila: Imprenta del Colegio de Santo Tomás, 1879), 207-09; Pedro Herce, "The Recollects in the Philippines," *Boletin Eclesiástico de Filipinas* 39 (January/February 1965), 241-43.

25 Rodríguez, "Un buen religioso," 25-26; Felix Sales, *Ang Sugbu sa Karaang Panahon* (Cebu, c.1935), 124-34; Fe Susan Go, *"Ang Sugbu sa Karaang Panahon:* An Annotated Translation of the 1935 History of Cebu," (MA thesis, University of San Carlos, 1976), 419-20; Vicente Rama, "Kinsa si 'Juan Diyong'?" *Bag-ong Kusog* (27 April 1923), 5, 8; Manuel Enriquez de la Calzada, *Legends of "Santo Niño de Cebu"* (Cebu City, 1965), 95-96.

26 This information is derived mainly from PNA, Protocolos, Cebu, 1818-1860.

27 *Reseña histórica del Seminario-colegio de San Carlos*, 6.

28 Salvador P. Escoto, "The Ecclesiastical Controversy of 1767-1776: A Catalyst of Philippine Nationalism," *Journal of Asian History* 10 (1976), 129; MAA, "Mapa de Almas del Opsipado de Zebú, ano de 1834 . . . Provincia de Zebú . . . parroquia de la Cuidad".

29 Wickberg, *The Chinese*, 93-94; AHN, 2174, P-5, "Ynforme de Yllmo. Sr. Obispo de Cebú al Superior Gobierno," 7 March 1833, 30-33; Encabo de la Virgen de Sopetran, 390-92, 396-97.

30 Fajardo d'Almeida, "Fundación," 16; AHN, 2174, P-1, "Oficio del Alc^e. m$\bar{o}$r. al Exm$\bar{o}$. S$\bar{o}$r. Capitan Gr$\bar{a}$l.," 22 July 1830, 29-32; P-5, "Ynforme del Yllmo. Sr. Obispo de Cebú al Superior Gobierno," 7 March 1833, 41-42; P-8, "Ynforme del R. P^e. Prior de San Sebastian," 1 September 1836, 2-3; *Mapa general de las almas que administran los padres agustinos calzados . . . 1820*, 5; Sales, *Ang Sugbu*, 98-99, (a slightly touched-up photograph of the Parian church can be found between pages 110 and 111); Buzeta and Bravo, *Diccionario geográfico*, 1:554; Martínez de Zúñiga, *Status*, 433.

31 Encabo de la Virgen de Sopetran, 390; AHN, 2174, P-5, "Ynforme del Yllmo. Sr. Obispo de Cebú al Superior Gobierno," 7 March 1833, 31.

32 These estimates were calculated from data derived from two maps of the city proper, one dated in 1699 and the other in 1826. The former is included in AHN, 2174, P-1, and the latter has been copied from a copy housed in the archives of the Ateneo de Manila University in Quezon City, Philippines, and was dated 25 August 1826, and signed by Miguel de Rojas. I wish to thank Fe Susan Go for permission to use her copy of the 1826 map. Ownership over the other lots in Cebu will be discussed briefly later in this essay.

33 Juan Francisco de San Antonio, "The religious estate in the Philippines," in Blair and Robertson, *Philippine Islands,* 28:150-51; calculations with regard to the declining numbers of Augustinians in the urban area derive from data in Elviro J. Pérez, *Catálogo bio-bibliográfico de los religioso agustinos de la provincia del Santísimo Nombre de Jesús de las islas Filipinas desde fundacion hasta nuestros dias* (Manila: Estab. Tipo. de Col. de Sto. Tomás, 1901); a somewhat similar view is expressed for the Franciscans in Samar at about the same period, see, Bruce Cruikshank, "An Essay on the Franciscans on Samar Island, the Philippines, 1768-1898," *Archivo Ibero-Americano* 38 (1978), 249, 262-63.

34 Pérez, *Catálogo,* 376-78; Rodríguez, "Un buen religioso," 16-26; the impact of these changes for Cebu's east coast will be more graphically described in a forthcoming monograph, based on the analysis of population and vital statistics, by Peter C. Smith and Michael Cullinane on population change in 19th century Cebu.

35 Although most local accounts stress that the central issue was one of jealousy on the part of the Spanish Bishop and his Augustinian and other allies (that the other urban dwellers despised the mestizos due to their wealth), the question of civil and ecclesiastical jurisdiction over several barrios and much of the land contiguous to the city was clearly the major concern that emerges from the documentation. Two important local accounts are those by Fajardo d'Almeida and Sales. All the documentation is found in the very large collection of materials on this subject in AHN, 2174.

36 AHN, 2174, P-1, "Oficio contestación del Sōr. Obispo," n.d., 26-28; "Oficio del Alcᵉ. mōr. al Exmͦ. Sōr. Capital Grāl.," 22 July 1830, 29-32; "Oficio del Sōr. Obispo al Exmͦ Sōr. Capitan General," 21 July 1830, 32-35; P-3, "Escrito del apoderado del los comunidades de los barrios de Parian y Lutaos," n.d., 24-45; P-5, "Contestación del Fr. [Mateo] Perez," 28 January 1833, 10-13; "Ynforme del Yllmo. Sr. Obispo de Cebú al Superior Gobierno," 7 March 1833, 24-49; P-7, "Recurso del los principales de la Cuidad de Zebú sobre prision impuesta por el Diocesano a su Cura parroco Dⁿ. José Hilarion Corvera," 7 October 1833, 1-11; P-9, "Escrito del Sr. Obispo de Zebú," 21 March 1838, 50-64.

37 AHN, 2174, P-1, "Ynforme del Cura de la Catedral de Zebú," 28 August 1828, 9-11; "Ynforme del Cura de Pueᵒ. de la Purísima Concepcion jurisdicción de la Ciudad de Sebú," 1 October 1828, 13-17; "Oficio del Cura de Boljoon," 10 September 1828, 12-13.

38 AHN, 2174, P-1, "Oficio del Sor. Obispo al Exmͦ. Sōr. Capitan General," 21 July 1830, 32-35; "Oficio del Alcᵉ. mōr. al Exmͦ. Sōr. Capitan Grāl.," 22 July 1830, 29-32; Pérez, *Catálogo,* 358-59.

39 AHN, 2174, P-1, "Dto. de S. E.," 11 December 1830, 36-37; P-3, "Escrito del apoderado de los comunidades de los barrios de Parian y Lutaos," n.d., 5-7, 24-45; P-10, "Ynforme de Y.S. Obispo de Cebú," 18 August 1838, 3.

40 AHN, 2174, P-2, "Comunicacion del Yllmo. Sr. Obispo de Cebú," 16 August 1831, 1-3; "Acta sobre la publicacion del edito del Sr. Obispo de Cebú, relativo a la union del Parian a la parroquia de Cebú," 15 July 1831, 4; P-3, "Decreto," 28 July 1831, 8.

41 AHN, 2174, P-2, "Representación de los gob^llos. del Parian y Lutaos . . .," 5 August 1831, 9.

42 AHN, 2174, P-5, "Ynforme del Yllmo. Sr. Obispo de Cebú al Superior Gobierno," 7 March 1833, 24-49; P-8, "Ynforme del R. P^e. Prov^l. de Recoletos," 1 September 1836, 2; "Ynforme del R. P^e. de San Sebastian," 1 September 1836, 2-3.

43 AHN, 2174, P-5, "Oficio del Alc^de. mor. de Cebú al Illmo. Sr. Obispo," 15 and 19 February 1833, 23-24; P-10, "Escrito del apoderado del pueblo de Talamban," n.d., 1.

44 AHN, 2174, P-10, "Ynforme del Y.S. Obispo de Cebú," 18 August 1838, 2-7; "Decreto conformatorio separando el Parian de la Catedral de Cebú," 13 November 1838, 13; P-11, "Nueva representacion del apoderado del Parian y Lutaos en Cebú sobre la separacion de su parroquia de aquella Catedral," 17 December 1838.

45 AHN, 2174, P-12, "Copia de un escrito del Obispo de Cebú," 26 August 1840, 9-11; Felipe Redondo y Sendino, compiler, *Pastorales y demas disposiciones circuladas a los parrocos de esta diócesis de Cebú (y tambien a los de la Jaro antes de su separacion)* (Manila: Establecimiento Tipográfico del Colegio de Santo Tomás, 1883-1884), 1:28-29.

46 *Ibid.*; AHN, 2174, P-11, "Nueva representacion del apoderado del Parian y Lutaos en Cebú sobre la separacion de su parroquia de aquella Catedral," 17 December 1838; P-12, "Testimonio del escrito del apoderado del Parian y Lutaos en queja de los procedimientos del Yllmo. Sr. Obispo de Cebú," 30 September 1840, 1-6; "Ynforme del Cura interino del Parian," 5 December 1840, 12-13; "Recurso del apoderado de los principales del Parian y Lutaos contra los procedimientos del Diocesano de Cebú," 6 September 1840, 1-22; "Recurso del cura parroco de la Catedral de Zebú contra las procedimientos de su Diocesano," 1 April 1841, 1-4.

47 Wickberg, *The Chinese*, 90; José Montero y Vidal, *Historia general de Filipinas desde el descubrimiento de dichas Islas hasta nuestros dias* (Madrid: M. Tello, 1895), 3:153.

48 Wickberg, *The Chinese*, 88.

49 Sinibaldo de Mas, *Report on the Conditions of the Philippines* (Manila: Historical Conservation Society, 1963), 163.

50 AHN, 2174, P-17, "Vista Fiscal," 19 July 1849, 75.

51 AHN, 2174, P-16, "Consulta del Gob.[or]. Yntendente de Bisayas sobre la necesidad y conveniencia de refundir en la Ciudad de Cebú los pueblos de Parian y Lutaos, acompañando al efecto un plano," 10 September 1847, 1-10.

52 AHN, 2174, P-16, "Ynforme del Y. Sr. Obispo de Cebú," 19 June 1848, 13-14; "Vista Fiscal," 15 December 1848, 16; "Decreto conformatorio," 30 January 1849, 34-38; P-17, "Decreto del Sup[r]. Gov[o]. de 31 de enero de 1849 trascrito por el Gov[or]. Yn[te] de Visayas al Alcalde mayor de Zebú," 9 February 1849, 1-6.

53 AHN, 2174, P-17, "Oficio del Ylmo. Sr. Obispo de Cebú," 19 March 1849, 64-70; "Oficio del Y.S. Obispo de Zebú," 25 May 1849, 71-73.

54 AHN, 2174, P-17, "Vista Fiscal," 19 July 1849, 84-85.

55 *Ibid.*, 72-95; AHN, 2174, P-17, "Decreto, definitivo reformando el de 31 de enero de 1849," 18 December 1849, 97-99; "Recurso del R. Parroco de Talamban," 13 February 1849, 12-14; "Recurso de los prales. de Talamban," 15 February 1849.

56 AHN, 2174, P-19, "El apoderado de los prales. del Parian y Lutaos pide testimonio de los expedientes instruidos sobre la incorporacion de dhōs. pueblos a la Catedral de Cebu para acudir a S.M.," 5 March 1850.

57 Fajardo d'Almeida, "Fundación,"; Sales, *Ang Sugbu,* 104-11; Go, "*Ang Sugbu,*" 415.

58 Fenner, "Colonial Cebu," 109.

59 Fenner, "Colonial Cebu," 109-19; Rafael Díaz Arenas, *Memoria sobre el comercio y navegacion de las islas Filipinas* (Cádiz: Imprenta de D. Domingo Féros, 1838), 49-50; Buzeta and Bravo, *Diccionario geográfico,* 1:553; PNA, Erecciones de pueblos, Cebu province, "Comunicación del Alcalde Mayor . . .," 13 September 1847.

60 Fenner, "Colonial Cebu," 110-13.

61 The major Spanish merchants in Cebu at this time can be clearly identified in PNA, Protocolos, Cebu province, 1830-1860; see also, Fenner, "Colonial Cebu," 113-14.

62 Fenner, "Colonial Cebu," 117, 119; PNA, Protocolos, Cebu province, 1830-1860; see also, note number 56.

63 Fenner, "Colonial Cebu," 113, 127.

64 The distribution of mestizo tributes throughout the province can be found in *Guía de Forasteros. . . 1852, 1853, 1856, 1857, 1859, 1861, 1863, 1864* (Manila, 1853-1865).

65 These comments are based on a detailed analysis of PNA, Protocolos, Cebu province, 1840-1860, and of the existing parish records of all of the east coast parishes of Cebu from Boljoon to Sogod.

66 Fenner, "Colonial Cebu," 125-28.

67 PNA, Protocolos, Cebu (on Veloso see, 25 August 1858, 29 November 1861, 22 August 1863, 28 December 1865, 30 June 1866); Fenner, "Colonial Cebu," 130.

68 Fenner, "Colonial Cebu," 119-22; Gregorio Sancianco y Goson, *The Progress of the Philippines* (Manila: National Historical Institute, 1975), 155; for an example of a *pacto de retrovento* in Cebu, see, PNA, Protocolos, Cebu, 1308-15, 13 April 1847.

69 PNA, Protocolos, Cebu, 1840-1860; Go, *"Ang Sugbu,"* 430-31.

70 Montero y Vidal, *Historia general,* 3:308, 310.

71 Azcarraga y Palermo, *La Libertad,* 171-73; Fenner, "Colonial Cebu," 144-49 (the quote is from page 146); Great Britain, Parliament, *Accounts and Papers. . . Commercial Reports, 1878-1879,* 72:1607.

72 Fenner, "Colonial Cebu," 149, 158-61.

73 Fenner, "Colonial Cebu," 150-51; a description of the *personero's* functions can be found in John Bowring, *A Visit to the Philippine Islands* (London: Smith, Elder and Co., 1859), 392-93.

74 Great Britain, Parliament, *Accounts and Papers. . . ,* 72:1607.

75 These conclusions derive from analysis of PNA, Protocolos, Cebu province, 1860-1898; see also, Fenner, "Colonial Cebu," 165-70, 177, 185-86, 209-10.

76 *Revista de Filipinas* (15 November 1976), 145; Sancianco, *Progress,* 155; Feodor Jagor, *Travels in the Philippines* (London: Chapman and Hall, 1875), 302. (Jagor cites for this information an undated "English Consular Report".)

77 Vandermeer, "Population Patterns," 318, 333; information on Carcar and its leading families derives from PNA, Protocolos, Cebu, 1860-1898, the Carcar parish records and a detailed study of late 19th and early 20th century newspapers and local histories.

78 Sancianco, 155; *Revista de Filipinas* (15 November 1876), 145.

79 Vandermeer, "Population Patterns," 318, 333; Fenner, "Colonial Cebu," 175-77; PNA, Protocolos, Cebu province, 1860-1898; Dean C. Worcester, *The Philippine Islands and Their People* (London: Macmillan, 1899), 309-12.

80 These comments are all based on a detailed study of PNA, Protocolos, Cebu province, especially 1890-1898, and the existing parish records of Cebu province, numerous local histories and several oral histories.

81 Wickberg, *The Chinese,* 54-55.

82 MAA, "Plan general de almas formado de los del año 1857. . . Provincia de Cebú. . . Ciudad"; Javier de Tiscar and José de la Peña, *Guía de empleados de*

Hacienda de Filipinas (Manila: Estab. Tip. de Amigos del País, 1866), 389; Agustín de la Cavada y Méndez de Vigo, *Historia geográfica, geológica, y estadística de Filipinas* (Manila: Imp. de Ramírez y Giraudier, 1876), 2:155.

83 PNA, Chinos en Provincia, Cebu province, 1885-1886; PNA, Padron de Chinos, Cebu province, 1891 and 1893. I wish to thank Fe Susan Go for providing me with access to her notes on the latter collection of documents.

84 PNA, Padron de Chinos, Cebu province, 1891 and 1893; PNA, Protocolos, Cebu province, 1890-1898; *El Oriente* (22 October 1876), 9; John Foreman, *The Philippine Islands* (London: S. Low, Marston, 1890), 477.

85 Great Britain, Parliament, *Accounts and Papers*. . . , Volume 72:1609; see also, Jagor, *Travels,* 302.

86 The quote is from Wickberg, *The Chinese,* 77. The continued commercial activity of many of Cebu's mestizos can be observed in PNA, Protocolos, Cebu province, 1860-1898; even as late as the 1890s at least "a half dozen" mestizos were still considered to be among the major merchants of Cebu, according to Velasco, *Isla de Cebu,* 16.

87 MAA, "Plan general de almas formado de los del año 1857. . . Provincia de Cebú. . . Ciudad".

88 Cavada, *Historia geográfica,* 2:159, 179; *Guía de forasteros*. . . 1857, 1863; *Guía oficial de las islas Filipinas*. . . 1879, 1892-1898; Ramon González Fernández and Federico Moreno Jérez, compilers, *Manual del viajero en Filipinas* (Manila: Establecimiento tipográfico de Santo Tomás, 1875), 421-25, and *Anuario Filipino para 1877* (Manila: Esta. tipo de Plana y Cª., 1877), 376-79; Velasco, *Isla de Cebu,* 16-22; Fenner, "Colonial Cebu," 203-04.

89 See, PNA Protocolos, Cebu, 1890-1898; *El Comercio* (Manila), 1869-1897; Go, *"Ang Sugbu,"* 57-119, 416-33; Fenner, "Colonial Cebu," 204-05.

90 Seminary of Cebu (Mabolo, Cebu City), "Libros de matrícula" (for the Seminario-Colegio de San Carlos), 1880-1900; University of Santo Tomás, Matriculation records for the Colegio de San Juan de Letrán and Universidad de Santo Tomás, 1865-1900; PNA, Protocolos, Cebu province, 1860-1898; *Guía oficial de las islas Filipinas*. . . *1892-1898;* Sales, *passim*; numerous accounts of Cebu and lists of appointments published in *El Comercio,* 1869-1897; Michael Cullinane, "Cebu-born students attending Manila schools during the late 19th century" (research project funded by the University of San Carlos Office of Research and Scholarships), typescript housed at the Cebuano Studies Center, University of San Carlos, Cebu City; *Reseña histórica del Seminario-colegio de San Carlos,* 103-13, 134-36, 175-78.

91 The quote is from Dale S. Miyagi, "Neo-caciquismo: Origin of Philippine Boss Politics, 1875-1896," *Pacific Asian Studies* 1 (April 1976), 27.

92 Data on the Veloso case comes from Miyagi, "Neo-caciquismo," 20-34, and
    AHN, Ultramar, Filipinas, Gobierno, 1899, legajo 5344; I wish to express my
    appreciation to the late Dale Miyagi, who kindly gave me his research notes
    from AHN on this controversy.

93 See, for instance, G.B. Francisco, *Fulgencia Galbillo* (Maynila: Lim. ng Ang
    Kapatid ng Bayan, 1907), 118-19; I wish to thank Resil B. Mojares for this
    reference.

94 *El Pueblo* (Cebu City) 26 October 1902; *El Comercio,* 4 February 1881.

95 The information here derives from a reading of notices on Cebu in *El Comer-
    cio,* 1869-1897; Sales, *Ang Sugbu, passim; Reseña histórica del Seminario-
    colegio de San Carlos,* 9-22, 55-64; Velasco, *Isla de Cebu,* 11-24; José Montero
    y Vidal, *El archipélago filipino y las islas Marianas, Carolinas, y Palaos*
    (Madrid: M. Tello, 1886), 356-57. The reference to Cebu as a "nice little
    place" is from George Campbell, *Log Letters from "The Challenger"* (London:
    Macmillan and Co., 1876), 232.

96 The figure of "less than 75 families" has been calculated by a detailed effort
    to reconstruct elite family genealogies from PNA, Protocolos, Cebu province,
    1860-1898; existing parish records of Cebu province; and oral histories. The
    socio-economic status of these families and many of their members has been
    derived from PNA, Protocolos, Elecciones de gobernadorcillos, Cabezas de
    barangay and Provincias, Cebu province, 1860-1898; Sales, *Ang Sugbu,
    passim; El Comercio,* 1869-1897; *Guia oficial de las islas Filipinas . . . ,
    1892-1898;* Gonzalez Fernández and Moreno Jerez, *Manual del viajero; El
    Pueblo,* 1902-1904.

97 *El Pueblo* (11 January 1903). Antolin Frias, who wrote under the pseudonym
    of "Juvenal", was a Spaniard and an ex-Augustinian, who remained in Cebu
    as a writer; he was a regular contributor to the early Filipino Spanish-
    medium press of Cebu in the first decades of the 20th century. Between Oc-
    tober 1902 and January 1904 he wrote a series of articles (under the heading
    "Galeria") on the prominent residents of Cebu City and province.
    Throughout the series he referred to the "Cebuano aristocracy", "aristocratic
    families", "that class, no less illustrious than favoured by wealth", and those
    whose position "was based on wealth and talent".

98 The "30 to 40 interrelated Chinese mestizo families" refers to the families
    that dominated the old Parian parish prior to 1849 (see note number 19).
    Although a few of these families did not appear to be particularly wealthy
    prior to 1860, all appeared to be in 1890. These comments are based on the
    same sources cited in note number 96. Lists of *principales* of the Parian and
    the *gremio de mestizos* for 1848 to 1852 can be found in PNA, Protocolos,
    Cebu province, 9 August 1848; AHN, 2174, P-18, 2-6; PNA, Provincias,
    Cebu province, 1852. Similar lists for the 1890s can be found in PNA, Elec-
    ciones de gobernadorcillos, Cebu province, 1890-1896, see especially the

1896 election for *gobernadorcillo* of the *gremio de mestizos; El Comercio,* 1890-1896; *Guia oficial de las islas Filipinas, 1890-1898;* Velasco, *Isla de Cebu,* 14; Fenner, "Colonial Cebu," 196.

99 These comments are based on PNA, Protocolos, Cebu province, 1840-1860, 1890-1898; and PNA, Elecciones de gobernadorcillos, 1890-1896.

100 Information on these immigrants derives mainly from PNA, Protocolos, Cebu province, 1890-1898, Elecciones de gobernadorcillos, 1890-1896 (*gremio de naturales*); and many of the existing parish records of Cebu province.

101 For information on Cebuanos see *ibid.;* for the Chinese and Spaniards: PNA, Padrones de Chinos, Cebu province, 1891 and 1893; various articles in *El Comercio,* 1865-1897; Go, *"Ang Sugbu,"* 422-24; Fenner, "Colonial Cebu," 196-202.

102 Velasco, *Isla de Cebu,* 18-19; *El Comercio,* 5 February 1890.

103 Information on the councillors is from *Guía oficial de las islas Filipinas . . . ,* 1892-1898; various articles in *El Comercio,* 1890-1897; Sales, *Ang Sugbu,* 252-53; Go, *"Ang Sugbu,"* 452, 519-22; information on occupations is mainly from PNA, Protocolos, Cebu province, 1890-1898.

104 Worcester, *Philippine Islands,* 299.

105 *El Pueblo* (26 October 1902); general observations on late 19th century life style of the Cebuano elite derive from *El Comercio,* 1880-1897; Sales, *Ang Sugbu, passim;* and numerous reports of social activities in the first few decades of this century in the local press: *Ang Suga,* 1902-1910; *Ang Camatuoran,* 1903-1911; *El Pueblo,* 1901-1904, and others.

106 Elecciones de gobernadorcillos, Cebu province, 1890-1896.

107 Sales, *Ang Sugbu,* 168-81; and numerous articles in *El Comercio,* 1880-1897.

108 *Reseña histórica del Seminario-colegio de San Carlos,* 55-64; *Breve Reseña del Colegio de la Inmaculada Concepción y de otras obras beneficas, 1880-1930* (Cebu City, 1930); Fenner, "Colonial Cebu," 221-22.

109 The information for these comments derives from PNA, Protocolos, Cebu province, 1890-1898; *El Comercio,* 1880-1897; early 20th century newspapers of Cebu (see note number 105); and *Escrito de conclusion presentado á nombre de Doña Damiana Veloso del Rosario y Siap en el juicio ordinario de mayor cuantia promovido contra la misma en el Juzgado de Cebú por la razon social Pedro Pladelloren y Compañía, de Barcelona, sobre cantidad de pesos* (Cebu City, 8 June 1895); see also, Fenner, "Colonial Cebu," 161.

110 Sales, *Ang Sugbu, passim; El Comercio,* 1880-1897; PNA, Protocolos, Cebu province, 1890-1898; Go, *"Ang Sugbu,"* 469.

111 *El Comercio,* 1896-1897; Sales, *Ang Sugbu,* 224-354; Manuel Enríquez de la
Calzada, *Ang Kagubut sa Sugbu* (Sugbu: Rotary Press, 1951); PNA, Protocolos, Cebu province, 1898; John Foreman, *The Philippine Islands* (New
York: Charles Scribner & Sons, 1899), 551-53; Go, "*Ang Sugbu,*" 433,
438-94.

112 Sales, *Ang Sugbu,* 376-592; National Library of the Philippines, Filipiniana
Section, "Documentos referentes a la toma por los americanos de la cuidad de
Cebu," 1899; Foreman, *Philippine Islands,* 553-54.

113 The information presented here derives from the author's work on the early
career of Sergio Osmeña.

114 It is interesting to note in this regard that the sharpest expression of anti-
Spanish sentiment among the Cebuano-educated elite (at the turn of the century) was also directed against Spanish friars and their extensive landholdings in Cebu. This sentiment, however, was not universally expressed
and the most dominant elements of the urban aristocracy did not participate
in any attacks on the friars or on the Spanish religious hierarchy.

A Queen Dies Slowly:
The Rise and Decline of Iloilo City

ALFRED W. McCOY

Modern day Iloilo City has many monuments to both its present economic plight and its past grandeur as the second city of the Philippine archipelago, the "Queen City of the South". Fronting the long arc of the city's once-busy waterfront are the ruins of British sugar warehouses bombed by Japanese aircraft during the opening months of World War II and left unrepaired in the decades since. Lining nearby Calle de la Rama, the epicentre of the prewar sugar trade, are the ruined shells of planters' mansions and corporate offices whose elegantly sculpted columns now frame pools of rainwater. Local fishermen mend their nets in the grand ballroom of the *Casino Español* where Spanish and Swiss merchants once danced the *rigodon* with the daughters of wealthy Visayan planters. Moving away from the waterfront, the signs of economic decay are more immediate. Crowds of young men "stand-by" outside corner stores during working hours. Horses graze on acres of grass growing over the rubble of a commercial district razed in a postwar fire. Squatters' shacks stand upon stilts over ponds of sewage near the heart of the city.

The remnants of Iloilo's elite are acutely aware of just how far the city's fortunes have fallen. Ignoring the shifting patterns of international trade which have rendered the city's once important role redundant, Iloilo's embittered elite have fashioned a narrative which reduces the complex historical causality of the city's rise and decline to the influence of just two men — the heroic British vice-consul Nicholas Loney who built Iloilo in the mid-19th century, and the demonic labour leader José Nava who destroyed it in the mid-20th. Described by one contemporary Filipino historian as the "Paladin of Philippine Economic Progress", Loney is credited with raising the city from a swamp, creating the region's modern export economy by establishing the sugar industry, and linking the city to international markets.[1] Something less than a century later, José Nava is supposed to have destroyed Loney's work of immaculate economic conception by unionizing the waterfront stevedores, holding the city to economic ransom, and forcing the flight of commerce to Manila and a rival Visayan port, Cebu.

The collective memory, like the individual's, is a selective instrument. Archival records reveal that Iloilo's export economy did not, Athena-like, spring full grown from the mind of Nicholas Loney. Iloilo began its rise in the mid-18th century, not the mid-19th, as a proto-industrial manufacturing centre for handwoven textiles. An agent of several Manchester textile firms, Loney's primary aim in coming to Iloilo was the destruction of the city's textile manufactures and their substitution by

British machine-woven cottons. His interest in sugar was an incidental one aimed largely at providing a return cargo for British freighters. If Loney was little more than an agent of the global expansion of 19th century British commerce, then José Nava was simply the representative of Iloilo's stevedores who refused to accept the wage reductions necessary to keep the city's port competitive once 20th century maritime technology rendered it redundant. Having devoted all its resources, human and financial, to the sugar trade for several generations, Iloilo City had lost its capacity for commercial innovation and begun its decline into economic miasma. If we are to simplify a complex causality, then Nicholas Loney was not the architect of Iloilo's prosperity, he was its assassin.

The local elite's misconception of their city's past is one shared by most Western social scientists who have studied the Asian city. Iloilo's selective memory may have forgotten the city's century of growth as a textile centre, but Western urbanization theory is hardly the key to its rediscovery. The traditional Asian city was supposed to have been a purely administrative centre, a parasitic adjunct to the totalitarian bureaucracy, lacking an independent bourgeoisie or the autonomous cultural life of Europe's chartered cities. The dynamic Asian commercial entrepôt did not develop until the mid-19th century when the rapid expansion of European trade required the creation of port cities from Bombay to Shanghai. If we accept the logic of this thesis, then 18th century Iloilo should not have existed, and much of its subsequent economic history should not have evolved as it did.[2]

Of more direct relevance to the study of Philippine social history, a fuller account of Iloilo's development raises issues with implications beyond the mere rectification of a local hagiography. The dichotomy of "Manila" and "the provinces" implicit in so much scholarly writing gives the impression of an historic primate, like Bangkok, which has dominated an archipelago-wide network of cities. Viewed from a provincial perspective, however, Manila is just one of four major regional primates whose trading network dominated its immediate hinterland, Central Luzon, but did not extend much further. While Manila's trade zone was by far the largest, other cities like Vigan and Cebu have a markedly similar entrepôt-hinterland structure. If Manila's size and density of data makes it a formidable, even impossible, research target for a thorough social history, the lesser cities are convenient microcosms for the study of Philippine urban history. Trends and problems concealed in the midst of Manila's complexity stand out far more clearly in the narrower confines of the archipelago's lesser cities.

The Setting

The history of Iloilo City is interwoven with that of two islands, Panay and Negros, known as the Western Visayas region. The area of longest continuous human settlement in the region, Panay has a distinct triangular shape flanked along its north-south axis by a non-volcanic mountain spine 1,728 metres at its peak. The island's five major rivers draining towards the north and south coasts from the Western Highlands have left wide alluvial plains suited to wet rice cultivation and made the island, particularly the Iloilo Plain, one of the archipelago's historic

Western Visayas Region circa 1940

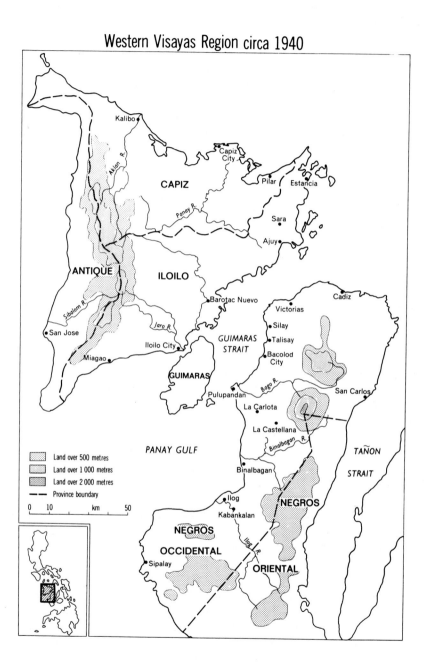

Kalibo

CAPIZ

Capiz City

Pilar

Estancia

Aklan R.

Panay R.

Sara

Ajuy

ANTIQUE

ILOILO

Cadiz

Sibalom R.

Barotac Nuevo

Victorias

Silay

San Jose

Jaro R.

GUIMARAS
STRAIT

Talisay

Iloilo City

Bacolod City

Miagao

GUIMARAS

San Carlos

Pulupandan

Bago R.

La Carlota

La Castellana

Binalbagan R.

TAÑON

STRAIT

PANAY GULF

Land over 500 metres
Land over 1 000 metres
Land over 2 000 metres
Province boundary

0   10   km   50

Binalbagan

NEGROS

Ilog

Kabankalan

NEGROS

OCCIDENTAL

Ilog R.

Sipalay

ORIENTAL

granaries. In 1939, for example, Iloilo Province had 92,235 hectares of rice under cultivation, constituting 56 percent of its arable land and the third largest area in the Philippines.[3]

Facing Iloilo only 30 kilometres away across the Guimaras Strait, Negros Island is geologically younger and is still shaken on occasion by minor eruptions from Mt. Kanlaon, a 2,465 metre volcano located at about midpoint along its mountain spine. Bisecting the boot-shaped island in a generally north–south direction, Negros' rugged cordillera, whose watershed demarcates the boundary between the island's two provinces, made overland communication almost impossible until the 1920s when autobuses began operating along newly constructed coastal highways. Populated by Cebuano migrants and oriented largely towards Cebu City's trade network, Negros Oriental has become an integral part of the Central Visayas region. Readily accessible from Iloilo across the generally calm waters of the Guimaras Strait, Negros Occidental's history has been shaped by the migration of capital and labour from Panay. Unified by a common language called Hiligaynon or Ilongo, a shared history, and commercial networks radiating outward from Iloilo City, Panay Island and Negros Occidental comprise a coherent region, a serviceable microcosm for the study of Philippine social history.

While Iloilo's agricultural economy has been based largely on rice cultivation, Negros Occ.'s has been dominated by plantation sugar production since the mid-19th century. The central cordillera is located slightly to the east of the island's centre and leaves wide plains fronting the western and northern coasts with a rolling topography ideal for sugar-cane. The province emerged as the archipelago's premier sugar producer in the late 19th century, and in 1938, for example, had 49 percent of its cultivated land planted to sugar, accounting for over half the Philippines' total production.[4]

The Western Visayas region has undergone three major economic transformations in the past two centuries, each with profound consequences for Iloilo City. The first major change occurred in the mid-18th century when the region began a transition from a largely subsistence economy to commercial textile production. Next, in the decade following the opening of Iloilo's port to direct foreign trade in 1855, the handicraft weaving industry failed in the face of competition from English manufactures and sugar produced on Negros plantations became the region's major export. Finally, foreign capital investments during World War I provided the finance for construction of large centrifugal sugar factories, called centrals, and effectively industrialized the milling sector of the region's sugar industry — with far-reaching consequences for all other aspects of production, including the transport and warehousing functions performed by Iloilo City.

Located on Panay's southeastern coast facing Negros Occ., Iloilo City has served as the region's paramount administrative and commercial centre since the start of Spanish rule in the 16th century. With the only protected anchorage of any size on the Guimaras Strait, Iloilo City is the optimal site for a major port. Throughout the four centuries of Philippine colonial history, Iloilo City was the commercial and cultural centre of the three provinces fronting on the Guimaras Strait — Antique,

Iloilo and Negros Occ. During its century as a textile centre, the city's trade networks were integrated with the weaving villages of Panay's southern and western coasts. At its peak during the 1850s Iloilo's textile industry sustained an urban area population of 71,060, making it a city of the same proportions as Sydney (54,000 in 1851), Chicago (84,000 in 1856), Buenos Aires (91,000 in 1855) or Valparaiso (52,000 in 1854).[5]

After Iloilo's port was opened to direct foreign trade in 1855, the city became a colonial entrepôt absorbed in the transport and warehousing of the Negros sugar crop. Although still the nominal capital of Iloilo Province, the city's logistic infrastructure was now completely integrated with the Negros hacienda complex. The front cover of the 1930 Iloilo City telephone directory shows, for example, that one could not telephone anywhere in Iloilo Province outside the city except the golf course a few kilometres away, but could call direct to almost any sugar plantation along the whole of the Negros Occ. coastline through an undersea cable across the Guimaras Strait. Emphasis on the formal geographical boundaries, Iloilo City and Province, would be a positive barrier to an understanding of the city's history. It is, in fact, the successive expansion and contraction of Iloilo City's trading boundaries that have determined the course of its commercial fortunes.

The Textile Era

The 18th century textile industry evolved from a highly developed rural economy with a centuries-long tradition of frame loom weaving as an integral part of woman's household work. From the 14th century, if not earlier, the Visayan region was involved in a regular trade with Chinese merchant fleets that passed through the islands enroute to the Sulu Sea and the Moluccas. The large volume of trade is evidenced by the considerable amount of Ming pottery shards recovered whenever contemporary farmers put fresh fields to the plough in southern Panay or when archaeological digs uncover pre-Hispanic grave sites. In addition to the obvious products like sandalwood, there is some evidence that handwoven cotton goods may have been bartered by Filipinos. At the time of Spanish contact in the 1560s the Ilongos had a highly developed material civilization and were already skilled weavers.[6]

During its first century of colonial settlement the Iloilo urban area served largely as an administrative centre and naval dockyard for Spanish campaigns of conquest. In 1571 the Spanish established a permanent garrison in the villages of Arevalo and Oton, now suburbs of Iloilo City, and later opened a shipyard to construct galleys for their expeditions to the Moluccas. Writing in the 1590s, the Spanish official Antonio de Morga reported that Oton had "many natives who are masters in building all kinds of ships" and nearby Guimaras was "thickly populated by natives all of whom are highly skilled carpenters".[7] After the Dutch razed Arevalo in 1618, the region's urban centre shifted a few kilometres east to the village of Iloilo where the major anchorage was located and there were "more than 100 Chinese married to native women".[8]

Iloilo remained a missionary and administrative centre until the mid-18th century when the city's Chinese mestizo merchants began to export the region's handicraft textiles.[9] We have, unfortunately, little data and only a few descriptions of the Iloilo weaving industry as it developed in the 18th century.[10]

The French scholar Mallat visited the Western Visayas in the early 1840s and published the first systematic survey of the Philippine weaving industry, giving the impression that Iloilo's had achieved a remarkable level of commercial sophistication. "The province of Iloilo," wrote Mallat, "is also renowned for its cloth called *sinamays* and *piña* . . .; the combination of their designs and colours is so bright and varied that they have the admiration of the whole world." Of the 52 varieties of Philippine textiles he was able to identify, Mallat found ten different mixtures of cotton, silk, pineapple and hemp fibres woven in Iloilo. While the cotton and pineapple fibres were grown locally, the abaca was imported from the Bikol region of southern Luzon and the silk from China. Produced at the rate of half an inch per day, the better weaves had "an admirable beauty which is impossible to imitate in Europe because the cost of production would be prohibitive". A total of 248,000 francs' worth of cloth was exported via Manila in 1842, and Iloilo's production found markets in Asia, Europe and the Americas.[11]

The growth of Iloilo's cloth industry appears to have had a marked impact on the demography and morphology of the six towns which comprised the urban area. Population data for 1760 indicate that these were still small towns — Jaro had 2,531 residents, Molo 2,343, and Iloilo only 835.[12] The rural town of Dumangas just to the north, for example, had a total of 7,021 inhabitants in 1732. During the next four decades Jaro's population increased slowly to only 5,890 in 1797.[13]

Despite the slow rate of population growth, several urban area municipalities were developing characteristics which would survive the 19th century. Records of tax payers (*tributos*) for the 1809-1818 period show that the great majority of urban-area Chinese and Chinese mestizos were living in Molo, the Ilongo *parian* (ghetto) where the Chinese had historically been required to reside.[14]

As the weaving industry boomed in the late 18th century, Jaro began a period of exceptionally rapid growth, and its total population increased from 5,890 in 1797, to 23,583 in 1834, and 30,208 in 1856. Much of the increase was no doubt due to migration, but the number of live births in Jaro was also going up. The aggregate number of baptisms registered in Jaro's parish indicates a strong upward trend: during 1700-1719, only 2,999 baptisms were recorded; 1800-1819, a marked increase to 11,598; and 1840-1859, a total of 23,282 baptized, indicating a large population of young females.[15]

Contemporary historians have been nearly unanimous in their assessments that the year 1855, the year Iloilo was opened to foreign commerce, marks the start of a new era in Philippine economic history. On 31 July 1856 the new British vice-consul, Mr. Nicholas Loney, landed at Iloilo to begin a 13-year residence in the city that was to have a major impact on the region's economy. As commercial agent for British and American firms, Loney dedicated himself to the promotion of cheap British cottons as a substitute for Ilongo productions and the encouragement of sugar production as a return cargo — in short, the extension of Manchester's trading sphere to the Visayas.16

Although Loney was the architect of the industry's demise, he had a high opinion of Iloilo's textile industry and has given us, in his consular reports, a detailed portrait. In his first report, dated April 1857, Loney estimated that fabrics accounted for $400,000 (Mexican) out of the province's total 1855 exports of $720,500. His observations indicated that small factories had been established, specialized job descriptions had developed, and the urban elite practised a form of debt bondage to maintain control over their weavers:

> Considering that the Philippines are essentially an agricultural rather than a manufacturing region, the textile productions of Iloilo may be said to have reached a remarkable degree of development. Nothing strikes the attention at the weekly fairs held at the different towns more than the attendance of native-made goods offered for sale; and the number of looms at work in most of the towns and villages also affords matter for surprise. Almost every family possesses one or two of these primitive-looking machines, with a simple apparatus formed of pieces of bamboo. In the majority of the houses of the mestizos, and the more well-to-do Bisayans, from six to a dozen looms are kept at work. I have heard the total number in this province computed at 60,000, and though these figures may rather over-represent the actual quantity, they cannot be much beyond it. All the weaving is done by women whose wages usually amounted to from 75 cents to $1.50 per month. In general — a practice unfortunately too prevalent among the natives in every branch of labour — these wages are received for many months in advance, and the operatives frequently spend years — become in fact virtually slaves for a long period — before paying off an originally trifling debt. There are other work-women employed at intervals to "set up" the pattern in the looms, who earn from $1 to $1½ per day in this manner. I should add that Capiz and Antique produce in a lesser degree than Iloilo a proportion of manufactured goods.17

If Loney's figure of 60,000 looms is accurate it would mean that almost one-half of the province's potential female labour force was employed in the textile industry.18

Loney indicated that British cotton manufactures had already made inroads. After collecting shipments of fabric, the Chinese mestizo merchants of Molo and Jaro sailed for the Manila market on sailcraft less than 50 tons deadweight. With their profits from the sale of native fabrics, the mestizo traders purchased raw materials, Chinese silk and Batangas cotton, since Iloilo's weavers required 300 tons of this latter fibre annually. Alternatively, the merchants bought cheap British manufactured cloth "from the large Chinese shopkeepers at Manila". Since "the mestizo dealers look for their principal profit to the *piña* goods", the British fabrics were sold at a low mark-up and enjoyed a growing market among Iloilo's "labouring population". British cloth imports to Iloilo were valued at $360,000 to $480,000 per year, roughly equivalent in value to Iloilo's cloth exports to Manila, and Loney expected further advances once Iloilo cargoes were no longer transited

Iloilo City in

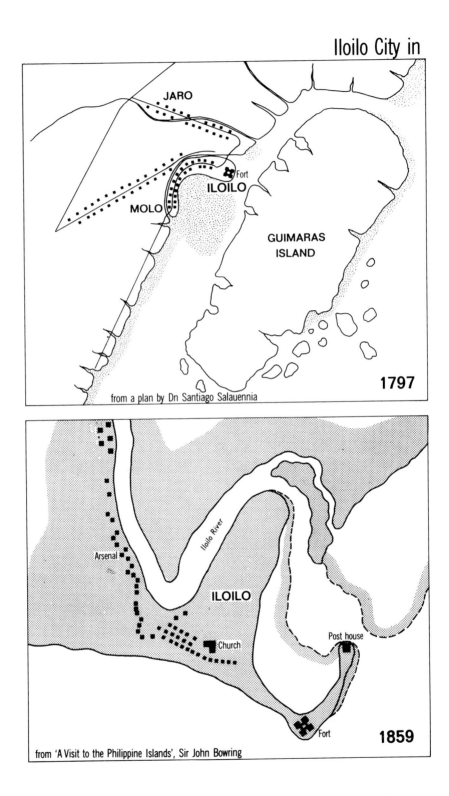

JARO

ILOILO
Fort

MOLO

GUIMARAS
ISLAND

1797

from a plan by Dn Santiago Salauennia

Arsenal

Iloilo River

ILOILO

Church

Post house

Fort

1859

from 'A Visit to the Philippine Islands', Sir John Bowring

Maps 1797 to 1956

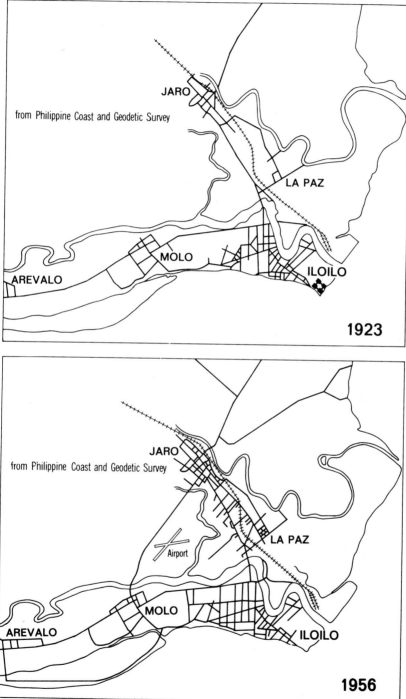

from Philippine Coast and Geodetic Survey

JARO

LA PAZ

MOLO

AREVALO

ILOILO

1923

from Philippine Coast and Geodetic Survey

JARO

LA PAZ

Airport

MOLO

AREVALO

ILOILO

1956

through Manila.[19]

In his 1858 report Loney described his efforts to promote direct shipping links between Britain and Iloilo which would increase the competitiveness of British cloth. To provide a return cargo for vessels arriving from Liverpool, Loney was encouraging sugar production on the island of Negros:

> I have no hesitation in affirming it to be much more than probable, that in the course of two years . . . the sugar crop be raised to a point which will render it easy for the vessels arriving with piece goods [cloth] to obtain return cargoes of sugar.[20]

The outbreak of the American Civil War (1861-1865) produced a Manchester "cotton famine" and slowed its exports, allowing Iloilo's weavers a temporary respite from the inevitable onslaught. In July 1861 Loney reported that native cloth exports had grown from $400,000 (Mexican) in 1855 to over $1 million per annum in the current year, and still comprised over half of the region's exports.[21] The following year cloth exports from Panay Island were considerably higher, totalling some 151,826 *piezas,* a minimum of 696,836 metres of handwoven fabrics. Exports to Manila totalling 141,420 *piezas* in 1863 arrived in 29 separate

Changing Patterns of Export Trade, Western Visayas, 1855–1890

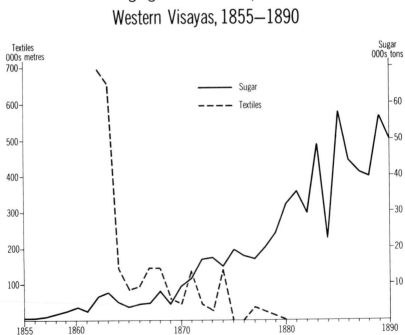

shipments from 13 towns along Panay's heavily populated western coast — 125,200 *piezas* from the Iloilo port area, 3,150 from the Guimbal-Miagao area, 900 from Antique Province, and 12,150 from the Capiz coast.[22]

As Manchester's production revived in 1864-65, Panay's cloth exports declined steadily, and within a of the decade had been reduced to a minor factor in the region's economy — from 30,673 *piezas* in 1864, to 12,700 in 1869, and 5,100 in 1873.[23] The British vice-consul at Iloilo reported in 1879 that: "The trade in *sinamay* fabric, which used to be very large with the island of Luzon, and was a great industry in this province, has dwindled down to a mere nothing."[24] In his annual report for the year 1892, the Spanish governor of Iloilo recalled the weaving industry's demise in the early 1870s:

> It was not long ago that Iloilo had considerable importance as an industrial centre: even the poorest houses farthest from the populated centres had one or more looms in production . . . But 20 years ago manufactured cloth from Europe and America was introduced into the market gradually at the outset, and then, produced to look like the native varieties and sold in the market at much lower prices, it provided severe competition for the native textiles.[25]

Sugar Entrepôt

The shift from textile to sugar exports had a profound impact on almost every aspect of Iloilo City's economic and social organization. The capital, commercial skills and labour dislocated by the precipitous decline of the weaving industry were quickly absorbed into Negros' expanding sugar economy. Deprived of its original economic base in the weaving industry, Iloilo's urban area suffered a steady loss of population and the city did not recover its 1859 population level until the sugar boom of World War I. As the city's mestizo entrepreneurs moved across the Guimaras Strait to take up sugar lands, the urban districts of Jaro and Molo lost their dynamism and became quiet suburbs of the foreign entrepôt that began to grow at the mouth of the Iloilo River. Jaro's population plummeted from 30,200 in 1856 to only 11,200 some 30 years later. Protected by the high limestone cliffs of Guimaras Island and afforded an extensive waterfront by the winding Iloilo River, the quiet fishing village of Iloilo became the safe harbour for the Negros sugar trade. Although the soils of Negros Occ. were ideal for sugar cultivation, the province's open coastline and shallow littoral were exposed to the periodic storms that swept down the Guimaras Strait.

As the quantities of Negros sugar passing through Iloilo's port grew with each successive harvest, from 12,000 piculs in 1855 to 2,470,400 in 1898, British and Spanish firms filled in the marshy soil along the river's edge and built an impressive colonial entrepôt. During the 1850s and 1860s they constructed stone warehouses fronting the Iloilo River. From the 1870s onward, foreign firms built permanent offices, banks, residences and retail shops along the streets paralleling the waterfront. The annual harvest cycle of the sugar-cane set the rhythm of the city's commercial activity. From September to April the foreign traders filled their riverfront warehouses as the fleets of light *lorcha* sailcraft delivered bagged sugar from hundreds of steam mills dotting the Negros sugar districts. From January to August foreign freighters tied up to unload finished goods — cheap cloth for the workers, luxury goods for the planters, farm equipment for the plantations — and take on cargoes of sugar for Europe, America or China.

While Negros produced the sugar, Iloilo City performed all of the industry's support functions. Banks, social clubs, warehouses, machine shops, printing presses, retail shops, commercial firms, educational institutions and medical services were only to be found in the city. Iloilo City's prosperity was based upon serving the needs of the Negros sugar planter, his foreign patrons, and, perhaps most importantly, its own population of stevedores.

To move the sugar from *lorcha* sailcraft into the warehouse and from the warehouse into the foreign bottoms, Iloilo City maintained a substantial population of resident and migratory stevedores that replaced the women weavers as the basis of the city's working class. During September and October as the mills began grinding in Negros, an estimated 2,000 to 3,000 seasonal stevedores migrated into the city to handle cargo until the bulk of the foreign vessels had finished loading in May or June.[26] Paid daily in cash and often unburdened by family responsibilities, the Ilongo stevedore, or *jornal,* was a potent consumer. The stevedores' wages injected a substantial amount of cash into the city's economy and supported its bars and restaurants, its retail *bazars* and its vernacular drama, the *zarzuela,* whose "golden age" was the city's supreme cultural triumph.

Despite its more impressive appearance, the reborn City of Iloilo had lost its essential economic dynamism. No longer the home of an independent mercantile elite who controlled their own capital, equipment and transport, Iloilo had become a satellite of the London and New York sugar markets subject to all the vagaries of the global commodities trade. Indicative of its weakened economy, the city's population dropped from 71,060 in 1859 to 43,300 in 1878, a net loss of some 40 percent. With the exception of the very largest merchants, the mestizos had become planters dependent upon the foreign firms for their capital, market and transport. No longer an independent commercial centre, Iloilo became a regional break-and-bulk port — bulking up sugar for export and breaking up larger import cargoes of finished imports for regional–local distribution.

Simultaneous with his destruction of the weaving industry, Vice-Consul Loney played an important catalytic role in the emergence of Iloilo as a sugar entrepôt. Believing that an efficient port was of paramount importance to the growth of the region's foreign trade, Loney devoted considerable efforts to improving the shipping, warehousing and commercial facilities at Iloilo. Loney's initiatives can be divided into two categories: first, a comprehensive effort to develop the infrastructure for a colonial entrepôt; and, second, a parallel attempt to foster the inter-island and international shipping connections which would vitalize his developing entrepôt.

At the time of Loney's arrival in 1856 the village of Iloilo was the smallest of the six which comprised the urban area. The French scholar Mallat had described it as "poor and lightly inhabited" during his 1840 visit and Loney found it little changed 15 years later.[27] Most of the town's area was tidal marshland which left only a "narrow tongue of land" suitable for permanent construction. In his 1859 travel memoir, British diplomat Sir John Bowring published a map of Iloilo Town which shows its few houses strung out in a row over a distance of 1.5 kilometres paralleling the river, and the entire riverfront area, which later developed into the city's waterfront, as an uninhabited swamp.[28] The Spanish government took few positive steps to improve the port, leaving Loney and his fellow foreign merchants to develop Iloilo's waterfront on their own. With an advance of $15,000 from the American firm Russell & Sturgis, Loney constructed a stone warehouse along the swampy riverfront in 1857,[29] and later reported that vessels of 300 tons "load inside the river, at jetties communicating with the warehouse".[30] Other foreign and local merchants followed Loney in constructing warehouses and jetties along the Iloilo River.[31] The foreign mercantile community continued to play a dominant role in the development of Iloilo's port throughout the remainder of the Spanish period. In 1890, for example, all warehouse owners along the Iloilo riverfront contributed funds for the widening of the waterfront, construction of "a good quay wall" along the river, and purchase of a "dredging machine" from England.[32]

An import merchant above all, Loney devoted much of his energy to the promotion of British goods and the establishment of direct Iloilo-England shipping lines to reduce transport costs. In June 1860 Mr. J.W. Farren, the senior British diplomat in the islands, reported that Loney had personally sold $300,000 of British imports, nearly equivalent to the total sold at the time of his arrival. To achieve his ultimate goal of direct import of Manchester textiles to Iloilo, Loney applied for a 12-month home leave to England in 1861 to meet with manufacturers, insurers and shippers about establishing the direct trade.[33]

Another of Loney's interests was the promotion of inter-island steam shipping. During his home leave in 1863 he was "chiefly employed while in London in forming a small steam company for the internal navigation of the Philippines — a matter which is of importance as respects their future commercial progress".[34] Although Loney's project was eventually blocked by Spanish law, his efforts "had the effect of drawing attention to the matter", and by September 1864 a Clyde-built steamer was "on her way out" for the Iloilo-Cebu-Manila route. It would be the second inter-island steamer sailing between Manila and the Visayas.[35]

The growth of inter-island steam shipping promoted Iloilo City's growth as the dominant regional port in the Western Visayas. Inter-island shipping before 1865 was characterized by irregular, direct sailcraft voyages from a dozen or more small towns along Panay's western coasts. Less than 50 tons deadweight, sailcraft had travelled according to the season, sailed directly to the port of destination without passing through Iloilo City, and were owned by local merchants. Between 1860 and 1880, however, shipping patterns changed markedly. In 1861 only one steamer entered Manila from Iloilo compared to 25 sailcraft arriving from a number of Panay ports. But 20 years later steam arrivals outnumbered sail 70 to two. As steamship connections on the Iloilo-Manila route approached two per week, sailcraft were reduced to a feeder role linking Iloilo City with small ports along the Guimaras Strait. Instead of proceeding direct to Manila on sailcraft, cargoes were shipped to Iloilo City by sail where they were warehoused in bulk for direct export or shipment to Manila on the twice-weekly steamers. As Iloilo City emerged as the region's break-and-bulk port, the number of local sailcraft entering her port shot upward. Between 1862 and 1871 the number of vessels entering Iloilo increased from 254 to 1,122 per annum, and the number of sailcraft arriving from Negros Island jumped from 75 to 405 during the same period. While 370 of the vessels arriving from Negros in 1871 contained sugar or rice, those departing Iloilo either carried finished goods, imported and domestic, or were in ballast. Clearly, Iloilo City had replaced Manila as the regional centre for the distribution of foreign imports.[36] (See map, pages 312-13.)

To handle the growing trade a community of Chinese and Europeans developed at Iloilo, giving the town the character of a foreign enclave. In 1863 the largest American company in Manila, Russell & Sturgis, opened a branch office at Iloilo, and was soon followed by other foreign firms.[37] A British handbook published in 1878 listed 42 European–American merchants and professionals in residence and 11 commercial houses or branches.[38] Foreign banks soon followed the merchants. In 1875 the Hong Kong and Shanghai Bank's Court of Directors appointed Mr. C.J. Barnes, manager of its Siam Sugar Factory, to the newly created post of Special Agent in Manila, and he opened an agency at Iloilo in 1883 "to prevent the Chartered Bank from getting all the business there". Until a branch of the Spanish colonial bank, Banco de Las Islas Filipinas, was established in March 1897, the Hong Kong and The Chartered Bank, both British firms, remained the only two banks in Iloilo.[39]

While the Europeans managed Iloilo's import–export firms, the Chinese population controlled the region's retail trade. Loney counted only 32 Chinese in the urban area in 1857. Thirty years later — after Spain readmitted Chinese to the colony — Iloilo was the centre of a substantial Chinese male community. According to an 1895 tax roll, Iloilo's urban area had 1,995 Chinese adult males, 79 children, and ten women concentrated around a few city blocks between J.M. Basa and Iznart Streets — the location of the city's Chinatown until the present. In the Iloilo provincial towns outside the city there were another 250 men and six women, and in Negros Occ. there were 821 Chinese males in 1891. Investing infrequently in sugar lands, the Chinese concentrated on retail trading from rented premises along Iloilo's main streets or in the provincial towns. Notarial documents registered during the 1884-1894 period indicate that there was only one Chinese Don Francisco Yap-Tico, equal in stature to the major European or mestizo merchants.[40]

Although Iloilo City was obviously more "developed" by 1890 than it had been in 1855, it had in many ways a far weaker and less coherent economy. During the textile era Jaro and Molo were proto-industrial towns adequately provisioned by the rice farms of the Iloilo plain. By the 1880s Iloilo City had traded its industrial economy for one dependent upon sugar handling, and was now forced to consume most of its surplus to purchase products, cloth and rice, which it had once produced in quantities sufficient for both local consumption and export. While sugar comprised well over 90 percent of exports from the 1870s onward, imports consisted largely of rice and finished goods — steam sugar mills, machine-made textiles from Great Britain, luxury goods and miscellaneous farm implements. In 1888, for example, Iloilo earned ₱4.8 million in exports, ₱4.7 million of that from sugar, but also spent ₱4.7 million on imports — ₱3.3 million for textiles, and ₱708,000 in rice.[41]

Despite the export boom, the region was no longer able to feed itself adequately. There is evidence that the periodic food shortages which appeared after 1870 were the result of the transfer of labour from Panay's rice farms to Negros' sugar plantations. As early as 1878 the British vice-consul at Iloilo reported that "many deaths have occurred from starvation" because of a poor rice harvest.[42] Five years later another consular report noted: "The natives having turned all their attention to planting sugar-cane and the native rice crop being a failure, a large quantity of foreign rice had to be imported which has caused a great drain on the resources of this province." This latter report showed foreign rice imports of 466,184 piculs in 1884 as against 150,000 piculs the preceding year — in addition to substantial quantities purchased in Central Luzon.[43] While sugar production climbed steadily upwards, shortages of labour and capital in the subsistence sector produced recurring famines.

The Negros Plantation Frontier

The opening of the Negros plantation frontier is one of the major events in the modern social history of the Philippines. Within the space of a half-century, the fertile coastal plain of Negros Occ. was transformed from a sparsely populated rain forest into the most productive agricultural area in the archipelago. The population of Negros Occ. increased from 18,805 to 308,272, while that of Iloilo Province across the Guimaras Strait remained relatively stable — 321,049 in 1849 and 410,315 in 1903. A contemporary observer, the Spanish lawyer Robustiano Echauz, described the transformation as follows:[44]

Negros Island	1850	1880	1893
Population	30,000	200,000	320,606
Sugar (piculs)	3,000	618,120	1,800,000
Rice (cavans)	10,000	659,330	430,000
Sugar Mills	7	571	821

In the half-century that followed the opening of the Negros plantation frontier, the sugar industry's development was largely extensive in nature. That is, the rapid increase in production was sustained by depressing wages and constantly acquiring new lands, rather than by investing capital in new technology for more intensive and efficient cultivation of existing plantations.

Changing Inter-Island Shipping Patterns,

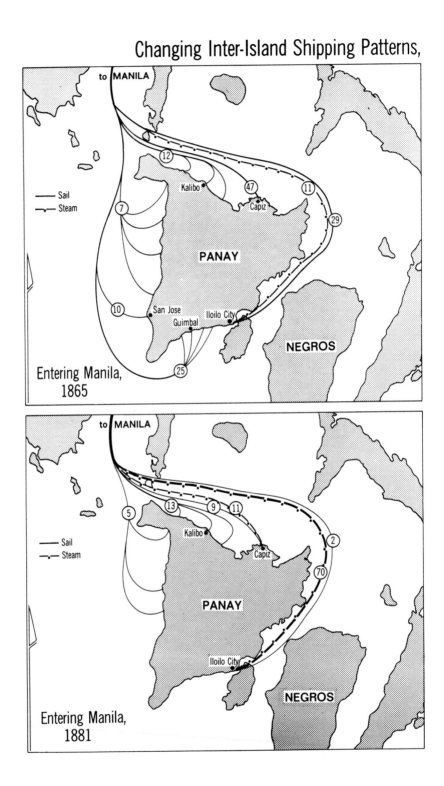

to MANILA

Sail
Steam

Kalibo

Capiz

11

47

29

12

7

10

San Jose
Guimbal

Iloilo City

25

PANAY

NEGROS

Entering Manila,
1865

to MANILA

Sail
Steam

5

13

9

11

Kalibo

Capiz

2

70

PANAY

Iloilo City

NEGROS

Entering Manila,
1881

Western Visayas Region, 1862-1894

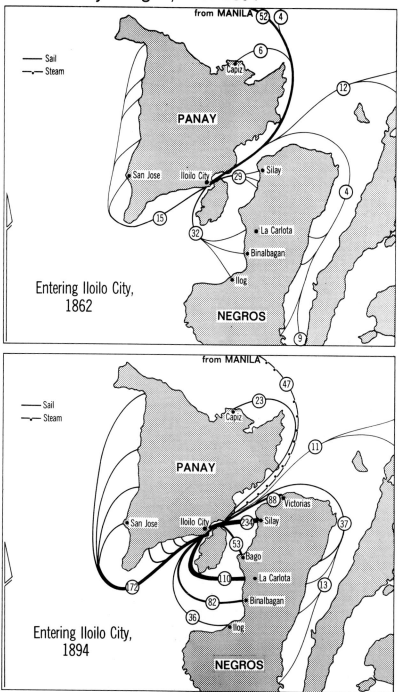

The most significant feature of this growth, one completely overlooked by historians, is the close relationship between the de-industrialization of Iloilo City and the development of Negros' sugar industry. The three critical elements in the rapid expansion of sugar production — plantation management, capital and agricultural labour — were largely derivative from the Ilongo textile industry. The mestizo merchants from Jaro and Molo who built their fortunes in the textile trade shifted their capital and entrepreneurial skills into the Negros sugar industry. Most plantation labour came from the overpopulated weaving villages of western Panay, and the mass migration across the Guimaras Strait was one of three major population shifts which shaped the social history of the 19th century Philippines. Indeed, it is no exaggeration to say that Negros' sugar plantations were, almost literally, built upon the ruins of Panay's weaving industry.

With the exception of some Spanish pioneers, Iloilo's expatriate Chinese and European communities played a secondary role in acquiring land for haciendas. This aspect was dominated by three segments of the Ilongo elite which had controlled the weaving industry — the Molo mestizos, Jaro's mixed mestizo-Ilongo merchants, and a smaller but still significant group of elite from the Guimbal-Miagao area on Iloilo's southern coast, a weaving district second only to Iloilo City in output during the 1860s. Jaro itself was located at the fringe of Iloilo's central plain and had several extensive agricultural barrios which were the first area of significant sugar plantation in the region. A survey of Augustinian parishes in 1845 reported that Jaro had 80 sugar mills in operation — as opposed to seven for all of Negros in 1850 — while none of Iloilo's other towns had any.[45]

In his 1861 consular report, Nicholas Loney emphasized the role of Chinese mestizos — whom he described as "a remarkable commercial, industrial and speculative race" — in the rapid growth of sugar production:

> A great number of Yloilo mestizos have also invested in the large tracts of fertile and well-situated land on the coast of Negros, each taking with them several families from Molo, Jaro, Miagao and other *pueblos* of this province to settle on their estates and work on the usual system of proportionate share of profits. Most of these mestizos have hitherto been engaged in the piece goods [textile] (wholesale and retail) trade in this province, but finding that the importation of goods at Yloilo from first hand at Manila interfered with their usual practice of obtaining them from the Manila shops for subsequent sale here, and that the increasing number of Chinese shopkeepers rendered their retail sale of goods at the different markets much more difficult, precarious and unremunerative, they have directed their attention to agriculture in preference. The new tendency thus given to their capital and industry will, by increasing the area of cultivation and amount of production, be much more beneficial than their former employment in a branch of commerce where they had become superfluous.[46]

Loney's impression of the mestizo merchants' role in the Negros economy is borne out by archival evidence. In 1897 the Spanish colonial government conducted a survey of 27 of Negros Occ.'s 33 municipalities which reveals two important trends: first, the bulk of prime sugarland had been partitioned into large plantations; and, second, many of these plantations were owned by mestizo families originally from Jaro or Molo. Of the six landowners in the whole of the province who owned over 1,000 hectares, two were Spanish; one was the Jaro mestizo merchant, Don Teodoro Benedicto; and three were the Molo mestizos Ysidro de la Rama with 1,525 hectares, Lucio Lacson with 1,067, and Teodoro Yulo with 2,525. Illustrating the dominance of large plantations, the town of La Carlota in central Negros had 4,359 hectares of land under cultivation, mainly sugar, which was divided into 33 plantations ranging from 30 to 400 hectares with an average holding of 132 hectares.[47] To demonstrate the continuity between Molo's pre-1865 elite and the Negros planter class, the simplest method is to compare a list of Molo's *gobernadorcillos* (town mayors) between 1841 and 1865 with the family names that appear on the 1897 Negros Occ. land lists. Significantly, 18 of the 22 men who served as *gobernadorcillo* of Molo during this period have family names that appear on the Negros land lists, and their average holding is 774 hectares, a substantial land area when one considers farm sizes in Iloilo Province. An 1896 survey of Miagao, a weaving town on Iloilo's southern coast, showed that only 12 of the town's 222 landowners had more than 10 hectares, while the great majority of the town's farms were less than two hectares. Similarly, 45 of Jaro's 124 *cabezas de barangay* (neighbourhood captains) listed for 1852 had surnames which correspond to those of Negros landowners whose holdings average 640 hectares in 1897.[48]

There are a number of known genealogical ties which indicate a direct line of descent from the Jaro–Molo elite of the 1850s to the Negros planters of the 1890s. *Cabeza* Basilio Lopez, for example, appears on the Jaro list for 1852, and in 1896 his son Claudio Lopez, the vice-consul for Portugal at Iloilo, owned three haciendas in La Carlota totalling 550 hectares. Another of *Cabeza* Basilio's sons was Eugenio Lopez, grandfather of Philippine Vice-President Fernando Lopez, who owned 11 haciendas in Negros and Iloilo totalling 2,592 hectares in 1887.[49]

Documents in the Philippine National Archives provide additional evidence of close links between Iloilo City's mestizo merchants and the development of the sugar industry. In 1863, for example, planter Yves Gaston filed his will with the courts showing ₱53,030, an enormous capital for the day, invested in loans. A French colonial planter from Mauritius, Gaston had migrated to Negros in 1846 and opened the first commercial cane plantation on the island. With the exception of ₱9,000 invested with the English firm Loney & Ker at Iloilo, all of the loans had been made to Molo mestizos currently occupying haciendas in Negros — Lucas Locsin owed ₱27,000, Pio Sian ₱4,400, Alejandro Montelibano ₱4,630, Damaso Lacson ₱2,000, and Vicente Locsin Gonzaga ₱1,000. The largest loan, ₱27,000, had been extended to Lucas Locsin, a native of Molo residing in Silay, Negros, to enable him to purchase Gaston's Hacienda Buenretiro in Silay and was guaranteed by Locsin's brother, Ramon, a former *gobernadorcillo* of Molo. It is extremely significant that these men, who were founders of some of Negros' wealthiest families, were already credit-worthy for such substantial loans in the late 1850s, well before the

Negros sugar industry was operating at any significant level.[50]

While large plantations dominated northern and central Negros Occ., there were a substantial number of small-holders in the southern portion of the province. In La Carlota there were a total of 33 land holdings in 1897 averaging 132 hectares each, but a southern town of similar size, Hinigaran, had over 250 farms most of which were smaller than 10 hectares and occupied by migrants from the Guimbal–Miagao area on Iloilo's southern coast. There is no direct evidence of causality, but it is nonetheless interesting that Panay's major weaving district outside the Iloilo urban area should have been the source of Negros Occ.'s only significant concentration of small-holders.[51]

While there is a clear continuity in entrepreneurial elite during the transition from the textiles to sugar, the lines of capital flow between the two industries are somewhat less direct. Although sufficient to finance the labour-intensive weaving industry, local capital was inadequate for the demands of the sugar industry and turned to foreign export firms for additional finance. In December 1883 the British vice-consul reported:

> The three great obstacles to a more rapid development of the sugar lands of Negros are want of capital, want of labour, want of roads. The planters, unless they have, as is rarely the case, sufficient capital to start the estate themselves, are obliged to borrow money on most onerous terms from sugar dealers or others, as the want of any system of registration of mortgages renders almost impossible the establishment of any properly constituted agricultural bank.[52]

The primary aim of Iloilo's major creditors, the foreign commercial houses and two English banks, was control over the region's sugar exports. Loans were, therefore, tied primarily to the standing crops and only secondarily to the land. Iloilo's two English banks loaned their money to European–American commercial firms at interest rates that started at eight percent. The major commercial firms, in turn, advanced crop loans to the larger hacienda owners for 12–15 percent interest and a guarantee that the sugar produced on the plantation would be delivered to the foreign firm's Iloilo warehouses for sale abroad with an additional two percent commission charge.[53]

Since there was usually a close correlation between the amount loaned and sugar exported, the statistics on sugar exports from Iloilo by the various firms indicate the growing importance of the foreign commercial houses in the capitalization of the Visayan sugar industry. In 1881 and 1886 seven Anglo-American and one Swiss firm controlled all of the port's sugar exports. By 1919 Chinese firms had taken over the export of sugar to China and two Ilongo merchants — Esteban de la Rama of Molo and Julio Javellana of Jaro — had made a minor entry into the market. But the Anglo-American houses still controlled 1.5 million out of Iloilo's 2.2 million tons of sugar exports.[54]

While the banks and foreign firms were the region's major source of capital, the Jaro–Molo elite were also active as financiers. Most of the urban elite were also plantation owners who had access to credit from the foreign firms at 12 percent, and made their loans at correspondingly higher rates ranging from 15 to 30 percent.[55] Several property inventories indicate the extent of the urban elite's involvement in credit operations. The inventory of the deceased Clara Lopez, daughter of Jaro *cabeza* Basilio Lopez, made in 1887 showed that of her estate valued at ₱126,175.50 only ₱55,000.00 was invested in agricultural lands, and ₱42,053.50, a full one-third of her assets, was on loan to 29 creditors.[56] Similarly, the contemporaneous settlement of the estate of Cirilo Corteza, a prominent mestizo resident of Molo, showed that close to one-half his total assets of ₱198,288.14 were involved in credit activities — ₱77,000.00 was invested in two Negros haciendas totalling about 350 hectares, ₱14,000.00 in six *lorcha* sailcraft of 700 to 1,200 piculs' cargo capacity each, and ₱90,359.60 in 61 loans ranging from ₱127.00 to ₱7,828.33.[57]

Although the Jaro–Molo mestizos held title to much of Negros Occ.'s prime sugarlands by the 1890s, extant archival records indicate that it was not they who had originally cleared and settled the land during the 1850s and 1860s. Judging from notarial records of land sales and court hearings into elite landgrabbing, it appears that much of Negros Occ. was initially cleared and settled by peasant migrants from the weaving villages along Panay's western coast. Migration began slowly in the 1850s, but accelerated in later decades following the decline of the region's weaving industry. Baptismal records in the parishes of Negros Occ. indicate that most migrants originated in overcrowded weaving towns such as Miagao on Iloilo's southern coast whose fragmented land holdings and poor agricultural conditions, similar in several respects to those on the Ilocos coast, required income from women's handicrafts to sustain their large populations. Travelling in light sailcraft, Panay migrants sailed directly across the Guimaras Strait and usually settled in districts opposite their home villages. Northern Negros was settled by migrants from Cebu and central Iloilo, while the province's more expansive central and southern plains were populated by a massive migration from the densely populated towns of southern Iloilo and Antique provinces.[58]

As they pushed inward from the narrow strip of coastal settlements, the early Negros migrants encountered uncleared forests inhabited by the region's last significant concentrations of non-Christian Ilongos still outside the reach of Spanish colonial government. When peasant migrants and land speculators began to push into the province's interior during the 1850s, they met some resistance from the non-Christians, ruled by traditional chiefs, and the Spanish governor mounted a series of pacification campaigns which produced systematic slaughters and forced the non-Christians deep into the highlands.[59]

While there remained land for the taking on the Negros frontier until the century's turn, labour remained in short supply until the mid-1920s. The mestizo planters were, in essence, trying to establish a labour-intensive industry in a labour-deficit area, a basic fact that forced them to devise a complex of labour-control strategies. Iloilo's mestizo merchants used three basic tactics to acquire an adequate supply of labour and *cleared* land: forced expropriation of peasant farms

Number and Origins of Migrants to Negros Towns

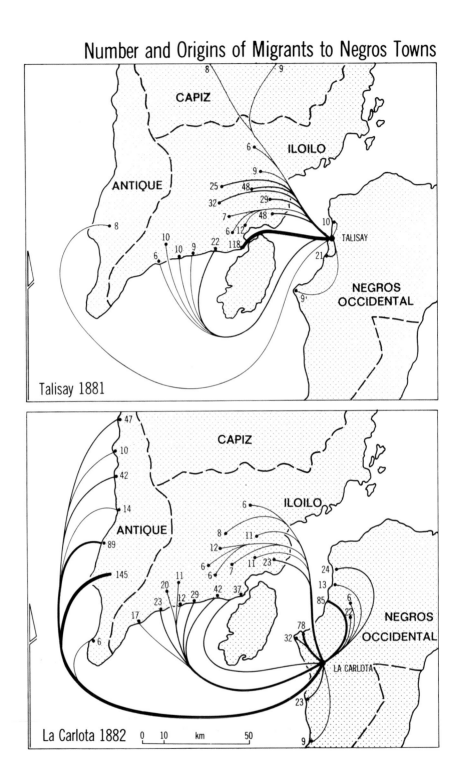

During Years of Peak Influx, 1868–1900

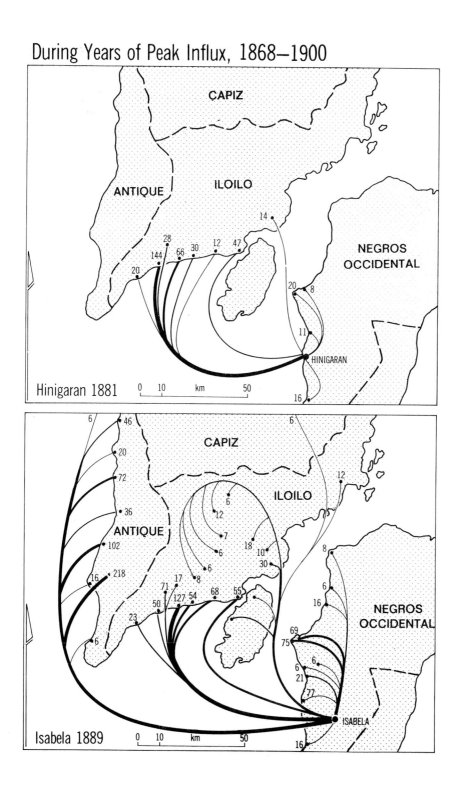

later legitimized by legal documentation; cash purchase of small peasant farms to form a plantation; and high interest loans to peasant proprietors with default provisions requiring forfeiture of land and years of debt bondage. Once the haciendas were cleared and titled, the planters employed a variety of tactics to maintain their workforce — contract migrant labour recruited annually in western Panay (the *sacadas*), cash advances to encourage migration by permanent workers, and debt bonding of resident labourers. Lacking any other incentive to motivate their debt-bonded work gangs, plantation foremen made regular use of corporal punishment. Workers often absconded from their debts and fled the plantations, compelling planters to devise a complex system of security patrols and passes to return runaways to their home plantations. The result was a social system marked by a high level of fraud and coercion.

The inadequacies of Spanish land law contributed markedly to the exploitative conditions on the Negros frontier. During the first three centuries of Spanish rule, native Filipinos, or *indios,* were generally barred from titling land outside their town of residence, a law which prevented the early peasant pioneers from registering their claims. What one Filipino forestry official called the "period of modern legislation" began with a Royal Decree dated June 1880 which established general procedures for confirming title to occupied lands and acquisition of empty lands. Flooded with an enormous backlog of land claims, Spanish colonials were able to collect substantial bribes for processing land titles. In an effort to accelerate the process, the Spanish government devolved the adjudication of all claims under 10 hectares to municipal land committees and those below 50 hectares to a provincial committee, a procedure which conceded entrenched elites a virtual monopoly on acquisition of new sugar lands in Negros Occ. The high level of corruption among Spanish and Filipino officials worked to the advantage of the Ilongo planters who had ample cash reserves to secure *post-facto* approval of their fraudulent and forced acquisitions.[60]

Two investigations of illegal land expropriations conducted by the *Inspeccion general de Montes* — those against Teodoro Benedicto and Gavino Gasataya — reveal the dimensions of illegal land expropriation by the Ilongo elite. Born in 1835 into a Chinese mestizo family residing in Jaro, Teodoro Benedicto began his career as a petty cloth merchant before the growth of the sugar industry. Described as "the personification of the grandiose, the ceremonious, the ostentatious", Benedicto was the founder of one of the region's major family lines, a conclusion evidenced by his daughter's later marriage to Senator Ruperto Montinola, Iloilo's leading politician for most of the American colonial period. In 1871 he purchased Hacienda San Bernardino in La Carlota, Negros Occ. for ₱1,871 from a family who had acquired the land in 1855. During the five years following Benedicto's acquisition, the hacienda grew from its original 300 hectares to 1,120.09 hectares — a progress which aroused the anger of Don Teodoro's Spanish neighbours.

Writing to the Superior Civil Governor in August 1876, 11 Spanish planters in the La Carlota district described the "evils which accompanied the acquisition of lands in Negros". They began with an evocation of the peasant pioneers who had migrated from Panay 20 years before to clear small farms from the forest:

> The first house was followed by the construction of another by a friend or
> relative of the first settler, and was followed by another and another to form a
> barrio and then a town in a place which not long before was unpopulated. But
> neither the first nor any of the others who followed held a title to the land they
> were cultivating, nor any other right to it at all. This mode of possession, this
> manner of acquiring property, is totally unrecognized by the Laws of the Indies...

The small-holders of Negros were being victimized by a few men with an "insatiable desire to possess". The Spanish petitioners went on to discuss in detail the
man they alleged was the most notorious of these — Don Teodoro Benedicto.
Claiming that Benedicto had acquired a total of 7,000 hectares in the La Carlota
district through his questionable methods, the Spaniards charged that he had occupied an "immense property" on the slopes of Mt. Kanlaon by "the expulsion from
his properties of poor *indios* who had from time immemorial cultivated small plots
of coffee and cocoa sufficient to cover the cost of their basic necessities . . ." Aside
from the 7,000 hectares Benedicto had expropriated in La Carlota, the Spaniards
charged that he had "usurped" 2,600 hectares in Bo. Bungayin, Isabela belonging
to a village of Christianized mountaineers; the entire barrio of Antipolo in
Pontevedra; and approximately 1,600 hectares in Bo. La Castellana, Pontevedra.
The original inhabitants of these barrios were forced off their lands and compelled
to "quietly retreat to the mountains with their families where they are relegated to
a miserable life". The Spaniards claimed that Benedicto had corrupted the *gobernadorcillo* of Pontevedra, leaving the poor dispossessed no official recourse.
Benedicto was not without his "imitators", however, and the Spaniards alleged
that the creole Spaniard Bonifacio Montilla was responsible for similar abuses in
Bago, a town adjoining La Carlota to the north.

These charges prompted a full investigation of Teodoro Benedicto's title to Hda.
San Bernardino in La Carlota. In March 1877 officials of the *Inspeccion general de
Montes* convened a hearing in La Carlota at which they interviewed the Spanish
petitioners, 21 small-holders expelled from Benedicto's hacienda, and Don Teodoro
himself. A creole Spaniard, Alejandro de la Viña, testified that Benedicto's armed
men drove small-holders off their land, depriving them of "all their properties even
the harvest". A peninsular Spaniard, José Domingo Frias, owner of the 163 hectare
Hda. Candaguit, testified that Benedicto's *encargado* (foreman), the *gobernadorcillo* of Pontevedra, sent armed men to occupy small-holder farms "and in case the
owners refused to turn over their lands they were driven off with violence". The
testimony taken from the 21 small-farmers expelled from Hda. San Bernardino
reveals the process through which Negros' peasant pioneers were dispossessed. All
migrants from Antique during the 1850s and 1860s, they had cleared the land and
established small-holdings ranging from one to 18 hectares several years before
Benedicto began investing in sugar lands. Once they were driven off, their combined holdings totalled some 256 hectares — a substantial addition to Benedicto's

hacienda.

The official government prosecutor charged with completing the review of the case ruled that "in the investigation of the methods employed by Dn. Teodoro Benedicto for the acquisition of lands there is a criminal liability on the part of him and his accomplices . . . ", and recommended that the files be forwarded to the Negros Court of First Instance for trial.[61]

Fifteen years later a less prominent Negros landowner, Gavino Gasataya of Guimbal on Iloilo's southern coast, was accused of a variant form of corruption. During his term as *gobernadorcillo* of Isabela in 1886-1887, Gasataya had made loans totalling ₱3,374 to the municipality's 52 *cabezas de barangay* to help them cover shortages in the payments of their constituents' personal taxes. Gasataya required each *cabeza* to sign a lien on personal real estate and livestock worth up to ten times the value of the initial loan, and when they failed to meet their repayment schedules he foreclosed on their property. In April 1891, however, the new *gobernadorcillo* of Isabela, a Molo mestizo, solicited a petition from all the incumbent *cabezas* charging that Gasataya had "reduced to poverty fathers of families, more correctly labelled the robbery of an entire community". Despite supporting petitions from towns along Iloilo's southern coast, Gasataya was remanded to Bilibid Prison for several years.[62]

Using a variant form of the same tactic, many elite planters acquired both land and labour by making loans to peasant pioneers who had completed the labour-intensive task of clearing working farms from the dense Negros forests. Notarial records indicate that loan contracts often contained clauses requiring forfeiture of land upon non-payment and subsequent debt bondage to the lender's hacienda for an unlimited period until the balance was worked off. In their mortgage and sale agreements, planters listed such debts as a part of the hacienda's assets together with plough, work animals, implements and buildings. A good example of the means by which planters used debts to secure labour was a series of eight contracts signed between the Spanish planter Adolfo Lazarte and peasants from the Bacolod area in 1871. To repay debts ranging from ₱50 to ₱85, these eight peasants agreed to work for an indefinite period on Lazarte's Hda. Agravante. In exchange for a half-share of sugar produced, the debtors were responsible for cultivating an assigned plot on the hacienda, cutting and hauling the cane to the hacienda's mill, providing half the firewood to boil the cane from their fields, and, most significantly, contributing one day of free labour per week to the hacienda. Within a decade, however, similar contracts dropped their share tenancy clauses and required daily labour at fixed wage rates — indication of a fundamental change from a preliminary tenancy system to the work gang system that characterized Negros' haciendas at the century's turn.[63] Viewed in retrospect, the one day per week of free labour in the Lazarte contracts represents a transitional device in the shift from tenanted to administered haciendas.

Another elite tactic for the establishment of a *cleared* sugar plantation was cash purchase of small parcels from contiguous peasant farmers. Using capital acquired from urban mercantile activities or loans, planters were able to offer cash for a dozen or more small parcels of less than 10 hectares each to form a working hacienda. For the capitalist unwilling to meet the high cost of clearing land with wage labour, outright purchase of small working farms was an economical strategy. For example, between March 1850 and August 1856 the French planter Yves Gaston, the first large planter in the Silay district, purchased ten parcels of land from small farmers to form a hacienda of some 200 hectares.[64]

While these strategies provided adequate labour for the clearing and cultivation of land, they were incapable of supplying sufficient workers for the most labour-intensive phase of the sugar-cane cycle — the cutting at harvest time. Writing in 1883, the British vice-consul at Iloilo described the antecedents of the contemporary *sacada* or contract labour system: "Labour is exceedingly scarce, and at crop time men are brought over from Antique on the west coast of this island to work on the plantations of Negros."[65]

Under the labour deficit circumstances that prevailed in Negros Occ. during the late 19th century, workers had an advantage that they would later lose. While workers were not able to voice grievances about their treatment, they could, and often did, default on their debts to the planter by fleeing to another hacienda where the conditions were better or by becoming pioneers in some of the more remote districts.[66] Writing in 1894 in a Spanish agricultural journal, one commentator claimed that two-thirds of the recent harvest was lost on some Negros haciendas because of labour shortages, and suggested special tribunals for the trial of workers who fled a hacienda without paying off their debts.[67] The problem became a subject of interminable newspaper commentary and editorial correspondence during the 1890s. In January 1896, for example, the Iloilo newspaper *El Porvenir de Bisayas* advocated accelerated Chinese immigration as one possible solution.[68] No positive steps were taken to resolve the problem, and labour shortages continued until the construction of the modern centrifugal mills reduced the demand for labour.

Confronted with a difficult labour problem, the province's planters used corporal punishment to maintain discipline and elaborate security procedures to prevent flight. After work each day, plantation labourers returned to the barracks inside the hacienda compound. During the night hacienda guards patrolled the perimeter to prevent flight and *Guardia Civil* troopers monitored the roads to catch fleeing workers. Workers leaving a plantation had to carry a pass, and those who absconded were subject to arrest by the *Guardia Civil*. A U.S. Constabulary officer who served in Negros at the century's turn painted Negros plantation life in the darkest of hues:

Each hacienda was a community in itself — a feudal community of which the *hacendero* was the overlord. The *hacendero*'s house, like a baron's fortress of the Middle Ages, stood in the centre of the buildings and dependants' huts. Many miles of almost uninhabited country might separate one hacienda from the next or from the nearest *pueblo*. The labourers, men, women and children . . . might be said to belong to the *hacendero,* for they were usually so deep in debt for the clothing and food advanced that escape was well-nigh impossible. And the *hacendero* would tell you that unless the peasants were in his debt they would not work.

This officer compared the Negros plantations to those of "our own south before the war when slavery fostered brutality". And he noted that each foreman carried a "stout club made of the heaviest and hardest wood found in the islands", and used it without effective legal prohibition to inflict injury or death on offending workers. Other sources indicate that whipping remained a standard practice in Negros until the 1920s when it was curtailed by the union movement.[69]

Volatile labour relations on the Negros frontier exploded in the Papa Isio revolt which started as a messianic, nationalist peasant uprising against Spanish rule and ended in class warfare between workers and planters. The most formidable peasant movement in the region's history, the Papa Isio revolt began on the western slopes of Mt. Kanlaon volcano (2,645 metres) overlooking the La Carlota sugar district in late 1896. Its leader was Dionisio Sigobela, popularly known as "Papa Isio", a 50-year-old plantation labourer who had been born in San Joaquin, Iloilo but later migrated to Negros. After losing his farm to a large planter, Papa Isio worked on a Spanish-owned plantation at La Carlota but later fled to the mountains after an attempt on the life of the proprietor. Whatever his origins, which are the subject of contradictory accounts, Papa Isio's movement was, in its early stages, a fusion of nationalist aspirations and traditional *babaylan,* or spirit-medium, religious practices.[70]

Fighting broke out in December 1896 when Spanish authorities began receiving reports that labourers were fleeing the plantations to join Papa Isio in the mountains. Spanish expeditions into the mountains throughout 1897 encountered fierce resistance and were always forced to withdraw after inflicting heavy casualties upon rebel forces numbering some 1,500.[71] Following the collapse of Spanish rule in September 1898, the Negros planters, who had remained loyal to Spain, declared their sympathy with the new Philippine Republic and forged a brief alliance with Papa Isio.[72]

Concerned about the maintenance of "internal order", the Negros planters decided after only three months of independence to seek a formal protectorate under the United States, their main sugar market for several decades.[73] Within a matter of weeks Papa Isio denounced the planters as traitors and returned to the heights of Mt. Kanlaon. The conflict now took on the character of a class war.[74] The American commander on Negros, Col. James Smith, reported in July 1899 that most of the insurgents were former plantation labourers who were fighting for the destruction of the sugar industry and the redivision of the haciendas into small rice farms.[75]

Papa Isio's 1899 campaign in the La Carlota–Isabela area of central Negros seemed the fulfilment of those aims. From his camps on Mt. Kanlaon, Papa Isio directed a mass uprising in the haciendas along the volcano's western slopes. In a four-month period several towns were attacked and razed; 40 Spanish planters fled the district; 56 plantations, mainly Ilongo-owned, were burnt out; and 12 Ilongo planters were murdered.[76] In 1901 the American commander in La Carlota reported that "this is not an insurrection against the United States but against the property owners".[77]

Although his guerilla warfare crippled the sugar industry in southern Negros Occ. for several years, Papa Isio's repeated mass assaults on U.S. Army garrisons guarding the plantations and the provincial capital were repulsed in furious fighting which left his forces with hundreds of casualties. Gradually forced to withdraw deeper into the interior of the island's mountain fastness, Papa Isio's forces were generally inactive from 1902 to 1906. After a final offensive in 1907, Papa Isio surrendered himself to the provincial governor.[78] He was sentenced to death in 1908, but the U.S. governor-general granted a reprieve upon advice that Papa Isio's execution would encourage belief in his immortality and spark a revival of the revolt.[79]

By the century's turn the Negros plantation economy had evolved into a social system without parallel elsewhere in the Philippines or Southeast Asia. Unlike the tenanted sugar plantations of Central Luzon, Negros haciendas were cultivated by supervised work-gangs paid a nominal daily wage. The Kapampangan sugar tenant of Central Luzon lived in his own freestanding house, worked some four to ten hectares of plantation land on a sharecrop arrangement, and was responsible for supplying his own work animals and implements. The Kapampangan tenant was, in short, the planter-capitalist's industrial partner responsible for managing his own farm. The Negros hacienda worker was, by contrast, a wage or debt slave who owned, quite literally, nothing more than his clothes and cooking utensils. Worked in teams under the supervision of a foreman like open-air factory workers, the Ilongo plantation hand was paid an inadequate daily wage which left him constantly in debt to the planter.

Unlike most provinces, autonomous villages were few and the planter served as the agent of the Spanish colonial regime with the *de facto* power to administer justice and call upon *Guardia Civil* troopers to enforce his authority. Having used debt bondage to keep women weavers at their looms in Iloilo City's primitive textile factories during earlier decades, the planters replicated this system in the canefields. Influenced by their antecedent experience as textile entrepreneurs, the Negros planters managed their haciendas like factories in the field.

Viewed from a comparative perspective, Negros planters demonstrated few of the "rent capitalist" attributes that McLennan and Fegan ascribe to the hacienda owners of Central Luzon. Unlike "true" capitalists, the *hacenderos* of Bulacan and Nueva Ecija did not attempt to increase the profitability of their holdings by imposing more direct managerial controls. Instead of placing operations under their direct supervision, Central Luzon rent capitalists divided their haciendas into tenanted farms of usually less than five hectares each and increased their incomes over the decades by devising elaborate means of squeezing their tenants. As in Central Luzon, Negros *hacenderos* used tenants to clear the land during the mid-19th century. From the very beginning, however, Negros *hacenderos* avoided the less profitable fixed-rent tenancies adopted on the early Central Luzon haciendas and employed the closely supervised share tenancy system. Central Luzon later shifted from fixed-rent (*canon*) to share tenancy in the first two decades of the 20th century, a half-century after Negros had moved beyond share tenancy to directly administered plantations. Rather than allowing tenancy to evolve into a permanent social institution, Negros *hacenderos* demonstrated far more advanced capitalist instincts by shifting to work-gang plantations as soon as the pioneering work was done. The transition from tenanted hacienda to directly administered plantation began in Negros Occ. during the 1870s and was largely complete within 20 years. During the same period, Central Luzon, in contrast, moved from fixed-rent to the beginnings of share tenancy. How do we explain why two regional elites sharing nearly identical cultural origins, Chinese mestizo, and producing the same crop, sugar, adopted such divergent economic strategies — rent capitalism in Central Luzon and a purer capitalism in the Western Visayas? Clearly, the difference lies in the Negros *hacenderos'* antecedent experience in the Iloilo textile industry. While Ilongo entrepreneurs gained a substantial fund of capital and experience from the proto-industrial textile trade, Central Luzon merchants had been limited to a petty buy-and-sell trade that left them incapable of anything but a more crude variety of operation — rent capitalism.

Advent of the Centrifugal Sugar Factory

While the initial half-century of sugar exports made Iloilo City the premier port of the Visayan Islands and earned it the title "Queen City of the South", the construction of the modern centrifugal mill ultimately transformed the radiant Queen into a decaying dowager. From 1914 to 1927 local and foreign capitalists invested sufficient funds to replace some 820 plantation steam mills with 17 centrifugal factories. The industrialization of the milling sector soon affected every other aspect of production and eventually produced a transformation of the region's economy. Most importantly, this technological change rendered Iloilo's port redundant and ultimately brought about its decline as the entrepôt of the Visayan sugar trade.

In their initial decade the centrifugal mills augmented Iloilo's prosperity and enabled the city to achieve a level of economic activity that far exceeded its earlier peak of the 1890s. The centrifugal mills increased the percentage of sugar juice extracted from the cane, and with it the margin of profit of the individual planters, thereby prompting a boom in construction, conspicuous consumption and commerce. The prosperity was, however, illusory. As the basic structural changes in the economy began to be felt, the amount of sugar transiting through the city's warehouses decreased and the long downward slide in the city's economic fortunes began.

With their initial capital and profits, the mill owners financed the construction of rail grids, usually several hundred kilometres in length, to link the individual haciendas with the centrifugal factory. As their profits, which were enormous, accumulated with each milling season, the centrals completed their rail grids and constructed modern piers along the Negros coastline. While the plantation steam

Sugar Industry Logistics, Western Visayas, 1937

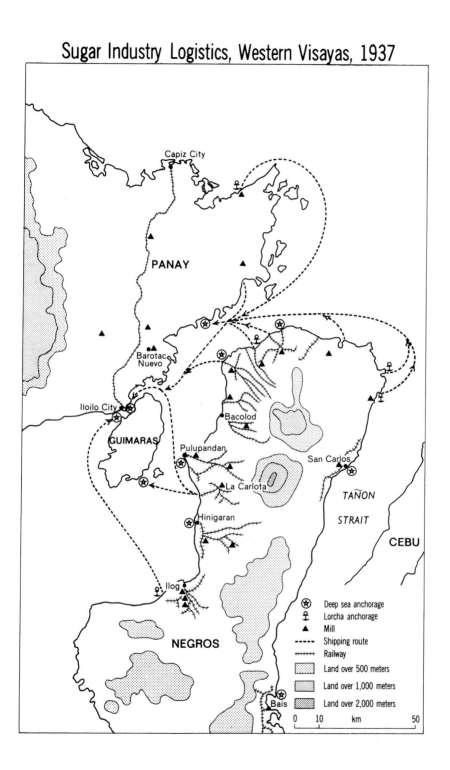

Capiz City

PANAY

Barotac
Nuevo

Iloilo City

GUIMARAS

Pulupandan

Bacolod

San Carlos

La Carlota

TAÑON

STRAIT

Hinigaran

CEBU

Ilog

NEGROS

Bais

⊛	Deep sea anchorage	
⚓	Lorcha anchorage	
▲	Mill	
- - -	Shipping route	
┼┼┼┼	Railway	
	Land over 500 meters	
	Land over 1,000 meters	
	Land over 2,000 meters	

0   10   km   50

mills had loaded their output at hundreds of scattered landings along Negros' streams and rivers, the centrals now dispatched their sugar from the modern docks.

The other significant development in the industry's maritime sector was the establishment of the Visayan Stevedore Transportation Company (Vistranco) in Iloilo City in 1920. Utilizing the growing complex of docking facilities, Vistranco employed the tug-and-lighter system as a more economic means of hauling the sugar from Negros to the Iloilo waterfront. Instead of loading 300 to 400 bags of sugar into an individual *lorcha* sailcraft, Vistranco used steam, and later diesel, tugboats to tow a string of steel-hulled lighters across the Guimaras Strait each loaded with several thousand bags of sugar. By 1930 Vistranco had enough tonnage to haul nearly the entire Negros sugar crop and held a virtual monopoly over transport across the Guimaras Strait.

These changes in local maritime technology complemented the modern ocean-going freighters of the international sugar trade, creating for the first time the potential for direct off-shore loading along the Negros coast. Once the centrals consolidated the loading points at ten docks along the coast, it became possible for a steel-hulled, steam-powered freighter to anchor off one or two of Negros' piers and take on a full load of sugar from lighters towed alongside by Vistranco's tugs. Not only was such a procedure feasible, it was far more economical. By loading directly off the central's Negros dock, the shipper saved the entire expense involved in moving the sugar across the Guimaras Strait into Iloilo's warehouses, thereby reducing transport and stevedore labour costs by half.

During most of the 1920s the potential for direct off-shore loading remained largely unexploited. With the exception of San Carlos central on the eastern side of Negros, most of the mills and exporters were content with the old system and continued to load sugar from their Iloilo warehouses. A string of disruptive strikes, accelerated by the Depression, ultimately forced the major sugar exporters to exercise the option created by the new technology and abandon Iloilo City's warehouses in favour of direct off-shore loading.

The far-reaching ramifications of these technological changes created both the need and opportunity for unionization in every sector of the sugar industry. In Negros the new mills facilitated a rapid expansion of the region's sugar exports from 1.7 million tons in 1913 to 10.3 million in 1932 and required a radical reorganization of the industry's internal structure which ultimately facilitated unionization. After the construction of the new mills, the Negros cane fields were no longer a structurally uniform patchwork of self-contained plantations ruled by authoritarian planters. Employing over a thousand workers, the centrals spawned mill towns in the heart of the sugar districts outside the control of the planters. Moreover, the 30-year milling contracts sparked strong conflicts between the planters and mill owners over the sharing of processed sugar, and thereby produced a cleavage in the elite which could be exploited by a labour movement. While the mill town became something akin to a free city set down midst the baronial oppression of the hacienda communities, the mill's industrial labour force was a proper proletariat and ideal target for union organizers. Although plantation workers were initially less open to unionization, the industrialization of milling and mechanization of much farm work during the 1920s reduced the demand for agricultural labour for the first time in the province's history, creating a surplus and depressing wages.

The map of the La Carlota sugar district is an apt illustration of the impact that the new central mills had upon the organization of sugar production in Negros. After the La Carlota Sugar Mill began operating in 1919-1920, the district's planters shut down some 55 smaller steam mills and began shipping their cane to the central mill on a network of over 200 kilometres of narrow gauge rails.

The new mills also produced major structural changes in stevedoring work, depressing both wages and working conditions on the Iloilo waterfront. Moreover, as the demand for stevedoring labour increased in close relation to the rise in sugar exports unmediated by any basic technological change, the city's population grew from 52,400 in 1903 to 77,900 in 1918 in bursts of 2,000 to 3,000 at the start of each milling season after five decades of decline or stagnation.[80] Unprotected by worker's compensation, minimum wages or meaningful labour laws, the city's expanded workforce turned first to mutual aid societies for security in case of death or illness and, later, joined labour unions to demand increased wages and improved working conditions. Propelled by these changes, Iloilo City's union movement evolved quickly from impotence to militance, passing through three stages between 1902 and 1932. Seeking to strengthen the anti-colonial movement by extending its base into the working class, elite nationalists encouraged the city's labour movement from 1902 to 1913 but met with little response. During the second phase, the city's workers joined neighbourhood mutual aid societies to secure a form of insurance in case of illness or death. Simultaneously, Iloilo's stevedores joined localized unions and mounted abortive strikes against individual warehouses. Finally, the union movement entered its militant phase in 1928 when working class leaders formed a city-wide union, the *Federacion Obrera de Filipinas* (FOF), and then launched a series of general strikes in 1930-1931. With each successive phase, the impetus for organization moved downward on the social scale and working class consciousness grew increasingly militant.

The introduction of tug-and-lighter stevedoring was perhaps the greatest single factor in changing working conditions on the Iloilo waterfront. Under the hacienda regime before 1914, small semi-permanent stevedore gangs of 20 to 40 men had handled the unloading of the *lorcha* sailcraft under the supervision of foremen, *cabecilla,* who were also responsible for the group's mutual aid activities. The progressive introduction of the tug-and-lighter system during the early decades of this century increased peak labour demand and amplified the scale of work-gang organization. In December 1906, for example, Iloilo's vernacular newspaper *Kadapig Sg Banwa* published a fictional dialogue, "A Discussion Between Two Workers", which was presented as an accurate representation of conditions aboard the lighters:

La Carlota Sugar Milling District , 1930

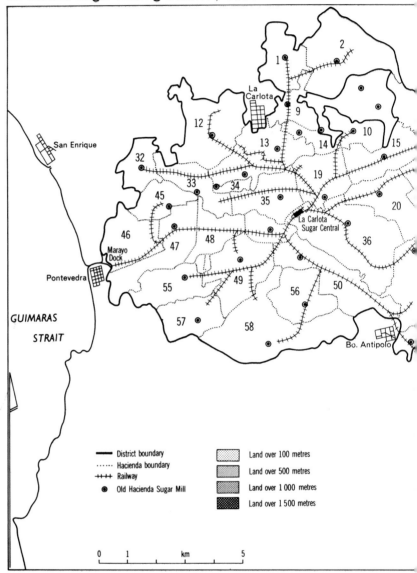

—	District boundary	
.....	Hacienda boundary	
+++++	Railway	
⊙	Old Hacienda Sugar Mill	

	Land over 100 metres
	Land over 500 metres
	Land over 1 000 metres
	Land over 1 500 metres

0   1   km   5

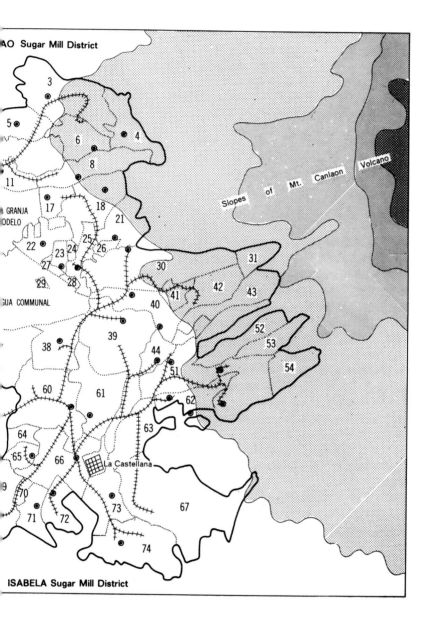

AO Sugar Mill District

3

5

6 4

8

11

GRANJA
ODELO 17 18

21

22 25 26

23 24

27 31

29 28 30

GUA COMMUNAL 41 42 43

40

52

39 53

38 54

44

51

60 61

62

64 63

65 66

La Castellana

70 67

9

71 72 73

74

Slopes of Mt. Canlaon Volcano

ISABELA Sugar Mill District

Oyong encourages Abog to load cargo on a ship anchored in the strait, but Abog answers he would work the docks even if they are only paying three pesetas a day.

OYONG: So where are you going to work? Just stand around here?

ABOG: Those *cabos* [foremen] on the freighters are really cruel; and even if you make a peso a day, the sweat is almost squeezed out of you.

OYONG: Even so the pay is high and you get free meals.

ABOG: What a fool this man is. How good is it if the food arrives when your ears are ringing with hunger and the men fight over it out of hunger, and there are no plates so they just pour the rice and vegetables into the men's dirty hats, and if you don't have a hat just get used to eating your rice and vegetables off the dirty deck mat? And no matter how much you drink the sweat is wrung out by the *cabo* driving the work.[81]

The rapid increase of employment in the tug-and-lighter sector following construction of the sugar centrals made such conditions the plight of most Iloilo stevedores. Instead of working in permanent crews of 20 to 40 men, Vistranco's stevedores were herded about in groups of several hundred under the direction of company *cabos*. Typical of waterfront conditions in most Pacific ports before unionization, Iloilo's stevedores were selected every morning at 5.00 a.m. by company foremen (*cabos*) out of a crowd of hundreds that gathered outside Vistranco's waterfront offices. When the company launch pulled alongside the freighter at anchor in the strait, the stevedores fought, clawed and kicked their way up the ropes to win a place at the winch and earn a slight increment in pay. A shift was 12 hours of hauling 60-kilogram sacks, heavier than many of the stevedores themselves, under the tropical sun and prodded by the curses and kicks of the *cabos* who usually undermanned the crews to pocket the wages of ghost workers. The only break in the working day was lunch, and it was the ultimate indignity. Under the gaze and laughter of foreign seamen, the stevedores squatted on the deck as their lunch was shovelled into their hats or onto the deck matting. Vistranco's stevedores felt a loss of dignity and to this day use an animal imagery to describe working conditions of the 1920s — "we were worked like cattle" or "we were fed the way a farmer slops his hogs".[82]

Very few of the city's union leaders were actually members of the working class. During the union movement's first decade from 1903 to 1913, most working class organizations were led by elite nationalists seeking to strengthen the independence movement by extending its base into the working class. Nationalist leaders founded two kinds of workers' organizations — labour unions attracting members on the basis of work-related issues, and mutual aid societies, specific to a particular neighbourhood, which provided a collective insurance for members' widows and a guarantee of a decent funeral. Iloilo's first labour union, the *Union Obrera,* was organized in 1903 by Julio P. Hernandez, a wealthy sugar planter and former Secretary of War in the local revolutionary government. Hernandez was a social conservative who publicly advocated Draconian laws to prevent Negros plantation labourers from absconding on their debts, and his union, not surprisingly, was short lived.[83] The earliest mutual aid society of any significance, *Mga Baybayanon* (The Shore Dwellers), was established at Molo in 1905 by Rosendo Mejica, founder of the Negros branch of *Union Obrera* in 1903 who was now editing a vernacular newspaper in Iloilo.[84] The society remained a fixture in Molo's coastal neighbourhoods for decades, but it attracted few imitators. Unlike Manila where parallel elite efforts laid the basis for later movements, there was little continuous organizational activity among the Iloilo's working class before 1914 and these early efforts were of little lasting consequence.

While Julio Hernandez typified the landed nationalists who led the city's early unions, leaders of the unions and societies formed after 1913 were usually local literati, journalists and dramatists, of middle and working class origins. In an age when subscriptions, not advertising, paid for the press, the flowering of popular journalism in the early decades of American rule created an economic basis for independence from retaliation by planters or foreign commercial firms, an important factor in a city dominated by a single industry. Aware of working class problems through their work as newspaper reporters, Iloilo's literati were actively involved in the lives of the city's poor as municipal politicians, neighbourhood leaders or fiesta patrons. Recognition from achievements on the stage or in press columns earned a writer a following among the lower class and inspired confidence when he aspired to leadership. The role of literati in working class mobilization was not unique to Iloilo. Cebu City unions were led by journalists in prewar decades; and the leaders of Manila's *Congreso Obrero* during the 1920s included the journalist Francisco Varona, poet Joaquin Balmori and printer Crisanto Evangelista.

Iloilo's working class mobilization during the period 1914 to 1927 has the quality of an inter-class dialogue between a chiding literati leadership moving upwards toward the middle of the society and an impoverished working class who attended their plays, read their newspapers and joined their unions. While this trend was evident in other Philippine cities, Iloilo's peculiar urban morphology reinforced this quality and gave it a special resonance. Instead of being divided into class-segregated neighbourhoods, Iloilo was a city of hollow squares, each with its localized class gradient. Built largely on a swamp since the 1860s, the commercial centre of Iloilo proper had grown by using earth fill to form roadbeds elevated above the estuaries' high watermark. First-class commercial and residential structures were built upon the roadway's elevated frontage, establishing two criteria for prime real estate — locality *and* proximity to the roadway. While the cement and brick structures fronting the roadways remained dry throughout the year, the interior of Iloilo's large city blocks filled with up to a metre of standing rainwater and sewage during every rainy season. Forced away from prime frontage land by the prohibitive cost of rentals, the city's working class rented small plots and erected temporary bamboo and *nipa*-thatch stilt houses inside the city's hollow squares. Most city streets had two kinds of addresses — for example, "no. 3 Valeria Street" indicating a wooden or concrete house fronting the roadway, and "no. 3 Valeria Interior" indicating a bamboo house inside the hollow square. Iloilo's peculiar mor-

Iloilo City Land Use, 1934

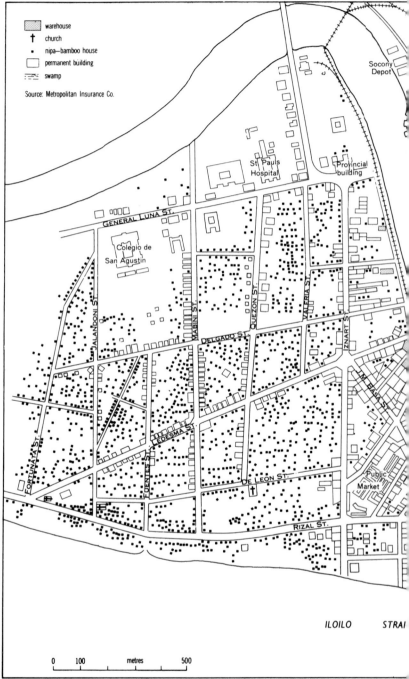

warehouse
† church
. nipa—bamboo house
□ permanent building
swamp

Source: Metropolitan Insurance Co.

Socony Depot

St Pauls Hospital

Provincial building

GENERAL LUNA ST.

Colegio de San Agustin

JALANDONI ST.

MABINI ST.

QUEZON ST.

VALERIA ST.

IZNART ST.

DELGADO ST.

FORTUNATA ST.

FUENTES ST.

LEDESMA ST.

DE LEON ST.

M. BASA ST.

Public Market

RIZAL ST.

ILOILO   STRAI

0   100   metres   500

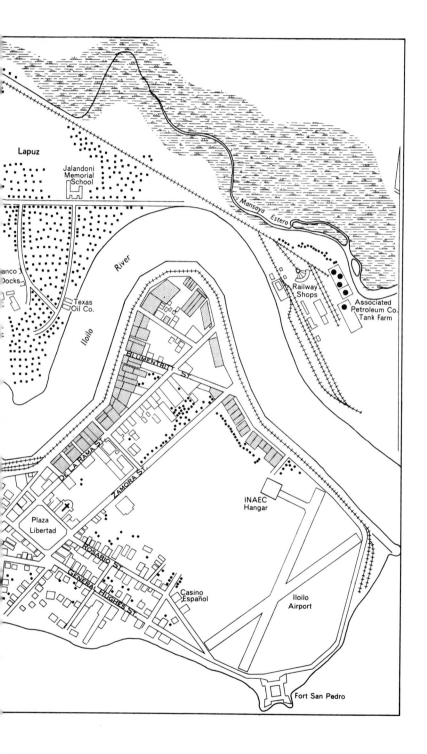

Lapuz

Jalandoni
Memorial
School

River

Iloilo

anco
Docks

Texas
Oil Co.

Mansaya Estero

Railway
Shops

Associated
Petroleum Co.
Tank Farm

BLUMENTRITT ST.

DE LA RAMA ST.

ZAMORA ST.

ROSARIO ST.

GENERAL HUGHES ST.

Plaza
Libertad

Casino
Español

INAEC
Hangar

Iloilo
Airport

Fort San Pedro

phology brought the city's working class "interiors" into almost daily contact with their social superiors who lived in the better housing along the street frontage. Sympathetic elite were drawn into a patronage relationship with their poorer neighbours through roles as fiesta patrons, godfathers, political aspirants or friends. When changing work conditions created problems for the city's labourers, it was not difficult for them to turn to literati or local elite who had demonstrated their sympathy as neighbourhood patrons.

This middle economic position of the literati and other working class leaders can best be demonstrated by an examination of urban housing valuations during the 1920s. My computer sorting of all available valuations for the 1920s and 1930s reveals three broad social strata, illustrated here by sample properties: in the upper level (above ₱10,000), Fernando Lopez, planter and local newspaper publisher who later served three terms as Philippine Vice-President, owned a house valued at ₱11,994.63 in 1931; in the middle stratum (₱500 to ₱10,000), José Nava, founder of the city's most militant union, owned a house worth ₱3,730.00 in 1924; and in the lower stratum (below ₱500) Leon Mata, founder of the Iloilo branch of the Philippine Communist Party, owned a ₱70.00 house, and Teofilo Castilo, a waterfront foreman and FOF founder, had a house valued at ₱105.00.[85]

The most important labour leader to emerge from the ranks of Iloilo's literati was José Maria Nava, the reputed assassin of the city's prosperity and a major figure in the history of Philippine trade unionism. Unlike most of the city's literati, Nava was born into a prosperous merchant family and his union activities were largely the outgrowth of his work as a journalist. At the time of his birth in 1891, Nava's family had been established as urban merchants for at least three generations and traced its origins to the Chinese mestizo community of Binondo in Manila.[86] His father Mariano had married the daughter of another local merchant family and built his home on Iznart Street at the heart of the city's non-European commercial district. It was there that José was born in August 1891 and spent the next 26 years until the house was destroyed by fire in 1917.[87] Mariano served as an officer in the Revolution and lived out his days as a respected member of the community— municipal councillor, accountant for the city's Chinese, and treasurer of the city's annual Rizal day celebrations.[88]

Although raised in a Spanish-speaking household, José attended the English-medium public schools through high school level. At 16 he revealed his combative disposition by heading a student delegation which filed a court action against an American teacher who made racist remarks about Filipinos in class.[89] After several years in Manila studying painting and sculpture, Nava returned to Iloilo where he became active in both Spanish and vernacular theatre and produced his first Ilongo zarzuela in 1912. Although he had written eight zarzuelas by 1917, he began to devote most of his time to journalism, working as editor of several of the city's leading English and Spanish dailies. With financial support from his father, Nava purchased his own press in 1922 and began publication of a militant Spanish daily, La Prensa Libre, which achieved a circulation of 3,027 by 1931, the second largest in the city.[90] Prospering from his various commercial ventures, Nava married, fathered nine children and settled into a rambling, wooden house on Valeria Street behind the Chinese Chamber of Commerce. Proceeds from the newspaper and his father's old accountancy firm remained the basis of his income until the mid-1930s and gave him the financial independence to establish the region's largest labour union.

After the collapse of the early unions, there was little activity until 1914 when vernacular newspaper publisher Rosendo Mejica tried to revive the *Union Obrera*. The union's first meeting at the Teatro Malhabour was convened by Mejica, two other newspaper editors, and the province's most famous revolutionary hero, Colonel Quintin Salas. Although it attracted a "monstrous" crowd, the *Union Obrera* was controlled by an elite executive with no branch components and soon collapsed.[91]

In November 1917, however, José Nava and his close *compadre* Vicente Ybiernas, son of the upper stratum merchant Matias Ybiernas, called a meeting at a city cock-pit to form a far more active union, the *Union Obrera de Iloilo*. In addition to a central executive headed by Ybiernas, the union established workplace branches, called *gremios*, of 50 to 100 members for seamen, warehouse stevedores, casual stevedores, and mechanics. In 1921 many of Iloilo's warehouses announced mass dismissals of waterfront workers, and the union responded with the city's first dock strike.[92] Pressed by the postwar decline in sugar prices, the exporting firms that owned Iloilo's warehouses decreased wages and dismissed their weighing crews, one of three work gangs in each warehouse. Under the hacienda regime, each warehouse had employed three stevedore gangs: the *banda descargada* which hauled the sugar sacks from the *lorcha's* hold to the warehouse entrance; the *banda pesada* which weighed every sack to make sure that the plantation mills had adhered to standard weight; and the *banda pasaka* which carried the sacks from the scales to the top of the 10-metre pile inside the warehouse. Instead of using handwoven, palmleaf sacks packed unevenly by hundreds of different haciendas, the modern centrifugal mills used standard jute bags machine-woven in Calcutta and filled to a uniform weight under precision factory conditions. The *banda pesada* had become redundant and was abolished, reducing permanent waterfront employment by a factor of almost one third.[93] After a two-week strike restricted to those warehouses involved in dismissals, the *Union Obrera* was forced to accept terms which appear to be a compromise. The union was a reasonably effective one and won important concessions, most notably the right of Vistranco stevedores to be provided a plate at mealtimes.[94]

At the peak of its influence the *Union Obrera* collapsed, largely as a result of political factionalism. Ybiernas was elected municipal mayor of Iloilo in 1918 as the union's official candidate, but as the 1922 elections approached he claimed that his earlier victory was the result of his individual efforts. Nava broke with Ybiernas over the issue, and the union collapsed amid bitter recriminations.[95]

With the exception of several conservative craft unions organized in the early 1920s, the next major labour union was not established until 1925. Organized largely among the stevedores living in the Blumentritt Street area just behind the sugar warehouses, the union, known as *Balhas Sang Mamumugon* (Sweat of the Workers), had a mixed leadership characteristic of this period — dock *cabecilla* (foreman) José Espinosa, Spanish language newspaper editor Lucio Fernandez, who lived in the area, and vernacular newspaper editor Victorino Guadarrama. In 1925 *Balhas* declared a strike against Vistranco, demanding that wages be raised and all workers loading in the Strait be provided a plate at mealtimes, a concession that had lapsed following the collapse of the *Union Obrera* in 1922. The strike was short lived since Vistranco management recruited the Molo mutual aid society, *Mainawaon*, as strikebreakers and fired the incumbent workers. The new workers became members of a company union, *Tres Triangulos*, and *Balhas* soon faded.[96]

During most of the decade, the trade union concept lost influence to mutual aid societies which were based in the city's neighbourhoods and were generally conservative on industrial issues. Responding to the 1919 rice crisis and the rapid growth of unregulated industrial employment, wage labourers throughout the archipelago formed mutual aid societies during the 1919-1926 period which were similar in conception to Iloilo's earliest society, *Mga Baybayanon*. At their peak in the mid-1920s, these societies demonstrated marked differences in Iloilo and Negros Occ. While Iloilo's societies restricted themselves to local concerns, the Negros Occ. organizations became embroiled in the politics of the province's sugar industry. The most radical Negros society, *Kusog Sang Imol* (Strength of the Poor), was comprised of plantation workers who united to retaliate against foremen who whipped their workers. Nominally led by a Bacolod journalist, Felix Severino, *Kusog* was in fact controlled by a centrifugal mill owner, Gil Montilla, who used it as a base for winning the 1922 election for provincial governor and as a weapon in his battle with planters over the terms of the milling contracts. Resentful of the mill owners and jealous of their disciplinary prerogatives, the planters organized a counter society, *Mainawaon* (The Compassionate), headed by another Bacolod journalist, Esteban Vasquez.[97] While Negros' societies were, then, a product of the province's gathering conflict between planters and millers, Iloilo's were largely an expression of neighbourhood and factional ties. Each Iloilo City neighbourhood had its own society, usually sponsored by wealthy local patrons. In October 1922, for example, the Iloilo Branch of *Mainawaon* celebrated the unfurling of its banner at a ceremony hosted by Governor Ruperto Montinola, Mayor Serapion Torre and Vistranco owner Cesar Barrios.[98]

After less than two years of peak activity, the mutual aid movement began to collapse in 1924. Conflicts between rival local societies intensified and physical violence, with occasional fatalities, became commonplace. Concerned over the rising tide of violence and mounting allegations of corruption, the colonial government began to apply pressure by auditing society accounts, confiscating arms, and barring members from the Insular civil service. The Cebu branch of the largest national brotherhood, *Legionarios del Trabajo,* broke away from the national organization over allegations of corruption, and in 1927 the Insular Treasurer discovered massive theft of membership contributions from the society's national accounts.[99] The most powerful society in the Western Visayas, *Kusog,* collapsed in

1925 when its president, Felix Severino, was sentenced to three years in prison on adultery charges.[100] Although the societies were relatively short lived, they represented an important transition phase in the growth of worker consciousness.

Iloilo's labour movement entered its final phase in July 1928 when a group of local leaders from the working class neighbourhood of Lapuz approached José Nava and asked him to assume the presidency of a union they were organizing. Squeezed between the Vistranco dry dock and the Philippine Railway yards just across the river from the sugar warehouses, Lapuz, an exception to the city's hollow square pattern, had the highest density of working class residents in the city and lacked a local streetfront elite. Although a patron to the interior cluster of lumber and copra stevedores who lived just opposite his Valeria Street home, Nava had no contact with Lapuz until January 1928 when a resident employed at the Vistranco dry dock called at his newspaper offices. Blinded in one eye by an industrial accident, the worker sought Nava's assistance in pressing his claim for compensation. Nava eventually won the worker ₱1,700 from Vistranco, and refused the ₱400 the man offered as payment. Several weeks later the worker returned with 50 fellow Lapuz residents and a petition signed by 470 dry dock and waterfront workers "advocating the organization of a legitimate labour union". Nava accepted the offer of leadership and proclaimed the new union, the *Federacion Obrera de Filipinas* (FOF), at a public ceremony several days later. The union grew steadily, gaining its early membership in Lapuz and the interior housing clusters surrounding Valeria Street where Nava already had a strong personal following.[101]

As his union expanded in the coming months, Nava developed a two-tier organization that remained the union's basic structure until the outbreak of the war. To administer the disparate branches, Nava recruited a small central executive from the upper strata of the city's working class — men with some secondary education and mixed incomes from sources such as gambling, petty commerce or clerical work.[102] The union's strength lay in its network of workplace branches, or *gremios,* which elected their own officers and maintained separate treasuries.

Although the FOF grew into the Philippines' largest labour union with 185,000 members divided into some 200 *gremios* covering the whole of the Visayas and Mindanao, its financial base remained the score of stevedore and transport *gremios* that controlled the Iloilo waterfront. Unlike the central or railway *gremios* which were organized on proper trade union principles, the stevedore *gremios* represented a taut compromise between the FOF executive, the elected *gremio* officials, and the *cabecilla.* While Nava and his union won the unqualified support of the working stevedores and their elected officers, his relations with their supervisors, the *cabecillas,* was one of mutual need and distrust. Something of a Janus-faced figure, the Iloilo *cabecilla* was by definition a labour contractor who agreed to supply men for the movement of cargo in and out of a given warehouse for a set rate per sack. Although he was, in a certain sense, an employer whose interests corresponded with those of the warehouse, the *cabecilla* also had strong motives for favouring the interests of his men over those of the warehouse since his own income was a fixed percentage of their piece-rate earnings. After the warehouse paid the *cabecilla* a lump sum for all sacks moved by the end of the day, he then took his 25 to 50 percent share of the total, paid the two crew foremen (*cabos*) their shares, and divided the balance evenly among the men. In cases where the difficulty of the work demanded an increment — if, for example, the ship was docked 100 metres from the warehouse — the *cabecilla* had a strong vested interest in demanding an increased piece-rate, but was often reluctant to do so out of fear of losing the labour contract. When the FOF began organizing the warehouse stevedores, the *cabecillas* supported the union and later conceded a share of their percentage to pay the wages of two FOF inspectors. Unwilling to press the warehouses about increments on their own, the *cabecillas* welcomed the union as a blind through which they could push their demands anonymously.[103]

The advent of the Depression in October 1929 sparked a confrontation between the new union and the city's sugar exporters. Pressed by the sudden collapse of the world sugar price, export houses tried to economize by reducing stevedore rates and dismissing redundant workers. Although Nava later claimed that the general strike was his initiative, oral and documentary sources indicate that the response originated at the sugar warehouse of the venerable Spanish firm, *Compañia General de Tabacos,* better known as *Tabacalera.* Several unusual organizational features made the *Tabacalera* stevedores uniquely capable of such an initiative. Other warehouses had eliminated the *banda pesada* ten years earlier, but *Tabacalera* retained its weighing crew until the Depression forced the move as an economy measure. If the sudden dismissals provided cause, it was the warehouse's exceptional *cabecilla* structure which gave its workers the capacity to initiate the general strike. Unlike the other *cabos* who were primarily labour contractors, the *cabos* of *Tabacalera's banda pasaka* worked along with their crew and took no extra share of the group's earnings. Under the leadership of a Lapuz *cabo* named Teofilo Castilo, *Tabacalera's banda pasaka* developed an esprit based on a strongly masculine pride in their abilities at moving the 60-kilo sacks up the 10-metre pile two at a time and evolved mutual aid mechanisms that became a model for other FOF *gremios.*[104] Acting upon representations from the *Tabacalera cabos,* Nava pressed the city's ten major exporters for concessions and when rebuffed called for a general waterfront strike in May 1930. Over 10,000 workers joined the pickets, and for 20 days at the height of the milling season not a single vessel was loaded on the Iloilo waterfront.[105]

The union's timing was perfect and its strike threatened a costly disruption of the entire sugar industry. Lacking anything more than a temporary holding capacity in Negros itself, the province's 17 sugar mills depended upon the uninterrupted flow of sugar across the Guimaras Strait into Iloilo's export warehouses. A prolonged closure of Iloilo's warehouse capacity would eventually force the centrals to suspend milling, and in turn force the planters to stop harvesting — a decision that would soon become costly for both as juice began to dry in the cane under the hot tropical sun. Incapable of mounting an effective counter-attack, Iloilo's export firms were forced to capitulate and grant many union demands.[106]

The union hailed the settlement as a major victory, but soon came to realize that its triumph was Pyrrhic. As Vistranco expanded its off-shore loading operations, cargo volume in the city warehouses covered by the bargaining agreement plummeted and the union's members drifted away to Vistranco and the Negros docks to find work. Only three months after the dock strike had been settled, Nava organized a walk-out at Vistranco. Embittered by the same abusive conditions that had characterized the company's operations for over a decade, Vistranco's workers responded enthusiastically to a strike call. Vistranco repeated the tactics it had

Iloilo City Sugar Warehouses, 1937

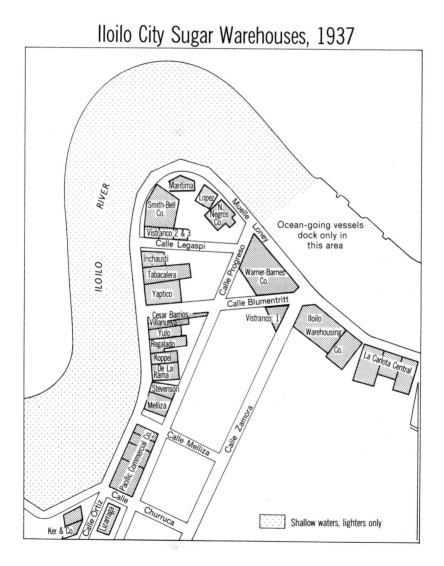

used to break the 1925 *Balhas* strike and formed a rival union, *Inanak Sang Pangabudlay* (Children of Toil). The new union was an *ad hoc* alliance of available forces — ex-Mayor Serapion Torre, a sponsor of the *Mainawaon* society; Anselmo Panaguiton, president of Vistranco's conservative seamen and mechanics' unions; the founder of the second *Union Obrera,* Rosendo Mejica; and the city's most famous entrepreneurs in violence. Most importantly, almost all of Vistranco's *cabecillas,* unlike their waterfront counterparts, remained loyal to the company. While the waterfront *cabecillas* had a strong stake in the union's success, Vistranco's *cabecillas* were salaried employees whose only increment came from padding the work crew lists and pocketing the wages of the ghost workers. After its victory in the May strike, FOF had taken control of the stevedoring work at Vistranco and instituted a roster system which eliminated the *cabecillas'* discretion at the 5.00 a.m. shape-up and the opportunities for pocketing ghost workers' wages. Embittered towards the FOF on both counts, Vistranco's *cabecillas* supported the company union, and their leader José Espinosa, an influential Blumentritt Street resident who had led the 1925 *Balhas* strike, became a member of the *Inanak* executive.[107]

After mobilizing substitute work crews from the villages and city slums, the hired gladiators and *cabecillas* led their followers in assaults on the FOF picket lines and eventually succeeded in breaking the strike. Nava and Panaguiton agreed to divide the city's stevedoring labour — all work on the waterfront was to be done by Nava's FOF and work on water by Panaguiton's *Inanak.*[108]

Despite the defeat, the FOF's reputation grew and Negros workers began sending delegations to Iloilo to seek affiliation. After months of organization, Nava launched the Western Visayas general strike in January 1931 and an estimated 50,000 workers went out at seven major Negros docks, five sugar mills and the Iloilo waterfront. Although Nava was able to use his political and media contacts to win public support for the strike in Iloilo, he met with strong opposition from the Negros provincial governor who was closely allied to the centrals. Philippine Constabulary troopers were again dispatched, but on this occasion, supported by the Negros provincial government, they broke the strike at bayonet point.[109] The mills and major exporters were willing to concede Iloilo City to the union since it was already redundant, but fought with far greater tenacity when Nava threatened their control over Negros Occ.'s mills and docks, the indispensable heart of the sugar industry. As the crisis mounted, all Negros mill owners met in secret to discuss ways to crush the union and collected a substantial anti-union war chest by tithing each central on the basis of its milling capacity. Funds were channelled to Esteban Vasquez, a former mutual aid society leader, and he established a company union which soon won bargaining contracts with the Negros mills.[110]

With vast quantities of sugar stored in Iloilo's warehouses and shipping commitments to fulfil, the exporters were still forced to challenge Nava's control of the city. Iloilo's export houses refused, once again, to discuss union demands and tried to break the strike by force. A panic-stricken call to the colony's governor-general brought several companies of Philippine Constabulary to patrol the Iloilo waterfront with fixed bayonets. Through Don Ramon Aboitiz, one of Cebu City's leading Spanish merchants, some 300 Cebuano workers were brought into Iloilo to move the sugar out of the warehouses under Constabulary protection.[111] Wielding like a knight's mace their *caburata,* a lead-tipped rope used by stevedores to bind up their lower stomachs, Iloilo's workers assaulted the Cebuano crews and forced them to cease work. The strike became a test of endurance, and Nava mobilized his allies to support the union — his Chinese clients contributed food, the Spanish and vernacular press declared their support, political leaders in Manila pressed the colonial government to take a more impartial stance, and FOF *gremios* not on strike contributed generously.[112]

Unable to break the strike, the foreign commercial houses decided to abandon Iloilo City as a sugar entrepôt. At a series of emergency conferences with Vistranco's management, the exporters implemented a plan, initiated in the wake of earlier FOF strikes, for by-passing Iloilo and loading the sugar off the Negros coast at selected anchorages. Insurers in the City of London approved the plan by telegram, and at the height of the strike Vistranco began loading the sugar from the mills at sea off the Negros coastline.[113]

Although initially defeated in Negros, Nava played upon the planter–miller fissure and ultimately succeeded in organizing several of the Negros mills. Invited to participate in the 1931 meeting of mill owners, the Negros planters' association walked out and pointedly refused to contribute to the anti-union war chest. During the strike itself many plantations ignored the centrals' request for strike breakers, and tried to remain neutral.[114] Finding themselves weak before a common enemy, the planters and the union formed an alliance in the 1931 provincial elections and succeeded in defeating the provincial governor instrumental in breaking the Negros strike. Building his strength gradually in Negros during the mid-1930s, Nava eventually won several contracts at mills in the southern portion of the province and used them as bases to launch strikes in the plantations.[115]

Despite the FOF's aggressive campaigns throughout the decade, it was the outcome of its first three strikes in 1930-1931 that laid the basis for a new social settlement in the Western Visayas. The union's May 1930 strike established it as the master of the Iloilo waterfront, but the failure of later strikes against Vistranco and the sugar centrals denied it control over most of the region's sugar handling. Unable to defeat the union in Iloilo City, the region's major sugar exporters decided to abandon a port which had already become redundant. The volume of sugar loaded off the Negros coast rose markedly from 89,765 tons in 1924, to 237,478 tons in 1931, to 488,358 tons in 1933. This latter figure represented 76 percent of Negros Occ.'s harvest of 640,388 tons, indicating that Iloilo was now handling less than a quarter of the province's sugar exports. As the volume of sugar passing through the city's warehouses plummeted, Iloilo City began the long economic decline from which it has never recovered. Iloilo Province's total personal income declined correspondingly from ₱6.0 million in 1929 to ₱4.8 million in 1936, while Negros Occ.'s increased from ₱10.9 to ₱17.6 million during the same period.[116]

The decline in the city's share of the region's sugar exports was dramatic but still not complete. Elizalde & Co., owners of the La Carlota mill, and some of the smaller Spanish mills continued to warehouse their sugar exports on the Iloilo waterfront until the start of World War II. Despite the early antagonism, the union managed to reach an understanding with the remaining Spanish export firms and became accepted as an integral component of the city's stevedoring industry.[117]

After its victory in the Iloilo dock strike, the FOF became one of the prime beneficiaries of an exploitative waterfront institution, the *cabo* or *cabecilla* system. Superseding the old *cabecillas* who were incorporated into the new union structure, the FOF negotiated new labour contracts with the warehouses and became, in strict trade union terms, a labour contractor, not a labour representative. During the 1920s most *cabecillas* had collected 20 to 50 percent of their labourers' piece-work earnings. After the FOF won contracts with the warehouses in the 1930 dock strike, the *cabecillas* conceded the union executive 3 percent of piece-work earnings from their share to pay the wages of union inspectors. Although initially dependent on the *cabecillas,* Nava was aware of their excesses and tried to reduce their shares gradually. Recalcitrant *cabecillas* who insisted on the 50 percent share were dismissed, and those remaining agreed to a revised sharing formula — 77 percent for the stevedores, 20 percent for the *cabecilla* and his *cabos,* and 3 percent for the union executive. Since the *gremios* outside the city never contributed to the central treasury, that 3 percent provided the FOF with a financial base for the organization of strikes in Cebu City, union campaigns in remote areas of Mindanao, and constant pressures on the Negros mill owners.[118]

Death of a Queen

After the war all shipments of Negros sugar from Iloilo City ceased, and the economic bond between the city and sugar industry, attenuated during the 1930s, was now severed. During the war many Negros centrals were destroyed and much of the Iloilo waterfront was levelled by Japanese bombing. Postwar reconstruction provided a chance for a radical restructuring of the industry, and the result was the end of Iloilo's role as a sugar port. The abrupt termination of sugar and related fertilizer shipments produced a sharp contraction in the demand for waterfront labour and revived the prewar conflict between the city's two dominant unions. No longer content to restrict its activities to waterwork, Vistranco's company union, renamed the Consolidated Labor Union of the Philippines (CLUP) and headed by José Espinosa's son Pascual, launched a direct challenge to FOF's dominance of waterfront work. As the conflict for control of remaining stevedoring work intensified, both unions armed themselves with surplus U.S. weapons. A spectacular waterfront war erupted involving hand grenades, submachine guns, .45 calibre pistols and armoured vehicles.

The opening battle set the tone for the next five years of Iloilo's commercial history. Determined to break FOF's hold on the waterfront, Vistranco violated the prewar agreement in March 1946 by awarding Espinosa's CLUP a contract for unloading 5,332 gasoline drums from a lighter moored alongside the California-Texas Oil Co. (Caltex) riverfront depot in Lapuz. When Caltex refused to reinstate the FOF men, a union gunman, acting on Nava's orders, swam alongside the lighter and pitched a grenade into the hold, sending up a towering column of flames which drew thousands of spectators from the city's business district.[119] The gathering violence accelerated the flight of business, sending Iloilo into a downward spiral of declining cargo volume and escalating union warfare.

Although the FOF won almost all of the early battles, it eventually lost this five-year war for control of the waterfront. The causes of the union's defeat were a complex combination of adverse long-term trends and short-term tactical blunders. Espinosa's CLUP lost its bid for the Iloilo waterfront, but was rewarded with a lucrative Vistranco contract recruiting labour to work on U.S. Navy installations in the Western Pacific, largely on Guam. Between 1946 and 1953 CLUP collected ₱1.5 million in dues and fees from the 4,000 Ilongo stevedores based on Guam, an enormous sum compared to the FOF's maximum annual income from the Iloilo waterfront of ₱9,000.[120] With his vast financial resources, Pascual Espinosa was able to mobilize superior military and political forces against Nava and by 1949 had emerged as a leading figure in city politics. Espinosa was a pure labour entrepreneur who won strong allies among the city's conservative commercial interests. Nava remained a relentless advocate of his members' interests and forced the city's shippers to pay wage rates several times higher than those at any other port in the Philippines.

While his militance soon cost him allies among the city's elites, Nava's management of the union's internal affairs alienated him from much of the membership. By the end of the war nine of his children had come of age and sought their fortunes within the union structure. Exploiting the union's anti-*cabecilla* campaign, Nava's sons ousted veteran waterfront leaders from the union and expropriated their positions. Unable to pay proper wages to the gunmen employed to fight the Espinosas, Nava enrolled them nominally in the stevedore gangs and paid their guard-duty service with shares from stevedore wages, a policy which aroused hostility in the waterfront *gremios*.[121]

Compounding his already considerable problems, Nava decided to gamble his dwindling political capital on a communist victory, and sent his sons into the hills of Panay in 1949 to join the Huk guerillas. The revolt was a premature one for Panay's traditional peasantry, and within two years collapsed under the weight of a government counter-insurgency effort. At the height of the rebellion fires swept the city's central business district and rumours circulated that Nava's union had set them to prepare for a communist assault on the city. In 1951 Nava was arrested for his role in the Huk insurgency and his union was dissolved on military orders.[122] Politically isolated and alienated from his union membership, Nava was sentenced to death. Three years later he died in prison awaiting execution.[123]

Should we then, as does the majority of intelligent opinion in Iloilo today, consider José Nava author of this regicide? Although a militant union leader, Nava was never anything more than the duly elected agent of the Ilongo working class. The city's workers selected him in 1928 and abandoned him in 1950 when he was too weak to lead them well. His strikes and high cargo charges were the results of demands from the *gremios,* and were presented at the insistence of his membership.

If Iloilo were to have survived the transition to centrifugal milling, its stevedores would have been forced to absorb the cost of the city's inefficiencies in lower wages, longer hours and depressed working conditions. The Ilongo stevedore's rejection of these terms was not only an indication of his growing class consciousness, but strong evidence that Iloilo's prosperity was based on the peculiar requirements of the hacienda regime. Its popular culture, newspapers and theatre fostered a working class consciousness that was far in advance of Iloilo's role in the global hierarchy of cities. While its stevedores demonstrated the militance and solidarity of an industrial proletariat, the city itself was an expendable entrepôt at the bottom rung of the transport chain, not an indispensable industrial centre. The pressures of a competitive international sugar market dictated a reduction in local handling costs after the 1929 Depression. When Iloilo's stevedores refused to accept these dictates and held the city against the onslaughts of both financiers and government, the sugar industry simply abandoned the city.

Sugar transport had become Iloilo's only significant economic activity after 1870, and its loss was a blow from which the city could not recover. Recalling the outline of the city's commercial history, it is perhaps simplest to conceive of Iloilo's urban economy as a metaphoric sugar warehouse. As the cargo volume passing through the warehouse increases, higher wages are paid to the city's stevedores and correspondingly greater amounts of cash are injected into its economy to sustain its commerce, construction and culture. Correspondingly, as the amount of sugar entering the warehouse dwindles, the cash flow necessary to support the city's economy slows and then nearly disappears.

So it happened in Iloilo City during the 1930s and 1940s. As sugar handling shifted to Negros, the decline began. Stevedores' wages dropped, commercial activity slowed and major firms shifted personnel and resources to Bacolod, Cebu and Manila. Finding no work available, 4,000 Iloilo stevedores, an approximate majority of the waterside labour force, left for Guam and returned a decade later to find the city's waterfront moribund. The leading Ilongo families, whose wealth had lent the city social glitter and economic substance for the better part of two centuries, quit the city to build their new sugar palaces at Bacolod and Manila. No longer the dynamic entrepreneurs who built the textile and sugar industries, the Visayan planters had become wards of the state, dependent upon the low interest finance of the Philippine National Bank and guaranteed access to the American sugar market. Ostentatious, wealthy and generally indolent, Iloilo's surviving urban elite were uninterested in alternatives to the sugar industry and generally lacked the capital and managerial skills to implement any plans they might devise.

The Queen was dead.

NOTES

The author would like to thank Glenita Formoso McCoy for her considerable assistance in the preparation of this essay during both the research and writing. Among the many participants in this narrative who were generous with their time and counsel were Ignacio "Lagoy" Montinola, Alfredo Palemjar, and the many sons of José Nava, particularly Flavio. Elizalde & Co. were uncommonly generous in granting access to their records, and their employees Domingo Itchon, Antonio Beltran and Mr. Espinal were ideal hosts. Iloilo historian Demy Sonza provided both introductions and insight throughout my stay in Iloilo, as did Mr. and Mrs. Rosario Formoso. Finally, Dr. Doreen Fernandez of Ateneo University generously shared information about the *zarzuela* theatre.

1 Dr. Gregorio F. Zaide, "Nicholas Loney: Paladin of Philippine Economic Progress," and, Demy P. Sonza, "Nicholas Loney: Best Friend of Iloilo" (National Conference of Historians, 120th Anniversary of the Opening of the Port of Iloilo to International Trade, 27-28 September 1975).

2 In sharp contrast with the enormously detailed studies completed on Europe and the Americas, research on Asian cities is still at a rudimentary level. This lack of data has not discouraged generalizations about the comparative quality of Asian urbanization, but has, in fact, encouraged sweeping conclusions that European urbanists, with denser data and greater awareness of the complex issues involved, are more reluctant to make. The geographer Rhoads Murphey has been one of the more articulate exponents of the view that the pre-modern Asian city was non-entrepreneurial and has made a very forceful argument that the Asian maritime trading city — from India to Japan — was a product of the late 19th century expansion of Europe.

While Murphey's conclusions may have validity for China, where they have also been challenged, they seem particularly inappropriate in the context of insular Southeast Asia. Through its own commercial and cultural resources, Iloilo City spawned the proto-industrial weaving economy of the mid-18th century and formed its own group of local capitalists with minimal European support or involvement. Even the spectacular growth of the sugar export industry in the mid-19th century was a direct product of the antecedent century of textile development. British capital or entrepreneurship played a largely secondary role. Finally, the city's waterfront unions and working class consciousness were the product of the city's autonomous intellectual and cultural life, expressed in the *zarzuela* and its trilingual press.

See, Rhoads Murphey, "The Treaty Ports and China's Modernization," in, M. Elvin and G.W. Skinner, eds., *The Chinese City Between Two Worlds* (Stanford: Stanford University Press, 1974); Rhoads Murphey, "Traditionalism and Colonialism; Changing Urban Roles in Asia," *Journal of Asian Studies* 29 (November 1969); Rhoads Murphey, *Shanghai: Key to Modern China* (Cambridge, Mass.: Harvard University Press, 1953); Rhoads Murphey, "Urbanization in Asia," in, Gerald Breese, ed., *Urbanization in Newly*

Developing Countries: Readings on Urbanism and Urbanization (Englewood Cliffs, N.J.: Prentice-Hall, 1969); Max Weber, *The City* (Glencoe: Free Press, 1958); Philip M. Hauser, ed., *Urbanization in Asia and The Far East* (Calcutta: UNESCO, 1957); Louis T. Sigel, "Urbanization, Modernity and Identity in Asia: An Historical Perspective," *Modern China* 4 (October 1978).

3 Commonwealth of the Philippines, Commission of the Census, *Census of the Philippines, 1939: Summary for the Philippines and General Report for the Censuses of Population and Agriculture* (Manila: Bureau of Printing, 1941), 2:42-46, 1184; M.M. Alicante, et al., *Soil Survey of Iloilo Province* (Manila: Bureau of Printing, 1947), 14-16, 22-46.

4 M.M. Alicante, et al., *Soil Survey of Negros Occidental Province* (Manila: Bureau of Printing, 1951), 86-115; Commission of the Census, *Census of the Philippines, 1939*, 2:1260.

5 Patronatos de Yloilo, 1859, Manila Archdiocesan Archives (hereafter, MAA); J.W. McCarty, "Australian Capital Cities in the Nineteenth Century," in, J.W. McCarty & C.B. Schedvin, eds., *Australian Capital Cities* (Sydney: Sydney University Press, 1978), 20-21; E. Chamberlain, *Chicago and its Suburbs* (Chicago: A.T. Hungerford, 1874), 279; Richard M. Morse, ed., *The Urban Development of Latin America, 1750-1920* (Stanford: Center for Latin American Studies, Stanford University, 1971), 23, 54, 111.

6 Emma Blair & James Robertson, *The Philippine Islands* (Cleveland: Arthur H. Clark Co., 1903), 3:194-95.

7 Antonio de Morga, *Sucesos de las Islas Filipinas* (Cambridge: The University Press, 1971), 267-68.

8 Blair & Robertson, *The Philippine Islands,* 17:102-03; 23:167,216-19.

9 Don Fernando Fulgosio, "Cronica de las Islas Filipinas," in, Jacobo de la Pezuela, *Cronica de las Antilles* (Madrid: Rubio, Grilo, & Vitturi, 1871), 77-78.

10 Blair & Robertson, *The Philippine Islands,* 4:37-38.

11 J. Mallat, *Les Philippines: Histoire, Géographie, Moeurs, Agriculture, Industrie et Comerce des Colonies Espagnoles dan l'Océanie* (Paris: Arthur Bertrand, Editeur, 1846), 295-97, 300-06, 315-20, 346-53.

12 Padrones de Yloilo, 1760-1765, MAA.

13 El R.P. Comisario, *Memoria Acerca de Los Misiones de Los P.P. Augustinos Calzados Presentado Al Exomo. Sr. Ministero de Ultramar en 1880* (Madrid: Imprenta de Alejandro Gomez Fuentenebro), III, Cuadro Estadistico.

14 Varias Provincias, Resumen General del numero de Tributos, Yloilo, 1809-1818, Philippine National Archives (hereafter, PNA).

15 Libros de Bautismos, 1696-1900, Jaro Parish, Iloilo City; Planes de Almas, Yloilo, 1797 & 1834, MAA.

16 Letter from Nicholas Loney, 10 September 1864, F.O. 72/1087, Public Records Office (hereafter, PRO), London.

17 Letter from Nicholas Loney to Farren, 12 April 1857, F.O. 72/927, PRO.

18 Planes de Almas, Provincia de Yloilo, 1857, MAA.

19 Loney to Farren, 12 April 1857, PRO.

20 Sir John Bowring, *A Visit to the Philippine Islands* (London: Smith, Elder & Co., 1859), 411.

21 Nicholas Loney to Farren, 10 July 1861, F.O. 72/1017, PRO.

22 *Gaceta de Manila* (Manila), 7ª Seccion, Movimiento Maritimo, 1861-1880. During this 20-year period, the *Gaceta* published a daily record of all ships entering Manila from inter-island and international ports with a detailed description of their cargoes. To compile these totals, the author read through the *Gaceta*'s shipping columns for this 20-year period noting each shipment from the Western Visayas and then compiled the data from these note cards.

23 *Ibid.*

24 Great Britain, Parliamentary Papers, Vol. LXXII (*Accounts and Papers,* Vol. XXXI), "Commercial Reports," Yloilo, 1 January 1879, 1666-67.

25 Memoria de la Provincia de Yloilo, Año de 1892, Varias Provincias, PNA.

26 This estimate is based on interviews with veteran union leaders who worked the waterfront during the period immediately following World War I. There is some indication in Iloilo City's monthly municipal census reports for 1912 that much of the city's stevedore population was migratory. During January to August 1911 Iloilo's Filipino population hovered at 38,000. In October, the start of sugar milling in Negros, it jumped to 39,974 and again in November to 40,339, but then remained stable during the first months of 1912. *El Adalid* (Iloilo) 13 January, 10 February, 12 April, 12 June, 12 August, 13 September, 18 October, 9 November, 12 December 1911; 6 January, 12 February 1912.

27 Mallat, *Les Philippines,* 302-03.

28 Bowring, *A Visit to the Philippine Islands,* 354.

29 Nicholas Loney, *A Britisher in the Philippines: The Letters of Nicholas Loney* (Manila: National Library, 1964), 66-68.

30 Loney to Farren, 10 July 1861, PRO.

31 *Gaceta de Manila,* 26 November 1873, 16 February 1875.

32 Great Britain, Parliamentary Papers, Vol. LXXXVII (*Accounts and Papers,* Vol. XL), Manila, 1890, pp. 8-9.

33 Letter from J.W. Farren, 16 June 1860, F.O. 72/990, PRO; Loney to Farren, 16 May 1860, F.O. 72/990; Letter from Farren, 31 August 1861, F.O. 72/1017, PRO; Letter from Loney to Undersecretary of State for Foreign Affairs, 21 November 1861, F.O. 72/1017, PRO.

34 Loney, *A Britisher in the Philippines,* 89; Letter from Nicholas Loney, 15 August 1863, F.O. 72/1070, PRO.

35 Letter from Nicholas Loney, 10 September 1864, F.O. 72/1087, PRO.

36 *Gaceta de Manila,* Seccion 7ª, Movimiento Maritimo, Yloilo, 1861-1880.

37 Letter from Nicholas Loney, 15 April 1863, F.O. 72/1070, PRO; Circular, Ker & Co., Precios Corrientes (Manila), Essex Institute.

38 *The Chronicle and Directory for China, Japan, & The Philippines for the Year 1878* (Hong Kong: The "Daily" Office, 1878), 44-185.

39 Court of Directors, Hong Kong and Shanghai Banking Corp., Minutes, 25 March 1865, 11 November 1875, 15 March 1883, 12 April 1883, 31 December 1885, Hong Kong; Bank of the Philippine Islands, *Souvenir of the First Bank Established in the Far East* (Manila, 1928), 45-46; Great Britain, Parliamentary Papers, Vol. LXXX, (*Accounts and Papers,* XXXIV), "Commercial Reports," Iloilo, 31 December 1883, 562-65.

40 Padron General de Chinos, Yloilo 1895, Negros Occ. 1891, PNA.

41 *Estadistica General del Comercio Exterior de las Islas Filipinas de Año de 1888* (Manila: Manuel Perez, hijo, 1890).

42 Great Britain, Parliamentary Papers, Vol. LXXII (*Accounts and Papers,* Vol. XXXI), "Commercial Reports," Iloilo, 1 January 1879.

43 Great Britain, Parliamentary Papers, Vol. LXXVIII (*Accounts and Papers,* Vol. XXXIV), "Commercial Reports," Iloilo, 31 December 1884, 939-40; Great Britain, Parliamentary Papers, Vol. LXXXVI (*Accounts and Papers,* XXXVIII), "Commercial Reports," Manila, 31 January 1887, 3; Vol. XCIII (*Accounts and Papers,* XLII), "Commercial Reports," Iloilo 1897, 9-10.

44 Robustiano Echauz, *Apuntes de la Isla de Negros* (Manila: Tipo-Litografia de Chofre y Compania, 1894), 33-37.

45 *Mapa General de las Almas que Administran los P.P. Agustinos en Estas Islas Filipinas* (Manila: Imprenta de D. Manuel Sanchez, 1845), 51-52.

46 Loney to Farren, 10 July 1861, PRO.

47 Estadisticas de los Terrenos Agricolas, Negros Occ. 1897, PNA; Tributos de Iloilo 1852, PNA; "Historical Data of Iloilo," *Historical Data Papers* (hereafter, *HDP*).

48 Estadisticas de los Terrenos Agricolas, Yloilo & Negros Occ., 1897, PNA: Tributos de Iloilo, 1852, PNA; "Historical Data of Iloilo," *HDP.*

49 Relacion Nominal de los Indios Reservados, Jaro, Iloilo, 1852, Varias Provincias, PNA; Estadisticas de los Terrenos Agricolas, Silay, Negros Occ., 1897, Varias Provincias, PNA; Eugenio Lopez y Jalandoni, Reconocimiento de Obligacion, Protocolos Yloilo 1603, 30 August 1887, PNA.

50 Testamento de Yves Leopoldo German Gaston, no. 491, Protocolos Negros 1724, n.d., PNA; Ma. Fe Hernaez Romero, *Negros Occidental Between Two Foreign Powers (1888-1909)* (Bacolod: Negros Occidental Historical Commission, 1974), 33-34.

51 Estadisticas de los Terrenos Agricolas, La Carlota and Hinigaran, Negros Occidental, 1897, Varias Provincias, PNA.

52 Great Britain, Parliamentary Papers, Vol. LXXX (*Accounts and Papers,* Vol. XXXIX), "Commercial Reports," Iloilo, 31 December 1883, 562-65.

53 Ynchausti & Co., Caja Mayor No. 1, Ynchausti Co., (hereafter, YCO); Protocolos Yloilo 1592, 28 May 1885, PNA; Protocolos Yloilo 1592, 1 August 1885, PNA.

54 Shippers of Sugar from the Philippine Islands for 1881 and 1886, Peele-Hubbell & Co., R.D. Tucker Papers, Peabody Museum; *Sugar Central and Planters News* (Manila), January 1920; *El Porvenir de Bisayas* (Iloilo), 5 June 1896.

55 Protocolos Yloilo 1600, 30 June 1887, PNA.

56 Protocolos Yloilo 1600, Appendix, 47, PNA.

57 Protocolos Yloilo 1599, Appendix, 129, PNA.

58 These conclusions are based on an enumeration of baptismal records surveyed in the towns of central and southern Negros Occidental covering the years 1868 to 1900. Beginning in 1868 it was the practice in most parishes to record the town of origin of the parents of a baptized child. Lacking any other form of systematic survey of the origins of Negros pioneers in the latter half of the 19th century, we decided to survey these records with a view to determining migration patterns. This method eliminates migratory cane cutters who have usually left their families at home in Antique and probably represents the more stable elements of the permanent labour force. Young adults in their prime are probably the most likely candidates for both procreation and migration. Compiled daily with the voluntary support of rural residents, these records are a remarkably sensitive, and largely unexplored, statistical index of population movements in the late 19th century Philippines.

59 Robustiano Echauz, *Sketches of the Island of Negros* (Athens, Ohio: Ohio University Center for International Studies, Southeast Asia Program, 1978), 73-74.

60 D. Joaquin Rodriguez San Pedro, *Legislacion Ultramarina Concordada y Anotada* (Madrid: José Fernandez Cancela, 1865), 4:669, 673-77, 688-89; Miguel Rodriguez Berriz, *Guia del Comprador de Terrenos Baldios y Realengos de Filipinas* (Manila: Manuel Perez, hijo, 1886), 12-16, 51-52, 71-80, 338-39; Capt. George P. Ahern & Gregorio Basa, *Spanish Public Land Laws in the Philippine Islands and Their History to August 13, 1898* (Washington, D.C.: Government Printing Office, 1901), 19-54; *Gaceta de Manila,* 9 November, 8 November 1887, 1 November, 20 December 1888; Libro 2°, Junta Provincial de Composicion de Terrenos de Esta Provincia de Negros Occidental, December 1890 to June 1891, Negros Occidental, Provincial Building.

61 Francisco Varona, *Negros: Historica Anectodica de su Riqueza y sus Hombres* (Manila: General Printing Press, 1938), 130-31; Real Audiencia Territorial de Filipinas, Tribunal Pleno, Expediente sobre desline de los Montes del Estado . . . con la hacienda de Sn. Bernardino, Ysla de Negros, legajo 58, no. 1195, 1887, PNA.

62 Secretario del Gobierno General de Filipinas, Expediente exterior contra el vecino del pueblo de la Ysabela . . . Dn. Gavino Gasataya, No. 1127, April 1891, PNA.

63 Reconocimiento de deuda y obligacion al pago a Adolfo Lazarte por Rito Miranda, nos. 218-252, Protocolos Negros 1736, 5 May 1871, PNA.

64 Alejo Severino y Leopoldo Gaston, Venta de Hacienda, no. 376, Protocolos Negros 1724, 1 October 1861, PNA.

65 Great Britain, Parliamentary Papers, "Commercial Reports," Iloilo, 31 December 1883, 31 December 1884.

66 Letter from Nicholas Loney to Lord Stanley, 31 January 1867, F.O. 72/1155, PRO.

67 *Boletin Oficial Agricola de Filipinas* (Malabon) 1 December 1894, 35.

68 *El Porvenir de Bisayas,* 4 October, 6 November, 18 November, 20 November 1895; 22 January 1896.

69 John R. White, *Bullets and Bolos: Fifteen Years in the Philippine Islands* (New York: Century Co., 1928), 111-18.

70 F.R. Fabie, no. 3871, R-642, Philippine Insurgent Records (hereafter, PIR); Dionisio Papa, Letter 9 August 1899, RG 395, E-2619, U.S. National Archives and Records Service (hereafter, NARS); *The Iloilo Enterprise,* 7 April 1909; *La Libertad* (Bacolod), 25 July 1899; *El Tiempo* (Iloilo), 21 September, 23 September 1907.

71 Guardia Civil, *Sucesos de Negros* (Manila, n.d.), 20-23.

72 Delegacion Policia Aduana, 13 December 1898, RG-395, E-2624, NARS; General Juan Araneta, Letter 19 December 1898, R-642, PIR; Remegio Montilla, Letter 28 November 1898, R-649, PIR.

73 *La Libertad,* 5 November 1899; Acta, 18 February 1898, no. 4201, P-642, PIR.

74 Acta, 2 March 1899, PR-58, PIR, Philippine National Library (hereafter, PNL).

75 General James F. Smith, Report, 31 July 1899, U.S. War Department, *Annual Report of the War Department* (Washington, D.C.: GPO, 1899), 344-46.

76 *La Libertad,* 25 July 1899; Telex, To: Smith, 17 June 1899, RG-395, E-2619, NARS; Telex, To: Smith, 21 March 1899, RG-395, E-2619, NARS: Lt. Victor D. Duboce, Letter 3 May 1899, RG-395, E-2619, NARS.

77 Telex, To: Poore, Bacolod, 7 September 1901, RG-395, E-2619, NARS.

78 *El Tiempo,* 8 August 1907.

79 *Kadapig Sg Banwa* (Iloilo), 10 October 1907; *El Nuevo Heraldo* (Iloilo), 18 March 1909.

80 *El Adalid,* 13 January 1911 to 12 February 1912.

81 *Kadapig Sg Banwa,* 27 December 1906.

82 Interviews with José Quilantang, Vistranco Stevedore, 3 December 1974; Serafin Roga, Vistranco Stevedore, 3 December 1974; José Suberano, Vistranco Stevedore, 21 January 1975; and Josef Tamayo, Vistranco Stevedore, 17 January 1975.

83 *El Tiempo* (Iloilo), 7 March 1903; *Kadapig Sg Banwa,* 12 June 1907; *Nuevo Heraldo,* 10 December 1908; 4 March 1899, Commision de Guerra, Julio Hernandez, Vol. 24, R-642, PIR, NARS.

84 *Pamatanon* (Iloilo), 2 August 1906; "Tilipigan Sang mga Anak . . . Sang Mga Baybayanon," (Mejica Collection, Molo, Iloilo), 1906.

85 Property Assessments, Office of the City Assessor, 1907-1940, Iloilo City.

86 Interview with Mariano Nava, Jr., brother of José Nava, Iloilo City, 20 April 1974; Alfredo Palejar, FOF Treasurer and son-in-law of José Nava, 9 December 1973; Flavio Nava, son of José and FOF General Inspector, 19 August 1974; Don Mariano Nava, Poder à Don Severino Nava, Protocolos Yloilo 1593, 17 October 1885, PNA; Doña Timotea Legaspi, Venta Real à Don Vicente Gay, Protocolo Yloilo 1589, 20 February 1884, PNA.

87 José Maria Nava, Libro de Bautismos, Vol. 11, 15 August 1891, San José Parish Church, Iloilo City; *Makinaugalingon* (Iloilo), 18 April 1917.

88 *Porvenir de Bisayas,* 21 November 1893, 15 November 1894; *Makinaugalingon,* 10 May 1927, 13 May 1927; *El Adalid,* 19 June 1911.

89 Federacion Obrera de Filipinas, *FOF: 20 Years Struggle for Democracy* (Iloilo, 1949), 23-24; *Liberator* (Iloilo), 28 May 1949.

90 Andres R. Camasura, *Cebu-Visayas Directory* (Manila: Camasura, 1932), 51, 399.

91 *Makinaugalingon,* 19 March, 28 March, 16 April 1914; *Nuevo Heraldo,* 2 May 1914.

92 *Liberator,* 28 May 1949; *Makinaugalingon,* 14 November, 17 November 1917, 24 September 1919, 28 November 1921.

93 *Makinaugalingon,* 28 November 1921; interviews with 28 surviving members of FOF *Gremio Tabacalera* cited below, Note 104.

94 *Makinaugalingon,* 8 December 1921.

95 *Makinaugalingon,* 14 August 1918, 30 May 1922, 12 January 1923; *Liberator,* 28 May 1949.

96 *Makinaugalingon,* 14 November, 21 November 1924, 21 August 1925; Interview with José Quilantang, Vistranco Stevedore, 3 December 1974; Serafin Roga, *Balhas* member and Vistranco Stevedore, 6 December 1974; Jacinto "Caburata" Falospero, *Balhas* member and later FOF bodyguard, 28 December 1974.

97 *Makinaugalingon,* 2 March 1918, 24 December 1919, 21 July 1922, 15 April, 6 May 1924; *The Independent* (Manila), 12 April 1924; interview with Vicente Jimenez-Yanson, organizer of *Kusog Sang Imol,* La Carlota, 2 August 1975.

98 *Makinaugalingon,* 31 October 1922.

99 *Makinaugalingon,* 28 March, 15 April, 6 May, 30 May, 4 July, 25 July, 29 August, 4 November, 11 November, 13 January 1924, 29 October 1926, 1 March 1927.

100 *Makinaugalingon,* 1 May 1925, 1 March 1927.

101 José Ma. Nava, "The Federacion Obrera de Filipinas — A Potent Factor in Philippine Labor," in, Federacion Obrera de Filipinas, *Ivory Book: 13th Anniversary Souvenir, Federacion Obrera de Filipinas (July 31 1928 — July 31 1941)* (Manila: FOF, 1941), 17-18; interview with Alfredo Palmejar, 9 December 1973; Pablo Asegurado, prewar Valeria Street resident and FOF bodyguard, 25 January 1975; Epifanio Solis, prewar Valeria Street resident and *zarzuela* author, 23 May 1976; Narciso Parreño, prewar resident of the Quezon-Delgado Streets area and FOF official, 12 January 1975.

102 Nava, "The Federacion Obrera de Filipinas," 17-20; interview with Alfredo Palmejar, son of Alfonso Palmejar, 9 December 1973; Ruperto Mijares, son of FOF founder Mariano Mijares, 27 November 1974; FOF, "20 Years Struggle," 6-7; *Prensa Libre* (Iloilo), 5 April 1929.

103 Interview with Julio Salvo, member of FOF *Gremio Pinggadores,* 13 January 1975; Narciso Parreño, official of *Gremio Talisay,* 12 January 1975; Ignacio Montinola, *cabecilla* at *Gremio Tabacalera,* 1 September 1974; Aurelio Mateo, FOF inspector at *Gremio* Caltex, 9 January 1974; and others.

104 These conclusions are based on intensive interviews with 28 surviving members of *Gremio Tabacalera,* most importantly those with Ignacio Montinola, postwar *cabecilla,* 1 September 1974; Vicente Espinosa, longest serving member, 3 January 1975; Demetrio Gonzaga, former member of *Tabacalera banda pesada,* 29 December 1974; Anselmo Desabal, worker in *banda descargada,* 2 January 1975.

105 Nava, "The Federacion Obrera de Filipinas," 18, 20; *Makinaugalingon,* 2 May, 9 May, 14 May, 16 May 1930; *Tribune* (Manila), 14 May, 18 May 1930.

106 In 1936 the Philippine Sugar Association published a series of maps showing milling capacities of the centrals and Iloilo's warehouses which made this point clearly; *Makinaugalingon,* 26 May 1930.

107 *Makinaugalingon,* 13 August, 20 August, 22 August, 25 August 1930; *Progress* (Cebu), 19 August, 24 August 1930; *Tribune,* 17 August 1930; interview with Cipriano Espinosa, Vistranco stevedore and brother of José Espinosa, 30 April 1974; José Quilantang, Vistranco stevedore, 3 December 1974; Antonio Pineda, Vistranco employee, 28 August 1974; Fermin Zapanta, official of *Katilingbang sang Inanak sang Pangabudlay,* 4 December 1974; and others.

108 Interview with Alfredo Palmejar, FOF Treasurer, 9 December 1973.

109 Nava, "The Federacion Obrera de Filipinas," 20, 22.

110 Letter to Joaquin M. Elizalde, 24 January 1931, Ynchausti & Co., Iloilo, YCO.

111 Letter to Fritz von Kauffmann, Sr., 7 February 1931, YCO.

112 Interview with Jacinto "Caburata" Falospero, FOF bodyguard, 28 December 1974; Alfredo Palmejar, FOF Treasurer, 9 December 1973.

113 Letter from Mr. A.H. Taylor, Vistranco, to Philippine Sugar Central Agency, 3 December 1930, YCO; Letter to Fritz von Kauffmann, 6 January, 14 January, 21 January 1931, YCO; Letter from C.C. Barnes, Warner-Barnes & Co., to Ynchausti Manila, 1 July 1931, YCO.

114 Letter from Central Azucarera de la Carlota to Joaquin Elizalde, 19 January 1931, YCO; Telex to Ynchausti Manila, 17 January 1931, YCO; Letter to Joaquin Elizalde, 24 January 1931, YCO.

115 Nava, "The Federacion Obrera de Filipinas," 20, 22-30, 35-39, 46.

116 Philippine Islands, Bureau of Customs, *Annual Report of the Collector of Customs* (Manila: Bureau of Printing, 1925, 1932, 1934); Philippine Islands, Collector of Internal Revenue, *Annual Report of the Collector of Internal Revenue* (Manila: Bureau of Printing, 1929, 1936).

117 Interview with Alfredo Palmejar, FOF Treasurer, 9 December 1973; Flavio Nava, FOF General Inspector, 19 August 1974; Percentage Liquidation, 1 March — 15 May 1949, Federacion Obrera de Filipinas, José Nava Papers Iloilo City.

118 This conclusion is based on a number of interviews with surviving *cabos* and *cabecillas* conducted between 1973 and 1975 (see, Note 103); Alfredo Palmejar, FOF Treasurer, 9 December 1973; Flavio Nava, FOF General Inspector, 19 August 1974.

119 *People v. Restituto Sumili,* Iloilo Court of First Instance, Criminal Case 463 (1946); interview with Flavio Nava, FOF General Inspector, 19 August 1974. For a detailed description of the war on the Iloilo waterfront see, Alfred W. McCoy, "Ylo-ilo: Factional Conflict in a Colonial Economy, Iloilo Province, Philippines, 1937-1955" (doctoral dissertation, Yale University, 1977), 568-672.

120 *The Philippines Free Press* (Manila), 10 July 1954; Alfredo Palmejar, Treasurer, Statement of Income and Expenses, 1 January 1948 to 31 December 1948, Federacion Obrera de Filipinas, Flavio Nava Papers, Iloilo City; *Eustaquio Marañon, et al. v. Luzon Stevedoring Corporation,* Iloilo CFI, Case 3375, 3405, 3424, 3505.

121 Much of the impetus for the postwar reform of the *cabecilla* system came from the FOF's General Inspector Guillermo Capadocia, prewar Secretary General of the Philippine Communist Party. His efforts were ultimately defeated by the union's financial imperatives and the personal interests of the Nava family. In preparation for the April 1947 FOF Convention, Capadocia wrote a new constitution which stated that it was "the goal of the Federacion . . . to organize the following industrial unions". The document then listed 26 types of industrial labour unions, including the proposed "Longshoremens and Warehousemens' Union (WU)", but nowhere mentioned the *gremio* — the basic organizational unit of the FOF on the Iloilo waterfront. Capadocia was trying to transform the FOF's internal organizational structure from one based on "feudal" relations between *cabecilla* and stevedore into a modern trade union organized according to objective principles of work classification. Although Capadocia lobbied successfully for approval of the new constitution at the union's 1947 convention, Supremo Nava refused to apply its organizational principles to the Iloilo waterfront. In an August 1974 interview, Flavio Nava recalled his father's reasoning:

 You must have noticed that FOF was more of a contracting union rather than a regular trade union. It was FOF who held a contract with a company for the work, not the labourers. And it was through the *cabecilla* that FOF managed this contract with the company. In Manila the CLO [Congress of Labor Organizations] was a regular trade union, but here in Iloilo FOF was more of a contracting union.

 It was Capadocia who tried to change FOF into a regular trade union. Capadocia was telling us over and over that we had to keep up with the times and transform the FOF from a contract union to a real trade union. My father assigned Capadocia to write the new 1947 FOF Constitution. And in his writing . . . , Capadocia laid the basis for these changes into a regular union.

The constitution required that the branches send a certain percentage of their 50 *centavos* monthly dues for the expenses of the Iloilo Central Office. In exchange, FOF Central Office was supposed to manage strikes, pay legal fees, pay the salaries of organizers sent to Negros and Mindanao. But the branches were always behind on their dues so it was the 10 percent share from the 6,000 labourers on the Iloilo waterfront that supported the FOF.

During the FOF discussion about the *cabecilla*'s percentage, I also wanted to reduce the percentage of the FOF Central Office. But my father answered me, saying: "You don't understand our situation. Cebu, Mindanao, and Negros are not paying us their dues and it's the percentage from the Iloilo waterfront that is supporting the Central Office. We are running out of money."

I found out from [FOF Treasurer Alfredo] Palmejar that the branches in Negros, Cebu, and Mindanao were behind in their dues. In fact, Cebu was the worst — it was paying very little. So in fact it was the poor dockworkers here in Iloilo who were supporting the entire structure of the union. Yes, it was the 10 percent share from the *bodegas* that supported the whole FOF. For example, as a National Inspector of the FOF I was supposed to receive a certain share from the union's Central Office. But my salary as a national inspector was never paid. I supported myself from my *cabecilla*'s percentage at *Gremio* Everett and *Gremio* Olizen.

Because the waterfront in Iloilo was supporting the entire organization, we often had to send around circulars ordering a special dues payment of one peso from each stevedore. There was a time when we were sending a circular every month. During the strikes at [Central] La Carlota and the other centrals as well as the Mindanao strikes, we had huge legal expenses and travel expenses of sending delegations out. For example, if we needed money for a delegation to go to Negros we would send a circular to the *bodegas* that had work. If there was work at Tabacalera, the Central office would type up a circular to the *cabecilla* saying: "There is a one peso payment at the end of the day for this work." And so the *cabecilla* would deduct one peso from the pay of the men when he gave them their share.

If we relied on the monthly dues, we would have been broke, so we had to send out circulars. We knew that the waterfront workers were complaining, but what could we do?

Capadocia's reforms did, however, have the unintended consequence of providing a rationale for the expropriation of the *cabecillas'* positions by members of the Nava family. Nava employed seven sons and two sons-in-law in the FOF Central Office, and most of these were unable to support their families on union salaries. Between 1946 and 1949, therefore, Nava's sons tried to take control of four of the union's 26 waterfront *gremios*. In March 1950 these conflicts between FOF Central Office and the *gremios* culminated in the murder of veteran *cabecilla* Alipio Villar by gunmen loyal to Flavio Nava. Although the causes of the incident were complex, most of the union membership blamed the killing on Nava's sons and felt even more alienated from the FOF leadership. The *cabecilla* of *Gremio* Tabacalera, Ignacio Montinola, recalled his reaction in an April 1974 interview:

> In the early days we could speak directly to old man Nava about all our complaints. Whatever our complaints were we could go directly to the old man and feel his concern for the justice of our complaints. But after the war Nava began to run the union by remote control. No longer could we go directly to the old man, but we had to see [FOF Secretary Alfredo] Palmejar. The Central Office began sending out circulars replacing the old *cabecilla* with new men who were sons and relatives of Nava. When the old men of the union tried to complain they were not able to see Nava. Gradually, the old fire began to die out in the men's hearts and they lost their loyalty to the FOF. When Flavio [Nava] tried to take away the work of Villar, head of *Gremio* Manug-Kahoi, and killed him . . . the feelings of loyalty began to die.

For a more detailed discussion of this conflict and its impact on the union, see, McCoy, "Ylo-ilo," 688-717.

122 *People v. José Ma. Nava et al.,* CFI Iloilo, Criminal Case 2878, Judge Magno S. Gatmaitan, Decision, 1952; McCoy, "Ylo-ilo," 717-38.

123 *The Times* (Iloilo), 15 January 1954.

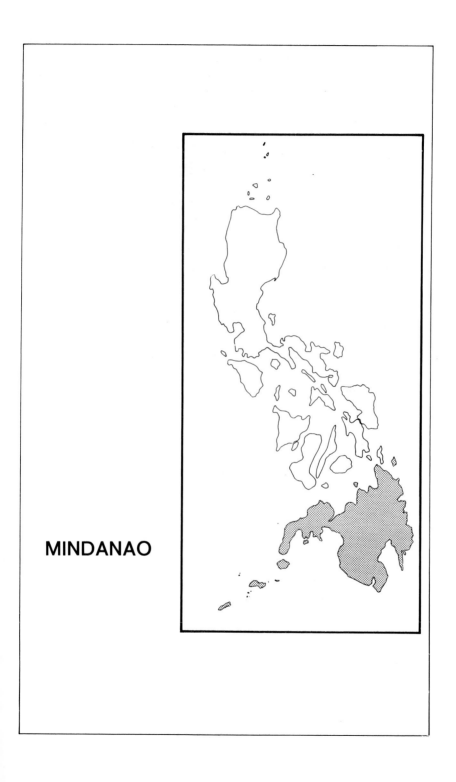

MINDANAO

Frontier Society on the Bukidnon Plateau: 1870—1941

RONALD K. EDGERTON

B etween the mountains of central Mindanao and the north coast of that island lies a spacious plateau of rolling grasslands. On this plateau people of the mountains, the Bukidnon, met and interacted with the *dumagats,* people of the coast. Not until after World War II did the plateau cease to offer an atmosphere conducive to accommodation and gradual acculturation, for not until then, when the trickle of migrants became a flood, did *dumagats* become a majority of the resident population. In the 70 or so years before, the plateau remained an open frontier. Settlers and ranchers slowly moved south — away from proximity to the north coast, and out onto the grasslands — away from the principal towns. Bukidnons moved back and forth between the towns and their hillside swidden plots, back and forth, as it were, between the locus points of two culture worlds. In these years, as migrants ceased to return regularly for visits to their provinces of origin, so Bukidnons gradually stopped attending the ancient tribal harvest festivals held annually in their old familiar havens. In both cases, migrants and Bukidnons grew to feel at home on the plateau.[1]

The study of social development on the Bukidnon plateau during the frontier years from the 1870s to the 1940s raises a number of important questions about this process of change. Were these decades of low-level immigration marked by conflict between lowland migrants and Bukidnon, or, in contrast, did the frontier setting somehow promote a more positive interaction? Did the frontier allow significant social and economic mobility for both groups, and, simultaneously, lead to a change in political orientations from local to national by uprooting the migrants and mixing these peoples in the new towns of the plateau?

The Environment

The Bukidnon plateau, like the Deccan highlands of India, has been a region both of relative isolation and of transition between cultural centres. Covering most of Bukidnon Province, which measures 803,840 hectares today, it separates the Muslim world of Cotabato from the Hispanicized culture of Mindanao's north coast. Bordered on the east by a densely forested mountain chain separating it from the Agusan River valley, and on the west by the rugged high country of Lanao, the plateau has been, despite its obstacles, the most natural path of communication between the Magindanao and the Visayan cultural worlds. Across its sweep of grasslands traders travelled for centuries, those going north climbing very gradually until they crossed the low divide at Dalwangan (at least 800 metres high), and then descending imperceptibly to 500 metres before they reached the rim of the plateau just inland from the sea at Macajalar Bay.[2]

But while the plateau posed no impenetrable barrier between coastal worlds, travelling across it remained a long and arduous endeavour undertaken by few prior to World War II.[3] This is perhaps why trade across the plateau never constituted a preliminary to political control by either north or south. From the north the traveller had to cross deep and precipitous canyons cut by swift-flowing streams into the long, gently sloping lava flows from Mt. Kitanglad.[4] Like spokes on a wagon-wheel, the rivers and their tributaries radiate from this great mountain, cutting deep gorges through the volcanic soil. Not only do they inhibit travel overland; their rushing currents make river travel hazardous too. North of the Dalwangan divide most of these streams comprise two major river systems — the Cagayan and the Tagoloan which empty into Macajalar Bay. South of the divide they flow into the Pulangi (or Rio Grande de Mindanao) which originates in the mountains of northeastern Bukidnon, sweeps majestically across the eighth parallel, and then plunges through treacherous rapids before evening out in Cotabato and debouching in the Cotabato gulf.[5]

Approaching the plateau from the south was even more difficult than from the north, for the Pulangi is "one continuous series of rapids" as it plunges down into Cotabato.[6] In 1902, *Datu* Masaloot, "the last Moro *datu* on the river" going north into Manobo country, "knew of no trail up the Rio Grande River". He told First Lieutenant R.O. Van Horn, leader of an American exploratory expedition from Cotabato to Cagayan de Oro that year, that "there was no trade in that direction with the Manobos". They would have to take the Mulita River and then go by trail overland through the Manobo area. Proceeding by this route, Van Horn found the going slow and exhausting although the Mulita River trail was "quite plain" and evidently"fairly well travelled". The Manobos in this region collected rubber and gutta-percha which they sold to *Datu* Ali of Magindanao. In so far as they were in contact with the world outside their immediate environs, it was the Muslim world of the south with which they traded.[7]

While the Manobo along the Mulita River were within the Muslim trading orbit, peoples on the plateau to their immediate north were clearly more influenced by the Visayan world of the north coast. Leaving wooded terrain near Maramag, Van Horn and his party emerged "into open, rolling country" where the grass was "knee high". Thereafter they found the trail, by comparison with the one along the Mulita, to be in excellent shape all the way north to Cagayan de Oro, making travel easier as they moved north, and hence contact greater in that direction. Immediately after starting across the grasslands, they discovered "half cast Manobos, mixed with Filipino blood", who had "been under the Jesuits' influence . . . and were converted, thus getting the name 'Tlandig', either by intermarriage or mixture of so many kinds of blood . . .". From that point on, Van Horn's Manobo packers "did not care to go any farther".[8]

Inhibited by canyons in the north and by turbulent rains and wooded terrain in the south, travellers were also kept away by the lack of any strong lure of profits to

The Bukidnon Plateau, 1941

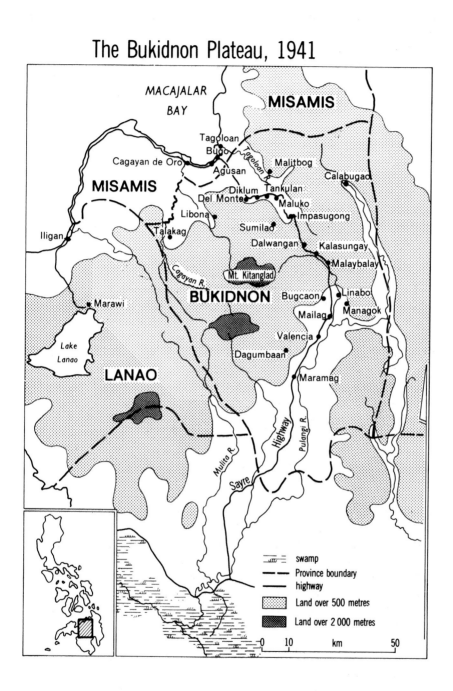

MACAJALAR BAY

MISAMIS

MISAMIS

Tagoloan
Bugo
Cagayan de Oro
Agusan
Malitbog
Calabugao
Diklum Tankulan
Del Monte
Maluko
Libona
Impasugong
Talakag
Sumilao
Iligan
Dalwangan
Kalasungay
Mt. Kitanglad
Malaybalay
BUKIDNON
Bugcaon
Linabo
Marawi
Mailag
Managok
Valencia
Lake Lanao
Dagumbaan
LANAO
Maramag

Tagoloan R.
Cagayan R.
Mulita R.
Sayre
Highway
Pulangi R.

swamp
- - - Province boundary
——— highway
Land over 500 metres
Land over 2 000 metres

0   10   km   50

be made among the inhabitants of the plateau itself. Numbering no more than 20,000 "pagans" and perhaps an equal number of Muslims, these inhabitants were concentrated in small and widely dispersed swidden agricultural settlements in the mountains and along the rivers. The Muslims were primarily Maranaos concentrated in the west along the Lanao border. The Bukidnons and Manobos — racially similar to Visayans but linguistically and culturally distinct — lived in three nuclear areas: Manobos along the middle Pulangi and Mulita south to Cotabato, and Bukidnons in the northeast along the Tagoloan and upper Pulangi rivers and, to a lesser extent, on the upper Cagayan bordering Lanao. Few people lived on the grass plain itself, but there were settlements along the edge of the forest. In fact, the slash-and-burn agricultural methods of these people may well have created that constantly receding edge. Settlement on the grasslands became a reasonably attractive alternative for them only when plough agriculture was introduced to the plateau in the early 20th century.[9]

Neither a lure nor an easy communication route, the plateau remained unconquered by lowlanders in the 1870s. Bukidnons and Manobos recall in their shared oral epic a tradition in which their common ancestors (among whom Agyu is best remembered) fought long and terrible battles along the coast before retiring inland to Nalandangan, their fortress high in the mountains, from which they stood ready to repel invading *dumagats*. Although many variations exist in the retelling of this epic by *datus* (chiefs) from different corners of Bukidnon today, all are agreed that their people originated along the coast but retired to the interior seeking freedom from domination by coastal peoples. Whereas Manobos equate the trek inland with liberation from slavery by the Magindanao to their south, Bukidnons living in the northeast equate it with redemption from Hispanic influence to their north. In either case the connection between their move to the mountains and retention of their own culture is a strong one. In this context their flight into the forest becomes a pilgrimage back into their own culture, and the mountains become not only places of refuge but symbols of the ageless strength of an ancient tradition.[10]

Bukidnons in the 1870s

Bukidnons do not appear to have possessed a high degree of political organization in the 1870s. There was no overarching political structure and no chief *datu* to whom all gave fealty by that time.[11] And yet the loosely structured nature of their political system in the 1870s may have been a change from earlier years. Bukidnon epic literature, despite local variations, depicts a past in which Bukidnons, descended from a common mother and father, were led by common heroes.[12] Whether or not the epics reflect historical reality is difficult to say. But in 1754, Sr. D. Joseph Romo, Governor of the Province of Cebu, granted to Lingaon Binoni, a Bukidnon *datu*, the title of *Maestre de Campo* of the *monteses*, and conferred on him the symbol of office, an ebony, silver-topped cane or *bastun*, in recognition of Binoni's assistance to Father Ducos in battle against Moro raiders of northern Mindanao.[13] The tradition of a supreme high *datu*, known to Bukidnons as *Masikampu* or *Masalicampo*, lingers today, for the term was recently used by a Bukidnon *datu* in explaining how there had once been such a "high *datu*" over all Bukidnons.[14] However, according to Fr. José Maria Clotet, S.J., the title *Maestre de Campo* was conferred by the Spanish not necessarily on one high chief, but rather on Bukidnons who had distinguished themselves by some service for Spain.[15] Likewise, it should be noted that this was a title bestowed upon Bukidnons by the Spanish, not by their own people, and it may never have been honoured by people beyond their immediate control. It appears likely, in fact, that the concept of a supreme high *datu* operated only on a regional level, with each of the major Bukidnon regions (the upper Tagoloan, Pulangi and Cagayan) having once had such a recognized leader. Thus Fay-Cooper Cole reported that "a chief *datu* was recognized" in the central district of Bukidnon but not in the Cagayan River area in 1910, and William E. Biernatzki concluded that the "high *datu*" (*dadatu-on*) of northeastern Bukidnon, who possessed a *giling* or "black stick the length of one's forearm and hand", enjoyed territorial jurisdiction over "all or portions of several river valleys occupied by the bands of subordinate *datus*".[16]

The next level below the *Masalicampu* or the *dadatu-on* (where these in fact were recognized) was occupied by settlement chiefs presiding over areas called *tulugan*. Such areas were usually confined to one river valley and its surrounding hillsides, but for chiefs living at the forest edge the grass plains (which they used for hunting, not agriculture) formed part of their *tulugan*. Their say extended to 40 or so nuclear families (never more than 100) which were interrelated by marriage or blood and which lived in rooms tacked onto their chief's large house (also called a *tulugan*).[17] These chiefs controlled the land and its use in their immediate environs, determining which families would work which swidden plots.[18] Bukidnon social structure at this, the *tulugan*, level was not democratic, but neither was it brutally authoritarian. *Datu*-ship was not confined to the head *datu*'s immediate family, a fact which permitted a degree of social mobility within the group. Below the head *datu* there were lesser *datus,* the people themselves, and then slaves taken in raids on other *tulugan*. To become a *datu,* a man had to win recognition for his ability to settle disputes among tribesmen. Success as an arbiter (or counsellor, as Clotet called the *datu*) presupposed knowledge of customary law, and, to a lesser degree, of the epics. Ultimately it is also required financial resources with which to soothe hurt feelings and effect payment for wrongs done. Given these requirements, the son of a *datu* certainly had an advantage over others. And yet the position was not hereditary. Neither was it filled by appointment. There were as many *datus* in a settlement as there were arbiters who inspired respect among their tribesmen for their ability to settle disputes.[19]

Bukidnon Society, 1870–1900

Bukidnon society in the late 19th century thus was characterized by swidden farmers cultivating widely separated upland regions, some of which had supra-local leaders, and residing in scattered settlements of interrelated families presided over by *tulugan* chiefs and a number of lesser *datus*. In the last decades of the century these people were drawn more and more tightly into the web of northcoast culture by traders anxious to barter for their produce; by Augustinian, Recollect and Jesuit priests concerned for their souls; and by the Spanish government determined to halt the spread of Islam in Mindanao. Together, these outside forces effected change in Bukidnon economic life and in settlement patterns, and they speeded up the process of acculturation as well.

Bukidnons grew a variety of crops which wealthy Visayan and Chinese merchants in coastal towns took in exchange for sugar, salt, cloth and liquor. Abaca constituted their principal export. Fr. Clotet remarked in 1889 that among them there was "widespread interest in the harvesting of abaca, for they know the high price this fibre brings in the market". Of the 30,243 piculs (valued at ₱128,532) exported from Misamis Province in 1870, most came from the plateau region which was then part of that province. Other crops cultivated for export included coffee, rice, cacao and copra. The tobacco, which Clotet rated as "top quality", they grew themselves and sold "in large quantity at Cagayan". Although they grew corn principally for their own consumption, this was still another cash crop.[20] Finally, the gutta-percha shipped from Misamis was virtually all harvested by Bukidnons, and these people began to raise cattle for export too.[21]

As trade between Bukidnons and Visayans or Chinese expanded, the former adopted the role of middlemen in a marketing system linking the coast with the Manobo peoples farther to the south. Bukidnons, for example, obtained the *balarao*, their "most commonly used weapon . . . , in trade from the Manobos of the Agusan River in exchange for cloth, corn, camotes, salt, etc." [22] Both as middlemen and producers of export commodities sold on the coast, Bukidnons thus became participants in a much wider trading system than they had known before. And more than before, their lives were influenced by market forces beyond their control.

Linked to the north coast and the Visayas as traders, Bukidnons were further influenced by Philippine lowland culture when Jesuits began making regular visits to their settlements in the 1870s.[23] They created the first mission inland from the coast at Sumilao in 1890, adding another at Linabo in 1894.[24] In their effort to save souls the Jesuits significantly affected the plateau's settlement pattern, for they were able to persuade many Bukidnons to settle on the grasslands in *reducciones*. Villages which "in general . . . differed but little from the Visayan towns along the coast" thus grew up on the plateau. Principal among these were Malaybalay (then called Oroquieta by the Spaniards), Sumilao, Bugcaon and Linabo, with populations respectively of 1,439, 1,340, 1,083 and 790 in 1892.[25] In these and other still smaller settlements the Jesuits were certain of having baptized at least 4,992 Bukidnons by 1900.[26]

The new towns differed from the old settlements both in their pattern of settlement (individual dwellings rather than the old *tulugan* grouping) and in the extent to which Christianity reached their residents.[27] What was more, they were all linked together by the trail which meandered from Cagayan to Agusan town, then up onto the plateau and south to Linabo and Maramag. Along this path moved Jesuit priests and a growing number of traders and Bukidnons with their forest products.

Reflecting the increased movement and activity, many of the new settlements took names expressive of a traveller's point of view. Tankulan (now renamed Manolo Fortich) was the first town a trader riding south from Cagayan or Agusan would reach after a day's journey. Its name may have come from the Binukid word "tangkul" — a one-node bamboo musical instrument which is strummed; Tankulan was thus a place where people made these instruments or where they could be found in abundance. Following the trail south, the trader next came to Dalirig, meaning "to pass by the side, not through", a *sitio* very near the impressive Tagoloan Canyon. Maluko was "a peaceful place where animals could lie down", and Silipon (later Dalwangan) meant "to look through". Situated on the divide formed by the lava flows of Mt. Kitanglad, this last community was indeed a place where travellers could finally look through to the heart of the expansive Bukidnon plateau.[28]

Not all the plateau settlements came to have principally a trading function. Bugcaon, for example, was established in 1888-1889 as a Spanish garrison to turn back Maranao Muslim influence on the plateau. There, an outpost of 30 *Guardia Civil* led by a Spanish officer brought greater security to the settlements of Mailag, Linabo and Malaybalay. Then in the 1890s, Bukidnons who had settled in those communities were organized by the Jesuits into a militia, and, with the governor-general's approval, supplied with guns and used to push the Maranaos back west of the Cagayan River headwaters and south of the Manupali. By the turn of the century Maranao influence was minimal on the plateau, and it virtually ceased to exist there in the decades before World War II.[29]

Bukidnon Society at the Turn of the Century

The ties forged between Bukidnons and lowlanders in the late 19th century — ties which, as we have seen, were having a marked effect on Bukidnon religious practices, economic development and demographic patterns — were temporarily severed at the turn of the century. First the Philippine Revolution brought a halt to Jesuit activity on the plateau.[30] Then the Philippine–American War completely disrupted life in the new settlements. Finally, Americans arrived and set in motion an effort to free Bukidnon society permanently from dominance by powerful interests in the coastal city of Cagayan de Oro.

Bukidnons played only a peripheral role in the Philippine–American War. While Filipinos on the coast reported in large numbers to fight under the leadership of Nicolas Capistrano and Apolinar Velez, in the highlands few people took part in the fighting. The exception to this rule occurred when General Capistrano retreated to the interior in December 1900. American troops pursuing him were assaulted by "heavy logs and stones rolled down from above" at one point when they were making their way through a canyon near Sumilao.[31] Those rolling the logs and stones were believed to have been "monteses" (i.e., Bukidnons), six to eight of whom were shot by the Americans before the others mounted "small native ponies" and got away.[32] Major E.F. Taggart of the Twenty-eighth Infantry, USV, later remarked that "every man of military age from Sumilao south . . . [was]

enrolled as a *machetero* and [was] under the military orders of Capistrano". He reported, however, that they had joined Capistrano not because of patriotism, but because "they will obey any organization which is supported by guns", including the Americans.[33]

In the opinion of American officers, Capistrano's forces did not feel any more at home on the plateau than Americans did. Colonel William E. Birkhimer, also of the Twenty-eighth Infantry, regarded the Filipino retreat to the interior as a measure of his success. For the "rebels" to abandon the coast for the plateau "would be to abandon the Garden of Eden of the Bay district for a most uninviting and poverty-stricken country". Predicting that the upland environment would quickly destroy the morale of the Filipino troops, he adopted a policy of denying the coast to all armed men. "I shall permit families of women and children to come into their old houses and resorts, and [even] encourage them; but with men of military capacities, every one of whom almost was out against us . . . , I shall not permit these military availables to come in now and enjoy the sweets of Bay country life unless they surrender their arms."[34] This policy, together with Major Taggart's rapid advance and surprise attack of 28 February 1901 on Capistrano's headquarters at Malaybalay, persuaded Capistrano to call an end to the fighting. Of the 191 men who surrendered at Sumilao on 27 March 1901, not a single one listed a plateau settlement as his home.[35]

The war, though only briefly fought in the interior, thoroughly disrupted life on the plateau. This was so despite American efforts to separate "monteses" from *dumagats* and treat them as nonbelligerents. Major Taggart, for example, referring to his attack on Sumilao, noted that "twenty-one of the bolomen [Bukidnons] were captured and their weapons turned over to the *presidente* with instructions to return them. These men were released and told that the Americans did not wish to harm them, and that they should tell all bolomen the same".[36] Despite this policy, Bukidnons felt compelled by the American advance and by the fighting between Sumilao and Mailag "to flee to the mountains and to abandon the settlements, many of which were destroyed".[37]

Americans who arrived in northern Mindanao during the war became quickly convinced that "monteses" had fallen victim to a "hemp trust" headed by influential families residing in Cagayan de Oro. They set about to protect Bukidnons from the machinations of their coastal trading contacts. As early as March 1901, Major Taggart alluded to such a "trust". He argued that leaders of the Filipino forces were using their power and the funds of their government to purchase abaca from "monteses" at cut-rate prices. "The price which Capistrano has paid for hemp stored at Oroquieta [Malaybalay], and which I shall burn, is . . . $1.50 (Mexican) per pico, which is about one-twentieth part of what they sell it for in Cebu."[38] Furthermore, each *presidente* (chief of a settlement) has been ordered "to furnish Capistrano (for military purposes) 50 cavans of corn and palay". As a result of these exactions and conditions, the "natives" had told Taggart that if they were "not soon . . . permitted to go to Tagoloan or Cagayan, they must starve".[39]

Although it is difficult to measure the extent to which Visayans of the north coast actually were taking advantage of Bukidnons, there can be little question that the relationship between these two peoples was not an equal one in 1900. "It is probably true," wrote Dean Conant Worcester, "that in no part of the Philippine Islands were members of the non-Christian tribes so robbed and oppressed as were the Bukidnon people."[40] Bukidnons were especially at a disadvantage because of the linkage which existed between the trading community and the power structure of Misamis Province. In the words of William Cameron Forbes, "Governor [Manuel] Corrales, who looked a thorough scoundrel and didn't belie his looks, had a ring with a couple of scalawags . . . [which] compelled everyone who came from the interior to sell their produce to them, paying them some trifle for it." And "if the unfortunate from the interior objected, he was charged with sedition and thrown into jail".[41] Captain John J. Gallant, Senior Inspector of Constabulary for the province, concurred in this assessment in 1906, maintaining that "a ring . . . existed about Cagayan which controlled all features of administration and conduct of the province, and that the governor [Apolinar Velez] was not only a member of, but a strong factor in, this ring".[42]

The "hemp trust" or "ring" operated to diminish the power of Bukidnon *datus,* thereby further disrupting Bukidnon society at the turn of the century. Throughout Misamis Province, barrio *presidentes* were appointed by the governor in Cagayan de Oro. In the interior these appointments were made "mainly through *commissionados* or agents of the principal *commerciante*". In return for their appointment, *presidentes* (favoured *datus,* most likely) "handled their . . . dependants according to the will of the . . . [*commerciante*] who controlled them". Thus the Cagayan River section of the province was controlled in actuality not by the *datus* of that region, but by "Señor Vamenta, one-time *presidente* of Cagayan and *commerciante*", whose power was so absolute that the people "could not sell their products to anyone but him or his agents".[43] Because few Bukidnons understood the intricacies of the Spanish legal system, few had recourse to the courts for redress of grievance. When they fell into debt to the *commerciantes,* therefore, "many ran away from the settlements in order to escape the pressure that was brought to bear in their collection".[44] Still others fell into debt bondage. There is, for example, the case of two young Bukidnon males who were forced to work off the debts of their father upon his death. Taken to Cagayan de Oro, they were compelled to labour without pay for the man to whom their father had owed money, and they were, according to their testimony, whipped often during their involuntary servitude.[45]

The American Impact

Although many Americans were disturbed by the evidence that *commerciantes* in Cagayan de Oro were taking advantage of Bukidnons in 1900, no American was more outraged by such reports than the Secretary of the Interior, Dean Worcester. Worcester visited the plateau in 1907 and thereafter developed a special interest in the Bukidnon frontier and the people living there. What Rajah Brooke had done for upland peoples in Sarawak, Dean Worcester determined to do for hill tribes in the Philippines.[46]

The American effort, which began formally among Bukidnons in 1907 and which was led by Worcester, sought to provide protection for Bukidnons against *dumagat* dominance while educating and training them to a point where they could function as equals in the rapidly expanding world of lowland Philipine culture. To achieve these goals, Americans in northern Mindanao instituted a number of policies: first, administrative separation of the plateau from the coast; second, appointment of vigorous administrators independent of control by the Misamis elite; third, resettlement of Bukidnons once again on the plateau; fourth, justice for all, but particularly for Bukidnons, in the courts; fifth, economic protection for them through the establishment of government trading posts as alternatives to rapacious private traders; sixth, employment of Bukidnons in municipal and provincial offices; seventh, public education for them, especially in methods of lowland agriculture; and last, utilization of as much of the land as possible by Bukidnons and by cattle ranchers rather than by crowds of migrant homesteaders.

In 1907, at Secretary Worcester's initiative, the plateau and bordering mountains north of the eighth parallel were designated as the Sub-Province of Bukidnon, within the Special Province of Agusan, and were placed under the jurisdiction not of the old Misamis elite but of an American appointee. The governor of Agusan was selected by Worcester and resided in Butuan, Agusan, leaving the new sub-province to be administered by a lieutenant governor residing in Malaybalay. For the next seven years virtually all Bukidnons came directly under American administrative control in the persons of Lt. Governors Frederick Lewis and Manuel Fortich. Then in 1914, Bukidnon became a full-fledged province, separate from Agusan as well as from Misamis, with new boundaries encompassing not just the Bukidnon population but many Manobos living south of the eighth parallel as well.[47]

The mission to develop Bukidnons to a point where they could compete economically and educationally with lowlanders began soon after 1907. As a first step, they had to be resettled on the plateau. A vigorous campaign, led at first by Frederick Lewis and later by Manuel Fortich, was inaugurated to bring them back down out of the hills to where they could be managed more easily. Fortich, whom Worcester had discovered in 1907, was especially forceful in this effort. A former Constabulary officer who hailed from a highly placed Cebu family, Fortich rode across the plateau as much as 600 miles a month, pressing Bukidnons and Manobos to settle on the grasslands, begin plough agriculture, and have their children attend the settlement schools. He impressed Worcester as a man absolutely without fear who "shoots with extraordinary accuracy, and rides like Jehu". A "tremendously energetic" man, he was also "reputed to have a vicious temper", so that "the good people are very fond of him, and the evil-doers deathly afraid of him".[48]

Bukidnons who spurned Fortich's overtures and resolved to continue dwelling in the mountains ran the risk of being attacked by Constabulary soldiers as *magahats,* a term which meant blood-avengers but which came to be applied to all lawless elements in the mountains. "The old people vowed not to send their children to school," recalled Albino Pensahan, a Bukidnon whose tribal group held out against relocation until approximately 1913 when he was ten years old. Then one morning they were awakened near Calabugao in the northeast:

> We left the house that dawn. I . . . cannot forget . . . My father said: 'What is this noise which seems like . . . burning *kaingin?*' It was similar to a bamboo cannon . . . My mother said: 'Who would burn [*kaingin*] when it is still early?' Afterwards our followers [*sakop*] arrived and said: 'Soldiers have reached us; they are already shooting.' Those who died were a cousin and my aunt, and my uncle [Manustil, the chief *datu*] was captured . . . All in all there were four who died [and Manustil was imprisoned until his father gave himself up]. That is why we were forced to live in the town [of Kalasungay]. When we reached the town, . . . they said that Manpensajan [his father] would [also] be placed in prison because he had a gun. [Another Bukidnon, however, who was close to Fortich, persuaded him to free Manpensajan.] We children then went to school, and we stopped being 'magahats'.[49]

Whether by luring or by browbeating them, Lewis and Fortich succeeded in effecting the resettlement of Bukidnons on the plateau between 1907 and 1914. Bukidnons from the upper Pulangi and the middle Tagoloan settled in Maluko, Impasugong and Kalasungay especially, while those from the upper Tagoloan settled in Malaybalay.[50] They did not abandon their hillside plots completely, preferring on the basis of past experience to keep a hand in both camps.[51] But, in the words of Agusan Governor Frederick Johnson, "new men are continually arriving from the hitherto unoccupied districts, [and] towns are being built where before the people lived entirely wild and beyond control".[52]

It is little wonder that the years of greatest pressure for resettlement were also the years of greatest conflict prior to World War II. In 1907 Manobos on the border between Bukidnon and Butuan sub-provinces killed an American official of the Bureau of Science.[53] Extant court records for the years immediately following clearly evidence extensive *magahat* violence among other Manobo groups closer to the plateau.[54] One group, for example, attacked the store of Eugene and Richard Barton, Americans living and trading with Manobos in Mailag. Although these Manobos were moved to action specifically by the Bartons' failure to pay them fairly for logs they had delivered, their leader, Banao, claimed to be able to catch bullets in his shirt, a circumstance which suggests that the movement may have had millenarian overtones.[55] To the extent that this was the case, the incident at the Barton store might be tied to the larger Manobo *Tungud* movement which, according to Cole, started in eastern Mindanao in 1908 and began attracting Manobo followers in Bukidnon two years later. While Cole deemed the movement to have "had only minor influence in Bukidnon", and concluded that "the acculturational pressures were less in the Bukidnon region", he noted that Frederick Lewis had at first considered it "to be a reaction against his attempts to locate all the Bukidnon in model villages".[56]

It need hardly be noted that all of the above-mentioned movements and incidents took place among Manobos rather than Bukidnons, a circumstance doubtless owing to the fact that they had not previously been exposed to the powerful outside forces which their Bukidnon neighbours had experienced earlier. This is not, however, to suggest that Bukidnon society remained completely unshaken. While court records indicate only isolated acts of violence among Bukidnons, open resistance to government resettlement efforts was not confined just to *Datus* Manpensajan and Manustil.[57] Indeed resettlement must have been a traumatic experience for most Bukidnons. Even as early as 1910, Cole noted a significant shift in their social and political hierarchy which he attributed to "the aggressive intervention in [their] daily affairs by the American governor — Frederick Lewis". What Cole attributed to Lewis — namely the weakening of *datu* leadership — seems, in fact, to have been due equally to pressures emanating from the coast and dating back to the late 19th century. And as the status of *datus* declined, that of *baylans* or religious mediums increased. Although there were few known religious movements among Bukidnons in 1910, "the ceremonies which the mediums conducted were assuming increasing importance to the extent that they dominated the social and religious life. As other aspects of the old life weakened, interest in the spirit world increased".[58]

The success of the resettlement effort depended to a degree on an absence of violence, for, in the words of Johnson, "if a murder occurs in a town, the whole town will probably go into the wilderness rather than expose the murderer to danger of punishment".[59] The justice of the peace court begun in Malaybalay in 1907 was intended to offer a less traumatic alternative. And yet, for Bukidnon *datus* accustomed to mediating disputes and meting out justice, nothing could have been more threatening. That few of the court's cases over the next decade were between Bukidnons (rather than between them and migrants) suggests that *datus* continued to function as arbiters in most disputes among their own people. But by 1914 an occasional case did appear on the court docket involving a dispute between two or more Bukidnons, a fact which indicates that some were beginning to have faith in the new system or that they were prepared to have recourse to the court when their *datu* failed them. In either case, this use of the court implied a further diminution in the power and prestige of the *datu*-ship.[60]

Once administrative independence had been won, resettlement begun and a court opened, the next step in the American effort to protect and manage Bukidnon development concerned the problem of Visayan and Chinese control over economic life on the plateau. Merchants along the coast had, as we have seen, enjoyed an upper hand in trading with Bukidnons who were paid minimally for their products and then charged high prices for coastal goods. To remedy this situation the American governor of Agusan began a system of government exchanges or trading posts in 1910. These stores sold cloth, utensils, needles, salt, blankets, ornaments and sugar to Bukidnons and Manobos for curios, handicrafts, abaca, timber, coffee, cacao and other forest products.[61] By 1915 the government store in Malaybalay, capitalized at ₱1,000, had average daily sales of ₱25.[62]

The government exchanges not only offered competition to Visayan and Chinese traders, they also provided jobs for Bukidnons.[63] Bukidnons also found employment in the new government offices and services. By 1934, Governor Antonio Rubin estimated that "about 99.8 percent of our local police force[s] are natives", while ten of 11 municipal *presidentes* were Bukidnons. In contrast to the situation at the municipal level, jobs open to Bukidnons in provincial offices tended to be menial. Alluding to the fact that "natives" on the provincial payroll typically held jobs as clerks, janitors, telephone linesmen, guards, letter carriers, messengers and locust inspectors, Rubin (a Tagalog) declared that "very few" were as yet "qualified for appointment". Nevertheless, he counted 20 working in the Division Superintendent of Schools Office, 15 in the Treasurer's office, and seven more in his own. And of the 115 teachers in 1933, 17 were Bukidnons, or almost 15 percent.[64]

Beginning in 1908, Bukidnons who resettled in the plateau towns were exposed to education in English. In that year four primary schools were erected in as many communities, "with a teaching force of nine native teachers and an American supervising teacher".[65] By 1911 the number of primary schools had grown to 14 and an agricultural high school had been established in Mailag.[66] And by 1916 there were 1,766 pupils enrolled in 22 settlement schools plus the high school.[67] While it was not until 1924 that a normal school was opened, Bukidnon men and women as early as 1912 had been sent as government *pensionados* to study at the Philippine Normal College in Manila or at the agricultural school in Muñoz, Nueva Ecija.[68]

One of the most important tasks assigned the schools was to teach students up-to-date agricultural techniques, including the use of a wooden, iron-tipped plough introduced to Bukidnon between 1910 and 1914.[69] The work of the settlement schools was, according to a Bureau of Education report, "to demonstrate that this rolling grassy land can be more successfully cultivated than the mountain sides can be by the 'kaingin' system".[70] Students spent half the day in class and half engaged in farm work. That the new techniques began to catch on is suggested by comparing descriptions of Bukidnon land use in 1915, 1918 and 1933. The first of these declared that "most of the crops are grown on the distant mountain sides or along the sides of cañons". The second remarked on "the beautiful fields of corn surrounding their settlements" and also on the increased plantings of rice and *camotes*. And the third reported that "the people are fast replacing their old caiñgin instinct with the productive methods of lowland cultivation".[71]

Production of corn did increase in Bukidnon, from 10,000 *cavans* in 1910 to 16,881 in 1918. In that same period rice production went from 16,000 *cavans* to 25,376. Meanwhile, traditional hillside-grown export crops such as coffee and cacao did not increase as much: 3,500 *cavans* of coffee were exported in 1911 and 3,752 in 1918, and 500 *cavans* of cacao were exported in 1911 and only 247 eight years later. As for abaca, the principal export in the 19th century, it fluctuated wildly from 4,000 *cavans* exported in 1910 to 65,000 in 1913 and then down to 5,719 in 1918.[72]

The increased production of staples, when weighed against the less impressive gains for exports, lends support to the thesis that Bukidnons were rapidly becoming plough rather than slash-and-burn agriculturists. Indeed, there can be little question but that Bukidnons were beginning to farm the grasslands in this period, although most families continued to maintain hillside plots at the same time.[73] At no time before World War II, however, did they produce staples in large quantities. In fact, during some prewar years they did not grow enough rice for their own consumption and had to import this staple. In 1909 Lt. Governor Lewis commented on food shortages. The following year the sub-province had to import "only 1,000 piculs" of rice. And in 1911, Lt. Governor Fortich reported that inhabitants of settlements just south of Malaybalay had "suffered a good deal from hunger". Although the following years brought some improvement, the province began to import rice again in the 1930s.[74]

Part of the problem concerned yields which were lower in Bukidnon (12.75 *cavans* of rice per hectare) than in any other province of the Philippines in 1918. To be sure, none of the province's farm land was irrigated in that year. But a still more telling reason for the low production was the extremely limited amount of plateau land actually being utilized for farming. Of the 1,002,589 hectares inside Bukidnon's boundaries in 1918, only 15,656 hectares were designated as farms, a mere 1.6 percent. And of these 15,656 hectares, only 49 percent (7,679) were actually cultivated. What is still more remarkable, of the land cultivated, only 1,991 hectares (one-fifth of one percent of the province's total land area) were utilized for rice production, and only 1,139 hectares were cultivated in corn.[75]

The plateau itself was thus still comparatively open and uncultivated in 1918. "Except for small patches of abaca, rice, corn and various other food crops and some pasturage, the land is still unoccupied and open for settlement," reported an American observer two years later.[76] There were only 4,337 farms, and virtually all of these (4,124) were in the northern half of the province between Malaybalay municipality and the coast.[77] Land surveys had not been initiated except in the *poblaciones* of Malaybalay, Libona and a few other towns where a cadastral survey was completed in 1912.[78] Hence of all the farms enumerated in the 1918 Census, only one was officially titled; the rest awaited survey before they could be registered under Torrens title, private deed or another form of ownership.[79] And even when people did begin to take formal ownership of farm land after 1918, they were very slow to do so. In the next two decades only 816 titles were issued — 461 as free patent, 255 by judicial decree, and 100 as homestead patents. This compares with 956 homestead and free patent titles issued in 1948-1949 alone, and 15,429 original titles (mostly free patent and homestead) issued between 1945 and 1977.[80]

Why was such a small percentage of the plateau land divided up into privately owned and cultivated farm plots before 1941? To begin with, Bukidnons, who had shied away from the grasslands before, continued to keep at least one foot in the hillside soil which had sustained their people for generations.[81] Then, too, the slow progress in opening up lands to plough agriculture conformed with the American design for this frontier region. While Americans like Worcester initiated policies to promote the relocation of Bukidnons on the plateau, they did not encourage the spread of coastal migrants there. Thus when Frank Carpenter, Director of the

Department of Mindanao and Sulu, allowed that he "was inclined to reserve the great plateau . . . and [to] cut it up into homesteads for colonists from the north", Worcester criticized him sharply for views of such a "socialistic character relative to land tenure".[82]

Still another reason for the slow progress of farm agriculture in Bukidnon can also be traced back to the Americans, for it was they who pre-empted much of the rolling grassland for their own entrepreneurial ventures. Philippine Packing Corporation, a subsidiary of Del Monte Corporation, provides an insightful example. In the late 1920s PPC discovered that rainfall and soil conditions along the northern edge of the plateau would be superb for growing pineapples. Limited by law to a plantation of no more than 1,024 hectares, the American directors of PPC turned to Governor-General Dwight F. Davis for help. When Davis converted public lands west of Maluko into a large naval reservation, PPC was able to sub-lease almost 20,000 hectares from the United States Navy. Then in 1935, when this hectarage reverted to the Philippine Commonwealth, PPC succeeded in persuading President Manuel Quezon to declare it a National Development Company lease. It is from this public company that PPC continues to sub-lease land for pineapple production today.[83]

While pineapple growing was one important American venture in Bukidnon, far more significant in terms of land-use was the emergence of an extensive cattle-ranching industry under American tutelage. Beginning in 1913-14, thousands of hectares were leased by Americans and their Filipino allies as pasture land. Bukidnon began to develop as the premier cattle-ranching province of the entire Philippines.[84]

Cattle had been virtually eliminated in Bukidnon between 1890 and 1905 when rinderpest decimated the native stock. By 1911, when the quarantine effort had begun to bring the disease under control, cattle in the province numbered only 159.[85] Dean Worcester, upon his retirement as Secretary of the Interior in 1913, imported the first disease-resistant Nellore Brahmin bulls. As Vice-President and General Manager of the American-Philippine Company, he then provided the impetus for that company's subsidiary, the Agusan Coconut Company, to establish Bukidnon's first big ranch. By 1920 the Diklum Ranch, as this came to be known, maintained a herd of 6,000 head. Worcester in the meantime set up his own Nellore Ranch near Mailag, and before the outset of World War II this 7,000-hectare spread supported a herd of 2,500. Other early cattlemen, all of whom were close associates of the Secretary, were also Americans. Together with Manuel Fortich, whom Worcester deeply admired and who built up a herd of 4,000, they were the pioneers in cattle ranching on the Bukidnon frontier.[86]

In so far as Bukidnons participated in the new cattle-ranching industry, they did so not as ranchers or managers but as cowboys. Like their American counterparts they were at the bottom of the ranching social structure. But unlike American cowboys, they never became folk heroes of a romanticized frontier ethos. "Anybody could be a cowboy," said former ranch manager Manuel Fortich, Jr., referring to the fact that the eight cowboys under his management at Diklum had all been Bukidnons. The Bukidnon cowboy was merely a "muchacho", a boy, paid ₱30 a month to rope and brand cattle and ride herd. Most depended solely on their wages for a livelihood, and few wanted their children to follow the same profession. They never evolved a cowboy ethic of mobility, self-reliance and straight-talk. To the contrary, they tended to fall into debt to their managers and otherwise to become dependent clients of their manager–patron. At best they regarded their work as a vehicle for social mobility, but from their point of view even becoming a land-owning peasant signified a definite step upward.[87]

The new ranch-cattle industry succeeded in pre-empting land for pasture rather than for private farms, and in doing this it discouraged large numbers of Filipinos from homesteading in Bukidnon before the war. It did not, however, provide much of an avenue of socio-economic mobility for Bukidnons. As we shall see, the industry passed through its pioneering stage in the early 1920s. By that time, American influence which had been important in the creation of Bukidnon — in education, and in land use as well as in economic development — had begun to diminish. Bewailing this trend, Worcester in 1921 reported that there had been "a good deal of unfortunate retrogression in the work for the non-Christian tribes". Bukidnon had, he said, "held together longer than any other part of the wild man's territory, owing to the continuance in office of Governor Manuel Fortich, one of my old men". Even here, though, lowlanders were encroaching all the time. Indeed, at the insistence of powerful interests in Cagayan de Oro, the northeastern section of Bukidnon (including the settlement of Claveria) had reverted to Misamis Province, and there was growing pressure to take back the rest of Bukidnon as well.[88]

Bukidnon in the 1920s and 1930s

Reduction of the American presence in Bukidnon ushered in a period of increased *dumagat* influence. Worcester died in 1924, and although his son continued to operate the Worcester ranch until World War II, other American-operated spreads were sold to wealthy Filipinos. The Agusan Coconut Company ranch in Diklum, for example, was bought by Angel Elizalde, and the government's experimental ranch in Dagumbaan went to Alejandro Roces. Ranching thus became a business for rich absentee owners who lived in Manila and Cebu and who rarely visited their spreads.[89] At the same time the road from Cagayan de Oro to Malaybalay was finally completed, making automobile traffic possible between the two towns. The closer ties which developed between the plateau and the coast can be measured in the increased number of migrants who swelled Bukidnon's population to 57,561 by 1939.[90] But a still better indicator of the nature of these ties was provided by Manuel Fortich when he opted to build his family home not in Malaybalay but in Dalirig, close to Cagayan de Oro City. Thereafter, the Fortich family, which had personified Bukidnon's struggle for independence from Misamis, became more and more closely associated with the Misamis elite.[91]

Renewal of coastal influence on the plateau between 1920 and 1941 was manifested in Bukidnon's economic enterprises as well. Most of the retail stores, for example, came to be capitalized by Chinese living in Cagayan de Oro or Agusan town, especially after the government exchanges folded in the early 1920s.[92] Bukidnons once again brought their abaca to these stores or directly to the store owners on the coast, and bartered for coastal products such as salt, sugar and cloth. But in one important respect the plateau economy remained independent from merchants of the coast. Cattle, the principal export of the province, were not marketed through Cagayan de Oro or Agusan. Rather, they were moved in cattle drives direct from the range to Bugo (on the coast), from where they were shipped direct to the slaughterhouse in Manila.[93] Although some Cagayan de Oro families (Chavez, Neri, Roa and Alquitela, among them) operated ranches of their own, the ranch-cattle industry of the plateau never fell under their control.

In other, perhaps even more important ways, Bukidnon developed independently from the coast in the two decades before World War II. What is most striking about Bukidnon society as it evolved in these years is the emergence of a new elite comprised of civil-servant migrants. Attracted to Bukidnon originally by the availability of civil service jobs in 1907-1920, most of these migrants settled in Malaybalay where the provincial government was located and where they worked as sanitary inspectors, nurses, teachers and so forth. They came from many provinces but especially from the Ilocos region. Most possessed at least a secondary school diploma, and all indicated by their very presence in Bukidnon a readiness to set out on their own and seek their fortune on the frontier, independent from their families and factions at home. They arrived with no special attachment to the north coast of Mindanao, but rather with an identity to their home provinces or even to the ideal of nationhood. By the 1920s many of these migrant public employees had become small entrepreneurs — store-keepers and ranchers especially. Pasture leases, costing only ₱0.20 a hectare and good for 25 years, were especially attractive investments for this group. Some began with only a handful of cattle, watched these multiply into a herd, and then moved out onto the range to become serious ranchers. Among the biggest ranchers (other than the absentee owners already referred to) on the plateau itself in the 1930s, most — perhaps all — had originally come to the province as civil service employees.[94]

Malaybalay, where they settled originally, became a frontier town with an ambience all its own. Here, in the words of the parish priest, were: "Government officials, Constabulary and School teachers from every Province, who themselves ask for the sermon in English or Spanish. Side by side with them are Bukidnon Government Officials who prefer Visayan, and then the poorer class Bukidnons who only understand Binukid."[95] Here many Bukidnons continued to hold positions in the provincial government.[96] Here they continued to own some of the most desirable land around the plaza and along the main street.[97] And here they were able to elect a Binukid-speaking mayor in every election until 1971. Bukidnons in Malaybalay came to recognize their own elite of landed, educated, acculturated families. Members of these families held salaried jobs in government offices, spoke English and Visayan as well as Binukid, and married into migrant families.[98] They attended the big social events — especially receptions at the Government Rest House — where they mixed freely with non-Bukidnons.[99] And they joined the churches in the *poblacion* — a Catholic church constructed permanently when Malaybalay became a parish in 1934, and a Baptist one organized in the early 1920s — which became meeting grounds for people from all linguistic groups. By 1938 there were "about 1,500 Catholics" in the *poblacion* and "two nearby barrios", and some 400-500 Protestants.[100] Malaybalay thus developed as a frontier town in which there occurred before 1941 sufficient socio-economic mobility and group interaction to break through class and linguistic barriers which were such important elements of lowland society elsewhere in the islands.

Malaybalay, however, in the words of Fr. Joseph Lucas, was "the one grand exception to everything".[101] Elsewhere on the plateau much less cross-cultural interaction took place. In the vicinity of Malaybalay (the barrios of Kalasungay and Casisang in particular), and in barrios to the immediate south (especially Linabo), where contacts with the capital were extensive daily and where many migrants bought land and began growing rice and corn, Bukidnons were drawn into the pattern of life of the capital.[102] But even here they remained on the periphery of that social world, due to the scarcity of salaried jobs which left them no alternative but to remain closely tied to the land. Farther away from Malaybalay, in barrios such as Sumilao, Bukidnons typically remained poor peasants who continued to employ swidden techniques (now in tandem with plough agriculture) and who continued to depend on *dumagats* in trading their crops. Despite the availability of primary education for these people, they continued to use Binukid in their homes (although most learned Visayan as well), and rarely intermarried with non-Bukidnons.[103] Although many became Catholics, they were, according to Fr. Lucas, "for the most part . . . baptized Pagans".[104] This is not to suggest that Bukidnons in these barrios cherished as ever their ancient traditions. While they did recognize *datus* as their local leaders, and did perform traditional ceremonies for marriages and the like, little power accrued anymore to the *datu*-ship other than that delegated by Governor Fortich and the official government.[105] Bukidnons fell to regarding themselves as second-class citizens in their barrios distant from the provincial capital.

Conclusion

The years before World War II thus witnessed, on one hand, the emergence of a community of highly acculturated Bukidnons in Malaybalay, and on the other, a disintegration of traditional culture without compensating socio-economic mobility among Bukidnons elsewhere on the plateau.[106] The establishment of administrative independence, of a public education system, of a better road network, of a new ranch-cattle industry, and of active Catholic and Protestant churches operated to change the Bukidnons' way of life. But the extensive resettlement effort, when not combined with provision for widespread employment opportunities among Bukidnons, left these people in a state of limbo. Only in the provincial capital and its environs did there emerge a new, more fluid, more integrated and more cosmopolitan culture. So long as the pace of immigration remained slow and the space for accommodation wide, conflict between Bukidnons and migrants would not characterize life on the plateau. But when these conditions changed after the war, when Bukidnon's population grew from 63,470 to 532,818 in just 27 years, society there would become fraught with tension and smouldering conflict.[107] With an expanding Philippine majority culture that had run out of space and a vulnerable minority culture that had run out of time, the frontier had closed on the Bukidnon Plateau.

NOTES

1 The dates 1870-1941 encompass a period in which the Bukidnon plateau became a frontier for the expanding Philippine culture. As such, these dates are somewhat arbitrary, for the plateau did not suddenly become a frontier in 1870 any more than it suddenly ceased being this in 1941. But while Philippine lowland culture had made itself felt before 1870, forces of acculturation personified by traders, priests and government officials were much more in evidence on the plateau after that date. Likewise, while 1941 did not mark an end to frontier life, it did mark an end to prewar society in which Bukidnons had been the most populous group on the plateau. After the war, when the influx of migrants burgeoned, Bukidnons became a minority group even in this their traditional domain. The year 1941 thus marks the beginning of a new period of social and economic change for this area, and this period must be dealt with separately.

2 The elevation estimates are taken from Map No. NC 51-52, U.S. Army Map Services (PV), Corps of Engineers, 1956-1957, 1:1,000,000.

3 Travelling across the plateau was made somewhat easier when, on 2 September 1940, the Sayre Highway linking Misamis Province to Cotabato and running the length of Bukidnon was officially opened by President Manuel Quezon and High Commissioner Francis B. Sayre. Santiago Artiaga, Governor of Bukidnon, to M.E. Cooley, 8 October 1940, Michigan Historical Collections, Ann Arbor, Michigan, Santiago Artiaga Papers, folder marked "Papers, September-December, 1940".

4 Mt. Kitanglad (or Katanglad), at 2,938 metres (9,639 ft.), is, next to Mt. Apo, the highest peak in the archipelago. See, Francis C. Madigan, S.J., *Mindanao's Inland Province: A Socio-Economic Survey of Bukidnon* (Cagayan de Oro: Xavier University, Research Institute for Mindanao Culture, 1969) 1:55; and F.L. Wernstedt and J.E. Spencer, *The Philippine Island World, A Physical, Cultural and Regional Geography* (Berkeley: University of California Press, 1967), 560.

5 Juan A. Mariano, *Soil Survey of Bukidnon Province Philippines* (Manila: Department of Agriculture and Natural Resources, 1955), 5.

6 H. Gilsheuser, Governor, Davao District, Moro Province, "Report of an exploring expedition from Cagayan–Misamis across the Kalatungan mountain

range to Davao", 12 September 1911, University of Michigan Library, Department of Rare Books and Special Collections, Worcester's Philippine Collection, Documents and Papers, 4:21.

7 R.O. Van Horn, "Exploring Expedition, Cotabato to Cagayan, Mindanao," 18 March 1902, in U.S. War Department, *Annual Reports of the War Department for the fiscal year ended June 30, 1902* (Washington: GPO, 1902), 9:586-88.

8 *Ibid.*, 588-89.

9 Population figures for the plateau area in the 19th century are estimates at best. The figure cited here is from Agustín de la Cavada y Mendez de Vigo, *Historia geográfica, geologica y estadística de Filipinas* (Manila: Imp. de Ramirez y Girandier, 1876), 2:197. Because Bukidnon Province was not created until the 20th century, the figure is for the "Monteses and Manobos" and "Moros" in Misamis Province which then subsumed what is Bukidnon Province today. Other estimates indicate that this figure was reasonably accurate. José Maria Clotet, S.J. estimated "more than 13,000" Bukidnons in 1889. His letter of 11 May 1889 has been translated and edited by Frank Lynch, "The Bukidnon of North-Central Mindanao in 1889," *Philippine Studies* 15 (July 1967), 466. The 1903 Census estimated the "pagan" population of Misamis Province to be 21,163. Republic of the Philippines, National Census and Statistics Office, *1975 Integrated Census of the Population and Its Economic Activities: Population, Bukidnon* (Manila: National Census and Statistics Office, 1975), 1.

10 The ancient epic is called the "Ulaguing" by Bukidnons and the "Ulahingan" by Manobos. Only fragments of this lengthy narrative poem which is chanted in archaic Binukid and Minanobo have been recorded and transcribed so far. For the "Ulaguing," see, Carmen Ch. Unabia, "The Bukidnon Oral Traditions" (M.A. thesis, Xavier University, Cagayan de Oro City, 1977). For the "Ulahingan," see, the articles by Elena G. Maquiso, "The Ulahingan Episodes: The Creativity of the Manobos," *Silliman Journal* 16 (1969), 360-74; and "The Ulahingan: A Manobo Epic," *Silliman Journal* 14 (1969), 227-38. See also, Langkan and Santiago Abod, "The Visit of Lagabaan to Nelendangan," trans. by Elena G. Maquiso and Abraham Saliling, *Silliman Journal* 17 (1970), 19-39. The Manobo retreat from the Magindanao is discussed by Maquiso in the last of these articles, 19-20. The Bukidnon retreat from Hispanic influence is best remembered in the story of "Kumbalan and Tawaga," discussed by William E. Biernatzki, "Bukidnon Datuship in the Upper Pulangi River Valley," in, Alfonso de Guzman II and Esther M. Pacheco, eds., *Bukidnon Politics and Religion* (Quezon City: IPC Papers No. 11, Institute of Philippine Culture, Ateneo de Manila University Press, 1973), 21-23.

11 According to Fay-Cooper Cole, "during the 1880s Jesuit missionaries . . . found the grass plain mostly unsettled, while the people lived in scattered isolated villages along the edge of the forest or in small settlements bordering the water courses". *The Bukidnon of Mindanao,* in *Fieldiana: Anthropology* (Chicago: No. 46, Chicago Natural History Museum, 1956), 14.

12 Information on their origins is from Gervacio Libertad, interview, Malaybalay, Bukidnon, 14 May 1977. Information on their heroes is from Unabia, "The Bukidnon Oral Traditions". One Bukidnon story specifically mentions a "high *datu*" named Pabulusen who ruled over "all the inland Bukidnon on the central plain of Bukidnon province, in the upper Pulangi River valley, and in the western tributaries of the lower and middle Agusan River" during the time when two Bukidnon *datus* — Kumbalan and Tawaga — were retreating to the interior from Hispanic influence along the coast. See, Biernatzki, "Bukidnon Datuship," 22.

13 See the appendix to Clotet's letter of 11 May 1889, as described by Lynch in "The Bukidnon of North-Central Mindanao in 1889," 473.

14 Unabia, "The Bukidnon Oral Traditions". *Datu* Sangkuan, one of Unabia's informants, spoke of a "Masikampu" as the highest *datu* whose symbol of power was a *giling* or a stick with inscriptions on it. Some of Clotet's informants almost 90 years earlier referred to a "Masalicampo". See, Lynch, "The Bukidnon of North-Central Mindanao in 1889," 472-73.

15 Clotet, in Lynch, "The Bukidnon of North-Central Mindanao in 1889," 473.

16 Cole, *The Bukidnon of Mindanao,* 18, 79-80. Biernatzki, "Bukidnon Datuship," 15-16, 19.

17 Information on the *tulugan* is from Gervacio Libertad, interview, Malaybalay, Bukidnon, 18 May 1977; and Vincent G. Cullen, S.J., personal communication, 16 September 1979. Libertad, a former *datu,* insisted that there were no higher *datus* than *tulugan datus* in 1900 when he was born. The "datto superiors" mentioned by Clotet appear to have been the same as these *tulugan datus.* See, Lynch, "The Bukidnon of North-Central Mindanao in 1889," 478. Concerning the number of people living in these *tulugan* clusters, Libertad recalls about 36 to 40 families in one at the turn of the century. In his account of the "Talaandig" people (i.e., Bukidnons living in the high country between Mt. Kitanglad and Mt. Kalatungan to its south), *Datu* Kinulintang (Anastacio Saway) counts ten *tulugan datus.* See, the "Map of the Early 'Tulugan' (districts) of the Talaandigs according to the Historical Account of A. Saway," in Unabia, "The Bukidnon Oral Traditions". Cole commented that "it is claimed that in former times each district had a petty ruler or *dato* who lived in a large house raised high on stilts. Such dwellings did not exist in 1910 . . ." *The Bukidnon of Mindanao,* 18.

18 Cole, *The Bukidnon of Mindanao,* 79; Biernatzki, "Bukidnon Datuship," 43-44.

19 Biernatzki, "Bukidnon Datuship," 29-37; Gervacio Libertad, interview, Malaybalay, Bukidnon, 18 and 19 May 1977; Unabia, "The Bukidnon Oral Traditions"; Cole, *The Bukidnon of Mindanao,* 79-88.

20 Clotet, in Lynch, "The Bukidnon of North-Central Mindanao in 1889," 476-77; Cavada, *Historia geográfica,* 2:201.

21 Dean C. Worcester, "The Non-Christian Tribes of the Philippine Islands and What the United States Has Done for Them" (manuscript, Worcester's Philippine Collection, Documents and Papers), 4:40, 36. Cavada, *Historia geográfica,* 2:351, estimates that there were 10,039 cattle in Misamis Province in 1870. An indication that most of these were grazed up on the plateau is provided by Colonel H.R. Andreas who discovered "tens of thousands of cattle" there (south to Dalwangan) in 1900-1901. Andreas, "Harking Back," *American Oldtimer* 2 (November 1934), 24.

22 Clotet, in Lynch, "The Bukidnon of North-Central Mindanao in 1889," 474.

23 It is not clear exactly when the religious orders began to have an impact on Bukidnon society. Austin Dowd, S.J., states that the Recollects came to Bukidnon in 1867. ("Questionnaire of the History of San Isidro Church, Malaybalay," 7 April 1938, Ateneo de Manila University, Jesuit Archives, 8:10, Sevilla, Bukidnon Mission, 1890-1899.) In the town of Impasugong today there is a "very large bronze church bell . . . [which] gives the date 1880 — Sumilao, and the Patron del Pilar", suggesting that Sumilao was at least a *visita* for the Jesuits from the coast by that time. Vincent G. Cullen, S.J., letter to the author, 2 October 1978. It is this author's belief that the Jesuits became especially active in visiting settlements on the plateau after they set up a mission at Tagoloan in 1888.

24 *Catalogus Provinciae Aragoniae Societatis Jesu* (Manila: IHS Matriti, 1859-1920). The Sumilao baptismal books begin in 1890. The Linabo mission was absorbed into Sumilao in 1896-1899. It is important to note that this Linabo mission was officially called Sevilla at first. But Sevilla, the Spanish name for Mailag, proved too small a settlement for the Jesuits, who thus located in Linabo instead. See, "The Society of Jesus in the Philippines," *El Archipielago Filipino* (Washington: GPO, 1900), 1:128.

25 Cole, *The Bukidnon of Mindanao,* 36; *Cartas de los Padres de la Compañía de Jesus de la Mision de Filipinas* (Manila: Imprenta y Litografia de M. Perez, Hijo, 1892), 9:677.

26 Frederick Henfling, S.J., "A Short History of the Parish of Sumilao, Bukidnon," 28 June 1938, Ateneo de Manila University, Jesuit Archives, 8:15. The number 4,992 which is based upon the Sumilao parish records begun in 1890 probably does not include baptisms in the Linabo (Sevilla) mission before it was absorbed into Sumilao in 1896. This would explain Henfling's remark later in the same letter, that "50 years ago the Priests from the Jasa-an

parish often visited the Province of Bukidnon and during their visits they baptized almost 10,000".

27 Cole, *The Bukidnon of Mindanao,* 6, 35-36.

28 Gervacio Libertad, interview, Malaybalay, Bukidnon, 14 May 1977, and (for Tankulan) Vincente G. Cullen, personal communication, 16 September 1979.

29 P. Pablo Pastells, S.J., "Informe sobre la Isla de Mindanao presentado al su Exlmo. Gobernador Gral. de las Islas Filipinas, D. Valeriano Weyler, por el R.R. Superior de la Misión de la Companía de Jesus," 15 August 1888, Ateneo de Manila University, Jesuit Archives, 7; Secretary of the Governor-General to the Superior, S.J., 4 October 1889, Ateneo de Manila University, Jesuit Archives, 8:9; Governor-General to the Superior, S.J., 20 August 1894, Ateneo de Manila University, Jesuit Archives, 8:9; and Thomas B. Cannon, S.J., "History of the Jesuits in the Philippines," *Woodstock Letters* (Woodstock, Maryland: Woodstock College Press, 1872-1951), 66:145-46.

30 Sumilao, the only parish on the plateau in 1898, recorded 501 baptisms in 1898. That number dropped to 65 in 1899 and to one in 1901, before rising to 393 in 1902, the year the Tagoloan residence was re-established. Frederick Henfling, S.J., "A Short History of the Parish of Sumilao, Bukidnon," 28 June 1938, Ateneo de Manila University, Jesuit Archives, 8:15. In the *Catalogus Provinciae Aragoniae Societatis Jesu,* Sumilao is mentioned as a residence from 1890 to 1899, but then not again until 1908.

31 Andreas, "Harking Back," *American Oldtimer* 2 (December 1934), 19-20.

32 *Ibid.*

33 E.F. Taggart to the Adjutant-General, Provisional District of Mindanao and Jolo, 2 March 1901, U.S. War Department, *Annual Reports of the War Department, Fiscal Year Ended June 30, 1901* (Washington: GPO, 1901), 1:6:315.

34 William E. Birkhimer to the Adjutant-General, Department of Mindanao and Jolo, 29 December 1900, National Archives and Records Service (hereafter, NARS), Washington, D.C., RG 395, No. 2105, Department of Mindanao and Jolo, General Correspondence, 1900-1905, Box 4, document 2063.

35 "List of Insurgents Surrendered," NARS, RG 395, No. 2105, Box 6, document 3973.

36 Taggart, 2 March 1901, War Department, *Annual Reports,* 1:6:312.

37 Frederick Lewis, "Report of the Lieutenant-Governor of the Sub-Province of Bukidnon," 1908, NARS, RG 350, Bureau of Insular Affairs, Philippine Commission Manuscript Reports, 1908, 1:796.

38 Taggart, 2 March 1901, War Department, *Annual Reports,* 1:6:315.

39 *Ibid.*

40 Dean Conant Worcester, "Report of the Secretary of the Interior,"in U.S., Philippine Commission, *Report of the Philippine Commission to the Secretary of War for the Year ended June 30, 1910* (Washington, D.C.: GPO, 1911), 71.

41 25 November 1904 entry, Forbes Journal, 1:108, Harvard University, Houghton Library, W. Cameron Forbes MSS.

42 W.S. Scott, "Report of the District Director, Fifth District, Bureau of Constabulary," 1 August 1906, in U.S., War Department, Bureau of Insular Affairs, *Seventh Annual Report of the Philippine Commission, 1906* (Washington: GPO, 1907), 307.

43 Frederick Lewis, "Report of the Lieutenant-Governor," NARS, RG 350, Philippine Commission Manuscript Reports, 1908, 1:796-98.

44 *Ibid.*

45 The Case of Florencio Racines, No. 24, Proceedings of the Justice of the Peace Court, Malaybalay, Bukidnon, Agusan, January 1913. This case was later dismissed because "the house in which Ramon Pitoy and Toto Pitoy were held in slavery by defendant is and was within the jurisdiction of the Province of Misamis to which Act No. 2071 [making slavery illegal in non-Christian provinces] is not applicable". Case No. 2119, Proceedings of the Court of First Instance for Misamis, 19 July 1913.

46 Worcester expressed his admiration for Brooke in his letter to Frank Carpenter, 7 August 1914, Michigan Historical Collections, Worcester Papers, Box 1, folder marked "Correspondence, July-December, 1914".

47 Worcester's initiative in cutting Bukidnon out of Misamis and putting it under the jurisdiction of an American appointee is discussed by W. Cameron Forbes in his Journal, 3:446, footnote 145.

48 Dean C. Worcester, "Memorandum Relative to Men and Conditions in the Special Government Provinces, for the Governor-General," n.d., Worcester's Philippine Collection, Documents and Papers, 4:41.

49 Albino Pensahan, interviews, Malaybalay, Bukidnon, 8 and 15 January 1977. It should be noted that Pensahan harbours no grudge against Fortich, for had Fortich's soldiers not uprooted him and his family, "then we would not be educated".

50 Gervacio Libertad, interview, Malaybalay, Bukidnon, 14 May 1977. It is not suggested here that all Bukidnons from the upper Tagoloan settled in Malaybalay municipality or that other Bukidnons settled only in a predetermined location, but rather that they tended to move from certain settlements to certain other settlements.

51 Cole, *The Bukidnon of Mindanao,* 34.

52 Frederick Johnson, "Report of the Governor of Agusan," 30 June 1909, NARS, RG 350, Philippine Commission Manuscript Reports, 1909, Vol. 2.

53 John R. White, "Report of the Governor of Agusan," 8 August 1911, NARS, RG 350, Philippine Commission Manuscript Reports, 1911, Vol. 2.

54 The Docket for the Justice of the Peace Court, Malaybalay, lists four murder or manslaughter cases for the years 1907-1909 (two convictions, one dismissal, one unknown); eight murder or manslaughter cases for the years 1910-1912 (six convictions, two unknown); and three murder or manslaughter cases for the years 1913-1916 (all convictions). In all of these cases the charges were brought against either Manobos or Bukidnons. In this same decade there were also two manslaughter cases brought against lowlanders, but there were no murder cases in which a lowlander was charged.

55 For extensive documentation on this incident, see, Worcester's Philippine Collection, Documents and Papers, 21:2.

56 Cole, *The Bukidnon of Mindanao,* 118.

57 Manuel Fortich reported that in April 1910 there was "a fanatical outbreak" in Sumilao in which "more than a hundred families went to the Kitanglad Mountain to worship the so-called 'bailan'". "Annual Report of the Lieutenant-Governor, Sub-Province of Bukidnon," NARS, RG 350, Philippine Commission Manuscript Reports, 1910, Vol. 1.

58 Cole, *The Bukidnon of Mindanao,* 6.

59 Frederick Johnson, "Report of the Governor of Agusan," 30 June 1909, NARS, RG 350, Philippine Commission Manuscript Reports, 1909, Vol. 2.

60 The case of Jacinto Idoria (a Bukidnon), in which the girl he was accused of raping (Marqueza Dialong, another Bukidnon) reported her situation to Fortich, is perhaps the best example. Criminal Case No. 2510, Proceedings of the Court of First Instance for the Province of Bukidnon, 23 September 1914.

61 Frederick Johnson, "Annual Report of the Governor of Agusan," NARS, RG 350, Philippine Commission Manuscript Reports, 1910, Vol. 1; and Dean Worcester, "The Non-Christian Tribes of the Philippine Islands," 38.

62 Manuel Fortich, "Annual Report of the Governor of Bukidnon," 1 January 1916, NARS, RG 350, Philippine Commission Manuscript Reports, 1915.

63 Juanito Junlaan, interview, Malaybalay, Bukidnon, 29 January 1977. Junlaan was manager of the government exchange in Impasugong.

64 Antonio Rubin, "Annual Report, Office of the Provincial Governor, Bukidnon," 31 December 1933, Michigan Historical Collections, Joseph Ralston Hayden Papers, Box 27, folder 27.

65 Frederick Lewis, "Report of the Lieutenant-Governor," NARS, RG 350,

Philippine Commission Manuscript Reports, 1908, 1:817-18.

66 Manuel Fortich, "Annual Report of Bukidnon Sub-Province," 15 July 1911, NARS, RG 350, Philippine Commission Manuscript Reports, 1911, Vol. 2. The agricultural high school was later moved to Managok.

67 Manuel Fortich, "Annual Report of the Governor of Bukidnon," 1 January 1916, NARS, RG 350, Philippine Commission Manuscript Reports, 1915.

68 Fortunato Carbajal, interview, Malaybalay, 29 December 1976; Pacifico Ramos, interview, Malaybalay, 14 October 1976; Marcela Abello Cudal, interview, Malaybalay.

69 Cesar Fortich, interview, Cagayan de Oro, Misamis Oriental, 26 March 1977; Remigio Casinabe, interview, Kalasungay, Bukidnon, 20 March 1977; and Marcela Abello Cudal, interviews, Malaybalay, 23 November 1976 and 11 January 1977.

70 Bureau of Education, "Local Geographical and Historical Notes [on Agusan, including the sub-provinces of Butuan and Bukidnon]," a circular, n.d. (received by the Bureau of Insular Affairs, 15 September 1914), NARS, RG 350, Bureau of Insular Affairs Document 16898-8.

71 For 1915, *ibid.* For 1918, P.J. Wester, "Mindanao and the Sulu Archipelago: Their Natural Resources and opportunities for development," in Government of the Philippine Islands, Department of Agriculture and Natural Resources, Bureau of Agriculture, *Bulletin* 38 (Manila: Bureau of Printing, 1922). For 1933, Antonio Rubin, "Annual Report," 31 December 1933, Michigan Historical Collections, Hayden Papers, Box 27, folder 27.

72 These production and export figures are taken from: Frederick Johnson, "Annual Report of the Governor of Agusan," NARS, RG 350, Philippine Commission Manuscript Reports, 1910, Vol. 1; Manuel Fortich, "Annual Report of Bukidnon Sub-Province," 15 July 1911, NARS, RG 350, Philippine Commission Manuscript Reports, 1911, Vol. 2; Manuel Fortich, "Annual Report for the Sub-Province of Bukidnon," 31 May 1913, NARS, RG 350, Philippine Commission Manuscript Reports, 1913, Vol. 1, and Census Office, *Census of the Philippine Islands: Taken Under the Direction of the Philippine Legislature in the Year 1918* (Manila: Bureau of Printing, 1920-1921), 3:338-39, 348-49, 352, 374-75, 380-81.

73 The family of Juan Paresco Melendez was one of the early Bukidnon families to begin farming the fertile plateau lands near Managok, but they also maintained close ties to their ancestral lands near the headwaters of the Tagoloan. Pedro Melendez, interview, Malaybalay, 4 January 1977.

74 Frederick Lewis, "Report of the Lt. Governor," 1909; Frederick Johnson, "Annual Report," 1909; and Manuel Fortich, "Annual Report," 1911, Philippine Commission Manuscript Reports, NARS, RG 350. In 1933, when "production was more than that of last year, although far less than that of 1931," 2,150 *cavans* of rice were imported. Antonio Rubin, "Annual Report," 19, 24.

75 *Census Year 1918,* 3:338-39, 236-37, 51, 348. In Table No. 17, "Comparative table of the cultivation and production of rice in 1918 and 1903, by provinces and subprovinces," the figure of 1,091 hectares in column 1 is a misprint and should read 1,991.

76 P.J. Wester, "Bukidnon: Its Natural Resources and Opportunities for Development," *The Philippine Agricultural Review* 13 (1920), 241.

77 *Census Year 1918,* 3:58.

78 Felicisimo S. Santiago, Registrar of Deeds for Bukidnon, interview, Malaybalay, 11 May 1977.

79 *Census Year 1918,* 3:202-03.

80 Felicisimo S. Santiago, Registrar of Deeds for Bukidnon, interview, Malaybalay, 11 May 1977; and Timoteo Quimpo, "111,742.88 Hectares for You," in, Cris S. Turrecha, ed., *Bukidnon Agricultural, Commercial and Industrial Carnival and Exposition* (Malaybalay, Bukidnon: The Lions Club of Bukidnon, 1951), 39-40.

81 Fortunato Moreno, interview, Kalasungay, 17 April 1977. Moreno, a Bukidnon farmer in Kalasungay, confirmed that it was (and to some extent still is) common practice for Bukidnons to practise slash-and-burn agriculture in their hillside plots while using a plough for their plateau land, and to use both methods at the same time.

82 Frank Carpenter to Worcester, 13 May 1914, Michigan Historical Collections, Worcester Papers, Box 1, "Correspondence, Jan.-June, 1914"; and Worcester to Carpenter, 7 August 1914, Michigan Historical Collections, Worcester Papers, Box 1, "Correspondence, July-Dec., 1914".

83 Information on PPC sub-leases from the Navy and the National Development Company is from Cesar Fortich, interview, Cagayan de Oro, 17 November 1976, and Cesar and Manuel Fortich, Jr., interview, Cagayan de Oro, 26 March 1977.

84 The author has done a more detailed analysis of cattle-ranching and cowboy culture in Bukidnon in his forthcoming article, "Americans, Cowboys and Cattlemen on the Mindanao Frontier".

85 Manuel Fortich, "Annual Report," Philippine Commission Manuscript Reports, 1911, Vol. 2, NARS.

86 Estimates on the sizes of prewar herds vary greatly. I have chosen as a rule the more conservative estimates, in interviews with Manuel Fortich, Jr., Cagayan de Oro, 13 March 1977; Cesar Fortich, Cagayan de Oro, 26 March 1977; and Carlos and Remedios Fortich, Dabongdabong, Bukidnon, 18 February 1977.

87 Manuel Fortich, Jr., interview, Cagayan de Oro, 12 May 1977.

88 Worcester to the Wood-Forbes Mission, 4 August 1921, Michigan Historical Collections, Worcester Papers, Box 1, "Papers, 1921-1922, Concerning Wood-Forbes Mission".

89 José Sanvictores, interview, Quezon City, 17 June 1977. Sanvictores was manager of the Roces ranch in the 1920s.

90 *1975 Integrated Census Bukidnon,* 1. It should be noted that the road between Cagayan de Oro and Malaybalay had been completed before the 1920s except for a number of bridges the absence of which restricted automobile traffic between these towns.

91 Benjamin Tabios, interview, Manila, 22 June 1977.

92 Dolores Suclatan Tan Nery, interview, Malaybalay, 18 May 1977.

93 Cesar and Manuel Fortich, Jr., interview, Cagayan de Oro, 26 March 1977.

94 This information is based on interviews with many migrant families including those of Benjamin and Guillermo Tabios, Julian Rubio, Edilberto Mamawag, Bartolome and Adoracion Rubin Mendoza, Esteban Sanchez, and Santos Cudal.

95 Joseph Lucas, S.J., to Willmann, 4 May 1934, Ateneo de Manila University, Jesuit Archives, 8:10.

96 Antonio Rubin, "Annual Report," 31 December 1933.

97 Casiano Litanon, interview, Malaybalay, 27-29 December 1976.

98 This information is based on extensive data collected in interviews with Bukidnons in Malaybalay, including the following: Pedro Melendez, Fortunato Carbajal, Casiano Litanon, Marcus Reciña and Catalino Damasco.

99 Pacita MacFarlane Cid, interview, Cagayan de Oro, 12 May 1977.

100 Austin Dowd, S.J., "Questionnaire of the History of San Isidro Church, Malaybalay," 7 April 1938, Jesuit Archives, 8:10.

101 Joseph Lucas, S.J., to Willmann, 4 May 1934, Jesuit Archives, 8:10.

102 This information is based on data collected in interviews with Bukidnons in Kalasungay, including the following: Remigio Casinabe, Fortunato Moreno, Pedro Moreno, Roque Sario, German Berial, Florencia Moreno and Pio Binayao.

103 This information is based on data collected in interviews with Bukidnons in Sumilao and in interior settlements including Silae, Calabugao and Miarayon, Bukidnon.

104 Lucas to Willmann, 4 May 1934, Jesuit Archives, 8:10. Many Bukidnons continue even now to hold on to some animistic religious practices. In the words of one Jesuit today, "the early priests may have tried to stop it [animistic religion] or substitute something else for it, but in my experience

it merely became more private — marriages, healing, rites of the dead, while the new thing [Catholicism] was the more public practice". Vincent G. Cullen, personal communication, 16 September 1979.

105 Fortich selected certain *datus* as his *liders,* and these often became municipal presidents.

106 It should be noted that PANAMIN has recently been very active in, among other things, heightening awareness of traditional Bukidnon culture.

107 *1975 Integrated Census . . . Bukidnon,* 1.

The Defiant and the Compliant: The Datus of Magindanao under Colonial Rule

JEREMY BECKETT

The local elite, whether indigenous or creole, is a problematic element in any colonial system. To the extent that it controls the lower orders it may be either an ally of the regime or its enemy. And to the extent that it exploits them it may be either a partner or a competitor. Whichever course it follows there are dangers. If it is defiant it risks destruction, and at very least jeopardizes the protection given by its masters. If it is compliant it may jeopardize its legitimacy among the common folk. Either way it risks displacement by an alternative elite, more responsive to the situation. Elite groups and families, then, are sensitive indicators of changing conditions; and their fluctuating fortunes deserve close attention.

The Philippines is a particularly interesting case in this respect because, despite four changes of regime in the 50 years between 1898 and 1948, its elite remained substantially intact. The degree of continuity among the *principalia* from the conquest to the early 19th century is hard to establish, but it seems that thereafter the growth of export industries caused a good deal of upward and downward mobility.[1] In Pampanga, for example, Chinese mestizos who had prospered in the burgeoning sugar industry either displaced or married into the old landed elite.[2] What Owen has called the super-*principalia* attained in Bikol, as in Pampanga, a level of affluence far greater than their predecessors had enjoyed.[3] The Revolution, the American take-over, the explosion of public education, even the Japanese occupation, seem by comparison to have caused little mobility. Individuals rose and fell, but the family coalitions that dominated the early years of the Republic were in many cases the same that had composed the elite of the late Spanish period. The 1950s and 1960s saw a good deal of mobility, with the growth of a national elite focused on Manila, and the increasingly turbulent and costly electoral politics.[4] However, these developments lie outside the scope of the present study.

The Muslim areas of the south had a different history. Maintaining a fierce resistance, they managed to remain outside the Spanish pale until the second half of the 19th century. Even by 1898 the ordinary folk were barely integrated with the rest of Philippine society, but certain of their *datus* had found a foothold in the colonial order. By the end of the American period these same *datus* had come to occupy much the same position as the big landlords of Luzon and the Visayas, despite continuing cultural differences.

Islam and Malay versions of Islamic political institutions were established in the south by the time the Spaniards came. Majul has argued that these provided the framework for resistance on a scale far greater than non-Muslim Filipinos could achieve.[5] Exploiting their position on the peripheries of several colonial domains, the so-called Moros were able to carry on a profitable commerce with European and Chinese merchants. This they augmented by yearly raids on Spanish-occupied territory. Magindanao and Sulu became centres of sufficient importance to support sultanates with more than a semblance of centralization and hierarchy.[6]

As the 19th century wore on, Spain's naval blockade deprived the sultans of their economic support; then, in the second half, she began undermining their authority through a series of military and diplomatic campaigns. By 1898 they were effectively neutralized, but this did not mean the end of indigenous leadership. The sultanates had always been segmentary states, in which a good deal of the power remained with local *datus*.[7] These now had to choose between defiance and compliance, with the latter proving the wiser course in the long run.

The Spanish withdrawal and the subsequent American take-over set off a further period of instability, but with much the same outcome. The *datus* who came through these upheavals with their followings intact became key elements in the *pax Americana,* and therefore were well placed to reconstitute their hegemony, in local government and in the expanding economy. When independence offered further opportunities for aggrandizement, they were again well placed to take advantage.

An elaborate ideology of rank, grounded in Islamic belief, had supported political authority, and the historical record suggests that the power holders and leaders usually were of the nobility, until the Spanish invasion. The upheavals of the late Spanish period broke the connection, however, leaving the new generation of *datus* to command recognition on pragmatic grounds such as the use of force and access to the colonial authorities. With the years certain *datu* lines acquired a born-to-rule reputation, but still without the old trappings of rank and title. The literature on the Christian Philippines is remarkably vague on the subject of political legitimacy and ideology, but there would appear to be little more than personalistic ties of the patron–client type.[8] The new Magindanao *datus,* however, were in some sense heirs to the old; moreover they were Muslims who stood between their people and alien domination.

Documents and Oral Sources

The sources on Cotabato history are extensive.[9] Apart from the Spaniards, who assiduously gathered intelligence from the late 16th century, the British and Dutch had a passing interest in Magindanao and sent home occasional reports. A good deal of this material was published, either at the time or subsequently, though there is no telling what remains undiscovered in the archives. At the beginning of the American period, Najeeb Saleeby produced his *Studies in Moro History, Law and Religion,* based on an examination of Magindanao manuscripts; but thereafter published sources yield little of consequence beside statistical data and short routine reports.[10] There is more to be got from the papers of General Wood and Joseph Hayden, but Cotabato engaged their interest less than Sulu or Lanao, perhaps because it was the most peaceful of the Moro provinces.[11]

Karl Pelzer, the geographer, carried out a study of Christian settlement in Cotabato in 1940,[12] and Chester Hunt, a sociologist, worked in Cotabato City in 1953.[13] Otherwise there was little academic interest until the end of the 1960s when there was a sudden, though unco-ordinated, burst of activity. Majul's *Muslims in the Philippines,* though only published in 1973, was the fruit of many years of research.[14] Pressing its enquiry back to the pre-Spanish period, it traced the history of the Magindanao and Sulu sultanates through to their collapse in the mid-19th century. Meanwhile, Reynaldo Ileto had completed a study of the final phase of Magindanao resistance to Spain during the second half of the 19th century.[15] A little earlier, in 1968, Peter Gowing completed a study of the American administration of the "Moro Provinces" up to 1920;[16] and a little later Ralph Thomas carried the story through to 1946 focusing on the theme of national integration.[17] At about the same time Samuel Tan was exploring the particular theme of Muslim armed resistance between 1900 and 1941.[18]

The writer's interest in the Magindanao stems from a short reconnaissance in 1969. It was intended that the six months' anthropological field work carried out in 1971 would be the first of several such periods. In the event, only two short visits have been possible since. The situation and the culture demanded a historical orientation: in 1971 the Magindanao were in the throes of a profound upheaval; however, this was but the latest of a series of upheavals, going back more than a century. Informants were very much aware of these changes and readily retailed stories of *datus* such as Ali and Utu who had died long before they were born. Members of the old nobility could discuss dynastic disputes of the 1830s and kept genealogies going back to the 16th century. This traditionalism seemed to mitigate the realities of change.

It soon became clear that an understanding of the contemporary situation, and of the people's perception of it, could only be achieved through an investigation of the historical record. This paper is an outcome of these investigations, a historical account informed by some first hand acquaintance with the Magindanao and their oral traditions. It owes much to the work of the professional historians whose names have been cited already, but is written from a somewhat different perspective. Excellent as these studies are, they are not well co-ordinated. For example, Ileto's impressive grasp of Magindanao social structure is not shared by those who cover the later period, whose interest is, in any case, in colonial policy rather than indigenous elites. Again, it is difficult to link the last phase of the Spanish period, as described by Ileto, with the first phase of the American period as described by Gowing, who completed his work about the time Ileto was beginning. Only Tan had the chance to refer to all the other writers. As a result, the element of continuity is muted. To take just one example, one would not know that the *Datu* Ayunan who figures largely in Ileto's narrative was the founder of the Sinsuat "clan" that has played a major role in provincial affairs ever since. This essay, then, attempts an overview of the colonial period from the vantage point of contemporary Cotabato.

The Region

The region known to the Spaniards and the Americans as Cotabato occupies almost the whole of southwestern Mindanao. As defined by the latter, it covered an area of some 2,491,580 hectares of which approximately a quarter was level valley land, ascending almost imperceptibly to an elevation of 35 metres some 80 kilometres inland; a half undulating plateau lands at an average elevation of about 300 metres, mostly forest; and a quarter mountainous, covered with heavy stands of virgin forest. The valley is that of the Pulangi or Rio Grande, which almost bisects the region, separating the coastal Cordillera or Tiruray Highlands from the Central Mindanao Highlands. Wernstedt and Spencer describe it as follows:

> This extensive, low-lying, swampy plain . . . includes a lowland area of well over 1,000 square miles. Recent uplift across the mouth of the river, which has formed the low Cotabato and Timaco hills, has resulted in the impounding of river waters and the creation of two large swamp areas, the Libungan Marsh and the Liguasan Swamp. Together these two swamps cover a combined area of 450 square miles during normal water levels; however, the swamplands expand well beyond these limits when heavy seasonal rains and river floods inundate additional areas of the valley floor, and indeed, during heavy rains, all of the lowland downstream from Lake Buluan looks like a vast lake from the air.[19]

This valley is the homeland of the Magindanao ethno-linguistic group, the name referring, appropriately, to its tendency to flood. At various times in the past, small numbers have settled along the coast or pressed on into the Koronadal valley, but until the recent build-up of population through immigration they did not attempt to occupy the uplands. These were populated by Muslim Iranun and Maranao in the north, and by pagan groups such as the Tiruray, Manobo and Bila'an in the coastal and central parts.

The indigenous population was for the most part agricultural, but there was no shortage of land until large-scale immigration began towards the middle of the 20th century. When the Americans conducted the first census in 1903, they reported a total of 125,875, of which 113,875 were Muslims and the balance pagan.[20] This was a sparse population for such a vast region, and inevitably posed the possibility of immigration from the overcrowded islands, once peace and order could be established. Christian immigrants and their descendants now heavily outnumber the indigenous peoples, but at the last American census, conducted in 1940, Muslims numbered 162,996 out of a total of 298,935, and pagans 70,493.[21] Cotabato City remains the only settlement of any size, with a population of some 60,000. However, it amounted to only a few hundreds at the beginning of the century and had reached only 10,000 by the end of the American period.

Magindanao Political Organization

Although the Sultans of Magindanao have pride of place in the historical record, they were not the only title-holders in the valley. As Ileto notes, the upper valley

Rajahs of Buayan were probably of more consequence when the Spaniards first visited in the late 16th century; and even at its height Magindanao did not claim sovereignty over them.[22] As it slid into decline through the 18th century, several of the Rajahs assumed the title of sultan, as though to assert equality.

The notion of sultanate is, in any case, an inadequate tool for understanding Magindanao political organization, referring as it does to form rather than reality. The centralization it suggests could scarcely be realized among a homesteading population, widely dispersed over difficult terrain, with primitive communications.[23] While a sultan might have sanctity, magical powers and exalted rank, he

Southwestern Mindanao Region

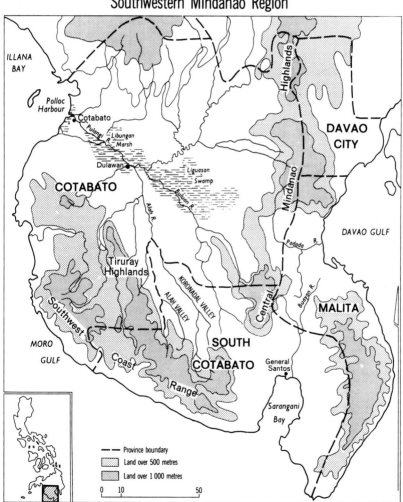

was just another *datu* when it came to politics. The basic building blocks of the system were the local *datus,* autonomous in theory, but often dependent on others for access to resources such as salt and iron, and intermittently articulated into wider alliances for attack or defence.

The primary meaning of *datu* is ruler, a concept standing opposed to that of *lukas,* or elder who merely reflected the will of his group. The *datu* represented the centralizing principle in a volatile society in which centrifugal forces were strong. In his struggle to maintain his following, against disintegration on the one hand, and against predatory *datus* on the other, his personal attributes were recognized to be critical, above all his ability to command fear and respect. Thus elevated, personal power could never be contained by notions of order or legitimacy; to a degree power became its own legitimation. If a *datu* were strong enough to enforce folk-Islamic or *adat* law, he was also strong enough to transgress it. If he could command the goods of his followers, he could refuse to redistribute them, as a kind *datu* was supposed to do. The followers might be entitled to leave him, but the likelihood of their doing so was in inverse proportion to the fear in which they held him. Thus, finally, a *datu* was what a *datu* did.

The size of a *datu*'s following depended on his personal qualities, combined with the control of some economic resource. The power of the upper valley *datus* seems to have been based on the production of rice with slave labour, the collection of dues from Muslim peasants and the taking of tribute from upland pagans. As one proceeded downriver, however, the exploitation of trade became increasingly important, with *datus* controlling strategic points from which they could exact tolls. The Sultans of Magindanao derived their unusual importance from their control of the region's principal entrepôt, just inside the northern mouth of the river. The same location served as the rallying point for the large fleets that raided the Spanish Philippines, year after year, under the Sultan's aegis.[24] Ileto shows how Magindanao declined with the reduction in raiding and trading, while the upper valley prospered on the traffic in slaves taken from the pagan groups. It is difficult to assess the size of a *datu*'s following, which no doubt varied a good deal; in the 1870s two upper valley *datus,* Utu of Buayan and the Sultan of Kabuntalan, were each reported to have several thousand slaves, apart from other followers.[25] However, as *Datu* Piang explained in an interview early in the American period, such estimates varied according to whether one included the followers of lesser *datus* who attached themselves to the more important ones.[26]

At one level one could regard the Magindanao as living in a state of perfect political competition for followers, slaves and resources. And to judge by the accounts of petty feuding and confrontation, this was indeed a tendency within the system; but it was mitigated by certain ideological principles. The secondary meaning of *datu* was one entitled to rule on account of his descent from *datus.* Not all such *datus* would in fact rule, but their *maratabat* or honour gave them something to live up to.[27] Thus certain ruling lines were associated with a particular place, called *ingod,* a title or *grar,* and servile groups called *ndatuan.*[28] Commoner groups might also be attached to them, either through a traditional agreement or as cadet lines of the one stock.

In the absence of a rule of primogeniture, the succession to a title was a matter for competition. No doubt the *datu* qualities of the claimants, who might be numerous given the prevalence of polygyny, were a major consideration. But here again ideological principles reduced the element of conflict. By taking into account the status of the mother as well as the father, it was possible to make fine distinctions of *maratabat.*

The ranking system is complex, and a full treatment must await another article; but it can be summarized by reference to the charter legend of *Sarip* Kabongsoan. The *Sarip,* which is the local form of the Arabic *sharif,* was the son of an Arab who had married the Sultan of Johore's daughter. Chance brought Kabongsoan to the mouth of the Rio Grande, where he began preaching Islam. He took wives from his converts, thus establishing a local stock that could claim descent from the Prophet Muhammad. The Sultans of Magindanao claimed descent from a son of Kabongsoan, the Rajahs of Buayan from a daughter, and most of the other Magindanao *datus* claimed membership of one or other of these stocks, and in some instances both. The Maranao *datus* also claim descent from the *Sarip,* while more elaborate versions of the legend assert a common origin for all the *datus* of Brunei, Sulu and Mindanao. Their relative nobility was assessed in terms of the number of links they could trace with the *Sarip,* and any *datu* line of consequence kept a written genealogy or *tarsila* indicating these links.[29] The Sultans of Magindanao seem to have been credited with the purest breeding, and reference is made to their light complexions and aquiline features as evidence of their Arab ancestry.

The legend not only provides a charter for the ranking system, and so of political authority; it also presents a model of political articulation through the transmission of nobility in marriage. It describes how a highborn stranger marries the daughter of a local chief, founding a line that is far superior in *maratabat* to any of the others, and so entitled to rule. The wife's kin gain from this arrangement a more prestigious line of rulers and connection with the nobility elsewhere. According to the *tarsila,* young *datus* often followed this strategy, probably after failing to gain the family title. The legend also describes Kabongsoan bestowing his daughter on a Rajah of Buayan, ennobling his descendants, though in a lesser degree since women transmitted less nobility than men. As Mastura has shown, marriages were regularly arranged in the process of alliance formation.[30]

Such marriages were governed by a complex calculus, for it was on such occasions that rival parties brought their respective claims to nobility into the open. The degree of nobility conferred by the bride, relative to that of the husband, determined the size of the bride price but also the importance of the alliance. Basic to the system was the principle of hypergamy, according to which a woman might marry a man of equal or higher, but not inferior rank. A man, on the other hand, might marry beneath him; indeed an important *datu* had wives of every degree, including concubines who were slaves. The sons of these unions were to be called *datu,* but they were not all of equal standing, and probably only a few would be entitled to claim the succession. In the same way, the rank of daughters varied, which was an advantage to their father since he could always find one to bestow on an ally, however lowborn. Because of her connection with himself he could claim a high bride price, but because of her mother's status he could claim she was not marrying beneath her.

The centralizing tendencies displayed by Magindanao society at certain points in its history are to be understood in terms of an interplay between economic and political factors on the one hand, and ideology on the other. It would seem that when material conditions became favourable, the hierarchical forms that came with Islam were there to give structure and legitimacy, lending themselves to elaboration as centralization continued. What would have happened without these forms is hard to say, but we can state that among the Maranao there was no tendency to centralization, although the forms were present, presumably because the material conditions were lacking in their landlocked situation.[31]

A reading of Magindanao history indicates that power and nobility tended to coincide. And while the system no doubt provided loopholes for *post hoc* ennoblement of the powerful, it nevertheless seems that society did focus on the sultanates of Magindanao, Buayan and, from the 18th century, Kabuntalan. At the same time, it is inconceivable that the highest-born *datu* was always the bravest; indeed the histories indicate that the titleholder was often either a child or an old man, leaving the real power in the hands of a close kinsman of lesser rank. The focus of political organization, then, was not the titleholder himself so much as the line to which he belonged.

The existence of a *datu* category had the effect of identifying those who were in reality powerless and dependent with the powerful. In the same way, commoners could identify with a line of *datus* by claiming descent from a cadet line that voluntarily "gave way" in the succession. For the lower orders the idiom was one of voluntary support. However, in assessing the factor of ideology, it must be remembered that those who were most exploited lived, or came from, outside the boundaries of Magindanao society. The followers of a forceful *datu,* even his slaves, might share in the plunder and captives taken from Christian settlements, or exact tribute from a group of pagans.[32]

The Datus Under Spain

Although Spain did not establish a presence in Cotabato until 1851, she had played a hand in Magindanao affairs from the outset. The sultanates were segmentary states, intermittently capable of uniting for offence or defence, but always liable to internal dissension. In conflict, factions readily accepted outside help, even from Holland and Spain.[33] The problem was, however, to prevent the allies from becoming masters, and it was just such a miscalculation that enabled the Spaniards to occupy the delta in 1861, without a shot being fired. Securing the upper valley was a less easy matter, requiring a series of campaigns over the next 25 years. Once again Spain exploited internal divisions, and as she demonstrated her superiority in the field more and more *datus* joined her camp. But when the last of her enemies had made his submission, she was left with allies whom she could scarcely control, and whose loyalty was very much in doubt. She had brought down the old political order, but a new style of *datu* had emerged in place of the old.

Since Ileto has described this period in rich detail, only a brief outline need be given here. Spain's first target was the Sultan of Magindanao. Having reduced him to penury by naval blockade, she set about determining the succession by exploiting dynastic rivalries. When the old Sultan, Kudarat II, died in 1857 — under suspicious circumstances, so it is said — Spain's nominee Makawa succeeded. Three years later he was forced to invite the Spanish into the delta to shore up his insecure position. In doing so he alienated what remained of his support, becoming largely dependent on the pension Spain allowed him. Spain may have intended to use the Sultan as an instrument of control, but she succeeded only in neutralizing him. He and his successors spent much of their time in the old tributary of Sibugay, in Zamboanga del Sur, avoiding involvement in the upheavals along the river.

Meanwhile, in the upper valley a powerful alliance was forming around Utu, highborn *datu* of the Rajah Buayan line. However, resistance to the Spaniards could only be sustained at the cost of severe strain: manpower losses were unprecedently heavy; pagan groups suffered repeated raids for slaves, to be traded for guns; ties of kinship and affinity were stretched to breaking point. Under such conditions an alliance could only be held together by terror. Seventy-seven years after his death, Utu remains vividly in the folk memory as a monster of cruelty, cunning and caprice.[34]

By 1888 Spain had broken the alliance, but did not attempt to remove Utu from his place in the upper valley. In 1890, however, he came downriver to spend his last years under Spanish protection. According to tradition, he woke one morning to find that his followers had all deserted during the night, seeking the protection of his onetime trusted servant, Piang.[35] According to tradition, the people were sickened with his cruelty, and finally angered at his refusal to open his granaries to them during a time of famine. *Datu* Piang is always described as "kind to the people", but he was no less ruthless in prosecuting independent-minded *datus,* displacing them or taking away their followers.[36] Though a Chinese mestizo with no claim to nobility, he replaced Utu as the most powerful *datu* in the upper valley, forming an alliance that included Utu's nephew and others of the Raja Buayan house.

Piang's alliance was not subjected to the strain of a war with Spain, however. Indeed, he declared himself her friend, and Saleeby supposed that his overthrow of Utu was effected with the approval of Spain. He certainly enriched himself by supplying food to the upriver garrison at Reina Regente, but also established useful ties with Chinese traders at the river mouth. Saleeby reported that "at the time of the Spanish evacuation he had become the richest Moro in Mindanao and the most influential chief of the island".[37]

Despite her superior firepower, Spain could scarcely have defeated Utu without Magindanao help. She needed not only additional manpower, but local knowledge, particularly of how to win over Utu's restive supporters. The Sultan and his kinsfolk either could not or would not intervene, but others came forward, most notably *Datu* Ayunan, whose career Ileto has traced in some detail.[38] Ayunan's origins are obscure, but he does not seem to have been of the high nobility. His base, a point of minor strategic importance some 12 miles upriver, became the front-line when the war with Utu began; but instead of fleeing he chose to stay, becoming the leader of a powerful alliance. He engineered a number of defections from Utu's ranks, and may have been behind the revolt of Piang, who had become his son-in-law. Spain viewed his aggrandizement with unease, and while conferring on him the title *gobernadorcillo,* took steps to curtail his influence once Utu had been defeated. He died in 1898, on the eve of the Spanish withdrawal, passing his title on to his brother Balabaran.

When the Spaniards withdrew at the beginning of 1899 they left Cotabato under a triumvirate, composed of *Datu* Piang, representing the Magindanao; Ramon Vilo, representing the 600 Christian Filipinos now living in the delta; and another, representing the Chinese trading community.[39] Within a few months the men of Piang and Ali had invaded the lower valley, seizing and later killing Vilo. The Chinese remained under Piang's protection, but the Filipinos were subject to various outrages and several *datus,* unfriendly to Piang, were forced to flee. Among these was Balabaran, which suggests that Piang had taken over what remained of his brother Ayunan's old alliance. In any case, when American troops arrived at the end of the year, the upriver *datus* promptly withdrew, offering their services to the new regime.

Although the Spaniards maintained sizeable garrisons on the coast and smaller establishments in the interior, they made little attempt to administer the population outside the small delta settlements at Tamontaca and Cotabato. Pursuing a "policy of attraction", they avoided interference in religious practices or the *datus'* rights over their followers. They formally abolished slavery, and a Jesuit establishment offered sanctuary to Utu's runaway slaves, but many *datus* still had theirs when the Americans arrived. In the lower valley even the highborn had dwindled into local dignitaries, and a number were seeking escape in opium and gambling. Political marriages were still contracted, but within a narrow span. In the hinterland, however, political alliances were still important, and reinforced by marriage, though the ranking system was already in disarray.

The Datus Under the United States

The Magindanao offered only one serious challenge to American rule, under the leadership of *Datu* Ali in 1903.[40] Ali was defeated and killed in the following year. Thereafter Cotabato was the most peaceable of the Moro provinces, with only occasional and localized outbreaks of disorder. Continuing the Spanish "policy of attraction", the Americans left the *datus* as they were, making friends out of former enemies.[41] But the end of fighting meant the end of alliances. The way to prosperity was now through cultivating the favour of the administration, or through participating in the development of the province as a major producer of rice and corn.

Ali initially confronted the Americans with a force of 15,000 men, but it was unable to withstand the Krag rifle and soon fragmented into guerilla bands. He remains a Magindanao hero, but mainly on account of his personal bravery. There was no question of his becoming another Utu, since it was not he but Piang who had inherited the political skills, and Piang did not support him. The latter professed friendship for the Americans, and supplied intelligence as to the rebels' whereabouts. It may also be true, as tradition asserts, that he simultaneously warned them to move on, and he would assuredly have joined the revolt had the Americans showed signs of weakening. But in the event Ali's death saw him on the winning side, the authorities in his debt, and his aristocratic rival out of the way.

Piang had impressed the Americans from the outset. In 1902 the following report was forwarded to the Philippine Commission:

He is very shrewd, has brains and is self made, being now quite wealthy and a power in the valley, as he controls all of Dato Ali's influence over the tribes and adds to this his own brain. He is the only prominent Moro who seems to appreciate what the American invasion means and the business opportunities it brings with it. The Chinese blood in him makes him a shrewd business man, and he has accumulated quite a fortune and is daily adding to it. He practically controls all the business of Cotabato, especially exports, through his Chinese agents in that place; has complete control of the Moro productions, and working with the Chinese merchants makes it practically impossible for a white firm to enter into business in the Rio Grande Valley, even with much capital behind them.[42]

At an interview he guessed that he might have 15,000 people, but could not be sure because the followers of the upriver *datus* were all his followers since their masters were his friends.[43] Another military observer reported that:

. . . the control of Piang over his people is absolute and complete. All know the refusal to work or fetch materials as ordered would have resulted in a swift and sure chastisement which might be limited to a flogging with rattan, but possibly would not stop short of beheading.[44]

Although the Americans at various times declared their determination to break the hold of the *datus,* Piang retained much of his power to the end. In 1926, when he was in his late 70s, an American observer described him in the following terms:

In late years younger datus have striven to displace him, but although no longer supreme, he is still easily first in the valley . . . His slaves still surround him, his word is still law, and it is said, although probably could not be proved, that in accordance with the old Magindanao code he still has recalcitrants of certain sorts cast to the crocodiles. I know that he recently put an influential datu on the wood pile for two months for crossing him. Also the old fox has accumulated much wealth during the three or four decades of his power: 42,000 coconut trees (they are good for $1 per tree each year), thousands of carabao, thousands of hectares of rice, land, horses, cattle, buildings, boats, and what not — to say

nothing of the tithe paid him by his loyal subjects. He is also reputed to have a
huge hoard of gold coins . . .[45]

What the observer said for Piang went for other *datus* in lesser degree. He had retained his slaves and followers, his hold over land and those who cultivated it, and
his control of both force and legal sanctions.

At the outset it looked as though the American administration would break the
power of the *datus*; instead it came to rely on them. Cotabato's quiescence, compared with the other Moro provinces, was largely due to the influence of Piang and
his associates.[46] Moreover he was ever responsive to American programs.[47] He led
the way in developing commercial agriculture. He supported modern education to
the extent of sending his own sons to study in Manila, one becoming an
agriculturist, another an educationist, and a third the first Muslim attorney. He
gave his backing to settlement of immigrants from the Visayas, and — in the face
of nationalist opposition — to a proposal for massive American investment in Mindanao. The pro-Americanism of Piang and the other *datus* and their hostility to
Philippine nationalism also proved an asset in the earlier years, though something
of an embarrassment later, once independence had become a firm prospect.

The *datus,* for their part, found themselves well placed to take advantage of the
economic and political changes that were taking place. In the economic sphere this
meant intensifying the production of rice and corn. The Magindanao had, of
course, long lived by commerce; and while raiding and toll-taking might have been
more important sources of wealth at certain periods, agricultural produce had
always been important, particularly in the upper valley. With raiding suppressed
and the toll posts increasingly by-passed by the new overland routes, and with the
demand for forest products declining, they now became of prime importance. The
datus' task was to adapt their traditional rights over land and people to meet
modern conditions.

Spain's policy had been to choke off Magindanao commerce with other countries,
but not to stop trade as such. Ileto notes that the need of her establishments for
supplies stimulated local trade, and that rice and high quality cacao found their
way from the upper valley to Manila and Sulu, through Chinese intermediaries.[48]
In 1901 the Americans found some 204 Chinese in the town of Cotabato, mainly
engaged in the sale of rice, wax, coffee, rubber and gutta-percha, which last they
sent to Singapore.[49] They estimated the aggregate of exports at about $150,000
Mexican. The bulk of these products came from the upper valley, and so were subject to the control of *Datu* Piang. He personally organized the collection of forest
products, and maintained a virtual monopoly through his connections with the
Chinese merchants. He also extended his interests into rice-milling and lumber.
And as long as the river provided the means of transportation, his seat at Dulawan
exceeded Cotabato in commercial importance. However, business remained in
Chinese hands, and the Magindanao concerned themselves almost exclusively with
agricultural production.

Economic statistics occur irregularly. In 1908 the Governor of Moro Province reported the establishment of saw and rice mills, and exports to the value of ₱21,246.50.[50] By 1919 the figure had reached ₱760,428, exceeding imports by more than ₱200,000.[51] Rice had become the most important item, with copra coming second and corn third. In the years that followed, the area under rice increased from 1,864 hectares in 1920 to 24,630 hectares in 1935.[52] Cotabato was on its way to becoming the rice bowl of the Philippines.

It is difficult to locate the sources of this expansion. The handful of foreign concerns produced coconuts, rubber and cattle. The settlers who came from other parts of the Philippines were few in number until the 1930s, and would have been preoccupied with subsistence for several years after arrival. Thus it would seem that much of the increase came from Magindanao farmers. The bulk of these would have been small to middle-sized peasants, for relatively few of the *datus* emerged as major land owners or rural entrepreneurs.

While political change proceeded apace, agrarian change came slowly, and many *datus* made the mistake of supposing that their traditional rights over land and labour would remain effective. Hitherto, land had been plentiful and occupation shifting. *Datus* could claim more land than they had followers to settle on it, and so took no trouble setting boundaries to what had been given them by God. Their fields might be more extensive than those of the commoners, thanks to the work of slaves and servile adherents, but much of their wealth came in the form of tax and tribute. Even slaves, once married, maintained their own households, fed from their own fields.

The Spaniards had not attempted to register native landholdings, and the U.S. cadastral survey did not begin registration until 1926, leaving the task unfinished in 1941. Moreover, the less foresighted occupants failed to lodge claims, either through a trust in traditional rights or unwillingness to pay the tax. Some of these later discovered that their land had been registered in other names. As a rule the court recognized ownership only when there was actual occupation; consequently most of the titles were for less than five hectares, while few *datus* got more than 20 — holdings that became trifling when divided among numerous heirs. Areas above 100 hectares went mainly to a few large-scale agriculturalists, such as Piang's son Ugalingen, and *Datus* Sinsuat and Dilangalen. Some of the more adventurous among the younger generation took up large tracts of virgin land, as the interior was opened up.[53] However, most of the large estates of recent years were formed under the more liberal conditions of the Republic.

The account of Piang's domain in 1926, quoted above, indicates that at least some *datus* kept their slaves. Although the institution had been formally abolished, slaves, along with other servile and tributary groups, continued to observe their traditional obligations, at least till the old *datu* died. However, they tended to disperse before the new generation could succeed. A young *datu* could still build up a following, but defined in terms of personal service or contract. Tenancy also made its appearance, though with land plentiful and cultivators inclined to mobility, the rate remained low by Philippine standards, even as late as 1971.[54]

The Americans' policy of attraction entailed recognition of Moro customary and religious law. Thomas devotes some pages to this matter, describing how *datus* were brought in to advise the judges but pointing up the difficulty in getting Muslims to bring their cases to court rather than to the *datus,* and also in separating religious from secular cases.[55] There is little data on this topic from Cotabato, but it is suggestive that as late as the 1970s cases of murder were being settled by *datus* informally rather than in the courts. However, a circular from Governor Gutierrez, dated 1935, reveals further complexities.[56] He complained that in certain districts, provincial and municipal officials were adjudicating "so-called religious cases", appropriating the fines imposed and making prisoners work for their private benefit. An examination of the names of municipal presidents and other officials indicates that the *datus* monopolized these positions.

The American authorities were slow to give Muslims responsible political office; no Magindanao served as provincial governor until the Japanese occupation, though there was usually one on the provincial board. Piang was for some years a member of the National Assembly, but all that most *datus* could hope for was a municipal district presidency, an office carrying less power and reward than a full municipal presidency and a great deal less than a mayor under the Republic. Nevertheless, these administrative divisions placed a limit on the dominance of figures such as Piang by reserving office for local *datus.*

Until the 1930s all offices were appointive, so that advancement depended on the favour of the governor rather than ability to rally support. As long as he lived, Piang had first call on it, but he died in 1933 and his eldest son Abdullah, who had taken his place in the National Assembly, died a few months later. There were four other sons, well qualified in terms of education to succeed, but they now had to compete with Sinsuat, son of Balabaran, who had stood second to Piang for some years. He had already had some experience of national affairs when he was appointed senator in 1935.[57] Then in the first election for the National Assembly in 1936 he defeated Attorney Menandang Piang by 312 votes to 128. Ungalingen Piang regained the seat in the next election, when there was a franchise of more than 20,000 votes.[58] With this election Magindanao politics once again became a matter of large-scale alliance formation, though the contest did not begin in earnest until after the Japanese occupation.

The American records have surprisingly little to say about Sinsuat Balabaran.[59] Born in 1864, he had grown up during the ascendancy of his father's brother Ayunan. His father, Balabaran, succeeded to the title of *gobernadorcillo* on the eve of the Spanish withdrawal, and also proclaimed himself Sultan, but evidently lacked Ayunan's political strength for he was forced to flee Taviran for the delta in 1899 and again in 1901, for fear of Piang's men. A subsequent marriage between Sinsuat and the daughter of the Sultan of Kabuntalan suggests a recovery, but Balabaran died soon after and the importance of such alliances declined with the end of fighting. Sinsuat himself retired to the family bailiwick, where he was presently appointed Municipal President. Between 1923 and 1931 he served as special adviser to Governor Gutierrez, having already represented Mindanao and Sulu in the negotiation of the Jones Act of 1916. Throughout this period he must have been consolidating and extending his political base, for in a 'Who's Who Among the Datus', dated 1927, he is described as controlling territory from Tumbao to the southern mouth of the river, and having great influence over the Tiruray in the adjacent mountains.[60] Evidently he was also acquiring large tracts of land, worked by tenants, while his many brothers and sons were pushing back the frontier, establishing themselves along the coast and even in the growing town of Cotabato. Sinsuat's own move to the outskirts of town reflects his increasing rapport with the Governor and other Christian settlers, which was later to place the mayorship in family hands.

Another influential figure, whose descendants were to become powerful in the postwar period, was *Datu* Ampatuan. Claiming Arab ancestry, he sometimes styled himself *Sarip* and was accorded the same status as descendants of Kabongsoan.[61] A former lieutenant of *Datu* Ali, he had been won over to the American side by Piang, whom he succeeded on the Provincial Board in 1917. He is described as controlling 1,500 families in the upper valley.[62]

Compared with these three, the most prominent members of the royal houses were just local notables. A few, like *Datu* Dilangalen of the Rajah Buayan house, had wide lands and many followers; but many were left with little besides their nobility. Mastura, son of the last legitimate Sultan of Magindanao, succeeded to the title in 1926 and briefly revived its old dignity. But he was already very old, and when he died a few years later, it passed back to the Sibugay branch over the protests of his numerous descendants.

Aware, perhaps, of the changing conditions of political hegemony, Piang and Sinsuat took advantage of the colonial education program to advance some of their sons. Gumbay Piang trained as an educationist, Ugalingen as an agriculturalist, while Menandang became the first Magindanao attorney. Duma Sinsuat also became an attorney soon after, along with Salipada Pendatun. The latter was son of the upper valley Sultan of Barongis, but being orphaned and in poor circumstances he owed his advancement to the American teacher, Edward Kuder. Some of the old nobility also allowed their sons to go to school, but others rejected the opportunity for fear that it was covert Christianization. Some commoners were also able to take advantage of the program, but the mass of the population remained illiterate and ignorant of English, so that they were dependent on leaders who could deal with government on their behalf.

The Japanese Occupation and After

The Japanese record is poorly documented, but the oral record is relatively fresh.[63] In many respects, the war years recreated the conditions prevailing around the turn of the century, with the foreigners controlling the delta and a few upriver towns, with the nominal support of the *datus* thereabouts. In the hinterland, guerilla groups were in control, nominally under American command but in practice often independent and occasionally warring among themselves. *Datu* Mantil Dilangalen and Piang's son Gumbay headed small detachments, but Salipada Pendatun and his brother-in-law, *Datu* Ugtog Matalam, emerged as the major figures, laying the foundations for major political careers after the war. In Cotabato, as elsewhere, collaborators suffered internment during the liberation period, but were soon released and suffered no subsequent disadvantages.

One important consequence of the Japanese period was the release of large quantities of arms, which were never taken in after the war, and the formation of private armies. These became a major factor in the turbulent electoral politics of the Republic. It is not entirely fanciful to see this as a revival of traditional political forms; however, just as outside connections were important in the proto-colonial period, so connections with one or other national party were important under the Republic. Success depended on a combination of high-level connections in Manila and widely ramifying alliances in the provinces. These alliances must increasingly include Christian immigrants, who were soon to outnumber the Magindanao. It is a tribute to the skill and tenacity of the *datus* that they were able to keep hold of the principal positions until 1971.

Politics under the Republic proved a more difficult and costly business than it had been under the Americans, though the rewards were also greater. A number of notable families were eclipsed, most notably the Piangs with the death of Congressman Gumbay in 1949. They retained control of their home municipality, but it was several times subdivided to make room for expansive neighbours such as the Ampatuan family.

Salipada Pendatun remained Cotabato's principal representative in Manila up to the suspension of parliamentary government in 1972, first as senator, later as congressman. This removed him increasingly from provincial affairs, but his interests were protected by his brother-in-law, the resistance veteran *Datu* Ugtog Matalam, who held the governorship. Their control was repeatedly challenged, by the Sinsuats and Ampatuans, and various Christian aspirants. The Sinsuats gained the congressional position only once, in 1949, narrowly losing it in 1969. However, they have always retained their hold on their home municipality, which was recently subdivided, and only lost the predominantly Christian Cotabato City in 1968. In 1978 *Datu* Blah Sinsuat was among those representing Cotabato in the interim National Assembly, and a nephew joined the Regional Assembly in the following year. The record of this family is impressive, running as it does from the 1860s through to the present. However, it is not without parallel. Among the grandsons of Ampatuan there have been several municipal mayors, and a former provincial governor and regional commissioner. The descendants of Sultan Mastura likewise include a recent governor, several municipal mayors and a delegate to the Constitutional Convention of 1971.

A Colonial Elite

Najeeb Saleeby was the only member of the American occupying forces to achieve an understanding of the Magindanao, and his period of influence was brief. Already on the sidelines by 1913, he lamented what seemed to be the destruction of traditional authority:

A strong power was rising in the Mindanao valley and Datu Ali could have easily brought all the Magindanaw Moros under his sovereignty. He could easily have gotten complete control of all that territory now known as the district of Cotabato, and extending from the neighbourhood of Malabang to Sarangani Point. But since 1899 all Moro authority has been crushed. Every strong datu who was living then has either been killed or passed away, and the country is completely disrupted and disorganized.[64]

He continued:

The datu should . . . be respected and recognized as the chief of the datuship because he is our best agent for governing his people. The Moro masses are perfect strangers to us. We cannot speak their language nor can they speak ours. We do not understand their ways and ideas and they do not understand ours. We cannot manage them directly, and in person, nor do they lie within our immediate reach. We cannot rule them without an intermediary and we cannot force upon them measures which we cannot force upon the datus. Why should we not then accept the natural inter-agency of the datu and benefit by his position and influence. We cannot have another intermediary without rupture and we cannot accomplish much good without peace . . .[65]

Whether the government finally heeded Saleeby's words, or whether it was overtaken by the realities he had outlined, it came to rule through an indigenous elite. It by-passed the old sultanates, but relied on *datus* like Piang and Sinsuat, whose power pre-dated the *pax Americana* and was to some extent independent of it.

When the Spaniards invaded the delta in 1861 the *datus* had to choose between defiance and compliance. The defiant were eventually broken, but they continued long enough for the compliant to become indispensable to the colonial regime. The sequence was repeated under the Americans, with many of the same actors. But whereas the primary role of Spain's *datus* had been to keep her enemies in check, that of America's was to facilitate the economic exploitation of their region. In this latter process their part was important but limited. They became part of a composite elite, monopolizing political office and controlling the agrarian sector, but leaving commerce to the Chinese and public administration to the Christian Filipinos. Piang and his sons recognized these trends and made some effort to move into commerce and government, but few followed their example.

In the agrarian and political sectors the *datus'* importance depended on their conrol over the ordinary Magindanao. This was grounded in traditional forms of clientage and support, but took on new forms as the old weakened. The *datus* had always performed the function of political articulation, linking scattered homesteaders with civil authority and periodically mobilizing them as a military force. Now they organized access to the alien authority, which in turn relied on them for access to the masses. Established as gatekeepers, they could transform the rational–bureaucratic forms of legitimacy into quasi-traditional loyalties to their persons and families.

Despite the continuity of particular political families, and of elementary political structures, the traditional order had been destroyed forever. Whether defiant like Buayan or compliant like Magindanao, the high nobility became the principal casualties of colonial domination. They survived as dignitaries, perpetuating their rank through arranged marriages, but without even the semblance of authority outside the places where they lived.

The final separation of power and rank was made clear as early as 1902, when *Datu* Utu's death left the highborn Raja Putri, daughter of Sultan Kudarat II, a widow. An American official was given to understand that she would marry either *Datu* Ali or *Datu* Piang, both of whom would no doubt have welcomed the connection and access to Utu's fortune. But the former was of lesser rank, while the latter was a commoner; in the event she married the current Sultan of Magindanao, Mangigin, who was of suitable rank but a political cipher. With the Raja Putri's death, around 1919, there disappeared the last vestiges of courtly life.

Piang, as an unashamed commoner, was a living proof of the nobility's decline, and yet it never quite lost its lure. His own attitudes towards it are indicated in the following anecdote. Entertaining a party of hereditary *datus,* he withdrew when the food was served, as protocol required; pressed to stay, he replied with a nice turn of ambiguity that it would be better for him to eat with the dogs. However, even he married into the minor nobility, and others among the new *datus* sought high-ranking wives, "buying *maratabat*" for their children. Even today, those who can trace their descent to *Sarip* Kabongsoan and other men of importance assume the honorific *datu.*[66]

Earlier it was suggested that *datu* had ruler as a primary meaning and descendant of rulers as a secondary meaning. The latter, however, provided the basic principle for a notional order that bore some resemblance to reality before colonial rule. Spain and the United States destroyed that order, creating a new type of *datu* who formed a dependent elite within the colonial order. His position in it was essentially ambiguous. Seen from above he mediated the policies of the colonial government; seen from below he mediated the people's unarmed resistance to forces that were alien and infidel. Thus situated he prospered and his power became entrenched. The new *datus* of the Spanish period had created their own *maratabat;* by the end of the American period they were once again inheriting it, not unlike the old *datus,* but also not unlike the elite families of the Christian Philippines.

NOTES

The research for this essay was funded by the University of Sydney. Sponsorship in the Philippines was provided by the National Museum in 1971, and by the Ateneo de Manila's Institute of Philippine Culture in 1973 and 1979. In the course of my research I have been personally and intellectually indebted to *Datus* Nasrullah Glang and Mokamad Mamadra, Assistant Regional Commissioner Attorney Michael Mastura, Attorney Corocoy Moson and Governor Sandiale Sambolawan. They are not, however, responsible for anything written here.

1 See, for example, Renato Constantino, *The Philippines: A Past Revisited* (Quezon City: Tala Publishing Services, 1975), 127-28.

2 John Larkin, *The Pampangans: Colonial Society in a Philippine Province* (Berkeley: University of California Press, 1972).

3 Norman G. Owen, "The Principalia in Philippine History: Kabikolan, 1790-1878," *Philippine Studies* 22 (1974), 297-324.

4 See, for example, Kit Machado, "Changing Patterns of Leadership Recruitment and the Emergence of the Professional Politician in Philippine Local Politics," in, Benedict J. Kerkvliet, ed., *Political Change in the Philippines; Studies of Local Politics Preceding Martial Law* (Honolulu: University of Hawaii Press, 1974), 77-129; Mary Hollnsteiner, *Dynamics of Power in a Philippine Municipality* (Quezon City: Community Development Research Council, University of Philippines, 1963).

5 Cesar Adib Majul, *Muslims in the Philippines* (Quezon City: University of the Philippines Press, 1973), 78.

6 For an account of Magindanao in the 17th century, see, Francisco Combes, *Historia de las Islas de Mindanao, Iolo y sus Adyacentes* (Madrid: Viuda de M. Minuesa de los Rios, 1897), and for the 18th century, see, Thomas Forrest, *A Voyage to New Guinea and the Moluccas, from Balamabangan* (London: J. Robson, 1779).

7 For an analysis of segmentary state systems, see, J.M. Gullick, *Indigenous Political Systems of Western Malaysia* (London: Athlone Press, 1958). Also, Thomas Kiefer, "The Tausug Polity and the Sultanate of Sulu: A Segmentary State in the Southern Philippines," *Sulu Studies* 1 (1972), 19-64.

8 See particularly, Carl Landé, *Leaders, Factions and Parties: the Structure of Philippine Politics* (New Haven: Monograph Series No. 6, Southeast Asia Studies, Yale University, 1965). Also, James C. Scott, *The Moral Economy of the Peasant: Rebellion and Subsistence in Southeast Asia* (New Haven: Yale University Press, 1977).

9 For a comprehensive bibliography the reader is referred to Majul, *Muslims in the Philippines,* and Reynaldo Ileto, *Magindanao, 1860-1888: the Career of Dato Uto of Buayan,* (Ithaca, N.Y.: Data Paper No. 32, Southeast Asia Program, Cornell University, October 1971).

10 Najeeb Saleeby, *Studies in Moro History, Law and Religion* (Manila: Bureau of Public Printing, 1905).

11 Joseph Ralston Hayden Papers, Michigan Historical Collections, Ann Arbor, Michigan; Leonard Wood Papers, Manuscript Division, Library of Congress, Washington D.C.

12 Karl Pelzer, *Pioneer Settlement in the Asiatic Tropics: Studies in Land Utilization and Agricultural Colonization in Southeastern Asia* (New York: American Geographical Society, 1948), 127-59.

13 Chester L. Hunt, "Ethnic Stratification and Integration in Cotabato," *Philippine Sociological Review* 5 (1957), 13-38.

14 Majul, *Muslims in the Philippines.*

15 Ileto, *Magindanao.*

16 Peter Gowing, *Mandate in Moroland: the American Government of Muslim Filipinos, 1899-1921* (Quezon City: University of the Philippines Press, 1977).

17 Ralph Benjamin Thomas, "Muslim But Filipino: the Integration of Philippine Muslims, 1917-1946," (doctoral dissertation, University of Pennsylvania, 1971).

18 Samuel Kong Tan, "The Muslim Armed Struggle in the Philippines, 1900-1941" (doctoral dissertation, Syracuse University, 1973). Alunan Glang's *Muslim Secession or Integration* (Quezon City: R.P. Garcia, 1969) includes some historical pieces, based on the published sources, but is mainly concerned with contemporary problems. Michael O. Mastura's study, "The Condition, Status and Destiny of the Muslim South (Magindanao, Maranao, Tausug) 1880-1871," is in preparation.

19 Frederick L. Wernstedt and Joseph E. Spencer, *Philippine Island World: A Physical, Cultural and Regional Geography* (Berkeley: University of California Press, 1967), 545.

20 U.S. Philippine Commission, *Census of the Philippine Islands Taken in 1903* (Washington, D.C.: GPO, 1905). The estimates, particularly of the pagan population, were probably below the actual figure.

21 Philippine Commonwealth, *Census of the Philippines, 1939* (Manila: Bureau of Printing, 1940); Frederick L.Wernstedt and Paul D. Simpkins, "Migrations and the Settlement of Mindanao," *Journal of Asian Studies* 25 (November 1965), 83-102.

22 Ileto, *Magindanao,* 2.

23 Although the river was navigable for some 100 kilometres, such a journey would take several days paddling in a *banka.*

24 For an account from the Maranao perspective, see, Melvin Mednick, "Some Problems of Moro History and Political Organization," *Philippine Sociological Review* 5 (1957), 39-52.

25 Ileto, *Magindanao*, 35.

26 *Datu* Piang formulated this principle in an early interview with American personnel. See note 43 below.

27 Like the Mediterranean notion of honour (see, John Peristiani, ed., *Honour and Shame: The Values of Mediterranean Society* [London: Weidenfeld and Nicolson, 1965]) *maratabat* is inherited in varying degree but must also be vindicated by action whenever the occasion arises. The greater the hereditary *maratabat,* the more jealously must it be defended. See also, Mamitua Saber, Maugag Tamano and Charles A. Warriner, "The Maratabat of the Maranao," *Philippine Sociological Review* 8 (1960).

28 Unlike the Taosug and Maranao, but like some other lowland Philippine groups at first contact (see, Frank Lynch, "Trend Report on Studies in Social Stratification and Social Mobility in the Philippines," *East Asian Cultural Studies* 4 [1965], 163-91), the Magindanao recognized a four-tier stratification: *datus*; commoners as exemplified by the *donatos* and *Sapi*; *ndatuan* or serfs; and *baniaga* or chattel slaves. There were also *olipun* or bond slaves whose condition was created by debt, the clearance of which released them at least in theory. They emanated from, and presumably might return to any one of, the four strata. Membership of the four strata was hereditary, but groups acquired their status through a variety of historical or pseudo-historical events. Thus the cadet branch of a *datu* line might opt for *donato* status. Certain servile groups were descendants of Visayan captives and still called *Bisaya*. Others were associated with certain occupations such as potting. The *baniaga* seem mostly to have originated as captives from the pagan groups.

29 The term *tarsila* comes from the Arabic *silsilah,* which means a chain or link. Saleeby (*Studies in Moro History*) copied a number of such documents concerning the principal lines of Magindanao. However, I have transcribed a number of documents relating to other branches of the Buayan line. I have also seen booklets, printed in Arabic, outlining the legendary origin of the Sultans of Sulu, Magindanao, Maranao and Brunei. For a discussion of the analysis of such documents, see, Cesar Adib Majul, "An Analysis of the Genealogy of Sulu" (paper, Filipino-Muslim History and Culture Seminar-Workshop, Department of History, University of the East, Manila, 20 October 1977).

30 For an analysis of political marriages during the dynastic wars of the 19th century, see, Michael O. Mastura, "The Magindanao Core Lineage and the Dumatus," *Notre Dame Journal* 7 (1977).

31 Melvin Mednick, *Encampment of the Lake: the Social Organization of the Moslem-Philippine (Moro) People* (Chicago: Research Series No. 5, Philippine Studies Program, University of Chicago, 1965).

32 The following judgement of *Datu* Utu, whose career is discussed below, could in fact be applied in greater or less degree to any *datu*. "In effect his natural talent, his prestige, his riches, his supporters and above all his fiery despotism, had created around him a certain air of glory which made him like a feared idol or the compelled leader of whatever action took place in the basin of the Rio-grande." (Ileto, *Magindanao,* 35.)

33 Tan, "Muslim Armed Struggle," 132-33; Majul, *Muslims in the Philippines, passim.*

34 For a general discussion of the kind of conditions under which Utu was operating, see, E.V. Walter, *Terror and Resistance: a Study of Political Violence* (New York: Oxford University Press, 1969).

35 Regarding Piang's early career and overthrow of Utu, see, Ileto, *Magindanao,* 63. According to this account, Piang and others broke with Utu following a dispute over arms. According to oral tradition, which is still current, Utu's followers deserted him when he refused to open his granaries during a time of famine. See, Captain C. Mortera, "The Career of Bai Bagnogan of Buluan, Cotabato," MS, 1934, Hayden Papers.

36 U.S. War Department, *Annual Reports of the War Department for the Fiscal Year Ended June 30, 1902* (Washington, D.C.: GPO, 1902), 9:481, 578.

37 Najeeb Saleeby, *The History of Sulu* (Manila: Bureau of Printing, 1908), 262.

38 Ileto, *Magindanao,* 61-63.

39 U.S. War Department, *Annual Reports for 1902,* 522-24.

40 Gowing, *Mandate in Moroland,* 151-54; Tan, "Muslim Armed Struggle," 35-38.

41 This is particularly apparent in the case of *Datu* Alamada, who carried on a local resistance in the interior up to 1913, and *Datu* Ampatuan who briefly defied the regime in the same year. See, Tan, "Muslim Armed Struggle," 37-38, 62-148. Both leaders subsequently became part of the governmental system.

42 U.S. War Department, *Annual Reports for 1902,* 528.

43 Interview of Commandant with *Datu* Piang, Cotabato, 2 April 1901, in, U.S. War Department, *Annual Reports for 1902,* 105.

44 General G. Davis, "Notes on the Government of the Country Inhabited by non-Christians in Mindanao and the Neighbouring Islands," MS. (1902) in Dean Worcester Collection, University of Michigan Library, 256.

45 Letter, J.R. Hayden to Dr Barr, 21 September 1926, Hayden Papers.

46 See, Thomas, "Muslim but Filipino," 103; Tan, "Muslim Armed Struggle," 148.

47 See, for example, the report on Abdullah Piang's death in the *Philippine Herald,* 10 December 1933; Thomas ("Muslim but Filipino," 129) notes Piang's support for American investment, as proposed by Congressman Bacon in 1926.

48 Ileto, *Magindanao,* 23.

49 U.S. War Department, *Annual Reports for 1902,* 111.

50 U.S. Philippine Commission, *Report of the Philippine Commission to the Secretary of War, 1908* (Washington, D.C.: GPO, 1909), 1:360, 366.

51 Philippine Islands, *Reports of the Governor General of the Philippine Islands to the Secretary of War, 1919* (Washington, D.C.: GPO, 1920), 81.

52 P.J. Webster, "Mindanao and Sulu Archipelago: Their Natural Resources and Opportunities for Development," *Bureau of Agriculture Bulletin* 38 (1920), 41; *Statistical Bulletin of the Philippine Islands* (Manila: Bureau of Printing, 1936).

53 For an account of agrarian conditions in Cotabato during the American period, see, Pelzer, *Pioneer Settlement,* 127-59.

54 In 1939, the date of the earliest estimate, 23 percent of farms were operated by tenants; in 1960 the percentage — of a very much larger total — was 26 percent. It is doubtful whether these estimates took into account traditional relationships through which a *datu* received a percentage of the farmer's crop.

55 Gowing, *Mandate in Moroland,* 191-92; Thomas, "Muslim but Filipino," 65-70.

56 Provincial Circular, 98, 15 January 1935, Hayden Papers.

57 *Directorio Oficial de la Asemblea Nacional* (Manila: Bureau of Printing, 1938), 143-44.

58 *Ibid.,* 149-50.

59 Thus, Bureau of Insular Affairs Chief, Frank McIntyre, wrote, ". . . our record of Datu Sinsuat and my memory are not so detailed". Memorandum of 16 August 1926, Bureau of Insular Affairs, U.S. National Archives and Records Service (hereafter, NARS), 5828/42.

60 Major Carter, "Who's Who Among the Datus," MS, 1927, Bureau of Insular Affairs, NARS, 5075-147.

61 According to local sources, Ampatuan's great grandfather came to Mindanao from Arabia. But since neither he nor the intervening descendants are mentioned in the Spanish records it may be concluded that *Sarip* Ampatuan was the first to assume political importance.

62 Major Carter, "Who's Who Among the Datus".

63 Edward Haggerty describes a brief visit to Cotabato in his *Guerilla Padre in Mindanao* (New York: Longmans Green and Co., 1946). A mimeographed newspaper, *Mount Peris Echo,* published by Gumbay Piang during the war, has yet to be traced. Ralph Thomas has summarized the Japanese sources, with particular reference to collaboration, in "Asia for the Asiatics? Muslim Filipino Responses to Japanese Occupation and Propaganda During World War II," *Dansalan Research Center Occasional Papers* 7 (May 1977).

64 Najeeb M. Saleeby, *The Moro Problem: An Academic Discussion of the Government of the Moros of the Philippine Islands,* (Manila: E.C. Mc-Cullough & Co., 1913), 15.

65 *Ibid,* 18.

66 The Magindanao have, however, abandoned the use of titles, in marked contrast to the Maranao.

Slavery and the Impact of External Trade: The Sulu Sultanate in the 19th Century

JAMES WARREN

During the late 18th and 19th centuries, a strong state emerged within the Sulu trading zone,[1] an extensive region encompassing the southern rim of the Sulu Sea and the whole of the Celebes Sea basin. The formation and prosperity of the Sulu Sultanate, as this account of its social history indicates, was based above all else on slaves. It was the role of the Sulu state, within its larger trading zone, to maintain the material and social conditions for the recruitment and exploitation of slaves.[2]

The zone encompassing the Sulu Sultanate is the historic home of peoples, languages and cultures as varied as its landscape. The Taosug (people of the current), the dominant ethnic group in the Sulu Archipelago (now part of the Philippines), are the sole residents of Jolo Island, the historical seat of the Sultanate. Originally fishermen and traders with martial skills, numbers of them adopted agriculture.[3] With the introduction of Islam in about the 15th century, they evolved a highly organized political and economic system.[4] The institution of the Sultanate established formal dominance of the Taosug over indigenous Samalan speaking peoples and later migrants to Sulu.

The Samal, strand dwellers with close ties to the sea, possessed of highly developed boat-building techniques and sometimes practising simple garden agriculture, are the most widely dispersed of all ethno-linguistic groups in the Sulu chain. Manifesting the greatest degree of internal linguistic and cultural difference, Samal communities predominate on the coralline island clusters in the northern and southern part of the Sulu archipelago, Northern Borneo and Celebes. The Samal distinguish among themselves by dialect, locality and cultural-ecological factors (principally between sedentary, Muslim shore-dwellers and nomadic animistic boat-dwellers).[5]

Samals tend to identify themselves with a particular island, island cluster or regional orbit. In the late 18th and early 19th centuries they comprised several groups which occupied non-contiguous territories along the southern Mindanao shore, on the south coast and in the near interior of Basilan, and on the islands of the Tapian Tana group, Cagayan de Sulu and the Balangingi cluster. Expert voyagers at sea, particular Samal groups had fixed bases of operation on a series of low, coral and sand islands flanking the northeastern side of Jolo. This group of islands, named *Los Samales* by the Spanish, was a springboard for launching seasonal raids against coastal villages from Luzon to Celebes. The most important island was Balangingi, dwelling place and organizational centre of the major slave-retailing group for the Sulu Sultanate in the first half of the 19th century. A related group of marauders, the Iranun, Maranao-speaking migratory strand dwellers, established their principal settlements along the river mouths of the southern coast of Mindanao.

The Sulu Archipelago's location between the Asian mainland and the large islands of Mindanao, Borneo and Celebes, its varied and productive resource base, and its sizeable population early attracted merchants from south China and Makassarese-Buginese mariners from Celebes. The annual arrival of Chinese junks and Bugis *prahus* at Jolo reflected a regular demand for local products procured principally from the Sultanate's essential domain — the sea.[6] It is important to note, however, that this traditional trade between Southeast Asian ports and the world outside was limited in scale.

By 1800 regional redistribution had become the main pattern of the economy of the Sulu Sultanate. Indirectly, it was the insatiable demand for tea that initiated European interest in Sulu's natural products and its sudden rise to regional primacy. During the 18th century tea replaced ale as the national beverage in England and was especially popular among the poorer classes. China was almost the sole supplier of tea to England. These merchants were quick to recognize the potential of participation in the long-standing Sino–Sulu trade as a means of redressing the one-way flow of silver from India. Marine and jungle products, highly valued in China, were needed to stem it. Sulu's ascendancy towards the end of the 18th century developed out of the expanding trade between India, Southeast Asia and China.[7] Commercial and tributary activity became linked with long distance slave raiding and incorporation of captured peoples in a system which made Jolo a principal entrepôt for extracted produce for the China trade.

The first section of my study, revolving around the interrelated themes of external trade, slave raiding and state formation examines the need for Sulu's maritime products in the British China trade. By fitting into the patterns of European trade with China, the Sultanate established itself as a powerful commercial centre. The maritime and jungle products to be found within the Sulu zone and in the area of its trading partners — *tripang,* birds nest, wax, camphor, mother-of-pearl, tortoise shell — were new products for redressing the British East India Company's adverse trade balance with China.

Of importance for Sulu were textiles and other imported manufactures, opium and also guns and gunpowder which contributed to the Sultanate's physical power. Taosug merchants on the coast and their descendants developed an extensive redistributive trade in which they wrested the function of the collection and distribution of commodities from traditional competitors, the Sultanates of Brunei and Cotabato. This commerce — involving trade with the Bugis of Samarinda and Berau to the south, with Manila to the north, and with Singapore and Labuan to the west — formed a complex set of interrelationships through which the segmentary state of Sulu was able to consolidate its dominance over the outlying areas of the zone along the northeast Borneo and western Mindanao coasts.

As the Sultanate organized its economy around the collection and distribution of marine and jungle produce, there was an increased need for large-scale recruitment of manpower in Sulu's economy to do the labour-intensive work of procurement. Slaving activity developed to meet the accentuated demands of foreign trade. Jolo became the nerve centre for the co-ordination of slave raiding. The second part of the study analyzes the technical aspects of the seasonal raiding programs in search of additional manpower to service the procurement of trading produce.[8] The final section delineates the parameters of slavery as an institution in Sulu and describes in some detail how "slaves" who were captives served as dependants of the Sulu

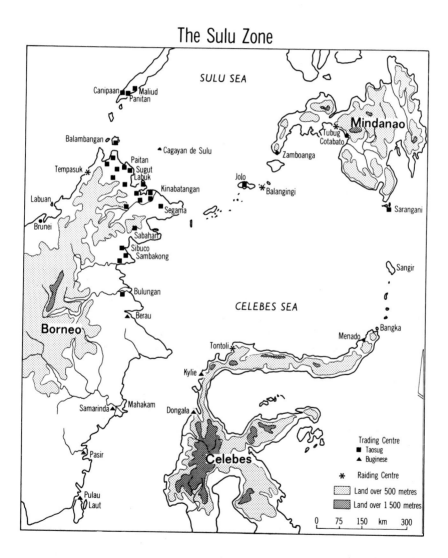

The Sulu Zone

elite and were able to better their condition and end up, at least in the second generation, as assimilated members of the Taosug and Samal population.[9]

I have drawn upon anthropological concepts, particularly the idea of a "segmentary state",[10] European documents in several languages with excerpts and examples from official reports, diaries, letters, journals and newspapers and local accounts to examine the economic vitality of the independent Sulu Sultanate's role as an entrepôt for European and Asian commerce in the China trade from the late 18th to the late 19th century, and its effect on the way slaves worked, lived and interacted with their masters.

Among the most important sources consulted are the manuscripts in the archives of Spain (principally Seville) on trade from Manila to the Sulu Sultanate between 1768 and 1848. When compiled and ordered as a time series these documents (particularly the *estados* and the *almojarifazgo*) suggest the overall level of commercial activity, shifts in market preferences, and the economic interdependence of Manila and Jolo in the period.[11] A careful reading of these documents thus reveals the level of economic integration achieved by Sulu and its Bornean dependencies in the wider island economy, the magnitude of the change that occurred after 1770, and possible reasons for shifts in the trade patterns over time. These data go far towards rounding out the detailed evidence which Van Leur saw to be lacking for maritime powers in the Indonesian archipelago.

In the late 18th and 19th centuries the population of Sulu was heterogeneous but changing — socially, economically and ethnically. This was a direct result of external trade. The populating of the Sulu zone by captives from the Philippines and various parts of the Malay world — primarily from Celebes and the Moluccas — and their role in the redistributional economy centred at Jolo cannot be underestimated. It has not been explored in detail. Previous historical studies of the Sultanate depended largely on published colonial records and accounts to understand the economic and social role played by the slaves in the economy, rather than on records produced by the slaves themselves. Slavery in Sulu was observed through the eyes and preconceptions of European observers and writers who viewed Sulu as the centre of a world fundamentally hostile to their interests — an Islamic world whose activities centred upon piracy and slavery.[12] Nevertheless, it is still possible to research aspects of the social history of the ethnically diverse slaves of the Sulu population.

I have drawn upon the statements of the fugitive slaves of the Sulu Sultanate which present a unique account from the perspective of the slaves themselves. From over 180 fugitive slave accounts, manuscript sources and travel literature, clear patterns of social life and economic activity can be constructed.[13] As a historical source the published and unpublished testimonies of the fugitive slaves of the Sulu Sultanate are both invaluable and neglected. The testimonies tell us much about the experience of slavery in Sulu that could never be found in more traditional sources. The experiences of captives from the moment of seizure, and their passage in the slave *prahus* to their settlement, life and labour in Sulu, emerge from anonymity in the slave testimonies. The total effect of these individual lives and cases of fugitive slaves is to throw very considerable light on the internal processes — the ethnic and social transformations — in the Sulu trading zone during the 19th century.[14]

The trade data and the statements of the fugitive slaves complement one another and together enable us to resolve many fundamental questions about the size of Sulu's indigenous trade and its flourishing slave population; about how these changed over time as a consequence of external trade; and where, how and in what quantities the natural produce was harvested.

Slavery and External Trade in Sulu

The impact of external trade on the pre-industrial economies of African kingdoms has received considerable attention from Catherine Coquery, Samir Amin and Yves Person.[15] In their analyses of indigenous African trade and markets they stress that the wealth and power of the aristocracy is based on the careful regulation of external trade in the form of rights and tolls. According to Emmanuel Terray, however, such a viewpoint which stresses the monopoly or highly centralized political control of the trade can underestimate the role of slave labour in producing the surplus which is the foundation of the social and political hegemony of the aristocracy. Terray shows that the central concern of the political leaders of the Abron kingdom of Gyaman was labour.[16] In this society external trade enabled the aristocracy to "realize" the surplus productivity extracted from the labour of its slaves. Above all, it was manpower and not foreign trade that was the direct and immediate foundation of the political economy of Gyaman.

The importance of a mode of production based on slave labour in the Sulu Sultanate is perhaps more apparent. Power and wealth in Sulu were defined only secondarily in terms of territory. A leader's power and status was based more on his control over personal dependants, either slaves or retainers, that he could mobilize at a given moment for what was deemed to be either commercially or politically expedient, than on the formal state structure. A report expressly prepared in 1812 for Sir Stamford Raffles, the Lieutenant Governor of Java, by J. Hunt, who lived in Jolo for six months, recognized the significance of the slave mode of production in Sulu's social formation: "The power and weight of the chiefs arise solely from their wealth, or like the Barons of old amongst us, from the number of *ambas* [slaves] or retainers each entertain."[17]

The accumulation of wealth and the transmission of power and privilege in Sulu was facilitated by the ownership of slaves. This was even more the case after the advent of European trade in the Sulu Archipelago in the late 18th century. The establishment of European and Asiatic enterprise and capital at Jolo on a hitherto unprecedented scale stimulated the production of *tripang* and other strand commodities and made labour the chief source of wealth. Slave labour in the *tripang* and pearl fisheries helped to provide the products introduced into the external trade. The expansion of slavery in Sulu occurs then as a direct consequence of developments similar to those in the Abron kingdom of Gyaman.

An abundant supply of labour was of considerable significance in producing power and wealth among the Taosug aristocracy. A *datu* who could acquire large numbers of slaves could engage more people in procurement activities and trade, and with the surplus wealth they produced attract others to him. The efforts of ambitious Sulu *datus* to participate in this burgeoning international trade, with its extraordinary profits, forced the demand for additional labour up and swelled the flow of external trade. The need for a reliable source of labour was met by the Iranun and Balangingi, the slave raiders of the Sulu zone. Indeed,the rapid growth of slave raiding was to keep pace with Sulu's foreign trade by providing the prime requisite for the continued growth and prosecution of the littoral and riverine procurement trade — manpower. Thus the Sulu state created and reproduced the material and social conditions for the recruitment and exploitation of slaves. More than anything else it was this source and application of labour that was to give Sulu its distinctive predatory character in the eyes of Europeans in the 19th century as a "pirate and slave state".

The Social Integration of Slaves in Sulu

The testimonies of fugitive slaves and historical accounts leave no doubt that slavery was an essential element in determining the economic, military and social patterns of the Sulu state. In large measure it was the slaves who held the fabric of Taosug society together in the period under consideration. In contrast to the industrial-plantation slavery of the West, slaves in Sulu were not solely defined in terms of their status as property. Slavery in Sulu as in other areas of Southeast Asia was primarily a property relation but not exclusively so, and a slave's social position was determined by a number of factors, often independent of his servile status.[18] In the Sulu Sultanate, *banyaga* (chattel-slaves) could have family roles as husband or wife, they could own property, and they often filled a variety of political and economic roles — as bureaucrats, farmers and raiders, as concubines and traders — by virtue of which they were entitled to certain rights and privileges accorded to other members of the community.

Slavery was a means of incorporating people into the Taosug social system. *Banyaga* were enrolled in the followings of *datus* for political support, but far more than anything else they were needed to labour in the fields and fisheries to maintain an expansive redistributional economy and the flow of external trade. They were predominantly Visayan, Tagalog, Minahassan and Buginese speakers, although almost every major ethnic group of insular Southeast Asia was to be found among their ranks. Some inherited their status. Others were obtained as a form of tax or in fulfilment of debt obligations. But all *banyaga* or their ancestors had been seized by professional slave raiders and retailed in communities throughout the Sulu zone.[19]

A distinction was drawn by Taosug between chattel-slaves (*banyaga, bisaya, ipun, ammas*) and bond-slaves (*kiapangdilihan*). *Banyaga* were either the victims or the offspring of victims of slave raids. *Kiapangdilihan* were persons from the ranks of commoner Taosug whose servility was the direct result of personal debt.[20] The familiar roads to recruitment into slavery were capture and birth. Capture in raiding was the principal mode of recruitment as the pressures of international trade sustained continued Balangingi slave raids throughout the first half of the 19th century. In addition, debt and fine obligations among the Taosug themselves provided a significant number of *kiapangdilihan*. A person might also be reduced to slavery by legal process. For example, conviction for criminal offences such as stealing and acts of sexual impropriety, particularly adultery, were punishable by heavy fines.[21] Inability to pay or offer some form of security for the fine imposed reduced people to the status of *kiapangdilihan*. *Kiapangdilihan* were an integral part of a creditor's following but with a lower status than freemen, who voluntarily

Slave Raiding in South East Asia

attached themselves to a leader. The creditor claimed rights over only a *kiapangdilihan*'s economic services and, in theory, was not allowed to harm him physically. In return for subsistence a *kiapangdilihan* was obliged to work for his creditor but his services did not generally count toward repayment of his debt. Many *kiapangdilihan* became dependants for life and their families might remain obligated for several generations. Indebtedness enabled *datus* to command the labour of Taosug commoners to ensure the manpower reserves they required in the functioning of the social formation. Debt bondage as an economic institution in Sulu was most fully developed at the end of the 19th century, when the Taosug could no longer rely on Balangingi raids to supply sufficient numbers of *banyaga* for their retinues, by increasing the amount of tribute ordinarily collected from clients and making the fines in the legal codes prohibitive.[22]

The legal position of a *banyaga* in the Sultanate of Sulu was determined by the Sulu code, a body of law codified from custom and precedent as well as Islamic law.[23] In theory, as defined in the Taosug codes, a *banyaga* had no legal personality; a *banyaga* could not hold property; a *banyaga* could be transferred, bought or sold at will; and a master held the power of life and death over a *banyaga* who could be punished for the slightest infraction of the law. The legal expression of social distinction is exemplified in the scale of penalties and fines in the codes for the offences of murder, adultery, theft and inheritance. Punishments were much more severe for *banyaga* than members of other social classes. For example, if a male *banyaga* had sexual intercourse with a free woman, he could either be killed outright or be severely punished and become the property of the woman's husband or family.[24] On the other hand, if a free man had sexual relations with a married female slave he need only pay a fine of 20 lengths of cotton cloth.[25] Less severe penalties for adultery between *banyaga* derived from their inferior social status. The Taosug commonly associated such degrading behaviour with slaves.

Although these laws provided institutional opinion on the debasement of people, and further reflected the low opinion of slaves held by masters, in fact *banyaga* were often socially and economically indistinguishable from freemen and in some respects more secure. The actual situation of many individual *banyaga* as revealed in their testimonies contradicted their legal status as a group. *Banyaga* were encouraged to adopt Islam and marry; some *banyaga* were permitted to purchase their freedom and assume a new status and ethnicity; the children of a female *banyaga* and a freeman inherited the status of their father; some *banyaga* could bear arms; any slave could own property which reverted to his master at death.

The basic differences between slavery among the Taosug and slavery as it was generally understood in the West was the variability of social distance that existed between slave and master. William Pryer stated that on the east coast of Borneo the relation was that of follower and lord rather than slave and master.[26]

The power and wealth of a *datu* was commensurate with the number of slaves he owned. The more slaves a *datu* acquired, the greater was his reputation and the willingness of people to seek protection within his settlement in return for services.

Banyaga were often well clothed, carried fine kris, and were entrusted with long journeys for their masters.[27] The personal and economic ties of slaves in the Sulu Sultanate "provided a sense of security which bound them to their masters and gave them identity and . . . [incentive] to labour".[28] A master was constrained to feed and clothe his slaves or give them sufficient opportunities to earn a living, otherwise his slaves might demand to be sold.[29] It appears to have been a common practice in the Sulu Sultanate to allow a *banyaga,* when he desired, to change masters rather than risk desertion.

Nevertheless there are statements of fugitive slaves and other reports which present the master–slave relationship in a much more severe light. In principle, the master's ownership was absolute and his authority unbounded. A *banyaga* could suffer bodily degradation and be put to death; he could be sold, bartered or given away if it served his master's interests.[30] Pryer noted the ambivalence in theory and practice that existed in the relationship between slave and master:

> Masters have the power of beating them [slaves] or even chopping them, but as a rule slavery here [Sandakan Bay and the coastal area] is regarded much as servantism is elsewhere . . . but a former Dato here cut one of his slaves to pieces for trying to escape.[31]

While there is evidence of contrasting degrees of benevolence and hardship, what is important to ascertain in assessing the system is whether cruelty and maltreatment were modal characteristics of slavery in the Sultanate. The fact that a *datu* defined his economic power in terms of the number of slaves he possessed, and that slaves were able to run away to another *datu* or try to escape to Zamboanga or Menado, placed important constraints on his actions. A purely antagonistic relation would little benefit a master if only because the successful exploitation of Sulu's natural produce hinged on the large-scale organization of the co-operation of the slaves and their dependants. In 1842, an American sailor who accompanied the Wilkes expedition wrote:

> We saw several captives here who had been captured among the islands in the Sooloo Sea [Visayas] or Philippine group. One was taken out of a fishing boat in the harbour of Batavia . . . This man, who belonged to Batavia, spoke some English, but very imperfectly. He states they were treated well by their masters, and did not seem anxious to obtain their freedom.[32]

A master was liable to neglect or mistreat a *banyaga* who was remiss in his duties, but the statements of escaped slaves and travel accounts of observers reveal that slaves, and especially those with knowledge and skills, had good relations with their masters and were not easily distinguished among his following.

Manumission was commonly practised in the Sulu Sultanate and freed slaves were merged into the general population, assuming a new ethnicity and status.[33] For *banyaga,* conversion and marriage were prerequisites to manumission. The process of manumission in the Taosug social system (occurring primarily among those *banyaga* in close contact with their masters), tended to be a gradual one in which incorporation was implicit.[34] An *indio* who altered his ethnic identity by becoming a Muslim and thereby achieving manumission found a new range of opportunities open to him as a freeman and a "Taosug".

A *banyaga* could purchase his freedom in the Sulu Sultanate.[35] This was frequently the case among those *banyaga* who had an aptitude for trade. Their owners often found it best to allow such slaves to acquire property so as to encourage initiative and establish their loyalty. In time the slave might purchase his freedom with his master's backing, having profited from participation in his commercial affairs. Once free, reciprocal obligations continued to bind them — now as patron and client instead of master and slave.

Manumission was an important feature of the Taosug social system. The steady leakage of manumitted slaves swelled the ranks of a *datu*'s retainers and hence increased his political hegemony and prestige. The likelihood of manumission was essentially a function of occupation. *Banyaga* who provided immediate and indispensable services to their masters, who served in their households or on their trading vessels, had better chances of manumission than those who laboured in the fields or fisheries.

But for many slaves among the Taosug and Samal, escape rather than manumission remained their central ambition. Naturally it was during the early years of captivity that the desire to escape was greatest. This was particularly the case of *indio* men who had been torn away from their homes and families and had experienced the hardships of the Balangingi traffic.[36] The initial social isolation created by differences in language, customs and status exacerbated the loneliness and yearning for the lost past. Some never did find the "indispensable margin of social and psychological space"[37] necessary to overcome the trauma of transition and settle down. They constantly reworked their past lives; the remembrance of their *pueblos* and *kampongs,* family and companions did not fade away.[38] One can feel in reading the statements of some of the fugitive slaves their desperation and incredible determination to secure freedom and reknit the fabric of their family and community life. All such *banyaga* lived in expectation of that eventual return.

The Taosug system was such that controls were difficult to apply, and 100 to 200 *banyaga* who chafed under oppression fled annually to foreign vessels at Jolo, to the interior of Jolo or some other island in the archipelago, or to Zamboanga and Menado.[39] Very little is known about the fate of those *indios* who actually managed to return to their *pueblos*. Undoubtedly, an *indio* sometimes reached home to find some or all of his family dead, his wife remarried, and outstanding debts and reciprocal obligations remaining to be fulfilled.[40] Many who escaped were left to make a new life, the reality of which was harsher than that which they had fled.

The Economic Integration of Slaves

Slavery, I have emphasized, became crucial to Sulu's economic and cultural life towards the end of the 18th century. Most accounts of the Sulu Sultanate written before 1780 indicate that the internal demand for slaves at Jolo was on a much smaller scale than it was destined to become in the 19th century.[41] The impact of the West's commercial intrusion in China was a watershed in the formation of the Sulu state. Slaves who were valuable for the variety of their labours essential to the growth of the state came to play a more avowedly important role in Sulu at this time. For example, among the Taosug, *banyaga* were used in trading ventures, in diplomatic negotiations, as slave raiders, as concubines and wet nurses, as tutors to their masters, as craftworkers and as peasants and fishermen.[42]

There was a clear division of labour between the work of male and female *banyaga*. Heavy work was performed generally by male slaves. Physically able men assisted their masters in clearing virgin forest, in ploughing, in harvesting timber, in building and maintaining boats, and hauling water.[43] Male *banyaga* also laboured in the fisheries in search of mother-of-pearl shell and *tripang*, manufactured salt, accompanied their masters on trading expeditions, and sailed as crew on Balangingi *prahus*. Included among the major tasks of female *banyaga* were: the sowing and weeding of rice fields; the pounding and threshing of rice; and the gathering and preparation of strand products.[44] Female *banyaga* were also included in the entourage of their mistresses as attendants, and some enjoyed positions of trust and some comfort as concubines of leading *datus*.

Mother-of-pearl shell became one of Sulu's most profitable exports by the beginning of the 19th century. Mother-of-pearl had previously been sought for the China market only on a limited scale.[45] The trade increased from 2,000 piculs in 1760 to an estimated 12,000 piculs per annum by 1835.[46] Once Asian and European traders realized the shell's value to manufacturers of jewelry, cutlery and furniture in Ceylon and Europe, they became the chief customers of this commodity,[47] which, with *tripang*, was among the most important items of export from Jolo. It can be roughly estimated from trade statistics that some 68,000 fishermen, slave and free, must have been engaged in diving for mother-of-pearl and fishing for *tripang* by hundreds of Taosug *datus* and Samal headmen during the 1830s.[48]

If the labour-intensive economy of the Sulu Sultanate relied on the sea as an abundant source of produce for external trade, the wilderness of Borneo was its second mainstay. It was principally from this environment that the Sultanate was supplied with specialties for the China trade.[49] Birds nest, procured primarily from limestone caves, and wax were obtained in abundance by thousands of slaves who initiated expansion of settlement and mined the riches of the forests of east Borneo for their Sulu overlords.[50]

Banyaga of initiative and energy were entrusted with their master's property and sent on trading voyages. Hunt noted that the Taosug employed slaves in their *prahus* not only as crewmen but as traders.[51] Slaves regularly traded from Jolo to Balangingi and Palawan on behalf of their masters in the 1830s.[52] The more capable *banyaga* were employed in trading excursions to the northeast coast:

> The most intelligent of them are picked out as traders and perform long journeys sometimes of months duration, trading to different ports without ever

Slave Raiding in the Philippines

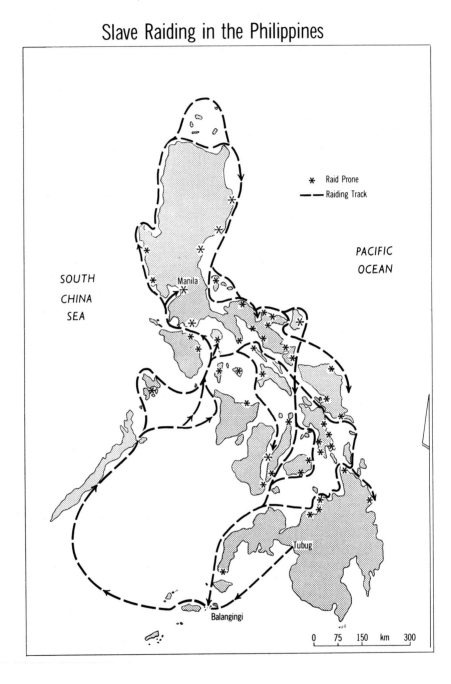

Raid Prone *

Raiding Track ---

PACIFIC OCEAN

SOUTH CHINA SEA

Manila

Tubug

Balangingi

0   75   150   km   300

thinking of running away. Many of these slaves amass considerable sums of money and have houses and belongings even finer than their masters . . .[53]

Aristocratic women were given *banyaga* to assist them in their business activities, primarily local marketing.[54] By the mid-19th century some of the leading local traders in Sulu were women:

> In Sulu the wives of the chiefs are entrusted with the principal management of accounts and carry on much of the trade; it is said that they have acquired considerable knowledge from the Manilla captives, who are often of a superior class.[55]

Ordinarily, the vending of cloth, vegetables and other trade goods in villages, at the open market, or to foreign vessels was done by *banyaga*. Noble women by virtue of their station lacked the liberty to barter produce, which entailed wandering amongst the houses, visiting the Chinese quarter, or rowing into the bay to a trading ship. It was common for Taosug women to send one or two Spanish-speaking slaves into the roadstead in small canoes on the arrival of a European vessel. The boats carried fruits, vegetables, coils of *tali lanun* (cheap rope of excellent quality), weapons and curiosities. Slave vendors were instructed to barter a specified minimum amount of produce by evening. They commonly accepted from European sailors only such trade items as cups and saucers, scissors, buttons empty bottles, tobacco and opium.[56] Slave hawkers were an important source of wealth to their mistresses. It was at the same time an attractive and profitable way of life for many:

> . . . one day I was talking to a Malay, of whom I had just bought some coconuts, when he informed me that he also was a captive . . . , upon which I enquired why he did not profit by the opportunity to escape, and revisit his country. "Why should I do so?" he replied, "there is something to regret everywhere; here I am well enough, my master treats me as if I were one of his kindred, I am well paid, and could save money if I wished; in my own country I know I could not do better, and perhaps should not fare as well; therefore, I prefer remaining here."[57]

The prosperity of the Sulu Sultanate depended to a large extent on the labour of the *banyaga* who manned the slave-raiding *prahus*. They augmented the strength of client communities that specialized in slaving, and as hirelings enriched their masters through active participation in raids. Wilkes observed that *datus* "receive a high price . . . for the services of their slaves".[58] The *banyaga* cooked, fetched water and firewood, and assisted the crew from time to time with their shipboard duties.[59] The *banyaga* were not armed but considered an integral part of the crew and it was their task to row, bail, clean and repair the *prahus*.[60] It was common for masters to send unaccompanied *banyaga* on these *prahus*, but fleet leaders (*nakodahs*) were reluctant to take those who objected to their master's wish.[61] Undoubtedly *datus* were constrained to reward such slaves, otherwise they would have been far more reluctant to participate in such a hazardous undertaking.

Under the Taosug some of these *banyaga* enjoyed considerable social mobility. The successful execution of a slave-raiding expedition was difficult and dangerous work and depended largely on the skill of its personnel. Proven ability and experience in raid was one of the most important criteria for leadership. Some *banyaga* held important positions as *nakodahs* and occasionally as squadron commanders in slaving expeditions, and in return they acquired wealth and slaves who complemented their personal followings. Visayan *indios* in particular demonstrated their talent and courage as *nakodahs* and developed a fearful reputation in the Philippines,[62] but *banyaga* from other parts of the Malay world, who had knowledge of dialects and of their former localities, proved equally skilful boat commanders.[63]

Raiding seems to have provided other such slaves with opportunities for modest social advance, especially if they showed a talent for fighting. Jadee, a Batak retailed to "Sulu pirates" for trade goods on the east Sumatran coast, was "made at first to row, and bale water out of their *prahus* [but] he gave such proofs of courage and address, that in a short time they advanced him to the rank of fighting man".[64]

Despite the emphasis placed upon external trade in the formation of the Sulu State, agriculture remained the main activity for the majority of Taosug who still resided inland on the volcanic high islands of the Tapul group and on Pata and Siassi.[65] The Sultanate needed a reliable source of food for its expanding population. The increased development of a slave mode of production conditioned the integration of the subsistence sector as a major component of the redistributive system. *Banyaga* employed in agriculture contributed towards providing the food supply which maintained the community and freed a *datu* and his retinue from subsistence pursuits, to devote their labour to trading and raiding.[66]

Small, dispersed farming communities comprised of *banyaga* dotted the interior of the larger fertile islands, especially on Jolo, Tapul and Pata. Masters allotted their *banyaga* a bamboo hut large enough to accommodate a single family and a farm plot.[67] The huts were scattered about over large tracts of land. The slave statements suggest that in at least some cases these subordinate agricultural settlements were homogeneous in language and religion. The size of such settlements is not known and would have depended on the number of farm slaves a *datu* owned, but they must have contained up to several hundred persons. These *banyaga* were encouraged by their masters to marry other *banyaga* and establish homesteads. Farm slaves were expected to provide for their own wants from the fields and gardens that had been given to them.[68] They were obligated to remit a fixed minimum portion of this produce to their master through the agency of the village headman, who could be of slave or non-slave origin. Farming was their major economic obligation, but *datus* demanded also that villages near the coast collect *tripang* and pearl shell for them, although for this they received barter goods in exchange. All were liable to be called upon for military services.[69]

In prominent trading centres like Jolo, Parang and Bual, where agriculture was of secondary importance, talented *banyaga* engaged in a wide range of activities and included among their numbers bureaucrats, tribute collectors, artisans, musicians, scribes and commercial agents. The opportunities for social mobility among these slaves stand in marked contrast to those of slaves engaged in farming or fishing.

Banyaga recruited by the Sultan as office holders enjoyed considerable prestige. The Sultan appointed them to administer trade and subject peoples in different parts of the zone in order to centralize his authority and thwart the ambitions of rival elements among Taosug aristocrats. Because of their inferior social status, *banyaga* did not have the political aspirations of the *datu* class, and the Sultan's power was strengthened by the use of such persons as administrators. The interests of these slaves by virtue of their elevation to political office lay unquestionably with the Sultan and they made loyal followers.

Banyaga played leading roles as bureaucrats on the Samal islands, acted as tribute collectors throughout the zone, and manned tariff stations on Bornean rivers.[70] Chrishaan Soerma commanded a large *prahu* that collected tribute from Parang, Tapul, Tawi-Tawi and Sandakan Bay in the 1830s.[71] A Chinese seized near Banjermasin by the Iranun named Banjer was a Sultan's man and had once been put on a trading station to control inland commerce along the Kinabatangan river.[72] The Sultan also made use of *banyaga* to exercise control over subject groups on the northeast coast of Borneo. In 1878 Pryer wrote, "it is not considered particularly degrading to be a slave, most of the leading men here have been so . . ."[73] One of the most influential of these slave headmen was Tuan Iman Gelanee who dominated the Samal Bajau Laut on the northeast coast after midcentury:

> Tuan Emum is a Bugis, he was captured when young by Sooloo pirates and taken over by the Sultan himself who finding him to be a man of ability sent him over here, Sandakan then apparently being pretty much in the hands of the Badjus, Emum married the queen of the Badjus, [and] became the headman amongst them.[74]

As Taosug trade became more complex and the political problems posed by the West grew, so did the amount of work which required literacy. The uses of written documents were no longer confined principally to the records of the genealogy of the Sultan, the appointment of officials, and the collection of tribute and legal fees. After 1770, writing was required for diplomatic and trade correspondence with the Spanish, Dutch and English, for recording grants of land and the terms of treaties of various sorts with the West, and to keep track of the accounts of *datus'* commercial enterprises.

Paradoxically, few Taosug aristocrats could read and write, and *banyaga* with education who could serve as scribes, interpreters and language tutors were much sought after.[75] The majority of these scribes were male slaves drawn from different parts of the Malay world, but female *indio* slaves served as the Sultan's secretary at different times.[76] While most other slave specialists — artisans and craftsmen — were more or less expendable, the skills of the educated *banyaga* could not easily be mastered by others and were considered indispensable to the business enterprise of *datus* who employed them. *Banyaga* who could speak or write one or more foreign languages were employed as trading agents by *datus*, enabling them to amass considerable personal wealth: "These [educated slaves] are not denied the right of holding property which they enjoy during their lives, but at their death it reverts to their master. Some of them are quite rich . . ."[77] Wilkes described such a *banyaga* who appears to have been of some assistance to his expedition:

> All accounts of the Datu of Soung are kept in Dutch, by a young Malay from Ternate, who writes a good hand, and speaks English, and whom we found exceedingly useful to us. He is a slave of the Datu who employs him for this purpose only. He told me he was captured in a brig by the pirates of Basilan and sold here as a slave, where he is likely to remain for life, although he says the Datu has promised to give him his freedom after ten years.[78]

The number of slave artisans — goldsmiths, silversmiths, blacksmiths and weavers — was never large, and comprised only a small fraction of the total slave population. Gifted *banyaga,* whose raw materials — brought by trade or tribute — were transformed into jewelry, tools, weapons and armour, were full-time artisans, while others who were less talented pursued their occupations on a part-time basis. Not surprisingly, the arbitrary distribution of *banyaga* left some talents wasted. José Ruedas, a silversmith, spent three years as a fisherman and gatherer of pearl shell before being taken by his master to be exchanged for a bundle of cotton cloth at Jolo, where he resumed his craft.[79] While some slaves found their skills superfluous in a particular island's economy, others appear to have had the opportunity to acquire training in critical occupations, especially as blacksmiths and armourers.[80]

It is clear from the accounts of Forrest, Hunt, D'Urville and Wilkes that slaves were called upon to perform instrumental music and sing, sometimes in Spanish, or recite Visayan poetry for religious festivals and when Europeans visited Jolo.[81] Under such circumstances, there was ample opportunity for *banyaga* with musical talents to improve their condition. Furthermore, some *datus* played the flute, violin or guitar and all were fond of Spanish songs and dances.[82] *Indio* slaves could and did act as their music instructors and entertained them at night while they smoked opium and discussed trade and politics.

I have emphasized that slave holding was the primary form of investment for the Taosug but have not yet mentioned the slave's significance as an object of exchange in a society and trade where general-purpose money was lacking. As a form of wealth, *banyaga* were a tangible asset in readily transferable form. In this context, *banyaga* were considered not only to be chattel but currency as well. For instance, the value of a *banyaga* in the 1850s, as an object of exchange in transactions between Taosug *datus* and Samal raiders, was equivalent roughly to ten *kayus* (pieces of coarse cotton cloth 20 fathoms in length), or two bundles of coarse *kain* (sarongs), or 200-300 *gantangs* of rice. *Prahus* could be purchased for six to eight slaves while boat rentals amounted to only two to three slaves. Portable cannon were loaned at the rate of one slave, and rifles (often defective) could be rented for five pieces of linen of 20 fathoms.[83] Slaves were exchanged over and over again. *Datus* rarely traded their own followers, especially the younger ones, who were considered more malleable and educable, but they trafficked extensively in slaves who were given to them by Iranun and Balangingi as tribute, in payment of debts and fines or as captives. It was not at all uncommon for a slave to have had two, three, and even possibly four masters in his lifetime, to have lived among several ethnic groups in very different parts of the zone, to have fulfilled a variety of economic functions and experienced varying degrees of hardship and servitude.[84] The ease with which slaves could be moved about reflects their centrality to the economic system.

Slavery then was of decisive importance in the economic and military organization of the Sulu Sultanate in the 19th century. *Banyaga* were encouraged to participate actively in the economic life of the state, and hence obtain a degree of social and cultural autonomy within the society:

> At Soung, business seems active, and all, slaves as well as masters, seem to engage in it . . . , these circumstances promote the industry of the community, and even that of the slave, for he too as before observed, has a life interest in what he earns.[85]

Many *banyaga* ultimately achieved a status and living standard that, though modest enough, was still in their view an improvement over their previous social condition under colonial overlords who did not scruple to thrust their own subjects into bondage. A minority were able to become wealthy; they maintained their own households in the principal towns, living out their lives in a style similar to that of their masters. Some of these *banyaga* who were wealthier than most Taosug commoners and even than some aristocrats owned mats, chests, fine clothes, brass utensils, weapons and gongs. A *banyaga* of standing had a *prahu* and owned a few other slaves to do his trading.[86] Of the condition of slaves in Jolo, Manuel de los Santos observed: ". . . those slaves who wish to marry can do so because there are many women. I have seen some of them bear arms. Others who were slaves formerly, now are wealthy and free."[87] José Ruedas stated: "There are many Christian captives in Jolo some of whom are happily married and wealthy . . ."[88]

The slave statements demonstrate that status discrepancy was common in 19th century Sulu. Among the hierarchy of *banyaga,* those who functioned as bureaucrats, artisans, scribes and concubines often had a greater degree of power and privilege than Taosug commoners. Wilkes remarked of such slaves: "Some of them are quite rich, and are invariably better off than the untitled freemen."[89]

There is some evidence illustrating that in rare instances *banyaga* of remarkable talent rose to the rank of *orang kaya* and *datu* as protégés of their masters.[90]

My discussion of slavery in Sulu thus far testifies to the view that the aristocracy were bent on attracting the flow of external trade to Jolo because it was the principal means of "realizing" the surplus they extracted from the labour of their slaves.[91] Slaves were what the *datus* needed in order to obtain the new luxury products brought by the trade. By the beginning of the 19th century the Jolo market offered British-manufactured brassware and glassware; Chinese earthenware and ceramics; fine muslins, silk and satin garments; Spanish tobacco and wines; and opium from India.[92] There was a constant increase not only in the variety but also in the quality of these objects of trade. These luxury goods for personal adornment and pleasure and for the household were translated into power and prestige factors by the aristocracy to form the material basis of their social superiority.

More important, the political and commercial growth of the Sulu state was reflected in the enormous increase in war stores in the Jolo market at the end of the 18th century — lead, iron, shot, gunpowder and cannon.[93] The Taosug aimed at monopolizing control over the exchange and distribution of these goods which, with slaves, enabled the reproduction of the social formation; the European firearms and gunpowder supplied by the international trade enabled coastal-dwelling Taosug to advance their commercial interests in the inter-societal exchange network, to promote raiding on a large scale and keep the zone free of undesirable intruders and competitors. As Terray emphasizes, it is only in this sense that external trade is a vital element in the overall functioning of the social formation: "Like every distributive mechanism, it created no wealth that was born in the process of production; but it gave a concrete form appropriate to the requirements of reproduction."[94]

It is worth emphasizing again the powerful economic forces that were pushing the Taosug aristocracy in the direction of acquiring more and more slaves; in the first place, their demands for all kinds of products coming in from external trade had to be satisfied — demands that were constantly increasing. These demands were both a consequence and cause of slavery. In order to trade, it was necessary for the Taosug to have something to give in exchange. Hence the collection and redistribution of produce was dominated by those *datus* with the largest number of slaves; that is by the Sultan and certain *datus* on the coast who were most directly involved in Sulu's external trade. Secondly, the more dependent Sulu's economy was on slaves, the larger loomed the question of its supply of slaves. The only way for the Taosug to obtain the raw materials which formed the basis of their commerce was to secure more slaves, by means of long-distance raiding.

In this period the rate of growth of the Sultanate's population had not kept pace with its expanding commercial economy. Since it was the labour of slaves that made possible external trade, slavery rose markedly from this time and became the dominant mode of production. This explains why Jolo quickly became the principal centre in the zone for the importation of slaves and the outfitting of marauders.[95] Slave raiding in the Sulu Sultanate was highly organized. There were several types of expeditions: those which were equipped by the Sultan and his kindred; those which were independently recruited with the encouragement of the Sultan; and those conducted without the sanction of the Sultan. While the right to organize raiding expeditions resided at all levels of the political system, the Sultan and certain *datus* on the coast were in the best position to do so by virtue of their control over external trade and their more expansive network of alliances.

The military and economic activities of Samal raiding populations were regulated closely by their Taosug patrons. They encouraged the Balangingi, an "emergent" community who themselves or their forbears had been captives, to become fishers of men.[96] To meet the West's insatiable demand for produce acceptable in Chinese gourmet markets and, hence, the increased demands for slave labour in the zone, *datus* not only equipped Samal vessels but also provided credit to the Iranun with advances in boats, powder and ball, cannon, rice, opium and additional crew.[97] Everything was to be repaid in captured slaves.[98] *Banyaga* familiar with distant costs and local conditions often accompanied the Balangingi on long slave raids southwards to Celebes and north to Luzon, raids which gave cause for considerable anxiety to colonial governments as late as the 1870s. Thus, the capture of slaves whose surplus labour could be converted into a source of wealth was the principal aim of Taosug-sponsored Iranun/Balangingi attacks on southeast Asian villages and *prahu* shipping.[99]

There are no statistics on the overall number of slaves imported into Jolo in the period under consideration, except for the divergent estimates of European observers. These range from 750 to as high as 4,000 captives per year from 1775 to 1848 for the Philippines alone. It is possible to reconstruct a clearer picture of the pattern of slave imports to the Sulu Sultanate on the basis of captives' statements and other sources. Slave imports to the Sulu Sultanate during the first 65 years (1780-1835) probably averaged between 2,000 to 3,000 per year. The steepest rise in the number of slaves brought annually to Sulu, between 3,000 and 4,000, occurred in the period from 1836 to 1848 when external trade was most intense at Jolo. The trade reached its apex in 1848 and slackened considerably in the next two decades with imports ranging between 1,200 to 2,000 slaves per year until it collapsed in the 1870s.[100] The figures appear to show that between 200,000 and 300,000 slaves were moved in Iranun and Samal vessels to the Sulu Sultanate in the period from 1770 to 1870.[101]

Conclusion

The second half of the 19th century proved to be a critical turning point in the history of the Sulu Sultanate, as it was in the rest of the non-Western world. Everywhere challenges arose to confront the Sulu state's ability to create and reproduce the material and social conditions for survival. With increased cooperation among Western navies and more effective use of steam vessels, the Sulu world began to shrink. The first signs came with the destruction of Balangingi and Jolo by the Spanish between 1846 and 1852.[102] The *datu*'s main source of wealth was his following. The destruction of Balangingi and Jolo placed serious constraints on the ability of the Taosug to retain control over the Balangingi Samal, their principal source of slaves. The grooved cannon and gunpowder of the West which had first attracted Iranun and Samal to Jolo as clients and suppliers of captives were now operating to drive them apart. There was a progressive fragmentation of Samal groups because of Spanish incursions and disruption of the Taosug economy. No longer could their harrying fleets expect to find coasts unprotected and towns defenceless. The era of long-range slave raiding was over.

The total collapse of the system only came with the concerted effort of Spain to end Sulu's autonomy. In the last three decades of the century the trade was destroyed by the Spanish naval campaign to annihilate systematically all *prahu* shipping in the Sulu Archipelago; by the development of a policy to compel the Taosug to settle down in villages as agriculturalists; and by the immigration of large numbers of Straits Chinese to Sulu in spite of, or perhaps because of, the naval campaign. Taosug control over the regulation of external trade collapsed, with drastic consequences. They were forced to curtail their commercial activities and become dependent on the merchant immigrants with contacts in Singapore. The traditional Taosug redistributive role was taken away, the zone disintegrated, and the pattern of life altered by the extinction of slavery. By the beginning of the 20th century, the demise of the trading and raiding system had left the former Sulu state bereft of its importance as a major commercial entrepôt in the wider island economy and confronted with severe internal social and economic problems.

Two major conclusions can be drawn from this discussion of the place of the slave in Sulu society in the 19th century. The first is the decisive importance of the exploitation of slaves in the functioning of the social formation in Sulu: "A social formation cannot be understood except by beginning with an analysis of the relation of productions which are at its base."[103] External trade spawned slavery in the Sulu Sultanate. The increase in external trade which affected state formation and economic integration made it necessary to import captives from the outside world to bolster the population. As goods from China, Europe and North America flowed to Jolo, the Taosug aristocrats thrived, and the Balangingi, a strong, skilled people who were the scourge of Southeast Asia, raiding in 60-foot-long *prahu*, emerged. The sea was the life force of the Sultanate, where tens of thousands of *banyaga* laboured annually to provide the specialties for external trade. The arrival of captive slaves on a hitherto unprecedented scale for intensive or skilled work and their gradual absorption into the lower levels of Taosug and Samal society was central to the development and expansion of the Sulu redistributive system.

Secondly, the rise of Sulu as the dominant state in the trading zone at the end of the 18th century conforms to the more general process of state formation and economic integration that begins with the introduction of external trade. The Sulu Sultanate's history thus parallels the evolution of independent states and stateless societies beyond Southeast Asia where slaves played economic and social roles similar to those in the Abron Kingdom of Gyaman.

NOTES

1 The zone comprising the Sulu Archipelago, the northeast coast of Borneo, the foreland of southern Mindanao and the western coast of Celebes set the geographical framework of the study.

2 My study, "Trade, Raid, Slave: The Socio-Economic Patterns of the Sulu Zone, 1770-1898" (doctoral dissertation, Australian National University, 1975), on which this paper is primarily based, stresses the impact of a rapidly expanding foreign trade on the economy and society of the Sulu zone, and provides a background to a discussion of slavery as an established feature of the Sulu Sultanate in this period.

3 Extensive ethnological research on the Taosug (Tausug, Tawsug, Suluk, Su'ug) conducted by Thomas Kiefer principally in the years 1966-1968 has been published in numerous articles and several monographs. See, Thomas Kiefer, *The Tausug: Violence and Law in a Philippine Moslem Society* (New York: Holt, Rinehart and Winston, 1972); "The Tausug Polity and the Sultanate of Sulu: A Segmentary State in the Southern Philippines," *Sulu Studies* 1 (1972), 19-64.

4 For a cogent discussion of the advent of Islam in Sulu and Mindanao, and its relationship to Southeast Asian Islam until the coming of the Spaniards in the 16th century, see, chapter 2 of Cesar Majul, *Muslims in the Philippines* (Quezon City: University of the Philippines Press, 1973).

5 William H. Geoghegan, "Balangingi," in, Frank M. Lebar, ed., *Ethnic Groups of Insular Southeast Asia* (New Haven: Human Relations Area Files Press, 1975), 2:6-9. Ethnographic studies of the Samal Bajau Laut, spanning nearly a decade, have been conducted in the environs of Tawi-Tawi in the Sulu Archipelago. See, Harry Arlo Nimmo, "The Structure of Bajau Society" (doctoral dissertation, Department of Anthropology, University of Hawaii, 1969); *The Sea People of Sulu* (San Francisco: Chandler Publishing Company, 1972).

6 For a detailed discussion of the traditional patterns of trade of the Sulu Sultanate, see, Warren, "The Sulu Zone," 16-35; see also my article, "Sino-Sulu Trade in the late Eighteenth and Nineteenth Centuries," *Philippine Studies* 25 (1977), 50-79.

7 See, James F. Warren, "Balambangan and the Rise of the Sulu Sultanate, 1772-1775," *Journal of the Malaysian Branch of the Royal Asiatic Society* 50 (1977), 73-93.

8 Warren, "The Sulu Zone," 245-47.

9 *Ibid.,* 348-408.

10 I rely heavily on the anthropological studies of Thomas Kiefer and also acknowledge the pioneering work of John Gullick and Melvin Mednick con-

cerned with the historical reconstruction of traditional Muslim political systems in Southeast Asia. See, Kiefer, *The Tausug,* 104-12; *idem,* "The Tausug Polity and the Sultanate of Sulu," 19-64; *idem,* "The Sultanate of Sulu: Problems in the Analysis of a Segmentary State"; *idem,* "Traditional States of Borneo and the Southern Philippines," in, Clifford Sather, ed., *Borneo Research Bulletin,* 111 (1971), 46-50; John Gullick, *Indigenous Political Systems of Western Malaya* (London: The Athlone Press, 1958); Melvin Mednick, "Some Problems of Moro History and Political Organization," *Philippine Sociological Review* 5 (1957), 39-52. See also, Donald Brown, *Brunei: The Structure and History of a Bornean Malay Sultanate* (Brunei: Brunei Museum, 1970).

11 See appendix V, "The Manila-Jolo Trade, 1786-1830," in Warren, "The Sulu Zone," 424-38.

12 In these Euro-centred histories the term "piracy" is conspicuously present in the titles. Vicente Barrantes, *Guerras Piraticas de Filipinas Contra Min- danaos y Joloanos* (Madrid: Imprenta de Manuel G. Hernandez, 1878),; José Montero y Vidal, *Historia de la Pirateria Malayo Mohomatana en Mindanao, Jolo y Borneo* (Madrid: M. Tello, 1882).

13 See, Blake to Maitland, 13 August 1838, Public Records Office, London (hereafter, PRO), Admiralty 125/133; Declaraciones de todos los cautivos fugados de Jolo y acogidos a los Buques de la expresada division, con objeto de averiguar los puntos de donde salen los pancos piratas, la clase de gente que los tripulan, la forma en que se hacen los armamentos y otros par- ticulares que arrogan los mismas declaraciones, Jolo, 4 October 1836, Philip- pine National Archives, Manila (hereafter, PNA) Mindanao/Sulu 1803-1890, 1-72; Relacion de los cuarenta y cinco cautivos venidos de Jolo sobre el bergantin Espanol *Cometa,* 19 March 1847, PNA, Piratas 3; Verklaringen van ontvlugten personen uit der handen der Zeeroovers van 1845-1849, Ar- sip Nasional Republik Indonesia, Jakarta, (hereafter, ANRI), Menado 37. Numerous statements and interrogations of freed slaves and captive marauders, recorded over several centuries and expressing their own at- titudes towards the place of slaves and raiding in the Sulu world, were also published occasionally in Dutch scholarly journals. See, A.J.F. Jansen "Aantekeningen omtrent Sollok en de Solloksche Zeeroovers," *Tijdschrift voor Indische Taal-, Land- en Volkenkunde, uitgegeven door het (Koninklyk) Bataviaasch Genootschap van Kunsten en Wetenschapen* (hereafter, *TBG*) 7 (1858), *TBG* 20 (1973), 302-06; W.R. Van Hoevell, "De Zeerooverijen der Soloerezen," *Tijdschrift voor Nederlandsch Indies* (hereafter, *TNI*) 2 (1850), 99-105.

14 See appendix XVIII, "The Statements of the Fugitive Captives of the Sulu Sultanate, 1836-1864," in Warren, "The Sulu Zone," 461-82.

15 C. Coquery - Vidrovitch, "An African Mode of Production," *Critique of Anthropology* 4 and 5 (1975), 37-71; *idem,* "Recherches sur un mode de production Africain," *La Pensée* 144 (1969), 61-78; Samir Amin, "Sousdéveloppement et dépendance en Afrique Noire," *Partisans* 64 (1972), 3-34; Yves Person, "Enquête D'Une Chronologie Ivoirienne," in, J. Vansina, R. Mauny and L.U. Thomas, eds., *The Historian in Tropical Africa* (London: Oxford University Press, 1964), 332. See also, Claude Meillassoux, ed., *The Development of Indigenous Trade and Markets in West Africa* (London: Oxford University Press, 1971).

16 Emmanuel Terray, "Long-distance exchange and the formation of the State: The case of the Abron Kingdom of Gyaman," *Economy and Society* 3 (1974), 315-45.

17 J. Hunt, "Some particulars relating to Sulo in the Archipelago of Felicia," in, J.H. Moor, ed., *Notices of the Indian Archipelago and Adjacent Countries* (London: Frank Cass and Co. Ltd., 1968), 37 (first edition 1837).

18 For an important article on the problems of defining slavery, see, E.R. Leach, "Caste, Class and Slavery — The Taxonomic Problem," in, A. de Reuck and J. Knight, eds., *Caste and Race: Comparative Approaches* (London: Churchill, 1967), 12-13. See also, Robert A. Padgug, "Problems in the Theory of Slavery and Slave Society," *Science and Society* 40 (1976), 3-27.

19 Diary of William Pryer, 25 November 1878; 26 June 1879, Colonial Office, London (hereafter, CO), 874/68.

20 Melvin Mednick, "Encampment of the Lake: The Social Organization of a Moslem Philippine (Moro) People," (doctoral dissertation, University of Chicago, 1965), 60-61; Kiefer, "The Tausug Polity and the Sultanate of Sulu," 30.

21 Beyer-Holleman collection of original sources in Philippine Customary Law (hereafter, BH-PCL), VI, paper 162, No. 16, Adolf Gunther, "Correspondence and Reports relating to the Sulu Moros," 10-12; paper 162, No. 25, Emerson B. Christie, "The Non-Christian Tribes of the Northern half of the Zamboanga Peninsula," 87; paper 162, No. 28, L.W.V. Kennon, David P. Barrows, John Pershing and C. Smith, "Census Report relating to the District of Lanao Mindanao," 4; Najeeb Saleeby, *Studies in Moro History, Law and Religion* (Manila: Bureau of Printing, 1905), 92-93.

22 Scott to Governor, 30 June 1904, H.L. Scott Papers, Library of Congress, Washington, D.C., Container 55; Saleeby, *Studies in Moro History,* 94.

23 Saleeby, *Studies in Moro History,* 65, 81, 89.

24 *Ibid.,* 71, 83, 93.

25 *Ibid.,* 93.

26 Diary of William Pryer, 14 March 1878, CO, 874/68.

27 William Pryer, "Notes on North Eastern Borneo and the Sulu Islands," *Royal Geographical Society* 5 (1883), 92-93.

28 John Keith Reynolds, "Towards an Account of Sulu and its Bornean Dependencies 1700-1878" (MA thesis, University of Wisconsin, 1970), 81.

29 Pryer, "Notes on North Eastern Borneo and the Sulu Islands," 92.

30 Thomas Forrest, *A Voyage to New Guinea and the Moluccas from Balambangan: including an account of Magindano, Sooloo and other islands* (London: F. Scott, 1779), 330.

31 Diary of William Pryer, 14 March 1878, CO, 874/68.

32 William Briskoe, Journal, Vol. 2, Department of the Navy, U.S. National Archives and Records Service, entry for 5 February 1842. See also statement of Vincente Santiago in Expediente 12, 4 October 1836, PNA, Mindanao/Sulu 1803-1890, 70.

33 Warren, "The Sulu Zone," 344-47; Mednick, "Some Problems of Moro History and Political Organization," 48.

34 See the statement of Francisco Enriquez in, Patricio de la Escosura, *Memoria sobre Filipinas y Jolo redactada en 1863 y 1864* (Madrid: Imprenta de Manuel G. Hernandez, 1882), 373.

35 BH-PCL, VI, Paper 163, No. 34, Oscar J.W. Scott and Ira C. Brown, "Ethnography of the Magandanaos of Parang," 16; Arturo Sociats y Garin, "Memoria sobre el Archipiélago de Jolo," *Boletin de al Sociedad geográfica de Madrid* 10 (1881), 171.

36 See the statements in, Relacion jurada de los individuos cautivos venidos en la Fragata de guerra Inglesa Samarang, 15 March 1845, PNA, Piratas 3; Hunt, "Some particulars relating to Sulu," 50.

37 Stanley Elkins, "Slavery and its Aftermath in the Western World," in, de Reuck and Knight, *Caste and Race,* 200.

38 Hunt, "Some particulars relating to Sulo," 50.

39 El Gobernador Capitan General a Señor Presidente del Consejo de Ministro de Guerra y Ultramar, 9 December 1858, Archivo Histórico Nacional, Madrid, Ultramar 5184; Hunt, "Some particulars relating to Sulo," 50.

40 Numero 133, Carlos Cuarteron, prefecto apostolico, a Señor Gobernador Politico y Militar de Jolo, 3 December 1878, PNA, Isla de Borneo.

41 Decreto numero 9, El Consejo de las Indias, 18 December 1775, Archivo General de Indias, Seville (hereafter, AGI), Filipinas 359; Pierre Vicomte de Pages, "Travels Round the World in the Years 1767, 1768, 1769, 1770, 1771," in, *Travel Accounts of the Islands 1513-1787* (Manila: The Filipiniana Book Guild, 1971), 156; Felix de Sainte-Croix Renouard, *Voyage Commercial et Politique aux Indes Orientales, aux Iles Philippines, à la Chine, avec*

des nations sur la Cochin Chine et le Touquin, pendant les années 1803, 1804, 1805, 1806 et 1807 (Paris: Clement, 1810), 2:275; Forrest, *Voyage to New Guinea,* 330; Barrantes, *Guerras Piraticas,* 160-61; Montero y Vidal, *Historia de Filipinas,* 2:369.

42 C. Wilkes, "Jolo and the Sulus," in, E.H. Blair and J.A. Robertson, *The Philippine Islands, 1493-1898* (Cleveland: A.H. Clark, 1903-1909), 43:128-42.

43 See statements of Mariano de la Cruz and Francisco Gregorio in, Expediente 12, 4 October 1836, PNA, Mindanao/Sulo 1803-1890; El Gobierno Politico y Militar del Zamboango a Gobernador Capitan General, 9 June 1847, PNA, Mindanao/Sulu 1838-1885.

44 Extracts from *Singapore Free Press,* 6 April 1847, PRO, Admiralty 125/133; BH-PCL, VI, Paper 162, No. 26, F.P. Williamson, "The Moros between Buluan and Punta Flecha," 103; Mednick, "Encampment of the Lake," 62.

45 The Chinese manufactured mother-of-pearl articles in the form of beads, fish counters, fans and combs. William Milburn, *Oriental Commerce; containing a geographical description of the principal places in the East Indies, China, and Japan, with their produce, manufactures and trade, including the coasting or country trade from port to port; also the rise and progress of the trade of the various European nations with the Eastern world, particularly that of the English East India Company from the Discovery of the passage round the Cape of Good Hope to the present period; with an account of the company's Establishments, Revenues, Debts, Assets, at home and abroad* (London: Black, Parry and Company, 1813), 2:513.

46 See, "List of Products of Sulu and its immediate dependencies," 26 February 1761, PRO, Egremont Papers, 30/47/20/1; "List of Goods to be had at Sooloo," MS, included with the log of the ship *Albree,* 656/1833A, Salem Peabody Museum, Salem, Massachusetts; Hunt, "Some particulars relating to Sulo," 48.

47 In 1859 the Singapore price of a picul of mother-of-pearl shell varied according to the quality between 300 and 600 dollars. It was not unusual to pay up to 850 dollars to re-export it to Ceylon. Numero 83, El Consul de España en Singapore a el primer Secretario de estado, 3 July 1860, Archivo de Ministerio de Asuntos Exteriores, Madrid (hereafter AMAE), Correspondencia Consulados Singapore 2067.

48 This estimate has been arrived at by using the few examples in the literature, archival documents and private manuscripts to provide ratios between the number of people involved in marine procurement and their annual output at small collecting centres in the zone. I have used these figures in conjunction with the statistic for the estimated volume of *tripang* (10,000 piculs) and mother-of-pearl (12,000 piculs) exported from Jolo in the 1830s to establish the relative size of the labour force. For example, Hunt wrote that at Towson

Duyon in Sandakan Bay [Northeast Borneo], "*A Hundred bajow or fishermen* [are] employed in catching and curing tripang; they obtain about *fifty piculs annually,*" and at Loo-Loo, "There are . . . *thirty to forty Bajow fishermen* employed in catching tripang; twenty or thirty piculs are cured here annually." On Tawi-Tawi there were "*eight hundred Islams,* chiefly the slaves [clients?] of Datu Mulut Mondarosa and Datu Adanan. They produce annually for the Sulo market *three hundred piculs of Kulit tepoy* [mother-of-pearl], *forty piculs of beche de mer* . . . and some very valuable pearls . . ." At Basilan, "*fifteen hundred Islams* produced *twenty piculs of black birds nest, three hundred piculs of Kulit tepoy,* a few pearls, some tortoise shell, and twenty or thirty prows of paddi for annual export". Hunt, "Some particulars relating to Sulo," 54-55, 59. (Emphasis added) These figures tend to support the conclusion that the collecting and curing of a picul of *tripang* or a picul of mother-of-pearl shell required the average labour of two men for *tripang* and four men for mother-of-pearl. This means that in the first half of the 19th century an estimated 68,000 men laboured in Sulu's fisheries. In 1880 a Spanish naval officer alluded to the size of the groups employed in Jolo's mother-of-pearl fisheries: ". . . in order to collect mother-of-pearl shell, they [the Taosug] assembled innumerable expeditions which are often led by a *datu.* (I guarded one [expedition] of 2,200 fishermen and three *datus.*)" Comision Reservada a Borneo y Jolo 1881-1882, bound Ms. Biblioteca de Palacio, Madrid, 38.

49 Warren, "The Sulu Zone," 128-57.

50 Crocker to Sir Rutherford Alcock, 10 September 1887, CO 874/243.

51 Hunt, "Some particulars relating to Sulo," 37.

52 Statements of Alex Quijano, Francisco Sacarias and Domingo Francisco in, Expediente 12, 4 October 1836, PNA, Mindanao/Sulu 1803-1890. See also statement of Juan Florentino in, Relacion jurada de los dos individuos cautivos venidos en la corbetta de guerra Francesa Salina procedente de Sumalasan en el Archipielago de Jolo, PNA, Piratas 3; Treacher to Sir Rutherford Alcock, 3 July 1884, CO, 874/237.

53 Pryer to Treacher, 5 October 1881, CO, 874/229; Pryer, "Notes on North Eastern Borneo and the Sulu Islands," 92.

54 Pryer, "Notes on North Eastern Borneo and the Sulu Islands," 93.

55 Spenser St. John, *Life in the Forests of the Far East* (London: Smith Elder and Company, 1862), 2:250.

56 Thomas Jefferson Jacobs, *Scenes, Incidents and Adventures in the Pacific Ocean, or the Islands of the Australasian Seas, during the cruise of the Clipper Margaret Oakley* (New York: Harper and Brothers, 1844), 335.

57 Melchior Yvan, *Six Months among the Malays and a Year in China* (London: James Blackwood, 1855), 258-59.

58 Wilkes, "Jolo and the Sulus," 181.

59 Statement of Alex Quijano in, Expediente 12, 4 October 1836, PNA, Mindanao/Sulu 1803-1890.

60 Jansen, "Aantekeningen omtrent sollok en de Solloksche Zeeroovers," 222; Bonham to Maitland, 28 June 1838, PRO, Admiralty 125.133.

61 Statements of Alex Quijano, Domingo Candelario and Mariano Sevilla in, Expediente 12, 4 October 1836, PNA, Mindanao/Sulu 1803-1890; statement of Mah Room, 2 June 1838, in, Bonham to Maitland, 28 June 1838, PRO, Admiralty 125/133.

62 Statements of Juan Florentino, Manuel Feliz, Domingo Francisco and Mariano Sevilla in, Expediente 12, 4 October 1836, PNA, Mindanao/Sulu 1803-1890; extracts from *Singapore Free Press,* 6 April 1847, PRO, Admiralty 125/133; Numero 137, Carlos Cuarteron, prefecto apostolico a Gobernador Capitan General, 12 August 1878, PNA, Isla de Borneo (2); Tomas de Comyn, *State of the Philippines in 1810 being an historical, statistical and descriptive account of the interesting portion on the Indian Archipelago* (Manila: Filipiniana Book Guild, 1969), 124.

63 Statements of Abdul and Sendi in, Verklaringen van ontvlugten personen uit de handen der Zeeroovers van 1845-1849, ANRI, Menado 37; Jansen, Aantekeningen omtrent Sollok en de Solloksche Zeeroovers, 225.

64 Sherard Osborn, *My Journal in Malayan Waters* (London: Routledge, Warne and Routledge, 1861), 41; in some instances slaves redeemed themselves by acts of bravery which indebted their masters to them. Slaves involved in raiding were most apt to receive their freedom under such circumstances. Witti to Treacher, November 1881, Co, 879/229; Cesar Majul, "Political and Historical Notes on the Old Sulu Sultanate," *Journal of the Malaysian Branch of the Royal Asiatic Society* 38 (1965), 35-36; Kiefer, *The Tausug,* 41. The following example illustrates the circumstances under which a master might have exercised the right of redemption by a sacred promise to God:

> Dato Meldrum of Johor states that he saw Pengeran Mahomet of Brunei wearing a *baju ranti* [chain mail] at Pandassan, in the early fifties. The Pengeran had married an Illanun wife who was settled there and who claimed rule over the river. Pengeran Mahomet said he had been pirating on the coast of China, more than once along with the Illanuns, on one occasion he fell into the sea with his *baju ranti* on but was saved by a slave who dived and fished him up . . .

British North Borneo Herald and Official Gazette (hereafter, NBH) 16 September 1895, 236.

65 Kiefer, *The Tausug,* 10.

66 Farren to Palmerston, 17 January 1851, CO, 144/8; Corbett to the Secretary of the Admiralty, 6 October 1862, Foreign Office, London (hereafter, FO), 71/1.

67 Statements of Pedro Antonio, Vincente Remigio, and Francisco Augustino in, Expediente 12, 4 October 1836, PNA, Mindanao/Sulu 1803-1890; Witti to Treacher, November 1881, CO, 874/229.

68 Statements of Vincente Remigio and Francisco Augustino in, Expediente 12, 4 October 1836, PNA, Mindanao/Sulu 1803-1890; Witti to Treacher, November 1881, CO, 874/229.

69 Statements of Juan Sabala and Vincente Remigio in, Expediente 12, 4 October 1836, PNA, Mindanao/Sulu 1803-1890.

70 Statements of Matias de la Cruz and Francisco Sacarias in, Expediente 12, 4 October 1836, PNA, Mindanao/Sulu 1803-1890; Verklaring van Chrishaan Soerma, 10 August 1846, ANRI, Menado 50; William Pryer, "Diary of a trip up the Kinabatangan," *Sabah Society Journal* 5 (1970), 119.

71 Verklaring van Chrishaan Soerma, 10 October 1846, ANRI, Menado 50.

72 Pryer, "Diary of a trip up the Kinabatangan," 119.

73 Diary of William Pryer, 14 March 1878, CO, 874/67.

74 *Ibid.*

75 Briskoe, Journal, Vol. 2, 5 February 1842; Diario de mi Comision a Jolo en el vapor Magallenes, José Maria Peñeranda, 19 March 1848, PNA, Mindanao/Sulu unclassified bundle; Jansen, "Aantekeningen omtrent Sollok en de Solloksche Zeeroovers," 214.

76 Escosura, *Memoria sobre Filipinas y Jolo redactada en 1863 y 1864,* 371; Diary of William Pryer, 8 March 1879, CO, 874/68.

77 Wilkes, "Jolo and the Sulus," 166; Jules Sebastion César Dumont D'Urville, *Voyages au pole sud et dans L'Océanie sur les corvettes L'Astrolabe et La Zélée . . . pendant les années 1837-1838-1839-1840* (Paris: Gide et J. Baudry, 1841-1846), 7:170.

78 Wilkes, "Jolo and the Sulus," 161.

79 Statement of José Ruedas in, Expediente 12, 4 October 1836, PNA, Mindanao/Sulu 1803-1890, 32.

80 Statement of Gabriel Francisco in, Expediente 12, 4 October 1836, PNA, Mindanao/Sulu 1803-1890, 71.

81 Forrest, *Voyage to New Guinea,* 330; Hunt, "Some particulars relating to Sulo," 40; D'Urville, *Voyage au pole sud et dans L'Océanie sur Les Corvettes L'Astrolabe et La Zélée* 7:308, 313; Wilkes, "Jolo and the Sulus," 165.

82 Forrest, *Voyage to New Guinea,* 330; Hunt, "Some particulars relating to Sulo," 40.

83 Jansen, "Aantekeningen omtrent Sollok en de Solloksche Zeeroovers," 216, 227.

84 Prefettura Apostolica de Labuan Su Dipendenze ECC. Nella Malesia Orientale, Carlos Curarteron, 10 November 1878, PNA, Isla de Borneo (1). See also statement of Simona Plasa in, Expediente 34, Gobernador Militar y Politico de la Provincia de Zamboanga a Gobernador Capitan General, 1 February 1852, PNA, Mindanao/Sulu 1838-1885; Verklaring van Chrishaan Soerma, 10 August 1846, ANRI, Menado 50.

85 Wilkes, "Jolo and the Sulus," 168.

86 Witti to Treacher, November 1881, CO, 874/229.

87 Statement of Manuel de los Santos in, Expediente 12, 4 October 1836, PNA, Mindanao/Sulu 1803-1890.

88 Statement of José Ruedas in, Expediente 12, 4 October 1836, PNA, Mindanao/Sulu 1803-1890.

89 Wilkes, "Jolo and the Sulus," 166.

90 Montero y Vidal, *Historia de la Pirateria Malayo — Mahometana en Mindanao Jolo y Borneo,* 69; in 1903 General Leonard Wood described Panglima Hassan as: "Originally a slave born on Pata island, and little by little has worked up until he is now the most important Chieftain in the island of Jolo, next to the Sultan and Datu Jokanian". Leonard Wood Papers, Library of Congress, Washington, D.C., container 3, Diary of Leonard Wood, 18 August 1903.

91 Terray, "Long-distance Exchange and the Formation of the State," 315, 344-45.

92 Warren, "The Sulu Zone," 74-76, 83-85, 103.

93 Warren, "The Sulu Zone," 39-52, 76-77. See also, Warren, "Balambangan and the Rise of the Sulu Sultanate, 1772-1775," 74-83.

94 Terray, "Long-distance Exchange and the Formation of the State: the case of the Abron Kingdom of Gyaman," 335-36.

95 James F. Warren, "Slave Markets and Exchange in the Malay World: The Sulu Sultanate, 1770-1878," *Journal of Southeast Asian Studies* 8 (1977), 162; "The Sulu Zone," 327-28.

96 *Ibid.,* 300-04.

97 Statements of Matias Domingo and Juan de la Cruz in, Expediente 12, 4 October 1836, PNA, Mindanao/Sulu 1803-1890; extract from *Singapore Free Press,* April 1847, PRO, Admiralty 125/133. Majul, *Muslims in the Philippines,* 285, fails to recognize the important redistributive role of the Taosug in raiding and its relationship to the reproduction of the social formation:

All the evidence points to the fact that the Sulu Sultan and chief datus never encouraged or approved of piracy by Samal or Iranun datus, for they were themselves traders having an interest that all shipping lanes be kept safe especially for traders going or coming from Jolo.

98 Statement of Juan de la Cruz in, Expediente 12, 4 October 1836, PNA, Mindanao/Sulu 1803-1890; El Gobierno Politico y Militar de Zamboanga a Gobernador Capitan General, 30 May 1842, PNA, Mindanao/Sulu 1838-1885.

99 Blake to Maitland, 8 August 1838, PRO, Admiralty 125/133; Jansen, "Aantekenigen omtrent Sollok en de Solloksche Zeeroovers," 217, 229.

100 Warren, "Slave Markets and Exchange in the Malay World: The Sulu Sultanate, 1770-1878," 174; "The Sulu Zone," 342.

101 Farren to Palmerston, 16 March 1851, CO, 144/8; Warren, "Slave Markets and Exchange in the Malay World: The Sulu Sultanate, 1770-1878," 174-75; "The Sulu Zone," 342-44. For a precise calculation on slave imports to Sulu 1770-1870, I have used the figure 20.5 slaves per boat based on the statements of slaves seized 1826-1847 minus 4,800 to 8,000 (1,200 to 2,000 per year) for the period 1848-1852. From the calculations it therefore follows that the number of slaves imported over the period 1770-1870 varied from a low estimate of 201,350 to a high estimate of 302,575. See table 4 in "Slave Markets and Exchange in the Malay World: The Sulu Sultanate, 1770-1878," 174.

102 Warren, "The Sulu Zone," 314-21.

103 Terray, "Long-distance Exchange and the Formation of the State," 340.

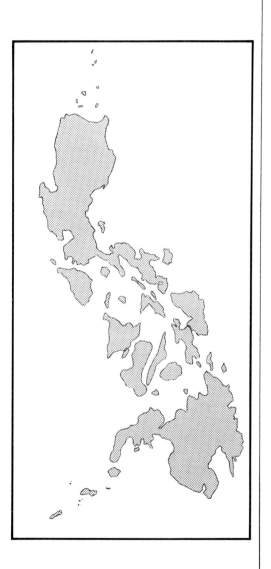

CONCLUSION

Conclusion:
An Agenda for Philippine Studies

ED. C. DE JESUS

The essays in this volume marshall information from a wide variety of sources, hitherto largely unexplored, to bring into sharper focus the political, economic and cultural variables shaping the evolution of specific Filipino communities. It seems almost perverse, therefore, or at least self-defeating, to strip away the layers of luminous detail in an attempt to reduce these studies to a set of general conclusions.

The primary concern of the contributors is clearly with the locality — city, province, region — they have chosen to study. Whether and to what extent local developments can shed light on broader national issues remains of secondary interest. To project to the national level conclusions reached at the local can be done at this stage only at some risk — one which the editors are not particularly eager to embrace. And yet, there is the equally real problem of the "neo-antiquarian swamp" that McCoy warns us about. Research on the Philippines could conceivably fall into the trap of endlessly churning out studies of increasingly smaller subnational units, a process of academic involution leading to our learning more and more about less and less.

McCoy has suggested a way of slipping past the two prongs of the problem. The option he offers is, in effect, to by-pass the local/national axis altogether and to focus on the linkages between sub-national units and centres of political and commercial power beyond the Philippines. Rather than merely providing inputs to national history or indulging purely pedantic interests, local studies would help clarify the patterns of relationship obtaining between primary exporting communities and world markets. Several studies in this collection confirm the explanatory power of this approach. Nearly half of the essays explicitly pursue the theme which has given the volume its title — local transformations provoked by the impact of global trade.

Our Western colleagues, it seems to me, are better positioned to continue exploring the ramifications of this theme. They have, to begin with, greater access to the literature on the history and historiography of other countries. Those holding teaching positions will rarely, if ever, offer a course exclusively focused on the Philippines. They will touch upon the Philippines as part of a larger geographic area such as Southeast Asia or the Pacific, as part of a broader economic-ideological category such as the Third World, or in the context of world movements such as colonial expansion or nationalism. Their particular circumstances facilitate the process of analyzing the Philippines or, more precisely, its constituent pieces, in terms of a broader conceptual framework.

In contrast, most Filipinos doing Philippine studies will have perhaps no more than a passing acquaintance with the experience of countries other than the Philippines. Those exposed to other cultures by graduate studies abroad come home to find limited opportunities for sustaining their interest in these areas. Their investigations, therefore, will tend to gravitate towards the local/national axis, an orientation strengthened by their proximity to archival and field data.

Quite apart from questions of training, resources and academic responsibilities, Filipinos will perhaps find a compelling psychological reason to force the leap from local to national history. It is more difficult for Filipinos to accept the reality that the nation-state is indeed a colonial creation. Even the geographical boundaries have been determined by the fortunes of colonial governments, not by the Filipinos themselves. Had the Spaniards been less energetic, the Sulu archipelago might have become part of another political unit. Had they been more enterprising, as some Filipinos wistfully observe, we would now be exploiting Borneo's oil deposits. The discomfort with the colonial burden is understandable even though it does manifest itself in such disconcerting ways as the periodic campaign to rectify history by changing the country's name. Similarly, there are periodic attempts at the use of terms plucked out of the pre-Hispanic past — such as *barangay* — to ennoble new instrumentalities of central government. But if the reality of the nation is indeed rooted in the ideas shared by the people from whom it claims allegiance, Filipinos ought to continue the search for the beliefs that give substance to Philippine nationalism. The local national axis remains a most promising point of departure for this search.

Current political developments provide the additional argument of contemporary relevance. The studies in this volume demonstrate how tenuous and uncertain has been Manila's control over the rest of the archipelago. The central government — whether operated by Spanish, American or Japanese imperialists or by duly elected Filipino leaders — has historically lacked the political-military strength, the economic resources and the administrative skills to enforce its will on the country's localities. Various regions developed their own resource bases and linkages with world markets. Enterprising "elites", often of Chinese or Spanish mestizo origins, parlayed profits from trade to gain control over crop lands and eventually over the people who worked them. Economic power became both an end to be protected by, as well as a means by which to attain, political power. Electoral politics institutionalized by the Americans allowed the more ambitious and the more skilful elites to extend and consolidate their leadership over increasingly larger geographical areas and electoral constituencies. Political alliances built on a network of patron–client relations and reinforced by marital connections and *compadrazgo* ties enabled them to compete for national office, from which they could then promote the interests of their own local base. Rather than the centre dominating the localities, the central government itself became a prize to be contested by shifting local alliances.

The imposition of Martial Law in 1972 marked the beginning of a determined attempt by one faction among the elite to establish the supremacy of the centre. The dissolution of private armies, the supervision of electoral politics and tighter government control over the economy — exemplified for instance by the law requiring all sugar exports to go through the government's National Sugar Trading Corporation — have effectively curbed the power of the rival elites whom Marcos has branded as the Old Society "Oligarchs". A new, post-Martial Law economic elite has emerged but, lacking an independent political base, exists on the sufferance and with the patronage of a regime which finds it useful as a medium for implementing economic policies and as a counterpoise to the established pillars of Philippine business.

The lifting of Martial Law did not spell the end of centralizing efforts, as witnessed by the successful manoeuvre to legitimize a strong president by constitutional amendment. The results of the April 1981 plebiscite on several such amendments showed that a few pockets of local strength — in Zamboanga, Misamis Oriental, Cebu, Catanduanes, Batangas — still exist. The tension between centrifugal and centripetal forces continues as a leitmotif in Philippine history.

For those who must continue to grapple with the issues revolving around the local/national axis, this volume uncovers the more treacherous pitfalls. The principal trap appears to be a matter of perspective. The materials presented here suggest that the conceptual filters through which we habitually sift our data require refinement. For conceptual clarity, as much perhaps as for ease of exposition, it has been convenient to organize the facts around sets of paired opposites — the elite and the masses, nationalist and colonialist, collaborator and patriot, pro- and anti-, Left and Right. But these Manichaean polarities conceal almost as much as they clarify. The categories we use are abstractions. Human beings demonstrate a remarkable capacity for reconciling apparently contradictory motives. It is risky to assume that people see only two sides of a question, or that they necessarily consider two options mutually incompatible.

Fegan's micro-study of Barrio Buga in San Miguel, Bulacan dramatizes the complex and conflicting claims to loyalty that an individual had to balance during the turbulent years of the Japanese occupation. Posing the problem in terms of whether a person was pro- or anti-American, pro- or anti-Japanese, pro- or anti-Huk, fails to capture the complexity of the equation that the individual had to resolve. The documentation on Bo. Buga during the war reveals patterns apparently duplicated on a broader canvas in the Western Visayas and perhaps also in Cotabato. The outbreak of the war introduced a new line of cleavage in a society already riven by conflict. The Japanese and the guerillas only represented new contenders in the ring, to be conciliated when necessary and exploited when possible.

In the absence of a dominant central authority to temper factionalism, individual leaders and/or families concentrated on protecting and expanding their own power base. The political decisions made during the war by Bo. Buga's de Guzman family were quite consistent with the positions they had taken before the war. Coincidentally, perhaps, rather than by deliberate design, these decisions also served to enhance the family's survival chances. The de Guzman family had all bets prudently covered, with one brother affiliating his personal following to the USAFFE, another brother commanding the local *Hukbalahap* unit and a relative, Dionisio Macapagal, joining the pro-Japanese *Ganap* Party.

Like the Japanese occupation, the Revolution against Spain and the Philippine–American War brought to the surface — in places like Cebu, Iloilo, Negros, Cotabato and Bukidnon — conflicts beyond those dividing pro-nationalist and pro-colonial. The ambivalence towards independence and Aguinaldo's government appeared most acute among those who recognized the linkages that had developed between their communities and world markets. The elite of Iloilo and Negros did desire independence — from Aguinaldo's government as much as from Spain.

Guerrero makes a persuasive case for the thesis that in Luzon and in the Western Visayas "the Filipino elite were the ultimate victors of the Revolution", while "the masses in town and countryside were the unwitting victims". Despite the dramatic rush of events which, within a span of four years, saw the overthrow of the Spaniards, the birth and death of a Philippine Republic and the establishment of an American colonial regime, political leadership at the local level remained essentially unaltered and reflected no discernible social change. This documentation of elite continuity through the years of revolutionary disorder is a significant contribution to our understanding of the period. Equally valuable are the leads that Guerrero and others provide for further research into the changing character of the 19th century *principalia*.

The elite during the period discussed by Guerrero seems characterized mainly by three things: possession of political office; an inordinate inclination to exploit their position to the detriment of the masses; and a compulsive, ruthless drive to preserve and expand their powers. Was there anything else — other shared attributes or interests, other bonds — that unified the elite and entitles us to speak of them as though they constituted, and acted as, a homogenous unit? If they did strive for common objectives, how did they articulate and promote them and resolve conflicts that might have impeded a concerted program of action? Or was there an Invisible Hand at work so that each civil or military official pursuing his narrow self-interest helped bring about the desired social order?

But perhaps, as these studies suggest, "elite" is too general a term to use without qualification. Guerrero herself writes of municipal elites, provincial elites and cosmopolitan elites, the last perhaps corresponding to Owen's super-*principales*. Relative power seems to be the element distinguishing one group from another, with the cosmopolitan elites able to exert a direct influence on national issues. It would be useful to learn more about the relationships among these different elite levels. McLennan notes, for instance, that the provincial elites of Nueva Ecija were migrants from other provinces, and Owen makes the same point regarding the provincial elites of Kabikolan. One might expect that their relationship with their respective municipal elites would differ from that obtaining in other areas where provincial elites had local roots.

Cullinane has traced the evolution of the Cebu Parian leadership from an ethnically distinct group dominating a ghetto community to a multi-ethnic urban aristocracy and thence to a province-wide, even region-wide, elite from which a genuine national leader like Sergio Osmeña emerged. More studies along this line would help us draw more substantial conclusions, or at least pose more meaningful questions about the nature of Philippine elites.

The term "masses" could also stand a measure of disaggregation. This convenient catch-all includes Bikol abaca-strippers and Bukidnon cowboys, Ilocano small-holders and Visayan *sacadas,* tenant farmers paying cash or sharing crops, landless agricultural labourers and waterfront stevedores, perhaps also *cabos* and *katiwalas.* The problems and the priorities of each group are not identical and their interests do not necessarily converge. Focusing on the poverty they share in common does not reduce the differences or make them less real. Although the poor themselves speak only of the distinction between "them" or "the others" and "us", recent studies indicate significant gradations of poverty from the marginally poor (*mahirap*) to the destitute (*dukha*).

The problem of the frontier is another theme central to several of these studies. Reflecting the colonial status of the 19th century Philippines, the term has two very different meanings: the colonial "frontier" inhabited by unsubjugated high-land *infieles* and southern Muslims; and the agricultural "frontier" of the Filipino peasant pioneers who cleared farms from the unpopulated forests of Luzon and the Visayas. Sulu and the Luzon Cordillera represented the first kind of frontier — areas at the outer reaches of Spanish and American control bitterly defended by hostile communities. Scott shows how colonial economic interests influenced the pace and pattern of the Spanish assault on the Cordillera. The actual process of highland pacification — combining skilful tactical adjustments and a ruthless use of force — bears scrutiny as a possible replay of Spain's 16th century campaigns against the lowland *indios.* The tragic legacy of the long history of hostility along this frontier has been the clouded relationship between lowland and highland Filipinos. The historical perspective should make authorities more sensitive to the anxieties provoked by central government projects, such as the Chico River Dam, among the highland peoples.

The other kind of frontier discussed in this volume deals with the areas of pioneer settlement — land cleared of forest growth and put to productive use by an expanding indigenous population. In other countries, most notably in the United States, an extensive literature has developed analyzing and celebrating the Fron-tier as both a physical and psychological reality, both a place and a frame of mind. In historiography and literature the American Frontier has figured as a central force shaping the character and the institutions of the people. The abundance of free land to move into, it has been claimed, provided a safety valve for class con-flict, fostered independence and individualism, promoted economic and social mobility and nurtured democracy.

The cost of occupying the frontier in the two countries was comparable. Like the winning of the American West, the settlement of Negros by the Ilongos, of Nueva Ecija by the Ilocanos and of the Bukidnon plateau by the coastal Visayans led to the disintegration of the culture of the areas' original inhabitants, if not to the ex-tinction of the communities themselves. But the pioneering process in the Philippines failed to create conditions conducive to the growth of egalitarian communities committed to democratic institutions. Whether it did produce communities with a stronger sense of nationhood (as perhaps happened in Bukidnon) remains an open question.

The articles in the volume suggest some of the reasons why the Philippine frontier environment did not generate socio-economic mobility or a more vigorous spirit of self-reliance. The process of settling the frontier did not really involve a radical break with tradition. As McCoy points out, the moribund Ilongo textile industry supplied the capital, labour and management required to open up the Negros frontier to sugar cultivation. It was not surprising then that the social structure in the sugar plantations should take on the same hierarchical cast as that which had obtained in the textile industry. And as McLennan recalls, the Ilocanos moved out from their hometowns not as individuals but as *barangays,* and arrived at the frontier with the web of established patron–client relationships intact.

The fact that the settlers were colonial subjects also placed sharp limits on the opportunities for social and political innovation. The American pioneers felt free to formulate laws suitable to the needs of their new environment. The Spanish colonial government could not in good conscience countenance any infringement of its legislative authority. Laws drafted in Manila and Madrid continued to govern the migrant wherever he might wander within the colony. This presumption effectively precluded the development of what Robin Winks has called "sociological jurisprudence".[1] Conditions on the frontier easily became exploitative because poor, unlettered migrants were left at the mercy of those who could use the land laws to their advantage.

Who makes what laws for whom and to what purpose? The study of the country's legal system, as it has evolved over time, and its changing functional relationships with the society it presumably serves ought to receive more serious attention. That it has not yet done so is, in retrospect, somewhat surprising. The Philippines seems to be a particularly litigious society, if the number of lawyers it has produced and the legal requirements for many activities serve as any indication. The law is a highly respected and much favoured profession in a society where a university degree is an essential mark of status. There is also a scrupulous concern for observing, and perhaps more important, being seen to observe the letter of the law. Witness, for instance, the elaborate efforts of the present government to ensure that its activities are within the bounds of the Constitution even if it means a periodic revision of that document.

Filipinos seem to regard the law with a curious mix of awe and contempt. On the one hand, there seems to be an almost mystical belief, perhaps inherited from Spanish colonial bureaucrats, that the mere act of promulgating a memorandum, ordinance or decree in the prescribed manner and form is sufficient by itself to resolve a problem. There is also, on the other hand, a cynical and quite callous willingness by those with power to manipulate the law for personal or partisan ends. Laws can be used to enslave as well as to liberate. The courts, as a number of these studies remind us, have not always served the cause of justice.

The experience of having been subjected for so many years to foreign legal systems constructed by colonial bureaucrats has perhaps influenced Filipino attitudes and responses to the law. Certainly the Filipinos quickly grasped the importance of learning the rules of the legal game. Cullinane offers us the instructive example of the Parian leadership holding governor and bishop at bay and protecting its interests through the adroit use of Spanish legal procedures and liberal recourse to bribery.

Like legal history, which received a boost with the awarding of the 1978 Bancroft Prize in American History to Morton J. Horwitz's *The Transformation of American Law*, the history of technology has also gained ground in the United States in recent years.[2] The contributions of McCoy and Owen, in particular, suggest that the impact of technological changes on Philippine economy and society deserve consideration as a new field of inquiry.

One technological innovation, the introduction of the steamer in the 1860s, altered shipping patterns in the Western Visayas and enabled Iloilo to replace Manila as the regional centre for the distribution of foreign imports. Other technological changes — the construction of centrifugal mills and the development of the tug-and-lighter system of moving cargo — eventually allowed mill-owners to build modern piers along the Negros coastline and to by-pass Iloilo as an entrepôt for the sugar trade, with far-reaching consequences for the city's waterfront workers and labour unionism in the region. Technological changes and the movement of international commodity markets, more than individual personalities, determined the duration of Iloilo's reign as the "Queen City of the South".

In a similar fashion, technology and the play of world markets governed the pattern of depression and prosperity in the abaca-dominated Bikol region. Owen has already traced for us the linkages among technological changes, the international price of abaca and the life of the region. But, as he points out, developments in the abaca industry did not necessarily determine how other commercial products, such as gold, textiles and coal, developed, and these commodities were just as sensitive to changing production and transport technologies. Opportunities for further research remain open even in the Bikol region.

It is in fact the opening up of new fields of investigation which we hope will be the main contribution of this volume. From the studies in this collection we can begin to draw a more rounded, more finely shaded picture of Philippine society. We hope that the wide range of questions they raise will suggest not only new areas for research but also new perspectives for action.

NOTES

1 Robin Winks, "The Myth of the American Frontier: Its Relevance to America, Canada and Australia" (Sir George Watson Lecture, University of Leicester, 21 January 1971).

2 Morton J. Horwitz, *The Transformation of American Law, 1780-1860* (Cambridge: Harvard University Press, 1977).

MEASURES

arroba   measure of weight equivalent to 11.5 kilograms.

cavan   measure of dry volume generally 75 litres with some local variation. Weight varies according to commodity, but a *cavan* of *palay* weighs 44 to 50 kilograms and one of milled rice about 57.5 kilograms.

peso, ₱   Philippine currency worth about US$1.00 during the mid-19th century, and about $0.50 from the 1890s until 1941.

picul   measure of weight ranging from 60 to 63.3 kilograms in most of the archipelago, but rising to 69 kilograms in late 19th century Leyte-Samar.

pieza   measure of cloth in the Western Visayas, ranging from 4.2 to 18.6 metres.

pilon   measure of weight used most often for sugar; 61.4 kilograms.

quiñon   Spanish areal measure, 5.76 hectares in the 18th century, but changed to 2.79 hectares in the 19th.

real   19th century Spanish currency worth one-eighth of a peso.

GLOSSARY

abaca: fibre of the plant *Musa textilis* spun into hemp and used for cordage and textile manufacture.

amo: master or leader; boss.

anting-anting: magic amulet that is supposed to grant immunity to weapons or illness.

Audiencia: the highest Spanish colonial court which heard important cases, advised the governor and occasionally initiated legislation.

ayuntamiento: Spanish colonial city council usually with Spanish representation.

babaylan, baylan: Filipino spirit medium believed capable of magical intervention.

banda descargada: stevedore crew that unloads vessels on Visayan waterfronts.

banda pasaka: stevedore crew that stacks sacks inside warehouses on Visayan waterfronts.

banda pesada: stevedore weighing crew on Visayan waterfronts.

banyaga: chattel slave in the Sulu sultanate; either captured in a slave-raid, or the children of those so captured.

barangay: a pre-Hispanic social unit of 30 to 100 families owing allegiance to one chief. Under the Spanish, each municipality (*pueblo*) was divided into tax collection units called *barangay* that did not necessarily coincide with local residential units, *barrios*.

barrio: roughly equivalent to village. Under the Spanish, each town (*pueblo*) was subdivided into smaller units designated according to a scale of decreasing population — *barrio, visita, sitio* and *rancheria*. During the 20th century the *barrio* has been the smallest government unit.

bolo: a generic term for bladed instrument designed variously for fighting and forest or farm work.

Bukidnon: people of the mountains; the name of an interior Mindanao province and region.

buri: palm used for weaving mats, hats and light containers; sap used to make sugar, alcohol and vinegar.

cabecera: administrative centre of a Spanish colonial town where market, church and town hall were located; equivalent to the term *población.* Alternatively, the term was used to mean provincial capital.

cabecilla: petty headman; 19th century Chinese chief agent in Manila who consigned goods to provincial sub-agents. Labour contractor and stevedore supervisor on Visayan waterfronts equivalent to *cabo* on the Manila docks. Also, foreman for agricultural work parties in Central Luzon and Negros Occidental.

cabeza de barangay: head of a collective tax-paying unit during the Spanish period.

cabo: foreman subordinate to a labour contractor (*cabecilla*) on Visayan waterfronts. On the Manila waterfront, a *cabo* is a labour contractor synonymous with the Visayan *cabecilla.*

cacique: a Spanish term for powerful local official *cum* property holder in Latin America and the Philippines. During the early decades of U.S. colonial rule, American officials used the term pejoratively.

camote: common root crop; a sweet potato.

canon: system of fixed-fee land rent paid in cash or in kind during the Spanish period.

capitán del pueblo: title for municipal mayors during the 18th century; equivalent to the later term *gobernadorcillo.*

carabao: a water buffalo.

casas de reservas: households exempted from corvée labour during Spanish period.

caudillo: used in the Tobacco Monopoly production areas for local officials, often *gobernadorcillos,* appointed to supervise cultivation and collection of the crop.

cédula personal: annual head tax under late Spanish and American regimes whose receipt served as an identification card.

Chinese mestizo: person of mixed Chinese and Filipino parentage. Generally, writers use the term "mestizo" to mean "Chinese mestizo", and are specific when denoting other mixtures — i.e. "Spanish mestizo" and "American mestizo".

cogon: high, dense grass.

colección: a cultivation region for the Spanish Tobacco Monopoly.

colegio: a secondary school.

comandancia politico-militar: Spanish term for province-sized area, usually at the frontier, requiring a military governor.

comerciante: a merchant or trader.

compadrazgo: a generic term describing the patterns of ritual brotherhood and sisterhood achieved by serving as sponsors in Church baptism, wedding or confirmation.

compadre, comadre: relationship and term of address for persons who have become siblings through sponsorship at Church wedding, baptism or confirmation.

conquistador: Spanish conqueror who establishes a colony.

creole: person born in the colonies both of whose parents were Spanish.

cuadrilleros: 19th century Spanish local police.

datu: pre-Hispanic local leader, usually the head of a *barangay.* Used in both pagan and Muslim areas of modern Mindanao-Sulu for a local man of influence, often with inherited status and usually controlling an area larger than a single village.

don, doña: formal titles awarded to the *principales* and their wives during the Spanish period. During the 20th century they have become informal terms of respect in the Christian areas for any person of outstanding wealth or status.

dumagat: a term used by the Bukidnon of Mindanao for lowlanders, usually referring to Cebuano-Visayans. Also, the name of a hunter-gatherer group in the Sierra Madre of Luzon.

encomienda: tribute-collection areas assigned to Spanish colonists during the 16th and 17th centuries which carried with them a nominal responsibility for providing protection and spiritual guidance.

estancia: a Spanish land grant of sparsely populated land usually intended for cattle ranching.

FOF: Federacion Obrera de Filipinas, a Visayan labour confederation based in Iloilo City, ca. 1928-1951.

Ganap: a pro-Japanese political party in Central Luzon during the late 1930s; later name of World War II para-military units of pro-Japanese Filipinos.

gobernadorcillo: Spanish administrative term used to designate native official assigned or elected to administer a town (*pueblo*). It replaced the term *capitan del pueblo.* Equivalent to municipal mayor.

gremio: under Spanish colonial law, a municipal ward or local administrative unit. Used by 20th century Filipinos for any branch or chapter of a private union or society.

gremio de mestizos: Spanish administrative unit for those of mixed Chinese-Filipino parentage resident in a city or major municipality.

gremio de naturales: Spanish administrative unit for those of Malay-Filipino descent resident in a city.

Guardia Civil: Spanish para-military constabulary established in the 19th century to maintain internal order.

Guardia del Honor: messianic peasant movement during the latter stages of the Philippine Revolution in Central Luzon.

hacendero, hacendado: proprietor of a large landed estate most often planted to sugar or rice.

hacienda: a large, unified agricultural property ranging from 50 to 1,000 hectares.

Huk, Hukbalahap: abbreviations for *Hukbo ng Bayan laban sa Hapon,* People's Anti-Japanese Army, organized by Communist and Socialist party supporters during World War II. Also used popularly for the *Hukbong Mapagpalaya ng Bayan,* the postwar anti-government guerillas active in Central Luzon and the Western Visayas.

ilustrado: a late 19th century term for any non-Spanish resident of the Philippines who had acquired some tertiary education, usually in Manila or Europe. Literally, means "enlightened".

indio: Spanish colonial term for any Christian of unadulterated Malay-Filipino descent; equivalent to the British term "native".

infieles: literally "non-believers"; used by Spanish colonials for non-Christian Filipinos usually found in mountains or Muslim south.

inquilino: lessee who pays fixed rent for a parcel of land which is often sub-divided among share tenants or *kasama.*

jornalero: a wage labourer.

Kabikolan: the Bikol region at the southeastern extremity of Luzon Island.

kaingin: a cultivated field or an agricultural method involving felling forest and burning off the dried timber.

kalayaan: freedom or independence.

Kapatiran Magsasaka: Brotherhood of Peasants, a Central Luzon peasant union, ca. 1918 to early 1930s.

kasama: literally "partner" in Tagalog; used to mean share tenant in Central Luzon.

kasugpon: literally "helper"; used for permanent labour on small family farms in Central Luzon.

Katipunan: abbreviation for *Kataastaasan Kagalanggalang na Katipunan ng mga Anak ng Bayan,* or Highest and Most Respectable Sons of the People, the revolutionary secret society organized by Andres Bonifacio in Manila in 1892.

Katipunan Mipanampon: a strike-breaking landlords' union active in Bulacan and Pampanga provinces during the 1920s and 1930s.

katiwala: an overseer on an estate in Central Luzon.

kiapangdilihan: bond-slaves in the Sulu sultanate whose status was the product of indebtedness.

KPMP: Kalipunang Pambansa ng mga Magsasaka sa Pilipinas, or National Society of Philippine Peasants, a large Central Luzon confederation of the 1930s.

lorcha: a single- or double-masted sailcraft of usually 30 to 50 tons deadweight in the Visayan coasting trade.

magahat: used in Bukidnon region of Mindanao to mean "blood avenger"; later meant all lawless elements in the mountains.

maratabat: Maranao term meaning a type of hereditary family honour.

mestizo: any person of mixed-racial parentage. Unless specified, term usually means those of Chinese mestizo descent.

Moro: Spanish term meaning Muslim, used specifically in the Philippines for Muslim residents of western Mindanao and the Sulu archipelago.

municipio: the administrative building for a municipality located in the *población.*

Nacionalista Party: Philippine political party formed in 1907 and one of two major postwar parties until the declaration of Martial Law in 1972.

naturales: a Spanish colonial term used most broadly to mean "natives" or *indios,* that is persons of pure Malay–Filipino descent. More precisely, it was used in legal and administrative documents with the connotation "born in the locality" and in that sense had no specific racial connotation.

nipa: a swamp palm whose fronds are used for roof thatching and the sap for alcohol and vinegar. The term "nipa house" usually means a structure of palm-thatch roof and bamboo walls.

pacto de retrovento or *pacto de retrovendendo:* a form of mortgage agreement used to secure loans and which facilitates foreclosure of the assigned property.

palay: the rice plant; harvested rice that has been threshed but not husked.

parang: grassland and scrub association, savannah.

parian: urban area designated by the Spanish regime as residence for Chinese.

Partido Federal: political party founded in 1900 by wealthy, educated Filipinos who favoured American statehood instead of independence.

pasion: Easter drama depicting the life and death of Jesus Christ, performed annually in the towns of the Tagalog region from the 18th century onwards.

peninsulares: Spaniards born in the peninsula, that is Spain.

personero: a local commercial agent for a Chinese or European trading firm.

PKM: Pambansang Kaisahan ng mga Magbubukid, or National Peasants Union, a Central Luzon organization of the 1940s.

población: the administrative centre of a municipality (*pueblo*), containing the market, church, town hall and major houses. Earlier accounts used the equivalent term *cabecera,* but contemporary documents almost always use *población.*

polista: anyone performing corvée labour services.

polo: corvée labour services required under the Spanish regime.

prahu: light sailcraft up to 25 metres long used for trade and slave raiding in the Sulu zone.

presidente: a municipal mayor during the American colonial period.

principalía, principales: a 19th century colonial term for the municipal political elite comprised of the incumbent *gobernadorcillo,* all those who had held the post, *cabezas de barangay* who had served ten years, and local school teachers.

pueblo: Spanish administrative term for municipality. Each *pueblo* was divided into *barrios* and *sitios,* and its administrative centre was the *población.*

pueblo de indios: from the 16th century onwards any Filipino municipality, and in later centuries a "native district" within a larger urban area.

pulajanes: term for messianic peasant movements in the Visayas. Literally, means "wearing red".

rancheria: the lowest, i.e. smallest, level of Spanish colonial administration.

Real Audiencia: see, *Audiencia.*

reservas: persons exempted from corvée labour during Spanish colonial period.

remontado: those subjects who fled the tax-paying villages for mountains or frontier areas.

sacada: seasonal worker recruited in western Panay to cut sugar cane in Negros.

Sakdal: a peasant nationalist union organized in the Tagalog-speaking provinces during the late 1920s and dissolved after its abortive revolt in 1935.

sinamay: type of handwoven Philippine fabric.

sitio: during the Spanish period, a small settlement loosely incorporated into the administration of a *pueblo.* During the 20th century this became the lowest administrative unit used for areas with only scattered settlement.

swidden: shifting cultivation of fields prepared by felling trees and burning off the dried underbrush. English equivalent of *kaingin.*

Tanggulan: abbreviated form of *Kapatiran Tanggulan Malayang Mamamayan,* or Brotherhood for the Defence of Free Citizens, a lower-class patriotic secret society, ca. 1928-1931.

tributo: Spanish adult head tax also used for census taking. Each married couple comprised one tribute, or *tributo,* and unmarried adults one-half tribute.

tripang: a type of sea cucumber or sea slug used in Chinese cusine. Alternative spelling *trepang;* equivalent term *balate.*

USAFFE: United States Armed Forces in the Far East, the U.S. Army command in the Philippines which included both American and Filipino detachments.

vagamundo: literally vagabonds, the Spanish colonial term for those without a fixed residence who avoided payment of tax.

visita: small settlement, usually larger than a *sitio* during the Spanish period. Originated as a term to indicate a settlement without a residential parish priest, but soon became the generic term for a settlement visited periodically by a priest from the nearest *población.* Also, a circuit chapel.

Zambals: a general term referring to inhabitants of Zambales Province on Luzon Island's western coast.

zarzuela: a Spanish dramatic form combining song and story that was borrowed by Filipino vernacular dramatists and dominated the theatre in the first three decades of the 20th century.

CONTRIBUTORS

JEREMY BECKETT is a Senior Lecturer in Anthropology at the University of Sydney. He has done field work in southwestern Mindanao and published extensively on Australian Aboriginal and Torres Strait island societies.

BRUCE CRUIKSHANK wrote his doctoral dissertation at the University of Wisconsin on Samar regional history in the 18th and 19th centuries. He has published a number of articles on Philippine history and is engaged in research on Spanish missionary efforts in East Asia.

MICHAEL CULLINANE is a doctoral candidate in Southeast Asian history at the University of Michigan and a Research Associate of its Center for South and Southeast Asia Studies. He has done extensive field and archival research into Cebu's history.

ED. C. DE JESUS is Associate Professor of Business History at the Asian Institute of Management in Manila. He has published articles on Philippine cultural history, did his doctoral dissertation at Yale University on the Tobacco Monopoly, and is engaged in research on the nation's economic history.

RONALD K. EDGERTON teaches history at the University of Northern Colorado and completed his doctoral dissertation at the University of Michigan on the politics of reconstruction in the postwar Philippines. His post-doctoral research has focused on the social history of the Bukidnon Plateau.

BRIAN FEGAN is a Research Fellow at the Australian National University. He did an ethnographic study of a Tagalog village in Central Luzon for his doctoral dissertation at Yale University and has conducted subsequent field research into the area's social and political history.

MILAGROS C. GUERRERO is Associate Professor of History at the University of the Philippines. She did her doctoral dissertation on the history of the Philippine Revolution at the University of Michigan and continued her work on that subject as a Research Fellow at the Australian National University.

ALFRED W. McCOY is a Senior Lecturer in History at the University of New South Wales in Sydney and did a doctoral dissertation at Yale University on the history of Iloilo Province. He is the author of *The Politics of Heroin in Southeast Asia*.

MARSHALL S. McLENNAN is Associate Professor of Geography at Eastern Michigan University. His doctoral dissertation at the University of California at Berkeley studied the socio-economic origins of commercial rice farming in Nueva Ecija Province.

NORMAN G. OWEN teaches history at the University of Michigan where he completed his doctoral dissertation on the socio-economic history of the Bikol region. He is author of *Prosperity Without Progress: Manila Hemp and Material Life in the Colonial Philippines* (forthcoming).

DENNIS M. ROTH is the Chief Historian of the U.S. Forest Service in Washington, D.C. and completed his doctorate in Anthropology at the University of Oregon. He is the author of *The Friar Estates of the Philippines.*

WILLIAM HENRY SCOTT teaches at the University of the Philippines and St. Andrew's Theological Seminary in Manila. He holds a doctorate in Philippine history from the University of Santo Tomas. His quarter century of involvement with the Cordillera as resident and researcher has produced a number of publications, most importantly his book, *The Discovery of the Igorots: Spanish Contacts with the Pagans of Northern Luzon.*

JAMES WARREN is Lecturer in Southeast Asian Modern History at Murdoch University in Western Australia. He is the author of *The Sulu Zone, 1768-1898: The Dynamics of External Trade, Slavery, and Ethnicity in the Transformation of a Southeast Asian Maritime State.*

INDEX

of Sulu, 433-34
pacto de retroventa, 69
Palaris, Juan de la Cruz, 27
Pampanga Province, 2-3, 58
   haciendas in, 67
   landlords in, 75
   rice exports from, 78
   sugar lands in, 148
   sugar planters in, 8
   sugar production in, 68, 325
Panaguiton, Anselmo, 342
Panay Island, 8, 10
   geography of, 298-300
Pangasinan Province,
   Ilocano migration into, 63
   Revolution in, 156, 173, 176-77
   rice production in, 75, 78
   rice exports to Bikol from, 200
Pansacula, Doroteo, 156
Pansacula, Teodoro, 156
Pantabangan Reservoir, 81
Papa Isio, 324-25
Pardo de Tavera, T.H., 158
Parian, 277, 282
Parian Church, 251
Parian district, 254, 257, 259-60, 262-68
Partido Federal, 101
pasion, 107
Paterno, Maximo, 158
Paterno, Pedro, 158, 167
patron-client relations, 13
   in Bikol, 207-8
   in Bukidnon, 376
   in Bulacan, 102, 119
   in Central Luzon, 66, 75
   in Cotabato, 392
   on friar estates, 145-46
   in Iloilo City, 336
   on Luzon frontier, 452
   on Samar, 236-38
   in Sulu, 424
pearl fisheries, 419, 425
peasant pioneers, 8-9
   in Bukidnon, 376-79
   in Bulacan, 92
   in Central Luzon, 63-66, 93-99
   on Samar, 219, 237-38
   in Western Visayas, 311-12, 317-26
peasant revolts, *see also* anti-colonial
      resistance, Huks
peasant revolts, 102
   in Bukidnon, 371
   in Cagayan Valley, 27-28
   in Cavite, 140-42
   in Cebu, 259, 262
   in Negros, 324-25
   by Sakdal, 111, 131
   on Samar, 219
   in San Miguel, 101

peasants, 4, 8
   alienation from Revolution by, 175-79
   in Bikol, 200-2
      abaca cultivation by, 195
   in Central Luzon, 63-66, 72-77
   on friar estates, 136-49
   in Negros, 317-26
   in Samar, 235-38
   in San Miguel, 91-129
   theories about, 95-98, 120-24
peasant unions, in Central Luzon, 107-12
Peele, Hubbell & Co., 195-96
Peirce, George, 196-97
Pelzer, Karl, 393
Peñalosa, Ronquillo, 24
Pendaton, Salipada, 405
Pensahan, Albino, 370
peonage, *see* debt bondage
Pérez, Fr. Angel, 52-53
Person, Yves, 419
Phelan, John, 21
Philip II, 134
Philippine-American War, 156-90, 450
   in Bukidnon, 367-68
Philippine Commission, 401
Philippine Constabulary, 342-43
Philippine Insurgent Records, 160, 168,
      171-72
Philippine Normal College, 373
Philippine Packing Corp., 375
Philippine Revolution, 2, 8, 148-49, 155-90,
      391, 450
   in Bukidnon, 367-68
   in Cebu, 281-82, 283-84
   on friar estates, 131
   in Negros, 324-25
   on Samar, 239
   in San Miguel, 100
Philippine studies, 2-3
Philippine values, 4
Piang, Gumbay, 405-6
Piang, Menandang, 404-5
Piang, Ugalingen, 403-5
Pickford, C.R.B., 272
piña, 302
pineapple, fibres from, 302
pineapple production, in Bukidnon, 375
pioneer settlement, in Central Luzon, 80
piracy, in Sulu, 420
plantations, *see* friar estates, haciendas,
      land titling
plantations
   in Bikol, 198
   in Bukidnon, 374-75
   in Bulacan, 101-6, 116-17, 120-23
   in Cebu, 269-70
   in Davao, 199
   in Negros, 10, 311-29, 338
   in Negros, Luzon, 325-26

ASIAN STUDIES ASSOCIATION OF AUSTRALIA
Southeast Asia Publications Series

EDITORIAL COMMITTEE

C/- Department of Pacific and Southeast Asian History
Australian National University, Canberra, A.C.T.
AUSTRALIA